D0909066

Studies in Eighteenth-Century Culture

VOLUME 7

Studies in Eighteenth-Century Culture VOLUME 7

EDITED BY *Roseann Runte*

Dalhousie University

PUBLISHED for the

AMERICAN SOCIETY FOR EIGHTEENTH-CENTURY STUDIES

by THE UNIVERSITY OF WISCONSIN PRESS

Published 1978
The University of Wisconsin Press
Box 1379, Madison, Wisconsin 53701

The University of Wisconsin Press, Ltd.
70 Great Russell St., London

First printing

Printed in the United States of America

LC 74-25572
ISBN 0-299-07400-5

Contents

Preface

Studies in Eighteenth-Century Culture publishes annually a selection of the papers read at regional and national conferences of the American Society for Eighteenth-Century Studies. The Editorial Board is honored to present the essays collected in volume seven which were carefully chosen from numerous and excellent submissions to represent the outstanding efforts of scholars from many fields in this bicentennial year.

With the exception of the ASECS prize article by Milton M. Klein, all of the papers in this volume were presented at the national conference of the ASECS held at the University of Virginia, April 8–10, 1976. Although the essays themselves have a common origin, the authors traveled from three countries and thirteen states to deliver them. In like fashion, although each paper contributes to the elucidation of some aspect of the eighteenth century, the topics covered and the critical approaches employed are widely divergent. This diversity is appropriate, not only because it represents the broad range of scholarship fostered by a multidisciplinary society, but because it reflects the complexity of the eighteenth century, a period rich in cultural and historical phenomena so varied that they often appear paradoxical. These phenomena are accompanied by a multiplicity of philosophical theories and concepts given voice by spokesmen of striking individuality in literary and artistic productions of abundant variety.

A philosopher is an observer and, in that sense, all of the contributors to this volume are philosophers who have recorded and interpreted their perceptions on some facet of the Enlightenment. Some deal with the printed word which is the external embodiment of thought; others with thought which, as Rivarol said, is itself a form of internalized expression. Perhaps the sole work which united eighteenth-century philosophers of disparate opinions and methods was the *Encyclopédie.* The present volume makes no pretense of establishing the internal relationships of human knowledge nor of recording or classifying all the essential details which form its substance. Rather than an aggregate of critical thought, the papers gathered here constitute a continuing discussion and often pose more questions than they resolve. Yet, like the editors of the *Encyclopédie,* the editor of *Studies in Eighteenth-Century Culture* is faced with the task of seeking a suitable order of presentation. In each case, the goals are the same. The parts must be related to the whole in such a manner as to communicate the ideas contained therein in a useful fashion. The editors of the *Encyclopédie* divided the objectives of human knowledge into three categories: history, philosophy, and the *beaux-arts,* which correspond to the different intellectual processes involved in their creation: memory, reason, and imagination. This volume follows this general outline to the extent that such a division is possible. However, overlap is inevitable and he who could separate objectively the gray areas in which thought, memory, and imagination intertwine, would undoubtedly be able to read the pages of the hermit's book which appeared blank even to Zadig, the most rational of men.

Professor Klein's article, "New York Lawyers and the Coming of the American Revolution," the ASECS prize essay, opens this volume and calls attention to a gap in the historical knowledge of the American Revolution. Professor Klein explains the reasons for the relative neglect of the vital role played by the lawyers, a signally important intellectual group, in the coming of the Revolution, both in terms of the actual historical phenomenon and in terms of the concepts of contemporary schools of historiography. He also supplies an excellent scenario which clarifies the influence of the lawyers on the drama in which they were actors, and the influence of the script on the actors. This article is followed by Professor Peterson's piece on "Thomas Jefferson's *Notes on the State of Virgina,*" which exposes the different aspects of Jefferson: philosopher, American, and eighteenth-century man. Professor Baeumer's article brings together aesthetic notions concerning the noble and simple from French sources and from Winckelmann. It shows that these strains exist in Jefferson as well. His thesis is that Jefferson may have acquired these notions partly under the influence of Winckelmann because of an acquaintance they held in common, C. L. Clérisseau. This paper acts as a bridge over the Atlantic, uniting the first two papers on American historical figures with the next three papers which deal with European history in general and the French Revolution in specific.

Professor Kurth-Voigt's historical and textual research broadens our understanding not only of the conflicts and unity of Wieland's version of an ideal method to be applied in man's search for truth when confronted with the complex historical developments of the time but also of Wieland's technique as writer of dialogues. Professor Racevskis's essay on the French Academy demonstrates the evolution of a concept from its expostulation to its application over a period of a century. Professor Rosenfeld's paper explains another evolution: the dramatic struggle for women's rights in the French Revolution. It is followed by Professor Shklar's piece, "Politics and the Intellect," which makes the appropriate suggestion that we discover ourselves in the eighteenth century and find the values the past has for us. The essay is a stimulating debate which is based on the ideas of Adams, Jefferson, and the French *philosophes*.

The three papers which follow were presented together at the Virginia conference in a session entitled "Stability and Innovation in Eighteenth-Century Science and Society." Professor Vartanian defines and clarifies an apparent paradox, one of the most gripping questions with which eighteenth-century philosophers such as La Mettrie, Diderot, and D'Holbach dealt. Professor Schofield provides a definition of what kind of authority Newton represented and what was genuinely Newtonian, extending the argument to different national settings and proposing the fundamental importance of Leibnitz in new ways. Professor Barnouw's paper is a commentary on the two preceding works and points out areas in which they agree and conflict.

The papers by Professors Livingston and Burke are both from the seminar devoted to Hume as a man of letters. Professor Livingston's work is a penetrating and informative description of Hume's conservatism and its situation in relation to both the history of conservatism and Hume's thought. Professor Burke's informative and argumentative contribution describes Hume's approach to history as parallel to his approach to philosophy. Professor Rex's essay which follows situates the articles by the Abbé Pestré both in the history of ideas and in the history of the *Encyclopédie.* In dealing with a philosopher who is also a member of the clergy, this essay leads to the next three, which deal with ideology and the French Catholic clergy and were delivered in a seminar with that title. Professor Plongeron analyzes the contradictions between the Christian morality of the Evangile and the *Declaration of the Rights of Man and of the Citizen.* He challenges the romantic theses of the nineteenth-century Christian socialists that the latter was the final consequence of the former. Professor Williams defines Jansenism and situates its transformation by the clergy in a historical perspective. Professor Tackett elucidates the interaction between ecclesiastical politics, socio-economic structures, and ideology in the context of one province, Dauphiné, and in the light of the critical role played by the curé deputies.

Professor Rogal's paper, "John Wesley on War and Peace," provides a helpful sidelight on one of the most eminent men of the century. It acts as transition between the study of religious beliefs and the tracing of a theme: that of peace, which is also the subject of the next essay by Professor Nelson. In his contribution, "War and Peace and the British Poets of Sensibility," Professor Nelson outlines the trends in eighteenth-century poetry and the extent to which peace was a coherent theme in that poetry.

Another thematic work by Professor Baird, "Cowper's Concept of Truth," describes the attitude of this poet toward salvation.

The two essays which follow both deal with Dryden. Professor Novak's comments on Dryden as imitator of Shakespeare make an original contribution to a much-studied subject. He considers the problem both in relation to the eighteenth-century reaction to Dryden and to modern scholarship. Professor Ormsby-Lennon's subject undertakes a purge of some misconceptions concerning Dryden and relates medical beliefs to a philosophical standpoint expressed in the literary text through medical analogies.

The next three papers deal with style and theory. Professor McCoy's essay discusses feminist criticism and its limitations, pointing out that Moll Flanders's character is determined more by class than by sex. Professor Corman's paper proposes a generic theory of Restoration comedy based on Crane's principles. Completing this trilogy, Professor Cohen studies the opposition between poet and philosopher in Diderot which results in a conflict between his theory and practice of style.

Professor Brady's paper stands alone in relating the philosophical standpoint of atomistic empiricism to its manifestations in art, architecture, interior decorating, literature, and life style.

The final two papers in this volume shed new light on several notable eighteenth-century figures by viewing them in retrospect. Professor Kenney describes the success and failure of the image of Johnson: his character, style, and thought. Professor Haac reveals how Michelet used Voltaire and Rousseau to illustrate his own moral objectives and to inspire social action.

The essays in this volume were selected and edited through the cooperative efforts of the following: A. Owen Aldridge, Paul Alkon, John Beattie, J. Laurnece Black, George Falle, Michael Fried, Gayle Garlock, Frank J. Garosi, Ruth Graham, James Gray, Robert Greaves, Roger Hahn, Frances L. Harrold, Henry Horwitz, Adrienne Hytier, David Jory, James King, Milton M. Klein, Paul J. Korshin, Victor Lange, John Loftis, Paul McIsaac, Michael Meyer, Walter Moser, Ronald C. Rosbottom, Eric Rothstein, Jean Sareil, Ambrose Saricks, Henry Snyder, Gerald Straka, and Rev. John M. Walker.

It is a great pleasure for me to thank these scholars for their time and careful thought as well as the gracious loan of their knowledge and expertise. My predecessor, Ronald C. Rosbottom, was of enormous assistance, and Paul J. Korshin and the Executive Board of the ASECS provided judicious advice and support.

ROSEANN RUNTE

Halifax, Nova Scotia
December 1976

Studies in Eighteenth-Century Culture

VOLUME 7

Reflections on the "Classical Age" of German Literature

VICTOR LANGE

I

The efflorescence of philosophical and literary energy at the end of the eighteenth century that drew the German men of letters into the mainstream of European modernism was the result of a remarkable variety of historical impulses, of an interplay of political, intellectual, and aesthetic experiences that gives to that period its especially fascinating character. Germany was a social entity far more heterogeneous and provincial than England or France: economically retarded, feudal in its power structure, and only slowly moving towards the emancipation of an effective middle class, dispersed over a barely surveyable plurality of regional forms of life and allegiances, and without the advantages of a center of cultural life. A community of language and of fervent if divided religious faith rather than of social or political solidarity, it was within a few decades forced to assess its potentialities, to abandon its peripheral role in Europe, to articulate its self-consciousness, and to create a philosophical and literary idiom of unmistakable native strength. From an experience of disparity, frustration, and vision, the most clear-sighted among its writers fashioned the language of modernism which in turn shaped the European imagination well into the nineteenth century.

Historians of culture have often enough described the features of this encounter, the state of mind which produced a canon of altogether unpredictably original works for which the term "German classicism" seemed appropriate. Ever since the demonstrated predilection of the age itself for definition and synthesis, ever since the efforts, in the writings of Herder or Goethe, at distinguishing their sense of radical modernity from that long tradition of mere modifications of established orthodoxies, the second half of the century seemed in Germany to reveal a pattern of purpose of truly revolutionary logic: beginning with the entry of Prussia into the concert of European powers and culminating at the moment of Napoleon's defeat, the epoch was understood as the record of an astonishing triumph of capabilities that had hitherto been scattered and merely emulative but that had now assumed a distinctive character of their own.

But this unitary view, so plausible to a nineteenth-century German society that revered the period as the ground on which its idealistic self-portrait could be traced, has in recent critical scholarship been dramatically challenged. It is this revision that I should like briefly to summarize.

The topography which is usually taken to encompass the German "classical" period is not easy to delimit: it includes some of the territorial landmarks of the more orthodox Enlightenment, the magisterial figures of Lessing, Mendelssohn, and Lichtenberg, the resonant work of Winckelmann, the philological genius of Hamann, the strange Miltonic view of Klopstock, and, above all, Hölderlin, barely acknowledged at the time, yet the greatest lyrical poet of the age. But in a narrower focus it extends roughly from Goethe's break with the political demands made upon him after 1775 by the provincial court in Weimar, that is, from his departure for Italy in 1786, to the death in 1805 of Schiller, for nearly ten years Goethe's closest collaborator. These two men, and a small group of congenial contributors, created not so much an aesthetic theory as a body of reflections on contemporary culture, a system of faith and action directed against the spiritual and political climate of the day, above all against the indications of sympathy, however disjointed, for the impulses and prospects of the French Revolution. It was this canon of writing and discourse, developed in Weimar and in the neighboring university town of Jena, that seemed at the time to offer to German and foreign observers a peculiarly impressive crystallization of widely admired contemporary and national convictions. If a number of German men of letters explicitly dissociated themselves from the Weimar establishment, and from the offered notions of the role of art in the shaping of a new society, they appeared nevertheless to many witnesses, for instance to Mme de Stael, to be part of a prevailing climate of opinion.

In Mme de Stael's enthusiastic, indeed, at times hysterical, account, the German literary establishment represented a rich and concerted effort of minds as dissimilar as Goethe and Jean Paul, to fulfill the historic thrust that was in philosophy begun by Leibnitz, in poetry by Klopstock, and was carried forward by powerful assertion of sectarian fervor and counter-orthodoxy. Mme de Stael, however limited her understanding, was determined to recognize (and in her book to construct) a design in which Enlightenment and Christianity, political conservatism and intellectual liberalism harmoniously coexisted. She had, after all, been expelled by Napoleon and was eager to discover, *outre-Rhin,* anti-revolutionary accomplices. Her account, *De l'Allemagne,* was banned in France and could not be published until 1813, ten years after her travels and interviews in Germany. Her summary of the German scene with its illuminating glow of transcendental thought was intended to offer an antidote to the materialism she so detested among the French revolutionaries. It was August Wilhelm Schlegel, her literary adviser, who by his tact and the range of his literary judgment saved her survey from being wholly willful or fatuous; it was in the end due to his intelligent coaching that the "classicist" Weimar world, and the Christian poets and critics elsewhere in Germany, were twenty years later to be hailed in France as the sources of the modern, now the "romantic," sensibility.

Mme de Stael's vision was blurred; she failed to differentiate. In her catalogue, the turbulent and the suave, the "Storm and Stress" voices and the urbane manner of Wieland, the scepticism of Lessing and the inwardness of German non-conformist belief were mere variants of a pervasive affirmation of humanism and integrity that she found most impressively manifest in Weimar.

This harmonious view was not only fascinating to contemporary French and English observers, but remained compelling throughout the subsequent historiography of German literature: a group of such indubitable intellectual energy—poets, dramatists, essayists and philosophers—was bound to produce the impression, or the illusion, of stylistic homogeneity and continuity. But it was a conspectus that could not for long remain unquestioned; its assumptions, both vaguely spiritual and nationalistic, were shown to rest on ideological preconceptions. From Heine to Lukács and more recent critics such as Werner Krauss, the monolithic appearance of the classical period has been denied, its heterogeneity demonstrated, and, above all, its philosophical antecedents differentiated. I can here touch on only a few significant aspects of this process of historical and conceptual reorientation.

II

The fundamental shift in our critical perspective has achieved a reassessment of the relative importance of the rationalistic as against the speculative disposition which in the view of earlier historians such as Dilthey sustained the intellectual (and political) history of the second half of the century. It has customarily been argued that the source of an indigenous German tradition was to be found in persistent currents of Renaissance neo-Platonism and metaphysical doctrine from Plotinus to Leibnitz. These, it has been thought, offered to the pre-Revolutionary generation in Germany—often in a theological syntax—a programmatic vocabulary with which to counter the emerging influence of French and English materialist or sensualist philosophies.

A pertinent sentence in Goethe's autobiography was for long regarded as the *locus classicus* for this view. In the third part of *Poetry and Truth,* Goethe suggests that in the days of his own fascination with Paracelsus and Böhme it was impossible for him and his friends to read

Holbach, La Mettrie or Helvétius without being chilled by their bleak empiricism. Ernst Cassirer was the first to modify this generalization by drawing attention to the lively interest of the "Storm and Stress" generation, of men such as Herder and Hamann, precisely in the French materialists, above all in Condillac and La Mettrie, but equally in English empiricist thought, in Hume, Locke, and Hartley. And it has been the work of men like Werner Krauss that has shown the overriding effect of the English deists, of Toland and Tindal, as well as the French *philosophes* upon the thinking of a large number of German writers, theorists, novelists, and pamphleteers prior to and during the French Revolution. We have been shown to what extent the satire of minor but widely circulated authors (such as J. C. Wezel) depended upon psychological and social theories supplied by Helvétius and Montesquieu or by Bonnet's or Tissot's analysis of pathological and neurological conditions; and how resolutely the metaphysical projections of Leibnitz and Wolff were countered by sceptical appeals, in the manner of Voltaire's *Candide*, to face life without comforting recourse to illusionary philosophical or theological speculations. The astonishing increase in the production of popular fiction during the last quarter of the eighteenth century in Germany is in large measure a reflection of that vast assortment of English and French novels in which a sensibility and an emotional energy, a concrete and critical rendering of the social setting, unknown in German religious and moral literature, became plausible and persuasive. The sympathies of novelists such as Nicolai, Musäus, Hippel, Thümmel, or Wieland with the pragmatic and sensualist convictions of their English and French models is unmistakable.

It is well to remember that, whether in fiction or in poetry, the anti-metaphysical ingredient in German pre-classical (and classical) literature has been demonstrated by specific investigations of the broadest possible spectrum of literary (and "sub-literary") production. Indeed, it is in part as the result of studies of the sociological realities of the literary life that attention has been directed to hitherto neglected patterns of taste, belief, and action. The social history of the book to which, happily, we are beginning to pay due attention, has provided extraordinarily useful information on the economic and social conditions of writers, patrons, and publishers, even in a setting so relatively underdeveloped as the German at the end of the eighteenth century. We have come to recognize the relationship between the modes of production, distribution, and reception of literature, German as well as foreign, of the politics of criticism, of the interplay of social and literary convictions, and the evolution of certain literary forms and genres designed to meet the expectations of an ever more closely organized market of producers and consumers. We have, at any rate, come to see that (to a much greater degree than had been assumed by historians primarily concerned with the philosophical predilections of conspicuous writers) it is by a measure of attention to the "function" of literature in Germany that we can most accurately differentiate the various impulses that give an heterogeneous cast to the period.

Empirical research has also been instrumental in providing an adequate assessment of the role, in shaping the intellectual and social disposition of a curiously interlocking audience, of such advocates of a rational humanism as the Freemasons, the *Illuminati,* or the Rosicrucians, all in certain territories clandestine but remarkably powerful organizations. Their cosmopolitan attachment to an anti-metaphysical sensibility contributed markedly to the creation of an effective community of political liberalism in which representatives of a feudal as well as a middle-class background joined in progressive debate. Frederick the Great, Lessing, Lenz, Wieland, Goethe, Herder, Fichte, Haydn, Mozart, and many less conspicuous but quietly effective public figures belonged to these influential groups.

I stress the impact of recent empirical investigations upon our view of the heterogeneous rather than the single-minded character of German "classicism" because it has, incidentally, led to a fresh examination of the effect of the most important foreign theorists upon German readers and writers. Roland Mortier, for instance, has unfolded, with admirable attention to detail, the social and literary context of Diderot's influence upon the German scene of the years before and, indeed, after the Revolution. Diderot's philosophical essays, which first appeared in Germany in 1774, were widely read and had, through Lessing, an extraordinary impact upon the development of an indigenous dramatic criticism as well as a German theory of fiction. When, in 1798, the German edition of his works appeared in fifteen volumes, and when, particularly, Goethe's translation of *Rameau's Nephew* was published in 1805, the discussion of the relationship between the *philosophes* and the Revolution received a substantial stimulus. It was Diderot, at any rate, more than any other French writer, whose insistence upon the connection between reflection and political action contributed to a strong, if localized, assertion of Jacobin sympathies among some of the most intelligent German writers of the period.

Curiously enough, there exists as yet no equally broad or illuminating investigation of the crucial role which Rousseau played in the self-definition of the period. We know, of course, how avidly he was read and absorbed by German writers, especially by members of the "Storm and Stress" group—among whom Herder maintained his attachment to Rousseau throughout his life. We know how significantly Rousseau affected Kant; we know to what extent his work encouraged the radically subjective speculations of Fichte, but we do not, in concrete terms, quite see the effect which a political tract like the *Contrat social* had upon the German writers before and after the Revolution. It was certainly in the spirit of Rousseau that men as different in their poetic purpose as Schiller and Hölderlin maintained and articulated their belief that, rather than direct political action or, as Diderot had hoped, the revolutionary effect of technology and the sciences, it was virtue and innocence alone that could in Germany effectively challenge and transform the fragmented state of its society. It was largely Rousseau's thinking that produced, as late as 1794, Schiller's programmatic essay *On the Aesthetic Education of Man*, an essay which, with full awareness of an unsatisfactory present, argued in radical terms the non-political, the anti-revolutionary position according to which masters and servants alike are at a moment of cultural crisis thrown back upon their natural, their authentic self.

The Rousseauian ideology, this much is clear, gained widely in appeal and legitimacy among German men of letters by being absorbed into the strong sectarian currents of pietism. This vehicle of Protestant anti-orthodoxy was instrumental in relating two kinds of total individual commitment to the emerging hopes of increased participation in the social process, both supported by feudal as well as middle-class interests: the one, more activist, invoked divine sanction for the reconstruction of society and, influenced by Jeremy Taylor, Richard Baxter, and Bunyan, formulated a severely puritanical work ethic; it sought the rebirth of man, the *homo novus,* in schools and in tightly organized communities in Germany and in the diaspora such as Pennsylvania and Georgia. The other, and for the structure of German classicism, more important, pietistic disposition was, on the contrary, entirely inward-directed, mystical in essence, attached to a dualistic theology which prescribed that the evils of this world were to be avoided and, in a state of primitive faith, the millennium to be awaited. This more introspective form of the movement was represented by two immensely productive and articulate Swabian theologians, Oettinger and Bengel, at Tübingen, whose hermeneutical work and whose *philosophia sacra,* a conglomeration of Bohemian mysticism, scientific speculation, and Swedenborgian faith in the "New Church" decisively influenced their pupils, the young Schiller, Hegel, Schelling, and Hölderlin. Their strong impact on Hölderlin's poetic language is sufficiently well known; what has only recently been stressed is the role which their insistence upon the *old law* played, in Württemberg and the Protestant German states, in the more or less open attacks upon the absolutist forms of government.

Nearly all those German poets who, in the decade immediately preceding the Revolution, groped for a system of social and political criticism embraced pietist principles. Another important effect of pietist thinking and feeling can be seen in the mass of "rebirth" testimonials, those sometimes agonizing accounts of an exemplary Christian life, which led in Germany, often under the influence of English puritan autobiographies, to the popular narratives of personal illumination and conversion, and to ever more elaborate and searching attempts at psychological fiction.

III

What has been the subject of a good deal of often partisan debate is the relationship of the philosophical and religious concerns to political thought and action in the final quarter of the century, and particularly after the French Revolution.

Of all the German pre-revolutionary manifestations of discontent with the existing social order, the anti-establishment outbursts of the late sixties and seventies, the "Storm and Stress" protests, however vague their intellectual or aesthetic convictions, have seemed to have the most striking polemical force and the greatest cohesion. "Storm and Stress" is certainly an important social phenomenon, but, under critical scrutiny, it can no longer be considered to have the character of a cohesive movement. Many of its features, the Rousseauian cultural pessimism, its populist sentiments, its apotheosis of national myths, its embrace of a certain historical relativism which Herder had learned from Montesquieu, its proclamation of the attributes of "enthusiasm" and of "genius" and its projection of these energies into poetic language, aesthetic theory, and the reading of the classics, Homer as well as Pindar—all these are the signatures of a generation that seemed to attack the larger frame of their social condition by challenging the formal and topical preferences of the rococo culture.

But recent criticism has seen in these demonstrations of discontent an unmistakable attachment to Enlightenment, if not Baroque, convictions rather than an early anticipation of romantic subjectivity. Lukács, as well as more formalist literary critics of "Storm and Stress" poetics and rhetoric, has shown the fundamentally conservative and unhistorical tenor of these evocations of past greatness or of present inhumanity. "Storm and Stress" dramaturgy, however opposed it may have been to any normative theory, tended to present the exceptional figure in mythical dimensions as a heroic counter-vision to the widely felt shortcomings of the contemporary social mechanisms; it had little interest in the kind of psychological analysis with which Lessing, and especially Goethe in his *Iphigenie* or *Tasso,* explicitly refuted the "Storm and Stress" partiality for demonstrative encounters between the Promethean genius and the established order. There is little of consequence in the theory of literature which the "Storm and Stress" playwrights—F. M. Klinger, H. L. Wagner, J. M. R. Lenz, F. Müller—offered; and it is not surprising that the early work of the poet who in his *Robbers* echoed the defiant pathos of that group most resoundingly, the young Schiller, is now placed in a different context altogether.

Almost ten years younger than Goethe, Schiller had as a graduation exercise composed a curious discourse on the relationship between the animal and the spiritual nature of man: it was a reflection at once of his interest in human pathology and of the pietistic teaching that had directed the course and the subject matter of his schooling. This dualism, which remained a basic impulse in Schiller's work as historian as well as dramatist and critic of culture, is in the early work sharply accented. *The Robbers,* his first play, was begun while he was still at school, published after much official hesitation, and produced in 1781 as the opening show of the carnival season; its topic is the melodramatic encounter between two brothers, one pathologically evil, the other driven to a life of banditry by his Rousseauian contempt for a society in which corruption is protected by the powers of convention. This almost Brechtian theme remained symptomatic of the unremitting moral exertions and the tremendous rhetoric with which Schiller continued throughout his life to seek a resolution of the tension between an inherently destructive natural disposition and the opportunities of salvation which a variety of intellectual and cultural models might offer.

In previous criticism, Schiller's *Robbers* and his subsequent drama, *Kabale und Liebe,* were sometimes interpreted as attacks on an obsolescent despotic order by its innocent victims; these plays have more recently been read as indications of that inflexible dichotomy between an inherently deficient human being and the immanent desire to transcend his weakness in a lyrical or utopian mood, or in the affirmation of a-historical myths of greatness.

In Schiller's early plays and poetry, this fundamental tension is repeatedly exemplified, but it was as historian, as professor at Jena, that he most consistently elaborated the Manichean thesis that world (or "universal") history is the court of judgment before which the great and insignificant alike must appear to face doom or receive grace. The French Revolution was therefore bound to be understood (and he shared this sentiment with the eloquent apologists of the events in America and France, with Thomas Paine and the Abbé Raynal) as a

"Crisis" that was the result primarily of moral rather than economic or social causes. As he saw it, the Revolution provided an opportunity to recover and to assert in freedom that state of innocence in which conflicting class interests do not exist. It was a perfectly appropriate gesture of reciprocity that acknowledged Schiller's apotheosis of freedom in a cosmopolitan society: in August 1972 the Paris Assembly made "le sieur Gille, publiciste allemande," together with Klopstock and Pestalozzi, George Washington, and his adjutant Kosciuszko, an honorary citizen of the Republic.

Enthusiasm for the French Revolution was shared by Kant and Herder alike: in the draft of his *Letters for the Advancement of Humanity*, Herder explicitly called it—again in religious terms—"the most important event in European history since the introduction of Christianity and the Reformation." He had not at that time come in contact with members of the Jacobin groups that had formed in some of the German cities along the Rhine. The activities of these groups and their spokesmen have now been assessed: they produced what is now regarded as an impressive body of uncompromising pamphlets and periodicals directed against aristocratic abuses and in support of the common cause which they hoped the German middle class might make with the Revolution.

This Jacobin ingredient in German thought and writing in the 1790s has been investigated and weighed with pardonable zeal on the part of politically minded literary historians; it is a factor of considerable importance and certainly present in Hölderlin (in whose work Pierre Bertaux has claimed to find an explicit ideological commitment), in men of letters such as George Forster, the writer and companion of James Cook, and even for a time in the young Schlegels. There can be no doubt that the Revolution and its aftermath, the campaigns of 1792 and 1793, forced the German advocates of freedom, equality, and humanity, of reconciliation and a new community, into tactical considerations and the resolve to secularize and activate a mass of hitherto religious and speculative impulses. And it was, on the other hand, the fear of partisan fervor, abhorent in its almost religious fanaticism and altogether uncontrolled by any articulate political or social theory, that persuaded the two conspicuous figures in Weimar,

Schiller and Goethe, to develop something like a carefully reasoned counter-program.

IV

Throughout the decades of political unrest, Saxe-Weimar had remained feudal in its basic assumptions, if liberal in its demonstrated concern for a constitutional form of government. Goethe, already a recognized man of letters, had become an increasingly effective official of that ducal court. He had survived the dubious fame of having written, in *Werther,* a critique not of any particular class but of an uncongenial social order. In the 1780s he had sketched a novel, *Wilhelm Meister's Theatrical Mission,* and drafts of *Tasso,* in which the conflict he himself felt between the claims of the imagination and its subordination to a self-confidently absolutist political system was the central theme. But he had left Weimar abruptly in 1786 and had returned after two years in Italy with a new sense of commitment now neither primarily to the court nor to the pursuit of letters, but to his interests in science, in optics, botany, and anatomy. When he met Schiller soon afterwards, he found himself gradually drawn into an exchange of ideas on the present and future state of what was clearly a disjointed but vigorous German literary and academic society. He had for some time distrusted Schiller's cerebral and radical cast of mind; but now the two men, of different social and intellectual backgrounds, joined almost at once in their rejection of the Revolution and its consequences.

They were convinced that the uprising had been premature and that by a demonstration of analysis and creative practice, the ground might be prepared for an eventual transformation of what both recognized as a politically and culturally unsatisfactory present. Each brought to this programmatic discourse his own complex of convictions and his own areas of preoccupation: Schiller, philosophical, relentless in his intellectual drive, eager to make use of literature and the theater as propagandistic vehicles; Goethe, on the other hand, far less single-minded, empirical in his scientific curiosity, urbane and conciliatory, and, in his literary production, altogether shrewd in balancing skepticism and resolute affirmation. They shared an admiration for facets of Greek antiquity: their early masters had been Winckelmann and the English and German philologists, and they were now determined to explicate, not for the cultivated, feudal readers of the past but for a middle class to be drawn into a new bourgeois culture, the substance of the classical achievement. They developed their "classicist" program not in conventional normative terms, but with an awareness of the impact of a century of European philosophical, political, and scientific experiences on a specifically modern consciousness.

Even before their collaboration in several short-lived journals and in the Weimar theater, Schiller had developed his thoughts on Kant's *Critique of Judgment* (1790) in a programmatic series of letters written (1793) for one of his noble patrons. Here, in an elaboration and extension of Kant's concluding paragraphs, he set forth his conviction that only the articulation of what he called the aesthetic sensibility can produce a responsible citizen, morally prepared to bring about a new society. He renounced the Revolution and explicitly withdrew his previous support for the Jacobin sympathizers. These letters are incomparably rich in analytical insight: they offer a modern theory not merely of poetics but of culture. The superb English translation by E. M. Wilkinson and Leonard Willoughby and their admirable commentary have made it clear that this work must be regarded as the cardinal text of the German classical era.

To Goethe this essay seemed excessively abstract and, in its severe philosophical vocabulary, altogether unattractive. His own disposition was pragmatic, he had his hands full with concrete ministerial responsibilities and, if he embraced any theoretical structure, it could only be derived from his scientific work. Yet he now joined Schiller in what was to be a strategy directed not merely at the political sympathizers with the Revolution, but the various forms of offered modernism, whether that of the belated rationalists in Berlin or the growing ground swell of Christian spiritualism in other parts of Germany.

In the essays published in Schiller's journal, *Die Horen,* and Goethe's *Propyläen,* and in their letters, their frequent meetings, and their creative work, they touched on political issues as such only by implication and offered instead an impressive canon of literary criticism and, altogether, discourse of a high order on the function of art and literature in a time of revolutionary transformation of social and intellectual values. They recognized that it is form that makes literature an institution, and were interested in evolving a modern theory of poetic conventions; for conventions in art, like theology in religion or codes and rules in law, insure the permanence of the institution. In this sense, their preoccupation with matters of genre suggests far more than a fascination with traditional technical devices; it was rather an attempt to demonstrate that a system of poetics need not be merely received truth but can be derived from modern anthropological premises. Epic, lyrical, and dramatic patterns were, so Goethe argued, "natural forms" which correspond to types of disposition and to the "gestural" projection of a given sensibility—a view of aesthetic action that revolved around notions of public effectiveness and intention rather than any normative principles.

The validity of their theory of genres was to be demonstrated in a series of appropriately organized works, because to write within a convention was to explore the underlying assumptions about life. In *Wilhelm Meister,* for instance, the model of a modern novel, the tenor of the epic progression was not to be practical but utopian—a process of development towards the receptive and informed personality whose aspirations were to be social in purpose and bourgeois in manner—that is to say, much like the character of the emancipated aristocrats who had contributed so much to Wilhelm's (and Goethe's own) education.

Schiller's chief undertaking, apart from his essayistic prose, was a theatrical treatment of two historical figures, Wallenstein and Mary Stuart. *Wallenstein* was begun in 1791 when Schiller still sympathized with the Revolution; its hero was to be a revolutionary figure who fought the prejudices of his age and who, as the enemy of the Jesuits and of Catholic machinations, had shown himself a representative of that liberty which is the hallmark of genius and greatness. The dramatic constellation in *Mary Stuart* was to be seen in much the same perspective: the play was to be a demonstration of Catholic-feudal plotting against Elizabethan England, the most progressive European state in the sixteenth century. Neither of these designs was executed;

when *Wallenstein* was completed in 1800, it was an incredibly well made modern tragedy, a formal exercise showing the eventual immobility of a character without true genius, greatness, or nobility, driven almost entirely by ambition, revenge, and egotistical calculation, whose downfall was brought about by forces that possess neither dignity nor historical importance. *Mary Stuart* similarly became, under the almost ruthless pressure of that formalism which now seemed to Schiller a prerequisite of the reader's education, a play in which all historical reason was sacrificed: Mary appears at the conclusion as the nobly suffering victim of an unyielding despot.

What continued to sustain Schiller's work was a philosophy of history derived from his early theological studies and again and again exemplified in dramatic and philosophical interpretations that took for granted the hubris of man in the face of a pitiless Fortuna. He held to the certainty of a transcendental judgment in which all but the highest ethical and intellectual exertions were declared futile. The tremendous exploration of this almost baroque proposition in the three awesome critiques of Kant was for Schiller the overwhelming proof of the limits of man, stated in the idiom of modern philosophy.

It is important to remember—and this is a further significant result of the critical reassessment that the "classical" movement or period has undergone—that in Weimar itself, the sense of dissatisfaction and disagreement with what seemed an esoteric cultural program was openly and stubbornly expressed by Herder, one of several nonconformists in the *ambiance* of the court. Herder's theory of history was in effect teleological, Goethe's and Schiller's, each for reasons of his own, altogether pessimistic; for them the accidents of history were to be transcended, for Herder they required the wholehearted application of the individual to realize their potentialities. Political action seemed to Goethe and Schiller a distracting and ephemeral activity; to Herder it offered an opportunity of contributing towards the progression in self-consciousness and purpose of the (national) communities that make up the society of man.

Fichte, too, for a few important years the spellbinding philosopher at Jena, continued to insist on a more directly political form of literary engagement. His last contribution to Schiller's journal was in 1795 rejected by the editor with a characteristic notation that the writer seemed to presuppose that "poetry must spring from life, and the age, from the concrete contemporary experience, and that it must ultimately affect the character of that experience." "This," Schiller added, "surely is a mistaken notion. At present the poetic genius has no choice but to withdraw from actuality and create its own world; by means of the metaphorical models of Greek myth it must strive to maintain itself heir of a distant, ideal age. Actuality," he concluded, "can only befoul it."

This rigorous aestheticism for which it would be easy to give other, equally uncompromising examples, Herder could only consider chilling and inhuman; he was joined in his anti-classicist views by Jean Paul, an increasingly popular writer, whose novel *The Titan* reflected a considered detachment from the quasi-aristocratic pretensions of *Wilhelm Meister.* Jean Paul's novels are masterpieces of detailed yet ironic reporting of petit-bourgeois life, far more trenchant in their critical assessment of contemporary life than anything Goethe and Schiller thought it appropriate to offer. But Jean Paul was wrong, as was Herder himself, if he thought of the classicist program as altogether aloof from the realities of the day. Despite their aversion to the Revolution, Goethe and Schiller were ready to argue that, politically, the only promising opportunities for developing a "progressive" social sensibility lay in the hands of that type of emerging bourgeois who, like the Girondist citizen, was to be economically free of oppressive feudal restrictions but capable of taking on the political role of the reduced aristocracy.

V

While Schiller after 1794 moved more and more into an abstract formalism, Goethe remained during that classicist decade (which roughly corresponds to the Directoire) more firmly committed to science than to literature. Indeed, science seemed to him the most effective instrument for the shaping not merely of an individual sensibility but of modern social institutions. Scientific traffic was bound to bring about a society which he envisaged as cosmopolitan not only in an elevated and formal sense, but in its most concrete and practical operations. The procedures of modern science and the necessary communication among scientists, he was convinced, would provide the means by which the universal preoccupation of the past century with religion and metaphysical speculation could be superseded. We have come to recognize that nothing is more important for the definition of Goethe's cultural intentions at the end of the century and later than an understanding of his attachment to scientific matters and to their implication for the shape of the future. Let me dwell on this issue for a moment. In looking back over his early life, he saw himself immersed in the tradition of those proto-scientific reflections on nature that were part of the pietist and Swedenborgian faith. The "Storm and Stress" view of the scientist as original genius had strongly appealed to him; but he was, even at that time, far from seeing in Newton, as Cowper put it, "the sagacious reader of the works of God," whom, in James Thompson's formula, "God to mortals lent to trace her boundless works." He turned now with extraordinary care to the history of the sciences and came to the conclusion that the pursuit of science had in the past proved more effective and was now more in keeping with modern needs than any traditional institution, church or state. The social and moral effect of scientific work struck him as immensely far-reaching; it was a source of meaning and stability far beyond its immediate application; as a system of order it was preferable, certainly, to any contemporary theory of political action. The central concept which he derived from his scientific studies, the principle of morphology, offered him descriptive and instrumental models in nearly all the spheres of his interest, anthropological, sociological, and poetological. To gain categories of such a comprehensive usefulness seemed to him amply to justify the enormous expense of time which, however amateurishly, he devoted to scientific inquiry.

His unyielding opposition to Newton, pushed to entirely unreasonable lengths, must be seen as a symbolic formula for two basic contentions which he defended vigorously at a time when, under the pressure of the Revolution, the issue of the social efficacy of science was widely discussed. The one was that a theory of physics such as Newton had proposed rested on mathematical and not on empirical premises, which in turn meant a denial of that concreteness of observation and reflection on which much of his own life and work had proceeded. Newtonian science, abstract and non-empirical, whatever its resultant technological achievements, meant, moreover, as he saw it, an abdication of an important kind of responsibility on the part of the inquiring mind. He was horrified to conclude that Newton's theories were likely to lead to "a discussion of color by blind physicists." His own science of color rested in large measure on physiological observations and on a high regard for the eye as an instrument centrally necessary at all stages of reflection. It was on that interplay between the physiological and the power of abstraction that not only his view of science but his conception of poetry ultimately depended.

His master was and remained Buffon; his most congenial allies were later to be Cuvier and Geoffroy de St. Hilaire. But it was another aspect of science that seemed to him of large philosophical and social consequence: its history offered, he thought, the only justification of a belief in progress. Political history struck him as largely an arbitrary and self-serving construct; the history of scientific effort, on the contrary, can only be read as an impressive chain of trial and error, of stubborn perseverance, of constant testing and revision. His own immensely rich and circumspect survey of those who had contributed to the evolution of the science of color confirmed this soberly optimistic view. It amounted to a counter-statement to Schiller's abstract eschatological concept of history.

Any just appraisal of Goethe's share in the classical epoch of German literature must recognize his acceptance of the conclusion, later so compellingly argued by Hegel, that the age of poetry, that is to say, the age in which the imagination could operate persuasively without a close awareness of contemporary thought and science, had come to an end. Science (and here Goethe continued resolutely in the mode of the *Encyclopédie* and of the Enlightenment) offered in its ever more cosmopolitan transnational operations the kind of institution which, like the comparable prospect of a world literature, had the unmistakable signature of modernism properly understood. The self-reflective subjectivism of the young Romantics was, he argued in an essay on

"Forced Talents," farther from an awareness of the modern temper than the hypotheses of scholars in biology, physiology, or mineralogy, who were united in a truly civilizing enterprise of modern scientific traffic.

Goethe's strong determination not to be drawn into spiritualist abstraction distinguished his own contribution to the Weimar program of anti-political, anti-revolutionary classicism from the retreat into aesthetic idealism which Schiller propounded as the core of his theory of culture. It was to be Schiller's advocacy of a radical, if at times utopian, idealism that inspired and ennobled the political protests of the nineteenth century. A year after his death, Prussia was defeated at Jena; by 1812, the historical constellation had taken on a new urgency for the German states. Patriotic and cultural nationalism, aroused by a conservative, Christian, neo-feudal philosophy (which Friedrich Schlegel helped to formulate after 1808 as a propagandist for the reactionary Austrian government) had made the classicist project at best a courageous experiment.

Our own critical views of that brilliant phase in European history have differentiated its presumed unity, have identified its several intellectual ingredients and recognized its role as one of several modes in which the contemporaneous experience shaped itself. We have come to see it as a relatively brief moment of spectacular creative abundance in which nearly all intellectual and aesthetic concerns of the eighteenth century converged and classical and romantic sensibilities sprang almost simultaneously from an awareness of revolutionary challenges. If in this complex of theories and styles, of proclamations and movements we focus on the special character of German classicism, we can best do it justice, beyond exploring the splendor of its poetic achievement, by recognizing it as one of the strategies by which, in a long-confined society, the modern "bourgeois" consciousness was articulated and brought into effective play, as an exemplary effort to give institutional legitimacy to the pursuit of art and literature at a time when the subjective imagination threatened to emancipate itself from its sustaining society.

New York Lawyers and the Coming of the American Revolution

MILTON M. KLEIN

In his famous Speech on Conciliation with America delivered in the House of Commons on March 22, 1775, Edmund Burke paid his respects to the colonial lawyers as one source of that "fierce spirit of liberty" which made the problem of easing the imperial crisis so difficult:

> In no country, perhaps, in the world is the law so general a study. The profession itself is numerous and powerful, and in most provinces it takes the lead. The greater number of deputies sent to the Congress were lawyers. But all who read, and most do read, endeavor to obtain some smattering in that science. I have been told by an eminent bookseller, that in no branch of his business, after tracts of popular devotion, were so many books as those on the law exported to the plantations.

Why, then, queried Burke, had not such knowledge taught the Americans more clearly the nature of their "obligations to obedience, and the penalties of rebellion"? Simply because Britain had not managed to win over such knowledge to the service of the Crown. Instead, study of the law rendered the colonists "stubborn and litigious . . .

From *New York History,* 55 (Oct. 1974).

dextrous, prompt in attack, [and] ready in defence" of their legal rights. A citizenry so well versed in law and led by lawyers did not await grievances to assay the evil of the principles on which they were grounded; rather it anticipated the evils of the grievances to the degree that they violated the principles which Americans held dear. Such a people "augur misgovernment at a distance, and sniff the approach of tyranny in every tainted breeze."[1]

At the turn of the nineteenth century, George Otto Trevelyan, the Whig historian of the Revolution, encapsulated Burke's sentiments in a neater exposition. Lawyers, he observed, should have been loyalists by and large since many of them held positions under the Crown, and all who practiced in the courts were, in effect, public servants of the royal governments; but instead, he noted, "most lawyers were patriots, for the same reason that . . . every patriot was, or thought himself, a lawyer."[2]

Subsequent historians have not capitalized on either Burke's or Trevelyan's perceptive observations, nor have numerous schools of historians since rendered any more tribute to the legal profession than did the revolutionary generation itself. Participants in the Revolution gave the leading role to lawyers by naming thirty members of the bar to the First Continental Congress (out of a total delegation of fifty-six), by having twenty-five lawyers affix their signatures to the Declaration of Independence (about half that constellation of immortals), and by sending no less than thirty-one of the profession (about half of all the delegates) to sit in Philadelphia during the summer of 1787 and organize that "more perfect union" which marked the close of the revolutionary era. Yet the task of appraising their role in these events and of elucidating its meaning has thus far eluded historiographical treatment.

Revolutions, of course, are very complex affairs, and their precise political and social anatomy has defied analysis despite generations of scholarly postmortems. The study of leadership in the making and shaping of revolutions is no less fascinating but equally elusive. Those of our own day that go by the name of "black revolution" or "student revolution" are illustrative case studies in the complexity of the problem. Intuitive and superficial examinations produced the hasty conclusion that these disruptions in the social order were led by the most disadvantaged elements in those communities, those elements most disturbed by the material deprivations of the system and hence reacting on the most personal of grounds—self-interest. Closer and more systematic analysis has disclosed a surprisingly different collective portrait—of individuals more rooted in the community than rootless, more prosperous than deprived, more fortunate than unsuccessful, and more disinterested than self-interested.

For that distant event called the American Revolution, we are indebted to two centuries of amateur and professional diagnosticians, but we are not much closer to concluding our postmortems as to the nature or the leadership of the affair. It is not likely that the approaching bicentennial celebration will complete the analysis or terminate the discussion; it will merely escalate the level of historiographical activity and proliferate the multiplicity of scholarly findings. Historians would not want it otherwise. How else would they find grist for their never-ending intellectual and literary mills? Carl Becker, who delighted in criticizing the historianship of others even more than he enjoyed writing history himself, once confessed that he secretly hoped the day would never come when "all fields of history having been 'definitely' done and presented in properly dull and documented monographs, the final synthesis could be made." What, he worried, would historians do then?[3] If Thomas Jefferson's forewarning was at all omniscient, we need not worry about the historiography of the Revolution. Responding in 1815 to John Adams's query, "Who shall write the history of the American revolution? Who can write it? Who will ever be able to write it?" Jefferson said:

> Nobody; except merely its external facts. All its councils, designs, and discussions, having been conducted by Congress with closed doors, and no members, as far as I know, having ever made notes of them, those, which are the life and soul of history must forever be unknown.[4]

Jefferson's gloomy forecast has not been entirely realized, although his warning may well give us pause as we immodestly attempt to confound it by the diligence and extent of our modern researches. But surely we have learned much about the American Revolution since its first chroniclers crudely narrated the event for posterity; and we are able with hindsight to diagnose somewhat better its anatomy. Crane Brinton's effort in 1938 to do just that for the American, French, Russian, and English Revolutions concluded that, as to leadership, all four revealed an extraordinary degree of moderation but that the American Revolution, particularly, was led by men who were of "striking respectability and excellent social standards."[5] More sophisticated and recent attempts to construct a theory of revolution modify Brinton's generalizations considerably but help little in understanding the American Revolution. Its leadership was not that of an aggrieved peasantry, a millenarian and charismatic single figure, a palace guard, a jacquerie, a nostalgic group of reactionaries, or a militarized mass in insurrection.[6] Its roots seem to have been less economic, sociological, or psychological than political, and central to any political revolution—in the view of today's theorists—is the role of an elite which feels itself alienated from the existing political order.[7]

If it is the anomie of the elite which caused the American Revolution—or which was its underlying imperative—then an analysis of the composition, nature, and mentality of this elite should tell us much of the character of the Revolution itself. That the colonies had developed such "stable, coherent, effective, and acknowledged local political and social elites," with considerable experience, visibility, authority, and broad public support seems amply demonstrable.[8] That astute if biased observer of events in colonial New York, Cadwallader Colden, adumbrated the findings of later social psychologists in noting, in 1732, that "few instances can be given where great changes were brought to effect, in any state, but when they were headed by Rich and powerful men; any other commotions generally only produced short lived disorders and Confusions."[9] It is a commonplace, too, to distinguish certain professional and occupational groups among this American elite: the merchants, the planters, the newspaper printers and editors, the clergy, and the lawyers; but the role of each of these groups in the leadership of the Revolution is not equally well known. Almost fifteen years ago, I called attention to the fact that while there were excellent monographs on the part played by the merchants, the clergy, and the press in the coming of the Revolution, there were none on the lawyers.[10] Since that time, we have had two more published studies on the influence of religion and the clergy but not one on the lawyers.[11] The neglect is not surprising when it is learned that between 1861 and 1972, of all the dissertations completed during that century—and there were over 400,000, some 14,000 of them in history—only 22 deal with law and lawyers and only 5 of them with members of the colonial or revolutionary bar. One treats of the relation of English law to the coming of the Revolution, one deals with Virginia lawyers, two with the Massachusetts bar, and only one covers the legal career of an early New York lawyer.[12]

The myopia of later Americans was not shared by the earliest historians of the Revolution on this side of the Atlantic. One of the first patriot accounts, that of David Ramsay, emphasized how much the event was a lawyer affair:

> Of the whole number of deputies which formed the Continental Congress of 1774, one half were lawyers. Gentlemen of that profession had acquired, the confidence of the inhabitants by their exertion in the common cause. The previous measures in the respective provinces had been planned and carried into effect, more by lawyers than by any other order of men. Professionally taught the rights of the people, they were among the foremost to decry every attack made on their liberties. Bred in the habits of public speaking, they made a distinguished figure in the meetings of the people, and were particularly able to explain to them the tendency of the late acts of Parliament. Exerting their abilities and influence in the cause of their country, they were rewarded with its confidence.[13]

If the Revolution was indeed precipitated by the actions of the colonies' social and political elite, then lawyers not unexpectedly took high rank in that privileged order. "Lawyer or merchant are the fairest titles our towns afford," wrote the Frenchman Crèvecoeur as he explained to his countrymen just what an American was like.[14] Of all the professional groups in the colonies—and they make up only 1–2 percent of the population—lawyers constituted the vast proportion, some 70 percent. And they were the wealthiest of all the professionals, earning as a group ten times as much as doctors and ministers and as much as the very wealthiest merchants and planters.[15] A recent study of some 231 high office holders in all the colonies finds that while planters and merchants included some who possessed average wealth only, all the lawyers in this group were wealthy or well-to-do.[16] Commenting on the economic status of lawyers in Virginia shortly after the Revolution, the French traveler La Rochefoucault-Liancourt observed: "The profession of a lawyer is here, as in every other part of America, one of the most profitable."[17]

How, then, are we to explain the relative inattention paid by historians to the vital role played by this signally important intellectual group in the coming of the Revolution? Apart from the sheer magnitude of the task—scores of important figures and hundreds of lesser ones must be dealt with—perhaps historiography and self-imagery suggest an explanation. The earliest historians of the Revolution represented the event as the rising of a united people, "under no general influence, but that of their personal feelings and opinions," led by no special powerful individuals, and motivated by democratic sentiments produced by "nature and society" with which they "grew up, from their earliest infancy."[18] George Bancroft, who fixed this view in our historiographical literature for more than a half-century, reiterated that the Revolution stemmed from "the excitement of a whole people." Each event in the unfolding process was ascribed to the efforts of a united citizenry. It was universal watchfulness that prevented Britain from eroding American rights and liberties by the Stamp Act; and the "whole continent" applauded the sacking of Hutchinson's house in Boston. Obviously, there was no need to stress the leadership role of any group in a movement which did not stem from the novelty of any single tax but was deeply rooted, divinely ordained, and one "which no human policy or force could hold back"—"as certain as the decrees of eternity."[19] This nationalist school of historians would have found it awkward to suggest that the American people had to be led into revolution by any elite segment rather than arising in righteous unity to achieve a heaven-sent mission.

The Progressive historians, who dominated American historiography at the beginning of the twentieth century, emphasized internal conflicts within the colonies and economic and social issues within the empire. For one of these, Louis Hacker, the contest was not at all over "high-sounding political and constitutional concepts: over the power of taxation and, in the final analysis, over natural rights." It was, rather, issues such as manufacturing, trade, currency, and western lands which lay at the heart of the struggle.[20] And to another historian of this persuasion, Arthur M. Schlesinger,

> The popular view of the Revolution as a great forensic controversy over abstract rights will not bear close scrutiny. . . . At best, an exposition of the political theories of the anti-parliamentary party is an account of their retreat from one strategic position to another. . . . it may as well be admitted that the colonists would have lost their case if the decision had turned upon an impartial consideration of the legal principles involved.[21]

To historians for whom principle was subordinate to material self-interest, and legal rhetoric a mere camouflage for more basic matters of economic and financial import, the role of lawyers was necessarily minimal. For the Progressives, the Revolution was made in the streets, not in the council chambers; and artisans, merchants, and planters were the protagonists, if not the heroes. Far from stressing the role of law in American history, the Progressives emphasized that "lawlessness has been and is one of the most distinctive American traits." In the dual movement which the Revolution represented to Carl Becker, legal resistance was employed in the contest with England; but in the more important struggle over who should rule at home, spontaneous explosions of popular feeling and outbursts of mass violence were more determinative of events than those petitions and resolves which bespoke constitutional and legal principles.[22]

Curiously, members of the legal profession did not fare much better with the neo-Conservative school of American historiography which flowered in the post-World War II era. For a principal spokesman of this school, Daniel Boorstin, what distinguished the American Revolution from others was its failure to give birth to a new political theory. Assuming that American history represented a continuity based upon those persistent values that were "givens" from the past, Boorstin stressed the failure of the Revolution to disrupt this continuity by producing any new dogma. At best, the event was for Americans merely an opportunity to affirm what was traditionally British in their heritage. If lawyers argued the case at all, it was not as theorists but merely as more articulate spokesmen of sentiments which all Americans understood—their English birthright. In a curious paradox, Boorstin concedes that what was at issue in 1776 was not a large political principle but merely a technical legal question, the constitution of the empire. The Declaration of Independence thus did not have to expound any new "high-flown political philosophy"; Americans already possessed it. Yet while one would have expected Boorstin thereupon to emphasize the role of the bar in expostulating the American legal position, he does not, escaping the dilemma by suggesting that since all Americans were versed in law, they required no specialists to speak for them. It was the "universal voice of our country" (quoting Jefferson) which responded to the British challenge. English principles did not have to be justified anew: they were already well known; no new American principles had to be explained: they were still to be discovered. In an era of law without lawyers, of institutions and principles so "given" that they need not be reduced to theoretical definition, there was obviously no call for lawyers to make the American case.[23]

One of the most recent schools of historiography, represented by Bernard Bailyn, stresses the centrality of the new world view which Americans developed by 1776 of their relationship with Great Britain. The sources of this general mood or "map of social reality," which Bailyn designated as ideology, were widespread; and they included the tradition of English common law. But, as Bailyn defined it, common law was less a collection of legal principles and experiences than "a form of history" which, presumably, was understood, appreciated, and cited by broader elements in the population than merely the practitioners of the law. Besides, common law as a source of American ideology ranked well below Enlightenment ideas and attitudes, the Classics, New England Puritan thought, and the political theories of the English "Commonwealthmen" in shaping American perceptions of themselves and their relationship with Britain. In any case, what moved Americans to action in 1776, according to Bailyn, was a cluster of fears, emotions, and convictions of almost evangelical fervor arising from their settled belief that the colonists' whole way of life was being endangered by British tyranny. Surely, the "abstruse points of constitutional law that so engaged the mind" of lawyers like John Adams did not propel Americans into revolution; implicitly, neither did the lawyers.[24]

For the most recent school of American historians, the angry young men of the profession and its "New Left," lawyers no less than merchants, planters, and clergymen represent skewed mirrors of the past. Our preoccupation with their thoughts and deeds has caused us to view history from the top down. These radical members of the profession would prefer an account from the other perspective, and although they have not yet drawn its outlines fully, it is clear that the history of the powerless and the inarticulate will not be exposited in their pages through the mouths of the lawyer class.[25]

Explanatory as our historiographical survey is for the neglect of the lawyers, it is insufficient; but it is buttressed by a historical phenomenon. The revolutionary generation may have been led by lawyers, but it was also suspicious of them. It was as much mistrustful of law as it was willing to employ the law in defense of its constitutional rights. The love-hate syndrome extended into the years of the early republic, when Jeffersonians attacked the common law for its intricacies and its authoritarianism, yet were unwilling to abandon it. The American constitutional system, it was clear, was based on principles of law, equity, and justice, but these principles ought to be so plain and simple that any man could understand them. The spirit of the law was the foundation of republican virtue; its letter must not be appropriated by shrewd lawyers as an instrument of antirepublican self-interest.[26] The ambivalence of early America was neatly expressed by James Fenimore Cooper's Natty Bumppo: "The law—'tis bad to have it, but I sometimes think it is worse to be entirely without it."[27]

The dualism was evident in colonial America. New York's merchant prince John Watts was an intimate of the colony's lawyers and employed them in his own business; yet he denounced the law as a "System of confounding other People and picking their Pockets." William Livingston studied the law and became a leading member of the profession, but he objected to many of its principles as against "Reason and common sense" and many of its practitioners as "unletter'd Blockheads."[28] The general attitude was early expressed by a Welshman after a fifteen-year residence in Pennsylvania: "Of Lawyers and Physicians I shall say nothing, because this Country is very Peaceable and Healthy; long may it so continue and never have occasion for the Tongue of the one, or the Pen of the other, both equally destructive of Men's Estates and Lives. . . ."[29] Governor Bellomont echoed the same complaint at almost the same time in New York, informing the British authorities at home that the province's lawyers bore such "a scandalous character" that it would grieve an Englishman to see his noble laws so "miserably managed and prophaned" in the colony.[30] Despite the increasing professionalization of the law by the eve of the Revolution, the rising social and economic status of the bar, and its improved qualifications for practice, the lawyer class remained publicly suspect. Elections, such as those in 1768 and 1769 in New York, could turn upon the success of one faction in persuading the public that its opponents were led by lawyers and by proposing for public debate the question "Whether a Lawyer could possibly be an honest Man."[31]

It is this double vision with regard to the law that explains why colonial Americans could permit the lawyers to be their spokesmen in the debate with the mother country without abandoning their intrinsic distrust of the profession, why they could continue to regard courts as sources of both protection and of persecution.[32] It also explains (or at least clarifies) why New York, which was the scene of some of the most turbulent lawlessness during the years 1765–1776, was at the same time under the leadership of lawyers.

In view of this confusion of public attitudes, the magnitude of the task, and the problem of inadequate sources of information, it would seem foolhardy and fatuous to define precisely what the role of the lawyers was. But a tentative hypothesis in the form of a paradigm is at hand. It is not even original but can be drawn almost intact from the paradigm which Arthur M. Schlesinger offered over fifty years ago to explain the evolution of merchant leadership during the revolutionary era. In his study, Schlesinger postulated that the merchants went through several fairly distinct phases of opposition to British measures after 1763. Basically conservative in temperament and socio-economic disposition, the merchants responded cautiously to the economic challenge of the Revenue Act of 1764, urging legislative protests and organizing local nonconsumption societies. The Stamp Act was broader in impact, affecting other than the commercial classes. It consequently elevated the controversy, provided a broader ground for opposition, and unfortunately enlisted the lower classes into the protest movement. While a "little mobbing" was useful to give point to the constitutional argument, violence was a two-edged sword, as dangerous to men of property as to the officers of the Crown. The merchants no less than the southern planters "lent the weight of their influence against popular demonstrations." Repeal of the Stamp Act obviated a confrontation between merchant leadership and the "rougher" elements who had intruded into the ranks of the antiparliamentary forces. The Townshend Acts revived both merchant countermeasures and the division within the American leadership. The commercial classes, repelled by their experience in 1765–1766, were more than ever resolved "to conduct their campaign for redress along legal and peaceful lines." The extended duration of this second contest with England made such a moderate course even more difficult than before, violence soon erupting in the form of smuggling, tarring and feathering of customs officials, and the destruction of royal naval vessels. By the end of the campaign against the Townshend Acts, the merchants were fully alienated from the more radical lower classes. In Cadwallader Colden's words, as men of property, they were "so sensible of their danger, from Riots and tumults" that they would not "readily be induced to enter into combinations, which may promote disorder for the future, but will endeavour to promote due subordination to legal authority."[33]

When the Tea Act and Boston's "tea party" revived the imperial crisis, the merchants were placed on the horns of a dilemma. The rising tide of radicalism threatened to change the character of the antiparliamentary opposition and to place its leadership in new hands. Some merchants withdrew entirely from the now extralegal movement, reflected in the actions of the First Continental Congress. These men ultimately became tories. Others among the moderates, equally disturbed by the changed complexion of the colonial protest movement, chose perforce to remain within its ranks in order to curb its temper and to control its course. While independence sheared off still additional moderates and made them active loyalists, those merchants who remained patriots exerted sufficient influence to insure the ultimate victory of conservative principles in the Federal Constitution of 1787.[34]

New York's lawyers fit Schlesinger's paradigm almost perfectly, but if anything, their role in each phase of its development is even more sharply etched and their imprint more deliberately impressed. And, more, the lawyers in New York began playing out their role even before the imperial crisis became full-blown. If the central question confronting colonists and Englishmen during the fateful decade after 1765 was the proper constitutional relationship between provinces and mother country, then lawyers in New York had defined the lines of disagreement years before. In response to the British contention that the plantations overseas were mere corporations of the Crown, ruled through royal instructions by the King's viceroys, the governors, three of New York's lawyers argued as early as 1754 that the colony possessed by virtue of long usage a "Political Frame and Constitution" that no royal instructions could "Destroy nor Restrain inlarge nor Abridge."[35] If the political ideology which nurtured the Revolution was the fear of encroaching prerogative power at the expense of popular liberties, then these same lawyers had given New Yorkers fair warning, as early as 1753, that an institution such as a college founded by royal charter stood on precarious grounds. If it was "the King's Prerogative, to grant a Charter," it was also his prerogative "to grant it upon certain Terms" and also to abrogate it for noncompliance. A college established by act of Assembly, in contrast, provided surety of its permanence and also of its representative character, since the Assembly which created it would itself be truly representative of the entire political community.[36]

If, as the Declaration of Independence put it, the Crown had sought to establish a tyranny over the colonies by making judges dependent upon the Crown for the tenure of their offices, then, again, New York's lawyers had made that point emphatically by their strenuous contest with Lieutenant Governor Colden over that very issue between 1760 and 1762. The Crown was victorious, but for two years lawyers reiterated to New Yorkers the danger to popular rights of a judiciary sitting at royal pleasure. More, New Yorkers had been assured that for English judges to serve on more secure terms than their American counterparts was to deprive Englishmen overseas of the "Liberties and Privileges" possessed by their countrymen at home, an invidious distinction. And, if the Declaration of Independence reminded Americans of the threat to their ancient right of trial by jury through the establishment of juryless Admiralty Courts in the colonies, New York's lawyers had already sounded that alarm in 1764, when Colden challenged the inviolability of the decision of a jury in a civil suit. With near unanimity, New York's bar insisted, in public and private, that Colden's action threatened "to deprive the Subject of his most valuable Rights" and to subvert the constitution of the province.[37]

Like the merchants, New York's lawyers responded to Britain's new imperial policy out of self-interest as well as principle; but unlike the former, principle was for the members of the bar neither adventitious nor supererogatory; it was both the language and the substance of their profession. Coke was "the lamp by which young [American] Aladdins of the law secured their juristic treasures," and Coke had been the champion of English opposition to the extension of royal prerogative and the source of the notion that there was a fundamental law controlling even the acts of Parliament.[38] New York's lawyers were undoubtedly social conservatives, linked by ties of blood, marriage, and economic interest to the ruling commercial and landed families; but, in the words of Richard B. Morris, they nevertheless "acted with plausible consistency in erecting a code of political liberalism upon the legal foundations of social reaction to which they were devoutly attached."[39] Three of the colony's young lawyers had gone beyond Coke, and in the pages of a popular journal of the mid-eighteenth century expounded in peculiarly American idiom the political philosophy of the English Commonwealthmen that ultimately became appropriated by the Americans for their own.[40]

In action, New York's lawyers behaved much like Schlesinger's merchants between 1764 and 1776. They protested the Revenue Act and the Stamp Act on constitutional grounds, penning the New York Assembly's petitions on the subject to King, Lords, and Commons. These legislative resolves, adopted on October 18, 1764, have been described by one modern historian as "among the great state papers of the pre-Revolutionary period."[41] They took an advanced position on the illegality of both the revenue measures and the contemplated stamp duties. Rejecting any distinction between external and internal taxes, the Assembly insisted that "all Impositions, whether they be internal Taxes, or Duties paid, for what we consume, equally diminish the Estates upon which they are charged." The new acts deprived New Yorkers not only of this birthright but also of the benefits of the common law, by placing enforcement in the hands of admiralty courts which "proceed not according [to] the old wholesom[e] laws of the land." Disclaiming any aspiration to independence, the Assembly nevertheless challenged all attempts to deprive the colonists of rights long enjoyed and "established in the first Dawn of our Constitution." And in an even more advanced statement of the American case, the petition to the House of Commons argued that the right to exemption from any but self-imposed taxes was a "natural Right of Mankind."[42]

In addition to their reactive measures in the halls of the legislature, the lawyers, like Schlesinger's merchants, were not unwilling to have opposition voiced in the streets as well; and a number of them were active members of the Sons of Liberty, both in New York City and in Albany. But as violence erupted and disobedience rather than non-compliance was urged upon them, the lawyers drew back, fearful—in the words of William Smith, Jr.—that "partial tumults" would escalate into "a general Civil War [that] will light up and rage all along the Continent" and lead to a "most Melancholy State of Anarchy under the Government of a Mob."[43] British officers were certain that the lawyers were the source from which the Stamp Act troubles flowed; the members of the bar were "at the bottom" of the "disloyal Insur[r]ection . . . the Hornets and Firebrands" of the violence.[44] What these observers did not record was the alacrity with which these same lawyers sought to quell the disorders and quiet public tempers and their refusal to accede to radical pressure that the courts be opened and legal business conducted without stamps. Lawyers instead took vacations; commercial litigation ceased; only criminal cases which did not require use of the hated stamps were tried between November 1765 and April 1766. The lawyers might pen fiery resolves and encourage the development of home industries through the establishment of a "Society for the Promotion of Arts, Agriculture and Oeconomy"; but they would not defy the law by doing business without stamps. As with the merchants, their separation from the radicals had begun.[45]

Lawyer William Smith, Jr., penned the Assembly's address of thanks to the Crown for the repeal of the Stamp Act. It emphasized both the "due subordination of the Colonies, to the Mother Country" and "an equal distribution of Rights" between the inhabitants of both. The sentiments were so unexceptionable that even the Council and the governor could endorse them. The moderation of the Assembly was revealed, too, in its action to erect an equestrian statue of George III and an "eloquent" one of Pitt in appreciation of their friendship for the American colonies.[46] The lawyers expressed their own conservatism by assuming leading roles in the prosecution of tenant rioters on the Hudson Valley estates who took violent action during the spring of 1766 to improve the terms of their leases. The bar's posture as advocates of law and order in this instant led one of the accused to sneer, at his trial, that if opposition to government constituted the crime for which he was being prosecuted, then none of the lawyers who sat on the court was himself guiltless.[47]

The Townshend Acts revived the estrangement between the lawyer-moderates and the more radical elements of the American opposition. Lawyer Robert R. Livingston's hopes that "our disputes will end, and the greatest harmony will subsist between us and our mother country" were shattered.[48] Again, the members of the bar sought to secure redress through lawful means, two of them penning "proper and constitutional Resolves" to the Crown and Parliament on the Assembly's behalf, late in 1768. The legislative addresses asserted "the Rights of his Majesty's Subjects within this Colony, which they conceive have been greatly abridged and infringed."[49] The abridgment to which the Assembly referred was not merely the new revenue measures but also the infamous suspension of the New York Assembly for failing to comply with the letter of the Quartering Act. When the legislature circumvented the act by a voluntary grant for troop support, the radicals accused it of kowtowing to Parliament and in the elections of 1768 and 1769 blasted the lawyers as "a pack of hipocritical, Cheating, Lying, canting, illdesigning Scoundrels."[50]

Nevertheless, the lawyers persisted in keeping the opposition to Britain within constitutional bounds, penning a second set of appeals, on the Assembly's behalf, to the Crown and the House of Lords in the spring of 1769. As in the earlier resolves, they disclaimed any notions of independence but stood firm on the right of New Yorkers "by uninterrupted Usage" to "a civil Constitution" and to an equality with Englishmen that "no Distance from the Mother Country" could diminish. Accepting general parliamentary authority, the Assembly rejected the idea of virtual representation as impractical and claimed exemption from all taxes not levied by the colonies' own legislatures. In blunter language than before, and reflective of the pressure of the more radical elements in the New York population, the address to the House of Lords noted gloomily that the colony's "confidence in the Tenderness of Great-Britain, seems to have suffered a very sensible Abatement." "We are Englishmen," the petitions declared, "and, as such, presume ourselves entitled to the Rights and Liberties, which have rendered the Subjects of *England* the Envy of All Nations."[51]

Britain's retreat in 1770 brought a three-year period of relief to New York's troubled legal profession. United in their insistence on colonial rights, they were already beginning to be divided in their view as to how best to assert those rights. Of the old triumvirate of lawyers who had led the constitutional opposition thus far, John Morin Scott became increasingly radical, William Smith, Jr., assumed a seat on the Governor's Council and turned increasingly conservative, and William Livingston, standing midway between them, abandoned the province for a country home in New Jersey. But the moderates were strengthened by the rise of a newer and younger group of attorneys, safely conservative, such as John Jay and James Duane. Political divisions were subordinated, however, as the members of the bar debated technical questions of law in their professional society, The Moot, where "any discourse about the Party Politics of this Province" was strictly forbidden. The differences could not be entirely ignored, and in a Debating Society, less restricted in its deliberations, lawyers Robert R. Livingston and Egbert Benson wrestled with the question of whether colonial liberties and the "just Ballance" of the constitution were more endangered by the "additional Weight of Influence . . . gained by the People" than by the increasingly oppressive conduct of the Crown.[52]

The tea episode of 1773 and its consequences confronted the New York bar with more than an academic exercise; and the lawyers, like the merchants, faced their penultimate dilemma. Future loyalists like William Smith, Jr., strove for accommodation with the Crown but took no part in the extralegal apparatus of committees and mass meetings created to pursue the contest. Other future loyalists like Peter Van Schaack were willing to serve in these extralegal bodies during the initial phases of their activity but then bowed out, not persuaded that British measures were "undue and oppressive" enough to constitute the "system of slavery" of which more militant patriots were already convinced.[53] Equally conservative lawyers like Robert R. Livingston, James Duane, and John Jay chose to remain within the revolutionary movement, despite their distaste for its excesses. Like William Smith, they dreaded "the Violence of the lower Sort"; but prudence dictated, in the words of Robert R. Livingston, "the propriety of swimming with a stream, which it is impossible to stem." Livingston's dictum explains the grounds on which many of the patriot lawyers made their ultimate decision for independence: "I long ago advised that they should yield to the torrent if they hoped to direct its course." James Duane thought similarly. The prospect of a permanent rupture with the mother country was a "most dangerous Extremity," but if the sword had to be drawn by the Americans, licentiousness must be prevented by placing command of the troops "in the hands of Men of property and Rank who, by that means, will preserve the same Authority over the Minds of the people which they enjoyed in the Hour of Tranquillity."[54] Duane's modern biographer notes that this New York patrician became a rebel "through necessity," that of keeping an independent state from surrendering to the dangers of mob rule, and "to save her from the excesses of democracy." The point was not missed by the mob leaders of 1776: rich and designing men were assuming active leadership of the movement for independence so that it would "not . . . go too fast and run into danger." William Gordon, the contemporary historian of the Revolution, confirmed the basis of the conservatives' seemingly paradoxical decision to join the revolutionary tide: "The people were ripe for it [i.e., independence]. Prudence dictated a compliance with their expectations and wishes. A disappointment might have disgusted, and produced disorder."[55]

Hence conservative lawyers like Duane, Livingston, and Jay attended the First Continental Congress as delegates from New York. Here they joined the conciliationists, fought for the Galloway Plan of union, and pursued every effort to end the "unnatural convulsions" by lawful means. As late as January 1776, they were hoping for reconciliation; and when in that month a self-styled Scottish nobleman, Lord Drummond, came to Philadelphia with a compromise peace plan, allegedly from Lord North himself, it was to Duane, Jay, and Livingston that he hurried, having been assured that the New Yorkers were most likely to be sympathetic to any plan for accommodation.[56] And it was New York's lawyer-led delegation which delayed the province's approval of the decision for independence so long that an irritated John Adams complained: "What is the reason that New York must continue to embarrass the Continent?"[57]

With independence effected, New York's conservative lawyers strove to insure that the new state constitution would retain power in the hands of those same men of rank and property who had held them in the earlier "Hour of Tranquillity." The constitution of 1777 was essentially the work of the lawyers Jay, Duane, Livingston, and Gouverneur Morris, with Jay playing the central role. Despite some democratic features, the constitution as adopted represented, on the whole, "a victory for the minority of stability and privilege."[58] New York's was one of the more conservative of the new state constitutions, yet it did not guarantee that permanency of control for the "better sort" that James Duane had hoped for. And herein lies the irony in the role played by the lawyers in this enigmatic drama. Devoted to conservatism but arguing their case against Britain on the highest grounds of legality and constitutionalism, they were driven by the logic of their exposition and the language of their rhetoric to become republicans despite themselves. The differences in temperament, social position, economic status, and political principles that made patriots of some lawyers and loyalists of others are barely discernible. The profession appears to have split almost evenly on the issue of independence. Of 36 lawyers practicing in the New York Supreme Court between 1762 and 1765, the position of 25 can be determined: 12 of these remained loyal, and 13 became patriots. A similar division marked the members of The Moot. Of 20 whose names are recorded in the club's minutes as members between 1770 and 1774, 9 can be identified as loyalists and 11 as patriots.[59]

What made republicans of some was neither change of economic and social position nor of principle; their "radical" posture after 1776 was rather the consequence of their earlier decision to swim with the tide in order to control its course. What the moderate men of the bar could not foresee was that their flaming rhetoric and high-sounding constitutionalism could be as useful in advancing democratic principles as in preserving conservative doctrines. The press, which moderate lawyers employed to plead for restraint and tempered action, made politics everyone's concern, especially in a province with a long history of political interest and dynamism such as New York; and whatever the intent, the language of moderation became the rhetoric of democracy.[60] The "new politics" that emerged in New York by 1776 was the lawyers' creation, but it could not remain their creature. Natural rights theory might be good old-fashioned English whiggism, but its limits far transcended Locke and limited monarchy when someone like Alexander Hamilton, perhaps innocently, converted it into words of timeless import:

> The sacred rights of mankind are not to be rummaged for, among old parchments, or musty records. They are written, as with a sun beam, in the whole *volume* of human nature, by the hand of the divinity itself; and can never be erased or obscured by mortal power.[61]

Nor could John Jay anticipate the implications of his reminder to the people of New York late in 1776 that "You and all men were created free, and . . . it is therefore . . . the duty of every man, to oppose and repell all those, by whatever name or title distinguished, who prostitute the powers of Government to destroy the happiness and freedom of the people over whom they may be appointed to rule."[62] Nor could William Livingston appreciate the infinitely prescient significance of his 1765 pronouncement that "Without liberty no man can be a subject. He is a slave."[63]

The republic which Americans finally fashioned in 1787 was not the one the lawyers anticipated in 1776, but it bore the stamp of their conservative legalism clothed in democratic dress, just as the moderate rebellion they visualized after 1765 became a revolution of transcending character by 1776. If their role in these events has not been better understood, it is perhaps because the lawyer class, as de Tocqueville observed in the 1830s,

> adapts itself with great flexibility to the exigencies of the time and accommodates itself without resistance to all the movements of the social body. But this party extends over the whole community and penetrates into all the classes which compose it; it acts upon the country imperceptibly, but finally fashions it to suit its own purposes.[64]

The lawyers who made the Revolution in New York accommodated themselves adroitly to its changing configurations, and in the process they fashioned it to suit their own purposes. But, ironically, and unperceived by the lawyers who were enacting the drama, they were also being acted upon by the force of events. They not only transformed the Revolution, they transformed themselves; and they became thereby bulwarks of constitutional republicanism as they had once been supporters of constitutional monarchy.

NOTES

1 *The Writings and Speeches of Edmund Burke*, 12 vols. (Boston, 1901), II, 124–25.

2 George O. Trevelyan, *The American Revolution*, new ed., 4 vols. (London, 1905–13), I, 73.

3 Review of J. B. Black, *The Art of History*, in *American Historical Review*, 32 (1927), 295.

4 John Adams to Thomas Jefferson, July 30, 1815, Jefferson to Adams, Aug. 10, 1815, *The Adams-Jefferson Letters,* ed. Lester Cappon, 2 vols. (Chapel Hill, 1959), II, 451–52.

5 Crane Brinton, *The Anatomy of Revolution* (1938; Vintage ed., New York, 1957), p. 107.

6 Lawrence Stone, "Theories of Revolution," *World Politics,* 18 (1966), 159–76, particularly 162–63. The typology summarized by Stone is that of Chalmers Johnson.

7 On this, see Stone, "Theories of Revolution," p. 165; Harry Eckstein, "On the Etiology of Internal War," *History and Theory,* 4 (1965), 133–63; and Isaac Kramnick, "Reflections on Revolution: Definition and Explanation in Recent Scholarship," ibid., 11 (1972), 26–63.

8 See Jack Greene, "An Uneasy Connection: An Analysis of the Preconditions of the American Revolution," in Stephen Kurtz and James Hutson, eds., *Essays on the American Revolution* (Chapel Hill, 1973), pp. 35–36, and Greene, "Changing Interpretations of Early American Politics," in Ray A. Billington, ed., *The Reinterpretation of Early American History* (San Marino, Cal., 1966), pp. 171–77.

9 "The State of the Lands in the Province of New York, in 1732," in E. B. O'Callaghan, ed., *Documentary History of the State of New York,* 4 vols. (Albany, 1849–51), I, 385.

10 Klein, "Prelude to Revolution in New York: Jury Trials and Judicial Tenure," *William and Mary Quarterly,* 17 (1960), 440. The monographs to which attention was called were Arthur M. Schlesinger, *The Colonial Merchants and the American Revolution* (New York, 1918); Alice M. Baldwin, *The New England Clergy and the American Revolution* (Durham, N.C., 1928); Philip Davidson, *Propaganda and the American Revolution* (Chapel Hill, 1941); and Schlesinger, *Prelude to Independence: The Newspaper War on Britain, 1764–1776* (New York, 1958).

11 Carl Bridenbaugh, *Mitre and Sceptre: Transatlantic Faiths, Ideas, Personalities, and Politics, 1689–1775* (New York, 1962); and Alan Heimert, *Religion and the American Mind from the Great Awakening to the Revolution* (Cambridge, Mass., 1966).

12 *Comprehensive Dissertation Index, 1861–1972,* 37 vols. (Ann Arbor, 1973), XXVIII, 430–31. The number of dissertations listed in these volumes is about 417,000. The figure of 13,579 in history is given in Warren F. Kuehl, *Dissertations in History* (Lexington, 1972), p. x. The total includes U.S. and Canadian dissertations completed between 1873 and 1970.

13 David Ramsay, *History of the American Revolution,* 2 vols. (London, 1793; reprinted, New York, 1968), I, 134.

14 J. Hector St. John de Crèvecoeur, *Letters from an American Farmer* (1782; Dutton Everyman ed., New York, 1957), p. 36.

15 James Kirby Martin, *Men in Rebellion* (New Brunswick, N.J., 1973), pp. 66, 68–69; Jackson T. Main, *The Social Structure of Revolutionary America* (Princeton, 1965), p. 101.

16 Martin, *Men in Rebellion,* p. 85.

17 Quoted in Main, *Social Structure,* p. 102.

18 Jeremy Belknap, *History of New Hampshire* (1812), III, 172, quoted in Arthur H.

Schaffer, "The Shaping of a National Tradition: Historical Writing in America, 1783–1820" (Diss. UCLA 1966), p. 69; Samuel Williams, *Natural and Civil History of Vermont* (Walpole, N.H., 1794), p. 376; Ramsay, *American Revolution,* I, 31.

19 George Bancroft, *History of the United States from the Discovery of the American Continent,* 10 vols. (Boston, 1870–79), V, 291, 313, 321; VII, 21.

20 Louis M. Hacker, "The First American Revolution," *Columbia University Quarterly,* 27 (1935), 290.

21 Arthur M. Schlesinger, *New Viewpoints in American History* (New York, 1922), p. 179.

22 James T. Adams, "Our Lawless Heritage," *Atlantic Monthly,* 145 (1928), 732; Carl Becker, *History of Political Parties in the Province of New York* (Madison, Wis., 1909), pp. 21–22, 26, 28, 79–80; Arthur M. Schlesinger, "Political Mobs and the American Revolution, 1765–1776," *Proceedings of the American Philosophical Society,* 99 (1955), 244–50.

23 For Boorstin's views, see his *Genius of American Politics* (Chicago, 1953), ch. 3, and *The Americans: The Colonial Experience* (New York, 1958), pp. 191–205. For other neo-Conservative historians, who see the Revolution essentially as a war of national liberation, the transition from colonial to national status required no special philosophical or legalistic justification. See, for example, Thomas C. Barrow, "The American Revolution as a Colonial War for Independence," *William and Mary Quarterly,* 25 (1968), 452–64.

24 For Bailyn's view, see his *Ideological Origins of the American Revolution* (Cambridge, Mass., 1967), ch. 2, and "The Central Themes of the American Revolution," in Kurtz and Hutson, eds., *Essays on the American Revolution,* pp. 3–31.

25 For the New Left view of the Revolution, see Jesse Lemisch, "Jack Tar in the Streets: Merchant Seamen in the Politics of Revolutionary America," *William and Mary Quarterly,* 25 (1968), 371–407; and his "The American Revolution Seen from the Bottom Up," in Barton J. Bernstein, ed., *Towards a New Past: Dissenting Essays in American History* (New York, 1968), pp. 3–45.

26 On early America's ambivalence about the law, see Gordon S. Wood, *The Creation of the American Republic* (Chapel Hill, 1969), pp. 303–5; Linda Kerber, *Federalists in Dissent* (Ithaca, 1970), ch. 5; and Richard E. Ellis, *The Jeffersonian Crisis: Courts and Politics in the Young Republic* (New York, 1971), ch. 8.

27 James Fenimore Cooper, *The Prairie* (1827), quoted in Perry Miller, *The Life of the Mind in America* (New York, 1965), p. 99.

28 Watts to Sir William Baker Knight, Jan. 22, 1762, *Letter Book of John Watts* (N.Y. Historical Society Collections, 1928 [New York, 1928]), p. 13; *New-York Weekly Post-Boy,* Aug. 19, 1745; [William Livingston], *The Art of Pleading* (New York, 1751), p. 7.

29 Gabriel Thomas, *An Historical and Geographical Account of Pennsylvania and of West-New-Jersey* (London, 1698), in A. C. Myers, ed., *Narratives of Early Pennsylvania, West New Jersey, and Delaware, 1630–1707* (New York, 1912), p. 328.

30 Bellomont to the Lords of Trade, Dec. 15, 1698, in E. B. O'Callaghan, ed., *Documents Relative to the Colonial History of the State of New York,* 15 vols. (Al-

bany, 1856–87), IV, 441–42. See also "Representation of the Lords of Trade on the Administration of Justice in New-York," Dec. 14, 1699, ibid., pp. 598–99.

31 *New-York Gazette,* Feb. 15, 1768.

32 This is one of the paradoxes which Michael Kammen describes so incisively in his *People of Paradox* (New York, 1972). See pp. 240–41 for his comments on the law and the courts.

33 Colden to the Earl of Hillsborough, July 7, 1770, *N.Y. Col. Docs.*, VIII, 217.

34 Schlesinger's theme is expounded throughout his *Colonial Merchants and the American Revolution,* but it is briefly summed up in pp. 591–606.

35 "Wm. Bryant agt. John Obriant, In Error," [1754], William Smith Papers, New York Public Library; William Smith, Jr., *History of the Late Province of New-York,* 2 vols. (New York, 1829), II, 204–5.

36 William Livingston and others, *The Independent Reflector,* ed. Milton M. Klein (Cambridge, Mass., 1963), pp. 195, 197 (April 12, 1753).

37 On these two issues, see Klein, "Prelude to Revolution . . . ," *William and Mary Quarterly,* 17 (1960), 439–62.

38 On Coke, see Charles F. Mullett, "Coke and the American Revolution," *Economica,* 12 (1932), 457–71. Coke had declared that "when an act of Parliament is against common right and reason . . . the common law will control it, and adjudge such act to be void." Americans may well have misinterpreted Coke's intention in his pronouncement in this case. See Bailyn, *Ideological Origins,* p. 177 n.

39 Richard B. Morris, "Legalism versus Revolutionary Doctrine in New England," *New England Quarterly,* 4 (1931), 214.

40 Bernard Bailyn, *The Origins of American Politics* (New York, 1968), pp. 114, 128. A recent student of colonial history observes that "the more I read the Livingston articles in *The Independent Reflector* . . . , the more certain I become that Livingston most clearly articulated a mature version of the political ideology that Bailyn describes." Joseph J. Ellis, *The New England Mind in Transition: Samuel Johnson of Connecticut* (New Haven and London, 1973), p. 284.

41 The estimate is that of Bernhard Knollenberg in his *Origin of the American Revolution* (New York, 1960), p. 205.

42 *Journal of the Votes and Proceedings of the General Assembly of the Colony of New-York,* [1691–1765], 2 vols. (New York, 1764–66), II, 769–79. The petition to the King was penned by John Morin Scott, that to the Lords by William Livingston, and the one to the Commons by William Smith, Jr. See William H. W. Sabine, ed., *Historical Memoirs . . . of William Smith,* 2 vols. (New York, 1956, 1958), I, 24.

43 William Smith, Jr., to General Robert Monckton, Nov. 8, 1765, Chalmers Papers, N.Y., IV, 19–20, New York Public Library. On lawyers and judges in the Sons of Liberty, see Beverly McAnear, "The Albany Stamp Act Riots," *William and Mary Quarterly,* 4 (1947), 486–98; Roger Champagne, "Liberty Boys and Mechanics in New York City, 1764–1774," *Labor History,* 8 (1967), 115–35; and Herbert Morais, "The Sons of Liberty in New York," in Richard B. Morris, ed., *The Era of the American Revolution* (New York, 1939), pp. 272–73.

44 Gage to Henry S. Conway, Dec. 21, 1765, in Clarence E. Carter, ed., *The Correspondence of General Thomas Gage with the Secretaries of State . . . 1763–1775,*

2 vols. (New Haven, 1931–33), I, 79; G. D. Scull, ed., *The Montresor Journals* (N.Y. Historical Society Collections, 1881 [New York, 1882]), p. 339.

45 Herbert A. Johnson, "John Jay, Colonial Lawyer" (Diss. Columbia 1965), pp. 29, 41–43, 53–58, 61.

46 *Journal of the Votes and Proceedings of the General Assembly . . ., June 11, 1766, to July 3, 1766* (New York, 1766), pp. 10, 11, 16; "Address to the King from the Governor, Council and Assembly of New-York," June 24, 1766, CO 5/1098, Public Record Office, London; *Smith Memoirs,* I, 32.

47 Irving Mark, *Agrarian Conflicts in Colonial New York* (New York, 1940), ch. 5; *Montresor Journals,* p. 384.

48 Livingston to John Sargent, May 2, 1766, Robert R. Livingston Papers, Bancroft Transcripts, NYPL.

49 *Journal of the Votes and Proceedings of the General Assembly. . . , Oct. 27, 1768, to January 2, 1769* (New York, 1769), p. 55; *Smith Memoirs*, I, 49.

50 John Wetherhead to Sir William Johnson, Jan. 9, 1769, Division of Archives and History, University of the State of New York, *Sir William Johnson Papers,* 14 vols. (Albany, 1921–65), VI, 575.

51 *Journals of the Votes and Proceedings of the General Assembly . . ., April 4, 1769, to May 20, 1769* (New York, 1769), pp. 12–16. William Livingston wrote the address to the King, William Smith, Jr., the one to the House of Lords.

52 Moot Club Papers, 1770–1775; Minutes of the Debating Society, [1768]; both in New York Historical Society.

53 Henry C. Van Schaack, *Life of Peter Van Schaack* (New York, 1842), 54–58.

54 *Smith Memoirs,* I, 186; Robert R. Livingston to William Duer, June 12, 1777, quoted in George Dangerfield, *Chancellor Robert R. Livingston of New York* (New York, 1960), p. 94; James Duane to Robert Livingston, June 7, 1775, Livingston-Redmond Papers, Franklin D. Roosevelt Library, Hyde Park, N.Y.

55 William Gordon, *History of the Rise, Progress, and Establishment of the Independence of the United States of America,* 3 vols. (London, 1788), II, 297; Edward P. Alexander, *A Revolutionary Conservative: James Duane of New York* (New York, 1938), p. 121; *American Archives,* ed. Peter Force, 9 vols. (Washington, D.C., 1837–53), 4 Series, VI, 996.

56 On this proposal, see Klein, "Failure of a Mission: The Drummond Peace Proposal of 1775," *Huntington Library Quarterly,* 35 (1972), 343–80.

57 John Adams to Samuel H. Parsons, June 22, 1776, in *The Works of John Adams,* ed. C. F. Adams, 10 vols. (Boston, 1850–56), IX, 407.

58 Richard B. Morris, *John Jay, the Nation, and the Courts* (Boston, 1967), pp. 10–14; Frank Monaghan, *John Jay* (New York and Indianapolis, 1935), p. 97.

59 The first computation is that of Johnson, "John Jay," Appendix A; the second is my own. For the bar generally, there are no adequate statistics as to the division between patriots and loyalists. Sabine, in 1864, estimated that a majority of the lawyers were patriots, but the "giants" of the law in all the colonies were loyalists. Wallace Brown, studying the loyalist claimants in England, concluded in 1965 that Sabine was probably right. Friedman, in his recent study, states casually that "many lawyers, if not most, were of the loyalist persuasion." In Massachusetts, Morris found that the bar split fairly evenly. Flick, in his volume on New York

loyalism, lumped lawyers with other professionals and concluded that a "very large proportion" of all of them were loyalists. However, he offers only seven names of New York City lawyers to illustrate his generalization and lists James Duane as a merchant rather than a lawyer. The fullest study of the early bar, that of Chroust, estimates that only one-fourth of the colonial legal profession left the country or retired from their practice because of their loyalty to the Crown. See Lorenzo Sabine, *Biographical Sketches of the Loyalists of the American Revolution,* 2 vols. (1864; rpt. Port Washington, N.Y., 1966), I, 59–60; Wallace Brown, *The King's Friends* (Providence, R.I., 1966), p. 265; Morris, "Legalism versus Revolutionary Doctrine," *New England Quarterly,* 4 (1931), 206–7; Alexander C. Flick, *Loyalism in New York during the American Revolution* (1901; rpt. New York, 1969), pp. 31–32; Lawrence M. Friedman, *A History of American Law* (New York, 1973), p. 88; Anton-Hermann Chroust, *The Rise of the Legal Profession in America,* 2 vols. (Norman, Okla., 1965), II, 11.

60 On this development, see Gary B. Nash, "The Transformation of Urban Politics, 1700–1765," *Journal of American History,* 60 (1973), 605–32.

61 *The Farmer Refuted* (1775), Harold C. Syrett, Jacob E. Cooke, and others, eds., *The Papers of Alexander Hamilton,* 19 vols. to date (New York, 1961–), I, 121–22.

62 Henry P. Johnston, ed., *The Correspondence and Public Papers of John Jay,* 4 vols. (New York and London, 1890–93), I, 103 (Dec. 23, 1776).

63 *New-York Gazette,* March 14, 1765.

64 Alexis de Tocqueville, *Democracy in America,* ed. Phillips Bradley, 2 vols. (New York, 1954), I, 290.

Thomas Jefferson's
Notes on the State of Virginia

MERRILL D. PETERSON

The American Revolution, which we commemorate in this bicentennial year, was a moral and philosophical adventure as well as a political one. "Never," as Herbert Schneider once observed, "was history made more consciously and conscientiously, and seldom since the days of classic Greece has philosophy enjoyed greater opportunity to exercise public responsibility."[1]

Foremost among the "philosopher-statesmen" of the new republic was Thomas Jefferson, whose first title to fame was the Declaration of Independence and whose last was the creation of the University of Virginia. The minds of most great men—someone has said—contract, like the pupil of an eye, the more light that is shed upon them. But Jefferson's mind dilates under the light of inquiry. As James Madison wrote after the death of his great friend, he was a man of wide learning and varied attainments who left "the philosophical impress" of his mind "on every subject which he touched."[2] Virtually nothing of human interest eluded his intelligence. From his youth he was "a hard student," zealous in the pursuit of knowledge. He had an insatiable appetite for books, the ancient with the modern, in half-a-dozen languages. By 1773, at thirty years of age, he boasted a library of 1200 volumes; and it had multiplied five or six times when, in 1815, his collection became the nucleus of the Library of Congress. Learning from books—how to design a house, measure an eclipse, form a just government—Jefferson extended his experience beyond the narrow range of colonial objects and gained a vantage point above time and place from which to perceive, as through the eye of reason, things as they ought to be. The Revolution freed his mind from provincial restraints, from what Jefferson called "the dull monotony of colonial subservience," and gave it generous scope for action. Perhaps he was always more at home in the world of ideas than in the world of affairs, but henceforth the effort of his life was to embody thought in conduct, theory in practice, vision in institutions. Ideas were meant to act on the world, to improve it, not to reflect it in some grand cosmic design. Caught up in the actions and passions of his time, he never enjoyed the luxury of cloistered philosophy; and, even supposing he felt the need, never found the occasion to reduce the totality of his thought to a system.

Jefferson did, nevertheless, manage to write one book, *Notes on the State of Virginia.*[3] Of all his voluminous writings it offers the best introduction to his mind. *Notes on Virginia* is a fascinating book, not alone for its information and opinions but also for what it reveals of the intellectual method and style of the author. A work of observation, it lays no claim to artistry or to philosophy, yet possesses both. It is, indeed, one of the rare literary monuments of the eighteenth-century Enlightenment in America. What Jefferson did in the *Notes* was to articulate a series of Enlightenment directives for the intelligence of the new American republic. More than that, he substantially met the desideratum of Lockean philosophy for a systematic account of the relationship between man and his environment. It is in this light, primarily, that Jefferson's book has significance for the emerging culture, society, and government in Revolutionary America.

In a sense, the book was a cultural accident. It was a by-product of revolutionary events and cannot be viewed in any other context. It had no prototype, belonged to no established genre, and answered to no speculative school. The very act of its creation expressed the amorphous and unpredictable character of American thought and imagination. Jefferson began the *Notes* in 1780, not with any idea of writing a book but in response to the more or less official request of the secretary of the French legation, François de Marbois, in Philadelphia, for information on the state of Virginia. Governor of Virginia at the time—a time of military catastrophe in the state—Jefferson was unable to return his answers to Marbois's queries until some months after his retirement the following year. That might have been the end of it, but Jefferson's philosophical friends in Philadelphia and elsewhere soon learned of the work and asked for copies. These he endeavored to supply, while at the same time he continued his investigations and kept adding to the manuscript until in 1784 it had "swelled to nearly treble bulk."[4] By then Jefferson had reluctantly consented to publication, though only in a small private edition and without ascription of authorship. The book was born in Paris, where Jefferson had succeeded Benjamin Franklin as American minister, in 1785. A French translation, then an English and an American edition, with his name on the title page, followed during the next three years. Such was the curious history of a book Jefferson had never meant to write and, having written it, tried to withhold from the world, yet a book that quickly earned for him international renown as an American *philosophe* second only to Franklin.

This came about because of Jefferson's imaginative response to the task presented to him. He might have answered Marbois's queries in a perfunctory fashion, as indeed they were answered, so far as answered at all, by informants in other states; but turning these questions into his own mind, Jefferson converted the task into an intellectual discovery of his native country, the greater Virginia of that day, reaching westward to the Mississippi or beyond. The country was still *terra incognita* to philosophy. The flora and fauna, the mountains and rivers, the natural resources and productions, the human inhabitants, laws, manners, institutions—the knowledge of these things wanted by a foreign ally and its philosophers was of infinitely greater value to enlightened Americans. In the act of writing *Notes on Virginia,* Jefferson sought to take intellectual possession of the country, to differentiate it from the Old World, define its special place in the order of creation, and vindicate the promise of independence. The work thus became a vehicle of American nationality.

The Frenchman's matter-of-fact queries were only the starting point for the work. The first thing Jefferson did was to sort them out, revise and rearrange the whole, under twenty-three topical headings, with a view to offering a systematic account of the country, proceeding from its natural situation, through considerations of its civil character, finally to questions of manners and morals. Although the formal queries placed Jefferson under constraint, he was not limited by them. A question on "the progress of human knowledge," for instance, was answered by an empirical essay on climate; and throughout the *Notes* Jefferson digressed freely, discussing subjects with a latitude congenial to his adventuresome mind.

As he gave his own design to the work, so did Jefferson impress upon it his own intelligence and sensibility. The operative mode of the inquiry was empirical; the purpose was fundamentally utilitarian; and the prose style was appropriately clear, crisp, and precise. Jefferson assumed the posture of the detached observer. His only conscious artistry lay in the ease and grace with which he conveyed masses of information without running into pedantry or bewildering the reader. He was a superb rhetorician, in the ancient usage of that term, more interested in communication of facts and ideas than in self-expression or literary effects. The book was distinguished beyond any previously written in America for its use of statistics. Although the word had not yet entered the language, Jefferson commanded the idea and presented much of his data in statistical form. In this respect the *Notes* reflected the "political arithmetic" abroad in the age, and also foreshadowed a modern faith, perhaps more widely held in America than anywhere else, in measurement and counting as the way to truth. Jefferson generally rose above the superficialities of this view, yet was not wholly free of the error, as is suggested by his refutation of Buffon's degeneracy theory with figures of weight and measure of American quadrupeds. His concern with classification—of birds, plants, Indians, and so on—disclosed a mind that placed priority on precision, order, and coherence. If the end of inquiry was to discover *how* things worked, it was first necessary to determine *what* they were within a rational scheme of nature, such as the science of the age delineated.

For all the impersonal factualism, taxonomy, and objectivity of the book, which gives its prevailing tone, there is another tone in which the manners and feelings of the observer shape the objects observed. Writing of such scenic wonders as the Natural Bridge and the passage of the Potomac through the Blue Ridge at Harper's Ferry, Jefferson expressed wildly subjective emotion, bordering on romantic rapture. Similarly, his denunciation of slavery and of a plan in war-torn Virginia to surrender the government to a military dictator drew upon depths of passion that belie any one-dimensional interpretation of the *Notes.* At this second level of consciousness, Jefferson appears, if only fleetingly, as a proto-romantic, more interested in self-expression than in the communication of useful knowledge, in the discovery of self than in the discovery of his native country. Perhaps no part of the *Notes,* not even its most statistical and taxonomic parts, can be fully understood without recognition of this self-conscious level; still, the fundamental assumptions, the method, the ideas, and the vision of the book belong to the science of the eighteenth-century Enlightenment whose geniuses were Bacon, Newton, and Locke, the three greatest men who ever lived, in Jefferson's opinion.[5]

The sense of the new, the undiscovered, and the boundless pervades the *Notes on Virginia.* This is one of the book's most striking characteristics, and it contributes to the air of contingency which is, of course, indicated by the title itself. Jefferson often apologized for the book's errors, omissions, and other imperfections. The evidence, from notations in his author's copy, suggests that he viewed the published work as only the first installment of an ongoing enterprise; and though he always meant to revise it, he never found the opportunity. "The work itself indeed is nothing more than the measure of a shadow," he wrote in 1814, "never stationary, but lengthening as the sun advances, and to be taken anew from hour to hour."[6] The image is a clue to the spirit of the work and suggests its significance for an American culture that possessed the qualities of the unknown, the unformed, and the unexpected. America was wide open to inquiry, from the standpoint of science still at the stage of infancy, with many gaps to fill up, errors to correct, and improvements to make. Repeatedly, in the *Notes,* Jefferson called attention to the uncertain state of knowledge. About some things ignorance was the only honest plea. The sources of the Missouri River, for instance, were unknown and the intervening country between the Missouri and the Rio Grande was a blank on the map. Inference and conjecture from remote facts permitted some tentative observations, and Jefferson made them, though he distrusted this method of reasoning. It was a goad to discovery. His early interest in the western reaches of the Missouri would lead, twenty years later, to the Lewis and Clark Expedition, which replaced speculative with exact knowledge.

On one subject after another Jefferson called for "more facts." "How unripe we yet are, for an accurate comparison of the animals of the two [continents]," he wrote even as he attempted to demolish Buffon.[7] The race of blacks, Americans by compulsion, he complained, "have never yet been viewed by us as subjects of natural history."[8] As for the natives of the New World, "nothing was truly known of them," Jefferson said, "for I would not honor with the appellation of knowledge . . . the fables published of them."[9] One of the sources of these fables was the Abbé Raynal's celebrated *History of the Two Indies,* which Jefferson once characterized as "the effusions of an imagination in deliris."[10] His own imagination could also run to the fabulous, of course, for how else is one to characterize his account of the American mammoth, that remarkable creature—"the largest of all terrestial beings"—vaguely known from Indian legend and a few fossil bones but believed by Jefferson still to roam the wild lands north of the Ohio?[11] The mammoth was evidence against Buffon, and more, a patriotic effusion in behalf of American grandeur. Jefferson could never wholly separate his science from his Americanism. But his persistent theme in the *Notes* was "more facts." "Ignorance is preferable to error; and he is less remote from the truth who believes nothing, than he who believes what is wrong."[12] Knowledge grounded in empirical fact alone had integrity, Jefferson insisted. "A patient pursuit of facts, and cautious combination and comparison of them, is the drudgery to which man is subjected by his Maker, if he wishes to attain sure knowledge."[13] And so, if it could be said that the logic of Descartes presided over

Montesquieu's *Spirit of the Laws,* it was the logic of Locke that presided over *Notes on Virginia.*

Viewed in the light of eighteenth-century knowledge, the book was primarily a work of natural history, secondarily of civil history. These were Baconian categories, and Jefferson was never more consciously a disciple of the Enlightenment than in the conviction derived from Bacon that man masters nature by discovering and obeying her laws, whether in the physical or in the social order. The object of studying nature was not to "know thyself" in some classical, Christian, or romantic sense, but to obtain useful knowledge for the good of mankind. As Dugald Stewart expressed it, "The more knowledge of this kind we acquire, the better can we accomodate our plans to the established order of things, and avail ourselves of natural powers for accomplishing our purposes."[14] Natural history comprehended the earth in time and space as the scene of life. It was the peculiar province of American science in the eighteenth century for a number of reasons. The physical sciences, which in Bacon's scheme belonged to the division of natural philosophy, were the same the world around; but America had its own natural history, and its discovery was a patriotic as well as a scientific obligation. Moreover, in an image the opposite of Buffon's, America was often perceived as "nature's nation," where everything still wore the innocent face of divine creation. With the Revolution, the conception of America as the favored place in the natural world, undefiled by the corruptions of civilization, unburdened by history, emboldened the hopes of enlightened philosophers in the new political experiment founded on the natural rights of man. "As America was the only spot in the political world where the principles of universal reformation could begin," Thomas Paine would write, "so also was it the best in the natural world."[15] America was a laboratory not only for enlightened ideas of government but also for the study of natural history—the features of the land, the kingdoms of plants and animals, the races and descent of man, the emergence of civilization out of nature. Jefferson treated all these matters in the *Notes,* and never ceased thinking about them.

The natural history approach led to a rather simplistic environmentalism. The century's fascination with "climate" as a cultural determinant, evident in Montesquieu's work as well as Buffon's, clashed with the century's penchant toward universality in the laws of nature. Jefferson was aware of the conflict yet never quite resolved it in his mind, insisting against Montesquieu, for instance, that the rights of man did not depend on the thermometer, but ascribing exceptional virtues to American nature. The natural environment provided the frame for understanding the system of things in America. This same environmentalism, in the hands of Buffon and others, had supported the denigration of American nature; but Jefferson, in refuting the theory, attacked Buffon's conclusions rather than his premises on the molding force of the environment. When he finished, the animals, the Indians, and the conquering white men of America were still contained within nature, only now that nature was read benevolently instead of malevolently. Among the benevolent features of the environment, ultimately traceable, with everything else, to the workmanship of a divine creator, were the rivers. Although the thirteen United States still hugged the Atlantic seaboard, Jefferson envisioned a country of little less than continental proportions. The mountains and vast distances might be overcome by laying hold of the rivers. The western waters of the Mississippi embraced five-eighths of the country in 1783—in time, would embrace more. Their navigation could be improved and by a series of canals they could be linked to the eastern rivers. The rivers and their characteristics were natural determinants of the nation's future, in Jefferson's view. Even the lines of political force were pre-ordained, in some part, by the rivers, for competition must arise between the eastern sections for control of the western waters.

In Jefferson's Lockean universe, time itself was comprehended in the natural environment. This was true in a geological sense. The passage of the Potomac through the Blue Ridge, said Jefferson, "hurries our senses into the opinion that this earth has been created in time."[16] It was also, and more significantly, true with regard to the progress of civilization in America, for that would come through the conquest of landed space. In a remarkable letter, written late in life, Jefferson observed that the whole history of the human race was recapitulated in America. He had himself observed all its stages from his

Virginia vantage point; and they might still be surveyed by the philosopher who proceeded from the Rocky Mountains eastward to the Atlantic, for this was a journey from primitive savagery through the pastoral state to the advanced state of civilization.[17] Nature was not static but developmental; it was realized not in some presocial "state of nature" but, humanistically, in the progress of civilization. Jefferson made his values explicit in his discussion of the Indians. Here, too, as against Buffon, he was seeking to vindicate American nature, which was incarnate in the aborigines. His standard, however, was not the present savagery of the Indians—a Rousseauistic standard Jefferson rejected—but their natural capacity for civilization. They were equal in body and mind to the white man; the lowly condition of the race was owing to circumstances rather than to nature. Jefferson proposed to elevate the Indians by gradually incorporating them into the conquerors' society. Paradoxically, the Indian would fulfill his nature, and at the same time save himself from extinction, by becoming civilized, in short, by ceasing to be an Indian in any ethnological sense. Jefferson's philosophy, with its egalitarian assumption about human nature, made no place for racism; nevertheless, when he came to treat the African, who lacked the virtues associated with American nature, prejudice eclipsed philosophy and he was unable to see this unfortunate race in the same developmental light as the Indian.[18]

Between the poles of nature and civilization, which would prove so important in American thought and imagination, Jefferson was not really ambivalent. The higher values were those of civilization; indeed, man fulfilled his nature only in the refined state. Jefferson's devotion to humanistic learning, his love of the ancients, his interest in the fine arts, above all the "elegant and useful art" of architecture—in these and other ways he declared himself a partisan of civilization. In the *Notes* he made a plea on behalf of "the genius of architecture," whose benefactions were thus far confined to the Old World.[19] It never occurred to him that the New World ought to have an indigenous architecture. In the arts and sciences he was a cosmopolitan, virtually untouched by the stirrings of romanticism and nationalism. Tilting with Buffon, even as he scored points with tales of American mammoth, Jefferson did not claim American superiority, only equality with the Old World, on the premise that nature is everywhere fundamentally the same. So, too, he did not aspire to an *American* art, but, rather, aspired to the elevation of American taste to the standards of excellence and beauty in Western civilization.

Yet, in other ways, the reality of American nature entered profoundly into Jefferson's humanism. Again, his observations on the Indians are suggestive. "Were it made a question," he wrote, "whether no law, as among the savage Americans, or too much law, as among the civilized Europeans, submits man to the greatest evil, one who has seen both conditions of existence would pronounce it to be the last: and that the sheep are happier of themselves, than under the care of wolves."[20] Fortunately, this was not a choice the Americans had to make. In a free and open environment, nature was constantly passing into civilization, constantly regenerating it, saving it from excesses; and the Americans might enjoy the blessings of both without the evils of either for an indeterminable future.

Jefferson's philosophy first conscripted man in the cause of nature and then—this was the trick—conscripted nature in the cause of mankind. The ideal state was one in which nature and civilization interpenetrated each other, and thus, as has been said, had the characteristics of the literary pastoral.[21] Perhaps it was exemplified in Jefferson's Monticello, brilliantly imaged by John Dos Passos as "a portico facing the wilderness."[22] In the *Notes* Jefferson defined the ideal in terms of the unique opportunities afforded by the American environment. Nature might be everywhere the same, but "the difference of circumstance" among countries should produce different results. "In Europe the lands are either cultivated, or locked up against the cultivator," Jefferson wrote. "Manufactures must therefore be resorted to of necessity, not of choice, to support the surplus of their people. But we have an immensity of land courting the industry of the husbandmen."[23] He went on to hymn the praise of agriculture. It put man into relationship with the natural world, through that to the Divine Creator; it nourished a virtuous way of life; it secured economic competency and that dignity and independence of character considered essential to republican government. "While we have land to labor then," he concluded, "let us never wish to see our citizens occupied at a work-bench, or twirling a distaff. . . . The mobs of great cities add just so much to the support of pure government, as sores do to the strength of the human body."[24] Jefferson's idealized American, no less than Emerson's at a later time and in a different philosophical context, was "timed to Nature, and not to city watches." And with this timing America's destiny might be different from Europe's. Peace, not war; free trade, not mercantilist selfishness; natural population increase, not immigration—these policy directives were also authorized by the American environment. Mastery of the continent was the first imperative. "Young as we are," Jefferson declared, "and with such a country before us to fill with people and with happiness, we should point in that direction the whole generative force of nature. . . ."[25]

Much of Jefferson's discussion of society and government in *Notes on Virginia* belonged to the realm of civil history; but so compelling were the naturalistic assumptions of his thought that it is impossible to understand his social and political ideas apart from them. Of course, the idea of natural rights had no dependence on American nature, nor did the idea of an innate moral sense. These were universal endowments, the property of "man in general," though America was the first place—as Paine said, "the best in the natural world"—where they could be fully recognized. The task of government in America was not to organize a just society, for the configuration of natural and social forces largely took care of that, but to give fair play to the capacities of free men. Adopting a benevolent rather than a selfish theory of human nature—a theory centered in the Scottish moral sense philosophy—Jefferson reasoned that man was naturally sociable, pursuing his own happiness by acting virtuously toward others. Because of this conception of a natural order of social life, the authority of the state, or of the church, was largely superseded by the self-regulating authority of moral man in a moral society. Society was natural, government was artificial. Although necessary to secure the rights of man, even the best government tended always to fall into corruption and tyranny. In the Jeffersonian elysium, government would be absorbed into society, becoming literally self-government.

Nowhere in the *Notes* did Jefferson articulate this political philosophy, but its outlines were implicit in chapters treating the constitution and laws of Virginia. He explained his efforts to wipe privilege from the land laws and to make landed property more accessible to the people. He described his plan for a comprehensive system of public education, one which would not only ensure the rudimentary education of all the people but also replace "the pseudo-aristocracy" of birth and wealth with "the natural aristocracy of talent."[26] The latter, destined by nature for leadership, were found among the poor as well as the rich and ought to be fully cultivated. Jefferson's decade-long campaign for religious liberty and equality culminated in the celebrated Statute for Religious Freedom in 1786. In the *Notes* Jefferson recapitulated the main arguments he had advanced for this revolutionary measure. Morality was sundered from its traditional dependence on religion. Coercion of belief could never be justified, nor could it ever finally succeed. Viewing religion as wholly a private concern, Jefferson denied the state authority even to adopt an opinion about it, any more than about physics or geometry, or to legislate in any manner. The fears so long entertained that without public sanctions religion would be subverted and the community reduced to moral anarchy had no credence with Jefferson. It was the nature of free men to live justly in society. As to religion, the Virginia Statute declared "that truth is great and will prevail if left to herself."[27] These views entered into the ascendant libertarian and egalitarian ideology in America.

At the outset I suggested that the American Revolution was a revolution of mind as well as of government. For Thomas Jefferson this larger revolution, prefigured in the philosophy of the Enlightenment, envisioned a more fruitful relationship between man and nature and looked to the building of civilization in the New World environment. "Light and liberty go together," Jefferson said. Science and freedom were companions, and with the American Revolution he hoped that the country might become—more than a free republic—"a republic of science" fulfilling the promise of Enlightenment dreams. His *Notes on Virginia* expressed this outlook, stimulated the work of discovery and understanding, and helped to form the still inchoate consciousness of American nationality. The book did not stand alone. For generations, almost from the moment the first of them stepped off the boat, Americans had been trying to comprehend their surroundings and to find their place within them. Jefferson himself was well versed in the literature that reflected this search. But his book was a landmark. Nothing like it had been seen before; and it set a new standard for American inquiry.

Among philosophical men the book sparked the excitement of new beginnings. As the venture in republican government was new, so, too, was the intellectual voyage of discovery in the American land. Nothing was finished in the *Notes;* it was all prologue to a drama only begun. In a letter from Paris in 1789 to Joseph Willard, President of Harvard, acknowledging receipt of the diploma of Doctor of Laws from the university, Jefferson recounted some of the current literary and scientific events in the French capital: Berthélemy's *Voyages of Anacharsis,* the collected works of Frederick the Great, a translation from the Greek of Ptolemy on the stars, La Grange's work on mechanics, a new history of Mexico, disputes in the infant science of chemistry, Thomas Paine's iron bridge, James Rumsey's experiments in steam navigation, and so on. Then, after this feast, and without blinking an eye, Jefferson turned enthusiastically to America.

> What a field have we at our door to signalize ourselves in! The botany of America is far from being exhausted; its mineralogy is untouched, and its . . . zoology totally mistaken and misrepresented. . . . It is for such institutions as that over which you preside so worthily, Sir, to do justice to our country, its productions, and its genius. It is the work to which young men whom you are forming, should lay their hands. We have spent the prime of our lives in procuring them the precious blessings of liberty. Let them spend theirs in shewing that it is the great parent of science and of virtue; and that a nation will be great in both always in proportion as it is free.[28]

The tense in America was the future, and the future would fulfill itself, above all, in the mastery of nature. How succeeding generations responded to Jefferson's challenge, or followed out the lines of thought and imagination plotted in the *Notes on Virginia,* is another story; but in its bearings for American culture Jefferson's book must be considered one of the most important literary and philosophical achievements of the eighteenth-century American mind.

NOTES

1 Herbert W. Schneider, *A History of American Philosophy* (New York, 1946), p. 35.
2 Quoted in Adrienne Koch, *Power, Morals, and the Founding Fathers* (Ithaca, N.Y., 1961), p. 23.
3 *Notes on the State of Virginia,* ed. William Peden (Chapel Hill, N.C., 1954). The citations which follow are to this edition.
4 Jefferson to Chastellux, January 16, 1784, *The Papers of Thomas Jefferson,* ed. Julian P. Boyd, 19 vols. to date (Princeton, 1950–74), VI, 467.
5 See his letter to John Trumball, February 15, 1789, *Papers,* ed. Boyd, XIV, 561.
6 *Notes,* p. xxi.
7 Ibid., pp. 54, 62.
8 Ibid., p. 143.
9 Ibid., p. 59.
10 Ibid., p. 257 n.
11 Ibid., pp. 43–47, 53–55.
12 Ibid., p. 33.
13 Ibid., p. 277 n.
14 Quoted in Gladys Bryson, *Man and Society: The Scottish Inquiry of the Eighteenth Century* (Princeton, 1945), p. 16.
15 *Rights of Man,* Part II, in *The Complete Writings of Thomas Paine,* ed. Philip S. Foner, 2 vols. (New York, 1945), I, 354.
16 *Notes,* p. 19.
17 Jefferson to William Ludlow, September 6, 1824, in *The Portable Thomas Jefferson,* ed. Merrill D. Peterson (New York, 1975), pp. 583–84.
18 See especially Bernard W. Sheehan, *Seeds of Extinction: Jeffersonian Philanthropy and the American Indian* (Chapel Hill, N.C., 1973).
19 *Notes,* p. 153.
20 Ibid., p. 93.
21 See especially Leo Marx, *The Machine in the Garden: Technology and the Pastoral Ideal* (New York, 1964), pp. 116–50.
22 In *Thomas Jefferson: A Profile,* ed. Merrill D. Peterson (New York, 1967), pp. 61–85.
23 *Notes,* p. 164.
24 Ibid., p. 165.
25 Ibid., p. 174.
26 Ibid., pp. 146–49.
27 In *The Portable Jefferson,* p. 253.
28 Jefferson to Joseph Willard, March 24, 1789, *Papers,* ed. Boyd, XIV, 699.

Simplicity and Grandeur: Winckelmann, French Classicism, and Jefferson

MAX L. BAEUMER

The American art historian John Ives Sewall remarked in 1953, "The man in the street who has never heard of Winckelmann will nevertheless quote him if asked to express an opinion about art. No other art historian has had a comparable influence. . . ."[1] Elisa Marian Butler, in her controversial book *The Tyranny of Greece over Germany,* written in the midst of Europe's experience with Nazi Germany, calls Winckelmann the "latter-day Greek . . . who summoned a submerged continent to the surface of eighteenth-century life." She continues: "The waves of the violent disturbance he created are still washing on to twentieth-century shores; for the labours he performed, in obedience to an instinct only partially understood, have had remarkable effects."[2] What Ms. Butler considered an "instinct" Harvard scholar Henry Hatfield calls a distorted vision of Greece, a pale and unreal concept, but one based on real knowledge, however limited, and on enthusiasm and love.[3]

The concept Mr. Hatfield refers to is Winckelmann's well-known formula for Greek art: "noble simplicity and quiet grandeur." This phrase, repeated again and again, "with the brutality of an erroneous headline,"[4] by generations of scholars and non-scholars alike, soon became an empty cliché that was largely responsible for the rejection and ridicule of classicism. Nevertheless, "noble simplicity and quiet grandeur," the maxim which Winckelmann used to characterize the beauty of Greek sculpture, became the byword of the Greek revival in German literature and the favorite formula for a doctrine of classical restraint in the arts. "Noble simplicity and quiet grandeur" ("edle Einfalt und stille Grösse") not only expressed the ideal of the Weimar classicism of Goethe and Schiller but also fascinated successive generations, persisting as a cult which "influenced the whole history of Western taste, not only in Europe" but in the New World as well.[5] Winckelmann, the man always connected with this phrase and its meaning, is not only the founder of classical aesthetics, but the father of both archaeology and art history as well. His *Geschichte der Kunst des Alterthums,*[6] with all its errors and its indebtedness to predecessors, divides art history into chronological periods founded, for the first time, on religious, political, social, and economic conditions, and it establishes new aesthetic norms for the interpretation of works of art. It is one of the works which appears on Thomas Jefferson's library list of 1815.[7] Winckelmann's last work is titled *Monumenti antichi inediti.*[8] In spite of its shortcomings, including the fact that it is based on inferior Roman copies of Greek originals, the *Monumenti* is a pioneering work of archaeological methodology which incorporates fresh evidence from the proving-ground of excavations at the newly discovered Pompeii and Herculaneum (since 1738 and 1748). The Winckelmann vogue in the Western world, however, cannot be explained away in terms of philological scholarship and archaeological innovations, but has its origin and expression in his concept that ideal beauty can be found only in Greek art and in its creative imitation.

This concept, I suggest, would directly influence Jefferson's aesthetic as he became more familiar with Continental thought, for while Winckelmann's ideas can be shown to be far less original than has generally been supposed, they were formulated in such a way that they were both memorable and all-pervasive. A little book, published in 1755, brought Winckelmann from obscurity into the limelight of the literary world; for his *Gedancken über die Nachahmung der Griechischen Wercke in der Mahlerey und Bildhauer-Kunst* contains his two principal aesthetic theses. The first of these is that "the only way for us to become great, or even inimitable if that is possible, is to imitate the Greeks."[9] A temperate climate, freedom from political restrictions, a natural way of life, health, and above all, gymnastics in the nude gave the Greeks their "beautiful nature," "the eminent beauty of their bodies," and "the noble souls of youth." In such an environment artists could create works of "ideal beauty." "Sensual beauty gave the artist the beautiful nature; ideal beauty rendered the sublime features; from the former he took the human, from the latter the divine" (*KS*, 35).

Although scholars have criticized Winckelmann for supposedly failing to provide a precise and consistent definition of what he means by "beauty"[10] when he discusses the properties of natural and of ideal beauty in Greek statues, he does formulate the general conception and distinguishing quality of beauty as follows: "The most significant characteristic [Das allgemeine vorzügliche Kennzeichen] that the Greek masterpieces have in common is in short a noble simplicity and quiet grandeur, both in posture and in expression. As the depths of the sea always remain calm, no matter how the surface may rage, just so does the expression of the Greek figures indicate among all passions a great and unruffled soul. Such a soul is portrayed in the face of Laocoon, despite his most violent suffering. . . . The expression of such a great soul exceeds the form of beautiful nature by far" (*KS*, 43). Not only is this a precise definition and one which controls all of his subsequent writings, but Winckelmann's central analogy of the calm sea is an image which achieves an equal popularity in successive writers.

"Noble simplicity and quiet grandeur," the second principle of Winckelmann's aesthetics, clearly defines his concept of classical beauty. It is widely agreed that the principles of imitation and beauty—beauty nobly simple and quietly grand—are more or less Winckelmann's own original concepts and contribution to aesthetics.[11] This claim, however, needs qualification. Winckelmann's first maxim, "The only way for us to become great . . . if possible, is to imitate the Greeks"—"the most original and daring thesis" of Winckelmann, according to Professor Hatfield[12]—can be found almost word for word in the first chapter to Jean de La Bruyère's book *Les Caractères* in 1688: "On ne saurait... rencontrer le parfait, et s'il se peut, surpasser les anciens que par leur imitation."[13] Winckelmann's *Gedancken über die Nachahmung der Griechischen Wercke* and his two maxims originate in the literary polemics of the "Querelle des Anciens et des Modernes," the quarrel among such ancient and modern writers of French classicism as Charles Perrault, Nicolas Boileau-Despréaux, Jean-Baptiste Dubos, and others in whose writings the idea of imitating the Greeks is expressed again and again. Winckelmann studied and copied passages from these polemics and from the writings of the art historians and painters André Félibien, Roland Fréart de Chambray, Roger de Piles, and Jonathan Richardson senior and junior during the years 1749 to 1754 before he wrote his own *Gedancken.*[14]

For example, Winckelmann could have found the same analogy of the calm sea virtually word for word in the Memoirs of Christina, Queen of Sweden, which appeared only four years before he wrote his *Gedancken:* "La mer est l'image des grandes âmes, quelque agitées qu'elles paraissent, leur fond est toujours tranquille."[15] In the same *Gedancken,* Winckelmann criticizes Christina for her handling of works of art (*KS,* 64).

I believe I can also demonstrate the source of the words "noble simplicity and quiet grandeur," which made Winckelmann so famous and which have been attributed to him since their appearance in his pamphlet more than 200 years ago. Lessing's use of them along with the image of the calm sea at the beginning of the *Laokoon: oder über die Grenzen der Mahlerey und Poesie* in 1766 only tended to popularize the notion that they originated with Winckelmann.[16] But they did not.

Later historians also err. Biographer Carl Justi (I, 410) mentioned in 1866 that Winckelmann, like Goethe, might have received his "gospel of the beautiful" (the ideal of "noble simplicity and quiet grandeur") from the painter Adam Friedrich Oeser. Historians of art and of literature subsequently asserted this mere possibility as a proven fact and maintained that, in the words of Hermann Hettner, "this unsurpassed slogan for characterizing the real essence of Greek art" was first given to Winckelmann by Oeser.[17] The Hungarian-born Adam Friedrich Oeser (1717–99) specialized in allegorical painting of simple figures moving naturally in large groups. He lived in Dresden and was (as much as Winckelmann and Goethe) an outspoken adversary of the ornate and elaborate style of baroque. In 1754–55 he taught his friend and house-guest Winckelmann the art of drawing. Twelve years later in Leipzig, the young Goethe was his modestly successful but enthusiastic student. Goethe remarks of Oeser, "He taught me that the ideal of beauty was simplicity and tranquillity."[18] After his Italian journey, Goethe turned critic and remarked that Oeser never studied the art of the classics in Italy, that he therefore lacked a knowledge of the strict rules of the highest art and followed merely the simple inspirations of his own talent, which enabled him to produce pleasing, if "nebulous," paintings (Dürr, pp. 132–33, 144). Oeser himself preferred in his own words "examples of simplicity and softness in art" ("des Einfachen und Sanften") and praised "cheerful tranquillity and gentle delight . . . in simplicity" as his beloved idea (Dürr, pp. 86, 147). Oeser didn't know "grandeur" and "nobility" at all. When he visited the Court of Weimar as a very welcome guest and painter, he was praised for his joyful and sincere scenes of simple nature but, at the same time, criticized for his lack of "great and tragic art" (Dürr, pp. 128–29).

It is obvious that Winckelmann found neither the Greeks nor noble grandeur in Oeser's art, but only simplicity and stillness of heart, the same qualities which, in a strictly religious context, he could have experienced in the strong contemporary movement of pietism.[19] But this poor son of a cobbler and unwilling former student of Lutheran theology had given up long ago what he considered the "nervous piety" of the conventicles[20] for the pursuit of classical beauty and of homoerotic intellectual friendships modelled on Plato's *Symposium*. Not only that: he had secretly become a convert to the Catholic faith in order to have the opportunity and financial means to study the heathen realms of classical antiquity in the shadow of the Vatican in Rome. "I see no other means of achieving my end but that of becoming a hypocrite for a time," he wrote to a friend in 1754.[21] Winckelmann's cavalier attitude towards formal religion and his willing hypocrisy in the cause of art force us to look elsewhere for the origins of this phrase.

Among the contemporary connoisseurs of classical antiquity discussed in Oeser's school of art, the French archaeologist Count Anne-Claude-Philippe de Caylus (1692–1765) was particularly praised (Dürr, p. 107). Justi asserts that Caylus' seven volumes on Egyptian, Greek, and Roman works of art, his *Recueil d'antiquités,* from 1752 to 1767, conform in many details with Winckelmann's *Geschichte der Kunst des Alterthums* of 1764 and that Winckelmann seemed to have intentionally forgotton to name Caylus among his sources.[22] Winckelmann and Caylus met and corresponded with each other. Winckelmann, on the one hand, praises Caylus for being the first to have recognized the characteristics of the antique style. On the other hand, he criticized Caylus bitterly and prevented him from gaining access to the newly discovered antique statues collected in the Villa Albani. Caylus not only preached the simplicity and greatness of the ancients against the corrupt taste of modern artists, he spoke in his first volume of 1752 (three years before Winckelmann formulated his maxim of classical beauty) of "cette noble simplicité" (I, xi) and of "la manière noble et simple du bel antique" (I, xiii).[23] Caylus emphasized the ideals of greatness, nobility and the sublime as the characteristics of ancient art. In his volume of 1756 (p. 127)—the same year that Winckelmann's *Gedancken* were translated into French—Caylus spoke of the noble simplicity which created greatness and the sublime in Greek works (Justi, II, iv, 93).

The idea that simplicity creates grandeur and the sublime leads directly to the common and original source of both Caylus and Winckelmann: Boileau's *Traité du Sublime ou du Merveilleux dans le Discours, Traduit du Grec de Longin* of 1674.[24] Here in his corrupt and falsifying translation of Pseudo-Longinus' rhetorical writing Περὶ ὕψους (*On the Sublime,* first century A.D.), Boileau states as a rule of style, cette simplicité même . . . en fait la sublimité" (I, 183–84), or in a more specific statement, "Le style dont la grandeur vient de celle des pensées que la simplicité de l'expression fait surtout ressortir" (I, 101–2). In another quotation, Boileau translates "φιλὴ καθ' ἑαυτὴν ἡ ἔννοια" ("the sole thought") from Περὶ ὕψους, IX, 2, as "une simple pensée" in order to make the statement that grandeur can be found in simplicity, "le Sublime se trouve quelquefois dans une simple pensée."[25] In order to avoid the exaggerations of the sublime style, which Pseudo-Longinus called "Parenthyrsus"—the excessive pathos of Dionysian passion—Boileau wants to combine Quintilian's "genus grande," "le style sublime," with the "genus subtile," "le style simple," simplicity with grandeur.[26] Basically, Boileau's concern is an old problem of rhetorical stylistics: the distinction and unification of two of the three styles of classical and medieval rhetoric, the "genus subtile" or "simplex," "medium," and "grande."[27] In addition, he defines the style of the Greeks and of classical tragedy as one which "consiste dans une simplicité noble et majestueuse" (IV, 146).

Caylus and Winckelmann, however, did not have to dig out these quotations from just one work of a single author. It was exactly that same problem of "simplicity and grandeur" in Boileau's *Traité du Sublime* which had become the subject of an extensive literary feud among Boileau, Michel Le Clerc, Pierre Daniel Huet, and others. The dispute had been in print since 1713 in the editions of Boileau's collected works, as the title indicates, "augmented by corresponding reports to his works in critical remarks and dissertations" (vol. V). The argument of these writers centers on Boileau's notion, based on Περὶ ὕψους, IX, 9, that Genesis I, 3, "God said: 'Let there be light': and there was light," is an excellent example of Moses' "expression sublime et . . . très simple" (V, 208). Not only did the pugnacious contenders argue the extremely important question whether or not Longinus could have had any previous knowledge of Moses' classical formulation of the sublime in the simple language of the Bible when he wrote his *Traité du Sublime,* they rather repeated and debated almost every utterance of "simplicity" and grandeur" expressed by Boileau, added new examples from the text of Greek tragedies and from the lines of heroic dramas by their contemporary writer Pierre Corneille, and finally agreed that they had given "enough quotations to prove once and for all that the simple and the sublime in rhetorical discourse by no means oppose each other."[28]

The conclusions from these findings are obvious: none of Winckelmann's famous concepts and formulations of classical beauty are original. They all come from the same source, from French classicism, or, to be more specific, from the authors participating in the "Querelle des

Anciens et des Modernes" mentioned before, from whose works Winckelmann made extracts and in whose works we find extensive arguments about noble simplicity and grandeur in the art of classical, biblical, and contemporary rhetoric. Caylus and Winckelmann transferred these concepts—as Félibien, de Piles, and Jonathan Richardson had done sporadically before them[29]—from rhetoric to the description and study of works of Greek and Roman art and architecture: Caylus, just a few years before Winckelmann, in rather dry and tedious archaeological explanations; Winckelmann for the formulation of the highest idea of art and in elegant, lively descriptions and enthusiastic essays on works of ancient sculpture like the statues of Apollo, Bacchus, Antinous, and Laocoon, which inspired his contemporaries with a new Grecomania and a new concept of aesthetics.

Winckelmann distinguishes "noble simplicity and quiet grandeur" from its opposite, the exaggerated style of "passions" which are "too fiery and too wild," "a fault, which the ancient artists called Parenthyrsis" (*KS*, 41–42). Winckelmann's authority, Boileau, using the same phraseology, substitutes in his main text for the word "Le Parenthirse" the expressions "fureur hors de saison," "emporter à des passions" and declares "Le Parenthirse" "un défaut opposé au Grand" (IV, 288). Therefore and for the reasons mentioned above, it is wrong to assume that Winckelmann adopted his expressions directly from the original work of Pseudo-Longinus.[30] He could easily have found the model of his combination of "quietness" and "grandeur" in Boileau's treatise, chapter VII, "De la Sublimité dans les pensées," where in reference to Περὶ ὕψους, IX, 2, the quietness, the silence of Ajax before Odysseus in the underworld (*Odyssey*, XI, 561), is given as an example—and consequently discussed and compared by Boileau's critics with the "quiet grandeur" of Jesus being condemned to death—as an example of the most elevating grandeur (IV, 314–16). Winckelmann refers to the same Ajax and his wild heroism in the state of madness, when he describes "grandeur in quietness" in opposition to "fiery passions" (*KS*, 44).

It is true that Winckelmann was also influenced by works of British writers which he quoted, like Anthony Shaftesbury's *Characteristics of Men, Manners, Opinions, Times* (1711), Alexander Pope's *Essay on*

Criticism (1711) and *Essay on Man* (1733), John Milton's *Paradise Lost* (1667), and Joseph Addison's *Spectator* of 1712 and his poem *The Campaign* of 1704, from which he quotes the line of the angel in battle: "Calm and serene he drives the furious blast."[31] Winckelmann's manuscript (vol. 66, p. 42) at the Bibliothèque Nationale in Paris contains excerpts from the works of Shaftesbury in which the British philosopher demands "a character of solemnity and simplicity" and of "extraordinary simplicity" in the art of painting.[32] In manuscript 66, p. 29, Winckelmann underlined in his extract from Shaftesbury, I, 119, the statement: "The true courage is the cool and calm." Furthermore he noted (on p. 40) Shaftesbury's remark about "the lofty, the sublime, the astonishing, and amazing" in Greek language (III, 140). Again it is obvious that Winckelmann transferred these formulations from single aspects of painting, ethics, and rhetoric to a new and general concept of art and Greek antiquity. And as for the dispute about "the sublime" among British writers, A. F. B. Clark concludes his book *Boileau and the French Classical Critics in England* with the statement, "It [the dispute] has forced upon Englishmen the view that 'the sublime' means the grandest thought expressed in the simplest language" (see n. 33).

But Winckelmann's actual and extensive sources are French works. In addition to Boileau, he copied from Dubos' *Réflexions critiques sur la poésie et la peinture* of 1709 expressions like "tranquillité d'âme" and "sérénité de l'imagination." He could find the connection "véritable Grandeur et . . . noble Simplicité" in the elder Jonathan Richardson's *Traité de la Peinture, et de la Sculpture* of 1728 which was in his possession and which he quotes (*KS*, 304–5, 342). Even if the single term "noble simplicity" can be traced to classical antiquity and the Middle Ages and to occurrences in German literature (sporadically and unconnected with art) since 1724,[33] its use, as in the case of Winckelmann, always leads back to the French.

France in the eighteenth century was the center of European intellectual activity, much of which drew on the past with an eye to the future. Thus it is not surprising that Winckelmann's ideas have their origins in the diverse writings of a variety of French intellectuals; nor should it be surprising that Jefferson would be intellectually drawn to

France in the 1780s in search of the best of the Old World for his new nation. What is surprising is the direct connection which can be established between Winckelmann and Jefferson. We do not know when Jefferson obtained his copy of the Italian translation of Winckelmann's *Geschichte der Kunst des Alterthums*: his interest in classical models during the early 1770s is evidenced by his plans for Monticello, but the list of books he recommends to Robert Skipwith in 1771 makes no mention of Winckelmann's works.[34] It is, however, reasonable to suppose that Thomas Jefferson's interest in Winckelmann dates from his trip to Europe (1784–89). He owned the works of Boileau and knew William Hogarth's *Analysis of Beauty* (1753), Henry Home's (Lord Kames) *Elements of Criticism* (1762–65), and Edmund Burke's *Essay on the Sublime and Beautiful* (1757), besides the more general works on painting, fine arts, and antiquity by Félibien and Richardson which were also familiar to Winckelmann. We can even assume that Jefferson, like Winckelmann before him, had probably read Addison's characterization of Boileau's works as "[a] treatise on the sublime in a grovelling style" (*Spectator,* No. 58) and his observation that Boileau's "sublime arises . . . from the nobleness of the thought, the magnificence of the words" (*Guardian,* no. 117). We also know that Jefferson was familiar with Henry Home's extensive treatment, in his *Elements of Criticism* (pp. 95, 103–4), of the "dispute about that passage ['Let there be light'] between two French critics [Boileau and Huet named at the same page], the one positively affirming it to be sublime, the other as positively denying."[35] Jefferson echoes Winckelmann in transferring the mostly rhetorical terms of Boileau to the realm of aesthetics when he called the late classical plaster-castings in the Düsseldorf art gallery "sublime" and remarked about his journey to the "Maison Carrée," the Roman temple (early first century A.D.) at Nîmes in Southern France: "From Lyons to Nîmes I have been nourished with the remains of Roman grandeur . . . [with] whatever is Roman and noble" (Berman, pp. 114–15). Of course, the aesthetic concepts of "grandeur" and "noble" are reminiscent of Winckelmann's innovation.

However, a direct connection between Winckelmann and Jefferson does exist in the person of the French architect and painter Charles-

Louis Clérisseau (1722–1820), a contemporary and friend of Winckelmann *and* of Jefferson.[36] Winckelmann and Clérisseau were close friends and frequent associates in Rome from 1762 until 1767, when Clérisseau returned to France. Before his arrival in Paris, he studied and surveyed Roman buildings in Southern France, above all the "Maison Carrée" in Nîmes; Winckelmann shared in Clérisseau's archaeological work at Nîmes through a lively correspondence terminated only by Winckelmann's death in 1768. In his letters Winckelmann is very enthusiastic and repeatedly states his intention to travel to Nîmes and to see "les monumens de l'ancienne grandeur Romaine." He also compares the "Maison Carrée" to a newly discovered temple of Isis at the excavation side of Pompeii.[37]

When Jefferson came to France in 1784, he had the form of an ancient temple in mind as the prototype for the planned State Capitol of Virginia.[38] Clérisseau's book *Antiquités de la France, première partie: Monumens de Nîmes* containing the results of Clérisseau's archaeological research on the "Maison Carrée" and influenced by Winckelmann's ideas, had been published in 1778. Jefferson and Clérisseau met personally and became friends and collaborators, for it was with the cooperation of Clérisseau that Jefferson was able to work out the detailed plan for the Virginia State Capitol on the model of the "Maison Carrée" (Lankheit, p. 74). He then characterized that edifice with the words of Winckelmann in this way: "It is very simple, but it is noble beyond expression" (Berman, p. 124). A few years later, in commenting on the competition for the design of the Capitol Building at Washington in 1792, Jefferson likewise gives preference to Dr. Thornton's plan because of its "grandeur, simplicity and beauty" (Berman, pp. 132–33). The conformity of these two quotations with Winckelmann's "noble simplicity and quiet grandeur" is obvious.

Winckelmann may have appropriated "noble simplicity" and "quiet grandeur" from his contemporaries' treatments of individual arts, but he was the first to apply them to the whole world of art. It is only natural, then, that this transcendent aesthetic should be carried into the evolving concept of the republic as well. Here too Jefferson can be said to have a direct connection with Winckelmann, for during his stay in Paris he met Jacques-Louis David (1748–1825), generally considered the founder and chief representative of French neoclassicism, as well as the cultural dictator and foremost painter of the French Revolution and Napoleon's favorite portraitist. Jefferson remarked in 1789: "I do not feel an interest in any pencil but that of David" (Berman, p. 83). David came to Rome in 1775, where he was introduced to the artists of the "School of Mengs."[39] The German Anton Raphael Mengs (1728–79), a leading classicist painter, was Winckelmann's closest friend and most influential collaborator in Rome. David studied the works of Winckelmann (Dowd, p. 11) and during his entire life spoke of him with great admiration.[40] He further described his drawing of the head of St. Michael by Guido Reni as expressing a "colère noble et élevée";[41] Winckelmann had praised the "greatness of expression" in Reni's painting (*KS*, 46).

A sense of an aesthetic very much akin to Winckelmann's maxim of classic art had also become the authoritative standard in Jefferson's private life. Before he went abroad, Jefferson had compiled a list of desirable objects for the adornment of Monticello, including the Apollo Belvedere, the Antinous, the Dancing Faunus, and the Hercules Farnese.[42] These were also the statues Winckelmann had described in his *Geschichte der Kunst des Alterthums* as the favorite examples of "simplicity and grandeur." William Hogarth, whose *Analysis of Beauty* was quite familiar to both Jefferson and Winckelmann, remarked eleven years before the publication of the latter's *Geschichte der Kunst des Alterthums,* "The Antinous fills the spectator with admiration only while the Apollo strikes him with surprise . . . of something more than human" (p. 146). Winckelmann, however, went on to explain that "something more than human" in his apotheosis of Apollo as "the highest ideal of art."[43] David, the revolutionary student of Winckelmann, selected the Apollo Belvedere as an example of the best of Greek art.[44] And Jefferson surely read, after his return from Europe and in his own copy of the *Geschichte der Kunst des Alterthums,* Winckelmann's enthusiastic revelation: "The highest conception of ideal manly beauty is especially expressed in Apollo, in whom the strength of mature years is united with the tender form of the most beautiful springtime of youth . . . befitting a noble youth, destined to great purposes. Hence Apollo was the most beautiful among the gods.

Health blooms in his youth, and strength manifests itself, like the ruddiness of morning on a beautiful day. . . . Here I wished that I could describe such beauty which can hardly have had human origin" (pp. 158–59).

There is another instance of the possible influence of Winckelmann on Jefferson. The latter, we know, not only participated in the favorite hobby in the second half of the eighteenth century, the collecting of engraved antique gems, cameos, and medallions carved in relief after classical models, but he asserted that coins and medals should be provided with appropriate emblems and be used to symbolize "the dignity of the young republic" (Berman, pp. 105–6). In a contemporary description of the drawing room at Jefferson's "classical" villa Monticello, "medallions and engravings in endless profusion" are mentioned.[45] It has not been ascertained whether Jefferson was in possession of, or knew of, the leading reference work on this subject, Winckelmann's second major publication, the *Description des pierres gravées du feu Baron de Stosch*, published in Florence in 1760. The political ramifications of Winckelmann's thought upon Jefferson's political theory is a subject for another paper (see n. 36). What we must note here in these examples is the depth, the directness, and the ubiquity of Jefferson's contact with the synthesizing aesthetic vision of Johann Joachim Winckelmann.

NOTES

1 *A History of Western Art* (New York: Holt, 1953).

2 1935; rpt. Boston: Beacon, 1958, p. 11.

3 Henry [C.] Hatfield, *Aesthetic Paganism in German Literature: From Winckelmann to the Death of Goethe* (Cambridge, Mass.: Harvard Univ. Press, 1964), p. 10.

4 Horst Rüdiger, "Winckelmann's Personality," *Johann Joachim Winckelmann, 1768–1968* (Bad Godesberg: Inter Nationes, 1968), p. 20.

5 Hatfield, *Aesthetic Paganism*, p. 5.

6 *Geschichte der Kunst des Alterthums*, 2 vols. in 1 (Dresden: Walther, 1764); trans. into French in 1766 (twice), into Italian in 1779, and into English in 1849.

7 E. Millicent Sowerby, *Catalogue of the Library of Thomas Jefferson*, vol. IV

(Washington: Library of Congress, 1955), no. 4247. Subsequent references as *Catalogue*. See William Bainter O'Neal, *Jefferson's Fine Arts Library* (Charlottesville: Univ. of Virginia Press, 1956), p. 53.

8 *Monumenti antichi inediti, spiegati ed illustrati da Giovanni Winckelmann,* 2 vols. (1767; 2nd ed., 3 vols., Rome: Mordacchini, 1821).

9 *Gedancken über die Nachahmung der Griechischen Wercke in der Mahlerey und Bildhauer-Kunst* (1755; rpt. in *Johann Joachim Winckelmann: Kleine Schriften, Vorreden, Entwürfe,* ed. Walther Rehm, Berlin: De Gruyter, 1968), p. 29. Subsequent references to this edition will appear in the text as *KS*.

10 Henry C. Hatfield, *Winckelmann and His German Critics, 1755–1781* (New York: Columbia Univ. Press, 1943), p. 13. Wolfgang Leppmann, *Winckelmann* (New York: Knopf, 1970), p. 114.

11 W. Leppmann, p. ix; Ludwig Curtius and Horst Rüdiger in *Johann Joachim Winckelmann, 1768–1968* (Bad Godesberg: Inter Nationes, 1968), pp. 12, 20; Hatfield, *Winckelmann and His German Critics,* pp. 7–8; Ingrid Kreuzer, *Studien zu Winckelmanns Ästhetik* (Berlin: Akademie-Verlag, 1959), p. 33.

12 *Winckelmann and His German Critics,* p. 7.

13 *Les Caractères de Théophraste, traduits du Grec, avec les caractères ou les moeurs de ce siècle* (Paris: Michallet, 1688). See Carl Justi, *Winckelmann: Sein Leben, seine Werke und seine Zeitgenossen,* 2 vols. in 3 (Leipzig: Vogel, 1866–72), I, 386. Subsequent references will appear in the text as Justi. See also Hans Robert Jauss, *Literaturgeschichte als Provokation* (Frankfurt: Suhrkamp, 1970), pp. 80–81.

14 *Manuscrits de Winckelmann,* Paris, Bibliothèque Nationale, Fonds allemand, vols. 61 and 62. See also Gottfried Baumecker, *Winckelmann in seinen Dresdner Schriften: Die Entstehung von Winckelmanns Kunstanschauung und ihr Verhältnis zur vorhergehenden Kunsttheoretik mit Benutzung der Pariser Manuskripte Winckelmanns dargestellt* (Berlin: Junker und Dünnhaupt, 1933); Jauss, pp. 80–82; and Martin Fontius, *Winckelmann und die französische Aufklärung* (Berlin: Akademie-Verlag, 1968).

15 *Memoiren der Königin Christine,* ed. Arckenholz, 4 vols. (Berlin, 1751–60); available to me only as quotation in Justi, I, 242.

16 Gotthold Ephraim Lessing, *Laokoon: oder über die Grenzen der Mahlerey und Poesie.* Erster Theil (Berlin: Voss, 1755), chap. 1.

17 See Hermann Hettner, *Geschichte der deutschen Literatur im achtzehnten Jahrhundert,* vol. III, part II (Braunschweig: Vieweg, 1869), p. 413; Alphons Dürr, *Adam Friedrich Oeser: Ein Beitrag zur Kunstgeschichte des achtzehnten Jahrhunderts* (Leipzig: Dürr, 1879), pp. 56–57. Subsequent references will appear in the text as Dürr.

18 Johann Wolfgang Goethe, *Weimarausgabe,* Abtheilung IV, vol. I, 22. Letter to Philipp Erasmus Reich, February 20, 1770.

19 For the pietist expressions "simplicity of heart" and "the quiet [people] in the country" see August Langen, *Der Wortschatz des deutschen Pietismus,* 2nd ed. (Tübingen: Niemeyer, 1968), pp. 178–82, 362–65.

20 See Richard Biedrzynski, "The eagerness to See and Observe," *Johann Joachim Winckelmann, 1768–1968* (Bad Godesberg: Inter Nationes, 1968), p. 44.

21 Biedrzynski, p. 46.

22 Count Anne-Claude-Philippe de Caylus, *Recueil d'antiquités égyptiennes, etrusques, grecques et romaines,* 7 vols. See Justi, II, ii, 86.

23 See Kreuzer, p. 33, n. 1.

24 Nicolas Boileau-Despreaux, *Traité du Sublime ou du Merveilleux dans le Discours, Traduit du Grec de Longin* (1674; et *Réflexions sur Longin,* 1694; ed. de Brossette, 2 vols. Amsterdam: Mortier, 1718). Subsequent references to this edition will be given in the text by volume and page numbers.

25 Vol. I, chap. x. See also I, 183–84: "N'y ayant rien quelquefois de plus sublime que simple même."

26 *Oeuvres de Boileau Despréaux,* Avec des éclaircissemens historiques donnés par lui-même, ed. de Saint-Marc (ed. Brossette, 1718; rpt. Amsterdam: Changuion, 1772), IV, 138–39. Subsequent references to this edition will be given in the text by volume and page numbers.

27 Quintilian, *Institutio oratorica,* XII, 10, 58.

28 *Oeuvres de Boileau,* V, 202, 208–18, 240–53.

29 See Baumecker, pp. 17–30.

30 Horst Rüdiger, "Winckelmann's Personality," *Johann Joachim Winckelmann, 1768–1968* (Bad Godesberg: Inter Nationes, 1968), p. 28.

31 *KS,* 46. See also Justi, I, 220–42.

32 Winckelmann copied from the 3 vols. of Shaftesbury's *Characteristics of Men,* 5th ed. (London: Purser, 1732); here III, 374–75. Subsequent references to this edition will be given in the text by volume and page numbers. For Winckelmann's copying from Shaftesbury see also Baumecker, pp. 39–68.

33 Wolfgang Stammler, "Edle Einfalt, Zur Geschichte eines kunsttheoretischen Topos," *Worte und Werke,* Bruno Markwardt zum 60. Geburtstag, ed. Gustav Erdmann, Alfons Eichstaedt (Berlin: De Gruyter, 1961), pp. 359–82; Winckelmann, *KS,* 342. For sources of Winckelmann's concept of art besides Boileau, see Gottfried Baumecker, *Winckelmann in seinen Dresdner Schriften* (Berlin: Junker and Dünnhaupt, 1933). For Winckelmann and Boileau, see Max L. Baeumer, "Winckelmanns Formulierung der klassischen Schönheit," *Monatshefte,* 65 (1973), 61–75. Boileau's *Traité du Sublime ou du Merveilleux dans le Discours, Traduit du Grec de Longin* of 1674 appeared until 1750 in more than fifteen editions. For Boileau's influence in England see Alexander Frederick Bruce Clark, *Boileau and the French Classical Critics in England, 1660–1830* (New York: Russell & Russell, 1963). Boileau's work was translated into German by the curator of the Dresden art galleries, Carl Heinrich von Heinecken in 1737. This very poor and clumsy translation, *Dionys Longinus vom Erhabenen, griechisch und teutsch,* appeared in Dresden in 1737 and 1742. Heinecken was ill-disposed toward Winckelmann and Winckelmann called him contemptuously a "feigned critic of art" (*KS,* 115). All eighteenth-century writings on the sublime depend on Boileau's *Treatise,* in particular Edmund Burke's *A Philosophical Enquiry into the Origin of our Ideas of the Sublime and Beautiful* (London, 1757) which, among others, influenced Thomas Jefferson's early concept of art, Moses Mendelssohn's *Betrachtungen über das Erhabene und das Naive in den schönen Wissenschaften* of 1758, and Immanuel Kant's *Beobachtungen über das Gefühl des Schönen und Erhabenen* of 1764. For the

further development and significance of the sublime in German literature, see Karl Vietor, "Die Idee des Erhabenen in der deutschen Literatur," in Karl Vietor, *Geist und Form, Aufsätze zur deutschen Literaturgeschichte* (Bern: Francke, 1952), pp. 234–66.

34 Eleanor Davidson Berman, *Thomas Jefferson among the Arts* (New York: Philosophical Library, 1947), p. 76. Subsequent references will appear in the text as Berman.

35 See n. 31; A. F. B. Clark, *Boileau and the French Classical Critics,* pp. 371–79. For works in Jefferson's possession see *Catalogue,* nos. 4236, 4248, 4491, 4546.

36 I have considered some of the connections between Winckelmann, Jefferson and contemporary French artists from a more political point of view in another study, submitted for publication elsewhere. Here the important relations are investigated in the broader context of the principal aesthetic ideas under which these connections were conceived and expressed by Winckelmann, Jefferson, and the artists themselves. For brief references to Clérisseau as a connecting link between Winckelmann and Jefferson see Karl Lehmann, *Thomas Jefferson: American Humanist* (Chicago: Univ. of Chicago Press, 1947; 2nd ed. 1965), pp. 55, 128.

37 See Johann Joachim Winckelmann, *Briefe,* ed. Walther Rehm, vol. III (Berlin, 1956), pp. 332–33.

38 Klaus Lankheit, *Revolution und Restauration: Kunst der Welt* (Baden-Baden: Holle, 1965), p. 74. Subsequent references will appear in the text as Lankheit.

39 David Lloyd Dowd, *Pageant-Master of the Republic: Jacques-Louis David and the French Revolution,* University of Nebraska Studies, new ser., no. 3 (Lincoln, Nebraska: Univ. of Nebraska Press, 1948), p. 8. Subsequent references will appear in the text as Dowd.

40 Klaus Holma, *David, son évolution et son style* (Paris, 1940), p. 16; as quoted by René Verbraeken, *Jacques-Louis David jugé par ses contemporains et par la postérité* (Paris: Laget, 1973), p. 171.

41 Helen Rosenau, *The Painter Jacques-Louis David* (London: Nicholson & Watson, 1948), p. 30.

42 Sidney Fiske Kimball, *Thomas Jefferson, Architect* (Cambridge: Riverside Press, 1916). See also Berman, p. 96.

43 See Winckelmann's "Description of the Apollo Belvedere," *KS,* 267.

44 See Sewall, p. 847.

45 William Wirt, *Eulogy on Jefferson,* in *The Writings of Thomas Jefferson,* Memorial Edition, XIII, xlvii. See also Berman, p. 79.

Wieland and the French Revolution: The Writings of the First Year

LIESELOTTE KURTH-VOIGT

Although the writings of Christoph Martin Wieland that treat, exclusively or incidentally, the French Revolution have received a fair share of scholarly attention ever since the first comprehensive study by Harald von Koskull appeared in 1901,[1] these works deserve still further analyses and interpretation. Close and detailed readings of the texts should prove particularly rewarding if significant factors of historical and literary contextuality are carefully considered, if the identities of the *personae* are meticulously analyzed, and if precise attention is given to the complex interrelation of these variants as they are uniquely combined in each of Wieland's relevant contributions. More specifically, every one of these pieces should be treated strictly in chronological order and in the context of the actual occurrences that are mirrored in the work. Furthermore, each work has to be viewed in its relation to contemporary publications, with which the author and his fictional figures were well acquainted; their critical reactions to crucial incidents and public documents always reach beyond the frame of a single work and must be understood as a participation in the continuing controversy of political reality. Most important, however, it is necessary to define the personalities of the fictional characters, their prejudices and idiosyncrasies, for Wieland created many of his figures with the distinct purpose of making them present subjective views on the controversial events of his time.[2]

Several of the relevant works are dialogues, and it is essential to remember Wieland's reasons for selecting a specific variant of this form for the treatment of political matters. From Cicero, Lucian, and, later, Shaftesbury he had learned that in contrast to Plato's biased characterizations, the creation of intelligent and well-informed interlocutors enables a writer to present various perspectives, each well-founded and seriously meant,[3] none necessarily revealing the author's personal stance. The resulting neutrality, so very carefully designed by Wieland, has often been violated by critics who interpret fictional statements as expressions of his own views, thus creating inconsistencies or contradictions which they then attack as evidence of his vacillation. Goethe, for one, knew better. Although he recognized the danger inherent in the artistic manipulation of opinions, he did not reject Wieland's intentions but defended them perceptively in one of his conversations with Falk: ". . . es war Wieland in allen Stücken weniger um einen festen Standpunkt als um eine geistreiche Debatte zu tun."[4] The undogmatic consideration of men and matters from different points of view was characteristic of Wieland,[5] and as he looks back upon his participation in the critical examination of historic events he admits these tendencies: "Meine natürliche Geneigtheit, Alles (Personen und Sachen) von allen Seiten und aus allen möglichen Gesichtspunkten anzusehen, und ein herzlicher Widerwille gegen das nur allzu gewöhnliche einseitige Urtheilen und Parteynehmen, ist ein wesentliches Stück meiner Individualität."[6]

In the analysis of his literary works it is necessary, of course, to distinguish carefully between the essays in which Wieland distinctly voices his own opinions and other writings in which mythological, historical, or invented figures express their personal convictions. Wieland, it will be remembered, was an acknowledged master of the art of characterization, and the literary figures he created were convincingly human, each unique in its make-up but at the same time frequently sharing the beliefs and antipathies of the groups they were meant to represent. Therefore, instead of seeing the individual spokesman as a mask for Wieland, it would be more enlightening to analyze each as an independent, self-determining personality with a well-defined part in the at times inharmonious chorus of voices that accompanied the events in France.

The first work directly concerned with the Revolution is the dialogue "Eine Unterredung über die Rechtmässigkeit des Gebrauchs, den die Französische Nazion dermahlen von ihrer Aufklärung und Stärke macht. Geschrieben im August 1789."[7] The identities of its participants are immediately established by carefully chosen, meaningful names: Walther, "ruler of the host," acts as a supporter of the people in rebellion, and Adelstan, "from the camp of the nobility," defends the position of the king and his loyal followers. Walther begins the dialogue with a diatribe against journalists who, he claims, defame the French people, and in support of his accusation he quotes a paragraph from the *Cahiers de Lecture* which had recently published what he considers a "hideous portrait of the moral depravity" of the capital of France. Walther, however, is an unreliable explicator who falsifies the document he is using to make his point. The title of the article, "Le camp des Tartares au Palais-royal, à Paris," circumscribes the "portrait," and, underlining this first impression, the detailed description of the notorious section surrounding the Palais explicitly states that among the crowd of young fools and their companions one will seldom find a sensible man and rarely a respectable woman or a decent girl.[8] But Walther could not have used such a discriminating depiction; he needed a grossly biased, generalizing account so that he could discredit the critics and replace their "portrait" by a more favorable image of the nation which, he believes, has astonished the whole of Europe with its "patriotism, wisdom, bravery, and perseverance."

It is at this moment that Adelstan interrupts Walther in mid-sentence and completes the statement with a contrasting characterization. Europe, he maintains, is filled with horror and loathing precisely because the anonymous author of the article in the *Cahiers de Lecture* has accurately described "terrible" and "cannibalistic" scenes that can be observed everywhere in France and are symptomatic of the lawless disorder that has spread through the entire country. Exploiting

Walther's distorting generalization and using it against him, Adelstan does not at all consider the unfavorable depiction an exaggeration, because the reality of the "outrageous arrogance of the National Assembly" and the "insane rage of the people" is actually still more sordid; in fact, it transcends the imagination of even the most severe critic.

Walther's reply to this indictment is an enthusiastic laudation of the French in which he expresses his compassion for a desperate people, a fierce contempt for the tyrants who enslave it, and an effusive admiration for the sound reason of the National Assembly, the manly spirit, enlightened minds, and the true nobility of its members. Adelstan is amused by the fervor of Walther's "recitation" and cautions him to remember that such excessive ardor coming from the heart may easily becloud the mind and impair the reason. Yet his own statements demonstrate that he is no less a *Schwärmer* than Walther as he defends the king and his cause with equal enthusiasm. And when he cites Mirabeau's famous address of July 10, he too changes the text of the speech to illustrate his own contentions more effectively.[9]

This first exchange of views establishes the basic positions of the two dialogists, and these remain unaltered throughout the conversation as they attempt to augment their arguments and to justify their stances.[10] The tactics they use to extol their ideals forcefully underscore their argumentation. Both men are skillful advocates of their causes and masters of the art of persuasion. They manipulate the language, carefully selecting a biased vocabulary, particularly when they discuss the contending parties, and they are sensitively aware of their linguistic subjectivity. For example, when Adelstan uses terms like *Pöbel, Aufruhr,* and *Anmassung,* Walther corrects him and suggests the use of less derisive terms, perhaps *Volk, Aufstand zu rechtmässiger Selbstverteidigung,* and *Behauptung seiner Würde,* which are of course equally slanted, with their emphasis on "rightful," "self-defense," and "dignity." The two men also use suggestive imagery and metaphors to reinforce their polemics. Walther has a preference for the vocabulary of steady, forward movement (*fester Gang, Schritt für Schritt*) and natural processes, seeing for example the outcome of the conflict as the rebirth of a monarchy that is at present struggling with political death. Adelstan intermittently uses the metaphors of the *theatrum mundi* and interprets the events as a "play" (*Schauspiel*), refers to the "place of action" (*Schauplatz*), mentions "scenes," and speaks of "appearances on the stage" (*Auftritte*). Although these phrases characterize the Revolution as a "drama," its merely "theatrical" aspects are later negated when he predicts that the princes of other nations will most certainly not idly witness the events as if they were nothing more than a stage tragedy (*Schauspielertragödie*).

Like most of Wieland's figures, Walther and Adelstan are well educated and at home with allusions to the classics, which lend their views an air of authority and establish meaningful perspectives in depth. When, for example, they discuss some of the recent motions and actions, but more important, the indecisiveness of the National Assembly, Adelstan fears that soon it will be too late for the new demagogues to turn from their abstract speculations to specific practical tasks, for the patient they wanted to "regenerate in Medea's magic kettle" may well have died meanwhile. The allusion is well chosen, because it carries appropriately political overtones and plays on the idea of rebirth Walther had previously introduced. Medea, legend relates, had cunningly convinced the daughters of Pelias that she knew how to rejuvenate their aging father. She suggested that they drug Pelias, cut him into small bits, and throw the pieces into a kettle of boiling water. She then would utter the magic charm and Pelias would emerge, younger and stronger. Trusting her promise, the women carry out these instructions, only Medea never speaks the magic words but disappears, and the king's daughters realize with horror that they have murdered their father. With his allusion to this event Adelstan establishes rather unflattering parallels: the naïve and unsuspecting among the French are duped into believing that there is a kind of magic cure for the ills of the nation. Misled by false promises, they share in sacrifices that seem necessary to bring about the rebirth or rejuvenation of their country, but they are betrayed and manoeuvered into disaster. Walther, of course, rejects these implications and believes that neither a *deus ex machina* nor Medea's magic kettle is needed to rescue a nation that in spirit, courage, and sense of honor surpasses all others and possesses effective means to help itself.

Through further allusions Adelstan contrasts Louis XVI with Dionysius and Aristion, suggesting characteristic differences between the modern French king, the ancient tyrant of Syracuse, whom Wieland had portrayed in *Agathon,* and the philosopher-king of Athens, whom he had depicted in an article published August 1781 in the *Teutsche Merkur.*

Walther's allusions establish equally important connections. His advice that a monarch should not object to a necessary curtailment of his powers but should recognize the wisdom of Hesiod, who maintained that a half is sometimes better than a whole, becomes even more meaningful when it is seen in the context of Hesiod's *Works and Days.* It immediately precedes the explanation that the dismal sorrows of mankind are the inescapable punishment of Zeus; man's misery is thus part of a larger design and not unique to the French condition.[11] A more significant context is evoked when Walther attempts to look at the conflict "aus dem gewöhnlichen Gesichtspunkte der Politiker, . . . wo Der Recht hat, für den sich der Erfolg, oder (wie Lukan sagt) die Götter erklären" (312). The reference is to the first book of the *Pharsalia,* and the reader familiar with the work (as Wieland's contemporaries were) will perceive ominous overtones.[12] The text immediately surrounding the quotation (126–29) questions the right of any party to involve another in a violent contest for superiority. Later lines indicate that the ancient rivals were ill matched, one representing an aging power, "tamed by declining years" (129), the other an ambitious, progressive, and easily challenged contestant who cleared "the way before him by destruction" (150). Lucan further suggests in this section that the division of power among "three masters"—a condition temporarily paralleled in France—precipitated the decline of a great nation and set the stage for a most horrible war, a "fierce orgy of slaughter" and fratricide (9). Of course, Walther would not have encouraged this kind of allusive speculation, for his position is severely jeopardized when the context of the reference is made to bear upon his interpretation of events. But Wieland no doubt hoped that the creative reader, his favorite reader, would accept the challenge of the allusion, establish its broader contextual meaning, and recognize the irony of reference by which the tenuousness of Walther's reasoning is exposed.

Adelstan and Walther are well informed on current publications and support their cases by citing relevant articles or by quoting distinguished orators who appeared before the National Assembly. They do not, however, use these documents with complete reliability, but adapt and supplement them, occasionally even falsifying the texts so that in their altered form they strengthen their arguments.

A characteristic example of their subjective exploitation of sources is provided by their use of the king's speech, delivered before the Estates-General on May 5, 1789.[13] Adelstan, a staunch advocate of Louis XVI, is fairly accurate when he combines the king's words with his own explanations as he attempts to prove that the deplorable state of the nation is not the sole responsibility of its present ruler. But ever so subtly he exonerates the king by interspersing a few phrases of his own into the indirect quotations from the speech. Whereas Louis had only mentioned "a costly, but honorable war" as part of the cause of the country's financial difficulties, Adelstan is more explicit as he speaks of the "American War" and reminds his opponent that this war "was enthusiastically supported by the entire nation." The king had merely mentioned the necessity for an increase in taxes, yet Adelstan does not allow Walther to forget that the burden of taxes had already been unbearable before Louis ascended the throne; and whereas Louis had only referred to the unequal distribution of taxes, Adelstan vindicates the king as he maintains that Louis was not at all responsible for this inequality in taxation but inherited it from his predecessors.

Walther is more overtly deceptive in his use of the address, as he supplements indirect quotations in such a fashion that all of it must be understood as the king's words. To be sure, he rephrases parts of the address correctly when he recalls that Louis had assembled the representatives to strengthen the nation and provide new sources for its monetary needs. But he clearly invents the continuation of this statement when he claims that the king had "admitted" the financial situation of France to be "a most miserable" one, never before encountered by this nation which under a wise government would have been destined to be "the very first in this world" but under his own rule is now "led to the brink of political destruction." Louis did not make these humble self-accusations, yet Walther needed this "confession" to build his case and did not hesitate to invent it.[14]

There are other moments of strong disagreement between the dialogists, and they clearly disclose the clashing views of these fictional yet plausibly real figures. Again and again Adelstan is convincingly characterized as a traditionalist and an "ardent royalist," and Walther is credibly portrayed as an enthusiastic progressive who zealously supports the Revolution against the Ancient Regime.

Wieland's second contribution, the "Kosmopolitische Addresse an die Französische Nazionalversammlung,"[15] has equally fictional qualities.[16] Its speaker, Eleutherius Filoceltes, looks at the events in France as an "individual unimportant *Weltbürger*," but he is identified as one who has, as his name indicates, a sincere affection for the French and who would be inclined to set free the enslaved.[17] The historical event that motivated the address was the crucial session of the National Assembly on the night of August 4, when inequalities were emotionally denounced and sweeping reforms, particularly the abolition of privileges in taxation, were initiated. Filoceltes assumes a moderate position between those of Walther and Adelstan as he examines recent decisions of the Assembly relating to the new constitution, the question of sovereignty, and the mounting national debt. Although he is less emotional and not as biased as his predecessors, he is as clever a disputant as they were. The address is well structured and carefully worded, and his case is convincingly argued, occasionally supported by appropriate references to published documents and by shrewdly chosen quotations.

His favorite device is the kind of rhetorical question that leads to a conditional supposition and finally implies exactly the answer he needs in order to make his point. The events of the night session and their aftermath have disenchanted Filoceltes, and he doubts that the French have chosen the proper methods to bring about the intended palingenesis of the monarchy. The first set of questions probes the right of the Assembly to overthrow the old constitution and establish a new one. He is critical of this action and hopes that the French will not claim to have based their decision on a "general, inalienable law of nature" that would apply to all nations and might thus encourage others to undertake similar steps whenever they have "the mood and inclination" (*Lust und Belieben*) to do so. Nor does he believe that dissatisfaction with imperfect conditions always justifies drastic measures. A change in constitution would then happen too frequently, for it is "fysisch und moralisch unmöglich . . ., dass eine Nazion im Ganzen und in allen ihren Theilen immer mit ihrem Zustande zufrieden sey" (319). He expects—and states this rather sarcastically—that the French will find "in den Archiven der grossen Göttin Natur . . . das Original eines Freybrietes" (320) establishing the exclusiveness of their right to select a new constitution whenever it would please their people—a unique privilege that should for the sake of peace and security not be granted to any other nation. Filoceltes does not deny the French the right to declare their opposition to monarchic and aristocratic despotism, but he questions their expectation that the type of "democratic despotism" they are about to establish will make the nation "happier, wealthier, and better." Until experience confirms the extent and duration of the national bliss of which the people in their intoxication with freedom sweetly dream, one should be permitted to doubt whether a realm that for centuries was one of the mightiest monarchies on earth can easily be transformed into a democracy.

To be sure, France still claims to be a monarchy, as was confirmed during the session of August 28, and although the Assembly declared Louis XVI the "restorer of French freedom," it also impaired his dignity by claiming sovereignty for the French people. All this has been done by those who call themselves "representatives of the people"; actually, Filoceltes believes, they are a small band of men who are at times as high-handed and demagogic as their opponents. Many of the reforms they introduced brought about "disorder, disadvantages, and abuses," and the most pressing problem, that of the heavy national debt, they not only neglected to solve but in fact seriously compounded. Why, Filoceltes asks, did they not simply reject financial responsibilities that are completely unrelated to the business of governing the nation and were caused by "excessive pomp, extravagance, and poor management at court"? How is it possible, he asks, that the representatives of the people who rejected so much of the past now "despotically" force them into a "scheme" that is clearly contrary to the principles of the new order?

In the final section of his address Filoceltes considers it necessary to identify and justify his position. He is neither a "Slave" nor a defender of the divine rights of kings, nor does he begrudge the French nation its newly found happiness and glory. He is, rather, as he had initially implied, the observer of a unique drama who in fairly objective conclusions sums up matters of which he approves and indicates actions he cannot possibly sanction. These latter aspects are often the subject of an unsparing satire that ridicules questionable decisions and dubious undertakings, occasionally with gentle irony—more often, however, with mocking sarcasm. The quarrel of the French over whether to call their new form of government "monarchic" reminds Filoceltes of Octavian who concealed the monarchical nature of his rule under the form of a republic, and he derisively asks: "Warum sollte die monarchische Form nicht eben so gut der neuen Demokratie in Frankreich zur Maske dienen können?" (323). Yet this is a minor matter; more serious disturbances seem to lie ahead, for the nation is apparently possessed by a strange kind of "freedom-fever" that is quite similar to the notorious *Abderitenfieber,* [18] an allusion obviously meant to imply that France is at the moment as much a republic of fools as Abdera was in ancient times. Continuing his satire, Filoceltes facetiously analyzes a statement contained in the "Declaration of the Rights of Man" which states that every citizen may either "personally or through a representative" participate in the enactment of legislation for the nation. He finds the implication of this statement ludicrous, for on the basis of this provision every one of about five million Frenchmen could "als eben so viele Solone und Lykurge" (325) appear in person in Versailles, though of course not all of them will come; many are too poor to dress appropriately, and it would simply not be decent to stand before the august body in wooden shoes and torn pants.

In his compassionate defense of Louis XVI, Filoceltes also scorns the "sentimental *Fastnachtsspiel*" the French have staged in the king's "honor"; the performance sadly reminds him of the cruel game the soldiers played with Christ when they draped him in a torn robe, placed a crown of thorns on his head, abused him, and mockingly proclaimed him King of the Jews.

Despite its at times severe criticism, the address concludes in an open-ended fashion and Filoceltes' final *subjectio* is slightly optimistic: "Wird die neue Ordnung, die aus diesem Chaos . . . entspringen wird, die unzähligen Wunden, welche der demokratische Kakodämon der freyheitstrunknen Nazion geschlagen hat, bald und gründlich genug heilen können, um als eine Vergütung so vielen Übels angesehen zu werden?

Die Zeit allein kann auf diese Fragen die wahre Antwort geben" (335).

The cautious attitude expressed in these lines is reminiscent of Adelstan's scepticism at the end of his dialogue with Walther. Yet despite some agreement, the views of these men on crucial matters are basically different, and although each of the three is depicted as having a distinctly individual personality, they also represent the ideals of larger segments of society and thus fulfill an important symbolic function.

Wieland's third contribution to the topic, "Unparteyische Betrachtungen über die dermalige Staats-Revolution in Frankreich," adds further perspectives.[19] The essay appeared in 1790 in the *Teutsche Merkur*, is signed with the initial W., and contains the author's personal views. Wieland begins his reflections with a quotation from one of his earlier works, "Eine Lustreise ins Elysium" (1787), in which he had assigned a role to himself, the *Ich* conversing with Menippus and Xenophon, and had virtually predicted the inevitability of the Revolution.[20] The *Unparteilichkeit* indicated in the title must be understood in a specific sense. It does not mean that Wieland is strictly neutral, but it implies that he is an outside observer who does not belong to either one of the parties in conflict. Yet these factions are so unequal, so different in their ideals and in the means they employ to achieve their goals, that it is impossible for a conscientious witness to remain impartial. The presentation that precedes this admission shows that Wieland's own sympathies lie with the people, "ein Jahrhunderte lang misshandeltes Volk" (336), and their representatives in the National Assembly. Although he finds it natural that the outsiders' points of view from which the Revolution is observed continue to shift, often as a reflection of the Assembly's actions which change its course, he does not approve of undiscerning judgments which, for example, label the Assembly "unjust" and "tyrannical" or claim that it merely replaces the despotic aristocratic and monarchic system by a democratic despotism. Wieland thus sets himself apart from Filoceltes who had voiced exactly this kind of censure.[21] But he is not as uncritically enthusiastic in his support of the king's opponents as Walther was and cautiously identifies his position: "Ich bin weit entfernt, mich zum schwärmerischen Lobredner der französischen National-Versammlung aufzuwerfen, und alle ihre Handlungen, alle ihre Decrete und Einrichtungen, ohne Ausnahme und Einschränkung, für die bestmöglichsten zu halten..." (350). He is aware of the fallibility of these men and of the haste with which they have reached certain decisions; he is conscious of the mixed character of this political body and therefore distinguishes carefully between destructive insurgents and the "most noble and enlightened" faction of the Assembly that possesses his regard.

The events in France are receiving much praise as well as a large share of criticism, some of it unjustly slanted. These prejudicial opinions, Wieland believes, are tolerable if they are expressed in a private manner. But distortingly subjective views become indefensible when they are maintained by well-known writers and published in widely read journals, for they then unfairly influence a public that trusts the author's judgment and has perhaps no other means to inform itself more objectively. Characteristic examples of such biased depictions had appeared in the *StatsAnzeigen*, a politically influential periodical whose editor was the renowned historian August Ludwig Schlözer, and a large portion of Wieland's "Betrachtungen" is a critical analysis of dubious views made public in this magazine. Although Schlözer had recently published a brief description of the disruption in France that was partly correct, he had supplemented it by a traveller's report which was unbelievably one-sided. As evidence of its irresponsible distortions Wieland reproduces a full page of the text and exposes the most blatant misrepresentations in extensive notes. These are often ironic, more frequently even sarcastic. When, for example, the traveller states that his searching inquiries about the reason and nature of the disruption in France were answered by "them"—"Und jedesmal antwortete m a n mir"—Wieland mockingly questions the precision of this identification: "Wer waren wohl diese wackern Leute, die dem ehrlichen (vermuthlich Teutschen) Frager eine so e i n h e l l i g e Antwort gaben?" (340). France, he believes, is too severely divided into many factions ever to have expressed agreement on all the topics the traveller claims to have discussed with its citizens.

The answers allegedly given seem equally ridiculous to Wieland. They attempt to place the blame for much of the disorder upon "a dozen most wicked villans," who follow in the footsteps of Cromwell, and fifty "second-rate villains" commanded by a man identified as M–, who manipulates the rabble of Paris as if they were marionettes. Wieland questions these insinuations; if the "villains" can be associated with Cromwell, at least they are "ganz respectable Bösewichter," although the English would rightfully resent any comparison of this nature. The puppeteer is obviously none other than Mirabeau, but Wieland ironically rejects this reading as erroneous: "Der Graf Mirabeau kann es wohl nicht seyn" (340), for he is by no means the kind of subordinate villain and inferior mind Schlözer's reporter makes him out to be. In this fashion Wieland's notes satirize other assertions of the speaker; they expose the prejudice of his report and caution the reader to doubt the reliability of similar vituperative articles in Schlözer's *StatsAnzeigen* and other contemporary periodicals with comparable tendencies.

Yet in his own documentation Wieland himself is not completely reliable. Like his fictional characters he also changes, albeit ever so slightly, the texts he uses. For instance, in one of his articles Schlözer quoted a French source that had stated: "Beim 'Schimmer der patriotischen Laternen in Paris,' lässt sich *noch* nicht eine Geschichte des dermaligen französischen ReichtsTags schreiben" (italics mine),[22] and he suggested to those who would like to contemplate the Revolution from a different point of view that they consider historical parallels that might reveal the better solutions earlier generations and other countries, particularly England, had found in the past. Although these thoughts are not alien to Wieland, he denies them an accurate representation. He only quotes the introductory sentence of the essay, thus treating it out of context; and by omitting the limiting particle *noch*, he converts the relative formulation into a dogmatic statement which he then rather unfairly analyzes as untenably doctrinaire.

The more broadly intended censure contained in Wieland's "Betrachtungen" is directed against those critics who draw their information from slanted sources, relying on the "ephemerischen Scarteken, womit der Parteygeist, zumal auf der missvergnügten Seite, Paris und die Provinzen überschwemmt" (355). Playing on words, Wieland does not consider such publications pure sources (*reine Quellen*), but dung puddles (*Mistpfützen*). The critic sincerely searching for the truth must consult other materials, public records, and official documents, and should rely on indisputable facts if he hopes to make a permanent contribution to the history of the Revolution.

To offset "one-sided" accounts Wieland will attempt to search more objectively for the truth, ". . . mit Beseitigung aller Vorurtheile, einseitiger Nachrichten, Anekdoten, angeblicher geheimer Aufschlüsse, and entweder wirklich passionierter oder absichtlich mit künstlicher Wärme geschriebener Declamationen" (342). The time for a conclusive judgment has not yet arrived; the outcome of the conflict is still uncertain; in fact, there is no doubt that the proponents of a counterrevolution are diligently at work. Wieland broadly indicates the direction toward which the nation should ideally be moving as he presents his characterization of the three factions involved in the struggle: the representatives of the people participating in the National Assembly, the aristocratic and court party, and the people themselves, who may profess loyalty to either of the groups but can be persuaded to alter their allegiance. Wieland's depiction of the two major parties is by no means as objective as one would have the right to expect on the basis of his promise to eliminate bias and prejudice. The comparison of the opponents is unfairly selective; the worst offenses of the "royal-aristocratic" party are contrasted with the achievements of the "most noble and enlightened part" of the National Assembly. The possible idealism of the royalists is lightly passed over, and the misdeeds of the people's party are understated or seen as regrettable exceptions. Language and images are shrewdly chosen and the *exempla* are cleverly designed to underline the contrast. Among those who are interested in a reactionary movement are the clergy and nobility, courtiers, parliamentarians, and financiers "mit dem ganzen ungeheuern Schweife, den dieser vielköpfige Drache nach sich schleppt" (344). They are constantly active with "unermüdeten, geheimen und zum Theil öffentlichen Machinationen" (344) trying to intimidate the true friends of freedom. They are politically clever enough to know, "dass man den Vögeln, die man locken will, liebliche Töne vorpfeifen muss" (347), and are patiently waiting for the moment at which they can spring the trap and lead the people back into slavery. If unchecked, this legion of evil spirits (*unsaubere Geister*) is bound to launch a civil war that will inflict intolerable misery on the French, cast the nation into anarchy, and cause its ruin and destruction.

Wieland is certain that in contrast to these "demons of doom," the noble members of the National Assembly will lead the French toward a better future. Guided by the benevolent genius of the nation, these patriotic men (he quotes Lafayette) "welche die Freyheit eben so gesetzt und entschlossen gegen die Licenz als gegen den Despotismus vertheidigten" (350), who possess the energies and the will to effect the best possible results, will surely accomplish the demanding task of providing France with an equitable constitution and an orderly system of finances. In an *exemplum* that leaves no doubt about Wieland's strong sympathies, he compares the National Assembly with a true physician able to cure his patient, though perhaps slowly and painfully, who is drawn into a contest with a charlatan, symbolizing the court party, who provides spectacular but temporary relief and is handsomely paid but who has with his magic *arcanum* actually hastened the death of his patient. In the final section of his "Unpartheyische Betrachtungen" Wieland discusses a particular aspect of the projected constitution in greater detail. He would not sanction the granting of exceptional privileges to any one Estate, because this might again cause the enslavement of other classes, but he expects that each of the three Estates will assume an important role under the new system. It is his hope that the French will follow the English model and establish a sound balance of power by creating two houses in which the representatives of the people together with the clergy and nobility will share in the government of the nation.

The National Assembly, however, was to move in a different direction. An initial step was taken on February 13 when the privileges of the clergy were curtailed and monastic vows and orders were abolished. Wieland, who in earlier works had occasionally satirized the *Mönchswesen,* did not voice any criticism of the Assembly's action but wholeheartedly supported the decision in his article "Die zwey wichtigsten Ereignisse des vorigen Monats," which was published in March 1790 in the *Teutsche Merkur.*[23] This is less an explanation of the edict than a defense of measures that must be taken to insure the efficacy of a new constitution. He admits that he cannot look at the consequences of the decree from the standpoint of those who suffer from the cancellation of privileges, but must see these matters in a larger perspective as an unavoidable move to "heal" the "ills and injuries of the nation."

Almost a third of the text is, by Wieland's own definition, an allegory poetically designed to persuade his readers of the justice of the edict. A perfect constitution is like a fine piece of architecture, he argues, and the process of its creation will delight an unbiased observer as much as if he were watching a skilled craftsman shape a work of art. The new constitution must be unencumbered by the rubble of the old "gothic monster" it is to replace; the ancient foundation must be razed. It is, of course, unavoidable that those who were securely and comfortably entrenched in the old structure—among them, according to a negatively selective listing by Wieland, mice and rats, spiders and sparrows—must be driven out when making room for the new building; and it would be unfair to accuse the craftsmen who perform the work and by necessity disturb these creatures of "ill will, secret envy, or other maliciousness." The constitution should not be a patchwork of the old and the new. By using the image of *Flickwerk* Wieland can even refer to an authority the bishops and monks affected by this measure are bound to accept, for it was Christ himself who had advised that "no man putteth a piece of a new garment upon an old; if otherwise, then both the new maketh a rent, and the piece that was *taken* out of the new agreeth not with the old" (Luke 5:36). The nation must free itself from the burden of obsolete customs if it wants to establish "the most rational constitution"; and France is indeed fortunate to have made great progress in the enlightenment of its people, most of whom enthusiastically welcome the reform of antiquated traditions, an undertaking which Wieland at this moment approves without reservations.

The next of his works concerned with the events in France is the essay "Zufällige Gedanken über die Abschaffung des Erbadels in Frankreich."[24] It expresses a much more critical attitude toward a new decree, an edict which shattered his confident hope that the French would establish the best possible form of government modeled after the English example. The introduction of these "Incidental Thoughts" reveals his disappointment: "Die Französische Nazionalversammlung," he writes, "hätte meiner politischen Sagacität keinen schlimmern Streich spielen können, als durch das schreckliche Dekret vom neunzehnten Junius, wodurch sie den erblichen Adel in Frankreich auf immer abgeschafft . . . hat" (363).

The presentation of arguments in this essay is more complex than in previous pieces. Before Wieland reaffirms his earlier judgment he pursues his intellectual habit of having an important matter viewed from multiple vantage points. During the debate preceding the formal motion, a man who would not have been affected by the decree, Abbé Maury, a zealous supporter of the monarchy, eloquently defended the privileges of the nobility, while ironically, Matthieu de Montmorency, a nobleman who stood to lose much, spoke strongly in favor of the edict. Since Wieland does not know the exact content of Montmorency's statement, he attempts to discover the reasons for his decision by borrowing an appropriate method from Shaftesbury, who in his "Advice to an Author" had recommended the soliloquy as a useful process of "Self-dissection" and an effective device for the analysis of a personal dilemma in need of a sensible solution. "By virtue of this SOLILOQUY" the man who practices it "becomes two distinct *Persons*. He is Pupil and Preceptor. He teaches, and he learns."[25] Every man has "two distinct separate souls," one good, the other evil, an inner state which Xenophon's Araspes, who is quoted in the "Advice," had much earlier discovered.[26] Since, according to Shaftesbury, this is true, a soliloquy will enable a troubled man to look at a problem from opposing points of view in a dialogue with himself as the rational soul argues with the irrational in search of satisfactory solutions.

In Wieland's essay it is Matthieu de Montmorency who by design of the author "divides" himself into "two Parties" and argues both sides of the question of whether or not hereditary nobility should be abolished. Significantly, this debate is the kind of Socratic dialogue of which Wieland himself did not fully approve, for it depicts poorly matched opponents. One of the interlocutors is unrealistically inarticulate, naive, and emotional; the other is unusually eloquent and mature. One could maintain, of course, that these characteristics accurately reflect the nature of the two souls performing their "Duodrama." However, the rational side of Montmorency is not completely reasonable, but overemphasizes the negative side of tradition and is occasionally even deceptive. He ridicules, for example, his opponent's pride in noble heritage and illustrious family tradition, and when he argues that such pride is comparable to the conceit of a wooden stick that carries the wig of the famous Marshal of Luxemburg, he exaggerates absurdly; when he further identifies the origin of noble privileges as the usurpation of rights cunningly taken away from the people during a time when murder and robbery were favorite pastimes of the nobility, he clearly overstates his case. Yet the irrational being does not perceive the sophistry of such arguments and is at the end of the soliloquy easily persuaded to agree.

In contrast to Montmorency, other noblemen had voiced different views on the significance of hereditary titles, and the Count of Landenberg-Vagginbourg spoke for many when he stated that no decree and no power in the world could prevent them from living and dying as *Gentilshommes*. The introduction of this term spurs Wieland to offer an ironic "explication de mot" in which he exposes the meaninglessness of mere titles when contrasted to the true essence of nobility.

The final section of the work contains Wieland's personal thoughts as he considers the "ticklish matter of nobility" from a "cosmopolitan point of view." For thousands of years humanity has nourished its superstitions and prejudices, and among these is the belief that noble birth endows a child with physical and moral superiority. To be sure, this conclusion is commonly recognized as a false assumption, and it could not survive if man were a creature of pure reason. Yet since human beings always participate, at least to a modest degree, in irrationality, they are inclined to subscribe to traditional prejudices, particularly if the underlying phenomenon has the appearance of being empirically true. Although the assumption is false, it does have certain advantages. Pride in one's heritage, for example, often quickens a desire to be worthy of one's name, and the dignity of a young nobleman who is heir to the distinguished achievements of an illustrious family may well inspire in others affection and respect. Wieland believes that a nation will not gain anything by suddenly effacing all consciousness of noble heritage or by striking all memories of fame and glory. The liberation of France from the despotism of an intolerable aristocratic monarchy was a splendid advancement of humanity. To replace it by a limited monarchy that insures the rights of all people would be equally laudable. But to establish in its place "a monstrous, immensely complicated, clumsy, and insecure democracy" seems to Wieland an inglorious undertaking that will no doubt demand many more tragic sacrifices of the French.

These "Incidental Thoughts" were recorded on July 12, 1790;[27] this, then, is the moment at which Wieland becomes disenchanted with the developments in France, and it is a specific incident, the abolition of hereditary nobility, which initiates a gradual change in his attitude. Two days later the nation was to celebrate the first anniversary of the storming of the Bastille, and despite his disappointment Wieland treated the events of the day in another work, albeit of quite a different nature, in the dialogue of the Gods, "Der vierzehnte Julius," which was published in September 1790 in the *Teutsche Mer-*

kur and depicts the celebration on the Field of Mars as it is observed from humorously "superior" points of view.[28]

The first scene opens with a conversation between Jupiter Olympius and Louis IX. Jupiter begins the dialogue with a question and is so carried away by his enthusiasm for the achievements of the French that he rudely interrupts Louis' answer in mid-sentence to continue his laudation. He is overwhelmed with amazement: "Hat man jemahls von einem so schnellen Uebergang von Knechtschaft zu Freyheit, einem raschern Sprung von der schmählichsten Herabwürdigung der Menschheit zum lebendigsten Bewustseyn ihrer ganzen Würde und zur glänzendsten Entfaltung ihrer edelsten Kräfte, gehört?" (59). Jupiter's language—carefully chosen by Wieland to underline his *Schwärmerei*—, his excessive use of superlatives, and his overemphasis on the rapidity of changes as well as his unquestioning approval of all that has happened, indicates a bias that is modestly corrected by Louis, who fears that in their eagerness to change matters the French might well have taken "ein paar gefährliche Sätze zuviel" (60).

The selection of Louis, the ideal French king of the Middle Ages, as a judge of modern France is particularly appropriate, since he too had ruled the nation during difficult times, but with greater success. As a peer of Louis XVI he is uniquely qualified to evaluate his performance. As he recalls how centuries ago he had kept rebellious nobility and clergy under control, emancipated scholars, burghers, and peasants, and promoted the welfare of the people, he suggests that Louis XVI might have avoided some of his problems by similar measures.

During the remainder of the scene the gods discuss the impending rains and hope that they may be averted so that Paris can hold its celebration in splendid weather. Jupiter Horkius is inordinately passionate in his praise of the French, and since it is usually easier to discover excessive ardor in others than in oneself, Jupiter Olympius is amused by the enthusiasm of Horkius and with a touch of satire, ironically reflecting back upon himself, praises the progress his "sub-delegate" has made in the study of rhetoric.

The course of the rains cannot be changed and gods and kings move onto a cloud above Paris where they continue their conversations. They are joined by Henry IV, perhaps the most popular of the French kings, who remembers the difficulties he had faced during his reign. He does not hesitate to give some of the credit for his success to the competent advisors he had chosen, among them d'Aubigné, the critical and outspoken member of his council, and the Duke of Sully, who had conducted the country's finances with exceptional skill. Thus Louis could have learned from Henry that a king must surround himself with frank, loyal, and resourceful counsellors, who are aware of the needs of the nation and introduce reforms before they are demanded. Jupiter, wishing to be fair, interjects a note of caution: In all these comparisons one must realize that Louis XVI is a man quite different from his predecessors and perhaps his unique personality is at least partly responsible for the misfortunes he is now suffering. Henry and Jupiter also exchange their views on political matters. Although Henry forcefully supports a "free constitution" and believes that sound attempts have already been made to establish one, he nevertheless fears that some serious and incorrigible mistakes have been committed because of hasty decisions and secret intrigues, that in fact the nation has by now gone too far in the wrong direction. Jupiter cannot deny these charges; yet he explains that previous excesses are responsible for present abuses, that the French went too far simply because they are human and thus imperfect. To live life properly is a difficult task and to govern a people is hardest of all. Even Jupiter admits that he has learned the best of what he knows from making mistakes.

A formidable duty the French still face is the enactment of an equitable and workable system of laws, a need Jupiter discusses with Numa Pompilius, the legendary lawgiver of ancient Rome, who would find it most troublesome if he had to devise legislation for a newly liberated people. Yet despite his misgivings he does suggest specific measures that would have prevented the embarrassing predicaments with which the French had to cope at the end of the century. His proposals for remedial legislation are so cleverly contrasted with things he would not do, but the French did, that concomitantly his advice is sarcastic criticism of their action; so much so in fact that Mercury is amused at the Satire Numa has, perhaps involuntarily, created.

The last to converse with Jupiter is Louis XIV, who recalls the power and honor of France during his own time, but not the unsettling crises toward the end of his reign that foreshadowed the decline of the nation. From his position of glory and dignity he can only despise the French for behaving like barbarians, and he is angry with Jupiter for his inactive observance of the degrading *Schauspiel,* which should not be viewed with compassionate understanding but should incite in other rulers the desire for revenge. He fears that the "demon of democracy" has conquered Olympus too, and that Jupiter, like Louis XVI, can do nothing but give in to everything his subjects demand.

The many and various opinions expressed in this dialogue are individually biased, but in its totality the work contains a fair balance of views, none of which, however, fully approves the actions of any of the contending parties. It is precisely this moderation and fairness that reflects Wieland's intentions, for all the dialogues of the Gods concerned with the Revolution are meant to convey "einen Geist von Mässigung und Billigkeit, der ihnen bei keiner Partei zur Empfehlung dient, aber desto gewisser auf den Beifall späterer Zeiten rechnet."[29]

These six works written during the first year of the Revolution establish formal patterns and literary techniques that foreshadow the artistic features of Wieland's later political contributions. In all of them different figures, usually characterized as intelligent and serious individuals who simultaneously serve as representatives of larger segments of society, are permitted to voice their opinions and to present a challenging variety of views, ranging from mutually supportive to clashingly contrasting positions, collectively reflecting the diversity of attitudes that existed in reality. Enthusiastic admirers of the Revolution, ardent royalists, and middle-of-the-road advocates; Frenchmen and foreigners; fictional figures and men of history or contemporary life—among them, of course, Wieland himself—judge the spectacular events of the time, some of them emotionally involved, others calmly observing. Taken together, these works are to be understood as a running commentary on intricate, complex, at times even irrational developments, and they should not be interpreted as evidence of Wieland's own vacillating attitude toward a single event, which the Revolution manifestly was *not.* The presentation of the many views contained in these writings affirms Wieland's vision of the ideal method to be applied in man's search for the truth.[30] It is the joining together of different perspectives that supplement and correct single fields of vision which is more informative and reliable than the isolated subjective perception of each individual observer.

NOTES

1 Harald von Koskull, *Wielands Aufsätze über die Französische Revolution* (Riga: W. F. Häcker, 1901). The following works are also importantly concerned with the topic: Klaus Bäppler, *Der philosophische Wieland* (Bern and Munich: Francke, 1974), pp. 86–115; Maurice Boucher, *La Révolution de 1789 vue par les écrivains allemands* (Paris: Marcel Didier, 1954), pp. 51–72; Jacques Droz, *L'Allemagne et la révolution française* (Paris: Presses Universitaires de France, 1949), pp. 320–31; Gonthier-Louis Fink, "Wieland und die Französische Revolution," in *Deutsche Literatur und Französische Revolution* (Göttingen: Vandenhoeck & Ruprecht, 1974), pp. 5–38; G. P. Gooch, *Germany and the French Revolution* (London: Longman, Green and Co., 1920), pp. 142–60; Enrico Rambaldi, "La crisi dell'illuminismo moderato di C. M. Wieland, di fronte alla rivoluzione francese," ACME, 19, No. 3 (Sept.-Dec. 1966), pp. 281–339; Friedrich Sengle, *Wieland* (Stuttgart: Metzler, 1949), pp. 440–53; Alfred Stern, "Wieland und die Französische Revolution," in *Reden, Vorträge und Abhandlungen* (Stuttgart and Berlin: Cotta, 1914), pp. 134–67; Alfred Stern, *Der Einfluss der Französischen Revolution auf das deutsche Geistesleben* (Stuttgart and Berlin: Cotta, 1928), pp. 108–19; Bernd Weyergraf, *Der skeptische Bürger, Wielands Schriften zur Französischen Revolution* (Stuttgart: Metzler, 1972); Hans Würzner, "Christoph Martin Wieland, Versuch einer politischen Deutung," Diss. Heidelberg 1957, pp. 95–120.

2 Although Wieland permits a variety of distinctly different and, in their individuality, masterfully characterized first-person speakers to voice their subjective prejudices, scholars have virtually disregarded the care with which he created these independent identities and have instead considered them as "masks" or "spokesmen" for Wieland. Indeed, some have stated explicitly that such fictional figures clearly reveal Wieland's own opinions (Koskull, p. 34) or are "relevante Hypostasierungen der Meinungsäusserung des Autors" (Bäppler, p. 106). It is almost customary to combine "Wieland" or "er"—the pronoun unmistakably referring to Wieland—with statements actually made by invented figures and to treat them as an expression of Wieland's personal views.

3 During a conversation with Goethe, Wieland expressed his preference for Lucian and Shaftesbury over Plato, whose dialogues, he felt, often suffered from an unfair bias against the interlocutors whose views Plato did not share; see *Literarische Zustände und Zeitgenossen,* In *Schilderungen aus Karl Aug. Böttiger's handschriftlichem Nachlasse,* ed. K. W. Böttiger (Leipzig: F. A. Brockhaus, 1838), I, 239.

4 *Goethes Gespräche,* ed. Wolfgang Pfeiffer-Belli, (Zurich: Artemis, 1949), I, 670.

5 For a more extensive study of these aspects, see my monograph *Perspectives and Points of View: The Early Works of Wieland and Their Background* (Baltimore and London: Johns Hopkins Univ. Press, 1974); pp. 174–80 contain a brief treatment of his writings concerned with the French Revolution.

6 *Der Neue Teutsche Merkur*, 1 (1800), 256. It is in this connection (p. 253) that Wieland himself cautions his reader to consider carefully the identities of the speakers in his dialogues so that he will not arrive at the wrong conclusions.

7 *Wielands Gesammelte Werke,* ed. Deutsche Kommission der Preussischen Akademie der Wissenschaften. Erste Abteilung: *Werke,* XV (Berlin: Weidmannsche Buchhandlung, 1930), ed. Wilhelm Kurrelmeyer, pp. 295–315. Subsequent parenthetical references are to this edition. Further references will be identified as *Werke, Akademieausgabe.* The dialogue was first published in Wieland's periodical *Der Teutsche Merkur*, 3 (1789), 225–62.

8 *Cahiers de Lecture,* 2 (1789), 97.

9 Adelstan's reference (p. 297) is no doubt to Mirabeau's speech "On the Removal of the Troops Concentrated Round Paris," read to the king on the evening of July 10 by the Comte de Clermont-Tonnere, on behalf of the National Assembly. For the complete text of the address see *The Principle Speeches of the Statesmen and Orators of the French Revolution 1789–1795,* ed. Morse Stephens (Oxford: Clarendon Press, 1892), pp. 91–95.

10 Walther does not really "convince" Adelstan of his views, nor does the dialogue end with a victory of "liberalism," as Koskull (p. 6) believes.

11 Hesiod, *The Works and Days,* trans. Richmond Lattimore (Ann Arbor: Univ. of Michigan Press, 1959), p. 23.

12 Lucan, *The Civil War,* trans. J. D. Duff, The Loeb Classical Library (Cambridge, Mass.: Harvard Univ. Press, 1951), pp. 3–13; parenthetical references are to the lines of the text.

13 The German version of the speech, which Wieland used (see *Werke, Akademieausgabe,* XV, 86A), was published in *Politisches Journal nebst Anzeige von gelehrten und andern Sachen,* 1 (1789), 605. The French text appeared in the *Gazette Nationale, ou Le Moniteur Universel,* No. 1. (1789), 1. Wieland was well acquainted with this paper and frequently used it as his source.

14 Neither the French original nor the German translation contains the statements Walther pretends to quote. In another connection Walther allegedly quotes from a "Mémoire" of the "Commission intermédiaire de Bretagne" (308) in support of his argument. Yet the published version of June 22, 1788, "Mémoire adressé au Roi par la Commission Intermédiaire" (Rennes: Nicolas-Paul Vatar, 1788), pp. 1–35, does not contain the statement Walther uses. For his edition of the *Werke* Kurrelmeyer was unable to locate the "Mémoire" (86A). One of its locations is the Archives d'Ille-et-Vilaine at Rennes; the *Directeur* of the Archives kindly made a copy of the document available to me.

15 *Werke, Akademieausgabe,* XV, 316–35. The work was first published in *Der Teutsche Merkur,* 4 (1789), 24–60.

16 The differences between the views of Filoceltes and those of Wieland himself as they are expressed in the "Unpartheyische Betrachtungen" (see pp. 86–90 of this

article) clearly reveal that Filoceltes' address is by no means "Wieland's political confession of faith" (*Glaubensbekenntnis*, Koskull, p. 17), nor is the name Eleutherius Filoceltes a "*nom de plume*" (Bäppler, p. 92) or a pseudonym (Rambaldi, p. 291) for Wieland.

17 *Eleutherius*, "the Deliverer," is an epithet of Dionysius, or of Zeus, as a god who sets free a slave or an enslaved people; *Filoceltes*, or *Philoceltes*, is one who has a love or fondness for the ancient Gauls or Britons.

18 Wieland's novel *Die Abderiten* was published in 1774 in the *Teutsche Merkur* and appeared in 1776 in book form (Weimar: Carl Ludolf Hoffmann, 1776). An expanded version, *Geschichte der Abderiten*, was published in 1781 in Leipzig.

19 *Werke, Akademieausgabe*, XV, 336–62. See also *Merkur*, 2 (1790), 40–69.

20 *Werke, Akademieausgabe*, XV, 92. Although the dialogue has three participants—Wieland, who explicitly identifies himself as *Ich*, Menippus, and Xenophon—critics usually ignore this meaningful division of views. Weyergraf, for example, repeatedly claims to cite Wieland when he actually quotes Xenophon (pp. 8–10).

21 See note 16 of this article.

22 *StatsAnzeigen*, 14, No. 53 (January 1790), 101.

23 *Weilands Gesammelte Werke*, ed. Deutsche Akademie der Wissenschaften zu Berlin. Erste Abteilung: *Werke*, ed. William Clark, (Berlin: Akademieverlag, 1969), XXIII, 307–15. See also *Merkur*, 2 (1790), 315–28.

24 *Werke, Akademieausgabe*, XV, 363–80. See also *Merkur*, 2 (1790), 392–424.

25 Anthony Ashley Cooper, Earl of Shaftesbury, *Characteristicks of Men, Manners, Opinions, Times*, 4th ed. (n.p., 1727), I, 158.

26 Shaftesbury, *Characteristicks*, I, 184.

27 *Werke, Akademieausgabe*, XV, 380.

28 *Der Neue Teutsche Merkur*, 4 (1790), 58–96; subsequent parenthetical references are to this edition.

29 *Wielands Werke* (Berlin: Gustav Hempel, 1879), IX, 6.

30 "Wahrheit," *Der Teutsche Merkur*, 2 (1778), 9–17.

The French Academy as a Proponent of Egalitarianism

KARLIS RACEVSKIS

When we consider the concept of equality in eighteenth-century thought, we are inevitably reminded of its appearance as the central term of the well-known revolutionary slogan. Nevertheless, while equality is a recurring topic in the eighteenth century, its manifestations are various, often ambiguous. The purpose of my paper is to study one particular strain of egalitarianism—the one promulgated by the French Academy. By tracing its evolution from the time of the Company's foundation to the interpretation it receives in philosophic discourses, I hope to bring out the complexity of the concept and to elucidate the special meaning it acquires for the *philosophes* who take over the Academy in the second half of the eighteenth century.

For the French Academy, the theme of egalitarianism is a part of a long-standing tradition that has always presented equality as a cornerstone of the Institution. Section XV of the statutes on which the Academy was founded in 1635 reads: "Celui qui présidera fera garder le bon ordre dans les assemblées le plus exactement et le plus civilement qu'il sera possible, et comme il se doit faire entre personnes égales."[1] The intention of this bylaw was twofold. It was meant, first, to abolish all social distinctions within the confines of the Academy, and second, to recognize achievement in the domain of letters. This had been the intention of the first protector, Richelieu, and was that of his successor, the chancellor Séguier, as well. Pellisson, the Academy's first official historian, gives us the following account of the chancellor's dealings with other members of the Company: "Il est impossible d'en user plus qu'il fait civilement avec tous les Académiciens . . . il préside avec la même familiarité que pourrait faire un d'entre eux, jusqu'à prendre plaisir qu'on l'arrête et qu'on l'interrompe, et à ne vouloir point être traité de *Monseigneur* par ceux-là même de ces Messieurs qui sont ses domestiques."[2]

When, following the death of Séguier, Louis XIV became the protector of the Company, the monarch showed himself just as desirous as his predecessors of maintaining the spirit of equality in the Academy. According to d'Olivet, when one of the older members of the Academy, the cardinal d'Estrées, requested that he be permitted to have a more comfortable *fauteuil* instead of the ordinary chair that the members had, Louis XIV, "prévoyant les conséquences d'une pareille distinction, ordonna à l'intendant du garde-meuble de faire porter quarante fauteuils à l'Académie."[3] This innovation remedied a situation that had not been entirely satisfactory, since "les Académiciens, ou Cardinaux, ou Ducs, ou en un mot d'un rang extrêmement distingué, étaient d'une manière peu convenable à leur rang, surtout dans les séances publiques." The king's action, therefore, "sauvait en même temps et les égards dus aux grands noms, et cette égalité flatteuse dont l'Académie se fit dès sa naissance une loi inviolable."[4]

The concept of equality implicit in these words and actions appears thus in a rather ambiguous light. It is obviously not understood to have a levelling effect, as it does not reduce anyone's stature but rather elevates the members in a symbolic fashion to the "highest common denominator." The inaugural discourses of the newly elected Academicians are revealing in this regard. A new member customarily recognizes the honor of belonging to an intellectual elite. But, in addition, he is obviously impressed by the realization that he finds himself on an equal footing with the bearers of the more illustrious names that decorate the membership list. Consequently, although Academicians speak of equality, their rhetoric betrays the awe they still feel in the presence of high rank or birth. In 1675 the *président* Rose expressed his amazement at being "transporté en un rang qui m'égale en quelque sorte, à ce qu'il y a de plus sublime dans l'Eglise, dans la Noblesse, dans la Cour même, et dans les plus célèbres professions de la vie civile."[5] On the occasion of the reception of the *président* de Mesmes in 1676, the director of the Academy, Benserade, invited the newcomer to consider his colleagues at the Academy and pointed out that "il y entre de ce que l'Eglise a d'auguste et d'éminent, de ce que la Cour et le reste du Royaume ont de Titres éclatants, et de Charges principales, de ce qu'il y a de savant et de poli parmi les gens de Lettres; ce mélange de conditions et d'esprits formant une société entre nous, où tout est égal, et sans aucune distinction de rang ni de préséance."[6] From these discourses, in which equality is presented as an almost miraculous phenomenon, it appears that the Academicians found it difficult to get accustomed to this concept. The strangeness of the notion is also apparent from the occasional contradiction of terms that stands out in some speeches. In 1671, for example, the Academy complimented Harlay de Chanvalon on his recent appointment as Archbishop of Paris. Speaking for the Company, the abbé Tallement assured the Archbishop that "tous les Académiciens, jusqu'aux moindres, ont triomphé de se voir en quelque sorte égaler à vous par cette qualité."[7] The qualification "en quelque sorte" strongly suggests that the "moindres" among the membership were not really forgetting their lesser status.

It is significant to note, however, that, as we near the end of the century, a growing emphasis seems to be placed on the distinction derived from intellectual achievement. The abbé de Choisy points out in 1687 that "ce n'est ni la naissance seule, ni les seules dignités qui rendent votre Compagnie si célèbre. Il ne suffirait pas pour entrer chez vous, d'avoir passé par les plus grands emplois; l'Esprit et le Savoir vous ont ouvert la porte de l'Académie."[8] The abbé Boileau makes the same point very eloquently in 1694 as he defines the special nature of the Academy: "Les personnes les plus éminentes n'y ont que des égaux, et les plus habiles y trouvent des maîtres. La dignité ne donne pas de rang, ni la réputation de supériorité. La littérature ennoblit, la critique égale, l'esprit brille, et le bon sens décide."[9]

By the eighteenth century, the theme of equality is thus a well-established tradition in the Academy. It remains to be seen what the *philosophes* did with it and in what manner they incorporated this theme within the more general program of philosophic propaganda.

The so-called philosophic conquest of the French Academy takes place during a period of time when the single most important position within the Society, that of *secrétaire perpétuel,* was occupied by Duclos. Without being a member of the philosophic sect himself, Duclos was helpful to its cause whenever the interests of the Academy coincided with those of the free-thinkers. More than anything else, Duclos was interested in reestablishing the Academy's literary reputation, which had suffered a considerable decline in the first part of the century. In addition to fulfilling the duties of secretary (from 1755 to 1772), Duclos was also the continuator of the official history of the Academy. His contribution is rather meager but is of special interest to us since most of it deals with the subject of Academic equality. It was a principle in which Duclos believed very strongly, the origins of which he traces back to the reign of Charlemagne. The emperor had founded a society of learned men in his palace and, Duclos tells us, "pour faire disparaître toute distinction de rang par une image d'égalité, il établit que, dans les conférences, chacun adopterait un nom académique. Il prit celui de David."[10] Turning to the history of the French Academy in the eighteenth century, Duclos notes with satisfaction that in the early years of the century the attempt to institute an honorary membership, "ce projet bourgeois," as he calls it, was rejected by the king. The historian then passes to the retelling of an incident in which he himself had become the champion of the principle of equality. It took place on the occasion of the election of the comte de Clermont, a prince of the blood. It was a candidacy that greatly honored the Company but, at the same time, it posed a threat to the egalitarian atmosphere that allegedly reigned in its assemblies. The threat became very real when Clermont's family made it known that "il ne convenait pas à un prince du sang d'entrer dans aucun corps sans y avoir un rang distingué, une préséance marquée." Duclos, very courageously, resisted this attempted infringement upon the traditional principle and in a memorandum addressed to the count explained: "Monseigneur, si vous confirmez par votre exemple respectable et décisif une égalité, qui d'ailleurs n'est que fictive, vous faites à l'académie le plus grand honneur qu'elle ait jamais reçu. Vous ne perdez rien de votre rang, et j'ose dire que vous ajoutez à votre gloire en élevant la nôtre."[11] Clermont very graciously acceded to the secretary's reasoning, and the matter of privilege within the Academy was settled once and for all. Equality was now solidly entrenched and, during the secretaryship of Duclos, was to acquire a theoretical structure that amounted to a political doctrine.

We do not have a single cohesive statement of this doctrine. It emerges only from reflections and observations scattered throughout the various academic discourses. On the other hand, there is a remarkable degree of uniformity in the attitudes of the various Academicians who broach the subject. As a result, it is possible to arrive at a fairly precise impression of what could be called the axiological frame of mind of the Institution.

The notion of equality manifests itself, as we have already seen for the seventeenth century, as a consciousness of belonging to a superior, highly select group of minds. It is this superiority which allows the *roturier* man of letters to consider himself the equal of his more aristocratic colleagues; the Academy is characterized as a place where "l'Esprit . . . est mis sur la même ligne avec la noblesse et les talents avec les dignités; les gens de Lettres y prononcent concurremment avec les premiers hommes de l'Etat et de l'Eglise."[12] However, the Academicians who deal with this subject, especially the *philosophes,* are quick to point out that this spirit of equality is not to have wider, political implications. Their intention is not to advocate "l'égalité des conditions"; they are, as d'Alembert emphasizes, "bien éloignés de Prêcher une pareille impertinence."[13] On the contrary, letters and philosophy can only contribute to strengthen existing political and religious institutions: "Le goût des Lettres, incompatible avec l'esprit de faction, est nécessairement l'ami de l'ordre, de la paix et des lois."[14] Similarly, Voisenon points out in 1762: "Les lettres forment une République qui est soumise aux Rois, et les immortalise."[15] The situation of the French Academy is thus seen as a paradox: it is a republic within a monarchy. According to the Academicians who perceive this reality, it is not in disagreement with the intentions of the founder of the Illustrious Society: "L'ardent promoteur de l'autorité monarchique, reconnut que la forme républicaine pouvait seule vous convenir." Richelieu had understood that "des esprits supérieurs, dont la communication mutuelle augmente encore les lumières, ne peuvent tendre au même but qu'en devenant égaux."[16] In 1771, Gaillard resolves the paradox in a similar fashion: "Richelieu voulut que les titres et talents réunis concourussent à la gloire des Lettres; il sentit que quand la liberté serait détruite dans l'Etat, elle devrait être l'âme d'une société littéraire."[17]

As befits a republic, then, titles and social distinctions lose their credit in the Academy: "L'Homme seul entre ici, et il n'y apporte avec lui que le mérite inséparable de sa personne."[18] The nobles within the Academy are constantly reminded of their new position, which is again presented as a paradox. They are assured that their dignity, far from being diminished, can only gain from this loss of aristocratic distinction. Thus, Voisenon: "Il faut que des Grands soient bien supérieurs à leur propre grandeur, quand ils peuvent deviner les plaisirs de l'égalité."[19] When the comte de Clermont dies in 1771, he is replaced by the dramatic author Belloy. The occasion does not fail to inspire the newly elected member with an appropriate observation, and he exclaims, "fut-il jamais un exemple plus éclatant de cette précieuse égalité?" Belloy then offers an explanation of the motives the nobles might have for seeking Academic honors: "Fatigués des respects et des hommages qui n'appartiennent qu'à leurs noms et à leurs dignités, ils cherchent dans l'assemblée des Sages, dans le Sanctuaire des Muses, la considération personnelle qu'on obtient par les vertus, et cette distinction si flatteuse qui récompense les talents."[20] Thomas, who earned a reputation as the most brilliant orator to promulgate the cause of the *philosophes* within the Academy, takes this line of thinking one step further. He clearly separates the two forms of dignity, the hereditary and the intellectual. His inaugural discourse considers the importance of the man of letters as a citizen. According to Thomas, a writer with a philosophical outlook "ne séparera point le respect qu'il doit aux titres, du respect que tout homme se doit. Il sait que la dignité des rangs est à un petit nombre de citoyens, mais que la dignité de l'âme est à tout le monde: que la première dégrade l'homme qui n'a qu'elle; que la seconde élève l'homme à qui tout le reste manque."[21] Stripped of the dignity that his aristocratic rank used to carry, what can the *grand* contribute to the Academy? "Quelques-uns pensent que c'est pour décorer les lettres," says Thomas. But letters and the Academy enjoy the prestige that an enlightened public and an enlightened age will inevitably bring them, indeed, "le peuple chez qui les lumières et le génie auraient besoin de ce secours pour être honorés, serait encore un peuple bien barbare." Fortunately, the nobleman can still be useful and can contribute to the glory of letters and the Academy by protecting the man of letters. "Quelle plus noble fonction, messieurs, que celle de repousser le calomniateur, de défendre le grand homme ou même l'homme estimable opprimé, d'épargner à l'autorité un crime, une honte à la nation, des malheurs à la vertu?"[22] Thomas attempts thus to bring some solace to the deflated self-esteem of the privileged Academician. This attitude is also shared by d'Alembert, the leader of the philosophic faction in the Academy and the engineer of the pro-philosophic campaign. The geometer finds that "un des plus nobles rôles que puissent jouer dans l'Académie les prélats qu'elle compte parmi ses membres, c'est de se rendre auprès du monarque les défenseurs des lettres calomniées et persécutées."[23] In his *Eloges,* d'Alembert often singles out the members of the higher clergy or of the nobility who have distinguished themselves in this protective function. In addition, the *philosophe* finds that the inclusion of the *grands* in the membership is useful "pour faire respecter la compagnie elle-même à cette multitude nombreuse, éblouie et subjuguée par les décorations extérieures, et à qui un cordon en impose plus qu'un bon ouvrage." At the same time, he finds it deplorable that his supposedly more enlightened colleagues would share this awe and should be "imbus d'une espèce de superstition pour ces fantômes de pouvoir et de grandeur qu'ils redoutent, comme un enfant a peur des ténèbres." Indeed, he would like to see the number of aristocratic members reduced as much as possible and finds that "ni la naissance seule, ni même le simple goût des lettres joints à la naissance, ne doivent être des passeports suffisants pour ouvrir l'entrée de cette compagnie."[24]

We have thus witnessed a gradual shift of emphasis in the manner in which the Academy has dealt with the subject of equality. While, in its beginnings, the men of letters felt flattered and privileged to be elevated to the level of their noble colleagues, the *roturier* Academicians of the philosophical era see themselves as the elite and feel that it is the aristocratic members who benefit from an elevation by virtue of the association. The principal justification for this reversal is found in a certain historical interpretation of the meaning of nobility. The fullest examination of this question appears in the reception discourse of the bishop of Autun, delivered in 1757. According to the prelate, the equality that once existed in some distant golden age vanished because men became unwilling or unable to recognize true merit; thus "l'ignorance et la corruption ne tardèrent pas à obscurcir l'idée, à affaiblir le goût de la véritable grandeur: la nécessité de la récompenser dans les uns, de l'encourager dans les autres, de la faire respecter par tous, entraîna celle d'y attacher des honneurs." "Les titres et les dignités," which were originally meant to reward merit and had therefore been established for the good of all, became "la proie des désirs particuliers: la faveur les a obtenus, la naissance les a perpétués; les voies les moins pénibles ont été bientôt les voies les plus ordinaries pour y arriver." As a consequence, rank and merit have become separated. Opposed to this deplorable state of affairs is the spirit that reigns in the French Academy, where there is no other superiority "que celle des connaissances et de la vertu,"[25] and where it is possible to discover the original notion of man's greatness, which used to be cultivated for its own intrinsic worth. "Oh! Déesse du siècle d'or, aimable égalité," exclaims Radonvilliers in 1763, "on ne vous trouve plus que dans ce sanctuaire. Le monde vous a bannie, la Philosophie vous regrette, l'Académie vous a rappelée et vous fait régner sur elle."[26]

The *philosophes* will adopt a similar line of thinking in an attempt to show that the nobility has abdicated the moral responsibility inherent in its rank. In his *Eloge du Dauphin,* Thomas asks: "Qu'était la noblesse dans son institution, que l'image et le symbole de la vertu même?" It therefore follows that "tout a été perdu, dès que ces deux choses ont été séparées."[27] Suard, elected to the Academy in 1774, traces the aristocratic decadence back, more specifically, to the early part of the eighteenth century, a time when "tous les liens de la morale se relâchèrent; toutes les âmes furent entraînées vers les jouissances de la mollesse et des voluptés; la débauche se montra sans voile; et cette moitié du genre humain, qui a tant d'influence sur les mœurs de l'autre, en perdant jusqu'au sentiment de la pudeur, perdit la plus grande partie de son empire. Les vertus domestiques furent non seulement abandonnées, elles devinrent ridicules; les pères furent étrangers à leurs enfants, les femmes à leurs maris." While showing that a void had been produced by the nobility's failure to fulfill its obligations, the *philosophes* were of course suggesting the need for a new guiding influence to replace the old. On a moral plane, according to Suard, philosophy had already assumed this function, and any progress made in the domain of ethics could be attributed to "cet esprit philosophique, qui, en répandant dans la société des idées plus saines des devoirs de l'homme, en poursuivant sans relâche le vice et la corruption . . . tend sans cesse à relever les âmes . . . et à fortifier les mœurs."[28] The moral superiority that the Academicians now attributed to themselves carried with it an obligation. It provided them with a new opportunity as well, since this awareness of a moral obligation was represented as a humanitarian concern for society and civilization. At the same time, we see the concept of equality undergo a corresponding transformation, and in the rhetoric of the *philosophes,* it becomes, in essence, an equality of opportunity.

Traditionally, men holding political power had always existed and acted separately from the thinkers and the writers. One of the principal aims of the philosophic campaign is to advocate a merger of the two groups in the interests of mankind. Thomas is gratified to find that "l'institution de l'Académie, et le mélange des lettres et des titres sert autant qu'il est possible à rapprocher ces deux classes."[29] It is even possible to see the foundation of the Academy as intended to serve this purpose. The historian Lacurne de Sainte-Palaye sees the creation of the Company as an integral part of the more general political design of Richelieu. The purpose of the cardinal had been to make "les routes de l'honneur également accessibles à tout Français." As a consequence, "les talents, le savoir et plus encore les vertus sont aujourd'hui des titres; . . . ces titres ont mis entre les Citoyens une proportion, un équilibre inconnus à des siècles barbares."[30] The Academy's claim to a role in the domain of ethics and politics is thus amply justified, and d'Alembert finds that the government should make use of literary societies such as the French Academy in order to "diriger les opinions vers le bien général de la nation et du souverain."[31] Saint-Lambert, elected to the Academy in 1770, finds that the Company already performs this useful function, since the principal goal of its members is "chercher, découvrir, inspirer des vérités utiles, . . . faire aimer le Prince, le travail et les lois."[32]

In practice, the influence which the Academy claimed it had a right to exert did not amount to much, but the theoretical distance that separates the original notion of Academic equality from the philosophical interpretation is considerable. It started out, as we have seen, as a vague and ambiguous ideal in the seventeenth century. During the reign of the *philosophes* it appears to serve two distinct and contradictory purposes. On the one hand, it is still an ideal, and the *philosophes*' claims to the contrary notwithstanding, it probably did contribute to undermine traditional class distinctions. However, as an ideal it is not very subversive and does not represent much more than the familiar notion of equality before the law. The levelling effect implicit in the concept of equality appears mainly as a rhetorical device. Thomas, for example, advocates an equitable system of laws by stating that "la justice rétablit l'équilibre entre les forces qui se combattent. C'est la justice qui crie à l'homme puissant: 'Tu es esclave de la loi.' C'est elle qui dit au riche: 'le pauvre est ton égal.'"[33] Yet it does not follow from this that the powerful man will become weaker or that the distance separating rich from poor will be reduced. In addition, the ideological force of the concept of equality loses much of its impact when we see the *philosophes* stressing the necessity of distinguishing "le public vraiment éclairé . . . d'avec cette multitude aveugle et bruyante."[34] The general feeling is that "ce qui pense ne peut être perdu dans la foule."[35]

Thus, fundamentally, the egalitarian rhetoric of the Academicians is self-serving; its purpose is to exalt their own status. While elevating themselves to a more prestigious social position and claiming equal standing with the upper ranks of society, the *philosophes* recognized and justified the distance that separated them from the general population. The double standard implicit in this attitude was not to go unnoticed, and in 1792 Robespierre pointed out that, "si les académiciens et les géomètres . . . ont combattu et ridiculisé les prêtres, ils n'en ont pas moins courtisé les grands et adoré les rois, dont ils ont tiré un assez bon parti."[36] One year later, the Academy was dissolved by a revolutionary decree. Its spirit and principles were considered those of an age that had come to a close.

NOTES

1 *Les Registres de l'Académie française* (Paris: Didot, 1895–1906), IV, 24. I have modernized the spelling in all of the quotations.

2 P. Pellisson-Fontanier and Pierre-Joseph Thoulier d'Olivet, *Histoire de l'Académie française par Pellisson et d'Olivet* (Paris: Livet, 1858), I, 71. We are told by d'Alembert that the only exception to this apparently traditional derogation from standard etiquette was the reception of Cardinal Dubois. The latter had insisted that he be addressed as *Monseigneur. Oeuvres complètes de d'Alembert* (Paris: Belin, 1821), III, 2–3.

3 Pellisson and d'Olivet, II, 479.

4 Ibid., II, 21–22. According to d'Alembert, "les Cardinaux Académiciens se dispensaient depuis longtemps d'assister aux séances, tant particulières que publiques, parcequ'ils croyaient des fauteuils indispensables à leur dignité." D'Alembert, III, 94. See also *Les Registres de l'Académie française*, I, 562, n. 1.

5 *Recueil des harangues prononcées par Messieurs de l'Académie françoise, dans leurs réceptions, et en d'autres occasions différentes, depuis l'establissement de l'Académie jusqu'à présent* (Amsterdam: aux dépens de la Compagnie, 1709), I, 380–81.

6 Ibid., I, 410.

7 Ibid., I, 212.

8 Ibid., II, 87.

9 Ibid., II, 335.

10 Charles Duclos, *Oeuvres complètes de Duclos* (Paris: Colnet, 1806), IX, 307–8.

11 Ibid., IX, 289, 294. On the subject of Clermont's election, see also d'Alembert, III, 676–79.

12 *Discours prononcés dans l'Académie françoise, le lundi 6 juillet 1772 à la réception de M. Beauzée* (Paris: J. B. Brunet, 1772), pp. 17–18.

13 D'Alembert, II, 570.

14 *Discours prononcés dans l'Académie françoise, le lundi 13 mai 1771 à la réception de M. l'abbé Arnaud* (Paris: la V. Regnard et Demonville, 1771), p. 20.

15 *Discours prononcés dans l'Académie françoise, le samedi 22 janvier 1763 à la réception de M. l'abbé de Voisenon* (Paris: la V. Brunet, 1763), p. 10.
16 *Discours prononcés dans l'Académie françoise, le lundi 12 janvier 1761 à la réception de M. de la Condamine* (Paris: la V. Brunet, 1761), p. 18.
17 *Discours prononcés dans l'Académie françoise, le jeudi 21 mars 1771 à la réception de M. Gaillard* (Paris: la V. Regnard et Demonville, 1771), p. 10.
18 *Discours prononcés dans l'Académie françoise, le samedi 26 mars 1763 à la réception de M. l'abbé de Radonvilliers, sous-Précepteur des Enfans de France* (Paris: la V. Brunet, 1763), p. 5.
19 Voisenon, p. 8.
20 *Discours prononcés dans l'Académie françoise, le jeudi 9 janvier 1772 à la réception de M. de Belloi* (Paris: la V. Regnard et Demonville, 1772), p. 4.
21 Antoine-Léonard Thomas, *Oeuvres complètes* (Paris: Verdière, 1825), IV, 208.
22 Ibid., IV, 232, 244.
23 D'Alembert, II, 478, n. 2.
24 Ibid., II, 290, 480.
25 *Recueil des pièces d'éloquence et de poésie qui ont remporté les prix de l'Académie françoise depuis 1753 jusqu'en 1759* (Paris: Brunet, 1760), pp. 224–27.
26 Radonvilliers, p. 5.
27 Thomas, II, 330.
28 *Discours prononcés dans l'Académie françoise, le jeudi 4 août 1774 à la réception de M. Suard* (Paris: Demonville, 1774), p. 19.
29 Thomas, IV, 242.
30 *Recueil des pièces d'éloquence*, pp. 324–25.
31 D'Alembert, II, 156.
32 *Discours prononcés dans l'Académie françoise, le samedi 23 juin 1770 à la réception de M. de Saint-Lambert, ci-devant Grand-Maître de la Garde-robe du feu Roi de Pologne, Mestre de Camp de Cavalerie* (Paris: la V. Regnard et Demonville, 1770), p. 15.
33 Thomas, II, 331.
34 D'Alembert, II, 155.
35 Thomas, II, 253.
36 Maximilien Robespierre, *Oeuvres de Maximilien Robespierre* (Paris: Presses Universitaires de France, 1950), VIII, 309.

The Rights of Women in the French Revolution

LEONORA COHEN ROSENFIELD

The Enlightenment's mounting but more or less sporadic defense of women in France[1] was metamorphosed by the French Revolution into a program, improvised, ill-coordinated, but broad-ranging and visionary. This was the first and most complete political drive for women's rights in any great modern nation. Within a few years it was all buried, and politically, women were worse off than ever before.

The struggle for "feminism," to use Fourier's word, may be viewed as a revolutionary drama with a poignant denouement. Condorcet and the melodramatic Olympe de Gouges played the leads in a large, often nameless cast.

In August 1788 France was in a ferment. Louis XVI, in order to levy new taxes in the financial crisis, had just convoked the States-General.

For the first time in its history, the mass of the nation was entering public life. Peasants, artisans, and parish priests, along with the bourgeoisie and the privileged classes, were allowed to vote for representatives. Lists of complaints and proposed reforms were being drawn up all over. Something electric seemed to sweep over the country. The

Count de Ségur, coming back to France after a five-year absence at the court of Catherine the Great, noted the transformation: "There is something alive, proud, and animated about the bourgeois, the peasants, even the women. A people that was bent under the yoke stands once more erect."[2]

"Even the women." Most women were denied the vote by the election regulations of January 24, 1789. Humbly, then boldly in pamphlets to the King or the States-General, then to the National Assembly, all classes of women protested, even the prostitutes.

In 1788, the author of the *Très-humbles Remontrances,* [3] an avowed monarchist, writes:

> In the midst of the general conversation being established between the Monarch and his people, it is impossible for the women of this Kingdom to remain silent. When all bodies from the clergy down make public their respectful remonstrances . . . it would be shameful for women not to speak up . . . We are monarchists [pp. 3–4]. . . . We formally request the Government to call up Deputies of our sex [p. 9]. . . . Public opinion is formed within our coteries [p. 10].

In her *Demande des femmes aux Etats Généraux,* Mme de Coicy reminds the States-General that women, publicly powerless in France, held official positions in the Middle Ages. Her conclusion is that "La gloire du Monarque n'est pas d'être Roi de France, mais d'être Roi des Françaises."[4]

A *Requête des femmes pour leur admission aux Etats-Généraux*[5] inquires how women should be represented in the soon-to-be convoked States-General. If their sex were to constitute a Fourth Estate, that would be contrary to historical precedent and unconstitutional. The alternative would be to divide women by rank among the three existing Estates. The august Assembly "ought to know how interested women are in redressing all abuses" (p. 6). ". . . the end of their slavery has arrived, & it will no longer be said that of the twenty-four million inhabitants who inhabit France, more than half will not have the right to be represented in the States-General" (p. 8). Women should be eligible to command armies and serve as ambassadors. Since the true wealth of a state is its population, the celibate should be taxed at double the ordinary rate. The reign of privilege is over. Tax the first two orders, and instead of twenty-four million Frenchmen the population will rise to thirty-six million (pp. 13–14). Girls should be given the vote at fifteen, and women with one child or more should be eligible to be deputies. Finally, "we promise to speak only in monosyllables" (p. 19).

The *Pétition du Tiers Etat au Roi*[6] addresses Louis XVI as a "tender Father." Women do not aspire to send deputies to the States-General. Rather they appeal to his Majesty for a free education so as to be able to earn a living in decency. Women of the Third Estate, without means, without any real education, beg that men leave them the traditional female occupations, sewing, embroidery, the dress and millinery trades. Establish free schooling so that women may be taught the French language, religion, and morals. Freed from ignorance, women will be able to furnish a "reasonable" education to the young.

Working women begged to be able to dispose of their own earnings when of age without accounting to their husbands. Ladies of the impoverished aristocracy requested situations compatible with their training in secretarial work, music, and art. The sixteen-page *Cahier des doléances et réclamations des femmes* of Mme B. B. argued in 1789 that since Negroes were going to be granted their emancipation, why not women too? And women can be represented only by women. Voltaire's and Condorcet's friend, the Marquis de Villette, called for training programs for unwed mothers. The abolition of the dowry system was often urged, for example in *Motions addressées à l'Assemblée nationale* (1789).

The *Requête des dames à l'Assemblée nationale* pointed out that the *Declaration of the Rights of Man* had proclaimed the rights of all men, including the poor, the serfs, and the slaves. The National Assembly had decreed the equality of all the French. Why then leave out one half of a nation? Guidelines for the emancipation of women were laid down, for thirteen million women's liberties:

1° Masculine privileges are to be irrevocably abolished in all France (p. 11).

2° Women have the same rights and liberties as men, and the right to the same honors (p. 12).

4° A woman's contractual rights should not have to be authorized by the husband (p. 12).

5° Pants will no longer be the exclusive prerogative of the male sex, but each sex will have the right to wear them (p. 12).
7° Qualified women are to be equally admissible to assemblies and municipal positions and as deputies to the National Assembly.
8° Women may be promoted to judgeships (p. 13).
9° Women may be admissible to all employment, recompenses, and military honors (p. 13).
10° Women may be eligible to the pupit—and promise not to preach at too great length (pp. 13–14).[7]

The *Requête* was officially ignored.

Among lower-class women and working women in guilds, there was no lack of direct action. Before the elections of deputies to the States-General, the women of Chevanceaux simply went ahead and voted in the primary assembly of 1789. The fishwives and female fruit sellers sent deputations to the Assembly of the Third Estate. Corporations of female workers which paid annual fees to the King protested their exclusion from representation in the Assembly of the Third Estate. Women went on the march in the provinces as well as in Paris. Bread riots were provoked on occasions when that dietary staple was particularly scarce. White bread was at times obtainable only on the black market. The shortages and spiralling costs of coffee, sugar, laundry soap, etc., speculation, hoarding, inflation, unemployment, and starvation in Paris precipitated incidents and even armed insurrection in which the women upon occasion proved more numerous and militant than the men.[8] But violent demonstrations provoked mounting repressive tactics by the authorities.

Already in 1789 women had been active in storming the Bastille; their participation (and not only by poorly dressed women) in the October 5 march on Versailles had been decisive; to prepare the *Fête de la Fédération,* on July 14, 1790, they dug in the Champ de Mars with pickaxe and shovel; when war was declared in April 1792 they volunteered as "Amazones" for military service; some served as canoneers, Reine Chappuy in the cavalry; the two Fernig sisters became officers of the General Staff and were cited for bravery. A petition of nine-hundred signatures, mostly from working girls and women of Paris, was delivered to the National Convention requesting the formation of five fully armed legions of two thousand women each.[9] To the tunes of *Ça Ira, La Carmagnole,* and *La Marseillaise,* patriotism was in the air.

The crusade for women's rights was spreading in the press. Each faction, each club, each leader had a newspaper. The "feminist press" of brief duration included political periodicals with woman editors and feminist journals run by men and women. The *Etrennes nationales des dames* called for the election of woman delegates to the National Assembly. The male-edited bi-weekly *Courrier de l'hymen ou Journal des dames* reported before it folded in the summer of 1791 that women were asking why they were left out of the powerful revolutionary *jurys d'accusation* and the *jurys de jugement.* "By what right are men the sole arbiters of our fate?"[10]

Perhaps the least ephemeral of the political magazines edited by women were the *Journal de l'Etat du Citoyen* (1789–90), which merged with the *Révolutions de l'Europe,* and the chief republican organ, the *Mercure national et étranger ou Journal politique de l'Europe,* both directed by the highly-educated writer Louise-Félicité de Keralio. In 1790 she married François Robert, the organizer and president of a Cercle central des sociétés fraternelles designed to centralize democratic forces throughout Paris. Mme Robert, who believed in working with men to further revolutionary causes, was one of the organizers of the Société fraternelle des deux sexes. Michelet deems her the author of the July 17, 1791 petition of the Champ de Mars to depose the King.

Labenette, editor of the *Journal du Diable,* contributed in 1791 to the daily *Journal des Droits de l'Homme* an article in which he reproached men for being ungrateful—they should extend those inalienable rights to the fair sex. However, the main feminist organ was the socialistic *Bouche de fer* that took its name from an iron box into which one could slip anonymous grievances. Edited by the abbé Claude Fauchet and Nicolas de Bonneville at the Imprimerie du Cercle social in 1790–91, it often published Condorcet and included among its collaborators Mme d'Aëlders.

Etta Lubina Johanna Desista Alders, born in 1743 and married at nineteen to Ferdinand Loderoyck Palm, who soon left her for the East Indies, came from her native Holland to Paris where she became known as the Baronne d'Aëlders. She wrote a *Discours sur l'injustice des lois en faveur des hommes aux dépens des femmes lu à l'Assemblée fédérative des amis de la vérité* (1790), which harangued the deputies in these terms. You admitted my sex to this patriotic organization. Why not give us the same education as yours? Of all despotisms, that to which women are subject is the most difficult to uproot. Yet "justice demands that laws be common to all beings . . . however everywhere the laws are in favor of men at the expense of women, because everywhere the power is in your hands."[11] She founded and was president of a women's club sponsored in February, 1791, by *La Bouche de fer,* the Club fédératif des citoyennes patriotes, also known as the Société patroitique et de bienfaisance des amies de la vérité. It aimed to further social security and assistance for the needy, to be administered through neighborhood Sociétés des citoyennes patriotiques. Each of the forty-eight sections of the capital was to have a branch, and the fraternal societies of the eighty-three Departments of France would be invited to be corresponding members. The plan aimed at a national federation of women's clubs for health, education, and welfare. At the first meeting, held in Paris on March 25, 1791, it was decided to use the local dues for workshop training for needy girls between the ages of seven and thirteen.

From her speeches at the Cercle social, this organizer issued in July 1791 a forty-five page *Appel aux Françaises sur la régénération des moeurs et nécessité de l'influence des femmes dans un gouvernement libre.* On April 1, 1792, she led a delegation of les Amies de la vérité to the Legislative Assembly to read a petition for civil and military employment for women, moral and national education for girls, majority for women at twenty-one years, equality of political liberty and of rights for both sexes, and a divorce law. The latter was granted, but as for the petition, it was sent to committee to be buried there. She had narrowly escaped imprisonment in July of 1791; in January 1793, Mme Palm, her head still intact on her shoulders, left France.

Women's clubs had been springing up in big and little towns; anti-aristocratic in origin, they introduced women to civic, educational, and public affairs as well as to social work. In Paris, clubs became co-ed. The spirited Théroigne de Méricourt, a native of Luxembourg, was a founder in January 1790 of the Parisian Club des amies de la loi. The Société fraternelle des patriotes de l'un et l'autre sexe was established the following month. It became the prototype for future societies that believed in social egalitarianism. The name "fraternal," used increasingly, usually meant open to both sexes. Such popular societies introduced women of the *menu peuple* to civic affairs and then, beginning especially in 1792, to active political interests. Delegations were dispatched to the Assembly. The words "patriotic" and "republican" came into use in club names, which shied away from saints' names. Thus the Société fraternelle de Ste Geneviève became the Société fraternelle des deux sexes du Panthéon français. Attendance there was at least as much by the *sans-jupons,* as by their male counterparts, the *sans-culottes.* The Union fraternelle de la section Gobelins, for one, granted full membership privileges to women, but some conservative sections of Paris refused to admit delegations of women.

Throughout France the women's clubs proved enormously helpful to the war effort, providing health services, collecting money, making clothes, shoes, bandages, obtaining saltpeter and guns, and so on. Women, without the church, were serving the State. A crisis developed after the fervent Société des républicaines révolutionaires was announced in Paris, May 13, 1793, with a membership sworn to live or die for the Revolution. Its leaders, Claire (Rose) Lacombe, a provincial actress who came to Paris in 1782, and the chocolatière Pauline Léon, served on successive months as presidents. Aligned with the extremist faction, *Les Enragés,* the Société failed to win the *sans-culottes* and alienated, even scared the Commune, the Convention, and the Jacobins. Worse, so far as Robespierre was concerned, Claire Lacombe called him "Monsieur Robespierre." Five stormy months after the founding of the Société, all women's clubs were disbanded by the Convention on 9 Brumaire (October 20), 1793. On 27 Brumaire, the *républicaines révolutionnaires,* wearing the *Phrygien* or red bonnet, burst into the Commune in protest, only to be ignominiously expelled. Claire Lacombe was imprisoned on April 2, 1794, by the Comité de sûreté général, a final irony, for the club of superpatroits had been founded to report spies and other enemies of the Republic. In the view of the authorities, the excesses of the *républicaines révolutionnaires* cast discredit on the women's movement.

Condorcet, the Enlightenment's most consistent champion of non-discrimination, was a mathematician, a forerunner of social science, a legislator, and a *philosophe*. His numerous writings sparked the feminist campaign. Foremost among the men of his time to apply the lessons of the new American polity to the problems of France, he valued the Declaration of Independence and the Virginia Declaration of Rights. He published in 1787 four *Lettres d'un bourgeois de New-Heaven* [*sic*] *à un citoyen de Virginie*, of which the second letter on "Les Droits de la femme" reasoned that since natural rights are the basis of human rights, one cannot logically deny equal rights to women who, just as men, are subject to feelings and capable of reason and moral ideas. Women, especially single women and widows, have the right to refuse to pay parliamentary taxes for which neither they nor their freely elected representatives have voted.[12] Equal rights include, besides the vote, eligibility, when qualified, for any position.

The next year his *Essai sur la constitution et les fonctions des Assemblées provinciales* held that "éducation commune aux hommes et aux femmes" (VIII, 474) is necessary for the enjoyment of the rights to be guaranteed to all citizens (VIII, 475). Women's full political and civil rights include voting and eligibility for election.

Sur l'admission des femmes au droit de cité asked how one can leave out half of humanity while proclaiming the rights of "man." Condorcet ridiculed the arguments of physical weakness (are men with gout or a cold left out of civil rights?) and domestic duties (are not workmen and farm hands tied down too?). "Either no individual of the human species has real rights, or all have the same; and he who votes against the rights of another, whatever be his religion, his color, or his sex, has from that moment abjured his own rights (X, 122). The essay, which first appeared in the *Journal de la Société de 1789* (No. 5, July 31, 1790), stirred up comment.

Condorcet's views on education for females were expounded especially in the first of five memoirs included in his *Sur l'instruction publique*, first published in 1791–92. Co-education is necessary, he explains, for women to keep up the education of their children and their men, and also for reasons of economy, for maintaining better manners and morals, and to prevent inequality in families. Women have the same right to public instruction as men (VII, 220). His committee report to the Legislative Assembly, *Rapport et projet de décret sur l'organisation générale de l'instruction publique* (VII, 449–573) would have established free, public co-education through the level of higher education, had it not been tabled. Its date, April 20–21, 1792, coincided with France's declaration of war against Austria.

From his hiding place in 1794 he wrote to his daughter Eliza that every girl must be trained to earn a living and be independent.[13] His *Esquisse d'un tableau historique des progrès de l'esprit humain,*[14] first published in 1795, a year after his death, held that no natural rights exist for man which woman should not share. The abolition of sexist prejudice will be one of the most important sources of progress. Full education for the two sexes will develop a more moral atmosphere and help create a better world (pp. 228–29). Some day, said he (three years before Malthus), to balance people against resources and maintain well-being for all, population might have to be limited (pp. 222–23).

To sum up, there was for Condorcet no dichotomy between woman's domestic and public roles. Discrimination against her, based on abuse of force and habit, hurts those who discriminate as well as society in general. Equality of women's rights should extend to education, civil and political life, and the functioning of society.

The female lead in the revolutionary drama was played as Olympe de Gouges flitted across the blood-spattered stage. Née Marie-Olympe Gouze in 1748, she established herself in Paris as the young widow of Louis-Yves Aubry. Her legal, if not natural, father in her native Montauban was a butcher. Spelling and handwriting were not her forte, and she preferred to dictate her copious works to secretaries, or even to the printer. Her one-act comedy, *Mirabeau aux Champs-Elisées,* was conceived and composed in four hours, she claimed,[15] and her play on Dumouriez in four days, but then this was a thirty-three page five-act drama. The author of numerous plays composed at this pace, she "was soon on quarreling terms with the whole of the Comédie Française,"[16] not to mention Beaumarchais. Still, the *Maison de Molière* did produce her *l'Esclavage des Nègres* in December 1789 (published in 1792).

Having caught "civisme," the public-spiritedness of the times, she brought out at her own expense an extensive series of patriotic revolutionary pamphlets ranging from one to fifty-six pages. Her *Lettre au peuple ou Projet d'une caisse patriotique* (1788) urged the alleviation of poverty. Later that year in her *Remarques patriotiques par la citoyenne auteur de la Lettre au peuple,* after calling for public work shops for the unemployed, she offered to lead women. "This sex too long oppressed is ready to shake off the yoke of shameful slavery. I place myself at its head."

Her feminism, touched on in earlier works, as well as in her *Mirabeau aux Champs-Elisées* of April 1791, was expanded by the Revolution. Her second Preface to the latter play mentions "a plan that I have conceived in favor of my sex, of my ungrateful sex. I know its defects, its foibles, but I also feel that some day it can arise; it is to that end that I wish to bend my efforts."[17]

The *Déclaration des droits de la femme et de la citoyenne,* a twenty-four page brochure signed "De Gouges," was undated but must have appeared shortly after September 14, 1791.[18] The dedication to the Queen predicts that if Marie-Antoinette supports the feminist cause she will soon have with her at least one-half of the Kingdom and at least one-third of the other half. Before the Preamble comes an introductory "Les Droits de la femme." The seventeen articles corresponding to those of the *Déclaration des droits de l'homme,* are followed by a postambule, then a "Forme du contrat social de l'homme et de la femme," and a postscript.

The Preamble declares that mothers, daughters, sisters asking to be represented in the National Assembly do solemnly declare the natural, inalienable, and sacred rights of woman.

> First Article. Woman is born free and remains equal to man in rights. . . .
>
> III. The principle of all sovereignty resides essentially in the nation which is only the assemblage of woman and man: no body, no individual, can exercise authority which does not emanate expressly from it.

VI. Law must be the expression of the general will; all female and male citizens must contribute personally, or by their representatives, to its formation; it must be the same for all: all female and male citizens, being equal in its eyes, must be equally admissible to all honors, positions, and public employment, according to their capacities, and without other distinctions than those of their virtues and talents.

X. . . . Woman has the right to mount the scaffold; she must have just the same right to mount the rostrum.

XI. The free communication of thought and of opinion is one of the most precious rights of woman, since this liberty assures the legitimacy of fathers toward children. Every *citoyenne* may then say freely, I am the mother of a child who belongs to you, without any barbarian prejudice forcing her to dissimulate the truth. . . .

XIII. For the maintenance of public force, & for the expenses of the administration, the contributions [taxes] of woman and man are equal; she participates in all the drudgery, and all the painful tasks; she must then have the same share in the distribution of positions, jobs, office, honor, and industry.

XIV. Female and male citizens have the right, either by themselves or through their representatives, to state the necessity of public contributions. Female citizens cannot join in this except through admittance into an equal share not only of the wealth but also of the public administration, and of determining the rate, the taxable income, the collection, and the duration of the tax.

XV. Women, *en masse,* whose contribution coalesces with that of men, have the right to demand of any public agent an accounting of his administration.

XVI. Any society in which the guaranty of rights is not assured, nor the separation of powers determined, has no constitution; the constitution is null and void if the majority of individuals who compose the nation has not cooperated in drawing it up.

XVII. Property is for all sexes, united or separate; it represents for everyone an inviolable and sacred right; . . .

The "Postambule" proclaims, "woman, awake; the tocsin of reason is being sounded throughout the whole universe. Recognize thy rights. . . . Man enslaved . . . has needed thy help to break his chains; free at last, he has become unjust toward his companion" (pp. 11–12).

Assorted reflections follow: ". . . the French government has depended for centuries on the noctural administration of women—

formerly worthy of scorn but respected; since the revolution respectable but scorned" (pp. 13–14).

Like her friend Mercier in his *L'An 2440* of 1770, Mme de Gouges then calls for the marriage of priests, and decries the efforts of the colonials within the National Assembly to stir up feelings against the colored people of the French Antilles. Such sparks, she predicts, must set fire to America (p. 20). Finally she recommends amalgamating the executive and legislative powers; otherwise France will lose her Empire.

Olympe de Gouges had dreamed of "a philosophic revolution, worthy of saintly humanity." "Blood, even of the guilty, eternally soils revolutions," she wrote. "Scaffolds, executioners, would this then be the result of a revolution that was to constitute the glory of France, to spread without distinction over both sexes and serve as a model for the Universe?"[19]

Opposing the death penalty for the deposed monarch, she addressed a petition in December 1792 to the president of the Convention, asking for the right to defend Louis Capet at his trial. She pressed his right to end his days in exile as an ex-monarch. If he's executed, he'll live on, but if he survives his fall from the throne, that's the end of him. As for Marie-Antoinette, she recalled in the Preface of her comedy *Mirabeau* (published in April 1791 before the royal flight to Varennes) that about fourteen years ago she had seen Marie-Antoinette at the door of the Comédie française. "I said out loud: 'Farewell, royal majesty, some day this Queen will shed tears of blood . . ." (XI, xiv).

A sort of female Cyrano de Bergerac, Olympe de Gouges defied Robespierre. She signed her *Pronostic sur Maximilien Robespierre par un animal amphibie* "Polyme." His throne would be the scafford, she prophesied. Receiving no response from him, she published a letter saying, "It is I, Maximilien, who am the author of thy *Pronostic,* I . . . Olympe de Gouges . . . . LET US PLUNGE INTO THE SEINE! Thou hast need of a bath to wash away the stains with which thou has covered thyself on the tenth [August 1792], thy death will calm things down, and as for myself, *the sacrifice of a pure life* will disarm the heavens . . . ."[20]

Les Trois Urnes ou le Salut de la Patrie was her last pamphlet. It proposed a plebiscite—the French should choose between an indivisible republic, a federation, and a monarchy. Just as she was arranging to pay a man to paste this up on the walls of Paris on July 20, 1793, she was arrested. Unbowed to the end, on the third of November, delivering her last lines, she mounted the inexorable guillotine, rostrum and scaffold achieved together. Her heart she willed to her country, her honesty to men, if they needed it, her soul to women.

Five days later, Mme Roland died on the guillotine. On July 28, 1794, it was Robespierre's turn. Some three months earlier, under mysterious circumstances, Condorcet had perished in prison.

A comparison between Condorcet and the more aggressive Olympe de Gouges illuminates different approaches to the common problem of woman's place. Her *Pronostic sur Maxilien Robespierre* reproached him with wanting to "assassinate Condorcet." Like Condorcet, she based her case on the Enlightenment principles. Equality, liberty, and justice, nature and reason, natural rights, the general will, the separation of powers, a constitution, and the social contract all figure in her Declaration. But whereas her predecessor Condorcet theorized, she added to his reasoning a note of political urgency—either the Constituent Assembly before its imminent expiration or the upcoming Legislative Assembly must proclaim her Declaration right away. Her second difference from Condorcet lies in the fact that she laid more detailed stress on the property rights and general economic rights of women. Wealth is to be shared between the sexes, she claims in her *Postambule*. Article XIII is pregnant with implications as to the value of women's labor, even menial or domestic labor. She seems more concerned than the Marquis de Condorcet with the interests of lower-class women. She states that women should personally profit from their labor which benefits others.[21] Women have property rights, according to Articles II, XIV, and XVII. Articles VI and XIII insist that women must be equally admissible to public employment and office as well as to jobs in industry. Since women pay taxes equally with men, she reasons in Articles XIV and XV, they must have an equal voice in determining taxation, another economic right of which they have been deprived. Like Flora Tristan, a nineteenth-century socialistic feminist, the author of the Declaration perceived or intuited the interactions between economic and political power, especially the usefulness of the latter to the former.

Last of all, by proposing a new form of free "mariage" bound only by a mutually revocable contract between the two principals, she was a forerunner of today's sexual revolution. At the same time she expressed disapproval of prostitution and sexual license.

Untutored and undisciplined as she was, she added social and political insights to the *Declaration of the Rights of Man* apart from extending it to her sex. Her Article XI claims that the father of natural issue may be duly named by the mother with no prejudice to anyone. A law to that effect was passed in France—in 1972. Olympe was the more concerned about illegitimacy, inasmuch as she purported to be the natural daughter of Le Franc de Pompignan. According to her Article XVI, any constitution is null and void if the majority of the nation has not participated in formulating it. This provision for implementing populist democracy was an addition to the *Déclaration des droits de l'homme.*

Condorcet was a pioneer in his project of free public co-education through higher education. Of greater stature than the uneducated Mme de Gouges, he encompassed feminism in a more complete fashion than she. They were in different ways too independent and uncompromising to be successful politicians, especially for those stormy times. But they were both idealists whose fertile concepts forecast future developments.

The Dénouement

After the Convention was established in 1792, every pretext was used to suppress the new political assertiveness of women that had been nurtured by the Revolution, which was devouring its progeny. A few prominent ladies were guillotined, others imprisoned, the rest intimidated. The formula of Terror worked. Scattered male protests failed to stem the tide. David Williams, called to Paris by the Girondins to help draft a constitution, was made an honorary French citizen. He published, in February 1793, *Observations sur la dernière constitution de la France avec des vues pour la formation de la nouvelle constitution.*[22] It granted limited rights to women, including juries of women in cases of women against women. Pierre Guyomar, deputy from the Côtes-du-Nord, affirmed in late April 1793 to the Convention that it would be shameful not to apply the *Declaration of the Rights of Man* to women. His plea, *Le Partisan de l'égalité politique entre les individus ou problème très important de l'égalité en droits et de l'inégalité en faits,* insisted that women should have the right to vote, to deliberate in primary assemblies, and to be elected, locally, so as not to have to travel. Another deputy, Charlier, protested against the Convention's denial of civil rights to the second sex: "Unless you contest the fact that women are part of the human species, can you deprive them of this right [peaceful assembly] common to all thinking beings?"[23]

The Jacobin Constitution of June 1793, by failing to classify women as citizens, excluded them from public rights along with criminals, minors, and the mentally incompetent. The dissolution of women's clubs in October was accompanied by the suppression of their newspapers. The Convention rejected the Comité de législation's code that would have granted married women a considerable measure of equality and independence. But the final touch to stop the feminist campaign was taken in Prairial of the year III (May 1795), when the Convention issued three decrees: women were forbidden to meet in groups of over five under penalty of arrest; they were excluded from political assemblies even as spectators; agitators among them were subject to trial. And they were barred from attending sessions of the Paris Commune.

"Tant que les femmes ne s'en mêlent pas," Mirabeau had proclaimed, "il n'y a pas de véritable révolution." The women of France had proved active in making a veritable revolution. In Michelet's words, "Les femmes furent à l'avant-garde de notre révolution."[24] In so doing they also endeavored to act as midwives to the women's revolution, predicted by Choderlos de Laclos in 1783: . . . apprenez qu'on ne sort de l'esclavage que par une grande révolution. Cette révolution est-elle possible? C'est à vous seule à le dire puisqu'elle dépend de votre courage. . . . sans liberté point de moralité et sans moralité point d'éducation. . . ."[25] His prophecy failed to come true. Woman's courage did not suffice to bring about the birth of female emancipation. The woman's revolution was stillborn.

What aborted it, despite the heroic labor of the feminists? The abuse of male brute force, as Condorcet claimed? The different classes of women were not united, nor do there seem to have been sustained ties between groups and among individual leaders. Women in politics were amateurs, outside of the system. Violence like that of a Charlotte Corday stabbing Marat, *l'Ami du Peuple,* in his Franklin bathtub furnished a good excuse after July 13, 1793, for keeping the fair sex in its place. The foolhardiness of some of the militants did not help ease their way into politics. Feminist activism went under in the backlash between Girondins, Jacobins, and *Enragés.* And the elimination of male social dominance could be deemed untimely in a nation reft by a split in the Church, bread shortages, runaway inflation, insurrections, invasions from within and without, not to speak of hysterical fears of enemies, spies, sell-outs, and treason, real or suspected, within the very army, navy, and civil government.

But unquestionably male chauvinism played a major role in the ruthless suppression of the drive for women's rights. Thus for example the popular but antifeminist journal *Les Révolutions de Paris* under Prudhomme's editorship stood for denying women the very right to petition. After Gouges' *Declaration* it stated: "Civil and political liberty is of no use to women and should therefore be kept from them. . . . A woman is acceptable only in the context of her father's or her husband's household. She needs to know nothing of what goes on outside, beyond what they may see fit to tell her."[26]

The Jacobins' *Journal de la Montagne* was more discrete. But Robespierre, Amar, and Chaumette, among others, were sexists if not misogynists. According to André Amar, women had neither the physical nor moral force nor the stability for judicious exercise of political discretion. Anaxagore Chaumette ordered the closing in 1793 of a play entitled *La Liberté des femmes.* Following Olympe's execution, he moralized in the *Moniteur universel*: "Olympe de Gouges . . . wanted to be a statesman [*homme d'Etat*] and it seems that . . . the law has punished this conspirator for having forgotten the virtues befitting her sex."[27]

The few gains made by women consisted mainly of their right to bear witness, cessation of sex discrimination in family inheritance, the sharing of the "biens communaux," and a divorce law passed in 1792, repealed in 1816 under the Restoration. The names of women, especially widows, with children to support and in need of social assistance were to be recorded on welfare rolls.

It remained for Bonaparte to give women, not just the movement, the *coup de grâce.* "The Code Napoléon established the political servitude of women worse than ever in the Middle Ages or under Royalty."[28] A married woman could not enter into any legal proceeding without her husband's consent; the father alone had authority over his child until its majority, and so on. "The relationship of husband and wife was one of the subjects in which Napoleon took a vivid interest when it was discussed at the time of the elaboration of the Civil Code. . . . on this subject his views prevailed. He wanted to introduce strict rules in order to keep wives in their place. . . . 'Nature has made our women our slaves. In other words, Madame, you belong to me body and soul.' "[29] The Code allowed husbands to kill, without trial, wives they accused of adultery.

The Civil Code of 1804 suppressed woman's civil rights. Participation in public affairs had already been forbidden her. She had been denied freedom of association, free speech, freedom of the press. According to Sullerot it took some forty years for the feminist press to recover. Despite Mme de Staël's spirited resistance in the Napoleonic era and the early Restoration, woman faced her darkest hour with respect to liberty. She was to find herself ill-equipped to face her urban exploitation in the nineteenth-century Industrial Revolution.

The movement for the equality of the female half of the French nation had been launched, as we have seen, in a spirit of exaltation. Its speedy downfall may be considered the most signal failure of the Revolution.[30] All public buildings in France, even the jails, are inscribed with the words "Liberté, Egalité, Fraternité." They might have added, "For men only."

Epilogue

All the figures viewed were in their different ways involved with politics, politics that was revolutionary in its urgency, in revolt against old traditions and new repression, in demands for immediate transformation of society's sex structure, in improvised solutions to newly developed crises, in fervor, moral convictions, and consciousness of starting anew.

What word best describes the politics of the feminists—philosophy or ideology? The women as a rule made ad hoc demands for practical legislation. Condorcet's philosophical approach to feminism was based on the logical application of natural rights to all, women as well as men. In a more inchoate way, the ideas of the generally less-educated woman feminists also had their basis in philosophy. Revolutionary politics, as they tried their hands at it, issued neither from the science of politics nor from an abstract philosophy so much as from a spirit, logical as well as idealistic, emotional and desperate, of justice and independence.

As for the term ideology, in its technical meaning, for Destutt de Tracy (Condorcet's comrade in the Société de 1789) and the other *idéologues* of the time, methodological analysis of man's sensations and ideas constituted the basis of social science. Olympe de Gouges and the other women feminists reviewed here, named and anonymous, were not in this sense ideologues. If, however, one means by the term an idealistic or visionary social or political doctrine, then, for the feminists of both sexes, ideology with moral and emotional overtones best describes their revolutionary quest for the application to the second sex of social egalitarianism, natural rights, liberty, equal justice, economic rights to subsistence, property, and jobs, and the elimination of discrimination.

The feminists of the Revolution fought and, in some cases, gave their lives for the generic sense of the word "man" in the proposition that all men are born and remain equal in rights. Their voices were stilled by an all-male régime that refused to follow the logic of its own premises. The Terror could extinguish their lives but not the sparks of their revolutionary ideas and claims.

NOTES

1 See David Williams, "The Politics of Feminism in the French Enlightenment," in Peter Hughes and David Williams, eds., *The Varied Pattern: Studies in the 18th Century* (Toronto: A. M. Hakkert, 1971).

2 Charles Seignobos, *Histoire sincère de la nation française* (Paris: Presses universitaires de France, 1946), p. 252. Here as elsewhere in this article the translation is my own.

3 *Très-humbles Remontrances des femmes françaises* (n.p., 1788). Such petitions are generally anonymous, without date or place of publication.

4 *Demande des femmes aux Etats-Généraux par l'auteur des* Femmes comme il convient de les voir (n.d., n.p.), p. 38. The author of the latter tract, hence of the former, is Mme de Coicy.

5 *Requête des femmes pour leur admission aux Etats-Généraux; à Messieurs composants l'Assemblée des Notables* (n.p., n.d.).

6 *Pétition des femmes du Tiers-Etat au Roi,* 1er Janvier, 1789. Another edition is dated 10 Janvier, 1789. Both contain eight pages, same text, but different size pages and different frontispiece designs.

7 Abridged and translated from *Requête des dames à l'Assemblée nationale* (Paris: Morin, 1789), pp. 11–14. Paule-Marie Duhet in her thoroughly documented *Les Femmes et la Révolution* (Paris: Coll. Archives Julliard, 1971), pp. 40–41, classes the above *Requête* among those suspected of being parodies. Its claims are, however, not out of line with others of the time. The wearing of pants by women had won them the right to be served in the cafés of Paris as far back as the 1730s. See Joseph Wechsberg, "The Historic Café Procope," *Gourmet,* 32 (Sept. 1972), 18ff. And red-and-white striped trousers appear in pictures of revolutionary women demonstrating in the streets of Paris.

8 George Rudé in *Paris and London in the 18th Century* (New York: Viking Press, 1970) says that "it was not only in the October days that women played so outstanding a part" (p. 114). He speaks of the "*menu peuple* of Revolutionary Paris, both men and women, the latter being more in evidence when the question of bread was to the fore" (p. 120). "A characteristic feature of the disorders was the prevalence of women among the rioters in the streets and in the Convention, a sure sign that the 'bread and butter' issue was to the fore" (p. 156). The food riots of February 1792 and 1793 as well as the risings of April–May 1795 were chiefly provoked by prices and supplies (p. 196). Michelet says that women were "plus violentes que les hommes. Marat est fort satisfait d'elles" (30 déc. 1790), *Les Femmes de la Révolution,* édition annotée par Pierre Labracherie et par Jean Dumont, Textes de présentation de P. Bessard-Massenet et de Pierre Labracherie (Paris: Hachette, n.d.), p. 84.

9 See Mary Jay Durham, "The Sans-Jupons' Crusade for Liberation during the French Revolution," Diss. Washington Univ., St. Louis, 1972), p. 187.

10 Translated from Evelyne Sullerot, *Histoire de la presse féminine en France des origines à 1848* (Paris: Colin, 1966), p. 43.

11 The National Union Catalogue lists no works by Etta Palm Alders or d'Aëlders. I have translated this passage from the extract in Marie Collins and Sylvie Weil-Sayre, *Les Femmes en France* (New York: Scribner's, 1974), p. 37.

12 *Oeuvres de Condorcet,* publiées par A. Condorcet O'Connor et M. F. Arago (Paris: Didot, 1847–49), IX, 15–16. Further Condorcet references will be to this edition unless otherwise noted.

13 *Conseils de Condorcet à sa fille,* I, 611–23.

14 Condorcet, *Esquisse d'un tableau historique des progrès de l'esprit humain,* nouvelle edition présentée par Yvon Belaval (Paris: Vrin, 1970), Dixième Époque.

15 *Mirabeau aux Champs-Elisées* [sic] in *Pièces de théâtre, Littérature patriotique* (Paris: Veuve Duchesne, 1791), XI, v.

16 Claire Tomalin, *The Life and Death of Mary Wollstonecraft,* (New York and London: Harcourt, 1974), p. 158.

17 *L'Entrée de Dumourier* [*sic*] *à Bruxelles ou les Vivandières,* in *Pièces de théâtre,* XXI, 10.

18 The National Union Catalog lists no copy of the *Déclaration.* Its subtitle states that it should be made into law by the National Assembly in its last sessions or in those of the approaching legislature (Oct. 1, 1791). The P.S. adds that the King has just accepted the Constitution (Sept. 14). A full English translation of the *Déclaration* has never been published. The present translation of its major articles is my own.

19 Quotations in this paragraph translated from E. Lairtullier, *Les Femmes célèbres de 1789 à 1795 et leur influence dans la Révolution* (Paris: Dondey Dupré, 1840), II, 61.

20 Translated from the text cited by Charles Monsalet, "Olympe de Gouges," in *Les Oubliés et les dédaignés* (Paris: Poulet Malassis et de Broise, 1861), p. 175.

21 See Barbara Woshinsky, "This awareness of the economic value of women's labor is one of Olympe de Gouges' most powerful insights," in "Olympe de Gouges' Declaration of the Rights of Women (1791)," *Mary Wollstonecraft Newsletter,* Dec. 1, 1973, 5.

22 See Alfred Dessens' *Les Revendications des droits de la femme au point de vue politique, civil, économique, pendant la Revolution* (Toulouse: thèse de droit, 1905), p. 95.

23 Cited by Duhet, *Les Femmes et la Revolution,* p. 157.

24 Michelet, *Les Femmes de la Révolution,* p. 51.

25 Laclos' *De l'éducation des femmes,* pp. 14–15. It was submitted in 1783 to the Académie de Châlons-sur-Marne for its essay contest on the question. However, having sponsored another contest on the "correction of abuses," the Académie was prevented from awarding any prizes. *De l'éducation des femmes* was not published until 1903, by Edouard Champion with "notes inédites de Baudelaire" (Paris: Vanier). See Madeleine Raaphorst, "Choderlos de Laclos et l'éducation des femmes au XVIIIe siècle," *Rice University Studies,* 53, No. 4 (1967), 33–41.

26 Tomalin, p. 155.

27 "Nonidi 29 brumaire an II [19 Nov. 1793] Aux Républicaines." Translated from Duhet, p. 205.

28 André Leclère, *Le Vote des femmes en France* (Paris: Librairie des sciences politiques et sociales, 1929), p. 44.

29 Pierre A. Picarda, "The Status of French Women in France," *Transactions of the Grotius Society,* 24 (1939), 73. It is only in very recent times that the last vestiges of the Code Civil's subjugation of women have been eliminated.

30 See Winifred Stephens Whale, *Women of the French Revolution* (London: Chapman and Hall, 1922), p. 274.

Politics and the Intellect

JUDITH N. SHKLAR

The question "Can eighteenth-century values be defended?" is often asked, especially during this bicentennial year. It cannot be answered because it is a badly put question. There was no single, self-consistent set of values in the eighteenth century, or indeed in any other country. Europe's intellectual tradition is one of multiplicity and conflict and no useful end is served by ignoring the diversity of the past. Even that part of the eighteenth century that we call "the Enlightenment" was a state of intellectual tension rather than a sequence of simple propositions. Not even its central significance, the emergence of the modern intellectuals as an identifiable social group, can be registered in terms of uniform individual experiences or responses. Indeed, the proper place of men of learning in society, the exact political location of the republic of letters, the duties of the educated and well-informed, in short, the right ethos for intellectuals, was the subject of considerable controversy. And it is one that still agitates us. We may therefore say with some confidence that the morals and mores of the eighteenth century need no defense today, since we still share them. It is the purpose of this essay to show that we may discover ourselves in the eighteenth century and that this is one of the values that any part of our past has for us.

Before turning to the debate about the political obligations of intellectuals one must ask why the picture of a monolithic Enlightenment remains so popular. For the notion of the uniformity of the "philosophes" depends on their having identical political and social aspirations. In spite of all the evidence to the contrary it is still assumed that the Enlightenment was "a movement among intellectuals to assert themselves as a social force and to introduce, or at least talk about, a new technique of social change."[1] But surely they did not say the same things. A sociological category, "intellectuals," tells us little about their thoughts. We remember that Diderot among others rejected Helvétius' over-confident "education can do everything." And Condorcet's vision of progress propelled by the twin engines of science and public education was indeed "as much a caricature of the Enlightenment as its testament."[2] Condorcet's rejection of the past, the need to forget in order to learn, the apparently unlimited hope for a future free from the errors of the ages was far from being the only mood of the age. It was shared by others, to be sure, as an essential aspect of the campaign against traditional religion. However, the very scepticism, eclecticism, and self-awareness that were needed for that struggle inspired doubt, pessimism, and self-criticism among some of the boldest prophets of the new age. It was a conflict within individual minds as much as between opponents. Sociological classifications should not blind us to such spiritual realities.

Sociological generalizing is not the only source of simplification. The two momentous revolutions that marked the final quarter of the century also tend to constrict our retrospective eyesight. We are too eager to reduce the "causes" of these events to manageable lists. The opinions and acts of the generation preceding these storms are seen as inexorable steps leading to a known finale. It will not do. We know how deeply the American revolutionaries differed from each other and from their fathers; the French were not different in this respect. It may be inconvenient for the historian, but Atlantic intellectuals were not a simple group. We cannot even follow de Tocqueville in ascribing the ambitions and opinions of the French men of letters to their complete lack of political experience. Jefferson shared most of their views and he was a very experienced public man.[3] Here the tendency to make a false uniformity is due to the demands imposed by a political theory. That also is deceptive.

Instead of a single-minded, power-and-reform-mad platoon of intellectuals, we in fact find an immense range of views about their own role. Condorcet's views are the ones usually identified with the age and are too well known to need reviewing. However we should recall that Montesquieu, Rousseau, and d'Alembert held quite different positions. These four constitute the best defined intellectual poles. In between these a very great number of degrees and combinations were possible, among them those chosen by John Adams and Jefferson.

Montesquieu argued that however great the merits of intellectual achievement were on their own account, they had no effect on a man's basic moral character. A despot is no less despotic because he is well read and patronizes scholars. On the contrary, learning not only fails to protect us against the temptations of power, it may even enhance them. Moreover, if the intellect has little moral force, it may, in the long run, also be insignificant socially. Men of letters may simply not be very significant on the great stage of history. It is a position of heroic moderation and surely as such, admirable. Most intellectuals tend to detest or worship their own caste, few will even consider the possibility of their own unimportance.

Oddly enough, Rousseau also did not grant the intellectuals a place of primary importance in the corruption of mankind; he rejected not only them, but all their works as well. At best they coated the pill of injustice. Perhaps the entertainment they offered prevented the worst degeneracies, but they could do no good. Moreover, they could do a lot of harm if they invaded relatively unspoiled places, like his native Geneva. Finally, there was d'Alembert's response to Rousseau's challenge. By separating the arts and sciences from those who practiced them he was able to cherish the former and reprove the latter for their moral defects, among which servility and vanity were the foremost. However, he did not despair. For if men of ideas were to stand outside the prevailing systems of power and prestige and adopt an ethic suitable only to their own, isolated vocation, they might yet serve as an inspiration to their fellow citizens and so, indirectly, be socially useful.

In the closing years of their lives and era John Adams and Jefferson also discussed the place of the educated man in the polity. Adams leaned more towards Montesquieu, Jefferson toward Condorcet. Yet both agreed that it was the new intellectual vigor and freedom that had made their century "the most honourable to Human Nature."[4] What gives their correspondence its particular interest in this debate is that they were not concerned with the moral hazards of the *ancien régime,* but with the services that educated men might render in a free, republican, and relatively egalitarian political order. Here again there was tension. For Adams spoke for the party of memory, remembering how power had depraved and been abused by the learned, no less than by the ignorant. Jefferson spoke for the party of hope, for those who looked to a new kind of public-spirited aristocrat, republican and decent as few had ever been before.

Let us, in honor of the Bicentennial year, begin at the end. The great problem to which both Adams and Jefferson turned in their last years was how to prevent the rise of political oppression in an inevitably inegalitarian society. They were entirely at one about what was most to be dreaded, but they differed greatly in their responses to their common fears. Jefferson, in spite of his practical involvements, was intellectually indifferent to politics. It bored him. He had none of Adams' passionate desire to create a science of politics. When his friend sent him an important book, he replied candidly, "but it is on politics, a subject I never loved and now hate. I will not promise therefore to read it thoroughly."[5] History was to him often, as in the case of his obsession with the ancient Anglo-Saxons, a source of mythology. At other times it was reduced to anthropology. The natural sciences alone claimed his full attention, especially those that might prove economically or educationally useful. In fact Jefferson wanted education to replace politics. Primary education would create citizens capable of protecting themselves against usurpation and governing themselves directly at the small, local "ward" level. Here education would render ruling superfluous. Secondary education, more selective, would presumably supply America with its skilled working force, capable of creating and maintaining an intelligent, well-administered economy and, above all, serve as a selection ground for the universities. Higher education open only to the few most able would provide the nation with a "natural aristocracy," an élite distinguished solely by its intellectual talents. True merit, as demonstrated by the capacity to learn and advance intellectual, and, especially, scientific disciplines, was to replace all other standards for distinguishing ranks in society.[6] It was simply assumed that intelligence and public virtue would always be joined among the well-educated. That this career open to natural talent would do nothing for equality did not trouble Jefferson, for that was not his aim. What such a system did ensure was change. It certainly does make sense for every generation to reject the political legacy of its predecessors, if scientific knowledge determined and measured all social values. As the former advanced, the latter would have to be adjusted.[7] In this way politics, the struggle of competing interests, the distribution of moral and tangible values, the relations between allies and enemies, all this becomes problem-solving by education and by the already educated. The expected certainty of knowledge replaces the turmoil of political passions.

In Europe this faith in perpetual, if not infinite, progress was largely supported by a Manichean view of history. Reason and superstition had fought an unequal war, until with the rise of science and the invention of printing, the tide of battle had turned and reason could now enjoy an irreversible victory. Such thoughts were far from alien to Adams and Jefferson also. It may well be that in America the concentration on scientific progress was peculiarly appropriate because the prevailing reality was the struggle between man and nature, rather than among men.[8] However, neither Adams nor Jefferson was blind to human hostility in general or to the part that organized religion played in it. It is in fact surprising to find Adams still so furious at religious dogmatism. Both looked upon Connecticut with contempt and dismay as if it were a veritable kingdom of darkness.[9] Adams, ever suspicious, sensed the resurgence of religious intolerance all about him.[10] These sons of the preceding century were, in fact, as anticlerical as the disciples of Voltaire, and while both were theists, they spent far more time discussing the political crimes of religious zealots than the benevolence of God. It was as an antidote to organized religion that Adams, just as much as Jefferson, valued the progress in the arts and sciences that both had witnessed in their lifetime. It was one of the strongest intellectual bonds uniting them and it allows one to treat their correspondence as the joint product of a single mentality.

The difference between them was, nevertheless, very real. It went well beyond the obvious one that Adams noted between his own fear of "the few," of aristocracy, and Jefferson's of "the one," of monarchy. We have here a conflict of intellectual inclinations. Adams believed that no kind of aristocracy, whether defined by intellect, wealth, or birth could be trusted with any degree of uncontrolled power. No one could be trusted to behave with self-control when the possibility of self-enrichment and aggrandizement arose. Jefferson was convinced that intellectual distinction was bound to express itself in public rectitude. Like many people of his age he assumed that when ignorance and superstition had been dispelled, their opposites, knowledge and enlightenment, would simply replace them to govern the new world. Adams was less sanguine. He was as suspicious of democratic egalitarianism as he was of aristocratic pretensions because all immoderate assertions worried him. Inequality was a political problem only because it invited imbalances in the distribution of power. Tyranny lurked everywhere, at least potentially.

It may well be that Adams saw everything through political lenses. He was certainly far more interested in political theory than Jefferson, as we saw, had ever been. History was Adams' source of political information and wisdom, and the very basis of his political science. Far from being a traditionalist, in the sense of revering the past with the piety due to one's ancestors, he looked back with the disenchanted eye of a social scientist. In this respect he was no less fact-minded than his friend who looked to nature. His whole disposition was to amass political examples so as to discover general political truths about recurrent political situations. Among these, mob attacks on the security of property and aristocratic oppression were the most threatening as well as the most common. What obstacles could be put in their path? Natural aristocracy he at once recognized as perfectly useless. Every sort of inequality may originate in natural superiority. Sooner or later it will translate itself into wealth, power, and prestige. If it be merely moral merit it cannot prevail against the real objects of ambition, good looks, wealth, and power. These give men reputation and these are the goals of ambition. All may be and are used to corrupt republics. In an electoral system an aristocrat is any man who controls more than a single vote.[11] In his native Massachusetts education was diligently pursued, and as a result generations of Harvard men, from father to son, could beguile lesser men and govern. Since Adams was just as eager to promote learning as Jefferson was, he encouraged the latter in all his projects. To other correspondents he did not hide his contempt for the competitive quarrels among scholars that made academies scenes of battle and served only to retard the advance of knowledge.[12] Knowledge in fact did not lesson political inequality and indeed had no effect on morals at all.[13] Only careful institutional engineering, the careful balancing and separating of constitutionally established powers, would protect the republic against aristocratic corruption. As we know, that was not the actual course of political history. It was rather, the theory and practice of Madison's organized political parties based on an extensive electorate that settled the relations between the few and the many. It was not a solution that would have appealed to the scientific or moral inclinations of either Adams or Jefferson, for this was no cure for factions but, in effect, a permanent dismissal of the idea of a principled and "true" public order. Jefferson's education and Adams' political science were designed to achieve a demonstrably right government, not a merely workable arrangement, however enduring. In that also they were in accord, even if one was of a hopeful and the other of a very wary disposition.

It has often been argued that Adams' undeniably grim view of human nature can be traced to his Puritan ancestors. That may be true, but perhaps no such explanation is necessary. A great many of Adams' contemporaries all over Europe, not only in Scotland, shared his attitudes to men and citizens. For all the differences in circumstances, style, in emphasis and character, they participated in the intellectual tensions of their whole age and not only in those peculiar to their own country. Montesquieu's name is one of the few that never appears on Adams' long litany of complaints against the *philosophes.* Nevertheless, he was also their most admired and influential writer. How to organize political élites for commercial Europe, given the decadence and incompetence of the hereditary nobility, was one of the central issues raised in *The Spirit of the Laws.* That is the burden of its pages devoted to republics and to Great Britain. Montesquieu's response was not precise, but it pointed to the approach Adams was to choose. Here there was no talk about "natural aristocracies," though much was said about religion and education. The conclusion one would, in any case, draw from that work is that the intellectuals of a society reflect rather than fashion prevailing régimes. Moreover, Montesquieu had earlier drawn a far from flattering portrait of the modern "natural aristocrat."

In the *Persian Letters* Montesquieu offers his readers a hero who is both an enlightened philosopher and a despot. Usbek, although he is in fact a nobleman in Persia, prefers to be a "natural" aristocrat. He despises the court and deliberately shakes off all his local ties to seek knowledge and enlightenment abroad.[14] He is of course a good deal less cosmopolitan when his personal interests are affected, for his harem is left to the strict and cruel care of his eunuchs.[15] That does not mean that his love of learning is insincere or superficial. It may have begun as a mere pretense but it is now perfectly genuine, and indeed Usbek *is* enlightened.[16] The perfectly detached outsider can see French customs and follies with a penetration not possible to others. His criticisms of the pettiness of every class of men, including the literati, of rituals and superstitions, of folly of every sort are supremely intelligent. His analysis of the slave trade and the commercial consequences of imperialism and bigotry is brilliant in every way.[17] Impartiality and a fine disinterestedness mark all his judgments of others. And, naturally, he is a defender of the arts and sciences as the greatest advantages of civilization. Without them we would revert to barbarism. It is his gentler friend Rhédi who worries about the tendency of knowledge to merely replace old evils with new.[18] In short, Usbek is the very model of a *philosophe.* His detachment, however, does have characteristic failings. He cannot feel anything.[19] He not only does not love his wives, he has no emotional life at all. When he is tempted by fatalism, by a belief in Providence, he rejects it as leading him to a loss of feeling, to insensibility. However the opposite belief has the same effect. Why not commit suicide when life ceases to please? Nature will not be affected and society is a mere contract for

among others. History, moreover, seemed to corroborate all these misgivings. In a finely reasoned history of royal policy and court culture, d'Alembert showed that in fact all along the king and the nobility had created, sustained, and dominated the world of the arts and letters. Reputations were still made in the ante-chambers of the great.[24] The response to this essay was, not surprisingly, cool. The "bragging of a young schoolboy" was a fair sample of opinion.[25]

D'Alembert's position was indeed a difficult one to maintain. Rousseau, by simply turning his back on civilization, had chosen an easier path. For d'Alembert, like Adams and their common master, Montesquieu, was utterly devoted to the life of learning and was an ardent promoter of every art and science. All worshipped knowledge. D'Alembert's ideas about a suitable modern education were just as science- and utility-oriented as Jefferson's were to be.[26] Adams had no objections at all to his enterprising friend's designs for instruction and indeed congratulated him warmly. The great division within these men's own minds, and between them and their more daring friends, was whether intellectual distinction, however great, was politically beneficial. For all the answer was far from being a simple yes or no. Enlightened views were clearly socially better than clerical and traditional lore. However, it was paradoxically only by withdrawing from the society and the mores of the political world that the men of learning could hope to advance either knowledge or its beneficial influence. Whether social or natural, the sciences could not create a politically superior "natural aristocracy" without corruption, both their own and that of the polity. Their avenue must be indirect.

It is worth remembering that eighteenth-century intellectuals were a pre-technological élite. They could not yet claim to be economically indispensable to society. They thought of themselves rather as teachers and guides, as the rulers of opinions and so, indirectly, of the polity. They would do well just what the clergy had, in their view, done so badly. It is not surprising that someone should rise to reject such enormous pretensions, whether clerical or anti-clerical. Rousseau's mission was all but inevitable and his day was to come, even in America. If the Revolutionary generation owed him little, later ones were to be much in his debt. Adams could only misquote him; Jefferson's agrarianism had other sources, but soon Americans were to be swept along by Rousseau. The apparent simplicity of his scorn appeals to many well-educated people who in a revulsion of self-hatred turn upon the "intellectual élite." Their often petulant and pseudo-democratic zeal is untempered by Rousseau's tragic insight into the insuperable moral limitations of man in society. Nor should we identify d'Alembert's rigorous self-judgment with the facile laments, so common today, about the disruptive impact of intellectuals upon liberal societies. Those who now express these fears would prefer the academy to conform more perfectly to the morals and manners of the market place and the bureaucracies. Theirs is in no sense a genuine self-criticism, nor do they offer insights into the real moral paradoxes of intellectual life. They merely want the "natural" aristocracy to become more conventional. As Adams saw, that happens in any case, inevitably. The prestige values and personal aspirations of intellectuals remain very stable. They are also adaptable generally. The reports of the dangers that they are likely to pose to an established order may well be greatly exaggerated. Flattery, especially, goes a long way here. The real and tormenting problems are those that were already plain at the moment when the modern world, both social and intellectual, was born. When the watchmen at the gate of the new age warned the men of letters to retreat to what is now often sneered at as the "ivory tower," they were not telling them to forget their obligations to society, but rather to assume them in a more respectable way. We might also ask ourselves, as some of them did, whether we really matter all that much. It is, after all, an open question.

NOTES

1 Charles Frankel, *The Faith of Reason* (New York: Columbia Univ. Press, 1948), p. 10.

2 Peter Gay, *The Enlightenment* (New York: Knopf, 1969), II, 122. Gay altogether offers a new and greatly improved account of the spirit of the age. See especially pp. 98–125.

3 Alexis de Tocqueville, *The Ancien Régime and the French Revolution,* trans. Stuart Gilbert (New York: Doubleday, Anchor, 1955), p. 13.
4 *The Adams-Jefferson Letters,* ed. Lester J. Cappon (New York: Simon and Schuster, 1971), p. 456.
5 Ibid., p. 259.
6 Ibid., pp. 387–92.
7 Letter to Samuel Kercheval, *The Portable Thomas Jefferson* (New York: Viking, 1975), pp. 559–61.
8 Daniel Boorstin, *The Lost World of Thomas Jefferson* (Boston: Beacon Press, 1960), *passim.*
9 *Letters,* pp. 510, 512.
10 Ibid., pp. 461–62, 607–8.
12 *The Political Writings of John Adams,* ed. George A. Peek, Jr. (Indianapolis: Bobbs-Merrill, 1954), pp. 184–85, 189–90, 198–99, 204–5.
13 Ibid., pp. 207–9.
14 *Lettres Persanes,* Lettre I. *Oeuvres Complètes de Montesquieu,* ed. André Masson (Paris: Nagel, 1950), I.
15 Ibid., II.
16 Ibid., VIII.
17 Ibid., CXVIII, CXXI.
18 Ibid., VI.
19 Ibid., LXXVI, CXIX.
20 *Oeuvres Complètes de d'Alembert* (Geneva: Slatkine, 1967), III, 442–43.
21 *Oeuvres Complètes* (Paris: Gallimard, 1959) III, 7, 21, 25, 49–50; I, 967–68.
22 D'Alembert, O.C., I, 82.
23 Ibid., IV, 474.
24 Ibid., I, 231–34; IV 335–73.
25 Ronald Grimsley, *Jean d'Alembert* (Oxford: Oxford Univ. Press, 1963), p. 127.
26 D'Alembert, O.C. IV, 481–89.

Necessity or Freedom? The Politics of an Eighteenth-Century Metaphysical Debate

ARAM VARTANIAN

The precise relationship between necessity as a metaphysical or moral concept and freedom as a civil and political principle is a subject open to speculation. While the one need not, in strict logic, preclude the other, there is at least plausibility in the common belief that a morally free agent is, by the nature of things, fit to be also (within prescribed limits) a politically free agent; and that, conversely, a human being incapable of free choice would have no true claim to the exercise of political liberty—indeed, that the notion of such liberty has something gratuitous and absurd about it when applied to a behavioral automaton. Thus, even if the ideas of metaphysical necessity and political freedom are not formally in contradiction, their incongruity is apparent to ordinary reasoning and is reinforced by semantic and psychological habit. If, to illustrate this point, we take the early case of Hobbes, we are impressed by the cogency of his general outlook. Anticipating several *philosophes* of the eighteenth century, Hobbes was, of course, a mechanical materialist who denied that thinking and action could in any proper sense be described as free. He argued, instead, that these resulted from corporeal movements that put the individual, whether he knew it or not, under ceaseless constraint. The Hobbesian politics turned out to be of a piece with his vision of a human nature ruled by necessity; for in that sphere, too, freedom became an idle word, and the outcome of all political initiatives was seen as determined by superior force among competing "bodies" in collective "motion." Compatibly with this, Hobbes left little or no place to any consideration that the subjects of his Leviathan might possess natural freedoms or inalienable rights. In taking a historical leap to modern times, a similar pattern of ideas may easily be observed. We find that apologists of dictatorial government prefer to picture men, not as metaphysically (and therefore immutably) free agents responsible for their choices, but rather as passive participants in politics, swayed and driven by a complex of external and impersonal causes—historical, national, economic, environmental, physiological, etc.—that dispose of their wills despite themselves. By contrast, in those societies where political liberty is a long-established fact, the dominant ideology, whatever its local version might be, takes for granted that human beings, despite all the pressures of circumstance acting on them, retain a margin of personal choice in their decisions. And one finds, in use among such peoples, an everyday rhetoric that intimately joins the notion of moral freedom to that of political and civil liberty.

I have insisted on what may seem an obvious thought-structure in order to set in sharper relief the *inversion* of this normal paradigm during the Enlightenment, particularly in France, where several *philosophes*—La Mettrie, Diderot, D'Holbach—who advocated, each in his way, freedom as an intellectual, religious, civil, or political goal, also categorically spurned it as a metaphysical and moral concept. The beginnings of this anomaly were in Spinoza. The great systematizer of determinism (or *fatalisme,* as it was called in eighteenth-century France) had, without any visible twinge of self-contradiction, warmly approved the Republican and liberalizing tendencies of Dutch politics in his day. A like paradox runs through the story of his life. One wonders why, if Spinoza was inclined to respect necessity in all things, he had not resigned himself to the fate of being a Jew. His excommunication was, in effect, a drastic act of liberation. In that case, did his later espousal of determinism, *inter alia,* spring from a desire to vindicate after the fact the course he had all too freely chosen? For, as everyone knows, the appeal to necessity is two-edged: when translated into practice, it can justify either submission to whatever situation is already given; or, retrospectively, rebellion against it and self-affirmation. If Spinoza was, so to speak, *forced* to be free, such a formula, which is not irrelevant to his influence on the Enlightenment, may be a key to understanding how he managed to lead as untrammeled an existence as possible while claiming that freedom was a vulgar illusion.

Another precursor of the fatalistic group of *philosophes,* the free-thinking priest Jean Meslier, offers a similar example. Though, unlike Spinoza, he did not overtly disavow his religion, Meslier's revolt against Catholicism was both fervent and total; but this became known only posthumously when his *Testament* was read. In its pages, his apostasy went together with a call for the radical economic and political emancipation of the "oppressed classes"—which, at the time, meant chiefly the peasantry. Yet, with Meslier too, the intransigeant will to be, for himself as for others, free from the multiple despotisms or repressions of Church and State found expression alongside a doctrine of philosophical necessity.

This anomalous paradigm grew and persisted, in varying degrees, during the Enlightenment. Montesquieu, for example, assumed that human behavior, at least in the realm of politics and law, was determined by the physical character of a nation's territory and by the psycho-physical influence of its climate on the inhabitants. Yet, despite the immobilizing effects of such a theory, the *Esprit des lois* also made, rather inconsistently, a strong case for introducing into France, on the model of an idealized British constitution, a whole program of political and civil liberties. Montesquieu's logic could, if impugned, be defended on the ground that his moral and political determinism was never intended as an all-embracing theory of human nature, and therefore left some room for political choice. Voltaire, on the other hand, whose many hopes and projects of reform were no less libertarian in spirit, straddled (as was his manner) the philosophical fence, not wishing to take a definite stand on the "necessity versus liberty" question. It was in the writings of the materialist *philosophes* that the concomitance of moral determinism and political liberalism showed up in a most striking form. La Mettrie's *l'Homme machine* was the earliest text to publicize a system of psycho-physiology which banished outright the notion of free will. Yet, though not a political author, La Mettrie preached freedom in its intellectual, religious, and ethical uses with a zeal that led to his being denounced as the arch-apologist of license at the time.[1] Diderot and D'Holbach also held that mental events in general, character-type, and all behavior were invariably determined by a combination of environmental and physiological causes—from which they concluded that freedom was a popular delusion entirely at odds with science. But this view of the human condition, drably fatalistic as it may seem, did not prevent Diderot and D'Holbach from being among the greatest liberal spokesmen for political, social, philosophical—even economic—change in eighteenth-century France. While maintaining that private and social man had of necessity become what he in fact was, they proclaimed that his bonds could be broken, and that he was at liberty to transform himself and his existence for the better. Students of the Enlightenment have long recognized, in this divergence between the theory of determinism and the practice of perfectibility, an unexplained contradiction among the materialist *philosophes*.[2]

For the sake of convenience, I will henceforth employ the term "man-machine" to designate the conception of human nature that La Mettrie, Diderot, and D'Holbach, notwithstanding differences of detail among them, professed in common. Despite—or rather because of—the puzzling relationship that occurred between the idea of necessity and that of freedom in the works of each, the purpose of this essay will be to ask what was the underlying socio-political meaning of the man-machine thesis in the milieu of the French Enlightenment. A thoroughly mechanistic approach was, at the time, a radical innovation in the still fledgling science of psychology. As such it clashed head-on with officially protected approaches that had always assumed man to be a composite of two substances, and had made free will the attribute of a soul described as essentially independent of the body.

The debate sustained during most of the century by these irreconcilable views of human nature had, for the parties involved, an obvious political dimension, although on the face of it a somewhat enigmatic one. What did it signify to envision, through a reform of the *Ancien Régime,* the liberation of a machine? Are we, perhaps, confronted here with merely an accidental configuration of disparate thought-elements? If (as it is likely) we are not, why should human beings have been represented, on the authority of science, as blind pawns of necessity, when the long-run aim was to render them consciously free agents? Or, as one suspects, did the man-machine, in some circuitous way, defy and dispute the absolutism of the existing order?

To these questions there is a deceptively simple answer, namely, that moral determinism, in controverting and effacing the spiritualist image of man, weakened the hold and prestige of religion and thereby sapped the ideological foundation of the *Ancien Régime.* In that case, the *philosophes* may be said to have used the argument as an anti-Christian ploy, without being much concerned about its other, boomeranging implications. This, however, would give narrowly irreligious motives to those who put forward the man-machine theory as a serious *critique* of dualism, which meanwhile had become a rationally and empirically dubious position, inviting attempts to analyze the mind and behavior anew by references to anatomical structure and physiological process. Having arrived along this route at the man-machine idea, the *philosophes*—particularly the extremists among them—did not hesitate, of course, to exploit its all too rich potential for disbelief and atheism. But it is evident from the works of La Mettrie, Diderot, and D'Holbach that they also, in all earnestness, held it to be scientifically valid. Thus it will not quite do to allege that their depiction of man as neither spiritual nor free was a propagandist manoeuver. It was that, too; but primarily it was a reasoned philosophical opinion. The traditionalists who took issue with it in a bitter and excited polemic also resorted to propaganda by announcing that determinism was not only an erroneous doctrine, but the product of depraved thinking and subversive designs. It was a commonplace with them to warn their readers that the false teachings of the "fatalists" would lead to the overthrow of political order and the dissolution of civil society. This readiness to politicize the free will question has usually been considered a tactic for oppressing or intimidating the *philosophes,* whose mechanistic psychology was in any case censurable on purely religious grounds. To find catastrophic dangers in the theory of determinism was, no doubt, an alarmist exaggeration. La Mettrie scoffed at such accusations: "Combien de disputes, d'erreurs, de haines et de contradictions a enfanté la fameuse question de la liberté, ou du fatalisme. Ce ne sont que des hypothèses cependant. L'esprit borné, ou illuminé, croyant à la doctrine de mauvais cahiers qu'il nous débite d'un air suffisant, s'imagine bonnement que tout est perdu, morale, religion, société, s'il est prouvé que l'homme n'est pas libre."[3] But one must also, to some extent, take the defenders of Church and State at their word and recognize that there was a measure of sincerity in their denunciations, and even, as they saw it, an element of truth. They were convinced, though for reasons they did not always make explicit or credible, that a merely theoretical denial of free will was inherently in conflict with any and all establishments of government and society. We believe that an explanation of the apparent paradox in the thought of the materialists will shed light also on the motives of the traditionalists who predicted that determinist philosophy would have the direst political consequences for France.

The historical setting in which the *philosophes* affirmed the man-machine thesis gave it a different significance from what we are likely to see in it today. For us, the man-machine idea is depressingly reductive because the mechanical is equated with what is lifeless, passive, regulated. To describe a human being as a machine evokes a robot-like figure—someone who, bereft of will and spontaneity, performs a monotonous and mindless task. It is natural enough that our own apprehension of the man-machine should be conditioned by the mechanized functions imposed on us in a highly industrialized economy, and by the various social and political extensions of the industrial model. Apart from its metaphysical or scientific bearing on the free will versus necessity problem, the man-machine is nowadays the practical and metaphoric antithesis of what a human being ought above all to resemble. But in the quite dissimilar socio-economic circumstances of eighteenth-century France, and in a culture dominated, often repressively, by a religious—that is, spiritualist—ideology, it could not, and did not, have the same connotations and associations. Yet, from the nineteenth century to the present, the *philosophes'* fondness for a mechanistic theory of man has been interpreted anachronistically in terms of what such an option came to mean to later generations. So modified, it has met frequently with strong distaste as the very negation of all truly human attributes and values.

The relative success in the Enlightenment of moral and metaphysical determinism leads one to suppose that, at the time, it signified something which has since become unfamiliar. That the *philosophes* who were the most attached to it were also the most liberal in their thinking about social and political issues has already been noted; but, more than that, their own temperaments were marked by qualities such as spontaneity, originality, rebelliousness, sensibility, even passion, rather than (as one might have expected) by the "mechanical" opposites of these traits. Surely, La Mettrie and Diderot, from everything that is known about them, exemplify the bill of particulars closely enough; but D'Holbach too, despite a sober and dry exterior, was an intellectual cauldron of unsubmissive energy. When such persons, whose impatience with conventional ways of belief and conduct makes them seem anything but manipulated and spiritless, proclaim that all human beings are ruled by the strictest necessity, there is reason to wonder what might be hidden behind the outward sense of their words. Moreover, it should be remarked that our three "fatalists" gave hardly any indication of a conflict in their minds between deterministic doctrine and libertarian aspirations. Many critics have taken this as a sign of illogicality, or dilettantism, on the part of would-be philosophers. The charge, though, is too facile. It is most improbable that three *philosophes,* however unsystematic their style of philosophizing, would in succession have failed to perceive a glaring and recurrent contradiction in their thinking—which, moreover, others were only too glad to point out to them. Had they perceived it as a contradiction, they would presumably have sought some conciliation, or compromise, between their notions of necessity and of freedom—certainly not an impossible task. But, except for Diderot, who would appear to have had some such purpose in writing his novel *Jacques le fataliste,* there was little acknowledgment by the materialists of the seeming paradox in their collective position. By way of accounting for their unconcern, one might venture the guess that they were far from convinced that the man-machine psychology negated their other opinions on behalf of liberty; and even that, on a deeper, in part unexamined level of awareness, they remained confident that it not only did not contradict but actually supported their program for the emancipation of mankind from age-old authoritarian bonds. Moral determinism may have been resented by many of their contemporaries as (among other things) an affront to human dignity. But it was also generally felt to be provocative, challenging, overlaid with irony, rich in scientific promise, and not unsuited to a display of wit. La Mettrie, in particular, was able to color the exposition of the *homme machine* with much of his own exuberant audacity, erotic innuendo, and speculative enthusiasm. The same affective traits, in a more dramatic and lyrical key, also characterize the *Rêve de D'Alembert,* the major work in which Diderot elaborated his own version of the man-machine. Offered in such literary contexts, it was meant to surprise, shock, stimulate, instruct, amuse, even bemuse, but certainly not to depress, stupefy, or dehumanize its readers. We must consider it an aspect of its meaning that the doctrine of necessity found expression through an idiom vibrant with imaginative and emotive unrestraint. But because La Mettrie and Diderot neglected to say on what their curiously sanguine trust in the man-machine was based, it would be difficult to quote them verbatim on that score. We are obliged, instead, to rely on less direct textual evidence, as well as on combined analysis and conjecture, in order to explain how the man-machine doctrine took its stand, implicitly, in the vanguard of the struggle for social and political liberty.

The anomalous relationship between the ideas of freedom and necessity in the French Enlightenment should, from the outset, be seen as the transposition of a pre-existing anomaly to which the *philosophes* could not but have reacted. This was the outlook of almost all traditionalists and conservatives at the time, who asserted, on the one hand, that metaphysically man possessed free will, but, on the other, upheld a regime that curtailed the exercise of freedom in the choice of his philosophical opinions, religious creed, ethical standards, or the government and laws under which he lived. Historians have not dwelt on this paradox in the thinking of those who opposed the Enlightenment, perhaps because it was something too banal and habitual to draw attention to itself. Although Christianity (except, perhaps, for Jansenism and Calvinism) had made a point of affirming man's freedom, its affirmation was in effect a disguised negation. The main role of such freedom was to render a culpable humanity responsible for its faults, thereby dissociating God from the presence of evil in the world. But in order not to sin, man had to obey God's will as voiced and enforced (in France) by the Catholic Church. Now, one can feel "free" to obey, provided there is no punishment—or at least no intolerable punishment—for disobedience. However, regarding the situation of the believer, for whom submission to divine commandments was an absolute imperative under pain of eternal damnation, it is hardly possible to talk meaningfully of being free to accept or refuse the authority of God and his representatives on Earth. One is "free" in the same way under the harshest tyranny, but one does not experience the yielding to threats as the exercise of freedom, even if one always remains "metaphysically" free to choose between compliance and retribution. It was in the midst of these consecrated ambiguities that the man-machine made its brash and disruptive appearance. Its authors, negatively conditioned by a longstanding equivocal and debased use of the notion of moral freedom, did not attach much practical value to theological pledges that man was a free being—a postulate which, historically, they had more reason to be suspicious of than to take hope from. As it turned out, they put greater trust in the counter-postulate that he was *not* free in order, by that reversal, to free him, not as a metaphysical entity but as a social and political agent. In this respect, the fatalist of the eighteenth century was a pious Christian turned inside out. For just as the latter could believe that he was free to do God's will under duress of an infinite penalty, the liberal-minded materialist could, with a cognate logic, imagine that mankind was destined by a universal necessity to enjoy freedom.

To see more clearly the dialectical matrix from which the *homme machine* sprang, it should be recognized that what was "mechanical" in eighteenth-century French culture was *spiritualism,* not literally of course, but in the more important sense that it served to keep the rank and file of the nation in the role of passive creatures of outworn and repressive habit—mere puppets of the *Régime* with little incentive to reshape the meaning, either public or private, of their lives. The "soul" had been spiritualized for so long and to such a degree that, in the end, it seemed quite depersonalized. Tending toward God as toward its source, it was perceived as irreversibly subject to the external power of the Church, which had it in her keeping; it resembled, so to speak, a collectively binding, undifferentiated Super-ego. As a result, the materialists had cause to view the free-willing soul of tradition not as an autonomous self, but as a captive and alienated portion of the self—as that part of the human being that was, in fact, least free and most controlled. For them it was no tragedy to lose such a soul, if in return a greater stake in the world might be gained; for what they were ready to sacrifice to the man-machine idea was only the heavily mortgaged soul claimed by religion and exploited by absolutism. One may wonder if the attribution of free will to the soul rather than to the *self* had not always been an adroit attempt to displace or ignore the real problem of liberty. The natural human desire for freedom had thereby been neutralized and "depoliticized" from the beginning—surely an advantage for those in religious and political authority, who could be expected to prize obedience over liberty in their followers or subjects.

But there was another, genuine "soul" by which the metaphysical-theological one might be replaced—a soul that would truly reflect the will and be the active principle of a concrete individual being. This soul, for which the *philosophes* had as yet no precise term, and of which they conceived somewhat gropingly, is what we would now call the psyche or personality—that is, the soul as the object of a science of psychology then still in the process of formation. In the eighteenth century, it was semantically—and therefore conceptually—difficult to make what for us seems an obvious distinction between a physiologically conditioned mind shaped by experience, and the abstract, disembodied, transcendant soul peculiar to theology or metaphysics. The word *âme* in French expressed both possibilities indiscriminately and confusingly. Prevented thus from thinking in terms either of a free-willing soul apart from its Christian spiritualist connotations, or of an individual psyche not determined in its operations by organic factors, La Mettrie, Diderot, and D'Holbach, theorizing perforce within the limits urged on them by the general background of dualism, had no alternative but to reject the "free" soul and to redefine the mind on the analogy of a living machine.[4] This, of course, entailed moral determinism. However, the framers of the man-machine theory denied freedom in merely one sense, while implying it more effectively in another. The mind, rendered functionally co-extensive with the organism, became the essence of an individualized self; and the man-machine served thereby as the ground of a personal autonomous will without which, in practice, political freedom could only prove futile. Whereas the doctrine of free will had traditionally been subordinated to conformism and passivity, determinism prefigured, in reversing the formula, self-determination. Divested of his immortal soul, man acquired in compensation a mortal personality that was, by contrast, truly and wholly his own. The man-machine thesis, all appearances to the contrary, could thus be offered confidently as a tacit step toward a new humanism redolent of libertarian overtones.

To appreciate better how this happened, it should be remembered that the concept of mechanism, as applied to human nature by certain *philosophes,* had a purpose and status that are not readily understood today. Just as we tend to think, biologically, in terms of vitalism versus mechanism, so in psychology we habitually oppose motivation and feeling to the merely mechanical or automatic, which by definition is assumed to preclude those capabilities. Whether or not such a dichotomy is ultimately valid, the point to be made is that it did not exist for La Mettrie, Diderot, and D'Holbach. The notion of the mechanical did not, in their view, diminish in any fundamental way the human attributes of consciousness, sensation, sentiment, thought, and will. When they spoke of the man-machine, their imaginations did not conjure up a degraded or "sub-human" species, but continued to behold flesh-and-blood beings with all the usual human characteristics. In the *homme machine* theory, mechanism was humanized in the same degree that man was mechanized. Thus we find that La Mettrie's living and conscious machine is not an automaton in the ordinary sense; but, possessed of an independent source of energy, it functions as a dynamic and self-regulating system. Its activities flow from its own vitality and initiative; it does not acquire them, as non-human machines do, from external agencies.[5]

Likewise, Diderot ascribed sensibility, intelligence, and volition, without decrease or prejudice, to the organization of matter. The mechanical necessity which, in the *Rêve de D'Alembert,* encompasses thinking and behavior is not "humanly" inferior to what conventionally was explained by reference to dualism. Moreover, it serves as a new and concrete basis for the unity of the self and the coherence of the individual will: "La volonté naît toujours de quelque motif intérieur ou extérieur, de quelque projet dans l'avenir. Après cela, je ne vous dirai de la liberté qu'un mot, c'est que la dernière de nos actions est l'effet nécessaire d'une cause une: nous, très compliquée, mais une."[6] The necessity that directs our every act, far from dissolving the self into anonymity, guarantees it a definite and unique identity: "Tâchez de concevoir la production d'une autre action, en supposant que l'être agissant soit le même. . . . Puisque c'est moi qui agis ainsi, celui qui peut agir autrement n'est plus moi; et assurer qu'au moment où je fais ou dis une chose, j'en puis dire ou faire une autre, c'est assurer que je suis moi et que je suis un autre."[7] Instead of speculating about a will that is free only in an impersonal void, the determinist doctrine starts by recognizing the reality of a positive individual will.[8]

Thus determinism becomes, for Diderot, auto-determinism, the basis of that autonomy of self thanks to which one is "free" to persist in one's own nature. If he did not employ the word "freedom" to describe this phenomenon, we are tempted to do so for him. In the *Réfutation d'Helvétius,* Diderot brought to light, however, the deeper, partly hidden meaning of his psycho-physical theory of man. Confronted by another kind of determinism, which made environmental necessity all-important in the science of behavior, he argued against Helvétius that everyone, precisely because he is a "machine," carries within himself the springs and motives that anticipate his unique reactions or adaptations to the environment. He rejected the postulate that in character, talents, and needs all human beings, sharing the same *sensibilité physique,* are initially alike, and can thereafter be conditioned in uniform ways by education and by a system of purely material rewards or punishments, as Helvétius had claimed. Diderot stressed, instead, an internalized necessity active in each person. Often resistant to ordinary criteria of self-interest or happiness, this self-directing necessity was the basis of what now would be called personal independence—of the will to be oneself in the teeth of risks, constraints, and seductions. The theme of individuality, which is the leitmotiv of the *Réfutation d'Helvétius,* finds illustration at one point in the life of Leibniz, who is shown to have behaved, not unlike one of his own monads, as a self-defining unit of force: "quand Leibnitz s'enferme à l'âge de vingt ans, et passe trente ans sous sa robe de chambre, enfoncé dans les profondeurs de la géométrie ou perdu dans les ténèbres de la métaphysique, il ne pense non plus à obtenir un poste, à coucher avec une femme, à remplir d'or un vieux bahut, que s'il touchait à son dernier moment. C'est une machine à réflexion, comme le métier à bas est une machine à ourdissage; c'est un être qui se plaît à méditer; c'est un sage ou un fou, comme il vous plaira, qui fait un cas infini de la louange de ses semblables, qui aime le son de l'éloge comme l'avare le son d'un écu; qui a aussi sa pierre de touche et son trébuchet pour la louange, comme l'autre a le sien pour l'or, et qui tente une grande découverte pour se faire un grand nom et éclipser par son éclat celui de ses rivaux, l'unique et le dernier terme de son désir."[9] In short, the crucial error of Helvétius (whatever one might think of Diderot's own account of the motives that determined Leibniz) was the failure to give due weight to the autonomy of the self rooted in the human machine—to the key role of that specific "machine à réflexion" which, in the case of the famous mathematician-philosopher, made necessity and self-realisation one and the same thing.[10] In the polemic against Helvétius and his schemes for psychosocial "programming," the relevance of the *homme machine* idea consisted, above all, in its potential for a liberal philosophy of man. The finality of the self-determining man-machine gave assurance of individual liberty in contrast to the "totalitarian" politics of human engineering and mass control towards which the teaching of Helvétius tended.

Seen from another angle, determinism was the natural basis of human diversification. Compared to both the featureless soul of metaphysical tradition and the *tabula rasa* of empiricist psychology, the "material soul" served *ab initio* as a principle of differentiation. Diderot declared: "Chaque homme est entraîné par son organisation, son caractère, son tempérament, son aptitude naturelle à combiner de préférence telles et telles idées plutôt que telles et telles autres."[11] Since no two human machines are, or could possibly be made, identical in structure and functioning, variations of personality are irreducible facts of nature. But this consequence of the *homme machine* theory has little in common with what mechanism came later to mean, namely, with its use as a general metaphor of dehumanized uniformity. The modern political analogue of the machine is regimentation, that is, a negation of individuality which is at the same time a denial of freedom; for, whatever freedom might mean to the metaphysician, politically it cannot be divorced from the expression of individual differences, which is its primary condition. In the Enlightenment, moral determinism implied the legitimization of everyone's idiosyncrasy, and to that extent it was a stumbling block to any political system founded on the belief that human beings should be coerced or modified in the interest of some Absolute.

The French materialists, it is true, liked to repeat that no one's will was free; but what they actually meant by this proposition (which explains their liking for it) was that one was not free to deny one's deepest convictions and strongest feelings. And inasmuch as the supreme object of such feelings and convictions was happiness, what determinism amounted to, when translated into ethical and political terms, was that everyone necessarily desired to be happy, and had, as it were, a physiologically inalienable right to pursue that goal, rather than the duty to make a "free choice" that would be incompatible—and free *because* incompatible—with the laws of his own being, that is, a choice of renunciation and submission. Thus interpreted, necessity wore the contented face of freedom, as we can see, for example, in La

Mettrie's comparison between the hedonistic morality of the man-machine and the official Christian ethics of the *Ancien Régime*: "Ici, il n'y a qu'à se laisser doucement aller aux agréables impulsions de la nature: là, il faut se roidir, se *regimber* contr'elle. Ici, il suffit de se conformer à soi-même, d'être ce qu'on est, et en quelque sorte de se ressembler; là, il faut ressembler aux autres malgré soi, vivre et presque penser comme eux. Quelle comédie!"[12] For, in the last analysis, each had to be happy in his own, not in a prescribed, manner. The man-machine theory laid stress on the infinite permutations of the common ideal of happiness: "Mais de toutes parts, quelle étonnante variété de Bonheur! Elle ressemble à celle des esprits et des visages: comme il n'y a pas deux semblables, il n'y a pas deux hommes également heureux, ni par les mêmes moyens; et d'où cela vient-il? si ce n'est de l'organisation, qui seule rend raison de tout: car par elle, par toutes ses variétés, sans entrer en aucun détail anatomique, qui serait ici superflu et déplacé, on conçoit pourquoi telle Nation sent mieux le plaisir, aime plus la volupté, et est en général plus heureuse, ou plus prête à l'être . . . que telle autre. Cette même variété de structure et de circulation de sang, de lymphe, et d'esprits, est la cause de la différente aptitude au Bonheur, qui se remarque non seulement entre différents peuples . . . mais entre les divers individus d'une même Nation, d'un même Climat, d'une même Province, d'une même ville."[13] In emphasizing this necessary diversity, the man-machine thesis laid down the psycho-physical prerequisite of political liberalism, for what, in fact, could have favored more the liberty of the citizen than the recognition, from the first, that government and laws ought not only to conform to the popular will, but should also accommodate, so far as possible, each person's separate pursuit of happiness? The logical bond between determinism and hedonism in the Enlightenment thus pointed toward the progressive "liberation" of an irrepressibly determined man-machine. Such, at least, must have been the dearest hope of the "fatalists."

The several themes so far discussed concerning the problem of necessity and freedom were recapitulated at length in D'Holbach's *Système de la nature.* But whereas until then the libertarian meaning of the man-machine had remained more or less implicit, in that work it was at last made explicit, and from it certain political conclusions were expressly drawn. In D'Holbach's eyes, too, determinism took on the aspect of self-fulfillment, inasmuch as it impelled man to change and perfect his way of life in order to attain happiness.[14] It was because this "natural necessity" had been obstructed by tyrannical rulers and suppressed in the public consciousness that "l'homme en société est tombé de la liberté dans l'esclavage."[15] Relearning and respecting the necessary laws of nature would, therefore, restore his lost liberty. But the necessity in question was also that of the endless diversification of human nature.[16] From this it followed, politically, that new laws should be framed and institutions remade in such a manner as to reflect the differences among individuals, so that finally "la morale et la politique pourraient retirer du *matérialisme* des avantages que le dogme de la spiritualité ne leur fournira jamais, et auxquels il les empêche même de songer."[17] Because, then, "le bonheur ne peut être le même pour tous les êtres de l'espèce humaine," and opinions inevitably vary from one person to another, the only practical and legitimate form of government will be *representative.*[18] Its aim should be, besides that of protecting life and property, to allow for the enjoyment of civil and private liberty, which D'Holbach defined in fairly generous terms: "La *liberté* est la faculté de faire pour son propre bonheur tout ce qui ne nuit pas au bonheur de ses associés."[19] Consequently, individual "passions," rather than needing to be curbed, deserve to have free expression while being directed, whenever possible, toward socially desirable and useful ends.[20] In all of this, we perceive clearly how the *homme machine* doctrine served as a rationale for radical criticism of the *Ancien Régime* and for a plan to replace absolutism by a political system conceived along familiarly liberal lines.

In sensing or supposing that there was an equation of some sort between necessity and freedom, the French materialists were not, of course, altogether original. Particularly important, in this regard, was the influence exerted on them by Spinoza, to whom they were in any case heavily indebted for the substance of their "fatalism." It could easily be shown, moreover, that their notion of self-determination—or the tendency of the human mechanism to persevere in its essence—had a similar origin. However, Spinoza's ideal of freedom as a purely intellectual attitude of acceptance based on a dispassionate grasp of the necessity of things remained typical of the contemplative mood of seventeenth-century metaphysics. Universal determinism, as reinterpreted by the *philosophes,* assumed a practical and secular thrust, in accordance with the pre-revolutionary tensions of their milieu. Understanding the necessity of things became, whether tacitly or openly, both the reason and the means for modifying them. In the noisy encounter between the man-machine and the subsisting order, the active will of the one was pitted, optimistically and even enthusiastically, against the weakening inertia of the other.

The maxim "To follow one's own will is liberty" had, in addition, an obvious background in Locke's *Essay.* In Book III, Chapter 21, the traditional notion of free will was abandoned in favor of the commonsense idea (given in experience) that to be "free" is simply to have the "power" to perform a particular action; and not to be free is to be impeded in its performance. Freedom, as a concept, thus refers properly not to the will, but to the act that is willed. The fact that the will is regularly determined by the mind's "uneasiness" to take some corrective action or other "is no restraint to liberty," stated Locke; on the contrary, "it is the end and use of our liberty." For to be free is to be able to pursue what we necessarily believe, on deliberation, would give us pleasure or make us happy. In view of such a willful and active definition of freedom, it is perhaps not surprising that, within the range of political choices available at the time, Locke was a "liberal" who opposed the increase of royal prerogatives attempted by the Stuarts.

Voltaire, among the *philosophes,* hewed closest to Locke's position, although with some wavering. To him, the main thing was that the man, not the will, should be free; and so the metaphysical dimension of the problem was sacrificed to its realistic meaning: "La liberté est uniquement le pouvoir d'agir."[21] Against the fatalists, he also invoked the hedonistic standard: "Ils ont beau dire, l'homme est déterminé par le plaisir; c'est confesser, sans qu'ils y pensent, la liberté; puisque faire ce qui fait plaisir, c'est être libre."[22] At times, he appeared to combine the Lockean view with that of his determinist colleagues: "En quoi consiste donc votre liberté, si ce n'est dans le pouvoir que votre individu a exercé de faire ce que votre volonté exigeait d'une nécessité absolue?"[23] But, in general, Voltaire remained wary of conceding too much to the man-machine theory, against which he even adopted on occasion a quite orthodox definition of free will.[24] While there was, then, some kinship between the Lockean-Voltairean treatment of the necessity-freedom question and that given by La Mettrie, Diderot, and D'Holbach, the difference was also significant. Although, in accord with the materialists, Voltaire objected that there could be no "liberty of indifference," and asserted that our every act, even the most seemingly arbitrary and unimportant, had a determining "cause" behind it, usually what he meant was a "motive" or "reason" rather than a physical or mechanical cause. Unlike the materialists, he was not much interested in the psycho-physiological basis of thought and behavior, and it was precisely this type of scientific interest that led to a deterministically inspired liberalism.

What has here been dealt with as the implicit and explicit politics of the doctrine of necessity was typical, by and large, of the French Enlightenment. Elsewhere, a similar nexus of ideas did not, as a rule, accompany "enlightened" thinking. This was because, in England as well as in Holland, religious belief and the related notion of a soul endowed with free will were not hindrances to a liberal or dissenting outlook; while in Germany there was neither enough political ferment, nor sufficient sympathy with materialistic and deterministic doctrines, to pose an ideological challenge to the conservatism that reigned in both politics and philosophy.[25] As a result of the French Revolution, the triumph, at least in part, of the reforms and freedoms sought by the *philosophes* divested the man-machine idea of its earlier revolutionary import. In the age of Romanticism, the soul was "rediscovered" and its emancipating powers universally acclaimed in philosophy and literature. But it was no longer the "alienated soul" of eighteenth-century metaphysical and theological convention that was thus reborn. Its new status might have been somewhat vague, elusive, and poetical, but despite (or perhaps because of) this ineffability, it was perceived again as a personal soul, that is, as the vital, active, sensitive, indestructible, and *free* essence of the human individual. So transformed and valorised, the notion of soul could ally itself easily with the natural aspiration to earthly happiness and the enjoyment of liberty in social and political life. After the joint rehabilitation of spirituality and free will in the nineteenth century, the man-machine (although its usefulness as a psycho-physical hypothesis remained intact) became at last a reductivist and dehumanizing concept—a change aided, no doubt, by economic and technological developments that turned human beings into machines with a literalness that had still been far from the imagination of the *philosophes.* One may conclude, nonetheless, that in the many-faceted quest for freedom which pervaded the Enlightenment even the man-machine made an important, albeit at times roundabout, contribution.

NOTES

1 He had said in self-exhortation: "Soyons donc libres dans nos écrits, comme dans nos actions; montrons-y la fière indépendance d'un républicain"; "Discours préliminaire," in *Oeuvres philosophiques* (Amsterdam, 1774), I, 59.

2 Ernst Cassirer, for instance, has said about the inconsistency between the determinism and the politics of the materialist school: "The doctrine of the absolute necessity of the events of nature gets caught in the net of its own reasoning. For on the basis of this doctrine what right have we to speak of norms at all, what right to demand and evaluate? Does not this doctrine see in every 'ought' a mere delusion which it transforms into a 'must'? And is there any alternative but to yield to this 'must'? Can we guide it and prescribe its course? Even eighteenth-century criticism of [D'Holbach's] System of Nature bared this fundamental weakness of its argument. Frederick the Great's reply to the book calls attention emphatically to this point. 'After the author has exhausted all evidence,' this reply objects, 'to show that men are guided by a fatalistic necessity in all their actions, he had to draw the conclusion that we are only a sort of machine, only marionettes moved by the hand of a blind power. And yet he flies into a passion against priests, governments, and against our whole educational system; he believes indeed that the men who exercise these functions are free, even while he proves to them that they are slaves. What foolishness and what nonsense!'" *The Philosophy of the Enlightenment* (Princeton: Princeton Univ. Press, 1951), p. 71. Like many critics before and after him, Cassirer takes this antinomy at face value, hardly attempting to explain or resolve it.

3 *Oeuv. phil.*, I, 20. In the *Encyclopédie* article "Liberté," which prudently took an unobjectionable tack, the alert reader could discover a veiled parody of the sort of

fanatical complaint to which determinism was vulnerable at the time: "Otez la liberté, toute la nature humaine est renversée, et il n'y a plus aucune trace d'ordre dans la société. Si les hommes ne sont pas libres dans ce qu'ils font de bien et de mal, le bien n'est plus bien, et le mal n'est plus mal. . . . La ruine de la liberté renverse avec elle tout ordre et toute police, confond le vice et la vertu, autorise toute infamie monstrueuse, éteint toute pudeur et tout remords, dégrade et défigure sans ressource tout le genre humain. Une doctrine si énorme ne doit point être examinée dans l'école, mais punie par les magistrats"; *Oeuvres* (Paris: Assézat-Tourneux, 1875–77), XV, 501. Of course, determinism as a theory of behavior could not possibly have had such baleful effects, because by itself it could not alter the given facts. If determinism was false, free will existed and would continue to exist; if it was true, it merely described the existing state of affairs; in either case, the socio-political order would not disintegrate from the loss of free will, as the critics of determinism feared. The impact of the man-machine idea on society and politics in the Enlightenment was no doubt real and subversive, but indirectly so: without changing the moral nature of human beings (i.e. from "free and responsible" to "unfree and irresponsible"), it did heighten, as we shall see, their consciousness of what was legitimately in their self-interest and effectively within their power under the *Ancien Régime*.

4 The semantics of philosophical discourse in eighteenth-century France offered no equivalents for *psyche, personality,* or *mind* as now used interchangeably or overlappingly in a psychological sense. *Esprit* was of limited applicability, and the use of it by Helvétius in the title of his *De l'Esprit* led to some uncertainty as to just what his book was about. The substantive *le moi* had not yet been adopted by philosophy. The word closest in meaning was *âme,* but it had a metaphysical aura, in particular that given to it by Descartes and his followers. This Cartesian "soul," held capable of willing freely, was defined by its own awareness that it existed as a "pure thinking substance." But by that very fact it remained a rational, undifferentiated entity. Descartes' dualism, moreover, left no middle ground between *âme* and *corps.* Therefore the notion of *âme* came progressively to signify in the Enlightenment an unqualified, self-identical substance whose concrete determinations and characterizations—in brief, the active psyche or individual mind—were discoverable in the mechanical and other modifications of the organism. As *âme,* in psychology, became an equivocal or superfluous term, the mind or psyche was represented more and more by means of bio-mechanistic language, imagery, and analogies. The will was thus materialized and its "freedom" assimilated to the necessity of bodily processes.

5 Typically, La Mettrie saw in physical dexterity and versatility proof that these qualities were owing to bodily mechanisms rather than to an immaterial soul (as claimed by the spiritualist medical philosopher Stahl): "Pour détruire l'hypothèse Staahlienne . . . il n'y a qu'à jeter les yeux sur un joueur de violon. Quelle souplesse! Quelle agilité dans les doigts! Les mouvements sont si prompts, qu'il ne paroît presque pas y avoir de succession. Or je prie, ou plutôt je défie les Staahliens de me dire, eux qui connoissent si bien tout ce que peut notre Ame, comment il seroit possible qu'elle exécutât si vite tant de mouvemens, des

mouvemens qui se passent si loin d'elle, & en tant d'endroits divers"; *La Mettrie's "L'Homme machine"*, ed. A. Vartanian (Princeton: Princeton Univ. Press, 1960), p. 187.

6 *Op. cit.*, in *Oeuvres philosophiques de Diderot,* ed. Vernière, (Paris: Garnier, 1956), p. 363.

7 Ibid., pp. 363–64.

8 In Diderot's view, the age-old controversy about free will had been kept alive by an imaginary notion of man: "Deux Philosophes disputent sans s'entendre, par exemple, sur la liberté de l'homme. L'un dit, l'homme est libre, je le sens. L'autre dit, l'homme n'est pas libre, je le sens. Le premier parle de l'homme abstrait, de l'homme qui n'est mû par aucun motif, de l'homme qui n'existe que dans le sommeil, ou dans l'entendement du disputeur. L'autre parle de l'homme réel, agissant, occupé et mû"; *Eléments de physiologie,* ed. J. Mayer (Paris: Didier, 1964), p. 264.

9 *Oeuvres,* II, 310–11.

10 A revealing association of ideas comes here to Diderot's mind. He compares himself and the leading Encyclopedists to Leibniz; for, being presumably also "machines à réflexion", each of them has fatefully followed, despite great risks, the commands of his intellectual conscience in joining battle with the *Ancien Regime* (Ibid., 314). In this allusion, we glimpse an intimate link between the man-machine philosophy and the "existential" sense of Diderot's career as a social and political reformer.

11 Ibid., 312.

12 *Oeuv. phil.*, I, 6.

13 *Discours sur le bonheur,* ed. J. Falvey, *Studies on Voltaire and the Eighteenth Century,* 134 (1975), 205. This train of thought leads La Mettrie to remark curiously on the resemblance between the book's outspokenness and his own "mechanically free" disposition: ". . . et j'ai si bien . . . imprimé mon caractère sur ce papier, que qui m'aura bien connu, reconnaîtra sans peine *les ressorts libres de ma Machine,* dans ceux de mon ouvrage" (italics added).

14 *Système de la nature, ou des lois du monde physique et du monde moral* (Paris, 1820), I, 67: "Tout ce que l'esprit humain a successivement inventé pour changer ou perfectionner sa façon d'être et pour la rendre plus heureuse, ne fut jamais qu'une conséquence nécessaire de l'essence propre de l'homme, et de celle des êtres qui agissent sur lui. Toutes nos institutions, nos réflexions, nos connaissances n'ont pour objet que de nous procurer un bonheur vers lequel notre propre nature nous force de tendre sans cesse."

15 Ibid., I, 71.

16 Ibid., I, 188: "Il n'est point, et il ne peut y avoir dans la nature deux êtres et deux combinaisons qui soient mathématiquement et rigoureusement les mêmes, vu que le lieu, les circonstances, les rapports, les proportions, les modifications n'étant jamais exactement semblables, les êtres qui en résultent ne peuvent point avoir entre eux une ressemblance parfaite. . . . En conséquence de ce principe, que tout conspire à nous prouver, il n'est pas deux individus de l'espèce humaine qui aient les mêmes traits, qui sentent précisément de la même manière, qui pensent d'une

façon conforme, qui voient les choses des mêmes yeux, qui aient les mêmes idées, ni par conséquent le même système de conduite."

17 Ibid., I, 193.

18 Ibid., I, 212.

19 Ibid., I, 213.

20 Ibid., I, 218.

21 *Traité de métaphysique,* in *Mélanges* (Paris: Gallimard, 1961), p. 187.

22 Ibid., p. 191.

23 Article "Liberté," *Dictionnaire philosophique,* ed. J. Benda (Paris: Garnier), II, 91. Compare: "Votre volonté n'est pas libre, mais vos actions le sont" (II, 93).

24 There is an example of this in the *Discours en vers sur l'homme* (IIe Discours, "De la liberté"), *Mélanges,* p. 217:

> "Ah! sans la liberté que seraient donc nos âmes?
> Mobiles agités par d'invisibles flammes,
> Nos voeux, nos actions, nos plaisirs, nos dégoûts,
> De notre être, en un mot, rien ne serait à nous:
> D'un artisan suprême impuissantes machines,
> Automates pensants, mus par des mains divines,
> Nous serions à jamais de mensonge occupés,
> Vils instruments d'un Dieu qui nous aurait trompés.
> Comment, sans liberté, serions-nous ses images?"

25 There were, to be sure, later British exponents of the determinist psychology that had begun with Hobbes and Locke. The freethinker Anthony Collins, whose *Philosophical Inquiry concerning Human Liberty* came out in 1715, was perhaps the most authoritative necessitarian of eighteenth-century England. Of hardly less importance in this respect was David Hartley's *Observations on Man* (1749). But whereas neither Collins nor Hartley exemplified the special paradigm studied in connection with the French Enlightenment, Joseph Priestley may be said to have offered a good instance of it. As the author of *The Doctrine of Philosophical Necessity Illustrated* (1777), and a staunch defender of civil liberties who welcomed the revolution in France, Priestley's thought showed a conjunction of moral determinism with political liberalism not unlike that of the French materialists. In the German States, notwithstanding Frederick II's patronage of several *philosophes* (including La Mettrie), and his flirtation with ideas considered hazardous to morals, religion, and society, the predominant temper of philosophy, owing mainly to the influence of Wolffianism, was quite unreceptive to denials of free will. This may be seen in the outpouring of antipathy for the man-machine thesis from all intellectual quarters in Germany (see, on this point, my *La Mettrie's "L'Homme Machine,"* pp. 99–105).

An Evolutionary Taxonomy of Eighteenth-Century Newtonianisms

ROBERT E. SCHOFIELD

Among the many misnomers for the eighteenth century, the "Age of Newton," perhaps, promises the most and provides the least insight into the thought of the period. For the use of that term implies a definable set of doctrines, or mode of investigation, of general influence on men of the Enlightenment, which can be identified with that of the great physicist. Yet the most cursory investigation of eighteenth-century thought will falsify each particular of that implication. We cannot identify, with any precision, *a* Newton doctrine; whatever Newtonian doctrines we can identify do not remain fixed, and however changing we permit our Newtonian doctrines to be, they are not of *general* influence.[1]

There is little doubt, for example, that a characteristic element in early eighteenth-century thought was a confidence in the power of human reason to solve human problems, a confidence justified, in large measure, by the example of the sciences. Nor is there *any* doubt that prominent advocates of that view came regularly to include Newton's name in their litany of exemplars. This does not, however, indicate with any surety the influence of Newton, for this faith in the generalizable virtues of the scientific method (whatever that might be) did not spring uniquely from Newton's successes, as the Cartesian Fontenelle and the Leibnizean Christian Wolff abundantly testified.[2] Here, as in the cosmological analogy of the world machine, Newton's name was substituted for that of earlier natural philosophers as its value in intellectual currency rose during the century. We are today too fully aware of the authoritative abuse of "Freudian" or "Darwinian" in current pop sociology to assign much significance to "Newtonian" abused in that manner in the eighteenth century. Yet surely its use, even in that manner, suggests that Newton had come to represent some kind of intellectual authority to a substantial portion of the learned world. What kind of authority did the term "Newtonian" represent and with what accuracy can one say it was genuinely Newtonian?

The task of identifying and tracing "influences" in the *full* range of problems and solutions considered by men of the Enlightenment is notoriously a difficult one, and one which I shall generally evade. But even in the sciences, where the authority of the "Incomparable Sir Isaac" ought to be clearest, the superficial validity of the term Newtonian (manifest in ritual obeisances to the grand master) obscures manifold national and temporal divergences and conceals a skein of variant Newtonianisms which must first be untangled before any genuine relevance of the description can emerge.

The obvious beginning to our task of disentanglement is with Newton, and his publication in 1687 of the *Philosophiae Naturalis Principia Mathematica.* Yet this *terminus a quo* does not, as one might hope, help to identify that Ur-Newtonianism from which all other forms of the doctrine might be presumed to have evolved. It has become clearer every recent year how very little is known of this man whose name has been borrowed for an age: in spite of scholarly effort so massive and sustained as to earn the title of the "Newton Industry," there has not yet been published a complete and critical edition of both of Newton's major published works—to say nothing of the minor publications; quantities of manuscripts still lie, essentially unstudied, in the archives of Trinity and King's Colleges, Cambridge; and the first edition of Newton's correspondence is still incomplete. For all its acknowledged inadequacies, the standard biography of Newton is the mid-nineteenth century version by David Brewster, whose pious and anachronistic version of the pseudo-Victorian gentleman ignores just those idiosyncratic psychological, sociological, Arian, neo-Platonic, and even hermetic considerations we need most to understand if we are to comprehend Newton's genius and the nature of its influence.[3] One might, however, argue that a knowledge of the "real" Newton is irrelevant to an apprehension of eighteenth-century thought—even to that of its sciences—for whatever else remains to be learned, it seems clear that Newton was not a Newtonian in any one of the many versions which can be identified.[4] The obvious lead into our tangle turns out to be a loose thread which pulls out too easily to be useful, and we must begin again.

Now copies of the first edition of the *Principia* were widely distributed and quickly found their way to Holland, Hanover, Paris, and Rome, where they were studied and reviewed. But the earliest stages of reception of Newton's ideas were, almost of necessity, limited to criticism and assimilation of the content of the *Principia* by the few mathematical philosophers competent to deal with the highly complex text in its own terms. The first suggestion of influence outside that context seems to be in Britain through the physico-theology of Richard Bentley, whose *Boyle Sermons* of 1692 includes two relating to Newton's ideas.[5] This theological Newtonianism continued in successive Boyle lectures by clergymen such as Samuel Clarke, whose letters in debate with Leibniz, first published in 1717, treated the same issues.[6] Here is one, rather muddled, stream of Newtonianism.

Fortunately, in its scientific implications, this theological Newtonianism differed but little from the earliest scientific Newtonianism represented, at first, by the Edinburgh-Oxford coterie of David Gregory, John and James Keill, John Freind, and Archibald Pitcairne. The influence of this group was scarcely apparent, however, prior to 1704 and the publication of Newton's *Opticks* and not until the publication of the first Latin edition of the *Opticks* in 1706 and the papers and texts on chemistry, pneumatics, and physiology which followed can there be said to be a pervasive Newtonianism in British science. It might, indeed, be said that the first scientific Newtonianism can only be defined a full quarter of a century after the publication of the *Principia.*

This Newtonianism I shall call a Newtonian Newtonianism, for it was derived out of the *Principia* and *Opticks* during Newton's lifetime and was given form by natural philosophers who were friendly with Newton—or as friendly, that is, as that notoriously prickly individual permitted anyone to be. In essentialist taxonomic terms, the characteristics of this Newtonian Newtonianism were (1) a vehement anti-Cartesianism; (2) a conviction that natural philosphy could be made mathematical (and therefore "true") by rigorous quantitative confirmation, via observation or experiment, of the deductions of mathematical natural laws; (3) a belief in the corpuscular nature of matter, whose homogeneous ultimate particles combined, or moved through the void, under the influence of forces of attraction or repulsion, forces *not* inherent in matter but the consequence, mediately or immediately, of the constantly exerted will of God; (4) an assumption of the absolute nature of space and time, guaranteed by Divine omnipotence and omnipresence. This action-at-a-distance Newtonian Newtonianism provided the basic structure for scientific speculation and explanation in Britain during the first decades of the 1700s, but the high point of its influence in eighteenth-century English science was reached in the *Vegetable Staticks* of the Rev. Dr. Stephen Hales, published in 1727, the year of Newton's death. Thereafter it submerged almost completely under the gradually increasing popularity of different Newtonianisms.[7]

The second Newtonianism to appear in Britain may also be called a Newtonian Newtonianism, for it too was derived from the *Principia* and *Opticks,* but from the second and subsequent editions of the *Principia* and from the second English edition of the *Opticks* and its subsequent editions. The essential characteristics of this second Newtonian Newtonianism differed little from those of the first (inclining me to think it might be a variety rather than a different species), except in the important consideration of action-at-a-distance. To the 1713 *Principia* Newton had added the so-called "General Scholium" in which he indignantly rejected the accusation that the forces of attraction and repulsion were "occult qualities," declared that the forces existed, though their causes were unknown, and, as to their causes, he would not feign an hypothesis—those fateful, often quoted (out of context) words: "*Hypothesis non fingo.*" He then proceeded to hypothesize the existence of an aether, whose subtle, elastic, and electric properties were just those which might cause the apparent action of those attractive and repulsive forces. Newton did not explain just what the properties of this aether might be, but the queries which he added to the 1717 *Opticks* employed the hypothesis of the aether as a possible mode of explaining certain phenomena—such as the periodicity of light and the transmission of heat through space—which had been observed since the appearance of the Latin *Opticks* of 1706. Because Newton did not explain, and no one else could explain (though several people tried) just how the aether might work, this aetherial Newtonian Newtonianism might rapidly have lost its struggle for existence save that it was crossed with another Newtonianism, and the hybrid vigor of the new form provided the justification for the imponderable-fluid explanations of electricity, magnetism, heat, and eventually, most other phenomena of experimental natural philosophy in Britain through most of the century after 1740.[8]

The newest Newtonianism was initially imported from Holland. By the first decade of the 1700s, Newton's ideas were being introduced into the medical schools of the Dutch universities, but there they were combined with a Baconian empiricism which was then next to ignored in Britain. It is worthy of note that during Newton's personal reign over British science, between 1687 and 1727, there were *no* editions of Bacon's philosophical works published in Britain, while the same period in Holland saw four editions of the *Opera Omnia* and separate editions of the *Sapientia Veterum,* the *Historia Ventorum,* the *Novum Organum,* and the *Augmentis Scientiarum.*[9] Obviously copies of these printings could have been, and probably were, distributed in Britain, but their publication in Holland suggests what the writing of Dutch scientists confirm, the empirical, pragmatic emphasis of Dutch science. From Boerhaave, from 'sGravesande, from Musschenbroek came texts on chemistry, on electricity and magnetism, or more generally on Newtonian science "confirmed by experiment." These Newtonian texts were widely used, in Britain as well as on the continent, and the message they carried was one of a Baconian Newtonianism, in which *Hypothesis non Fingo* was cited as demonstration of the non-metaphysical nature of Newtonian science. These texts also asserted their particular differences with Newton's results, based, they said, on a "more consistent application of Newton's methods" and they proposed the existence of a special substance of heat, whose properties were just those that could explain heat phenomena. It was by conflating the aether of Newton with this Dutch matter of heat that the notion of imponderable fluids as a Newtonian explanation began.[10]

But the influence of Baconian Newtonianism was more insidious than this alone. Fifty years ago Pierre Brunet described the Dutch physicians and their concern for the experimental method; some forty-five years ago he also described the introduction of Newton's theories into France by way of Holland.[11] It is not entirely clear that Brunet distinguished between the two phenomena. What is worse, it is not entirely clear that the French of the eighteenth century were more discriminating. It is time, then, to turn our attention to the subject of Newtonianism in French science.

In eighteenth-century France, the hegemony of Descartes was scarcely disturbed before the end of the third decade. Copies of the *Principia* and the *Opticks* had been sold in France and their contents discussed in the reviews. Pierre Coste had translated the *Opticks* into French in 1720, but, as the *Éloge* by Fontenelle will show, the image of Newton in France as late as 1728 was still but darkly reflected in a mirror of Cartesian design.[12] By 1732 Maupertuis had published his *Discours sur les différentes figures des astres* and begun, with Clairaut, the collection of a group of at least nominal Newtonians within the confines of the Académie des Sciences itself. There is no doubt but that Maupertuis and Clairaut were influential in the spread of Newtonian ideas—but there is equally no doubt that their direct influence was, at first, small and confined. Surely it is a sufficient commentary on the effectiveness of their Newtonian persuasion that the principal agents initiating the disturbance of Cartesian complacency in France should instead have been Voltaire and his mistress, Madame du Châtelet.[13]

Not even his most ardent admirers would claim for Voltaire any distinction as a scientist, yet it seems clear that the sections on Newton in his *Lettres philosophiques* of 1733 began the introduction of Newtonian ideas on a broad and popular level in France. Moreover, his *Eléments de la philosophie de Newton* of 1738 is at least comparable in value to the British popularizations by Pemberton and Maclaurin. It is, therefore, of more than minor interest to trace the process by which Voltaire obtained his "understanding" of Newton. And in doing so we discover the varied straïns which come together to form the peculiarly French species of Newtonianism.

Visiting England between May 1726 and February 1729, on one of his involuntary trips from France, Voltaire became one of the earliest and most fervent of the Anglophilic *philosophes.* Associating much of the charm of English "génie" to its philosophic and scientific proclivities, he determined to inform his countrymen of that national characteristic. There is little evidence, however, that he had much understanding of English philosophy and still less that he understood its science when he began seriously to construct the *Lettres philosophiques* on his return to France.

As early as 1724, Bolingbroke had urged him to read Locke and Newton, but that was for their deistic import and the steps toward philosophic self-education that Voltaire took while in England were in furtherance of that concern. He studied Locke and appears to have read the Clarke-Leibniz correspondence. He met Clarke and Bishop Berkeley, but did not meet Newton; he may also have read parts of Pemberton's *View of Sir Isaac Newton's Philosophy* in manuscript before leaving England. The most that can be affirmed, so far as his understanding of Newton at that time is concerned, is that he had attained an awareness (scarcely hard to come by in an England mourning Newton's death) that Newton and Descartes differed on nearly every evident essential interpretation of natural phenomena. As Newton's opinion seemed to him more consistent with philosophical Deism than that of Descartes, Voltaire declared for Newton.

The work on the *Lettres philosophiques* commenced almost as soon as Voltaire was resettled in France, and by late 1732 the only parts still needing work were those relating to Newton. Voltaire read, and re-

read, Pemberton's *View* and Fontenelle's *Éloge*; more particularly he read Maupertuis' *Discours sur les différentes figures des astres* and began an exchange of letters with its author for instruction and criticism on Newtonian science. These—Pemberton, Fontenelle, and Maupertuis—were to be his major sources for the Newtonianism of the *Lettres*.

With the publication of the *Lettres*, Voltaire appears to have thought longingly (perhaps desperately) of returning to poetry. A visit to Paris, however, revealed a popular enthusiasm for scientific philosophy ripe for his exploitation. But the controversies started over the Newtonianism of the *Lettres*, particularly that with his Cartesian former teacher, also revealed that his understanding was as yet too feeble a lance for any really heavy intellectual jousting. He left Paris with a determination to continue his study of Newton—and this was the state of his affairs when he found sanctuary in that curiously intellectualized *ménage d'amour* prepared for him by Madame du Châtelet.

Into some of the activities at Cirey we need not inquire too closely, but the château appears also to have become something of a Newtonian salon and workshop. Voltaire resumed and Madame commenced a correspondence with Maupertuis and soon both were receiving instruction in philosophy and mathematics from Clairaut as well. Toward the end of 1735, Francesco Algarotti visited Cirey and, during an extended stay, read to the company from his manuscript *Il Newtonianismo per le dame*, reinspiring Voltaire to write an essay on the philosophy of Newton and inspiring Madame du Châtelet to commence a treatise on natural philosophy in general. Voltaire's first draft of the *Eléments de la philosophie de Newton* was completed by December 1736, with the aid of Maupertuis and Clairaut. He had also read Coste's translation of the *Opticks* and adopted the form and structure of Pemberton's and Algarotti's popularizations.

Early in 1737 Voltaire travelled to Leyden, where he consulted 'sGravesande, and possibly Boerhaave and Musschenbroek, for constructive criticism of his work. The influence of the Dutch scientists on Voltaire and on other *philosophes* was to spread that empiricist or Baconian Newtonianism, later to be celebrated in the *Encyclopédie*. Voltaire, it seems, was strengthened in his opinion that Newton's physics was not a system of thought, but a method, combining experiment and mathematics to obtain correct answers. It was the Dutch who encouraged him in his almost embarrassing insistence on "*Hypothesis non Fingo*" as Newton's motto; and it was probably also from the Dutch that he acquired the view that light is the matter of fire itself.

Voltaire left a corrected manuscript of his *Eléments* with his printer in Leyden, with the understanding that he would shortly supply some additional chapters for a second part—and returned to Cirey. There, however, amidst the other diversions, he found himself involved in a metaphysical debate which delayed that "second part" beyond the first edition of 1738.[14] In 1736 Prince Frederick of Prussia had initiated an admiring correspondence with Voltaire, which had soon turned to philosophic matters and found Frederick pushing the claims of Leibniz to Voltaire's consideration. In 1737 Frederick commenced sending copies of a French translation of the works of Christian Wolff, the most prominent German philosopher of the period, a disciple of Leibniz and a protégé of Frederick. Voltaire and Madame du Châtelet read Wolff and were at first unimpressed, but early in 1738 Madame read Johannes (I) Bernoulli's *Discours sur les lois de la communication du mouvement* and, with Maupertuis' approval, adopted the Leibnizian view of *vis viva.* She then repeated her urgent request for assistance in the preparation of her natural philosophy text and Maupertuis visited Cirey early in 1739 on his return from Basle bringing with him Johann (II) Bernoulli and Samuel König, a fervent disciple of Leibniz whom Maupertuis had known as a fellow student of the Bernoullis in 1734.

At this point we must take a detour to consider the phenomenon of eighteenth-century Swiss science. It has scarcely been remarked how important the contributions of the Swiss were to the scientific thought of the eighteenth century. Not only was there the "school" of mathematical physicists, centering at Basle with the Bernoullis: Jacques I and II, Johannes I and II, Nicolas and Daniel, but also including Leonhard Euler, Johann Lambert, and Georges LeSage, among others; there was also a major collection of physiologists, botanists, and geologists, including Albrecht von Haller, Charles Bonnet, Abraham Trembley, Charles Senebier, Horace-Benedict De Saussure, and Jean

André DeLuc. Each of these men was aware of and, no doubt, made reference to the work of Newton. It would, however, be hard to demonstrate that any one of them was more than semi-Newtonian—and this is as true of the physical-sciences group as of those concerned with the life sciences.[15] The older Bernoullis had, in fact, been diverted from their strict Cartesianism only by personal correspondence with Leibniz; there is no marked form of Newtonianism in them at all. Daniel Bernoulli combined Leibniz' mathematics with Newton's laws of motion, but retained a fondness for Cartesian vortex whirls in what might be classed as Cartesian Leibnizean Newtonianism, while Euler's *Letters to a German Princess* stand as a monument to a positivist Leibnizean Newtonianism which he was to carry with him to Berlin and St. Petersburg.[16]

It was from this stronghold of Cartesian Leibnizeans that Madame du Châtelet was to obtain instruction. At Maupertuis' suggestion, König remained behind at Cirey to give lessons in mathematics, which, of course, he combined with exposition of Leibizean philosophy. Madame, dissatisfied with the lack of metaphysics in Newtonian philosophy as she understood it, recast her *Institutions de physique* in the form of a Leibnizean ontology grafted onto a Newtonian epistemology. Voltaire, unhappy with the turn of events and now convinced of the importance of metaphysical considerations, wrote his *Métaphysique de Newton,* contrasting Newton with Leibniz, to the former's advantage, for the 1740 edition of his *Eléments de la philosophie de Newton.*

Voltaire seems to have thought that Madame's flirtation with Leibnizean metaphysics ended with the publication of the *Institutions de physique* in 1740 and certainly her efforts, after 1745, in translation of Newton's *Principia* would seem to confirm that view. But Madame never understood the incongruity of combining Leibniz's relational space and time, his monads, and his principles of continuity, sufficient reason, and pre-established harmony with Newtonian corpuscularity, laws of motion in absolute space and time, Rules of Reasoning, and universal gravitation. With the aid of Clairaut, and regretting, in 1747, that her work on the *Principia* precluded her entering a contest in support of Leibniz's monads, she completed her French translation of the *Principia* just before her death.

We have, therefore, the incongruity that the two most extensive eighteenth-century works in French on Newton's physics: the second volume of Madame du Châtelet's *Institutions de physique* and her translation of the *Principia,* were prepared by a believer in Leibniz. And what of Voltaire? It is easy to assume from his *Candide* that he was always anti-Leibniz. Yet he appears, in correspondence with Frederick and after, to have adopted Leibnizean views of free will, and his persistence in defining Newton's attractive force as an inherent property of matter suggests that his Newtonianism was tainted with views sympathetic with the German's natural philosophy. Here then we have two avenues by which variant strains of Newtonianisms entered France: Baconian Newtonianism from Holland, via Voltaire, and Leibnizian Newtonianism from Switzerland via Madame du Châtelet and, possibly, a bit from Berlin via Voltaire.

What then of the influence of Maupertuis and Clairaut? On inspection it turns out there are reasons to suspect the purity of their Newtonianism as well. It would be absurd to expect an evolutionary development of French Newtonianism and require fixity of belief in French Newtonians. Maupertuis may, that is, have been a Newtonian in 1732 when he wrote the *Discours sur les différentes figures des astres,* but what kind of Newtonian? When he first declared his allegiance to Newtonianism, he did so in a revealing way. Descartes, he said, had demonstrated that the phenomena of the universe could all have been caused by extensive matter and motion. But Newton had demonstrated, "by experiment," Maupertuis declared, that attractive and repulsive forces were inherent in matter. The only reason for these otherwise unnecessary forces must be to demonstrate the existence and power of God; Newtonianism was, therefore, a support to Maupertuis' Deism—but what a curious support. For it inverts the Deistic arguments of British theological and action-at-a-distance Newtonian Newtonianism, which denies that the forces of attraction and repulsion are inherent in matter. Given Maupertuis' variety of Newtonianism, and his increasing association with the Basle Leibnizeans, the nature of

Maupertuis' "Newtonian" influence is questionable, particularly in light of his 1739 recommendation of the Leibnizean König as a teacher of natural philosophy for Cirey. Clearly by 1751 Maupertuis had adopted Leibnizean monadology in his *Essai sur la formation des corps organisés* and, by that time, must be included among the Berlin Leibnizean Newtonians.[17]

With Clairaut any transformation is, at the moment, less clear, but the original purity of the Newtonian strain is equally doubtful. Clairaut appears to have had little hesitancy in adopting Newton's inverse-square law of gravitation for computing planetary motions, but the moment that difficulties seemed to arise—in, e.g., correctly computing lunar motion—Clairaut had no qualms in tinkering, by trial and error, with that law to bring his calculations in line. Like most other French mathematical physicists—D'Alembert is another example—Clairaut seems to have felt that Newton's laws were empirical variations—minor Divine idiosyncracies—on an otherwise consistent system deducible from first principles. Whether these first principles were those of Descartes, I cannot yet say. Certainly, from D'Alembert down to the late nineteenth century, French mathematicians have found it hard to forgive God for not being a Cartesian.[18] But Clairaut may also be suspected ("guilt by association") of Leibnizean leanings, for all his closest friends—Maupertuis, Johannes (II) Bernoulli, Euler, and König—were, at best, Leibnizean Newtonians, and his favorite correspondent, Gabriel Cramer, was an adherent of the Basle "school," editing their work along with an edition of Christian Wolff's *Elementa* and two volumes of the correspondence of Johann (I) Bernoulli and Leibniz.

A rapid survey of the French experimental natural philosophers reveals similar anomalies demanding further attention. Neither Réaumur, nor Charles Du Fay, nor the Abbé Nollet—carrying us from the late seventeenth century to the 1770s—exhibit any evidence of Newtonian influence.

Buffon, nominated by Voltaire as the leader of young French Newtonians, combined Baconian rhetoric, Newtonian central (particularly gravitational) forces, and Leibnizean living atoms into a blend so uniquely his own that only recently, with Jacques Roger, has an attempt been made to untangle the consequences.[19] La Mettrie, friend of Madame du Châtelet, and protected by Frederick the Great at the suggestion of Maupertuis, denounced Leibniz in favor of Descartes, but built on the Swiss von Haller's concept of innate muscular irritability to create, in *L'Homme Machine,* an extension of the Cartesian animal-automaton through the use of dynamist concepts of matter later explicitly related (in *L'Homme plante*) to Christian Wolff.[20]

Meanwhile the introduction of animist physiology and materialist chemistry via the German Stahl, combined with translations of 'sGravesande and Musschenbroek, and Aristotelian essentialist taxonomy, via the Swede Linneaus, was producing curious hybrids among the nominal Newtonians of the *Encyclopédie.* Committed to the use of Newtonianism as a weapon against the Cartesian academic establishment, Macquer, d'Holbach, and initially Diderot supported an experimentalist, empirical-positivist Baconian Newtonianism. But Diderot, at least, soon concluded that Newton, had he wanted to, could have made his system easier (open, he said, to the simplest minds), and, by 1754 and his *Pensées sur l'interprétation de la nature,* already gives evidence of departure from Baconian Newtonian empiricism and corpuscularity. In *Le Rêve de D'Alembert* and even more in the *Principes philosophiques sur la matière et le mouvement* of 1770, we find Diderot maintaining that sensitivity is an inherent property of all matter, that it is activated by association with living animal substance, and forms, with inactivated matter, a holistic universe, which resembles at its worst a neo-Platonic living macrocosm and at its best a Leibnizean pre-established harmony of self-sufficient monads.[21]

With nearly every presumptive Newtonianism in France tainted with Baconianism, Cartesianism, Leibnizeanism, or combinations of the three in uniquely varying measure, the situation concerning the "Age of Newton" in France is clearly unclear. It seems possible reasonably to argue, however, that the first coherent body of French scientists for whom Newtonian Newtonianism ideas afforded a guide to research and interpretation might well have been that collected by Berthollet and LaPlace, as the Society of Arcueil, in the early years of the nineteenth century.[22] What then of other parts of Europe? My space is too limited and, more important, my research is still too incomplete to do more than suggest some of the problems facing the researcher in these areas.

The history of eighteenth-century Italian science has scarcely been studied (except, perhaps, in Italian) and the fate of Newtonianism there has not been traced.[23] One can note, however, that some of the professors of mathematical natural philosophy in Italian universities early in the eighteenth century were directly or indirectly disciples of Leibniz—such as Jacob Hermann and both Nicolas (I) and Daniel Bernoulli, at Padua and Venice. That such teaching had some influence may be reflected in the work of the Dalmation Roger Joseph Boscovich, one of the more imaginative Leibnizian Newtonians, who was educated in natural philosophy in Rome.[24] Later in the century (c. 1776) we find the experimental natural philosopher Giambattista Beccaria praising Newton and Hales, along with Galileo and Benjamin Franklin, as masters of experimental enquiry, the creators of a new science whose ornament was observation and experiment.[25] Italy, it appears, had both its Leibnizean and Baconian Newtonians. Eighteenth-century Scandanavian science seems, at the moment, to have come primarily out of Sweden. There, early in the century, Martin Triewald was, perhaps, some kind of Newtonian, as was Torbern Bergman late in the century, but the dominant figures through most of the period were Swedenborg, Anders Celsius, Samuel Klingenstierna, J. G. Wallerius, and Carl Linneaus. Swedenborg, so far as he heeded any earthly philosopher, was an admirer of Christian Wolff's metaphysics. Celsius and Klingenstierna were aware of Newton as an experimental empiricist (i.e. a Baconian), but in metaphysics they too were followers of the Leibnizean Christian Wolff. Wallerius was, at least late in life, a Paracelsian alchemist, while Linneaus, for all his studies in Holland during the period when Voltaire was investigating Newtonianism there, was an Aristoteleian essentialist taxonomist all his life. Not only did the Linnean taxonomic approach to science dominate the University of Uppsala for some thirty-five years, its popularity throughout Europe during the latter half of the century carried that approach from botany into mineralogy, geology, medicine, and even, with the Frenchman Lavoisier, for example, into chemistry. On the surface, at least, it is hard to see that Scandinavian science participated in the "Age of Newton" at all.[26]

In the German-speaking states, the situation was much the same. There is no suggestion of Newtonian science in Austria. The so-called Berlin *aufklärung* is characterized by the non-scientific writings of Moses Mendelssohn, who was a fervent disciple of Leibniz and of Christian Wolff, a vehement anti-Newtonian.[27] The chief center of organized science in the German states was the Berlin Academy of Sciences and the luminaries of that academy were Maupertuis, LaMettrie, Sulzer, and Euler—Leibnizean Newtonians representing, of all things, the *anti-Leibniz* coterie among the Berlin *aufklärung.* Only Immanuel Kant (and I concede the presumption of that *only*), among the major figures of eighteenth-century Germanic thought, appears to have had any favorable conception of the metaphysical implications of Newtonian science.[28] And Kant's natural philosophy, based on a force-oriented Newtonian Newtonianism, was transformed into a romantic idealism by anti-Newtonian *Natur-philosophen* such as Goethe, Franz von Baader, and Schelling.[29] Not until the reductionist, mechanist reaction against *Natur-philosophie* were German scientists such as Helmholtz seriously to confront the issues of Newtonianism. Finally, Euler and his friend Daniel Bernoulli also dominated the St. Petersburg Academy of Sciences, whose only native star was Michael Lomonosov, explicitly anti-Newtonian, educated in science at St. Petersburg under professors selected by Christian Wolff and in metaphysics at Marburg under Wolff himself.[30]

In this too rapid survey of the diffusion and diversification of the influence of Newton's ideas, I have adopted a taxonomy of Newtonianisms which has included: Baconian Newtonianism, Leibnizean Newtonianism, Cartesian Newtonianism, and at least two varieties of Newtonian Newtonianism. You will have noted that this employs the standard eighteenth-century binominal nomenclature, with the first term representing ontological distinctions. I do not intend by this, however, to emulate Linneaus or to suggest that this is a natural classification. Indeed it is clear that the system must be an artificial one, with so many hybrid forms typically confusing generic distinctions. But research on eighteenth-century Newtonianism is still too incomplete to have produced even its Jussieu or Candolle. All I have tried to do is to reveal those specific variations in time and geographical distributions which demonstrate that a study of the evolutionary diffusion of Newton's ideas through Britain and onto the continent ought to replace the static notion of a fixity of intellectual forms.

NOTES

1 This paper is a slightly revised version of that given at a plenary session of the seventh annual meeting of the American Society for Eighteenth-Century Studies, Charlottesville, Virginia, on April 8, 1976. The subject is, of course, one of perennial interest to students of eighteenth-century thought and a full bibliography would be impossible. In addition to the sources cited below, one might also name, as examples of recent studies, Gerd Buchdahl, *The Image of Newton and Locke in the Age of Reason* (London: Sheed and Ward, 1961); Henry Guerlac, especially his "Three Eighteenth-Century Social Philosophers: Scientific Influences on Their Thought," *Daedalus,* 82 (1958), 8–24; and Alan Charles Kors, *D'Holbach's Coterie: An Enlightenment in Paris* (Princeton: Princeton Univ. Press, 1975).

2 See, for example, Bernard Le Bovier de Fontenelle, "Sur l'utilité des mathématiques et de la physique," *Oeuvres* (Paris: Libraires Associés, 1766), VI, 67–68; and Christian Wolff, "Commentatio de studie matheseos recte instituendo," *Elementa Matheseos Universae* (Geneva: Henricum-Albertum Gosse & Socios., 1741), V, 129–32 and *passim.*

3 David Brewster, *Memoirs of the Life, Writings, and Discoveries of Sir Isaac Newton* (New York: Johnson Reprint Corporation, Sources of Science No. 14, from the Edinburgh 1855 ed., 1965).

4 Indeed, I have argued this in Robert E. Schofield, *Mechanism and Materialism: British Natural Philosophy in an Age of Reason* (Princeton: Princeton Univ. Press, 1970), pp. 4, 7n, and *passim.*

5 Richard Bentley, *Eight Sermons Preach'd at the Honourable Robert Boyle's Lecture, In the First Year, MDCXCII,* 5th ed., (Cambridge: Crownfield, Knapton, and Knopstock, 1724).

6 *Leibniz-Clarke Correspondence*, ed. H. G. Alexander (Manchester: Manchester Univ. Press, 1956), a modern edition of correspondence first published in 1717.

7 This is the type of "Newtonianism" called mechanism in Schofield, *Mechanism and Materialism,* and discussed there, pp. 19–87.

8 This second "Newtonianism" is discussed as Materialism in Schofield, *Mechanism and Materialism,* pp. 13–15, 96–231.

9 See Reginald Gibson, *Francis Bacon: A Bibliography of His Works and of Baconiana to the Year 1750* (Oxford: Scrivener Press, 1950).

10 For the Dutch "Newtonians," see Schofield, *Mechanism and Materialism,* pp. 135–54.

11 Pierre Brunet, *Les Physiciens hollandais et la méthode expérimentale en France au XVIIIe siècle* (Paris: Albert Blanchard, 1926); *L'Introduction des théories de Newton en France au XVIIIe siècle,* I: Avant 1738 (Paris: Albert Blanchard, 1931).

12 Fontenelle, "Éloge de Newton," *Oeuvres,* VI, 296–97. Aram Vartanian observes, in his *Diderot and Descartes: A Study of Scientific Naturalism in the Enlightenment* (Princeton: Princeton Univ. Press, 1953), pp. 60–62, that Fontenelle continued his defense of Cartesianism as late as 1751.

13 For the following treatment of Voltaire and Madame du Châtelet, I am chiefly indebted to Ira O. Wade, *Voltaire and Mme du Châtelet* (Princeton: Princeton Univ. Press, 1941) and *The Intellectual Development of Voltaire* (Princeton: Princeton Univ. Press, 1969), pp. 228, 265–91; and William H. Barber, "Mme du Châtelet and Leibnizianism: The Genesis of the Institutions de physique," *The Age of the Enlightenment: Studies Presented to T. Besterman* (Edinburgh: Oliver & Boyd, 1967), pp. 220–22.

14 This was published as a third part, entitled "métaphysique," in 1740, but is not included in the English translation, based on the 1738 edition.

15 Except for Aram Vartanian's "Trembley's Polyp, LaMettrie, and 18th-century French Materialism," *Journal of the History of Ideas,* 11 (1950), 259–86, there is no recent, truly analytical, historical study in English of these Swiss men of science, singly or collectively. The best present sources are the appropriate volumes of the *Dictionary of Scientific Biography.*

16 Leonhard Euler, *Letters . . . on Different Subjects in Natural Philosophy. Addressed to a German Princess,* trans. Henry Hunter (New York: Arno Press, 1975, reprt. of 1833 edn.).

17 On Maupertuis as Leibnizean, see the *Dictionary of Scientific Biography* and Ernst Cassirer, *The Philosophy of the Enlightenment* (Princeton: Princeton Univ. Press., 1951), pp. 86–87. His curiously inverted early deistical Newtonianism is treated in Colm Kiernan, "The Enlightenment and Science in Eighteenth-Century France," *Studies on Voltaire and the Eighteenth Century,* 59A (1973), 30.

18 On the continuation of Cartesianism in France, see Thomas L. Hankins, *Jean d'Alembert: Science and the Enlightenment* (Oxford: Clarendon Press, 1970); for Clairaut, see the *Dictionary of Scientific Biography.*

19 Jacques Roger, *Les Sciences de la vie dans la pensée française du 18e siècle* (Paris: A. Colin, 1963), pp. 527–84; also L. Hanks, *Buffon avant l'histoire naturelle* (Paris: Presses Universitaires de France, 1966).

20 Pierre Lemée, *Julien Offray de La Mettrie: St-Malo (1709)-Berlin (1751), médicin-philosophe-polémiste, sa vie, son oeuvre* (Mortain: Imprimerie du Mortainais, 1954), and Kiernan, "Enlightenment and Science."

21 Arthur M. Wilson, *Diderot* (New York: Oxford Univ. Press, 1972), pp. 380, 565, and *passim*; Kiernan, "Enlightenment and Science," *passim.*

22 For the "Newtonianism" at Arcueil, see Maurice Crosland, *The Society of Arcueil:*

A View of French Science at the Time of Napoleon I (Cambridge, Mass.: Harvard Univ. Press, 1967), pp. 259–60, 299–308.

23 See, however, Clelia Pighetti, "Per la storia del Newtonianesimo in Italia," *Rivista critica di storia della filosofia,* 16 (1961), 425–34.

24 *Roger Joseph Boscovich, S.J., F.R.S., 1711–1787,* ed. Lancelot Law Whyte (London: George Allen & Unwin, 1961).

25 Quoted by Beccaria's biographer in 1793 and cited by I. Bernard Cohen, *Franklin and Newton: An Inquiry into Speculative Newtonian Experimental Science and Franklin's Work in Electricity as an Example Thereof* (Philadelphia: Memoir 43, American Philosophical Society, 1956), pp. 279–310.

26 Hugo Lj. Odhner, "Christian Wolff and Swedenborg," *The New Philosophy* (1951), 237–51; Tore Frangsmyr, "Swedish Science in the Eighteenth Century," *History of Science,* 12 (1974), 29–42.

27 Alexander Altmann, *Moses Mendelssohn: A Biographical Study* (University, Alabama: Univ. of Alabama Press, 1973).

28 See, for example, Yehuda Elkana, "Scientific and Metaphysical Problems: Euler and Kant," *Boston Studies in the Philosophy of Science,* 14 (1974), 277–305; Irving Polonoff, "Newtonianism in Kant's cosmogony," *Proceedings of the Tenth International Congress of the History of Science* (1962), II, 747–50.

29 See, for example, L. Pearce Williams, "Kant, Naturphilosophie and Scientific Method," in *Foundations of Scientific Method: The Nineteenth Century,* ed. Ronald N. Giere and Richard S. Westfall (Bloomington, Ind.: Indiana Univ. Press, 1970), pp. 3–22.

30 *Mikhail Vasil'evich Lomonosov on the Corpuscular Theory,* trans. and intro. Henry M. Leicester (Cambridge, Mass.: Harvard Univ. Press, 1970), pp. 110–21.

Materialism and Freedom: Commentary on Papers by Robert E. Schofield and Aram Vartanian

JEFFREY BARNOUW

The two preceding papers touch, if they do not quite intersect, at the point where theories involved in the scientific understanding of the natural world are seen to have implications or consequences for human self-knowledge and conduct. I will try to comment on each paper with adequate attention to its specific concerns, without exaggerating the points of contact and possible conflict between them. But I would also like to attempt to sketch a framework which would allow us to consider the papers together in their bearing on the general intellectual and cultural importance and import of natural science in the eighteenth century.

Robert Schofield has traced for us the emergence of a series of relatively discrete and divergent Newtonianisms, with the intent of helping us to discard and guard against facile generalizations about the influence of Newton on an age that is sometimes named after him. In his introduction to Newton's letters to Bentley in connection with the first Boyle Lectures Perry Miller has suggested "that Newton was not quite a Newtonian. He was holding something in reserve, not giving himself entirely to his own discoveries." Miller points to the following sentence in the third letter as an index of Newton's distance from the Newtonianism of Bentley: "Gravity must be caused by an Agent acting constantly according to certain Laws; but whether this Agent be material or immaterial, I have left to the Consideration of my Readers."[1] This mental reservation means something more than Marx's "Je ne suis pas marxiste," for it points to an element in Newton's view of science that would seem to resist or repel the "ism."

Voltaire expressed something like this in his preface to Mme du Châtelet's French translation of the *Principia*: "If there were still somebody absurd enough to defend subtle and twisted (screw-formed) matter . . . as the cause of gravity, one would say: this man is a Cartesian; if he should believe in monads, one would say he is a Leibnizian. But there are no Newtonians, as there are no Euclidians. It is the privilege of error to give its name to a sect."[2] Voltaire was a "Newtonian," as Schofield has shown, and of a particular sort or sect. But the difference which Voltaire suggests here, between Cartesians and Newtonians like himself, is less a matter of disagreement on what the cause of gravity is than a radical divergence as to whether, or rather in what way, such causes are the concern of science. We must recognize this tactful or tactical reservation and self-limitation, paradoxically perhaps, as a powerfully attractive nucleus in Newtonian science for the formation of a new "ism."

Whether it was taken as freeing positive science from metaphysical presuppositions and pursuits, or as delimiting science to make room for such speculation and religious revelation and faith, or even as itself a vindication of and support for rational belief, Newtonianism of every variety in the eighteenth century drew significantly on the new conception and self-consciousness of modern science, which was seen as expressed in Newton's famous words "*Hypotheses non fingo.*" Much has been written on the meaning of this utterance,[3] and we must come back to try to assess the attitude which it suggests. But its various general misinterpretations are also significant for the cultural historian of science, for they were in many ways more influential.

The "ism" which is most frequently associated with this conception of science is positivism. "Positivism" is by now less a descriptive label than a term of opprobrium, in the social sciences and humanities at least, and it would be futile to try to rehabilitate it as a term here. But I do think that many of the problems attributed to materialism and mechanism, and to phenomenalism, as fundamental working assumptions within natural science and its philosophy, are actually the result of metaphysical backlash, which could be overcome if the "scientific attitude" were followed through more consistently and deeply in the social and human sciences.[4]

This needs to be pursued further in criticism both of reductive forms of positivism and of dogmatic forms of the "critique of positivism." Where positivism backs away from the commitment to science as a knowledge of reality, it is justly criticized, but this should not lead us to accept such criticism as a valid repudiation of the possibility that a philosophical, cultural, or social-practical orientation can be derived from the spirit of the Scientific Revolution of the seventeenth century and its first culmination in Newtonian Science. The task of carrying through the Scientific Revolution as a reorientation of men's thinking and relation to the world devolved, once the position of natural science was secure, on the Enlightenment, in fact, as the task of enlightenment.

One can appreciate the sceptical note in Schofield's reference to "this faith in the generalizable virtues of the scientific method (whatever that might be)," even while arguing that the task is still with us of understanding the New Science which emerged in the seventeenth century *as human science,* that is, in its historical-practical intentionality, and thus as containing the promise of human sciences as integral parts of a profession of science which would not be irrelevant to the problems of social enlightenment. As Bacon insisted, the dispelling of idols is an essential part of the growth of real knowledge, and if Schofield, by undermining the hypostatization of Newton's achievement and influence, has enabled us to see the eighteenth century as an Age of Newtonianisms, this is a step in the right direction.

His paper restricts itself generally to the scientific relevance of the various Newtonianisms he traces. As Exhibit A of his first species he refers to the physico-theology developed in the Boyle lectures first by Richard Bentley and then by Samuel Clarke, a "rather muddled stream of Newtonianism," which, however, Schofield says, is "fortunately, in its scientific implications," easily assimilated to "the earliest scientific Newtonianism" of David Gregory, the Keill brothers, and Archibald Pitcairne. The Boyle Lectures were, of course, established essentially for the sake of their theological, or more generally their religious, cultural implications. As Schofield relates in his book on "British Natural Philosophy in the Eighteenth Century," *Mechanism and Materialism,* Boyle's bequest "left an endowment for an annual series of eight sermons, or lectures, 'to prove the truth of the Christian religion against infidels, *viz.* Atheists, Theists, Pagans,' etc.,"[5] and Boyle's own example led lecturers like the classical scholar Bentley to draw primarily on science (and in fact on Newton) in their vindications of Christianity.

In a sense the Boyle Lectures represented the obverse and complement of the program of natural philosophy, that is, the experimental or mechanical philosophy, advanced by the Christian virtuosi and publicists (some of them Anglican bishops) who came together in the latter half of the seventeenth century in the Royal Society. A Boyle or Wilkins, Sprat or Glanville, was concerned to secure the advancement of science by showing that neither its discoveries nor the ideas of mechanism and materialism contained in it posed any threat to the Christian religion. This was probably the main source of their misgivings about Hobbes—who was excluded from the Royal Society—since his thought seemed to endanger precisely their containment of materialism and mechanism and thus to threaten the social acceptance of the New Science which they hoped to promote.

Hobbes's program of a science of man, to say nothing of his science of the citizen, was as ominous for them as the implications of atheism which they and others saw in *his* materialism. His denial of a separate spiritual substance was intimately connected with his extension of the idea of science, whereas the efforts of the Royal Society exerted an influence which tended to discourage or undermine the broad conception of science which Hobbes had taken over from Bacon. As a result, the Baconianism of the Royal Society exaggerated its utilitarian aspect, deriving the benefits for man which Bacon had envisaged not from science itself, as a discipline of human thinking, but only from its technical applications. This effectively impeded progress toward the Enlightenment.

Most thinkers of that time, for reasons other than scientific, felt that it was important or necessary to delimit the New Science to a knowledge of nature, and this tendency was reinforced from two directions. Either scientific knowledge, as derived from sense experience, was referred to mere appearances or phenomena, distinct from an underlying reality (an extension of the classical and scholastic conception of "saving the phenomena," which had been turned in a different direction by the nominalist movement), or it was referred exclusively to extended substance, as opposed to spiritual or thinking substance. In the first case the subjectivity of sensation and the conjectural nature of causal connections drawn from experience were taken as holding sceptical epistemological implications that could be used to fideist ends.

Hobbes, particularly where he was intent on showing and making use of the subjectivity of sense, opposed this sceptical phenomenalism, as he opposed Cartesian dualism, insisting on science as a knowledge of *reality*. His position is not irrelevant to Newton's own ideas. True, Newton began the first of the four letters he wrote to Bentley in preparation for the latter's inauguration of the Boyle Lectures, "When I wrote my treatise about our system, I had an eye upon such principles as might work with considering men for the belief of a deity; and nothing can rejoice me more than to find it useful for that purpose."[6]

But Hobbes, following Bacon, had himself consistently used arguments characteristic of the Ockhamite nominalist tradition to enforce a disjunction of the claims of knowledge and faith in our understanding of the world, in a way which imposed no barriers on the expansion of empirical science. Hobbes repeatedly shows that mixing the concerns of rational theology with scientific inquiry must work to pervert and undermine faith. This included all attempts "to prove the truth of the Christian religion."[7] Hobbes's vindication of the principle of faith involved no restriction of empirically rational science, but simply the critical dissolution of metaphysical pretensions.

A closer look at the difference between Newton's own intentions and the use that Bentley makes of them will lead us back into the core of Schofield's paper and its issues of scientific relevance. In that first letter Newton mentions various features of the cosmos which he does "not think explicable by mere natural causes" and is forced to ascribe "to the counsel and contrivance of a voluntary agent" (p. 282). "To make this system," he says, "required a cause which understood, and compared together, the quantities of matter in the several bodies of the sun and planets, and the gravitating powers resulting from thence, . . . that is, a cause not blind and fortuitous, but very well skilled in mechanics and geometry" (pp. 286ff.).

Beyond this version of an argument from 'design' (a significant pun which epitomizes the inference from pattern to intention, in the sense of conscious creation, not ulterior or utilitarian motive), Newton grants Bentley that one could also argue from the apparent adaptation of the world to the uses of human life, e.g. "the inclination of the earth's axis . . . as a contrivance for winter and summer, and for making the earth habitable toward the poles" (p. 289). But he is clearly lukewarm about such a teleological proof of deity in the style of physico-theology. Like Bacon, he resists the tendency of its anthropocentrism.

What is more, even in the argument from "order," that is, the evidence of divine intelligence in the universe, Newton does not see this as something separate from the tracing of the laws according to which nature is constituted or operates. He rejects the idea of gravity as an inherent property of matter, what he calls "Epicurean" gravitation, which would have attraction working across a vacuum, because it would force us to the assumption of the mediation of a non-material cause to take the place of mutual contact, and Newton does not want to be forced to such an assumption.

But that is exactly what Bentley wants us to be forced to, by *his* Newtonianism, as Schofield has suggested. Bentley rejects the "aetherial subtile matter" (p. 322) of the Cartesians by asserting that, as matter, it must weigh something—be "ponderable"—and thus could not play the sustaining role which the Cartesians claim for it in the causation of gravity. Rejecting both the Aether and (Gassendist) Effluvia or Spirits emitted from one body to another, Bentley affirms "that univeral gravitation is above all mechanism and material causes and proceeds from a higher principle, a divine energy and impression" (p. 344).

For Newton, however, "divine energy" must itself act "constantly according to certain laws" and it may yet be discovered to be material. It is the task of the scientist to try to discover the mode and law of such operation, even where this may lead—not beyond limits imposed by piety (I do not think Newton saw any great danger there)—but beyond the scope of the more or less established conception of mechanism. As a scientist, Newton is aware, as Bentley is not, how open and fluid the ideas of mechanism and materialism necessarily still are.[8]

As Schofield has emphasized, materialism and mechanism represent separable strands in Newtonian thought, and Newton himself later made public his own hypothesis of an Aether, describing it, in fact, allusively and elusively, in the final paragraph of the General Scholium he added to the *Principia* in 1713 immediately following the passage containing his famous words "*Hypotheses non fingo.*" Scrutiny of this passage may reveal certain affinities of Newton's materialism, not so much with that of Descartes as with that of Hobbes.

In the General Scholium Newton argues that "mere mechanical causes" are inadequate to account for either the origins of planetary motions or the cause of the observable (not occult) power of gravity. He links "mechanical causes" with the "outward surfaces" of bodies or particles, as opposed to their "inward substances." The latter are said "not to be known either by our sense, or by any reflex act of our minds," yet they are clearly intended by Newton's Aether-hypothesis, namely his supposedly necessary assumption of a "certain most subtle spirit which pervades and lies hid in all gross bodies."

By the forces and action of this spirit, not only are the phenomena of gravity, cohesion, light, heat, etc. produced, but also "all sensation is excited, and the members of animal bodies move at the command of the will, namely, by the vibrations of this spirit, mutually propagated along the solid filaments of the nerves, from the outward organs of sense to the brain, and from the brain to the muscles."[9] With this passage we can perhaps already glimpse a possible connection with the materialism of Aram Vartanian's French materialists. Newton's use of the Aether-hypothesis for a physiological conception of neural impulse and muscular innervation shows surprising proximity to the concerns of a La Mettrie or Diderot, precisely where physical causality or 'determinism' is claimed as the basis for understanding psychological processes and voluntary action.

I have claimed that this materialism in Newton is more Hobbesian than Cartesian, even though Descartes certainly contributed more to the speculative physiology of 'animal spirits'. A closer look at the final turn which Newton gives to his subtle spirit in the General Scholium, a text that went through eight drafts, will suggest a justification. The general conception of a physiology of will which Newton implies there is closely tied up with the idea of God's "dominion" in and over the world, an idea which is crucial to the earlier part of the Scholium with its counterattack to Cartesian, Leibnizian, and perhaps Berkeleyan insinuations that Newton's ideas entail atheism.

In a confrontation with Descartes dating from around 1670, in which he attacks not only the identification of matter and extension, but also the radical distinction of extended substance and spiritual or thinking substance, Newton writes, "It is clear that God created the world by no other action than that of willing in the same way as we also by the sole action of willing move our bodies."[10] This idea seems continuous with a conception of 'divine energy' that is not mechanical but may eventually be seen to be material and to operate according to some law.

Alexandre Koyré has shown that opposition to Descartes in an essential undercurrent of both the *Principia* and the *Optics,* intensifying in later editions. The implications of the physiology of will for human science might best be brought out by reference to the fifth of Newton's *regulae philosophandi,* quoted by Koyré from the manuscripts connected with the revisions of the *Principia.* This text is clearly aimed at reducing the Cartesian *cogito*—"the sensation of internal thoughts" as phenomena parallel to those of the external senses, or "that which we contemplate in our minds when thinking: such as, I am, I believe . . . I wish . . . I am thirsty . . . I rejoice, I suffer, etc."—to phenomena of inner experience accessible to empirical science as psychology.[11]

The influence of Locke may be apparent here, but I would argue that that of Hobbes is even more significant. Grounding the continuities of inner and external experience in the physiology of sense and a psychological epistemology, Hobbes provided a peculiar brand of materialism which was of far less use than the contained and segregated materialism of Descartes in establishing mechanism as a model, but was far more adequate to the problems of human sciences. This Hobbesian materialism, which had to be less rigorously reductive than Descartes' because it recognized no distinction between extended and spiritual substance, was to prove of greater value as soon as it became a question of moving beyond or opening up mechanistic ideas.[12]

In his paper here and in *Mechanism and Materialism,* Robert Schofield has distinguished two main waves of Newton's scientific influence in the eighteenth century: that of 'mechanism' or dynamic corpuscularism, and then, starting in about 1740, what he calls the 'materialism' of "the imponderable-fluid explanations of electricity, magnetism, heat, and eventually most other phenomena of experimental natural philosophy." His differentiation of this materialism, which it might be best to call 'qualitative', from the 'mechanical or corpuscular' theory, should help us to be more discriminating in our use of such terms, without leading us to project such a neat split back into Newton himself.

The break around 1740 has also been emphasized by Aran Vartanian as a "shift of accent . . . from the calculable laws of Newtonian mathematical science to the incalculable intricacies of organic nature."[13] It has been Vartanian's particular achievement to trace the emergence of conceptions and philosophies of the organism as a sort of machine in French materialism, and to trace their origins back to the materialism of Descartes. I am in substantial agreement with the main point made in Vartanian's paper. But I believe that the historical construction in which he situates his argument, and particularly the one-sided derivation of French materialism from Descartes and its polemical opposition to Hobbes' position, materially threatens to undermine that main point, namely the close connection between a certain strain of philosophical materialism and a particular conception and vindication of the reality of human volition and freedom.

I will concentrate on these disagreements, but this should not be allowed to obscure my basic agreement and my general debt to Vartanian's *Diderot and Descartes,* the concluding argument of which is resumed in his paper. With regard to the so-called free will vs. determinism controversy, a crucial passage in Diderot is the definition of will offered by Dr. Bordeu toward the end of the central section of *Le Rêve de d'Alembert,* that is, *Le Rêve de d'Alembert* proper. D'Alembert claims that sometimes in dreams we have not only a consciousness of ourselves, but of our will and freedom. What, he asks, is this will? It is the same, Bordeu answers, as that of a waking man: "the last impulse of desire or aversion, the final result of all that one has been from birth to the present moment."

You yourself have always acted without any separate act of will, he tells d'Alembert. "Can one simply will or wish on one's own? Will arises always from some motive, internal or external, a present impression, a reminiscence of the past, a passion, or a plan for the future. After this I need say only one word about freedom, that the last of our actions is the necessary effect of a single cause: ourselves, a very complicated yet integral cause."[14]

The attribution of sources is a tricky business, but I would risk the assertion that this conception shows the direct influence of Hobbes and his theory of willing and 'deliberation'. Deliberation, for Hobbes, is a process in which various motives contend, alternate, and interact; the last or resultant "appetite or aversion, immediately adhering to the action or to the omission thereof, is what we call the will."[15] Will is not to be hypostatized as a faculty, but is itself a form of desire which has been articulated by the processes of reflection and deliberation. Just as desire, for Hobbes, following Aristotle, is a passion rather than an action, since the active cause is the object of desire,[16] so too is will. This means that will is not voluntary.

In Chapter XII of *Human Nature,* which contains a full discussion of 'deliberation', Hobbes writes, "Appetite, fear, hope and the rest of the passions are not called voluntary; for they proceed not from, but are the will; and the will is not voluntary: for a man can no more say he will will than he will will will. . . ."[17] This is not a denial of the reality of willing, nor of human freedom. "This alternate succession of appetite and fear during all the time the action is in our power to do or not to do, is that we call *deliberation.*" This formulation implies the functional pun that Hobbes enjoys making: de-liberation as the process of putting an end (a determination, a goal?) to our freedom in any particular case. Freedom is involved in deliberation in the sense that the deliberated action must be a future and real possibility: "of *necessaries* therefore there is no deliberation."

But that one acts or refrains from acting is not the result of freedom, but always of an adequate cause, as the principle of sufficient reason would have it, namely that nothing happens without sufficient cause. In the case of deliberated or deliberate action this cause would include the reasons or motives that in fact move us to act.

Hobbes goes on immediately in that same chapter to make clear that this 'moral determinism', and not the supposition of a free or undetermined will, provides a rationale for punishment, since anticipations of the results of our environed actions are crucial to such motivation and determination of our willing.

> Forasmuch as will to do is appetite, and will to omit, fear; the cause of appetite and fear is the cause also of our will: but the propounding of the benefits and of harms, that is to say, of reward and punishment, is the cause of our appetite, and of our fears, and therefore also of our wills, so far forth as we believe that such rewards and benefits as are propounded, shall arrive unto us; and consequently, our wills follow our opinions, as our actions follow our wills; in which sense they say truly, and properly, that say the world is governed by opinion.

This is precisely the argument which Diderot's Bordeu goes on to make in the middle section of *Le Rêve de d'Alembert,* seeing rewards and punishments as the means of correcting that "modifiable being" man where he is evil and of encouraging him where he is good. There is no warrant for reducing this to totalitarian behavioristic conditioning in Hobbes any more than in Diderot. But by linking him with Helvétius, Vartanian gives this impression of Hobbes. In the opening paragraph of his paper Vartanian asserts that "Hobbes was a 'mechanical materialist' who denied that human thoughts and actions could in any rigorous sense be described as *free*; these appeared to him, on the contrary, to result from corporeal movements that placed the individual, whether he knew it or not, under constant physical constraint." Hobbes's materialism was in fact, however, far less 'mechanistic' than that of Descartes, and its ultimate function in

Hobbes's thought was to provide the basis for a compelling conception of obligation, which is to say, precisely *moral* constraint.

We can understand Hobbes's denial of free will as an important step in the vindication and articulation of real human freedom, only if we grasp the foundation which Hobbes secured for morality as well as for science in his physiological psychology of sense experience. The point of departure in Hobbes's theory is his understanding of *conatus,* of sensation and understanding, of desire and willing, as aspects of the "passive power" of the human mind, namely a capacity to be moved, which corresponds to an agent's capacity to move in the transitive sense. In voluntary action man becomes an agent, and Hobbes generally defines freedom as the absence of external restraints on such action.

As chapters 9 and 10 of *De Corpore,* "Of Cause and Effect" and "Of Power and Act," make clear, the requisite passive power or "power of the patient" is fully as necessary to any plenary or sufficient cause as the "power of the agent" which acts upon the patient, in our case, on the sentient subject. Free will in the sense of a volition without an adequate plenary or moving cause is, for Hobbes, simply an impossibility, a contradiction in terms. Through his psychological conception of *conatus,* 'endeavor' or urge, Hobbes is able to treat volitional or motive impulses as caused without assuming that such causation must lead to action. The perspective of *conatus* allows for an analysis of the process of willing in terms of infinitesimal and incremental components, and this offers a precise analogy to the contribution of Hobbes's concept of *conatus* in the analysis of external motion, his elaboration of Galilean mechanics that anticipated the development of infinitesimal calculus in Newton and Leibniz.

Writing to Landois on June 29, 1756, Diderot attributes the idea or illusion of free will to a natural habit of confusing the voluntary and the free.[18] For him too, denial of free will is a denial neither of the reality of will, nor, strictly speaking, of freedom, but simply a denial that the will can act from indeterminacy. Such gratuitous action, or freedom from all determining causation including that of rational motivation, would be destructive of all morality. This is the argument presented repeatedly by Hobbes. In his controversy with Bishop

Bramhall, beginning with "Of Liberty and Necessity," Hobbes maintained

> he is *free* to do a thing, that may do it if he have the will to do it, and may forbear, if he have the will to forbear. . . . The question therefore is not, whether a man be a *free agent,* that is to say, whether he can write or forbear, speak or be silent according to his *will;* but, whether the *will* to write, and the *will* to forbear, come upon him according to his will.[19] . . . it is the *consultation* that *causeth* a man, and *necessitateth* him to choose to do one thing rather than another. . . . and therefore consultation is not in vain, and indeed the less in vain by how much the election is more necessitated.[20]

Although Hobbes characteristically speaks of 'freedom' only in the sense of absence of external impediment to action, in this latter passage he clearly refers to what we could consider 'freedom' and relates it to the objective adequacy of motivation, that is, the degree to which an action is motivated by deliberation or consultation based on knowledge.

It is essential to any grasp of the continuity from Hobbes to the Enlightenment to understand the fundamental role he claims for empirical psychology. As the final item of the concluding section of his essay "Of Liberty and Necessity," under the heading "My Reasons," Hobbes writes with regard to "what liberty is":

> . . . there can no other proof be offered but every man's own experience, by reflection on himself, and remembering what he useth in his mind, that is, what he himself meaneth when he saith an action is *spontaneous,* a man *deliberates,* such as his *will,* that *agent* or that *action* is *free.* Now he that reflecteth so on himself, cannot but be satisfied, that deliberation is the consideration of the good and evil sequels of an action to come; that by spontaneity is meant inconsiderate [i.e. unpremeditated] action. . . . that will is the last act of our deliberation; that a free agent is he that can do if he will, and forbear if he will; and that liberty is the absence of external impediments. But to those that out of custom speak not what they conceive, but what they hear, and are not able, or will not take the pains to consider what they think when they hear such words, no argument can be sufficient, because experience and matter of fact are not verified by other men's arguments, but by every man's own sense and memory.[21]

The reference to his own inner experience, the appeal to that of the reader, and their possible consensus, is wholly characteristic of Hobbes, as the conclusion of the Introduction to *Leviathan,* the "Author's Epistle to the Reader" in *De Corpore* and the "Author's Preface to the Reader" in *De Cive* show. Fundamental to Hobbes's *empirical* psychology is this methodological recourse to self-consciousness, that is, to the awareness and analysis of inner experience. Consciousness is taken as the awareness in and of inner experience, much as in the passage quoted above from Newton's *regulae philosophandi,* which is to say, consciousness is expressly not taken as self-contained *cogito.*

That this methodological recourse to inner experience is taken above in the context of an argument for moral determinism should suggest that Hobbes intends no levelling of consciousness or will to mere epiphenomena of a "merely physical" universe. On the contrary, only from such a position, a non-dogmatic, psychologically self-aware materialism, can the reality, not only of drives, impulses and desires, but of motives and ideas, be grasped in a way that makes them more than epiphenomenal. To insist on their reality simply on the grounds of their immediacy "to consciousness," within the unextended substance of a *cogito* cut loose from practical life and reality by a stoic and sceptic *epochē,* is ultimately a self-defeating approach in which the supposedly immanent ideas would never be able to exert their influence intelligently in interaction with the 'extended' world, including one's body. This is particularly the case since that extended substance is to be thought of in terms of a far more reductive materialism that allows only for mechanical causes.

Vartanian has invoked Hobbes at the outset of his paper as a "mechanical materialist" whose "politics turned out to be of a piece with his vision of a human nature ruled by necessity; for there, too, 'freedom' became an idle word, and all political events, whether tending toward order or disorder in the state, were seen as determined by the relative strengths of competing 'bodies' in collective 'motion'." This seems to me to mistake Hobbes's diagnosis, or a parody of it, for a proposed solution and to ignore his constructive political thought altogether. Whatever the virtues of the implicit definition of 'liberalism', it is not legitimate to relate Hobbes to the "totalitarianizing behaviorism" of Helvétius as a foil for liberal political doctrines connected with the man-machine which Vartanian sees not only in La Mettrie but in Diderot.

There is nothing unique or anomalous about the combination of a commitment to human science in materialist terms and a concern for human self-determination in Diderot. Just this combination is to be found in Hobbes and, if we dig a little deeper, in Bacon. By conceding the framework of his argument to the widespread misapprehension of an inherent conflict between materialism or scientific determinism and the interests of human freedom—which he terms "our expectations of coherence" and a "normal paradigm"—Vartanian comes close to undermining his own central and well-taken point.

I have suggested that Hobbes's materialism is not mechanistic. This is as evident in his science of body as in that of man, both being built up from his conception of *conatus.* Although Descartes' *Traité des passions de l'âme* involves the affirmation of a fundamental integration of body and mind, which brings him closer to Hobbes than elsewhere, it was precisely the virtue of Cartesian materialism that it could afford to be rigorously reductive on a mechanist model because 'thinking substance' had been separated out and secured from the start.

But Hobbesian materialism had to deal with the workings of human impulse and thought at every stage, rendering his doctrine of body essentially epistemological in its basic character. Motion, for Hobbes, was philosophically conceived in terms of the ability to act, to have an effect. It was no less appropriate to the analysis of 'inner motions', motives and emotions, than to external, and Hobbes in fact showed that Galilean mechanics, with its introduction of the principle of inertia, had overcome the limitations of Aristotelian-scholastic mechanics by including in the analysis of motion an intensive factor that was not evident to the eye, but was experienced as impact or resistance to effort. In other words, our construction of external motions depended, instinctively and for an adequate natural science, on the extrapolation of the experience of resistance and effort from our awareness of inner experience.

Experientially, internal motions are more immediate (as we recognize only on reflection) than external motion. The motions of the mind must be caused, that is, provoked or called forth, by external motions but cannot be reduced to their level. They can be construed in terms of the operations of causality, but not of the same sort of causes as are appropriate to merely physical motion. The development of an organicist materialism which starts from irritibility or sensitivity is anticipated with far greater consistency in Hobbes's conception of *conatus* than in anything in Descartes, which is not to say, however, that such materialism is necessarily an improvement on Hobbes.

The constraints exercised by Vartanian's view that the materialism of the French Enlightenment derived primarily from Descartes are clear where he writes, "La Mettrie, Diderot, and D'Holbach, theorizing perforce within the limits urged on them by a dualist background, were left with no alternative but to reject the soul and to construe the psyche on the analogy of a machine. This, of course, entailed moral determinism." In fact, the moral determinism, at least of Diderot, could not have arisen on the foundation of a truncated Cartesianism in which only the material half remained from the dualism of substances. On the contrary, Diderot's materialism involves a repudiation of Cartesian dualism.

This is not to dispute the many instances of Descartes' influence, which Vartanian himself, in *Diderot and Descartes,* shows to have been made possible by Descartes' own inconsistencies and by creative misinterpretation on the part of the later materialists. But it should serve to suggest that we must not start by simply excluding the possible fundamental influence of a Hobbes, which would have offered affinities at a more basic level. To claim that no thinker of that time, including Hobbes, "had expressed, with the pertinence and effectiveness of Descartes, the ideological composite that was to comprise the very core of Diderot's attitudes,"[22] seems to me inappropriate.

It is a valuable contribution of Vartanian to have called attention to the rich possibilities of Cartesian materialism, particularly in its anticipations of a developmental or organic materialism.[23] Together with closer study of *Les Passions de l'âme* and the 'animal spirits' physiology of *De l'homme,* this aspect of *Le Monde* may eventually lead us to revise our conceptions both of the rationalist idealism of the *cogito* and of the mechanical materialism projected onto the extended world, disturbing the comfort of their discrete dualist coexistence. This would in effect show Descartes to be much closer to Hobbes than most of their readers (including Hobbes and Descartes, respectively) have imagined.

As Diderot wrote of Hobbes in volume VIII of the *Encylopédie,* most of those who cannot hear his name without shuddering have not read a page of his works and would scarcely be able to. Well into the eighteenth century people had a number of reasons for being unwilling to mention the name of Hobbes in a favorable context, and this makes an assessment of his not only provocative but positive influence difficult. That Descartes read him, and shuddered, and that Diderot read him, with sympathetic insight, and with profit for his own moral psychology, is evident. Hobbes is a legitimate forebear of Diderot's materialism, and perhaps, as well, of Newton's.

NOTES

1 *Issac Newton's Papers and Letters on Natural Philosophy and related documents,* ed. I. Bernard Cohen, assisted by Robert E. Schofield, with explanatory prefaces by Marie Boas, Charles Coulson Gillispie, Thomas S. Kuhn, and Perry Miller (Cambridge, Mass.: Harvard Univ. Press, 1958), p. 303. See Miller's remark, pp. 277f.

2 Quoted in Alexandre Koyré, *Newtonian Studies* (Chicago: Univ. of Chicago Press, Phoenix paperback ed., 1968), p. 62.

3 Beyond the second chapter in Koyré, *Newtonian Studies,* see I. Bernard Cohen, "Hypothesis in Newton's Philosophy," in *Boston Studies in the Philosophy of Science,* 5 (1969), 304–26, which grew out of his collaboration with Koyré in editing a "sort of variorum *Principia*."

4 John Dewey, in *The Quest for Certainty* (New York: G. P. Putnam, Capricorn paperback ed., 1960), makes this fundamental point very well.

5 Robert E. Schofield, *Mechanism and Materialism: British Natural Philosophy in An Age of Reason* (Princeton: Princeton Univ. Press, 1970), pp. 20f.

6 *Issac Newton's Papers and Letters on Natural Philosophy,* p. 280. Subsequent page references to this volume will be inserted in the text.

7 The recent publication of Thomas Hobbes, *Thomas White's* De Mundo *Examined* (London: Bradford Univ. Press, 1976), translated by Harold Whitmore Jones from the manuscript discovered and edited by Jean Jacquot, offers a rich new resource for study of this aspect of Hobbes. See pp. 38, 46, 54, 162f., 306–8, 346f., 385, 400f., 434, 443–45, 489f. At the conclusion of a discussion of gravity, p. 127, Hobbes writes, "So it seems to me, at any rate, to be impossible to describe

these motions of the parts in different kinds of bodies, i.e. to expose fully the nature of gravity." And he characteristically makes remarks such as this, p. 48, regarding the causes of rarity and density: "I myself affirm nothing, for I prefer ignorance to error." This does not mean he thinks an advance of knowledge in that particular field is impossible, but rather than it will be encouraged less by the dogmatic elaboration of conjectural constructions than by working from what we know. Cf. p. 87. This reservation vis-à-vis what he sees as metaphysical explanation is closely linked to the radical disjunction of scientific reasoning from matters of faith: ". . . the present world has been created in order that we may demonstrate *its own qualities* and those of its parts. And would that we were satisfied with this, and did not also proceed to demonstrate the properties of God himself" (p. 395).

8 In his *History of England* Hume makes the following comparison: "Boyle was a great partisan of the mechanical philosophy; a theory which, by discovering some of the secrets of nature, and allowing us to imagine the rest, is so agreeable to the natural vanity and curiosity of men. . . . While Newton seemed to draw off the veil from some of the mysteries of nature, he shewed at the same time the imperfections of the mechanical philosophy; and thereby restored her ultimate secrets to that obscurity in which they ever did and ever will remain." Quoted from Norman Kemp Smith, *The Philosophy of David Hume* (New York: St. Martin's Press, 1966), p. 52.

9 Newton, *Mathematical Principles of Natural Philosophy,* trans. Andrew Motte and rev. Florian Cajori (Berkeley: Univ. of California Press, paperback ed., 1966), II, 547.

10 Quoted by Koyré, *Newtonian Studies,* p. 93, from *Unpublished Scientific Papers of Isaac Newton,* ed. A. Rupert Hall and Marie Boas Hall (Cambridge: Cambridge Univ. Press, 1962), pp. 107f. See also the passage from the concluding pages of the *Opticks* quoted by Koyré, p. 109, from the *Opticks* (New York: Dover, 1952); cf. p. 403, relating the "active principles" of the universe, such as gravity, to the "powerful ever-living agent Who being in all places is more able by His will to move the bodies within His boundless uniform *Sensorium* and thereby to form and reform the parts of the Universe, than we are by our will to move the parts of our own bodies." Newton has explained, *Opticks,* pp. 401f., that he considers these principles "not as occult Qualities, supposed to result from the specifick Forms of Things, but as general Laws of Nature, by which the Things themselves are form'd; their Truth appearing to us by Phaenomena, though their Causes be not yet discover'd. For these are manifest Qualities, and their Causes only are occult. . . . And therefore I scruple not to propose the Principles of Motion abovemention'd . . . and leave their Causes to be found out."

11 Koyré, *Newtonian Studies,* p. 272, cf. p. 110. For its critique of Cartesian 'phenomenology' and its affinity to the materialism which Hobbes grounded in empirical psychology, the passage is worth quoting in full:

> Rule V. Whatever is not derived from things themselves, whether by the external senses or by the sensation of internal thoughts, is to be taken for a hypothesis. Thus I sense that I am thinking, which could not happen unless at the same time I were to sense that I am. But I do not sense that any idea

whatever may be innate. And I do not take for a phenomenon only that which is made known to us by the five external senses, but also that which we contemplate in our minds when thinking: such as, I am, I believe, I understand, I remember, I think, I am unwilling, I am thirsty, I am hungry, I rejoice, I suffer, etc. And those things which neither can be demonstrated from the phenomenon nor follow from it by the argument in induction, I hold as hypotheses.

12 The influence of Hobbes can be shown (above all through Schopenhauer) on those thinkers most responsible for the conceptual dissolution of the mechanicism and eventually the mechanics of the Newtonian 'paradigm', namely Helmholtz and then Mach.

13 Vartanian, "Trembley's Polyp, La Mettrie and Eighteenth-Century French Materialism," reprinted from the *Journal of the History of Ideas* in *Roots of Scientific Thought,* ed. Philip P. Wiener and Aaron Noland (New York: Basic Books, 1957), p. 505.

14 Diderot, *Oeuvres philosophiques* (Paris: Garnier, n.d.), pp. 362f. My own translation. In his notes, at this point, Paul Vernière remarks that much of this passage was reworked in Diderot's *Eléments de physiologie,* which may serve as a provisional justification for treating Bordeu as a vehicle of Diderot's own ideas in this passage.

15 Hobbes, *Leviathan,* ch. VI, in the edition of C. B. Macpherson (Baltimore: Penguin Books, 1968), p. 127. There are significant passages on 'deliberation' in Hobbes, *Thomas White's* De Mundo *Examined,* pp. 380ff., 386, 408, 447f., 452f.

16 See the seminal 'short treatise' of the 1630s, reprinted in Hobbes, *Body, Man, and Citizen,* ed. Richard S. Peters (New York: Collier Books, 1962) under the title "First Principles of Sense and Animal Motion," esp. pp. 177–80. In *Thomas White's* De Mundo *Examined,* p. 439, Hobbes relates the principles referred to in n. 7 above to the 'efficient cause' of sensation, desire, and willing: "God performs all natural actions, the voluntary no less than the involuntary, by means of second causes, namely the bodies constituting the universe. Therefore all actions should be equally pre-exist in second causes, and hence the appetites of animals, i.e. the wishes of men, should also possess their own causes composed of the gathering together of everything requisite to volition. That is, appetites should necessarily originate in second causes, be these animate or not-animate." This makes possible the definition of any *bonum* or *finis,* even an inanimate object, as the agent whose action constitutes desire and leads to voluntary and purposive action of the part of the subject.

17 Hobbes, *Body, Man, and Citizen,* pp. 237f.

18 Quoted in the notes to Diderot, *Oeuvres philosophiques,* p. 363.

19 *Body, Man, and Citizen,* p. 245.

20 Ibid., p. 256.

21 Ibid., pp. 271f.

22 *Diderot and Descartes* (Princeton: Princeton Univ. Press, 1953), p. 292. Cf. p. 316, claiming that both sought "a moral liberty subjective to man in the midst of an objective determinism."

23 See *Diderot and Descartes,* pp. 294f. When Vartanian contrasts the Cartesian speculations to Hobbes's position, as a consideration which serves "to relegate the influence of the English atheist to a secondary, and even peripheral, place," he misconstrues the attitude which was exemplified above (see n. 7), writing, p. 294, "Hobbes made no attempt to deduce from physical causation the emergence of the universe out of an initial chaos, but was satisfied to adhere, on that basic point, to the view of *Genesis.*" This was not simply the piety of an "atheist" but scientific scruple at work. The theme of organic development is certainly relevant to Diderot's differences with Helvétius, but its relation to the question of free will vs. 'moral determinism' is oblique at best. Diderot was arguing, against Helvétius' assumptions of the total uniformity and malleability of human nature, for the inclusion of biological as well as environmental factors in a more complicated, yet integral, complex of causation. The issue of totalitarianism seems also to be hardly pertinent here. In the denial of 'free will' in the interest of a better understanding of human willing and thus in the interest of the improvement and better use of freedom, Diderot follows no one more closely than Hobbes.

Hume's Conservatism

DONALD W. LIVINGSTON

Hume's political philosophy has generally been recognized as a form of conservatism, but its precise nature has yet to be stated. In this paper, I shall attempt a description of Hume's conservatism, the place it has in the history of conservatism, and how it is logically connected to his main philosophical doctrines of knowledge and existence.

I

The first barrier to appreciating Hume's conservatism is the term 'conservatism' itself. Partisan concepts like "liberalism," "conservatism," "Marxism," and "Christianity" are notoriously difficult to analyze not only because they have a history which changes but because they are *partisan* concepts, the understanding of which can hardly be free of value judgments. In understanding such terms, we must take account of what partisans think they mean by them as well as what the terms may be taken to mean on the basis of what partisans have actually done. To appreciate a partisan concept, then, we must take up both an internal partisan point of view and an external evaluative point of view. The difficulty in achieving a just appreciation of such concepts lies not so much in making the value judgment appropriate to the external point of view but in taking account of the partisan point of view. Conservatism more than other partisan concepts has not been appreciated from the internal point of view perhaps because, unlike other partisan concepts, it does not bear its minimal meaning on its face. The term 'Marxism', whatever it may mean, has to do with the teachings of Marx, 'Christianity' with the teachings of Christ, and 'liberalism' with a doctrine of liberty. But the term 'conservatism' appears to be vacuous, suggesting no substantial idea. It is for this reason, perhaps, that 'conservatism' is usually defined as an attitude or disposition: a conservative is one who has a disposition to defend the status quo and to look with suspicion on any significant change in the social and political order. But this definition applies to any ideology whatsoever: Marxists and Liberals in power, for instance, have a disposition to defend the status quo and to look with suspicion on any *significant* change in the going social and political order. Moreover, the history of self-professed conservatives shows that they are guided by a body of ideas and that they are capable of reformist and even radical action. So to appreciate the conservative mind and how Hume is connected to it, we must try to understand the ideas which conservatives think guide their own thought and action.

I shall begin with a statement by a contemporary Austrian conservative, Erik von Kuehnelt-Leddihn, who views conservatism as a resistance to what J. L. Talmon has called "totalitarian democracy," a turn of mind that it is convenient to date with the French Revolution. Kuehnelt-Leddihn writes:

> . . . the roots of the evil are historically-genetically the same all over the Western World. The fatal year is 1789, and the symbol of iniquity is the Jacobin Cap. Its heresy is the denial of personality and of personal liberty. Its concrete realizations are Jacobin mass democracy, all forms of national collectivism and statism, Marxism producing socialism and communism, fascism, and national socialism, leftism in all its modern guises and manifestations to which in America the good term "liberalism," perversely enough, is being applied.[1]

Although this particular manifestation of the conservative mind is shaped by twentieth-century conditions, it is essentially the mind of Edmund Burke who is usually considered the founder of modern conservatism. Conservatism so understood contains two important features: (1) it is a *historical* conception based on a doctrine of catastrophe, the fatal event being the French Revolution and the movements to which it allegedly gave rise. So conceived, conservatism is not a perennial outlook on things. It is a historically limited movement that appears on the scene only to combat a certain sort of enemy and to defend a certain sort of value; (2) conservatives have been clear about who the enemy is. Burke attacked the "adulterated metaphysics" of the Enlightenment which he thought informed the French Revolution.[2] This is paralleled by Hegel's rejection of the "alienated reason" and "absolute freedom" of the French Revolution and by Metternich's condemnation of "presumptuous man" who by reason alone seeks to understand and to reconstruct the foundations of social and political order.[3] Thus conservatives, from the first, were not so much concerned to defend the *ancien régime* as to rebut a certain sort of intellectual error which they saw as a threat to *any* legitimate social and political order whatsoever. It is for this reason that one can speak of a substantial conservative intellectual tradition.

Hume, of course, died prior to the French Revolution, and so it may appear improper to characterize him as a conservative. But since conservatism is mainly a criticism of certain *ideas* leading up to and following the French Revolution, Hume may be thought of as part of the conservative movement in so far as he identified those ideas and dealt with them in a characteristically conservative way. Indeed, Hume may be thought of as the first to give a *philosophic* defense of conservatism. Most conservatives have been either literary men, such as Johnson, Coleridge, and Eliot, or statesmen-philosophers, such as Burke, Metternich, and Disraeli. Excluding Hume and with the exception of Hegel (whose work, quite easily, can and has been put to revolutionary ends) there has been no deep philosophic articulation of the conservative view. For this reason, perhaps, conservatism is usually viewed as an anti-intellectual, anti-philosophical position. In Hume's philosophy, however, we find a conceptual structure designed to rebut revolutionary thought and capable of explaining in broad outline the conservative view of legitimate social and political order. This was dimly recognized by some of the first conservatives in France after the

Revolution who, as Professor Bongie has shown, took Hume's *History of England* and his political essays as founding documents of the Counter-Revolution.[4]

Conservatives agree that the common disaster is the intrusion of rationalistic metaphysics into the social and political affairs of common life. But they have disagreed on the precise nature of this error. In what follows, I shall give a general characterization of this alleged error, how Hume identified it, how he dealt with it, and how his position is different from most forms of conservatism. We shall see that Hume's critique of metaphysics in common life eliminates not only revolutionary thinking but most forms of conservatism as well.

II

The kind of revolutionary thinking which Burke thought he recognized in the French Revolution is a *total* rejection of existing social and political order. This total alienation is to be found in Rousseau's dictum that "Man is born free but everywhere he is in chains."[5] And later in Charles Fourier's condemnation of reform: "The vice of our so-called reformers is to indict this or that defect, instead of indicting civilization as a whole, inasmuch as it is nothing but a vicious circle of evil in all its parts; one must get out of this hell."[6] Bruno Bauer, a left-wing Hegelian, called for a "revolution against everything positive" and for the "terrorism of the true theory."[7] Later Marx was to say that revolutionary thinking is not directed against any "wrong in particular" but against "wrong in general."[8] And more recently, Herbert Marcuse, echoing the same pattern of thought, writes that "the true positive is the society of the future and therefore beyond definition and determination, while the existing positive is that which must be surmounted."[9] Albert Camus has aptly called this kind of a priori total criticism "metaphysical rebellion."[10] We must now determine the philosophical roots of such thinking.

It is convenient to begin with Descartes' conception of reason, which entails two principles, a methodological one and an ontological one. I shall begin with the methodological principle. To think rationally, we must treat as false all former opinions until it can be shown that they are, in some way, self-evidently true. Since few, if any, historical, social, and political norms are self-evident, this conception of reason requires that all existing social and political norms be treated as false. Descartes confined this method mainly to physics, mathematics, and metaphysics, but he presented it as a general feature of reason. And it was not long before thinkers such as Meslier, Morelley, and Mably began to apply its revolutionary consequences to affairs of common life.[11] What is important about this conception of reason and what has survived is not the criterion of truth as self-evidence, but the method of doubt: the methodological presumption that all former beliefs are false unless certified by something called reason. Bentham, for instance, did not accept the Cartesian doctrine of clear and distinct ideas, but he is still following the Cartesian method when he says that "Rude establishments" must be brought "to the test of polished reason."[12] And Marx is following the same principle when he writes in a letter to Ruge, "what we . . . have to achieve . . . is the ruthless criticism of all that exists. . . . Reason has always existed, but not always in reasonable form."[13]

Descartes' method can be stated as the maxim *dubito ut intelligam* which is contrary to the Augustinian and medieval maxim *credo ut intelligam.* Hume's conception of reason reflects something of the Augustinian principle, for it is tied essentially to a philosophy of *belief.* The sceptical ordeal at the end of Book I of the *Treatise* ends with an "indolent belief in the general maxims of the world," as a condition for understanding anything.[14] Of course once we have understanding, we may use it to modify the maxims of common life, but we can never rationally criticize the set as a whole. Philosophy for Hume and, hence, reason in its deepest sense is "nothing but the reflections of common life, methodized and corrected."[15] Hume and Descartes both hold that scepticism is internal to rational method, but they disagree on the function they give to scepticism. Descartes uses it as a way of purging thought of the prejudices of common life on behalf of theoretical and metaphysical certainty. Hume uses it to purge thought of metaphysical illusions on behalf of the lucidity of common life. If it is true that the philosophical ground for metaphysical rebellion was first sketched out in the *Discourse on Method,* it is also true that the philosophical ground for the corresponding counter-revolution was first sketched out in Book I of the *Treatise.*

The ontological principle entailed in Descartes' conception of reason can best be seen in his analysis of how knowledge of the physical world is possible. Like Galileo, Descartes believed that Nature is a book "written in the language of mathematics" and that physicists know the world through this special language.[16] Parallel to the theoretical language of physics is sensory language which, according to Descartes, is often confused with it. To say of a piece of wax that *it* has the sensory properties of yellow and sweetness is a mistake since sensory objects are private mental entities. Wax as it really is has only theoretical properties which are *logically* unobservable. Since in common life we invariably predicate sensory properties of material things, the sensory language of common life *as a whole* is illusory. Hume aptly called this the doctrine of "double existence" (a doctrine he did not share), which has continued down to our own time.[17] In a famous passage Sir Arthur Eddington explains that he is sitting down to *two* tables: one is the richly colored table of common life, the other is the table described by theoretical physics and having no sensory properties. Only the latter table is real, the table of common life being a "strange compound of external nature, mental imagery and inherited prejudice."[18] The doctrine of double existence is not simply a conclusion Descartes reached in his analysis of theoretical physics; it is entailed in his conception of reason: to understand anything, we must give two *prima facie* incompatible descriptions of it—an ordinary description from the language of common life and a theoretical description. Of Sir Arthur Eddington's table, we shall have to say both that it has color and that it has no color. The contradiction is avoided by *ontologizing* the theoretical description and declaring the ordinary description to be an illusory identification. But while there is no contradiction, there surely is a paradox, for we shall now have to say such things as "The brown table we see really has no color."

Applying this conception of theoretical reason to existing social and political norms yields paradoxical statements of the same type. Rousseau's dictum that man is born free but everywhere is in chains is parallel to Sir Arthur Eddington's invisible table that lies before our very eyes. There are two societies: the *natural* society discovered by theoretical reason and misidentified with the existing *historical* society of common life which is thought of as a total illusion. Similarly, Proudhon's statement that "Property is robbery" describes two systems of property relations: a self-evident theoretical system which alone is real and misidentified with the existing system of common life, which is illusory as a whole.[19] The habit of ontologizing theoretical language is deeply ingrained in modern philosophy and seems required by the concept of reason itself. It can lead to a profound alienation not only from the tables and chairs of common life but from its social and political norms as well. And when this occurs the mind is conceptually ready for metaphysical rebellion which must now appear as a demand of reason itself.

III

It is easy to confuse the modern doctrine of double existence with *idealism*. Plato, for instance, also conceived of society in two ways: the existing society and the Ideal of a Just Society. One might easily suppose, then, that Rousseau in the statement above is talking about the ideal of a natural society and that Proudhon is simply talking about an ideal for property relations. But this is mistaken twice over. First, Platonic Ideals and similar transcendent entities such as Natural Law and Kant's Categorical Imperative are not ontologically part of the world of facts they judge. Thus, although a historical society is a fact in the world, the Platonic Ideal of Justice is not another fact in the world but is a standard for measuring the success or failure with respect to justice of any existing society. Transcendent entities of this sort do not imply that the existing society is illusory as a whole but only that it may have failed in certain ways to have reached as high a degree of justice as possible. Transcendent standards, therefore, both affirm the reality of existing societies and make criticism of them possible. Second, the doctrine of double existence eliminates transcendent entities, entailing that the standard of judgment and the thing judged are *both* facts in the world. Thus theoretically conceived tables are simply facts in the world, and colors are simply private mental entities, also facts in the world. But the theoretical facts alone are judged to be real, which entails that the other set of facts are unreal as a class. Thus Rousseau's claim is not that it is a natural ideal that man should be born free; he is claiming that man is *in fact* born free but is artificially and, perhaps, perversely enslaved by historical society. Similarly, Marx is not saying that existing property relations fail to satisfy an ideal; he is saying that the right system of property relations is a *fact* locked into the class struggle, the outcome of which can be known with certainty through the science of dialectical materialism. Indeed, to talk of the "right set of property relations" is merely to talk about the set that is known to be *in fact* inevitable. (This is part of what is meant by saying that Marxism is scientific and not utopian.) There is nothing odd, of course, in taking one fact in the world to be a standard for judging other facts. The length of one's hand can be a standard of a system of measurement, but such standards are always recognized to be arbitrary and must be justified on pragmatic grounds. However, metaphysical rebels have not thought that the theoretical facts they have taken as standards are arbitrary and must be judged pragmatically; rather they have taken them as standards because they are thought to be *reality,* and they are thought to be reality because they are known through something called reason. And, as we have seen, the conception of reason can vary. For thinkers like Rousseau and Proudhon, the natural order of society is judged to be real because it satisfies the demands of reason, presumably viewed as self-evidence.[20] For Marx, reason is framed in the science of dialectical materialism.

In rejecting the Cartesian conception of reason, Hume also rejects the doctrine of double existence and with it the ontological alienation of reason from common life. At the end of the *Treatise,* Book I, he concludes that by a physical object we must mean what "any common man means by a hat or shoe," thus purging theoretical language of any ontological status.[21] Hume recognized that our basic common beliefs about the world (belief in the causal principle and in the existence of natural objects) are paradoxical. The most reason can do is point out the paradoxical character of our common beliefs, their natural necessity, and the futility and, hence, absurdity of ontologizing theoretical language. The Humean conception of reason, therefore, entails only that our common beliefs as a whole are *paradoxical*; it does not entail that they are *illusory.*[22]

What holds here for common judgments about the physical world holds also for common judgments about the moral world. What we must mean by social and political norms are basically what any common man in an actual society means by them. Thus, theft turns out to be not a metaphysical concept as it is for Proudhon, but simply taking someone's property, and there are no special *philosophical* problems in determining ownership. Such judgments, in particular, can always be modified by changing circumstances and reflection, but this can be done only by affirming as a whole an existing order of social and political norms. Hume did not, however, hold that all norms are historically immanent; his moral philosophy requires that in making judgments about the wrongness of acts in society, we assume the disciplined position of a disinterested ideal spectator. Moral norms, then, for Hume, transcend the world. In this his position is like the older philosophical tradition that posited the existence of transcendent entities such as Platonic Ideals, Natural Law, and God's Will as standards for judging the world. But Hume differs from this tradition in holding that moral norms have no ontological status: they are all abstractions from existing social and political norms. And on this point turns a great difference between Hume's conservatism and other forms. From the beginning, most conservatives sought to rebut metaphysical rebellion by instituting what might be called *metaphysical conservatism.* While agreeing that reform can go on *within* an existing social and political order, metaphysical conservatives hold that the order as a whole is certified by Divine Providence and cannot be criticized without implying a rebellion against God. Thus Samuel Johnson could say that "the Devil was the first Whig,"[23] and De-Maistre saw the entrance of Cartesian reason into politics as an instance of the "ferocious and rebellious pride" of the "intellectuals" whose "insolent doctrines . . . judge God without ceremony."[24] Burke interpreted the norms of historical society as the work of a "mysterious wisdom,"[25] and Coleridge taught that the first duty of the state is to make men "soberly and steadily religious."[26] Metaphysical conservatives, then, sought to do two things: (1) to limit the pretensions of reason to discern the foundations of social and political order and to construct it anew, and (2) to give historical society a transcendent, theological ground. Hume follows them in the first project, but the sceptical method he uses to accomplish it entails the elimination of the second project, that is, the elimination of any metaphysical ground for historical society whether sacred or secular: "the political interests of Society . . . [have no] connexion with the philosophical disputes concerning metaphysics and religion."[27]

It is perhaps worthwhile to point out, in passing, the close conceptual ties that exist between metaphysical rebellion and metaphysical conservatism. Descartes' revolutionary conception of reason was grounded on the supposition that the world just might be the creation of a perverse God; he eventually concluded, of course, that this supposition is false, but he still held that unless God exists and is not a deceiver, reason has no ground.[28] So Descartes' metaphysical rebellion ends in metaphysical conservatism, but it need not. Everything depends on establishing the crucial theological premise. The frame of mind here is well expressed in Ivan Karamazov's judgment that "if God does not exist, everything is permitted."[29] And it is a frame of mind to be found also in Marx's description of his own revolutionary thinking: "Thus the criticism of heaven is transformed into the criticism of earth, the *criticism of religion* into the *criticism of law,* and the *criticism of theology* into the *criticism of politics.*"[30] Marx has here tied his program for the metaphysical critique of existing society to the falsity of certain theological propositions. Should those propositions be true, metaphysical rebellion would be unjustified. Thus metaphysical revolution not only prompts metaphysical conservatism but logically feeds upon it and is the antagonistic reflection of it. Hume's conservatism, however, is not the result of any theistic or atheistic vision of the world; it is grounded in a purely philosophical analysis of the ideas of meaning, knowledge, and existence which, if sound, is compatible with theism or atheism. I shall briefly try to show how this is so.

IV

Hume's deepest philosophical doctrine is his theory of meaning, which is that all our simple ideas are derived from representative past impressions and that complex ideas are formed by natural associations of these simple ideas in the imagination. With the possible exception of Berkeley, Hume was the first philosopher to apply, systematically, a theory of meaning to philosophical problems. Prior to Hume, philosophical statements had been examined as to their *truth* or *falsity*, but Hume argued that some of the utterances of philosophers are cognitively *meaningless* and so neither true nor false: "What possibility then of answering the question, whether perceptions inhere in a material or immaterial substance, when we do not so much as understand the meaning of the question?"[31] This method of criticizing philosophical theories was exploited by later schools of empiricism, notably phenomenalism, pragmatism, and various forms of logical empiricism. But it is central in understanding Hume's conservatism to appreciate how his theory of meaning differs radically from that of later empiricists.

On Hume's theory, the meaning structure of an idea is at the very least a relation between a *past* and a present existent. Hume's theory takes as primitive the possibility of making true statements about the past. But the main forms of empiricism after Hume have constructed theories of meaning which entail that sentences purportedly about the past are *meaningless*. Phenomenalism ties the meaning of descriptive statements to actual or possible experiences in the *present*.[32] Pragmatism is the doctrine that the meaning of descriptive expressions is grounded in reference to *present* and *future* experiences. C. I. Lewis writes: "To ascribe an objective quality to a thing means implicitly the prediction that if I act in certain ways, specifiable experiences will eventuate," and that the "whole content of our knowledge of reality is the truth of such 'If-then' propositions."[33] If this account is right, then sentences purportedly about the past would have to be either meaningless or recast somehow into sentences about present and future experiences. A recent example of the pragmatic analysis of the idea of the past is Murray Murphy's thesis that "George Washington enjoys at present the epistemological status of an electron: each is an entity postulated for the purpose of giving coherence to our present experience, and each is unobservable by us."[34] Phenomenalism and pragmatism may be read as *tensed* theories of meaning in so far as they typically require the use of tensed expressions. But not all forms of empiricism are tensed. Various forms of logical empiricism explicate descriptive meaning by reference to *tenseless* expressions. Again expressions normally taken to be about the past are either meaningless or must be recast into some tenseless idiom. A. J. Ayer, for instance, once argued that "no sentence as such is about the past," on the ground that all tensed expressions must be reducible to tenseless expressions.[35]

Although quite different in other respects, absolute idealists share with logical empiricists the view that reality can be understood only through tenseless language and that statements purportedly about the past are philosophically defective. Thus Bosanquet thought that history, because it purports to be about the past, is "a hybrid form of experience incapable of any degree of 'being or trueness.'"[36] Similarly Oakeshott writes that "no fact, truth or reality is, or can be past," and that "there are no facts at all which are not present absolutely."[37] More recently, Jack Meiland has defended a version of the idealist view which he calls the "construction" theory of history, which holds that historians should not be thought of as making statements about the past because there is no past reality for their statements to be about. Rather, history is a study of the present understood in a tenseless way, the task of history being "to give a coherent account of the present world as a whole."[38]

We may refer to Hume's theory as a *past-entailing* theory of meaning because it requires that some statement about the past be true as a condition of our having an idea of something. But most important, there is a profound truth locked into Hume's past-entailing theory which is the conceptual foundation for his conservatism. We may begin with a recent criticism of the theory by Jonathan Bennett: "What someone understands now is not logically tied to what he underwent earlier: the account of 'newly born' adults in Shaw's *Back to Methusaleh* is a perfectly consistent fantasy."[39] Behind Bennett's criticism is presumably the view that our understanding of the world is tenseless, so that, even if somehow there were no past, our understanding of things in the present could be logically just as it is. If so, then Hume's past-entailing theory of meaning could throw no light at all on the nature of our concepts. At most, it could be considered an understandable confusion between the logical structure of a concept and its history. Now there certainly are concepts which support this criticism. Bennett's example is the possibility of "a newly born adult," that is, a being with no past but having all the observation and disposition properties of what would normally be called an adult man along with perhaps a coherent set of thoughts about his past all of which are false. Such a being is possible because "is a man" is an atemporal concept which does not require the truth of any statement about the past as a condition for its application to present existence. Much of our thinking about the world is through atemporal concepts such as "is red," "is elastic," "is a person," "is a house," and so on. There is no contradiction in holding that such concepts can apply to present existences even though no sentence about the past is true or even intelligible. But not all concepts are of this type: "is a nephew," "is a U.S. Senator," "is a friend," "is a priest," "is a Rembrandt" are concepts which logically cannot be applied to present existences unless certain statements about the past can be true. These we may call past-entailing concepts.

We are now in a position to deal with Bennett's criticism. Shaw's "newly born" adults without a past are logically possible, as is the older story of how God created Adam without a past from the dust of the earth. But not even God could create a nephew or a U.S. Senator without creating also a past of the appropriate length. Ontologically, there cannot *be* any U.S. Senators without a past stretching back at least to 1789 when the U.S. Constitution was ratified, and the concept of a U.S. Senator is unintelligible unless it is possible for sentences purportedly about the past to be true. Now the language of common life, constituting as it does a community of shared judgments, abounds in past-entailing concepts. Indeed, we may say that the language of common life is virtually constituted by past-entailing concepts. It is, of course, true that all past-entailing concepts presuppose atemporal concepts: if *x* is a Senator, then *x* is a man. So the individuals and institutions that make up common life have an atemporal structure, but in our common way of thinking they are of interest to us only under some past-entailing conception of them. And Hume was always one to take seriously our common way of thinking. Whatever difficulties there may be in Hume's theory of meaning, it is the only theory in the empirical tradition (and in most of the idealist tradition) that makes possible an account of the past-entailing character of common language and so in that respect is superior to the alternatives.

Why is Hume's empiricism unique in this regard? One reason is that phenomenalists, pragmatists, and logical empiricists have taken as their paradigm the language of theoretical science, which is not a past-entailing language. Hume is the only empiricist and, indeed, the only major modern philosopher to have made significant contributions to both philosophy and history, and history is written not in the tenseless idiom of theoretical science but in the past-entailing language of common life. As a moral philosopher, Hume's theory of meaning is designed primarily to account for the language of common life, which is why he had to consider references to the past as primitive. But perhaps the most important aspect of the theory is its *narrative* structure. Events take on narrative significance in a story when we view them in the light of temporally later events. To celebrate the birth of a great man, for instance, is to read a meaning into the event which those who lived through it could not have experienced. Similarly, a Humean impression of red on its first appearance is unintelligible; only after it has occurred can we have its idea. So the meaning structure of a simple Humean idea is narrative in form: a past existent is viewed in the light of a later existent which confers narrative significance on it and *because* of that fact is called an idea. Hume's paradigm of the narrative idea (in the case of simple ideas) is the *after-image*, which is a past-entailing concept. Once we have a set of simple narrative ideas we can, by ignoring their temporal features, construct in the standard Humean way an abstract, timeless idea of simple impressions. But our primordial way of understanding the world is narrative. All Humean ideas, therefore, are story-laden. Whether adequate or not, this account of simple ideas shows the lengths to which Hume is prepared to go to found a theory of meaning and understanding on narrative significance.

But as a moral philosopher, he is concerned mainly not with simple ideas but with complex ideas of reflection, and here the narrative paradigm of understanding is more in order. In *Treatise* II, III, VII–VIII, we learn that the self is essentially temporally reflective, being every moment aware of its location in the present and of its relation to ideas of temporally distant objects. The temporally reflective imagination logically weaves the idea of a past existence into the idea of a present existence and the idea of a present existence into the idea of a past existence. In short, the temporally reflective imagination structures the moral world narratively.

Although Hume holds that all our ideas are narratively structured, he does not hold that the existences corresponding to these ideas are narratively structured. The tenseless idea of red (which we abstract from the particular past-entailing idea of red) refers to red things which are conceived to have no tensed properties. Similarly, the abstract idea of time presented in *Treatise* I, II, III refers to a tenseless order of successive objects, and there Hume explicitly holds that real time exists under this tenseless conception of it. Indeed, his view appears to be that the entire physical world is to be thought of as ontologically tenseless. But the case is otherwise with what Hume calls "the moral world." The idea of the moral world is structured by the temporally reflective imagination, which necessarily conceives of objects in relation to the *self's* awareness of its position in tensed time. The conception of moral entities is, therefore, essentially tensed and narrative. And Hume is prepared to ontologize these narrative ideas. Thus corresponding to past-entailing ideas such as "is a Senator," and "is a Tudor Rose" are what we might call past-entailing existences, that is, real Senators and Tudor Roses that have the past built, ontologically, into their present existence. Such entities are real, however, only in the moral world which depends on the mind for its existence, since temporally complex ideas of reflection require reference to the self for their existence. Independent of the temporally reflective self, there are no tensed ideas, no narrative orders of existence, and no moral world.

V

Hume was the first modern philosopher to recognize the structure of metaphysical revolution in modern political parties. He distinguished within political parties those of interest and ambition and those of metaphysical principle. The former are "the most reasonable, and the most excusable." Parties of metaphysical principle, however, are conceptual absurdities and should be rejected a priori. Moreover, they are unique to modern times:

> Parties from *principle,* especially abstract speculative principle, are known only to modern times, and are, perhaps, the most extraordinary and unaccountable phenomenon that has yet appeared in human affairs. Where different principles beget a contrariety of conduct, which is the case with all different political principles, the matter may be more easily explained. . . . But where the difference of principle is attended with no contrariety of action . . . what madness, what fury, can beget such an unhappy and such fatal divisions?[40]

The argument against metaphysics in politics here is the same that Hume has urged elsewhere against metaphysics in general, namely, that contrary metaphysical principles do not entail contrary propositions that can be tested by experience and so are vacuous.

Hume's main examples of metaphysical political parties are religious ones, and his explanation of them is interesting. In barbarous times, before the appearance of philosophy, religious sects consisted mainly of "traditional tales and fictions" which may be different without being contrary and even when contrary:

> . . . every one adheres to the tradition of his own sect, without much reasoning or disputation. But as philosophy was widely spread over the world at the time when Christianity arose, the teachers of the new sect were obliged to form a system of speculative opinions, to divide . . . their articles of faith, and to explain, comment, confute, and defend, with all the subtlety of argument and science. Hence naturally arose keenness in dispute, when the Christian religion came to be split into new divisions and heresies; and this keenness assisted the priests in their policy of begetting a mutual hatred and antipathy among their deluded followers. Sects in philosophy, in the ancient world, were more zealous than parties of religion; but in modern times, parties of religion are more furious and enraged than the most cruel factions that ever arose from interest and ambition.[41]

Not having passed through the French Revolution and later attempts at total revolution, Hume could not have been aware that the same conceptual error that constitutes metaphysical religious parties would later constitute metaphysical secular parties, moving men and armies under such concepts as liberty, equality, and the historical class struggle. But his analysis of the error applies without conceptual remainder to the many secular forms of metaphysical revolution that appeared later. In the *Treatise,* Hume dryly remarked that "errors in religion are dangerous, those in philosophy only ridiculous."[42] But he later recognized in his discussion of Christian political parties that the errors in religion that are dangerous are *philosophic.* Burke saw the French Revolution as a unique intrusion of philosophy into politics and described it as an "armed doctrine." Later Marx was to make explicit the necessity of philosophy in politics: "The philosophers have only *interpreted* the world, in various ways; the point, however, is to *change* it."[43] And again in a letter to Ruge: "Philosophy has become secularized, and . . . the philosophical consciousness itself has been pulled into the torment of struggle not only externally but also internally. . . . what we must achieve is the *ruthless criticism of all that exists,* ruthless also in the sense that criticism does not fear its results and even less so a struggle with the existing powers."[44] By the ruthless criticism of all that exists, Marx meant the *conceptual* destruction of all existing social and political standards, and so by "philosophy," he is committed to a form of thinking which, in effect, embodies (1) the Cartesian method of doubt which requires a presumption against the reality of historical norms as a whole and (2) the doctrine of double existence which entails that those norms are *in fact* unreal, i.e., that they have no legitimate authority.[45] Not only does such thinking render the historical structure of common life illusory, as we have seen, it is *logically* incapable of discriminations between good and evil within that structure. Hume himself at times uses the term 'philosophy' in this negative way, as when he says that "philosophers are apt to bewilder themselves in the subtilty of their speculations; and we have seen some go so far as to deny the reality of all moral distinctions."

Hume argued that the evil done by factions of interest and ambition do not equal that done by the "deluded followers" of parties of religious metaphysical principle. Writing in the twentieth century, Albert Camus makes the same point about *secular* parties of metaphysical principle:

> There are crimes of passion and crimes of logic. . . . We are living in the era of . . . the perfect crime. Our criminals are no longer helpless children who could plead love as their excuse. On the contrary, they are adults, and they have a perfect alibi: philosophy, which can be used for any purpose—even for transforming murderers into judges. . . . In more ingenuous times, when the tyrant razed cities for his own greater glory, when the slave chained to the conqueror's chariot was dragged through the rejoicing streets . . . the mind did not reel before such unabashed crimes, and judgment remained unclouded. But slave camps under the flag of freedom, massacres justified by philanthropy . . . in one sense cripple judgment. On the day when crime dons the apparel of innocence—through a curious transposition peculiar to our times—it is innocence that is called upon to justify itself.[46]

The "curious transposition" of concepts to which Camus refers is not peculiar to the twentieth century. It is a transposition framed in a concept of reason worked out early in the modern period and of which I have taken Descartes' analysis of reason to be the paradigm. It is based on the methodological principle of doubting, a priori, all historical norms and on the doctrine of double existence. It was first identified and systematically challenged by Hume who offered an alternative conception of what it means to reason. Hume's conception of reason is based on a past-entailing theory of concept formation and on a theory of abstract moral ideals. Together they impose a formal limit on what can count as a valid criticism of any existing social and political order. We must first accept as a whole the historical norms internal to any existing society. These norms, in turn, can be criticized by abstract moral norms which both transcend the temporal provinciality of historical norms and are a reflection of them. In this way Humean conservatism makes possible both an affirmation of historical society and a criticism of it.

In this discussion I have tried to fix the general philosophic limits of Hume's conservatism, showing how it is grounded in key doctrines of his epistemology. To this end, no attempt has been made to discuss whatever conservative views Hume may have had regarding concrete political issues such as liberty, authority, political parties, and the like. (The most thorough discussion to date of Hume's views on the political issues of his time is Duncan Forbes, *Hume's Philosophical Politics,* Cambridge, 1975.) The philosophical conservatism I have attributed to Hume is purely *formal* and can be applied as a form of thought to any time and place. Thus Hume's views on particular political issues, whether defensible or not, are inessential features of his conservatism as I have described it. Since Hume's conservatism is formal, it may be easily underrated and considered empty; indeed much of his actual social and political criticism appears to have an air of vacuity about it. His usual method seems to be that of taking an impartial stance between factions, apportioning a fair amount of praise and blame to each side in the hope that impartial reason will prevail. Since in actual political disputes, one can hardly avoid taking sides, Hume's method of criticism appears to be unreal and even hypocritical. Or worse, it may appear the position of a total sceptic who has no convictions and is, amusingly, urging this vacuous position on others. This is how it appeared to Leslie Stephen, who accused Hume of a "cynical conservatism."[47] But what Hume is usually trying to do is to apply his formal conservatism to the issue at hand, and this consists, first, in purging political concepts of metaphysical meanings which always threaten to transform historical political reality into illusions and, second, to exhibit the actual historical norms men think by when they are not deluded by a metaphysical conception of them and, third, to evaluate these norms when necessary by abstract moral ideals. All of this is quite different from not taking a stand on political issues. Indeed, Hume thought that one could not rationally take a stand until this metaphysical cleansing had taken place.

NOTES

1 Erik von Kuehnelt-Liddihn, *Leftism* (New Rochelle: Arlington House, 1974), pp. 11–12.

2 Edmund Burke, *Reflections on the Revolution in France* (New Rochelle: Arlington House), p. 104. Peter Viereck, *Conservatism* (New York: Van Nostrand, 1956), p. 135.

3 G. W. F. Hegel, *The Phenomenology of Mind* (London: Allen and Unwin, 1964), pp. 599–610.
4 Laurence L. Bongie, *David Hume: Prophet of the Counter-Revolution* (Oxford: Clarendon Press, 1965), pp. 125–26.
5 Jean-Jacques Rousseau, *The Social Contract and Discourses* (New York: Everyman, 1950), p. 1.
6 Quoted in Gerhart Niemeyer, *Between Nothingness and Paradise* (Baton Rouge: Louisiana State Univ. Press, 1971), p. 64.
7 Ibid., p. 81.
8 *Marx and Engels, Basic Writings on Politics and Philosophy,* ed. Lewis S. Feuer (Garden City: Anchor Books, 1959), p. 265.
9 Herbert Marcuse, "Repressive Tolerance," in *A Critique of Pure Tolerance,* ed. Robert Paul Wolff (Boston: Beacon Press, 1965), p. 87.
10 Albert Camus, *The Rebel* (New York: Vintage Books, 1956), p. 23.
11 See Niemeyer, Chapter 1.
12 Quoted in Sheldon S. Wolin, "Hume and Conservatism," *The American Political Science Review,* 48 (1954), 1000. According to Mill, it was Bentham's *method,* not his opinions, that constituted the novelty and value of his work: "He begins all his inquiries by supposing nothing to be known on the subject, and reconstructs all philosophy *ab initio,* without reference to his predecessors." *Mill on Bentham and Coleridge,* ed. F. R. Leavis (New York: George W. Stewart, 1950), p. 57. The method described here is clearly Cartesian.
13 *Karl Marx on Revolution,* 13 vols., ed. and trans. Saul K. Padover (New York: McGraw-Hill, 1971), I, 516–17.
14 David Hume, *A Treatise of Human Nature,* ed. L. A. Selby-Bigge (Oxford: Clarendon Press, 1967), p. 269.
15 David Hume, *Enquiries,* ed. L. A. Selby-Bigge (Oxford: Clarendon Press, 1966), p. 162.
16 *The Philosophy of the 16th and 17th Centuries,* ed. Richard H. Popkin (New York: The Free Press, 1966), p. 65.
17 *Treatise,* p. 215.
18 Arthur Eddington, *The Nature of the Physical World* (Ann Arbor: Univ. of Michigan Press, 1958), p. xiv.
19 P. J. Proudhon, *What is Property?* (New York: Humbolt, 1893), p. 12.
20 Consider Proudhon's description of his own method: "If your will is untrammelled, if your conscience is free, if your mind can unite two propositions and deduce a third therefrom, my ideas will inevitably become yours." Ibid., p. 13.
21 *Treatise,* p. 202; *cf.* pp. 213–18.
22 Ibid., pp. 217–18.
23 *Boswell's Life of Johnson,* ed. George Birkbeck Hill, 2nd edition, 6 vols. (Oxford: Clarendon Press, 1964), III, 326.
24 Viereck, p. 132.
25 Burke, p. 94.
26 Viereck, p. 127.
27 *Enquiries,* p. 147.

28 René Descartes, *Meditations* in *The Philosophical Works of Descartes,* 2 vols., trans. Elizabeth S. Haldane and F. R. T. Ross (New York: Dover, 1955), I, 159.
29 Fyodor Dostoyevsky, *The Brothers Karamazov* (New York: Modern Library), p. 69.
30 *Marx and Engels,* p. 263.
31 *Treatise,* p. 234.
32 A. J. Ayer, *Language, Truth, and Logic* (London: Victor Gollancz, 1951), pp. 18–19.
33 C. I. Lewis, *Mind and the World Order* (New York: Dover, 1929), pp. 140, 142.
34 Murray G. Murphy, *Our Knowledge of the Historical Past* (New York: Bobbs-Merrill, 1973), p. 16.
35 A. J. Ayer, *The Problem of Knowledge* (New York: St. Martin's Press, 1956), p. 160.
36 Bernard Bosanquet, *The Principle of Individuality and Value* (London: Macmillan, 1912), pp. 146–47.
37 Michael Oakeshott, *Experience and Its Modes* (Cambridge: The University Press, 1966), pp. 146–47, 108.
38 Jack Meiland, *Scepticism and Historical Knowledge* (New York: Random House, 1965), p. 192.
39 Jonathan Bennett, *Locke, Berkeley, Hume* (Oxford: Clarendon Press, 1971), p. 228.
40 David Hume, *Essays, Moral, Political, and Literary* (Oxford: Clarendon Press, 1963), pp. 58–59.
41 Ibid., pp. 59–61.
42 *Treatise,* p. 272.
43 *Marx and Engels,* p. 245.
44 *Karl Marx on Revolution,* I, 516.
45 Since Marx held that all social and political norms are historical, it may appear inconsistent to say that he is committed to the unreality of historical norms. For Marx, however, present and past historical norms have authority to the degree that they are connected to norms constituting a *future* classless society. I have argued elsewhere that historical norms are relations between past and present existences and that the Marxian concept of a historical norm constituted by a relation to a future existent is inconsistent. But if the concept is inconsistent, and if the authority of historical norms is to be conceived in the Marxian way, then no historical norm can have authority. See my essay "Burke, Marcuse, and the Historical Justification for Revolution," *Studies in Burke and His Time,* Vol. XIV, Winter, 1972–73.
46 Camus, pp. 3 4.
47 Leslie Stephen, *History of English Thought in the Eighteenth Century* (New York: Harcourt, 1962), p. 181.

Hume's History of England: *Waking the English from a Dogmatic Slumber*

JOHN J. BURKE JR.

David Hume did not write history for the sake of history. He wrote his *History of England* to wake the English from their dogmatic slumber, the seventy-year slumber of Whiggery. Hume, who has so often been portrayed as a rationalist carving his history out of a ready-made Enlightenment mold,[1] in fact approached history as he had approached philosophy—as an iconoclast, as a skeptic. As Hume was not one to be satisfied with noisy assertions that the Whigs were wrong, he had to show both how and why they were wrong. He did this by re-examining the history which the Whigs claimed justified their political doctrines. He found an effective weapon for countering the Whigs in the arguments of historical relativism.

Because Hume was attacking the Whigs in his *History of England,* it has been widely assumed that he was therefore a Tory historian. That at least is what many prominent Whigs have thought. Not surprisingly, their comments on Hume have been acidulous. According to John Stuart Mill, "Hume possessed powers of a very high order [as a historian]: but regard for truth formed no part of his character."[2]

According to Thomas Babington Macaulay, Hume was the "skilled advocate of tyranny" whose *History of England* amounted to little more than "a vast mass of sophistry."[3] According to Thomas Jefferson, apprehensive about the stability of a youthful republic, Hume's *History of England* was Tory "poison."[4] Moreover, the politics of Hume's friends would seem to confirm the suspicions of the Whigs. According to Hume's own account in his brief autobiography, only two men in the whole of the British Isles dared a kind word in the midst of the storm which greeted his initial volumes on the Stuarts—the Anglican primates of England and Ireland. According to Professor Laurence Bongie, Hume's arguments in the *History* were later adopted by reactionaries in post-revolutionary France as a justification for political oppression.[5]

Nevertheless, Hume did not write a Tory history, however conservative his leanings.[6] He was at once too careful and too subtle a thinker for that. His emphasis on the theme of liberty in the *History*, particularly in forming the special character of England, could hardly be said to be the fulminations of the Tory stereotype fixed in the suspicious imaginations of the more violent Whigs. In fact, the early reaction to the Stuart and Tudor volumes only served to corroborate Hume's basic contention. So thoroughly had the English assimilated decades of Whig propaganda that they were utterly flabbergasted, when not outraged, that anyone would dare some words of sympathy for the Stuarts or suggest that the Tudors were something less than the patron saints of English liberty.

Perhaps, though, there is another alternative. If Hume was not a Tory—and he has seldom been mistaken for a Whig—perhaps he was recommending a golden mean between the two.[7] It could be that Hume's notion of the "mixed constitution" of England was at the heart of his historical thinking. It could be that his *History of England* amounts to a cautionary tale to both Whig and Tory, that he was warning one against the folly of a social contract and the other of the folly of divine right. All this sounds probable and is surely consistent with Hume's praise for "moderate opinion" and his repeated warnings against "extremes of all kinds." All this would be well and good if only there had been any Tory position to discredit. But the English of the mid-eighteenth century hardly needed David Hume to discredit the theory of divine right. John Locke, for one, had seen to that. There simply was no Tory position to discredit, at least not in David Hume's opinion. It was not Toryism which had a stranglehold on public discourse in Great Britain, it was Whiggery.

The political domination of the Whigs had become, in Hume's eyes, a form of intellectual tyranny and that triggered his innate iconoclasm. The Whig party, he reminds us more than once in *The History of England,* "for a course of near seventy years, has almost without interruption, enjoyed the whole authority of government."[8] Since "no honours or offices could be obtained but by their countenance and protection," they had the means for discouraging departures from the party line. Their historians—Algernon Sidney, John Locke, Paul de Rapin de Thoyras, Benjamin Hoadley—had one after another brought forth compositions which celebrated "only the partisans of [liberty], who pursued as their object the perfection of civil society," extolling them "at the expense of their antagonists, who maintained those maxims that are essential to its very existence." Though these compositions were "the most despicable, both for style and matter," they "had been extolled, and propagated, and read; as if they had equalled the most celebrated remains of antiquity" (VIII, lxxi, 310–11). Biases so often reiterated under the smile of the powers that be had acquired the aura of truth. Hume's purpose was to smash the golden calf of the Whig historians.

But not by way of direct assault. A direct assault on the Whigs would have undercut his effectiveness. It would have made it that much easier to make the label "Tory hack" stick. Moreover, Hume did not disagree with the Whigs on every issue. So he fashioned his narrative pose as that of an impartial judge, a man of moderation recommending the golden mean. If he would find fault with the Whigs, he would also find fault with the Tories. If he argued for stability and order, he would also praise the blessings of liberty. This pose was as much rhetorical as philosophical. The more he could convince his audience he was truly impartial, the more likely it would be they would attend to his arguments. His strategy was, in short: agree whenever possible in order to make the disagreements the more telling.

This strategy determined the structure of his work. A work of history, unlike, for instance, a work of fiction, does not allow the writer much control over his materials. In those areas where the historian has some discretion—what to include, what to omit, what to emphasize, what to subordinate—he must exercise his discretion within the narrow limits of inherited public materials. The man who would entitle his work "A History of England" cannot, for instance, decide to omit the Gunpowder Plot, never mind the reign of Elizabeth, if he expects his work to be taken seriously. Nevertheless, the historian does have some freedom in two areas: where to begin and where to end his narrative. For that reason, Hume's beginning and ending ought to provide further evidence of an anti-Whig strategy.

At first Hume's choices may seem meaningless, or innocuous, or simply conventional. He did have another plan in mind at first, but he changed his mind. Apparently, though, he had settled on the final plan before he began to compose in 1752, even though he did compose, so to speak, backwards.[9] What was important about English history, according to Hume, began with Julius Caesar's invasion of the island in 55 B.C. and ended with the Glorious Revolution in 1689. In other words, he began English history with the first reliable account of civilized men confronting and conquering a barbaric society. In so far as this beginning allowed him to dismiss the troublesome business of Britain's prehistory as "mere fable and mystery," this choice was as much convenient as philosophical. His choice for an ending proved less troublesome. What was important in English history had ended happily with the Glorious Revolution when the Parliament had acknowledged that England was to be a constitutional rather than a hereditary monarchy.

Hume's choice for an ending, however convenient or natural it may seem, argues something more. It structured English history as a success story. And Hume was eager to underscore this point. The Glorious Revolution, he tells us, decided once and for all that liberty was to be at the center of the English political experience. "And it may justly be affirmed, without any danger of exaggeration, that we, in this island, have ever since [that Revolution] enjoyed, if not the best system of government, at least the most entire system of liberty that was ever known amongst mankind" (VIII, lxxi, 308). Such an outburst of patriotic extravagance seems uncharacteristic, as though Hume had, for once, thrown caution to the winds. He asserts without qualification that the English enjoy "the most entire system of liberty that was ever known amongst mankind." If he does not also assert that the English enjoy "the best system of government" ever known amongst mankind, he encourages it as an inference. At least he conspicuously avoided offering examples of other systems of government that might tend to check such superlatives. It would seem that Hume was out-whigging the Whigs.

In a sense, he was. Hume did not disagree with every contention of the Whigs. His quarrel with them was not really a quarrel over the data of English history, nor even, in most instances, a quarrel with their interpretations of individual events such as the Glorious Revolution. Hume was no lover of tyranny, no contemner of liberty. He agrees that the Magna Carta was a needed check on rampaging royal power; he approves of Henry VIII's break with Rome; he applauds the passage of a bill of *habeas corpus*. Hume could and did agree with the Whigs on certain points, and he made considerable use of those points in his *History*.

But Hume did not agree with the Whig theory of history, that is, with how they linked together the events of English history in a meaningful pattern. In his view, the Whigs portrayed the Glorious Revolution, not simply as the happy outcome of English history, but as the climactic and necessary vindication of the political principles for which all right-minded Englishmen had always stood. According to them, the government of England had originated in a social contract whereby their sovereigns were granted certain prerogatives in exchange for their solemn promises to protect the lives, properties, and liberties of their subjects. Yet their heroic ancestors repeatedly had to fend off would-be tyrants attempting to encroach upon the civil rights of those whom they supposedly served. Sacred promises proved a feeble check on the lust for power. So their ancestors gradually made explicit what had always been implicit by forging institutions, such as the Constitution and the House of Commons, to safeguard their original liberties. Underlying such a view of the progress of English history Hume detected the assumption, if not the actual assertion, that this progress was the necessary or inevitable development of the special genius of the English people.

Hume could accept, with certain qualifications, the notion that the overall pattern of English history constituted a progress towards greater individual liberty, but he could not accept the corollary that this progress was necessary or inevitable, or, for that matter, any suggestion whatsoever that the data of English history could be linked together in a kind of metaphysical cause-and-effect relationship. For this reason and also because of his skeptical bent, he stresses the role of accidents in the making of English history. The fact of progress may be undeniable, but how that progress came to be was another question. For Hume, progress was fitful, uncertain, and unpredictable. First of all, "all advances towards reason and good sense are slow and gradual" (I, ix, 444). Moreover, English history teaches that "a great mixture of accident . . . commonly concurs with a small degree of wisdom and foresight, in erecting the complicated fabric of the most perfect government" (III, xxiii, 297). Ultimately, Hume was unwilling to admit in the *History* that the English had complete control over their destiny.

In this light, Hume's choice for a beginning takes on the usual anti-Whig coloring. The gradual advances of the English towards reason and good sense were the results of happy historical accidents, not of the choices of free men. The advance towards civilization began with the foreign conquest of the island. Other important advances were the results of similar accidents. Such favorite objects of Whig veneration as the Constitution and the House of Commons were not a legacy from their heroic ancestors, but the results of other conquests, and thus foreign contributions to English civilization. So Hume traces the origins of the Constitution back to the Germanic tribes who invaded England after the withdrawal of the Romans (I, Appendix, 202). The House of Commons proves to have been the contribution of the Norman French (II, Appendix, 113). Such observations clearly serve to discredit the Whig notion of a native English genius characterized by a special passion for liberty.

Hume uses such historical accidents to combat the Whigs on other fronts. He frequently, for instance, draws attention to the "might-have-beens" of English history with an eye to their effect on Whiggery. Consequently, there was nothing foreordained, to Hume's mind, about the ultimate victory of the adherents of Parliament in the seventeenth-century civil war. Had it not been for certain curious accidents, the final victory might have been the Royalists': "Had it not been for the garrison of Hull, which kept Yorkshire in awe, a conjunction of the northern forces, with the army in the south, had probably enabled [King Charles], instead of entering on the unfortunate, perhaps imprudent, enterprise of Gloucester, to march direct to London, and put an end to the war" (VI, lvi, 466). Even the "abdication" of King James II was far from a foregone conclusion at the time. Had it not been for the ambitions of William of Orange, the Catholic Stuarts might well have retained their hold on the English throne. "While every motive, civil and religious, concurred to alienate from [King James II] every rank and denomination of men, it might be expected that his throne would, without delay, fall to pieces of its weight: but such is the influence of established government—so averse are men from beginning hazardous enterprise, that, had not an attack been made from abroad, affairs might long have remained in their present delicate situation, and James at last have prevailed in his rash and ill-concerted projects" (VIII, lxxi, 264). Not only, according to Hume, did the future character of the English government depend to an important degree on the ambitions of a single individual, but England might also have become a Catholic country again because "men of education in England, were, many of them, retained in their religion more by honour than by principle; and that, though every one was ashamed to be the first proselyte, yet if the example were once set by some eminent persons, interest would every day make considerable conversions to a communion which was so zealously encouraged by the sovereign" (VIII, lxxi, 270). Such a speculation was hardly designed to flatter those Whigs who believed that the English took their Protestantism as a matter of principle or that a Protestant England was a matter of historical necessity.

The role of accidents is illustrated even more tellingly in the trivial. Small, almost unnoticed events can prove, with hindsight, to have been as decisive on the course of events as the more obvious factors typically cited by historians. For that reason Hume dwells occasionally on instances such as the following.

> The puritans, restrained in England, shipped themselves off for America, and laid there the foundation of a government which possessed all the liberty, both civil and religious, of which they found themselves deprived in their native country. But their enemies, unwilling that they should any where enjoy ease and contentment, and dreading, perhaps, the consequences of so disaffected a colony, prevailed with the King to issue a proclamation, debarring those devotees access even into those inhospitable desarts. Eight ships, lying in the Thames, and ready to sail, were stayed by the order of the council; and in these were embarked Sir Arthur Hazelrig, John Hambden, and Oliver Cromwell, who had resolved for ever to abandon their native country, and fly to the other extremity of the globe; where they might enjoy lectures and discourses of any length or form which pleased them. The King had afterwards full leisure to repent this exercise of his authority (VI, lii, 244–45).

It hardly needs to be said what a difference it might have made to the entire course of English history in the seventeenth century had those eight ships sailed off to the New World. It requires little guesswork to determine what King Charles' decision would have been, had he had the advantage of hindsight. The point is he did not. He was locked into his historical moment.

This, in Hume's eyes, was a major fallacy of Whig history: the failure to make the distinction between history as it appears to posterity and history as it really happened. In trying to establish the historical legitimacy of their favorite doctrines the Whigs persistently read the happenings of the past from the point of view of the present, history as they thought it should have been or wanted it to be, not as it actually was. The consequences of such historiography could be serious in the present. Because men would expect the future to observe the patterns they believed they had found in the past, they might foolishly apply the inapplicable. If, on the other hand, they learned to see history as often the result of baffling and unpredictable accidents, or at least allowed for them, they would be more flexible because more skeptical of their own certitudes, wise enough to expect everything or anything to happen, while hoping it would not.

The distinction between the past as it was and the past as it appears to have been led Hume to introduce a new criterion into his account of English history—the *situation,* a notion not unlike that of the *Zeitgeist* favored by later historians. The situation required a careful analysis of past events within the framework of space and time while allowing for the irrational. The whole would sometimes be larger than the sum of its parts. "Nothing will tend more to abate the acrimony of party-disputes than to show men, that those events, which they impute to their adversaries as the deepest crimes, were the natural, if not the necessary result of the situation, in which the nation was placed during any period" (VI, liii, 381).

Not surprisingly, the notion of the situation proved to be convenient to Hume's polemic. It allowed him to discredit Whig historiography by upending their tradition of heroes and villains, and that without ever having to discredit "the most perfect system of liberty that was ever known amongst mankind." Now a Whig villain like the first Charles Stuart could and should have been the most beloved of English monarchs. That he was not, that his actions led to disastrous results both for himself and for England, was due, not to any wickedness on Charles' part, but to the situation. "Neither the dissipation incident to youth, nor the pleasures attending a high fortune had been able to prevent this virtuous Prince from embracing the most sincere sentiments of religion; and that character, which in a religious age, should have been of infinite advantage to him, proved, in the end, the chief cause of his ruin: Merely, because the religion, adopted by him, was not of that precise mode and sect which began to prevail among his subjects" (VI, li, 210–11).

Hume uses this same procedure to reevaluate Whig heroes. His Henry VIII is not the familiar figure of the Whig historians. Instead of the selfless patriot bravely liberating the English from the shackles of Rome, daring what had never before been dared, Hume portrays a stubborn, greedy, witless, and ultimately dangerous man, whose overrated learning was little more than a foolish fondness for the opinions of the medieval theologian Thomas Aquinas, whose celebrated political acumen was no more than the result of his fortunate situation. "Both [Protestants and Catholics] hoped, by their unlimited compliance, to bring [King Henry] over to their party. The King meanwhile, who held the balance between the factions, was enabled by the courtship paid him both by Protestants and Catholics to assume an unbounded authority; and though in all his measures he was really driven by his ungoverned humour, he casually steered a course which led more certainly to arbitrary power, than any which the most profound politics could have traced out to him" (IV, xxxi, 99).

The same for another idol—William of Orange. The Dutchman's role in the Glorious Revolution is never questioned, the benefits of his actions to English liberty never doubted. However, William is said to have acted out his historic role, not because he had the interests of his future subjects at heart, but out of the needs of his situation in Holland. William knew he needed the English throne if he were ever to checkmate the ambitions of his hated rival, Louis XIV of France. The troubles of his father-in-law in England provided the opportunity. Accordingly Hume observes: "And thus, though [King William's] virtue, it is confessed, be not the purest which we meet with in history, it will be difficult to find any person whose actions and conduct have contributed more eminently to the general interest of society and mankind" (VIII, lxxi, 273).

Whatever Hume's motives for introducing the notion of the situation into his *History of England,* the fact is he did introduce it and use it. That necessarily raises questions about certain labels routinely assigned to Hume in discussions of his work as a historian. He is commonly, for example, described as a *rationalist.*[10] But if the term *rationalist* implies, as it usually does, that Hume believed that men could either control or shape history in a desired direction, then it would be hard to think of a more misleading label. A Henry VIII or a William of Orange was more the beneficiary than the cause of the historical event associated with his name. Hume simply did not believe that individuals rationally guided history in one direction rather than another. He was not a rationalist, he was a skeptic.

The term *rationalist* often implies, particularly in an eighteenth-century context, *uniformitarian,* another label which is attached to Hume with depressing frequency. It is, for instance, almost ritualistic in discussions of Hume as a historian to quote a passage from his *Enquiry Concerning the Human Understanding* as an unequivocal statement of his assumptions about the workings of history, along with the corollary that this passage contains the light in which his *History of England* should be read.[11]

> It is universally acknowledged that there is a great uniformity among the actions of men, in all nations and ages, and that human nature remains still the same, in its principles and operations. The same motives always produce the same actions. The same events follow from the same causes. Ambition, avarice, self-love, vanity, friendship, generosity, public spirit: these passions, mixed in various degrees, and distributed through society, have been, from the beginning of the world, and still are, the source of all the actions and enterprises, which have ever been observed among mankind. Would you know the sentiments, inclinations, and course of life of the Greeks and Romans? Study well the temper and life of the French and English: You cannot be much mistaken in transferring to the former *most* of the observations which you have made with regard to the latter. Mankind are so much the same, in all times and places, that history informs us of nothing new or strange in this particular. Its chief use is only to discover the constant and universal principles of human nature, by showing men in all varieties of circumstances and situations, and furnishing us with materials from which we may form our observations and become acquainted with the regular springs of human actions and behavior.[12]

Needless to say, the anti-historical character of this passage has been the source of endless merriment to Hume's enemies and of considerable embarrassment to his friends. Yet, even as little as a careful reading of the passage itself would argue for some caution. He did not say we could transfer all our observations from one period to another, only *most,* and the italics were his. More importantly, he qualified his assertion about the underlying uniformity of human nature more severely in a section which follows this passage: "We know, in general, that the characters of men are, to a certain degree, inconstant and irregular. That is, in a manner, the constant of human character."[13] Finally, given the pressure of his theme in the *Enquiry*—"to discover the constant and universal principles of human nature" as the basis for a science of mankind as distinct from but parallel to a Newtonian science of physical nature—a uniformitarian view of history was, if not actually necessary, at least highly desirable. No such pressure was at work when he began to compose *The History of England* four years later.[14]

This is not to say, however, that there are no uniformitarian elements in *The History of England.* There are, particularly in Hume's conception of character. Historical characters, for Hume, are forever acting out of ambition, or avarice, or self-love, or vanity—a scheme of the passions familiar to those who have read the *Enquiry.* He shows little interest in the personal lives of historical characters, though he often distinguishes between their public and their private selves, more often than not for an ironical effect. His three favorite verbs for describing human behavior seem to be "pretend," "affect," and "dissemble."

Yet, if to be uniformitarian implies a belief that history is somehow philosophy teaching by example, then Hume was not a uniformitarian. He was not because he believed that the circumstances of any given historical period created a situation. Consequently, the success or failure of an action could only be determined in that context.[15] The spectacular successes of Oliver Cromwell, for example, were due to the unique situation prevailing in seventeenth-century England. Cromwell's actions could never be successfully imitated because he was "suited to the age in which he lived, and to that alone" (VII, lxi, 156). The disasters which befell King Charles I, on the other hand, were due to the same unique situation from which his opponent benefited. Curiously, it was from Charles Stuart that the Whigs had the most to learn about the fallacy of historical analogy. Charles continued to imitate the model established by the Tudor monarchs when that model was no longer germane. He acted in the seventeenth century as though he were still living in the sixteenth.

> In every age, or nation, [King Charles I] had been secure of a prosperous and happy reign. But the high idea of his own authority, with which he had

> been imbued, made him incapable of submitting prudently to the spirit of liberty, which began to prevail among his subjects. His policies were not supported with such vigor and foresight as might enable him to subdue their privileges, and maintain his prerogative at the high pitch, to which he had raised it. And above all, the spirit of enthusiasm being universally diffused over the nation, disappointed all the views of human prudence and disturbed the operation of every motive, which usually influences society (VI, lii, 219).

Labels like *rationalist* and *uniformitarian* are ill-suited to the historian who perceives "a spirit" "universally diffused" over a nation, one that could disturb "the operation of every motive, which usually influences society." Such remarks are not consistent with the supposedly anti-historical historiography so often assigned to the Enlightenment in general and to David Hume in particular. Hume was not a uniformitarian, he was a relativist.[16]

So intrigued did Hume become with his notion of the situation that on occasions he, in his own words, "departs from the historical style." His departures consist of reserving the last parts of some chapters or even separate appendices for discussions of the manners which characterize an age, if not quite as unique, at least as different. They are in essence moments when he stops to consider which elements went into making up a particular historical situation. His surveys of manners can be wide-ranging, extending from examinations of the literature of a period to observations on fluctuations in real-estate values or even in the price of butcher meat. By and large, however, Hume concentrates on developments in commerce and changes in the relative position of the middle rank of men. In so far as Hume ever suggests cause-and-effect in history, he seems to have felt that the social and political changes in society were the results of antecedent economic changes. For instance, in his Appendix to the Tudor period he attributes the rise of political absolutism to the rise of luxury. The desire for ever more and better material goods indebted the nobles to the merchants. At the same time the change from wealth based on land to wealth based on commerce had succeeded in weakening the traditional leverage of those same nobles. But the middle class had not yet succeeded in gaining a political leverage commensurate with their new economic power. Royal power filled the vacuum, making the Tudor monarchs as nearly absolute as English monarchs have ever been before or after. Hence, Hume concludes: "The change of manners was the chief cause of the secret revolution of Government" (V, Appendix, 426).

But Hume's anti-Whig strategy is still in evidence even when his explanations have their most original ring. His sketch of the Tudor era is aimed again at various facets of the Whig myth of English history. The Whigs had stigmatized the Stuart monarchs by associating them with the hated and "un-English" system of political absolutism. But Hume counters with the argument that the Stuarts only talked absolutism, whereas the Tudors actually practiced it. If the Tudors were in fact autocrats, how then could they be revered as the patron saints of English civil liberties? The Whigs had argued that a "plan of liberty," however implicit, had always been evident in English history, even in the earliest times. Hume counters that anything resembling what the Whigs called a "plan of liberty" could only be traced back to the economic changes which took hold in the sixteenth century. When the "plan of liberty" emerged, it emerged as something *new.* For much the same reason Hume describes the Glorious Revolution of 1689 as forming "a new epoch in our constitution" (VIII, lxxi, 307), that is, as the accidental result of the situation prevailing at the time, not a validation of all that had gone before.

First and foremost, then, Hume's *History of England* was a tract for the times. Its purpose was iconoclastic: to wake the English from the dogmatic slumber of Whiggery. Hume's innovations in historiography may still be innovations, but they arose out of his polemical strategy. He aimed his historiography at the progressive theory of history the Whigs employed to justify their political convictions. He used the arguments of historical relativism—an emphasis on accidents, the notion of the situation—to counter the arguments of the Whigs. The ultimate point of Hume's historiography was that the lessons which should be taught to the English were far different from the lessons the Whigs had been teaching them for seventy years. "Above all, a civilized nation, like the English, who have happily established the most perfect and most accurate system of liberty that ever was found compatible with government, ought to be cautious in appealing to the practice of their ancestors, or regarding the maxims of uncultivated ages, as certain rules for their present conduct. An acquaintance with the ancient periods of their government is chiefly *useful* by instructing them to cherish their present constitution, from a comparison or consent with the condition of those distant times" (III, xxiii, 297). Just because Hume couches his conclusions in negative terms does not mean that he ended up a historical agnostic, as John Benjamin Stewart has argued.[17] His negative phrasing is simply consistent with his life-long habit of cautious skepticism. In his view, history was as unlikely to produce absolute truths as metaphysics. The danger was in thinking that it did. If Santayana could warn that "those who do not remember the past are condemned to relive it," then Hume was warning that those who remember the past, without taking into consideration the changes in circumstances, might be condemned to act out roles that are no longer relevant. History could be a trap as well as a guide.

NOTES

1 For some examples, see George Holland Sabine, "Hume's Contribution to the Historical Method," *Philosophical Review,* 15 (1906), 38; John Bennett Black, *The Art of History: A Study of Four Great Historians of the Eighteenth Century* (London: Methuen, 1926), p. 86; Ronald N. Stromberg, "History in the Eighteenth Century," *JHI,* 12 (1951), 297, 301.

2 Rev. of *A History of the British Empire,* by George Brodie, *Westminster Review*, 2 (October 1824), 346.

3 Rev. of *The Romance of History,* by Henry Neele, *Edinburgh Review,* 47 (May 1828), 360.

4 *The Life and Selected Writings of Thomas Jefferson,* ed. Adrienne Koch and William Peden (New York: Modern Library, 1944), p. 726.

5 *David Hume: The Prophet of the Counter-Revolution* (Oxford: Clarendon Press, 1965), pp. 167–72.

6 For earlier discussions of this matter, see Ernest Campbell Mossner, "Was Hume a Tory Historian? Facts and Considerations," *JHI,* 2 (1941), 225–36; Marjorie Grene, "Hume: Skeptic and Tory," *JHI,* 4 (1943), 338–48; Benjamin A. Ring, "David Hume: Historian or Tory Hack?" *North Dakota Quarterly,* 36 (1968), 50–59.

7 This is the argument of John Benjamin Stewart in *The Moral and Political Philosophy of David Hume* (New York: Columbia Univ. Press, 1963), pp. 224, 298–99.

8 *The History of England, from the Invasion of Julius Caesar to the Revolution of 1688,* 8 vols. (London: J. F. Dove, 1822), VIII, 310. Hereafter all references to *The History of England* will be to this edition and will be included in the text. Since a number of editions of *The History of England* are in use, my references will include the chapter numbers in small Roman numerals as well as the volume and page numbers to this edition.

9 Ernest Campbell Mossner, *The Life of David Hume* (Austin: Univ. of Texas Press, 1954), pp. 301–15.

10 Ernest Campbell Mossner has also taken up this point. See "An Apology for David Hume, Historian," *PMLA,* 56 (1941), 664.

11 A partial list of those who do so would include Sabine, p. 32; Black, p. 96; Mossner, "Apology," pp. 666–67; David Bayne Horne, "Some Scottish Writers of History in the Eighteenth Century," *Scottish Historical Review,* 40 (1961), 2; Leo Braudy, *Narrative Form in Fiction and History: Hume, Fielding, and Gibbon* (Princeton: Princeton Univ. Press, 1970), p. 56. Duncan Forbes once remarked that Hume's "alleged belief in the uniformity of human nature is almost universally misunderstood," but he did not elaborate. See "Politics and History in David Hume," *Historical Journal,* 6 (1962), 288.

12 *Enquiries: Concerning the Human Understanding and Concerning the Principles of Morals,* ed. L. A. Selby-Bigge, 2nd ed. (1902; rpt. Oxford: Clarendon Press, 1970), par. 65, p. 83.

13 *Concerning the Human Understanding,* par. 68, p. 88.

14 Paul H. Meyer has also noted the modification of Hume's views in this regard. See "Voltaire and Hume as Historians: A Comparative Study of *Essai sur les moeurs* and the *History of England,*" *PMLA,* 73 (1958), 55.

15 For a different discussion of this issue, see Catherine S. Frazer, "Pattern and Predictability in Hume's History," *Enlightenment Essays,* 1 (1970), 27–32.

16 Meyer too has seen "indications of historical relativism" in Hume's *History of England.* See "Voltaire and Hume," p. 55.

17 *The Moral and Political Philosophy of David Hume,* p. 299.

The Philosophical Articles by Abbé Pestré in Diderot's Encyclopédie

WALTER E. REX

It was a sobering experience to discover that d'Alembert had not told the truth about abbé Mallet.[1] The great mathematician had described this theologian—one of the original contributors to the *Encyclopédie,* the author of some 2,000 articles—as a broad-minded, philosophically oriented, tolerant, impartial churchman. Following this lead, later scholars thought they even detected in his work a delightful sense of humor and good fun. But the harsh reality is that abbé Mallet was a narrow-minded bigot, an enemy of religious toleration, an apologist for persecution,[2] mostly devoid of humor, usually against the Jansenists, by temperament distinctly bilious. His style of writing lacks elegance, character, or even moisture. Heaven knows why he was assigned the article "Harmonie de la prose" (VII, p. 52A–B), when his own prose lacked precisely the quality of harmony he was supposed to be so good at explaining.[3] Documents show that he was in league with the right wing of the French clergy, and circumstantial evidence suggests that he was a "plant," that is, someone the Assemblée du Clergé could count on to turn out pure orthodoxy by the columnful, to offset whatever poisonous impieties Diderot and his friends might be concocting. On d'Alembert's earliest list of contributors to the *Encyclopédie* his name appears second, and one suspects that he had been part of the original bargain, part of the price the *encyclopédistes* had to pay in order to get permission to operate.

To discover all this after having trusted in the flattering phrases of d'Alembert's eulogy of him is certainly enough to make one wary, not only of abbé Mallet's articles, but of all the clerics who contributed to the early volumes. If abbé Mallet was a right-wing "plant," so might others be. It is for this reason that I propose to place under close scrutiny one more of the churchmen who were among the original team of contributors to the *Encyclopédie.* His name is abbé Pestré, and he is something of a mystery.

In the first place we don't even know his Christian name(s) or the date of his birth. Robert Shackleton found out that he came from the Aveyron, that in the 1750s he was a "peripatetic private tutor," a man with a career to make, and finally, that he was "in a sense" a client of abbé Raynal.[4] Professor Lough adds that in the account books of the publishers of the *Encyclopédie* he was listed among those receiving payment.[5] But the most intriguing bits of information about abbé Pestré were discovered by Frank Kafker:[6] the police had taken note of abbé Pestré during the scandal over the thesis of the abbé de Prades, and although they did not think he had contributed to the actual writing of the condemned thesis, they were convinced that he had corrected the proofs of the *Apologie* for it. In any case, abbé Pestré was not forced into exile after this affair, as others were. Professor Kafker also tells us that abbé Pestré tutored children of the rich, that he was respected by both Turgot and abbé Raynal, and that he lived an almost unbelievably long time, until 1821. One source referred to by Professor Kafker claims that abbé Pestré also contributed some articles to Raynal's *Histoire . . . des deux Indes.* However, the articles in question are unfortunately not specified, and we have no way to test the truth of the allegation. Indeed, tantalizing though they are, these facts only give us hints of possibilities. They do not bring us close enough to the man or his work to characterize them.

Nor is d'Alembert very informative in his *Discours préliminaire*: he refers to abbé Pestré's "savoir" and his "mérite"; he states that abbé Pestré had helped abbé Yvon with several articles on ethics;[7] finally, he promises that the philosophical *mémoires* prepared by abbé Pestré will appear in later volumes.[8] Thus we are left with no idea of how he came to be chosen as an *encyclopédiste.* Diderot never mentions him in the surviving correspondence; neither does Voltaire, nor anyone else, so far as scholars have been able to ascertain. All the rest of abbé Pestré's existence which, according to the date proposed by Professor Kafker, must have lasted well over ninety years, is a total blank—except for the philosophical articles he signed in the *Encyclopédie.*

There are just nine of them, all but one appearing in volume II.[9] Perhaps the number seems slight, when compared to abbé Mallet's imposing 2,000. Yet their subject matter makes them especially interesting; in fact abbé Pestré was allotted some of the greatest topics of the Enlightenment—far more significant than many of those later doled out to Voltaire. "Baconisme" is the best known of them, but he was also allowed to do "Bonheur," an article that created something of a stir in its day, and "Cartésianisme," a topic of obvious importance. Add to these a long article on the Jewish Cabala, two more on the notorious philosophers Cardano and Campanella, a very curious article on "Canadiens," which will be discussed later, plus two minor pieces, and abbé Pestré begins to look like one of the more significant contributors to Diderot's enterprise.

Happily for the editors, abbé Pestré was not a "plant" as abbé Mallet had been. Far from it; in his articles he is faithful to the highest ideals of the *Encyclopédie* as defined by Diderot and d'Alembert, perhaps even more faithful than the editors-in-chief chose to be. Let us consider, for example, the article on Chancellor Bacon (II, 8B–10A). Admittedly it is not particularly original in its insights, in fact it contains references to Voltaire, d'Alembert and Condillac, all of whom had discussed the great Chancellor before.[10] However, if one wants to learn what it was the French Enlightenment found so compelling in Francis Bacon, this is one of the best places to look. An excellent vulgarizer, abbé Pestré has an easy, economical style and a sure sense of the importance of his topic. Most of his discussion involves short aphorisms and résumés of Bacon's thought, but there are longer quotations in French, too, conveying with something of Bacon's incomparable eloquence the philosophy that, by the admission of the *encyclopédistes,* had been a starting-point for their movement. The following quotation in which Bacon speaks of the quest for truth is a good example: "Il faut se flatter qu'on réussira dans la découverte de la vérité, et qu'on hâtera les progrès de l'esprit, pourvu que, quittant les notions abstraites, les spéculations métaphysiques, on ait recours à l'analyse, qu'on décompose les idées particulières, qu'on s'aide de l'expérience, et qu'on apporte à l'étude un jugement mûr, un esprit droit et libre de tout préjugé. . . . On ne doit espérer de voir renaître les Arts et les Sciences, qu'autant qu'on refondra entièrement ses premières idées, et que l'expérience sera le flambeau qui nous guidera dans les routes obscures de la vérité [. . .]" (II, 9B).[11]

It will be obvious that many of the great *topoi* of the Enlightenment are brought together in these quotations. Moreover, the stress on "expérience" in the final sentence runs exactly parallel to Diderot's famous prophetic allegory in the thirty-second chapter of *Les Bijoux indiscrets* (1748). In Diderot's vision, a temple representing traditional philosophy is overthrown and laid waste by an ever-expanding figure personifying "Expérience." Just as Bacon had suggested, "Expérience" bears a torch, and he is carrying out Bacon's program for the renewal of the arts and sciences by lighting up the whole universe. I don't believe there can be any question of Diderot having influenced abbé Pestré's article; in fact Diderot's novel is clearly *not* the source of "Baconisme." It is rather that abbé Pestré shared with all the enlightened *encyclopédistes* the realization that Bacon had shown mankind the way, and that the time had come to celebrate the truth of his predictions.

There is something of the same excitement in abbé Pestré's article on Descartes (II, 716A–725B), another familiar forefather. His discussions of the *Discours de la méthode* and the *Meditationes* would have given the general, enlightened reader a good idea of the importance of these works, and everywhere he emphasizes the aspects of Cartesianism that still seemed valid in his own time. He lays particular stress on the uniqueness of Descartes' approach, which used the story of his own intellectual development as an instrument of persuasion:

> Nous reconnaîtrions facilement nos défauts, si nous pouvions remarquer que les plus grands hommes en ont eu de semblables. Les Philosophes

auraient suppléé à l'impuissance où nous sommes pour la plupart, de nous étudier nous-mêmes, s'ils nous avaient laissé l'histoire des progrès de leur esprit. Descartes l'a fait, et c'est un des grands avantages de sa méthode. Au lieu d'attaquer directement les scholastiques, il représente le temps où il était dans les mêmes préjugés: il ne cache point les obstacles qu'il a eu à surmonter pour s'en défaire; il donne les règles d'une méthode beaucoup plus simple qu'aucune de celles qui avaient été en usage jusqu'à lui, laisse entrevoir les découvertes qu'il croit avoir faites, et prépare par cette adresse les esprits à recevoir les nouvelles opinions qu'il se proposait d'établir. Il y a apparence que cette conduite a eu beaucoup de part à la révolution dont ce philosophe est l'auteur (II, 719A).

Again in this article there is little that is original. On the other hand, it has a certain vigor and liveliness because abbé Pestré chose to treat the aspects of Descartes' philosophy that he himself most admired and that seemed most relevant for his own age. This article, entitled "Cartésianisme," is indeed a monument testifying to the extraordinary importance of the Cartesian "revolution" in the Enlightenment. At the same time, abbé Pestré's approach is rather personal, and, despite its title, the article tells more about Descartes and his works than it does about his "school."

At the end of the article d'Alembert intervenes in an apostil to make a few points clear. (He regularly did this in the early volumes, especially with the musical articles of J. J. Rousseau.) D'Alembert reminds us that although Descartes' followers have been numerous, they generally did not follow him in all doctrines. He also points out that Cartesianism had much difficulty in gaining acceptance in France. Ironically, by the time his theories were received by the universities and academies they were already rendered obsolete by Newton, whose theories were resisted in turn. He maintains, however, that for the last eighteen years everyone has been for Newton.[12] D'Alembert also mentions Descartes' theory concerning animal souls, a matter that posed such thorny problems for Christians.[13] Finally, he speaks of the persecutions Descartes suffered in France, the same country in which he is now so honored.

I find these remarks curious: no doubt they fill in certain topics that abbé Pestré had neglected. They also bring out Descartes' inadequacies somewhat more than abbé Pestré had done, and, of course, they take a dig at Christianity. Above all, they stress philosophy's struggle for survival, which was such a favorite topic of the Enlightenment, and one with which the *encyclopédistes,* in particular, could identify. In other words, d'Alembert's remarks not only fill in gaps; they make the discussion of Cartesianism distinctly more polemical.

In the eighteenth century abbé Pestré's most notorious article was "Bonheur" (II, 322A–323A). It drew fire from the Jansenist critic, Chaumeix,[14] and for very good reasons. Abbé Pestré's idea of "bonheur" was the exact opposite of the Jansenist view, so contrary, in fact, that one suspects abbé Pestré of deliberately contriving it in order to give lasting indigestion to anyone who took his Pascal seriously. According to abbé Pestré, "bonheur" is a pleasant enough state to be in, but it becomes somewhat tedious ("triste") unless enlivened from time to time by "plaisir," by which he means, essentially, love-making—or so I infer from his prose rhythms:[15] "Pour remplir nos désirs, il faut nous tirer de cet assoupissement où nous languissons, il faut faire couler la joie jusqu'au plus intime de notre coeur, l'animer par des sentiments agréables, l'agiter par de douces secousses, lui imprimer des mouvements délicieux, l'enivrer des transports d'une volupté pure, que rien ne puisse altérer . . ." (II, 322A).

But abbé Pestré also recognizes that "bonheur" may be founded on a feeling of self-satisfaction.[16] Thus, he says, even the stoics can be happy, despite their austere disciplines, because their virtuous principles make them feel satisfied with themselves, and superior to others. The Jansenist who criticised abbé Pestré's article claimed that all this reduced happiness to the kind of pleasure principle espoused by Epicureans, which indeed it does. However, abbé Pestré preferred to cite St. Thomas in this connection, paraphrasing his famous statement that grace does not abolish nature, but perfects it.[17] Needless to say, he is quoting the Saint out of context. Moreover, when at last he comes to speak of Christian happiness, it sounds suspiciously like another form of self-satisfaction as he describes it, something, we infer, that may bring happiness to certain individuals (as stoicism does), but not perhaps to everyone. In other words, despite the deference he shows to Christianity in its brief appearance, and the theological justifications of his views, the general tone of the article is distinctly secular.[18]

The article "Cabale" (II, 475B–486A) raises special problems that go beyond the scope of this study. It is taken, abbé Pestré specifically informs the reader, from the Protestant writer, Jacques Basnage. Abbé Pestré is not very sympathetic to the cabala, regarding these doctrines as a kind of superstition which he criticizes in a rather Protestant fashion, doubtless following his Calvinist source. Towards the end of the article he discusses the allegedly Christian ingredients various churchmen have claimed to have found in cabalistic writings: intimations of the Trinity, and so on. There were even some persons who suggested that such writings might be useful in converting Jews to Christianity. Yet abbé Pestré—presumably drawing on Basnage—is not convinced: the cabala is fraudulent, he argues, and anyone who was converted to Christianity on such a basis would eventually discover the fraud and begin to have doubts about the religion that had used such dubious arguments. The conversion would not last, or, at least, the man's faith would be seriously undermined.

At this point, the article ends, and d'Alembert intervenes in an apostil again, to suggest that the history of philosophy is often the history of mankind's follies, as the foregoing article has shown. He uses the terms "chimères," "extravagances," "rêveries," and "visions" to stress the point and make sure the reader has understood his message. Again I find this intervention significant: abbé Pestré—doubtless following Basnage—had been seriously discussing the problem of conversion to Christianity. There was no irony in his approach; it was simply a matter of interest. One certainly couldn't prove that abbé Pestré was a believing Christian on the basis of such a passage. The point is, rather, that he was broad-minded enough to allow such a religious issue to be raised and discussed in a neutral tone. Probably that was why d'Alembert felt he ought to intervene; he wanted to brush it all aside—Jewish cabala and Christian conversion alike—dismissing everything as "chimères" and "visions."[19]

But the prize article, the one that was reprinted twice in eighteenth-century anthologies of *Encyclopédie* articles, was called "Canadiens, philosophie des" (II, 581B–582B).[20] What an intriguing title to appear in the 1750s! Were there really so many philosophers already residing in Canada as to warrant a special article? Well, indeed there were. For the philosophy of the Canadians in question is the philosophy of the Huron Indians. The cultural joke is on us, with our narrow, European-oriented frame of reference. Furthermore, Huron philosophy turns out to be quite fascinating, at least in this account which is based on La Hontan. Abbé Pestré warns us that this author had been suspected of trying to subvert Catholicism because the Indians he describes are so often the winners in their religious debates with the Christians. Having thus put us on the alert, abbé Pestré feels free to plunge ahead anyway, drawing not only on La Hontan, but on a curious combination of authors who supplied him with useful points of view.

When he discusses the moral qualities of the Hurons, their behavior suddenly begins to take on a suspicious resemblance to the Quakers in Voltaire's first *Philosophical Letter.* As we recall, Voltaire's Quaker was reserved in manner when greeting the narrator, not at all given to the Frenchman's effusions and elaborate compliments. Yet Voltaire shows that there was more sincere hospitality and goodwill in the Quaker's reserve than in the Frenchman's artful politeness.

Turning to abbé Pestré's Huron, we find that his manner, too, is so "simple," so "taciturne" that abbé Pestré says it is hard for a European who does not know the Hurons to realize that this is their way of politeness: "Ils sont peu caressants, et font peu de démonstrations; mais nonobstant cela ils sont bons et affables, et exercent envers les étrangers et les malheureux une charitable hospitalité, qui a de quoi confondre toutes les nations de l'Europe. . . ."

On the other hand when abbé Pestré praises their rusticity, their freedom from the corruptions of civilization, one wonders whether he hasn't been reading, or hearing of, Rousseau's *Premier Discours.* Finally, after quoting a particularly sage and ingenious morsel of Huron philosophy, abbé Pestré comments, "Cela n'est point si sauvage." All we need here is "Mais quoy, ils ne portent point de haut de chausses!" to have a perfect imitation of Montaigne's great essay on cannibals.[21]

What do we learn about the Canadians? First, we are informed that they are *not* covered with hair all over their body, the way most people think they are; they have no more hair than we do, and are very fastidious about plucking it out. Moreover they are born white, even as we are; it is only the action of the sun on the oils and paints of their unclad bodies that gradually darkens them. They have some unexpected virtues: "Ils ont l'imagination assez vive, ils pensent juste sur leurs affaires, ils vont à leur fin par des voies sûres; ils agissent de sang-froid, et avec un phlegme qui lasserait notre patience. Par raison d'honneur et par grandeur d'âme, ils ne se fâchent presque jamais. Ils ont le coeur haut et fier, un courage à l'épreuve, une valeur intrépide, une constance dans les tourments qui semble surpasser l'héroisme, et une égalité d'âme que ni l'adversité ni la prospérité n'altèrent jamais." In their religion we find some amazing insights, sometimes anticipating doctrines the Christians thought they had invented, sometimes going far beyond them in wisdom and originality—or at least so we infer.

Brief though it is, the article amounts to a minor *mise en question* of European values: it leads us to speculate about our assumptions, to ponder the disadvantages of civilization, to wonder how people who live so simply can have a philosophy and a theology that are so sophisticated. In all of this, abbé Pestré exemplifies the Enlightenment's fascination with "le sauvage", a topic that would later serve almost ubiquitously as a touchstone in eighteenth-century discussions of law and morality. Yet his article does not, as with J.-J. Rousseau, try to answer these questions and force us through our admiration of the savage to turn against civilization. Abbé Pestré is careful to point out what he, with his European outlook and prejudices, considers to be the serious defects of character in the Canadians, that counterbalance their virtues: ". . . ils sont légers et volages, fainéans au-delà de toute expression, ingrats avec excès, soupçonneux, traîtres, vindicatifs, et d'autant plus dangereux, qu'ils savent mieux couvrir et couvrent plus longtemps leurs ressentiments. Ils exercent envers leurs ennemis des cruautés si inouïes, qu'ils surpassent dans l'invention de leurs tourments tout ce que l'invention des anciens tyrans peut nous représenter de plus cruel. Ils sont brutaux dans leurs plaisirs, vicieux par ignorance et par malice; mais leur rusticité et la disette où ils sont de toutes choses, leur donne sur nous un avantage, qui est d'ignorer tous les raffinements du vice qu'ont introduit le luxe et l'abondance." Clearly, the article is an invitation to reflection, rather than a dogmatic statement.

Except for one brief article in volume III, abbé Pestré disappears without a ripple after volume II. Even if we did not have Professor Kafker's researches, we could have been sure that his disappearance was not brought about by death, for d'Alembert would never have let the occasion pass for another obituary, doubtless stressing his "savoir" and his "mérite" again. As for the probable causes of his departure, it would seem legitimate to speculate at least that abbé Pestré with his secular idea of "bonheur," his erotic "plaisir," his Protestant "cabale," his experimental Bacon, and his metaphysical Indians, cannot have given much pleasure to those right-wing clerics who had "planted" abbé Mallet among the contributors and who were determined to bring religion in the *Encyclopédie* under control. They probably had him dismissed. One may presume also that d'Alembert would not have put up much of a fight. Abbé Pestré was not really polemical enough to suit the axe-grinding mathematician, who had already had to intervene twice in order to give more of an edge to the abbé's open-minded, informative statements. D'Alembert may even have been secretly relieved at his departure. As for the pleasant, mild-tempered abbé, there may be one piece of evidence that hints at his own disposition of mind as he so soundlessly left the *Encyclopédie.* For the solitary, little article by him that appeared in volume III is entitled—fittingly enough?—"Complaisance," a virtue the author highly recommends.

NOTES

1 See my article "'Arche de Noé' and other Religious Articles by abbé Mallet in the *Encyclopédie,*" *Eighteenth-Century Studies,* 9 (1976), pp. 333–52. Post Office inefficiency prevented me from including therein two references, kindly supplied by Professor Paul Korshin: Benito Arias Montanus, "De Arche Noe," in his *Antiquitates Iudaicarum Libri IX* (Leyden, 1593), reprinted, with engraved illustrations, in *Critici Sacri,* ed. Joshua Poole, 9 vols. (London, 1660); Don Cameron Allen, *The Legend of Noah* (Urbana, Ill., 1949).

2 Having learned from the cancels published by Professor Schwab (see pp. 339–40 of the article referred to above, note 1) that abbé Mallet actually favored the Revocation of the Edict of Nantes, we may now safely attribute to him the unsigned *Encyclopédie* article "Calvinisme" (II, p. 566A) which states the same reactionary view. Abbé Mallet's signature appears at the end of the article following this one ("Calvinistes"), and it was not an uncommon practice in the *Encyclopédie* to let a single signature at the end of a series of articles represent authorship of all of them. See the first volume of R. N. Schwab's *Inventory of Diderot's Encyclopédie,* in *Studies on Voltaire and the Eighteenth Century,* 80 (1971), 22, 34, 47–48.

3 Actually, the reason for his being assigned this article was probably the numerous volumes he had already published that dealt with *belles-lettres.* For example: *Principes pour la lecture des poètes,* 2 vols. (Paris, 1745): *Essai sur l'étude des belles-lettres* (Paris, 1747); *Principes pour la lecture des orateurs,* 3 vols. (Paris, 1753).

4 *The* Encyclopédie *and the Clerks,* Zaharoff Lecture (Oxford, 1970), pp. 8–9.

5 *The Contributors to the* Encyclopédie (London: Grant & Cutler, 1973), p. 23.

6 Frank A. Kafker, "The Risks of Contributing to Diderot's Encyclopedia," *Diderot Studies,* 16, 119–43.

7 Sure identification of these articles is admittedly difficult, since they bear only abbé Yvon's signature. However, one likely possibility is the article "Bienheureux" (II, p. 245). It is signed by abbé Yvon, and the first of its two parts is theological. However, the second part is ethical, and contains a *renvoi* to the article "Bonheur," signed by abbé Pestré.

8 *Encyclopédie,* I (1751), xli, xliv. These texts are conveniently reprinted in Lough, *The Contributors . . . ,* p. 31.

9 An index to all his articles is in the sixth volume of R. N. Schwab's *Inventory of Diderot's* Encyclopédie, in *Studies on Voltaire and the Eighteenth Century,* 93 (1972), 220.

10 The passage from Condillac's *Essai sur l'origine des connaissances humaines* is in Part II, sect. II, ch. III, paragraph 44. The one by Voltaire, who is not designated by name, is from the twelfth *Lettre philosophique.*

11 The ideas expressed here are favorite topics with Bacon and they recur with great frequency in his writings. However, doubtless as punishment for the number and gravity of my sins, I am unable to give a precise reference for this particular passage.

12 1734 is the publication date of Voltaire's *Lettres philosophiques.*

13 See J. Ehrard, *L'Idée de nature en France . . . ,* 2 vols. (Paris, 1963), II, 679–90; L. C. Rosenfield, *From Beast-Machine to Man-Machine* (New York, 1941).

14 See John Lough, *Essays on the* Encyclopédie *of Diderot and d'Alembert* (Oxford, 1968), p. 293, p. 306.

15 This lively eroticism would seem to make abbé Pestré's view significantly different from Fontenelle's more placid conception, described in R. Mauzi, *L'Idée du bonheur au XVIIIe siècle* (Paris, 1969), pp. 222–27. However, cf. J. Ehrard, *L'Idée de nature . . . ,* II, 564–65.

16 For the contrary argument, sc. that self-satisfaction is a sin, see the satire of Father Garasse in Pascal, *Les Provinciales,* ed. L. Cognet (Paris, 1965), p. 161.

17 Pascal used essentially the same principle, for contrary purposes. See *Les Provinciales,* ed. Cognet, pp. 374ff.

18 However, given the latitude allowed in eighteenth-century discussions of the relationship between pleasure and religion, it would be difficult to prove, on the basis of this article alone, that abbé Pestré was a non-Christian.

19 I will not discuss the articles "Cardano" (II, 675B–676A), "Campanella" (II, 576B–578A), and "Calomnie" (II, 563B–564A). The first two are typical examples of abbé Pestré's fair-minded approach, since he distributes praise and blame with an even hand. They do not, so far as I am aware, contribute anything new to the treatment of these philosophers. It is not known whether the topic of "calumny" may have had some private significance for abbé Pestré. As it stands, the article is not particularly noteworthy.

20 On the background of the question of Canadians in the eighteenth century, Michèle Duchet, *Anthropologie et histoire au siècle des lumières* (Paris, 1971), Index, s. v. "Canada, Canadiens."

21 *Essais,* I, 31, at the end.

Permanence d'une idéologie de "civilisation chrétienne" dans le clergé constitutionnel

BERNARD PLONGERON

"La révolution française est la conséquence dernière et la plus avancée de la civilisation moderne, et la civilisation moderne est sortie tout entière de l'Evangile. C'est un fait irrécusable si l'on consulte l'histoire et particulièrement celle de notre pays. . . . C'est un fait encore incontestable si l'on examine et si l'on compare à la doctrine de Jésus, tous les principes que la révolution inscrivit sur ses drapeaux et dans ses codes; ces mots d'égalité et de fraternité qu'elle mit en tête de tous ses actes et avec lesquels elle justifia toutes ses oeuvres."[1]

Plus qu'un jugement, c'est par cette conviction qu'en 1833, Buchez inaugure son *Histoire parlementaire de la Révolution française* en quarante volumes. Conviction d'un socialisme chrétien qui s'inscrit dans le droit fil de la 'chrétienté républicaine," chère à Grégoire et à ses confrères du clergé constitutionnel. De Grégoire à Buchez s'exprime clairement la référence évangélique comme vision du politique et de l'engagement républicain. Cela suffit-il à lever les ambiguïtés, voire les contradictions latentes d'un discours apparemment sans faille? Une lecture plus attentive nous invite à penser le contraire.

Que signifie, en effet, une "civilisation moderne sortie tout entière de l'Evangile" sinon que, toute "moderne" qu'elle soit, elle devra répondre aux valeurs évangéliques, c'est-à-dire à une morale chrétienne et à ses interdits? En d'autres termes, fût-ce en régime démocratique, Buchez ne conçoit pas que la "civilisation moderne" puisse évacuer son déterminant chrétien. Pour ne pas employer l'expression "civilisation chrétienne," célébrée par ses contemporains romantiques (Guizot et Ozanam en France; Balmès en Espagne), Buchez s'approprierait volontiers celle de "chrétienté républicaine" dont l'évêque constitutionnel Grégoire entretient quelquefois ses diocésains de Blois après 1792. Or, l'évangile vécu selon une orthodoxie de "chrétienté" ne peut s'accommoder de toutes les valeurs révolutionnaires. On aura remarqué que si Buchez exalte l'égalité et surtout la fraternité, il omet la valeur première du trinôme républicain; celle de liberté. Précisément la liberté—impliquant le droit à la différence des hommes et à l'indifférence des cultes qu'ils professent—est la question quasi-insoluble et franchement scandaleuse pour une "chrétienté." Les catholiques libéraux du type Lamennais (comme naguère le clergé constitutionnel) s'évertuent à tourner la difficulté en prônant *des* libertés particulières au lieu de *la* liberté: plus encore ils la mettent en sourdine au profit de l'égalité et de la fraternité qui ont l'avantage de s'harmoniser avec une sociabilité chrétienne. Ce n'est point là un trait particulier à la mentalité catholique. Le protestant libéral Benjamin Constant veut bien proclamer que *les* libertés civiles et politiques sont inséparables, mais c'est la notion d'égalité qu'il élève au rang d'"idée-mère."[2] Pourquoi? Parce qu'explique-t-il, en épigraphe, dans son ouvrage posthume *Du Polythéisme romain* (1833), "l'époque où les idées religieuses disparaissent de l'âme des hommes est toujours voisine de la perte de la liberté; des peuples religieux ont pu être esclaves, aucun peuple incrédule n'a pu être libre." Il y avait longtemps que son ami Grégoire avait établi cette nécessité organique entre liberté et religion (chrétienne).

Le pouvoir révolutionnaire avait récusé cette nécessité et dès lors condamné les chrétiens-citoyens à l'écartèlement entre leurs convictions chrétiennes et leur loyalisme politique—Comment apparaît cet écartèlement dans le processus de la Révolution française? Quelle est sa nature, quel est son sens? En référence à une "civilisation chrétienne" faut-il parler d'un malentendu ou d'un double langage du clergé constitutionnel? Quels sont les repères historiques qui nous permettent de nous prononcer en faveur de l'une ou de l'autre hypothèse? Tels sont les points que nous voudrions évoquer brièvement en guise de lignes de réflexion pour de futures recherches.

I

Commençons par constater le silence de l'historiographie religieuse traditionnelle sur ce conflit de la religion et de la politique dans le clergé constitutionnel. Des auteurs comme A. Aulard et A. Mathiez se bornaient à célébrer le loyalisme des prêtres républicains face au clergé réfractaire et émigré, d'abord dans les péripéties de l'application de la Constitution civile du clergé et de la prestation du serment, ensuite dans l'adhésion des conformistes à ce qu'A. Mathiez nomma fort justement la "première séparation de l'Eglise et de l'Etat," lorsqu'en 1794 la Convention déclare ne plus reconnaître ni salarier aucun culte. Là n'est pas la pierre d'achoppement pour l'Eglise constitutionnelle qui, tout en regrettant cette Séparation, s'en accommode. Elle ne renie pas, sur ce point, le *Contrat Social,* bien au contraire. Sa théologie politique en est imbibée, d'après la thèse qu'exposait, dès 1791, H. Reymond, dans son *Analyse des Principes constitutifs des deux Puissances.* A cette date, H. Reymond n'a pas tout à fait calmé ses ardeurs presbytérianistes qui enflammaient son combat à la tête des curés du Dauphiné en 1789. Mais devenu évêque constitutionnel de l'Isère, il est assez bon théologien pour faire passer son point de vue en doctrine officielle du clergé républicain. Que tout pouvoir tire sa légitimité de l'assentiment du peuple[3] ne fait aucun doute pour les évêques assermentés. Cet assentiment populaire étant porté par les députés, la Convention était donc, à leurs yeux, habilitée à prononcer la séparation de l'Eglise et de l'Etat. Les historiens contemporains comme M. Reinhard, A. Soboul et R. Cobb se sont davantage préoccupés de la déchristianisation qui a, elle, des incidences proprement religieuses. La résistance du clergé constitutionnel à la persécution de l'an II, puis à l'anticléricalisme agressif du Directoire, manifeste cependant plus le droit à l'existence du christianisme que le conflit entre la religion et la politique. Quelques auteurs ont pensé assez logiquement que les "folies de l'an II" avaient contribué à un raidissement conservateur de l'Eglise républicaine qui ne se départit pas pour autant de sa fidélité à la Révolution. Ne serait-ce donc là, comme n'était pas loin de le penser Mathiez, qu'une péripétie, un accident de parcours, parmi d'autres, entre le pouvoir révolutionnaire et les prêtres conformistes?

A défaut d'une rupture, 1793 bientôt renforcé par la reprise de la persécution directoriale, au lendemain du 18 fructidor an V, marque la fin des illusions de 1789 et dès lors donne lieu à des exégèses de plus en plus nuancées du pouvoir révolutionnaire, de la part des autorités religieuses. Sans moyen d'action véritable, elles procèdent malgré tout, au long des *Lettres pastorales* et mandements, à des mises en garde qui s'assortissent de *non possumus,* au nom des chrétiens de France.

L'automne 1792 révèle la nature et le sens du conflit. Il y a plusieurs raisons qui se conjuguent: la loi du 20 septembre proclame le divorce et du même coup ouvre aux prêtres la possibilité de se marier; voilà deux atteintes profondes aux sacrements catholiques du mariage et de l'ordre, qui ne peuvent laisser indifférentes les autorités constitutionnelles. Autant elles admettaient la sécularisation de l'état civil et même applaudissaient à cette mesure, parce que disait le président Agier, juriste de l'Eglise constitutionnelle, "je crois voir dans l'affectation à garder ces registres de baptêmes, mariages, sépultures, par les curés plus d'habitude que de réflexion, plus de zèle que de prudence, plus de souvenir de l'état passé que d'attention à l'état présent . . . ,"[4] autant elles se doivent de réagir lorsque l'intégrité de la religion est mise en cause. Il n'est que de juger des effets de la loi. D'abord à travers les campagnes de presse. *La Feuille villageoise,* spécialisée dans les questions religieuses, déclenche l'attaque contre le célibat ecclésiastique dans trois numéros de mai et de juillet 1792. Une semaine après le vote de la loi du 20 septembre, le journal commente longuement la "conquête" du divorce, puis revient à la charge en faveur du mariage des prêtres: deux numéros en octobre 1792, un en décembre et quatre autres de janvier au 1er août 1793 ("Encore sur le mariage des prêtres"). La pression sécularisatrice se concentre donc dans les derniers mois de 1792 et précède largement la vague de déchristianisation. Le clergé constitutionnel ne reste pas insensible à cette pression et ressent le scandale provoqué par ses membres qui non seulement se marient, mais prétendent conserver leurs fonctions sacerdotales: Lindet, évêque de l'Eure, marié le 21 novembre 1792; un vicaire épiscopal du Nord au printemps 1793; Jean-François Aubert, marié au printemps de 1792 et intronisé solennellement comme curé de Saint-Augustin à Paris par l'évêque Gobel, le jour de l'Ascension 1793.

Devant ces affaires entourées d'une tapageuse publicité, le clergé constitutionnel réagit avec fermeté. Ainsi Lindet explique-t-il son geste et le justifie-t-il par des arguments théologiques dans une lettre aux habitants de l'Eure.[5] Aussitôt les évêques de la métropole des Côtes-de-la-Manche publient, chacun pour leur diocèse, en décembre 1792, lettres pastorales et mandements sur la nature du mariage chrétien et de la discipline ecclésiastique, constitutive du sacrement de l'Ordre: Becherel, évêque de la Manche (lettre du 8 décembre); Lefessier, évêque de l'Orne (mandement du 14 décembre et lettre du 1er janvier 1793); Fauchet, évêque du Calvados (lettres pastorales des 19 novembre et 21 décembre 1792); Massieu, évêque de l'Oise (mandement du 7 novembre).[6] Sur les quatre-vingt-cinq évêques constitutionnels encore en fonctions au 1er octobre 1793, nous avons pu relever les écrits divers de quarante-huit d'entr'eux portant sur l'atteinte aux sacrements par les lois sécularisatrices, dont seize—et ce n'est pas une liste complète—ont été publiés entre septembre 1792 et avril 1793. Certains sont de véritables traités de théologie politique, comme le manuscrit de vingt-cinq feuillets de Lacombe, le premier collaborateur de Pacareau, évêque de Bordeaux, auquel il succéda en 1798.[7] Ce qui peut paraître surprenant, à première vue, c'est qu'aucun de ces écrits défendant l'intégrité des dogmes chrétiens ne met en cause nommément la responsabilité de la législation républicaine.

Bien plus, on affecte de la comprendre dans le sens d'une liberté des cultes qui loin d'autoriser la licence devrait au contraire permettre à la "société religieuse" (L'Eglise) de retrouver la rigueur de ses lois internes et constitutives. Cette argumentation qui rallie la très grande majorité des positions du clergé constitutionnel est avancée dans la *Réclamation adressée aux évêques de France par des curés de Paris* . . . .[8] Cet écrit est important à un triple point de vue: d'abord en raison de la place faite dans l'opinion publique républicaine, constitutionnelle et même émigrée—à ce "scandale" dont l'auteur, Jean-François Aubert, ex-premier vicaire de Sainte-Marguerite à Paris, n'était pas un inconnu; ensuite parce que dans ces mois cruciaux de 1793 où l'Eglise constitutionnelle joue son existence, elle met pour la première fois à jour ses contestations internes au plus haut niveau: l'évêque Gobel censuré par ses curés. La notoriété républicaine et religieuse de quatre des signataires de la *Réclamation* ajoute un relief supplémentaire: encore que si Lemaire, curé de Sainte-Marguerite, et Mahieu, curé de Saint-Sulpice, sont loin de passer pour des personnages négligeables, ils n'ont pas pour autant le prestige de Leblanc de Beaulieu, curé de Saint-Séverin et futur évêque constitutionnel de Seine-Inférieure, ni celle de Brugière, curé de Saint-Paul, ces deux derniers étant considérés comme les chefs de file des jansénistes constitutionnels. L'évêque de Paris, prétendent les curés protestataires, a failli aux lois religieuses en introduisant comme curé un prêtre marié, mais il a aussi contrevenu aux lois de l'Etat, car: "la loi en proclamant la liberté des cultes, reconnaît l'existence des associations religieuses; or, il ne peut y avoir d'association qui n'ait ses loix, sa police, son gouvernement. Il faut donc, de toute nécessité, que l'Etat laisse aux sociétés religieuses le droit de se gouverner suivant leurs loix, pour tout ce qui est essentiel à leur existence, sans quoi ces mots ne seraient plus qu'une dérision, incapable de faire illusion à aucun homme sensé."[9]

Ce texte est d'une ambiguïté calculée: il prend pour constat la liberté des cultes d'où découle logiquement la neutralité religieuse de l'Etat; or, c'est à une toute autre logique que parvient la *Réclamation*: l'indépendance de l'Etat vis-à-vis de l'Eglise—qui n'est toujours pas proclamée en 1793—devrait conduire au renforcement des structures chrétiennes dans ce qu'elles ont d'essentiel pour la foi. Remarquons que les auteurs présentent leur déduction comme une étape de la sécularisation à atteindre, parce que nous n'en sommes pas là, et de beaucoup; ils font aussi de leur déduction un avertissement ou une invitation pressante aux autorités révolutionnaires à épouser leur conclusion.

Et même si, par extraordinaire, le régime républicain comblait ce voeu, les constitutionnels seraient-ils alors satisfaits? Autrement dit, sont-ils prêts à accepter une séparation de l'Eglise et de l'Etat aux conditions suggérées par eux? Cette question est au noeud du débat. Pour y répondre correctement, il faut distinguer le plan politique et le plan socio-religieux. Sur le plan politique, le clergé républicain n'a pas l'intention de revenir sur ce principe émis par le curé Brugière: "nous naissons dans l'Etat et non dans l'Eglise; nous sommes citoyens avant que d'être chrétiens. La religion est admise dans l'Etat, mais elle n'est point admise pour apporter le trouble, la discorde et la confusion."

C'est la raison pour laquelle, les constitutionnels n'attaqueront pas de front l'Etat, fût-il persécuteur, parce que tout citoyen lui doit obéissance civique. Mais cette obéissance civique, cette intransigeance dans le loyalisme républicain n'altère pas une vision sociologique du christianisme.

Celle-ci est parfaitement définie par l'évêque Grégoire, à l'heure où il célèbre avec ses diocésains de Blois l'abolition de la royauté, le 10 août 1792.[10] "Le christianisme doit consoler les peuples affaissés sous le despotisme: Il dit aux hommes que sortis du même limon, ils avaient les mêmes droits et les mêmes devoirs. En proclamant la liberté et la justice, il effraya les tyrans: il sera toujours la pierre angulaire sur laquelle doit reposer notre édifice social, si l'on veut qu'il soit durable. Plutarque disait qu'il serait plus facile de bâtir une ville en l'air que de maintenir un gouvernement sans culte. Combien il serait coupable dans ses motifs et rétréci dans ses vues, le législateur qui prétendrait consolider l'édifice social sans le concours des vertus religieuses: j'en appellerai à sa conduite; c'est la pierre de touche pour apprendre au peuple que si ses mandataires sont impies, ils sont immoraux et qu'il ne faut jamais compter sur la fidèlité envers les hommes, de la part de celui qui est infidèle à Dieu."

"La loi ne peut être impie": telle est et telle demeurera la conviction inébranlable et absolue du clergé républicain. Et si la loi tourne à l'impiété, en 1793, c'est précisément parce qu'il y a "anarchie," c'est-à-dire négation de l'édifice social. En cela, les constitutionnels rejoignent l'opinion des Thermidoriens et partagent leur animosité contre "la dictature de Robespierre."

Mais bien plus profondément qu'une inclination politique vers une république bourgeoise, le clergé républicain ne se départit guère d'une mentalité de "civilisation chrétienne." A la seule différence qu'ils répudient une monarchie sacralisée, les propos de Grégoire rejoignent ceux de Joseph de Maistre lorsqu'il écrit: "Pas de moeurs publiques ni de caractère national sans religion; pas de religion européenne sans christianisme. . . ."[11] On relève même cette référence à Plutarque sur la nécessité d'un culte pour un gouvernement qui devient un lieu commun de la justification d'une religion d'Etat. Avant Grégoire, Mgr. de Bonnal, évêque de Clermont et instigateur d'un tiers-parti dans l'option au serment constitutionnel, l'avait utilisée à l'Assemblée nationale, le 22 août 1789, dans la discussion sur la liberté des cultes: "L'on élèverait plutôt une ville dans les airs, comme l'a dit Plutarque, que de fonder une république qui n'aurait pas pour principe le culte des dieux. Je demande donc que les principes de la constitution française reposent sur la religion comme sur une base éternelle." Dans son *Instruction pastorale dogmatique* du 5 janvier 1792, Prudhomme, évêque de la Sarthe, recourt encore à Plutarque pour tenir le même raisonnement.

Dans leurs prises de position comme dans leur pensée politico-théologique, les constitutionnels participent donc bien à une mentalité de "chrétienté," héritage d'une éducation, certes, mais aussi stricte allégeance à une orthodoxie catholique dont ils ne contestent finalement que l'organisation des pouvoirs ecclésiaux. Leur projet s'inscrit toujours et encore dans une "chrétienté républicaine" et non dans une république chrétienne dont J.-J. Rousseau disait que "chacun de ces deux mots exclut l'autre."[12] Entre les deux existe une différence de nature qui ne fut pas toujours perçue comme telle par l'Eglise constitutionnelle, et qui dès lors prêta à des malentendus, voire à un double langage (politique et religieux). Là où Rousseau accordait une sociabilité politique à la religion *civile,* les constitutionnels répondent par la *vertu sociale* de la religion *chrétienne,* fondement même d'un régime de chrétienté.

II

Un récent ouvrage regroupe les premières recherches du Centre d'Histoire Religieuse de Paris sur le discours d'une "civilisation chrétienne" au XVIIIe siècle, dans l'organisation mentale qu'il implique, dans l'apologétique qu'il déploie, dans les idées-forces qui demeurent inaltérables de l'Ancien Régime à Napoléon.[13] Il n'est pas question, ici, d'analyser les composantes de ce discours d'une "civilisation chrétienne," mais d'en rappeler le principe de base avant d'en examiner les conséquences pour la politique religieuse de la Révolution.

Le principe d'une conscience de "chrétienté" peut s'énoncer comme suit: *la religion perfectionne la société civile; elle "civilise" le lien social.* Ceci peut s'entendre d'une manière très stricte et aboutir à une véritable subordination de la société civile à la religion, de type théocratique ou du type "augustinisme politique." Les monarchies de droit divin s'en inspirent; au nom de la sacralisation du pouvoir royal, elles enferment le civil sous le contrôle rigoureux de la religion dominante, c'est-à-dire le catholicisme romain, à l'exclusion des autres confessions. Certains juristes de la monarchie française ont tiré de l'image constantinienne du prince "évêque du dehors" la théorie de l'absolutisme que récuse Bossuet lui-même. Cette conception intégriste de la "chrétienté" est battue en brèche, au siècle des Lumières, par la "civilisation chrétienne." L'expression comme telle n'apparaîtra qu'à l'époque romantique, mais sa charge idéologique est pleinement assumée au moment où le mot "civilisation" fait son entrée dans les dictionnaires du XVIIIe siècle. Retenons celle du *Dictionnaire de Trévoux* en 1771: "L'Ami des hommes[14] a employé ce mot civilisation pour sociabilité. La religion est sans contredit le premier et le plus utile frein de l'humanité: c'est le premier ressort de la civilisation. Elle nous prêche et nous rappelle sans cesse la confraternité, adoucit notre coeur." A travers les couples sociologiques: civilisation/religion, civilisation/sociabilité, puis le trinôme: sociabilité/humanité/confraternité, se dessine une nouvelle stratégie de la société chrétienne. On abandonne aux théologiens le soin de déterminer la seule religion qui assure le salut éternel de l'homme et l'on insiste sur la valeur éminemment politique de la sociabilité du christianisme. La fonction de "douceur" du christianisme n'a rien de romantique ou du moins pas encore, avant l'instauration de la "religion du coeur" de Rousseau à Schliermacher.[15] Cette "douceur" transforme les moeurs sauvages en sociétés policées; elle est l'agent par excellence de la civilisation.

Dès lors la sociabilité du christianisme devient le background des rapports des pouvoirs civil et religieux en régime de chrétienté. Sans doute n'a-t-on pas encore suffisamment manifesté l'importance de cette optique infléchie par les Lumières. Cela signifie que l'*utilité sociale* de la religion l'emporte sur l'éternel et épineux débat de l'Eglise et de l'Etat. Désormais on peut dissocier les deux questions et restituer à chacune des deux sociétés civile et religieuse sa vocation propre, on peut faire cesser la confusion du civil et du religieux et s'en tenir à leur complémentarité. Telle est la vision du jansénisme politique au lendemain de l'Assemblée du clergé de 1760:

> Dieu a établi encore la société chrétienne, dont le but est tout différent de celui que se propose la société civile. Celle-ci ne tend qu'à entretenir parmi les citoyens l'ordre et la police extérieure et à les faire vivre paisibles et tranquilles; l'autre pénètre jusques dans les coeurs et va jusqu'à y faire régner la vertu et la justice. Ainsi quoiqu'elles résident dans le même lieu, loin qu'elles doivent jamais se trouver en contradiction dans leurs opérations, l'une perfectionne l'ouvrage que l'autre laisse imparfait. Celle-ci se contente de la soumission extérieure aux loix sans porter ses vues plus loin; l'autre règne jusques sur les intentions et veut que l'accomplissement du devoir n'ait d'autre source que l'amour du devoir. La contrainte dont la société civile est obligée de faire usage suffit pour maintenir dans l'ordre ceux qui y ont le moins de penchant, parce qu'il ne lui faut que l'exercice ou l'abstention de certains actes extérieurs, mais comme la société chrétienne ne se borne pas au dehors, qu'elle exige l'amour du devoir et qu'il est impossible de l'aimer sans la pratiquer, il sait que l'on peut être citoyen sans être chrétien, mais que l'on ne peut pas être chrétien sans être citoyen.[16]

Montesquieu, lui aussi fidèle lecteur de Plutarque, se risque à l'extrapolation: la vertu sociale du christianisme en Occident doit être étendue à la *religio,* dans son acception latine, large et diffuse. Ce qui l'incite à écrire dans *Mes Pensées* (n° 1344): "Je ne voudrais pas que l'on allât prêcher aux Chinois: car, comme il faut leur faire voir la fausseté de leur religion, ils sont mauvais citoyens avant que l'on puisse les faire chrétiens." Jugement à la limite de la boutade qu'il nuance par ses développements sur ce sujet aux chapitres XXIV et XXV de *L'Esprit des Lois.* Cela n'empêche nullement ce maître à penser des futurs Constituants, d'établir l'excellence du christianisme qui, à l'exemple des autres philosophes des Lumières, lui sert de prétexte à établir la prééminence politique de la France sur le monde. Au cours de son voyage dans les Etats Autrichiens, en 1728, il s'initie à la politique orientale. Le cardinal Fleury dont il espère un poste diplomatique au Levant tient à la conservation de toutes les frontières de l'empire ottoman. Or, Montesquieu conteste la politique française et s'en explique en termes aussi révélateurs de sa mentalité de "civilisation chrétienne" que peu courtisans: "Je ne sais comment la conscience des gens de notre Conseil de France peut jamais aller bien. Notre intérêt est d'empêcher qu'on ne détruise les protestants, les Turcs et les corsaires de Barbarie. Si l'Empereur envahissait le pays des Turcs, il y établirait des manufactures qui détruiraient notre commerce du Levant. Sans les Corsaires de Barbarie, les Hambourgeois et autres villes hanséatiques iraient faire le commerce du Levant. Nous sommes catholiques et chrétiens et nous avons à maintenir les plus mortels ennemis des uns et des autres."[17] Voilà qui peut nous rendre soupçonneux à l'égard d'une tolérance religieuse quand elle concourt à une realpolitik, fût-elle "chrétienne." Au demeurant, Montesquieu trace déjà la voie d'un double langage que pratiqueront volontiers les législateurs de 1789. Parce que, selon lui, "le salut de l'Etat est la suprême loi," et sans se douter que cette maxime conduira au gouvernement révolutionnaire, il entreprend en 1753 une défense des jansénistes persécutés. En réalité, il définit une tactique aux multiples rebondissements ultérieurs, en distinguant la tolérance intérieure et la tolérance extérieure. Celle-ci est nécessaire parfois à la politique, tandis que celle-là est interdite par la religion. "Quand un prince catholique dit qu'il n'a point et ne veut point qu'on ait de tolérance intérieure, c'est comme s'il disait: 'Je ne puis approuver intérieurement aucune secte dans mes Etats, parce qu'il n'y a que la religion catholique qui sauve; et si je croyais autrement, je ne serais point catholique.' Quand il a la tolérance extérieure, c'est comme s'il disait: 'Je suis établi de

Dieu pour maintenir dans mes Etats la paix... il faut donc que mes lois soient telles, dans certaines circonstances, qu'elles ne s'écartent pas de cet objet. Ma conscience me dit de ne point approuver intérieurement ceux qui ne pensent pas comme moi; mais ma conscience me dit aussi qu'il y a des cas où il est de mon devoir de les tolérer extérieurement. Ce n'est point toujours en conformité du principe théologique, lequel je crois, que mes lois doivent être faites; mais il y a des cas où elles doivent être faites en conformité des principes des lois politiques, sur lesquelles tous les gouvernements sont fondés.'"[18]

Avec cette casuistique politique, ne sommes-nous point à la genèse de la politique ecclésiastique, connue au XIXe siècle sous l'appellation de la "thèse" et de "l'hypothèse" et pratiquée par les constitutionnels lorsque la sécularisation révolutionnaire les presse de trop près? Il nous semble bien retrouver cette distinction entre l'intérieur (la thèse) et l'extérieur (l'hypothèse) dans la question âprement débattue, parmi les constitutionnels en 1798, sur les églises annexées comme propriétés nationales. Noël de Larrière, autre jurisconsulte des *Evêques réunis,* donne ainsi sa consultation aux chrétiens-citoyens. "... C'est à la loi de disposer d'une propriété nationale, sans qu'aucune classe de citoyens ait des droits particuliers à faire valoir [le fait]. Il est vrai que s'il s'agissait de discuter les principes sur lesquels on s'est fondé pour faire des églises des propriétés nationales, la question pourrait n'être pas aussi facile à résoudre en *théorie* qu'elle l'a été dans la *pratique* [thèse]. Mais [hypothèse] des citoyens ne discutent pas contre la loi, ils s'y soumettent."[19]

Pareille politique a toutefois ses limites: acceptable dans le domaine des institutions et des biens, elle n'est plus de mise lorsqu'elle met en cause la foi des fidèles. Sans doute faudra-t-il la cruelle expérience des événements de 1792 à 1795 pour que l'Eglise constitutionnelle perçoive les écueils théologiques de la sociabilité chrétienne. Celle-ci conduisait Montesquieu à conférer au catholicisme un rôle de morale politique dans le cadre d'une "civilisation chrétienne." L'utile, chez lui, l'emportait finalement sur le vrai, ce qu'il laissait adroitement entendre en comparant la religion chrétienne et la religion mahométane: "Sur le caractère de la religion chrétienne et celui de la mahométane, on doit, sans autre examen, embrasser l'une et rejeter l'autre: car il nous est bien plus évident qu'une religion doit adoucir les moeurs des hommes qu'il ne l'est qu'une religion soit vraie."[20] Il faudra surtout la naissance des cultes révolutionnaires pour que les constitutionnels finissent par comprendre qu'une utilité sociale de la religion pourrait se penser autrement qu'en termes de catholicisme. Ici commence leur refus de poursuivre avec Montesquieu, parce que la "vérité" chrétienne ne peut être étouffée au profit de l'utilité sociale de la religion.

III

L'idéal de 1789 permettait de croire qu'il n'y avait et qu'il n'y aurait aucune contradiction entre les exigences de la foi et la sociabilité chrétienne en régime révolutionnaire. Une illusion peut-être, mais partagée par la très grande majorité des membres de l'Assemblée Constituante, seule assemblée où le clergé put jouer un rôle d'importance dans l'élaboration des nouvelles lois. Or celles-ci ne restent-elles pas empreintes d'une mentalité de "civilisation chrétienne" dès la Déclaration des droits de l'homme et du citoyen? A titre d'exemples, prenons trois étapes significatives des discussions que suscitent ces "principes d'une architecture sociale," selon l'expression de B. Groethuysen:[21] le préambule; l'article X sur la liberté de conscience; l'article VI sur l'égalité civile qui ouvre le contentieux du statut des juifs, toujours en suspens jusqu'au décret du 27 septembre 1791 sur leur émancipation.

La question de savoir si Dieu serait invoqué et sous quelle nomination dans le préambule de la Déclaration des droits, n'est pas sans rappeler les discussions du Congrès de Philadelphie. Mais les débats français s'orientent autrement. Il s'agit moins pour les héritiers de l'Occident chrétien de se placer "en présence et sous les auspices de l'Etre Suprême"—selon les termes neutres de la rédaction définitive du préambule—que de déterminer le rôle de Dieu dans la société révolutionnaire. Le nouveau citoyen n'a-t-il que des droits, son self-arbitre n'a-t-il pour bornes que les règles du contrat social ou bien ce nouveau citoyen reste-t-il un chrétien et par conséquent sa liberté ne continue-t-elle pas à être soumise aux décrets de Dieu? Les théologiens catholiques ne cessent, depuis Rousseau, d'alerter l'opinion sur la gravité du dilemme. Si l'homme n'a plus que des droits, c'est-à-dire si son autonomie est entière, la Révélation chrétienne et le dogme du péché originel s'écroulent. Proclamer unilatéralement les droits de l'homme, c'est donner une anthropologie authentiquement révolutionnaire, puisque, pour la première fois, depuis dix-neuf siècles de christianisme, l'homme serait totalement et fondamentalement libre et non plus enfermé dans la dialectique du péché et de la grâce. L'abbé Bergier, le plus percutant des apologistes de la fin de l'Ancien Régime, a fort bien perçu le danger. L'autorité suprême de la société a pour auteur et instituteur: Dieu, répète-t-il dans un de ses derniers écrits,[22] qui n'a pas attendu le consentement de la société, n'a pas eu besoin non plus du bon vouloir de chaque particulier pour lui prescrire ses obligations. Si les Constituants n'ont pas vu tout l'enjeu du débat, si finalement ils jetteront les prémices d'une société sécularisée à rebours de leurs propres convictions, l'abbé Grégoire comprend très vite que laisser la Déclaration des droits sans autre contrepartie, c'est condamner à mort la "chrétienté." Bien qu'adversaire politique de Bergier, il fait sienne l'équation redoutable posée par lui: *la* liberté = indifférentisme religieux = anarchie sociale.

C'est pourquoi, le 18 août 1789, il plaide pour les droits de Dieu face aux droits de l'homme. L'intervention est célèbre: "L'homme n'a pas été jeté au hasard sur le coin de terre qu'il occupe. S'il a des droits, il faut parler de Celui dont il les tient; s'il a des devoirs, il faut lui rappeler Celui qui les lui prescrit. Quel nom plus auguste, plus grand peut-on placer à la tête de la déclaration, que celui de la Divinité, que ce nom qui retentit dans toute la nature, dans tous les coeurs, que l'on retrouve écrit sur la terre et que nos yeux fixent encore dans les cieux?" Le chartreux dom Gerle, qu'on ne peut suspecter d'intégrisme, avait été plus explicite en proposant d'inscrire dans la Déclaration "que la religion catholique, apostolique et romaine était et serait toujours la religion de l'Etat et que son culte serait seul public." Mirabeau écarte promptement ces rappels à l'ordre chrétien d'un ton sec: "Messieurs, nous quittons l'ordre du jour..." Subsistera à l'ordre du jour cet article premier "les hommes *naissent* et demeurent libres et égaux en droits..." qui ruinait idéologiquement un régime de chrétienté. Le clergé réfractaire et émigré ne s'y est pas trompé. Il est caractéristique dans les lettres et mandements des évêques "légitimes" de relever en premier lieu les furieuses attaques contre "cette philosophie détestable des droits de l'Homme" et seulement ensuite les polémiques contre la Constitution civile du clergé et les serments.[23] Cette liberté inconditionnelle de l'homme fera, à l'expérience, tellement peur que les Thermidoriens s'empresseront de supprimer l'article premier de la Déclaration de 1789 et feront précéder la constitution de l'an III d'une Déclaration des droits et des devoirs de l'homme "en présence de l'Etre Suprême." Retour à Montesquieu, après abandon de Rousseau; pour des raisons de stratégie politique et économique, comme on l'a dit? Sans doute, mais à travers la restauration d'une morale politique qui ne songerait à des relents de "civilisation chrétienne" dont demeurent imprégnés les législateurs influents de l'an III, tels Lanjuinais, jansénisant, fidèle ami de Grégoire, Boissy d'Anglas, le protestant Cévenol, et même Daunou, tous en amitié ouverte avec l'évêque constitutionnel de Blois?

L'épineux principe de *la* liberté étant mis en veilleuse, on n'en est que plus à l'aise pour défendre *les* libertés individuelles, c'est-à-dire les personnes, au nom de la tolérance. Au début d'août 1789, l'abbé Fauchet devenait la vedette des prêtres patriotes après son tonitruant sermon prononcé lors du service funèbre pour les morts de juillet, au district de Saint-Jacques-l'Hôpital à Paris.

"Les faux interprètes des divins oracles, s'écriait-il, ont voulu, au nom du ciel, faire ramper les peuples sous les volontés arbitraires des chefs! ils ont consacré le despotisme! ils ont rendu Dieu complice des tyrans! Ces faux docteurs triomphaient parce qu'il est écrit: *rendez à César ce qui est à César.* Mais ce qui n'est pas à César, faut-il aussi le lui rendre? Or, la liberté n'est point à César, elle est à la nature humaine." Ne soyons pas dupes de ce débordement oratoire, car c'est le même Fauchet qui retrouve son orthodoxie catholique dans son remarquable ouvrage *De la religion nationale.* Pesons bien déjà le titre: il est, à lui seul, tout un programme de "civilisation chrétienne" à la lumière de 1789. Pas question à la "nature humaine" de se reconnaître impie, si elle en a envie. Inutile de craindre que "la majorité des Représentants du peuple français soient des impies qui établiront en loi l'indifférence du culte (. . .). Bonnes gens, c'est impossible" (p. 185). Et en voici la raison idéologique que le député Fauchet érige en stratégie parlementaire: "la loi de tolérance a pour objet non les cultes *mais les personnes* qui assure à tous les hommes de quelque religion qu'ils soient ou ne soient pas accueil . . . tant qu'ils ne troubleront pas la société (p. 187)."

On ne peut mieux résumer le fond des débats souvent passionnés qui entourent le vote de l'article X: "Nul ne doit être inquiété pour ses opinions, même religieuses, pourvu que leur manifestation ne trouble pas l'ordre public établi par la loi." Le deuxième membre de la proposition est dû à Gobel, le futur évêque constitutionnel de Paris, qui avec la plupart de ses collègues de la Constituante, distingue la religion et le culte. Personne ne met en doute ce principe de "civilisation chrétienne" rappelé par l'évêque de Clermont, le 22 août: "la religion est la base des empires; c'est la raison éternelle qui veille à l'ordre des choses." Le comte de La Borde, de la tendance libérale, conclut son intervention dans le même sens, quoiqu'en inversant curieusement les termes: "Nous ne pouvons pas professer d'autres sentiments: notre culte catholique ne doit porter aucun empêchement à l'exercice des religions." Le fondement religieux de la nouvelle société, c'est-à-dire le politique chrétien, étant sauvegardé, la question à débattre revient à la conservation de l'ordre social par la *tolérance* d'autres cultes. En vain, Mirabeau, avec une rare clairvoyance, accuse-t-il l'emploi du mot tolérance: "Je ne viens pas prêcher la tolérance. La liberté la plus illimitée de religion est à mes yeux un droit si sacré, que le mot *tolérance,* qui essaie de l'exprimer, me paraît en quelque sorte tyrannique lui-même, puisque l'existence de l'autorité qui a le pouvoir de tolérer, attente à la liberté de penser, par cela même qu'elle tolère et qu'ainsi elle pourrait ne pas tolérer." Il est piquant de constater que c'est Mirabeau qui doit rappeler aux théologiens de l'Assemblée le principe *négatif* de la tolérance: on tolère un mal qu'on ne peut empêcher et c'est la justification de l'*hypothèse* d'une société dont il faudra supporter la sécularisation sans qu'elle devienne admissible pour la *thèse* chrétienne; la liberté est un principe *positif* et l'entériner reviendrait à ruiner l'essence d'un politique chrétien. C'est pourquoi tous les efforts se conjuguent à la Constituante pour définir une tolérance des cultes, avec cet aspect restrictif et oppressif que dénonce avec fougue le pasteur Rabaut-Saint-Etienne. Il s'insurge contre le statut privilégié, déjà reconnu aux catholiques, parce qu'il sait, au nom des protestants de Nîmes qu'il représente, que la religion est la source du droit public, en régime de chrétienté. "Je demande pour tous les non-catholiques ce que vous demandez pour vous: l'égalité des droits, la liberté. . . . L'erreur n'est pas un crime: quelle que soit la religion d'un homme, il ne doit pas pour cela être frustré de ses droits. Je demande la liberté pour ces peuples toujours proscrits, errants, vagabonds sur le globe; ces peuples voués à l'humiliation, les Juifs." Adroitement, Gobel esquive la question des juifs: il ne pense pas, dit-il, le 23 août, qu'on puisse refuser aux non-catholiques l'égalité civile, le culte en commun, la participation à tous les avantages civils . . . mais qu'on n'en fasse pas mention dans la constitution! C'était bien l'avis de Fauchet. Ne précisait-il pas dans *De la religion nationale* que les non-catholiques ne sauraient accéder aux grandes responsabilités nationales, parce qu' "ils ne sont et ne peuvent être *de* la famille mais ils sont *dans* la famille nationale et doivent y être bien-aimés. . . ." (p. 196)? A la même date, l'évêque de Tréguier, Mgr. Le Mintier, était poursuivi devant l'Assemblée Nationale, pour avoir publié un mandement fort réactionnaire dans lequel il osait écrire entre autres: "l'on veut que le disciple obstiné de Moïse, le sectaire de Mahomet, le voluptueux athée vivent avec le chrétien. . . ."

L'évêque réfractaire parlait-il vraiment un autre langage que celui du patriote Fauchet et de ses collègues du clergé rallié à la Révolution? On ne saurait l'affirmer quant à la conservation d'une "civilisation chrétienne." Les réticences et reculades de la Constituante à propos du vote de l'article VI qui déclarait admettre à tous les emplois et dignités les citoyens "sans autre distinction que celle de leurs vertus et de leurs talents" allaient prouver la persistance d'une mentalité commune de "civilisation chrétienne" qui a du mal à intégrer les minorités, surtout les juifs. Le 24 décembre, l'évêque de Clermont "a fait remarquer que la majeure partie de l'assemblée avait manifesté qu'elle n'avait aucune répugnance à accorder aux protestants tous les droits des autres citoyens mais qu'elle ne montrait pas la même disposition en faveur des juifs et des comédiens; en conséquence, il a proposé de diviser la question." Ce qui entraîne le rejet de la motion Brunet de la Tuque, présentée la veille, en faveur de l'éligibilité et de l'accession à tous les emplois civils et militaires des "non-catholiques." M. de La Galissionnière fait tout de suite remplacer l'expression "non-catholiques" par "chrétiens," ce qui renvoie une fois encore les juifs aux ténèbres de la société. En dépit de leur émancipation enfin obtenue sous la Révolution, l'originalité de la "nation" juive demeure comme une anomalie au coeur d'une "civilisation chrétienne." Bonaparte s'en fait l'écho inconscient lorsqu'il déclare, au Conseil d'Etat en 1801, lors de la discussion de la loi sur les cultes: "Quant aux juifs, c'est une nation à part, dont la secte ne se mêle à aucune autre; nous aurons donc le temps de nous en occuper plus tard."[24]

On peut d'ailleurs remarquer que les réactions de "civilisation chrétienne" l'emportent sur le libéralisme républicain des partis "patriotes" (clercs et laïcs) dans toute l'Europe révolutionnaire. A Bologne, par exemple, la République-soeur qui se constitue à l'ombre de la France du Directoire adopte le texte suivant dans sa constitution en août 1796: "La religion catholique romaine est la seule dans tout le territoire de la république. Nul ne peut être élu aux emplois établis par cette constitution s'il ne professe cette religion." On reconnaît, dans la seconde phrase de cet intitulé, une rédaction très proche des débats de la Constituante française en décembre 1789 à propos du vote de l'article VI. L'antisémitisme, parfois sanglant, comme à Gênes, qui anime les républiques-soeurs d'Italie, n'habite pas moins des pays à mentalité, cette fois, protestante. Ainsi la nouvelle République Batave, issue des Pays-Bas, proclame, le 5 août 1796, la séparation de l'Eglise et de l'Etat. Cela n'affecte guère la situation de l'Eglise réformée qui reposait déjà sur une structure quasi-républicaine des communautés calvinistes. En revanche, il est significatif que la minorité des catholiques néerlandais parle, dès le 6 août, de son "émancipation," terme que nous croyions jusqu'ici réservé aux juifs. Eux aussi sont, par la même proclamation, émancipés en Hollande. Ce que confirme une loi votée spécialement en leur faveur, le 3 octobre 1796, par la Convention Batave. A la différence des catholiques, les juifs accueillent cette émancipation sans enthousiasme. Ils craignent que la liberté amène à la longue la communauté israëlite à l'assimilation; ce dont ils ne veulent pas en Hollande comme dans les autres pays. De plus, l'émancipation des juifs déclenche une vague d'antisémitisme chez les *patriotes* (clercs et laïcs, catholiques et protestants qui ont oeuvré en faveur de la chute de la Maison d'Orange) dont beaucoup se recrutent dans le milieu des corporations, traditionnellement hostile à la concurrence juive.[25]

C'est l'honneur du clergé constitutionnel français d'avoir combattu sans relâche pour le droit à l'égalité des races et des confessions. On connaît mieux aujourd'hui l'action de Grégoire en faveur des juifs et des noirs, grâce aux travaux de Grunebaum-Ballin et surtout de Miss Ruth F. Necheles et de Patrick Girard.[26] Ce qua la défense d'une société chrétienne interdisait, croyaient-ils, aux prêtres patroites, c'est-à-dire la liberté religieuse, était compensé par le désir brûlant d'une fraternité. Nous savons que c'est en définitive le leitmotiv de Fauchet dans ses *Sermons patriotiques.* Dieu "a voulu les progrès naturels de la raison qui devaient enfin renouveler le monde et amener librement tous les hommes à la divine fraternité," s'exclame-t-il, le 4 février 1791, à Notre-Dame de Paris. Aux juifs de Paris venus exposer leur situation à la Commune, le 28 juillet 1790, le président Mulot, ex-moine de l'abbaye Saint Victor et futur assermenté, répond: "La distance de vos opinions religieuses avec la vérité que nous professons tous comme chrétiens ne peut pas nous empêcher comme hommes de nous rapprocher. Et si mutuellement nous nous croyons dans l'erreur, si mutuellement nous croyons devoir nous plaindre, nous pouvons nous aimer."

Quelques jours plus tard, nouvelles démarches, encore à l'Assemblée de la Commune de Paris. C'est l'abbé Bertolio, franc-maçon et scrutateur, le 30 janvier 1791, lors de l'élection des curés constitutionnels, qui répond cette fois: "la morale des Hébreux comme celle des chrétiens est fondée sur ces deux maximes: Aime ton prochain comme toi-même. Ne fais pas à autrui ce que tu ne voudrais pas qu'on te fît." Et prolongeant sa petite improvisation, il aborde un point qui avait souvent armé la chrétienté: la réprobation des juifs à cause du déicide. "On voudrait trouver la vengeance divine, dit-il; n'est-ce pas un faux-fuyant de notre amour-propre?"[27]

De son côté, Lamourette, bientôt évêque de Rhône-et-Loire, s'est refusé, en 1790, à ramener la question juive à des données économiques. Le droit des juifs à l'égalité ne peut être contesté, il est dû à leur "dignité d'hommes." Le même mouvement inspirait son élève Grégoire lorsqu'il intervint courageusement le 3 août 1789 en faveur des juifs victimes de persécutions antisémites dans l'Est, "comme ministre d'une religion qui regarde tous les hommes comme frères." Jamais l'Eglise constitutionnelle ne cessera de prêcher en actes et en paroles cette fraternité universelle qui s'enracine dans le précepte de charité: Dieu ne fait exception de personne.

Quelques historiens se sont montrés sceptiques sur la générosité sociale du clergé républicain et plus particulièrement sur Grégoire devant les juifs. On lui reproche de n'avoir pas abandonné sa mentalité de "convertisseur," ce qui nous apparaît aujourd'hui comme contraire à la liberté des consciences et au respect dû aux personnes.

La logique interne de la "civilisation chrétienne," telle que nous l'avons vue, au cours de cette étude, habiter les mentalités d'Ancien Régime, devrait rendre compte des contradictions sans recourir à l'hypothèse malveillante d'une conduite double. Grégoire entend convertir en "régénérant," comme il l'écrit tranquillement en 1788, dans son *Essai sur la régénération physique, morale et politique des Juifs*: "L'entière liberté accordée aux Juifs sera un grand pas en avant pour les réformer, les régénérer, et j'ose le dire, les convertir." Mais "régénérer" qui? Non pas des individus isolés, mais la "nation" juive en tant que corps étranger au politique chrétien, lequel ne peut être, répétons-le, d'essence pluraliste sous peine de perdre son identité. Il y a donc rejet des *institutions* comme des *principes* jugés nuisibles au caractère unitaire de la "civilisation chrétienne" et la "nation" juive est une de ces institutions. En revanche, il y a appel à naturaliser socialement des individus pour les rendre citoyens à part entière du Politique chrétien. A la fin de sa vie, Grégoire n'a pas varié dans son raisonnement qu'il reprend à propos des juifs polonais. Le 2 avril 1818, il écrit à son ami, le libraire Julien: "En assimilant à tous les Polonais les Juifs de leur pays, en leur assurant la jouissance égale des droits sociaux, on opérera leur régénération. Je joins ici un extrait de l'ouvrage que j'imprimai il y a trente ans sur cet objet: il présente en résumé mon opinion."[28] On observera que Grégoire maintient cette logique quand la situation devient défavorable pour les catholiques. Ainsi s'incline-t-il loyalement devant la séparation de l'Eglise et de l'Etat, dans son grand discours des 3 et 4 nivôse an III *Sur la liberté des cultes.* "Le Gouvernement ne doit adopter encore moins salarier aucun culte. . . ." Voilà un *principe,* qui tient au politique révolutionnaire, fût-il antinomique du politique chrétien, "quoiqu'il reconnaisse en chaque *individu* le droit d'avoir le sien." Et c'est aussi pour sauvegarder le droit des individus qu'il a lu à la Convention son *Projet de Déclaration du droit des gens,* le 18 juin 1793, comme étant la forme la plus achevée d'une charité évangélique, elle-même motrice du politique chrétien en régime républicain.

IV

Somme toute, pour des consciences de chrétiens-citoyens, la liberté et l'égalité, prises au niveau des principes, se concilient difficilement avec une idéologie de la "civilisation chrétienne" quand bien même subirait-elle une régénération révolutionnaire. Cette incompatibilité de nature était discernable dès l'élaboration de la Déclaration des droits, mais elle n'accuse sa rigueur qu'à travers les lois de sécularisation de 1792. La logique chrétienne et la logique républicaine entrent en conflit ouvert à propos des sacrements du mariage et de l'ordre. La persécution déchristianisatrice qui suit, s'efforce de dissocier définitivement le citoyen du chrétien. Le loyalisme civique du clergé républicain n'effacera pas les amertumes et le doute profond à l'heure de l'accalmie de Thermidor. Rousseau n'avait que trop eu raison en déclarant contradictoires dans les termes les mots "chrétienté républicaine." L'évêque d'Amiens, Desbois de Rochefort, exprime publiquement ses réticences qui ne seraient pas déplacées dans la bouche d'un prélat insermenté. Or, Desbois de Rochefort avait connu la prison pendant quatorze mois pour s'être opposé ouvertement aux lois du 20 septembre 1792. Mis en liberté en 1795, il fut appelé par

Grégoire à cette sorte de directoire de l'église constitutionnelle, le comité des *Evêques Réunis,* qui tenta de réorganiser le clergé républicain en convoquant deux conciles nationaux.

A ses diocésains de la Somme qu'il retrouve, l'évêque trace un bilan pessimiste dont il indique les causes.

> Les principes les plus vraisemblables en spéculation ont des dangers incalculables dans leur application indéfinie au régime de la société; par exemple, l'Egalité, si énergiquement gravée dans les besoins et les maux communs à tous les hommes et encore mieux démontrée par l'Evangile, ne peut être offerte au genre humain qu'avec a circonspection que l'Auteur de la nature et le Sauveur des hommes ont si habilement employée; que la *Liberté,* ce bien ineffable des enfants de Dieu devient la source des plus grands maux, dégénère dans la licence effrénée des passions, bouleverse les Gouvernements même qui se flattaient de l'avoir pour base si elle n'est restreinte par d'autres bornes que des axiomes métaphysiques et insignifiants, par d'autres règles mêmes que les lois.[29]

Clarifions le pensée de cet évêque rescapé de la Terreur: la liberté et l'égalité ont bien des racines dans l'Evangile, mais elles ne peuvent former le lien social que dans la cité chrétienne et non dans une pratique révolutionnaire où, à terme, elles conduisent à l'anarchie par la subversion des institutions les plus respectables.

En revanche, la fraternité universelle, fruit de la charité évangélique, s'harmonise à merveille avec la sociabilité chrétienne, celle-là même que la tradition "philosophique" de Montesquieu à Voltaire continuait de défendre. Plutôt que de raisonner sur le *principe* de tolérance, il leur semblait plus nécessaire de défendre les droits *individuels,* ce qui n'allait pas sans certaines libertés, et une égalité, laquelle est ressentie par le clergé constitutionnel comme la pratique de l'humilité évangélique. Ardents propagateurs de cette fraternité, discrètement tenue en réserve par les révolutionnaires de 1789, les prêtres patriotes auront à coeur de transmettre cette valeur au XIXe siècle. La jeune démocratie chrétienne, de Lamennais à Lacordaire en passant par Buchez, s'efforcera de montrer dans les enthousiasmes de 1848, que, par la fraternité, l'Evangile et la Révolution peuvent former une symbiose, cette fois, régénérante pour la "civilisation chrétienne."

Parce que la sécularisation depuis un siècle et demi a largement pénétré les institutions de l'Occident chrétien, nous avons peine à comprendre cet écartèlement du chrétien-citoyen sous la Révolution, tout en admettant qu'au niveau des principes s'affrontaient deux idéologies. Sans doute l'expérience américaine est-elle bien différente, surtout en cette terre de Virginie, exemplaire, depuis 1775, pour la liberté religieuse que ratifieront la Déclaration de 1776, puis la Constitution fédérale de 1787,[30] renforcée par le premier Amendement de 1791. Il est bien évident qu'une proclamation de la liberté religieuse, nette et complète, dans la Déclaration française de 1789, eût changé le cours des évènements et levé bien des équivoques en forme de guerres de religion (le problème scolaire par exemple) qui pèseront sur le XIXe siècle français.

Or, précisément, nous avons cherché à montrer pourquoi et comment la solution américaine n'était ni possible, ni souhaitée par les plus libéraux des Constituants. Leurs illusions, leurs restrictions, leurs blocages psychologiques montrent à l'envi que l'idéologie de "chrétienté," plus qu'un problème confessionnel, s'était mué au cours des siècles, en une culture enserrant les mentalités dans ces "prisons de longue durée" comme les a qualifiées l'historien F. Braudel. C'est du côté de ce problème des mentalités plus que dans la recherche des manoeuvres politiques—nullement absentes par ailleurs—que le siècle des Lumières dans sa "lecture" révolutionnaire peut, nous le croyons, nous révéler davantage et autre chose.

NOTES

1 Buchez et Roux, *Histoire parlementaire de la Révolution française* (Paris: Paulin, 1834), p. 1.

2 Dominique Bagge, *Les Idées politiques en France sous la Restauration* (Paris: Presses Universitaires de France, 1952), pp. 89–92.

3 *Analyse des principes constitutifs des deux Puissances précédée d'une adresse aux curés des départements de l'Isère, de la Drôme et des Hautes-Alpes et suivie des notes justificatives du Cahier des curés du Dauphiné* (Vienne et Embrun, 1791). Voir Jean Godel, "La Réforme de l'Eglise gallicane à la veille de la Révolution française, vue par le clergé de second ordre et particulièrement par le clergé dauphinois." *Etudes juridiques et historiques* (Grenoble: Presses Universitaires, 1971), LXXXIV, 83–91.

4 Pierre-Jean Agier, *Du mariage dans ses rapports avec la religion et avec les lois nouvelles de la France* (Paris, an IX), pp. 57, 110.
5 *Robert-Thomas Lindet, évêque du département de l'Eure, aux citoyens du même département* (Paris, 1792), p. 5.
6 Papers of Bayeux Library (Canonical House), cart. 304, 6e file (Constitutional bishops).
7 L'un des meilleurs connaisseurs et l'un des moins indulgents à l'égard du clergé constitutionnel, le chanoine Pisani, écrit à propos de l'évêque Lacombe: "Quand parut la loi qui faisait entrer le divorce dans les moeurs publiques, il consacra à cette question un écrit où il établit avec force et orthodoxie la doctrine de l'Eglise, mais il n'a pas un mot pour indiquer ensuite ce que les catholiques ont à faire, pour résister à cette loi anti-chrétienne et anti-sociale," *Répertoire biographique de l'épiscopat constitutionnel* (Paris: J. Picard, 1907), p. 411. Le chanoine Pisani prend pour une lâcheté ce qui relève, chez Lacombe, d'une attitude patriotique. Le mémoire de Lacombe, retrouvé dans les archives diocésaines d'Angoulême, est publié dans la *Revue d'histoire de l'Eglise de France,* 170 (janvier-juin 1977), 92–95.
8 *Réclamation adressée aux Evêques de France par des curés de Paris contre l'institution canonique accordée par* M. *Gobel, évêque métropolitain de Paris, à un Prêtre marié, élu à une cure de son diocèse* (Paris, 1793). On en trouvera d'importants fragments publiés dans les documents annexes (VII 343–45) de Bernard Plongeron, *Théologie et politique au siècle des Lumières 1770–1820* (Geneva: Droz, 1973). Nous nous permettons de renvoyer à cet ouvrage pour les analyses détaillées et les documents dont nous faisons ici la synthèse.
9 *Instructions choisies de* M. *Brugière, curé de Saint-Paul* (Paris, 1804).
10 Henri Grégoire, *Discours prononcé dans l'église-cathédrale de Blois... au service des citoyens morts à Paris, le 10 août 1792,* pp. 10–11.
11 Joseph de Maistre, *Lettre au comte de Blacas* (22 mai 1814), *Oeuvres complètes,* X, 103.
12 *Du Contrat Social,* ch. VIII, "De la religion civile."
13 Jean-René Derré, Bernard Plongeron, *Civilisation chrétienne. Approche historique d'une idéologie XVIIIe–XXe siècle* (Paris: Beauchesne, 1975).
14 Victor Riquetti, marquis de Mirabeau (père d'Honoré-Gabriel, comte de Mirabeau, député à l'Assemblée Constituante), *L'Ami des Hommes,* 5 vols. (Paris, 1755). Le livre fit sensation en France, en Angleterre, et en Italie et fut réédité, dès 1756, sous le titre de *L'Ami des Hommes ou Traité sur la Population*.
15 Bernard Plongeron, "Archetypal Christianity: The Models of 1770 and 1830," *Concilium,* 7, no. 7, (September 1971), 78–92.
16 *Extrait du procès-verbal de l'Assemblée générale du clergé tenue en 1760, suivi d'un examen des réclamations de la dite assemblée,* pp. 33, 71.
17 *Lettre au baron de Stain* du 20 octobre 1729.
18 *Mémoire sur la Constitution* (Unigenitus).
19 *Journal religieux ou Mémoires pour servir à l'histoire de l'Eglise* (Dir. M. Larrière; 8 nos. 25 ventôse—10 messidor an VI), n° II du 10 germinal an VI.
20 Montesquieu, *L'Esprit des Lois,* 5e partie, ch. XXIV, sect. 54.
21 Bernard Groethuysen, *Philosophie de la Révolution française* (Paris, 1956).

22 Anonymous Pamphlet intitulé: *Quelle est la source de toute autorité?* (Paris, 1789). See Bernard Plongeron, *Théologie et politique au siècle des Lumières* . . . pp. 115–20.
23 See Bernard Plongeron, *Conscience religieuse en Révolution* (Paris, 1969) pp. 211–26.
24 Jacques Godechot, *Les Institutions de la France sous la Révolution et l'Empire* (Paris: Presses Universitaires de France, 1951), p. 627.
25 Pierre Brachin et L. J. Rogier, *Histoire du Catholicisme hollandais depuis le XVIe siècle* (Paris, 1974), p. 75; Jacques Godechot, *La Grande Nation. L'expansion révolutionnaire de la France dans le Monde 1789–1799* (Paris: Aubier, 1956), II, ch. XV, "Les problèmes religieux," pp. 518–30.
26 Ruth F. Necheles, *The Abbé Grégoire 1787–1831: The Odyssey of an Egalitarian* (Westport, 1971); Richard H. Popkin "La Peyrère, The Abbé Grégoire and the Jewish Question in the Eighteenth Century," *Studies in Eighteenth-Century Culture,* IV (1975), 209–22; Patrick Girard, *Les Juifs de France de 1789 à 1860* (Paris: Calmann-Levy, 1976).
27 S. Lacroix, *Les Actes de la Commune de Paris pendant la Révolution,* 16 vols. (Paris 1894–1914); Marcel Reinhard, "Les Juifs et la Révolution française," *Facultés Catholiques de Lille,* 21e Année (1964), 157–69.
28 See Jacques Madaule, "Grégoire et les Juifs," *Europe,* 128–29 (1956), 77.
29 *Mandement de l'Evêque d'Amiens* (Amiens, 1795), pp. 17–18.
30 The Statute of Virginia for Religious Freedom drafted by T. Jefferson in 1777 and adopted by the General Assembly in 1786. See William Walter Hening, *The Statutes at Large* (1823) (Charlottesville, 1964), XII, 84–86.

The Significance of Jansenism in the History of the French Catholic Clergy in the Pre-Revolutionary Era

WILLIAM H. WILLIAMS

Traditionally, Jansenism has been considered one of the most interesting of the religious movements since the Protestant Reformation, and, to the ablest scholars attracted to its study, one of the most complex.[1] As Alexander Sedgwick has recently shown, the historiography of Jansenism provides an example of amazing vitality and intensity of debate,[2] a debate which echoes that over the Reformation itself except for its vastly reduced scale. Many writers—especially in the nineteenth-century—found an ideological touchstone in Jansenism as they traced the origins of their modern world to the Enlightenment, to the demise of the *ancien régime,* and to the revolutionary upheaval at the close of the eighteenth century. Their interpretations reflect their own widely dispersed positions across the political and religious spectrum, with Jansenism depicted as evil or constructive according to their viewpoint. The variety and complexity of Jansenism explain perhaps why of the more than 15,000 titles devoted to the phenomenon there exists no single work which adequately explains its rise, transformation, and dissolution.

Despite the current surge of interest in seventeenth- and early eighteenth-century Jansenism, there have been very few studies of Jansenism in France before the Revolution. Yet the profound mutation which occurred in the Jansenist phenomenon in the eighteenth century has opened serious problems of interpretation which have still to be fully explored. This essay examines the fundamental difficulties in interpreting the significance of Jansenism in the pre-Revolutionary period and suggests an essential context in which these can be resolved.

A principal part of the problem is the use of the terms Jansenist and Jansenism in the last third of the century, for they provide in themselves a continuing source of confusion. This confusion was apparent to thoughtful contemporaries observing the political and judicial activities of determined factions in Paris in the 1750s and 1760s.[3] The historian Jean Leflon, although referring to the history of Italian Jansenism after 1850, has aptly suggested the bankruptcy of this term when employed in a general sense in France in this period. Leflon states: "The word Jansenist contains so many different facets that it loses all meaning. We thus have the Jansenist who is anti-Jesuit, the Jansenist who is an Augustinian, the Jansenist who is a theologian of efficacious grace, the Jansenist who is an anarchist, the Jansenist who is a republican, the Jansenist who is a liberal. The word changes according to the context."[4] In the most competent studies of the last decade historians have begun to confront the problem posed so succinctly by Leflon. They have traced the course of the movement across the national frontiers of Catholicism and have emphasized the international significance of Jansenism. In the process they have provided new dimensions to its place in the intellectual history of the Age of the Enlightenment.[5]

Modern studies of French Jansenism in the eighteenth century date from the 1930s when Gabriel Le Bras published his earliest articles. In these he pioneered the regional examination of the conditions of Catholicism in France in the context of a quantitative study of the sociology of religious practices.[6] His investigations culminated in his seminal work *Etudes de sociologie religieuse* in 1956, in which he suggested a correlation between the penetration of Jansenism in some regions, the decline of religious practices, and the subsequent loss of faith in these areas.[7] As Le Bras' scholarship richly suggests, the future of Jansenist historiography lies clearly in comprehensive regional studies. More importantly, the findings of local religious history must be projected into the larger context of collective mentalities in France, for which Le Bras' important work provides only a partial illumination.

The continuing tradition of Le Bras' scholarship is reflected in the significant article of 1967 by Bernard Plongeron on the Jansenist image of the Catholic Church as seen in their famous publication the *Nouvelles ecclésiastiques.* This periodical, which appeared, at times sporadically, from 1728 to 1790, was the official journal of the movement on doctrinal and social issues. Plongeron argues cogently that we must recognize the plural nature of the Jansenist phenomenon, admitting that there were many "Jansenisms" in the eighteenth century. In the closing years of the *ancien régime* he notes an increasingly gloomy picture drawn in the pages of the *Nouvelles ecclésiastiques* for the outlook of the Catholic Church in France, implying that this sentiment of desperation was an important factor in the hasty and ill-advised involvement of the journal in the pre-Revolutionary political debate. With an admirable concern for a more nuanced historical synthesis of the course of the Christian religion, Plongeron was the first to indicate that Jansenism, like Calvinism, should be studied within the perspective of the European crisis of conscience of the period, a larger perspective which transcends the limited one presented in the official Jansenist periodical.[8]

Recently, the broad lines of the drastic transformation which took place in French Jansenism in the eighteenth century have become clear. Focusing mainly upon the dramatic politicization which took place, the expanding literature on the sect has gradually revealed the intricacies of the Jansenists' increased public involvement. Scholars have thus traced how the "classic" Jansenism associated with the *Augustinus* of Jansenius and its adherents at the reformed abbey of Port-Royal des Champs was transmuted into an elusive and pluralistic subject for historical study.[9] Only in the last few years have the political implications of the movement been explored, as suggested by J. A. G. Tans in his 1956 article on the ideas of the Jansenists.[10] In this study, Tans noted the need for a comprehensive survey of the political theory of the Jansenists since the *Fronde*, noting in the process that their political tone vis-à-vis authority was far from servile, although their ideas were not democratic.

Like the Protestant Reformation, Jansenism in France in its initial phase was a theological movement. But after the condemnation by Pope Innocent X in 1653 of five of Jansenius' propositions (the total depravity of human nature, the necessity of God's "efficacious" or "irresistible" grace, the loss of free will, predestination, and limited atonement for sin) Jansenism acquired a more varied character. In what have been termed its second and third generations, French Jansenism assumed social, political, economic, and popular theological colorations which were almost entirely lacking in its origins. In the face of increasingly virulent attacks in the seventeenth century, the Jansenists attempted to broaden the base of their support. In the process, they compromised the integrity of their austere and ascetic theological position. Viewing their history in retrospect, it is clear that as the Jansenists turned increasingly to the offensive against their archenemies the Molinist Jesuits, they were drawn proportionately into the bitter controversies at the end of the century over authority in the absolutist state.

The mutation which occurred in Jansenism at the end of the seventeenth century in France has traditionally been studied within the context of the struggle over different concepts of power. This struggle took place at three levels. In foreign affairs, it was the dramatic confrontation between the temporal power of the papacy and that of Louis XIV over Avignon, the Low Countries, Cologne, and other matters. In relations between the Apostolic See and the Gallican Church, it was the bitter dispute of 1673 over the *régale*, or the King's right to income from vacant bishoprics, a quarrel which produced the corollary one over the confirmation of French bishops. This controversy over the *régale* is usually labeled the dispute over the "Gallican liberties of the French Church." In this second confrontation the focus should be placed upon the General Assemblies of the French Clergy and their policies of careful mediation between the two parties in these troubled times.[11] Finally, in internal ecclesiastical affairs in the French

Church, the dispute took the form of the protracted controversy between the episcopacy and the lower clergy over power in Church affairs.

What is generally not understood in the tangle of conceptual arguments which these disputes over power entailed is the consistency and success of the policies of Louis XIV. Nor has the significance of these factors in the history of Jansenism been generally recognized. The element of continuity of royal policies with respect to all three of the levels of power confrontation needs to be stressed. During the twenty years of bitter quarrels from 1673 to 1693 between the Vatican and Versailles the French position was constant. It was founded upon the classical distinction between the temporal and spiritual leadership of the papacy. In this view, affairs between the two states were essentially temporal relations, governed by diplomatic procedures and divorced from canon law. As the capital of the Christian world, Rome possessed a unique international character which gave each prince the right to have a representative there and to share in the exercise of public power. Louis XIV and his secretary of state, Colbert de Croissy, thus maintained that there was no threat to the head of the Catholic Church contained in their belligerent policies toward papal territories nor in their assertion of certain privileges in the governance of the Eternal City. As the self-proclaimed leader of the Christian powers, Louis XIV declared himself to be the chief defender of the papacy's spiritual integrity.[12]

In their political manoeuvres in the later seventeenth century, the Jansenists continually placed themselves in opposition to royal policies. This is seen in their antagonism to the extension of the *régale*, their campaign against the Jesuits, and their alliance with members of the Parisian parliamentary milieu. The history of Jansenism was thus entangled with the long dispute which began with Louis XIV's first edict on the *régale* of February 10, 1673 and which ended with his conciliatory letter to Pope Innocent XII of September 14, 1693, which healed the breach between the two states with minimal concessions by the monarch. In the interim, the doctrine of parliamentary Gallicanism was given a new formulation. Embodied in the historic Four Articles of the Gallican Church of 1682, Gallicanism asserted that the French king's power in temporal matters was subject only to God. It further posited the right of the Gallican Church to govern itself and to receive no papal bulls or briefs without the consent of the French episcopacy. Finally, it declared the superiority of Church Councils in matters of faith.[13]

After 1693, when the Sun King had consolidated his diplomatic position through peace with the papacy and had strengthened his power internally through the affirmation of Gallicanism, he turned anew against the suspect Jansenist faction. For in his view the Jansenists were menacingly "republican" and potential *frondeurs.* In particular, he distrusted the Jansenists for the ties that had gradually developed between some of them and the *Parlement* of Paris, the allegiance of the judges being still suspect because of their involvement in the *Fronde.* Through their opposition to the *régale,* their connections with the *Parlement,* and their unorthodox religious views, the Jansenists in the eyes of the king were associated with the spirit of rebellion.

The combined opposition of Versailles and Rome to the Jansenists culminated in the Bull *Unigenitus* of 1713 which condemned 101 propositions in Pasquier Quesnel's influential Jansenist book *Réflexions morales.* Most specialists agree that this date marks the end of the transition of a movement in which central theological problems were replaced by a wide gamut of other concerns and of which its political activities, culminating in the expulsion of the Jesuits in 1762, were the most notorious. It is in the fragmentation of the sect after 1713 that the serious problems of interpretation noted by Leflon appear. For under the label of Jansenism there flourished many groups of diverse doctrinal beliefs. Most spectacular in the earlier century was the popular Jansenist movement that flowered in the parish of Saint-Médard of Paris. This was a colorful sect of a chiliastic and millenaristic basis, whose growth points up the radical transformation of the original doctrines of Port-Royal, which were incompatible with such principles. In a wider context, the followers of the deacon François de Pâris implicitly raised questions which would undermine the principles of both Church and State concerning order and hierarchy, authority, and corporate privilege. Under the banner of spiritual liberation, his disciples emphasized a new fraternal and egalitarian society. By implication the *frères* and *soeurs* of Saint-Médard questioned the nature of the structure of the Bourbon monarchy and the Gallican Church. The civil authorities recognized this threat in their rigorous suppression of the sect. Confronted with a similar opposition from the Gallican hierarchy, the popular Jansenists came to view the episcopate as an entrenched corporate élite, exalting in the process the role of the laity and the lower clergy in their vision of a more democratic, congressional polity in the Church.[14]

In the history of Jansenism in France, the focus now shifts to the lower clergy, the third level of the confrontation over authority. Here the standard account since its publication in 1929 has traditionally been Edmond Préclin's classic work *Les Jansénistes du XVIIIème siècle et la constitution civile du clergé,* a work universally cited and one which comprises a veritable keystone in the historiography of Jansenism in the eighteenth century. Most significantly, Préclin's book suggests that Jansenism was not merely a phantom in the eighteenth century, as previously thought, but developed and propagated within itself the germs of a second heresy, Richerism, which would in the end absorb if not devour it. This "second Jansenism," deprived of the support of many prelates, linked itself with the lower clergy and flattered their instincts of independence.

The question of central importance is the degree to which the doctrines of Edmond Richer (1560–1631) served the lower clergy as a vehicle for social and political protest within the Church. In the context of disputed authority between the episcopacy and the parochial clergy, some elements of Richer's ideas had an obvious appeal to the priests. Richer's writings were known in the seventeenth century, but the definitive synthesis of his ideas, formulated in his work *Histoire du syndicat d'Edmond Richer,* was not published until 1753. Generally labeled "Presbyterianism" in French accounts, the position of Richer's followers was that the power to make infallible laws rested with the Universal Church assembled in Council. For Richer the government of the Church was that of a tempered aristocracy in which the pope was subordinate to the episcopacy. Although the episcopacy embodied the principal authority of the Church, the parish priests, descendants of the seventy-two disciples, possessed a spiritual power equal to that of the bishops. Ideally, in the government of the Church, both in the dioceses and in Church councils, the curés should serve as the Senate, with a decisive consultative vote. In assessing Richer's influence on the so-called "revolt of the curés" in the pre-Revolutionary period, Préclin conceded that the program of temporal and economic demands of the French lower clergy developed independently of this influence in response to the unique conjuncture of events. But he argued that the spiritual convictions of what he termed the "Jansenist-Richerists" concerning the importance of the priest in the hierarchy provided, as it were, the audacity of conviction upon which the curé reform movement of the later eighteenth century was founded.[15]

According to Préclin's thesis, what appealed to the lower clergy was the unique fusion of Jansenism, Richerism, and Gallicanism—first in Quesnel's *Réflexions morales,* then, after mid-century, in the writings of the erudite curé Nicolas Travers of Nantes, the most vehement of Richer's followers. Based upon a study of the history of the primitive Church, Travers' works exalted the position of the lower clergy even further than Richer, stating that "the functions reserved today for bishops could be delegated to simple priests."[16] Travers would deprive the bishops of their special prerogatives—sacramental, disciplinary, and administrative. He would reduce them to the position of honorary presidents of the consistories of their dioceses, requiring them to obtain a majority of curé votes to enact regulations. More radical than this, Travers maintained that bishop and priest had an equal right to Church property. Significantly, this emergent creed extended far beyond conventional Gallicanism. For traditional Gallican liberties merely emphasized the independence of the French Church under a monarch possessing a bishop's powers. In this traditional scheme the king would be restrained in the exercise of his power by an episcopal aristocracy acting through the General Assemblies of the Clergy. In Travers' doctrine, by contrast, the Church was seen in terms of a clerical democracy with important internal political power for the curés.

Préclin's concern is to demonstrate significant Jansenist influence among the lower clergy. He maintained that the bitter disputes which occurred in certain dioceses during 1759–73 provided the context in which the non-Jansenist lower clergy, who sought theoretical justification for their resistance to excessive episcopal domination, turned to "Jansenist-Richerist" teachings. But in developing this thesis that the doctrines of Quesnel and Travers were persuasive among the lower clergy to 1790, he encountered a serious problem on the eve of the Revolution. As he admitted, during the years just before 1789 evidence of this influence vanishes from the contemporary literature of the parish priests. For there developed first among the curés of Dauphiné and then in Lorraine, Brittany, Berry, and other regions an ideology of revolt which was highly pragmatic and goal-oriented, especially after June 1788. Préclin explains that the "Jansenist-Richerist" current went underground during those critical years to re-emerge in 1790 with the Civil Constitution of the Clergy.

In the most important regional study of the French clergy yet produced, René Taveneaux follows the main lines of Préclin's thesis. In his work, *Le Jansénisme en Lorraine: 1640–1789,* he argues that after 1730 Jansenism was reduced to "*un fait de mentalité,*" or mental disposition, among the lower clergy, who were naturally disposed to exploit ideas favorable to their order. This disposition wrought a change in attitudes among them akin to class consciousness. The movement was strengthened among the priests by rising costs which made their lives more difficult and by the aristocratic reaction of an episcopacy that had become the refuge of the younger sons of the great families. For Taveneaux, Richerism, which had been "a simple doctrinal audacity" a few decades earlier, became integrated by the middle of the century in the drama of the daily life of the priest. "Felt and lived at the same time," he states, "it dominated a Jansenism whose theological structure was undergoing a change."[17]

In the pre-Revolutionary period, Taveneaux believes in a sort of "interior Jansenism," which manifests itself in an "ardent existence," passionate but without exterior sign. Thus: "Secular clerics themselves—by reason of temperament or social organisation—lived with Jansenism as an individual condition more than as a collective movement. At no time—except perhaps in the debased forms of Richerism on the eve of the Revolution—did it, as in France, get mixed up in episodes of class warfare or political revolt."[18]

Because of the peculiar nature of the religious and ecclesiastical character of Lorraine, lying as it does on the frontier of French Catholicism, it is difficult to generalize from Taveneaux's conclusions until further regional studies have been completed. Moreover, a more severe limitations on the acceptance of his general thesis of Jansenism and the lower clergy is the highly subjective nature of his interpretation. Like Préclin's contention that the "Jansenist-Richerist" movement went underground before the Revolution, Taveneaux's conception of the "interior condition" of Jansenism is impossible to verify.

Both the interpretations of Préclin and Taveneaux of the parish clergy in the last years of the *ancien régime* appear inadequate. They suffer from the problem of definition which Leflon has identified. To attribute to "neo-Jansenist," "para-Jansenist," or even "Jansenist-Richerist" ideas the ideological motivation behind the disaffection of the lower clergy in the later century is to endow the movement of curé reform with an almost mythological aspect. In Lorraine, for instance, the most distinguished leader of the curé movement was the abbé Henri Grégoire, the priest whose career as deputy to the National Assembly and later as bishop of the Department of Loire-et-Cher placed him among the most notable of the clerics who sought to reconcile Christianity and the Revolution. An immensely humane and tolerant clergyman with some Jansenist sympathies, Grégoire is best understood, however, as independent in his theology, not as a Jansenist.[19] Certainly his practical concerns in the pre-Revolutionary period were to organize and carry through pragmatic reforms to strengthen the position of the curés in the parish, in the councils of the Church, and in the States-General.[20] Nor in Dauphiné, a second major center of curé reform activities, is there evidence of significant Jansenist influence. As Préclin admits, the head of the curé movement there, the abbé Henri Reymond, was clearly not a Jansenist, and there is no evidence of significant Jansenist penetration in that province.[21] Clericogeographic studies of Jansenist influence in this period are still in their infancy, and general conclusions must await a general cartographic picture. In this context, Plongeron has suggested that the many-sided character of Jansenism requires studies of the social geography of the phenomenon. Thus, he maintains, the researcher must investigate such élite groups as the bourgeoisie and the higher clergy and correlate the findings with those from the third estate, the convents, the lower clergy, and the common people.[22] Certainly, with respect to the reform-minded lower clergy, considered a pivotal group by previous historians, the significance of Jansenism in the pre-Revolutionary period remains to be proven.

Central to the problem of investigating Jansenism after 1770 is the lack of doctrinal specificity, even as elaborated in the *Nouvelles ecclésiastiques.*[23] With the expulsion of the Jesuits in 1765, the Jansenist faction in Paris had achieved a victory which, paradoxically, resulted in its own self-destruction as a viable political force. In the course of a century's bitter controversy these Jansenists had defined their positions too exclusively in terms of their opposition to the Jesuits. "Like some parasitic creature," writes Dale Van Kley, who has chronicled their intricate and sustained campaign, "they had destroyed the substance upon which they depended for life."[24] With their archenemies expelled from France, the Jansenist faction voiced in the *Nouvelles ecclésiastiques* a desperate concern to combat incredulity and to defend the Christian religion as the vehicle of civilization. Religious quarrels were forgotten as the social utility of religion was extolled. Politically, after 1770, the pages of the official Jansenist journal reflect a switch from defiance to the defense of the Bourbon régime. The position of the Jansenist publication vis-à-vis the authority of the State had undergone a transformation. The Catholic cult became the expression of the identity of the nation. Now, as ardent partisans of the *ancien régime* and of the society of orders on which it rested, the spokesmen for Jansenism urged the clergy to "gather together its talents and virtues so that its ministers in their functions would contribute to the diffusion of respect for the social order and subordination . . . in a word, all which can serve to promote the luster, happiness and prosperity of the State. . . ."[25]

There appears to be little in the Jansenist message as seen in its most concrete form in the *Nouvelles ecclésiastiques which would shed light upon the growing movement of curé* disaffection in the waning years of the *ancien régime*. In place of those interpretations which attempt to explain the motivations of parish clergymen in terms of a transmuted Jansenist doctrinc should be substituted one placed in the context of the collective mentality of the parish priesthood, especially as it developed in the last third of the eighteenth century. Until exhaustive regional studies have been completed, the picture of this mentality will remain incomplete, but the broad lines of this collective outlook can be indicated.[26]

Chronologically, the starting point for the development of this curé mentality would be Louis XIV's edict of April 21, 1695, in which he granted increased diocesan powers to the French bishops, an act that was completely consonant with the doctrine of royal Gallicanism. This act alarmed many parish priests and may be seen as the commencement of the internal political struggle with the episcopacy which culminated in the resistance to the authority of the episcopate so characteristic of the curé movements in Dauphiné and Lorraine in 1787–89. Yet the political aspirations of the lower clergy in the later century took many forms; moreover, the specifically anti-episcopal nature of the curé reform movement has been overstated. The parish clergy were more consistently obsessed in the period 1776–89 with the political and economic predominance in the Church of the "intermediate" clergy, the canons, priors, and other benefice-holders without cure of souls.[27]

Furthermore, the political aspirations of the lower clergy must be seen in an economic context. The central target for the underpaid curés *conguistes,* that is, the one-third of the priests of the kingdom who were salaried, was the possessor of the parish tithe, generally a monastery or cathedral chapter, sometimes a bishop, and, occasionally, a layman who had acquired it. To offset the influence of the tithe owners and their allies in the levying of taxes, the curés strove to win representation on the ecclesiastical bureau of taxes. The curés *décimateurs,* who possessed the tithes, sought to acquire social recognition at least equal to that enjoyed by the intermediate clery. Finally, the parish priests shared the preoccupation among secular clergy with proprietary wealth. The curé's *congruistes* envied the more flexible *rentier* income which attachment of the tithe to their benefices would bring. Of equal significance in the collectivity of their outlook, the socioeconomic values of the parish priests linked them, however loosely, with the proprietary sector of the middle classes and even the nobility.[28] In sum, there is a striking continuity in the social and economic aspirations of the lower clergy in the pre-Revolutionary period which must be carefully related to their political activities. In so doing, a significant commonality of outlook begins to emerge.

It has not been generally recognized that the parish clergy constituted a veritable local élite by virtue of their education, their social prominence (which was obtained in many communities through their charitable works and their spiritual ministry), and, finally, their activities as heads of agricultural *entreprises.* In this respect, the curé reform movement after 1750 was marked by an increasing consciousness of the curé's utility based upon the value set upon their functions in society by Turgot and other government officials, upon the prevailing literary image of the "good curé" in the eighteenth century, and upon their own conviction that the *corps* of curés would provide the foundation for a rejuvenated Church.

The spiritual intensity which underlay the curé reform movement is an integral part of their collective mentality. The parochial ideal which emerged in their writing represented their own solution to the dilemma of Catholicism in their day. It blended the virtues of primitive Christianity, the concern for the welfare and happiness of their flocks, a pragmatic desire for more power in the hierarchy of the Church, and an effusive optimism about obtaining their goals through royal intervention. Based upon the day-to-day vicissitudes of the parish priest's life, and upon his increasing frustration with the aloof authority of the hierarchy, the curé's attempt to restore the parish as the central unit for a rejuvenated Church represents a sincere and effective response to the diatribes which Enlightenment thought launched against the Church.[29]

The spiritual mission of the curé was a fundamental theme of the work which became the handbook of the priest's reform movement, Abbé Henri Reymond's *Droits des curés et des paroisses, considérés sous leur double rapport, spirituel et temporel* of 1776. As one of his essential themes, Reymond stresses the idea that the curés, through their daily ministry, exert an important and salutary influence in maintaining order in France and in preserving and raising moral standards among the French people. Reymond argues that the happiness of the people is the object of the ministry of the curés.[30] The functions of the curé place him in intimate contact with the masses, and he is thus in a position to see the causes of good and evil in the lives of the people and to influence them for the better. "However little patriotism or intelligence he may have," writes Reymond, "the curé acquires easily an intimate knowledge of the condition of the people because this knowledge springs quite naturally from a reasoned observance of certain matters that occur under his eyes and of which he is obliged to take notice." In the course of his argument, Reymond speaks of the curés as "public persons," declaring that few such "public persons" know the people so well or are so well placed to influence them. Although only crudely developed in 1776, this element of the public service rendered by the curé as a royal agent is a significant dimension to the curé's collective self-image. For through this utility to the State the curés could justify their appeals to the various authorities in the monarchical structure of government.

From 1787 to 1789 the unique conjuncture of events in France forced the curés increasingly to resolve their discontents in a national political arena instead of the more familiar ground provided by the old régime institutions where regional influences, such as a friendly Parlement or benign Intendant, might aid their cause. The expressions of malaise among the lower clergy in the later eighteenth century which Grégoire and Reymond recorded with such clarity were less a result of the theological politics of the Jansenists—although the Jansenist tradition of opposition to authority in Church and State can not be discounted—than the reflection of a profound change of religious values. The political and social activities of diverse Jansenist factions, as revealed in recent historical studies, appear symptomatic rather than causative of this change. The problem of definition of Jansenism is but one aspect of that of the pluralism of the Christian religion in the eighteenth century. Whether it is labeled "secularization" or "Christian Enlightenment," the transformation within the clergy represented concessions to modernity, to criticism of the Church, and to social trends. As a spiritual movement, it expressed the purification of Christian ideals and traditions under way in the century in France. The parochial ideal which was so clearly stated in the literature of the curés in the pre-Revolutionary era and which mirrors this change took shape gradually as the priests grappled with their dual responsibilities as citizens and priests. As a collective outlook, the parochical ideal was the product of an élitist milieu, and, as such, it sought to reinforce the position of the curé in the parish as a good and respected citizen and as a beneficient spiritual leader. While it was plausible in the context of the monarchy of the *ancien régime,* this elevated concept of the curé's role in the parish would be deflated by the secularizing strength of a revolution antipathetic to the parochial power of the priest.

NOTES

1 This article is dedicated to Professor Harold T. Parker, who retires from Duke University in 1977 after thirty-eight years of association with that institution to become Professor Emeritus of History. His inspiration and guidance to the author as mentor and friend are gratefully acknowledged.

2 Alexander Sedgwick, "Perspectives on French Jansenism since the Seventeenth Century," paper delivered at the meeting of the American Catholic Historical Association in Boston, April 1975; "Seventeenth-Century French Jansenism and the Enlightenment," paper delivered at the European History Section, Southern Historical Association meeting in Atlanta, November 1973. In these important papers, Professor Sedgwick explores among other problems the relation of Enlightenment thought to Jansenism and traces in fascinating detail the differing views offered by historians of the relation of Jansenism to the undermining of the *ancien régime.*

3 For D'Argenson's interesting distinction between "Jansenists by profession" and "what they call Jansenists these days" (the former being intolerant, hateful people; the latter, those who offered the "counsels of clemency and reason" in the face of "Jesuitical and ultramontane persecution of the *Parlement* and the people"), see D'Argenson, *Journal et mémoires du marquis d'Argenson,* ed. E. Rathery (Paris: Reynouard, 1959–67), VIII, 101–11, 204; see also Barbier's dis-

tinction between a "Parliamentary fanatic" and a "Jansenist" in C.-J.-F. Barbier, *Chronique de la Régence et du régne de Louis XV: 1718–1763,* ed. Charpentier, (Paris: Charpentier, 1866), VI, 508–9. Both of these are cited by Dale Van Kley, *The Jansenists and the Expulsion of the Jesuits from France: 1757–1765* (New Haven & London: Yale Univ. Press, 1975), p. 29.

4 Jean Leflon, *Pie VII: Des abbayes bénédictines à la papauté* (Paris: Plon. 1958), I, 32–33.

5 See especially Emile Appolis, *Le 'Tiers Parti' catholique au XVIIIème siècle* (Paris: A. & J. Picard, 1960), and Pierre Chaunu, "Jansénisme et frontière de catholicité (XVIIème siècle)," *Revue historique,* 227 (January–March 1962), 115–38.

6 On the immense domain of religious sociology, Le Bras remarked that the ken of this discipline was enormous because "elle embrasse tous les temps, tous les pays, tous les songes des hommes sur l'éternel et l'infini." Gabriel Le Bras, *Etudes de sociologie religieuse* (Paris: Presses Universitaires, 1955–56), II, 416. On the interdisciplinary quality of religious sociology, he remarked, "A partir du moment où l'enquête sur un groupe—paroisse, quartier, ville, province, pays—parvient à définir les composantes d'une mentalité, les frontières entre les disciplines disparaissent. Sociologues et cliniciens de l'âme traitent en condominium le même objet. Le pluralisme de la science s'efface derrière l'unité des savants." Le Bras, *Etudes,* II, 777. The essential article of Le Bras which initiated the study of religious sociology was "Statistique et histoire religieuse: Pour un examen détaillé et pour une explication historique de l'état du Catholicisme dans les diverses régions de France," *Revue d'histoire de l'Eglise de France* (October 1931), 425–49.

7 Le Bras, *Etudes, passim.*

8 Bernard Plongeron, "Une image de l'église d'après les 'Nouvelles Ecclésiastiques': 1728–1790," *Revue d'histoire de l'Eglise de France,* 16 (1967), 241–68.

9 See especially Antoine Adam, *Du mysticisme à la révolte: Les Jansénistes du XVIIème siècle* (Paris: Fayard, 1968); the fundamental work remains Charles Augustin Sainte-Beuve, *Port Royal,* ed. Maxime Leroy (Paris 1952); and still valuable, although difficult to use because of the organization, is Augustin Gazier, *Histoire générale du mouvement janséniste depuis les origines jusqu'à nos jours,* 2 vols. (Paris: E. Champion, 1923). Also useful is Louis Cognet, *Le Jansénisme* (Paris: Presses Universitaires, 1964), and Geneviève Delassault, *Le Pensée janséniste en dehors de Pascal* (Paris: Buchet/Chastel, 1963).

10 J. A. G. Tans, "Les Idées politiques des Jansénistes," *Neophilogus* (January 1956), 1–18. See the significant article by B. Robert Kreiser on the popular Jansenism surrounding the convulsionary movement at the parish of Saint-Médard, "Religious Enthusiasm in Early Eighteenth-Century Paris: The Convulsionaries of Saint-Médard," *Catholic Historical Review,* 61 (July 1975), 353–85. Also of importance is the forthcoming article by Richard M. Golden in the *Catholic Historical Review,* "The Mentality of Opposition: The Jansenism of the Parisian Curés." Armand Arnauld's position making legitimate a passive resistance to the sovereign is elaborated in René Taveneaux, *Jansénisme et politique* (Paris: Armand Colin, 1965), p. 27. This problem is treated with great lucidity by Bernard Plongeron in *Théologie et politique au siècle des lumières: 1770–1820* (Geneva: Droz,

1973), pp. 102–8, and, for a masterful treatment of political Jansenism by the same author, see "Une image de l'église," pp. 240–47, 249–51.

11 The indispensable study in this area is the definitive account by Pierre Blet, *Les Assemblées du clergé et Louis XIV de 1670 à 1693* (Rome, 1972); note also my review in *Catholic Historical Review*, 60 (July 1974), 285–87.

12 See Cognet, *Le Jansénism*; the recently published source which is essential for an understanding of relations between the Vatican and Versailles is Bruno Neveu's edition of the correspondence of Angelo Ranuzzi, papal nunciary at the court of Louis XIV. See *Correspondance du Nonce en France Angelo Ranuzzi: 1638–1689*, 2 vols., ed. Bruno Neveu [Acta Nuntiaturae Gallicae] 10 and 11 (Rome: Imprimerie de l'Université Grégorienne, n.d.).

13 The standard works, now somewhat dated, are Charles Gérin, *Louis XIV et le Saint-Siège*, 3 vols. (Paris: V. Lecoffre, 1893–94); Edmond Michaud, *Louis XIV et Innocent XI*, 4 vols. (Paris: Didier, 1883); and, among the numerous articles, the most useful is Marc Dubruel, "La querelle de la régale sous Louis XIV: 1673–1673, *Revue de questions historiques*, 3 (1922), 257–311.

14 See Kreiser, "Religious Enthusiasm," 384–85.

15 Edmond Préclin, *Les Jansénistes du XVIIIème siècle et la constitution civile du clergé* (Paris: J. Gamber, 1929). See especially pp. 1–2, 66, 106, 342–45, 361–62, 364–65, 379–80, and 459–60.

16 Nicolas Travers, *Pouvoirs légitimes du premier et du second ordre dans l'administration des sacrements et le gouvernement de l'Eglise* (n.p., 1774), p. 566. Taveneaux suggests that Richerist ideas had blended with Jansenist doctrines as early as the middle of the seventeenth century. Following Préclin's interpretation, he stressed that the economic and social gulf between curé and bishop in the eighteenth century made them receptive to the Richerist doctrines diffused in Quesnel's writings. He concludes: "Le nivellement idéologique issu de Richer se trouve ainsi porté par un phénomène de 'lutte de classé'. Le quesnellisme n'établit pas un système politique, mais il crée une conscience 'démocratique': chez les clercs du second ordre et chez les fidèles, le passage sera aisé du plan religieux au plan politique; la coutume s'établit de juger les choses d'Eglise en référence à la société civile." René Taveneaux, *La Jansénisme et politique*, p. 40.

17 René Taveneaux, *Le Jansénisme en Lorraine: 1630–1789* (Paris: J. Vrin, 1960), pp. 691–92.

18 Taveneaux, *Le Jansénisme en Lorraine*, p. 7.

19 Some significant new studies of Grégoire have altered our understanding of Grégoire. Cf. Ruth F. Necheles, *The Abbé Grégoire: 1787–1831* (Westport: Greenwood Press, 1971), pp. 10–13; and by the same author, "The Abbé Grégoire's Work in Behalf of the Jews: 1788–1791," *French Historical Studies*, 6 (Fall 1969), 172–84; also P. Grunebaum-Ballin, "Grégoire convertisseur? ou, La croyance de retour d'Israel," *Revue des études juives*, 21 (1962), 389–96.

20 For a clear concept of the specific goals of Grégoire and his fellow curés in Lorraine, see A MM. *les curés lorrains et autres ecclésiastiques seculiers du diocèse de Metz* (n.p., n.d.). This bears the date January 22, 1789, and is signed by Grégoire, curé d'Emberménil; Valentin, curé de Leyr; and Didry, curé de Parroy.

21 Préclin concedes "aucun de ces écrits n'autorise l'historien de lui attribuer les idées théologiques chères aux appelants." Préclin, *Les Jansénistes*, p. 400. On the paucity of evidence of Jansenist influence in Dauphiné in the later century, see Timothy Tackett, "The Citizen-Priest: Politics and Ideology among the Parish Clergy of Dauphiné in the Eighteenth Century," see pp. 307–28.

22 Plongeron, "Une image de l'église," 242.

23 The problem of this lack of specificity is developed in the succinct article by Daniel Blackstone, "A la recherche du lien social: Incredulité et religion d'après le discours Janséniste à la fin du dix-huitième siècle," in *Civilisation chrétienne: Approche historique d'une idéologie XVIIIe–XXe siècle* (Paris: Beauchesne, 1975), especially pp. 85–87.

24 Van Kley, *The Jansenists and the Expulsion of the Jesuits from France*, p. 228.

25 *Nouvelles ecclésiastiques*, 1790, p. 115.

26 The emergence of the collective mentality can be followed in William H. Williams, "The Priest in History: A Study of Divided Loyalties in the French Lower Clergy from 1776 to 1789," diss. Duke University 1965. See also Maurice G. Hutt, "The Curés and the Third Estate: The Ideas of Reform in the Pamphlets of the French Lower Clergy in the Period 1787–1789," *Journal of Ecclesiastical History*, 7 (1957), 74–92.

27 See especially my forthcoming article, "Perspectives on the French Parish Clergy on the Eve of the Revolution," *Proceedings of the Fourth Annual Consortium on Revolutionary Europe: 1750–1850* (University Press of Florida, 1977).

28 For the important development of this concept of non-capitalist proprietary wealth, see the pioneering article by Georges V. Taylor, "Noncapitalist Wealth and the Origins of the French Revolution," *American Historical Review*, 72 (January 1967), 469–96.

29 For a development of this topic, see William H. Williams, "Voltaire and the Utility of the Lower Clergy," *Studies on Voltaire and the Eighteenth Century*, 58 (1967), 1869–91.

30 Henri Reymond, *Droits des curés et des paroisses considerés sous leur double rapport, spirituel et temporel* (Paris 1776), I, 35–37.

The Citizen Priest: Politics and Ideology among the Parish Clergy of Eighteenth-Century Dauphiné

TIMOTHY TACKETT

Historians have long been aware of the widespread disaffection of the French parish clergy at the end of the Old Régime. The critical role played by the majority of curé deputies in the formation of the National Assembly of 1789 was, in many respects, the culmination of a developing "revolt of the curés" against many of the ecclesiastical and economic institutions of the eighteenth-century Gallican Church.[1] The purpose of the present study[2] is to examine this phenomenon in the context of one French province, Dauphiné, and to trace the interaction at the local level between ecclesiastical politics, socio-economic structures, and ideology. By all previous accounts, the curés of Dauphiné had been at the forefront of the clerical revolt throughout the period just prior to the Revolution.[3] The curés of this province present the additional interest of a clergy which did not withdraw its support of the Revolution after the enactment of the revolutionary reorganization of the French Church: between eighty and ninety percent would affirm their acceptance of the Civil Constitution of the Clergy, among the highest proportions of any region in France.[4]

I

In the emergence of a revolutionary ideology among this corps of curés perhaps no factor was more important than a regional peculiarity in the mode of distribution of the Church's revenues. The principal sources of income for most parish priests in France were the tithes and the beneficed lands or glebe. In some parishes, however, these ecclesiastical revenues were not controlled by the curés themselves, but rather by non-resident tithe-owners—clergymen or even laymen—who paid only a set salary, the so-called *portion congrue,* to the residing clergyman. This distinction between tithe-owning and "congruist" curés is well known to historians of the Old Régime. Less commonly known is the geographical distribution of the salaried parish priests. In most of the dioceses of northern and western France, they represented from about twenty-five to as little as five percent of the total number of curés; and many of those who were congruists received all or part of their salaries in kind—the *gros* as it was called in many areas. But the proportion increased considerably to the south and southeast. In the seven principal dioceses of Dauphiné, the congruists represented about seventy-five percent of the whole—and of these, the near totality received only a fixed money payment.[5]

The effects of these economic structures on curé attitudes in Dauphiné were far-reaching. The fixed salary of from 300 to 700 livres—depending on the period—was decidedly mediocre and well below that of the various lay notables of the rural community. During periods of inflation, such as the early seventeenth century and the last two-thirds of the eighteenth century, the great majority of the parish clergy of Dauphiné found their ecclesiastical income continually eroding in its real value. Whatever the diversity of their backgrounds and educational experiences, they all found themselves bound together before the common problem of financial insecurity. This economic homogeneity of the curés of the Southeast formed a stark contrast to the situation in many dioceses of northern and western France, in which curé incomes typically spread across the entire gamut from a few hundred to several thousand livres per year—and in which the median income might be two or three times greater than the median income in Dauphiné.[6] The nature of the congruists' income also led to difficulties over the *décime,* the ecclesiastical tax which the French clergy levied on its members. Many curés were convinced that, while their own income had been established by royal edict and was thus public knowledge, the revenue declarations of tithe holders were systematically undervalued.[7] Thus, adequate representation for the curés on the diocesan tax assessment boards seemed especially critical in Dauphiné.

But it was not only a question of the curé's personal financial position. Additional problems arose over a number of incidental expenses in the parishes for which the tithe owners in Dauphiné were responsible: the upkeep of part of the Church, the replacement of clerical vestments and sacred vessels, as well as oil and candles for lighting and bread and wine for the communion.[8] Many tithe owners traditionally employed every conceivable pretext to avoid payment for such items. In an age when external splendor in religion was widely considered to be essential for the propagation of the faith, the parsimonious attitude of many non-resident tithe owners seemed to work to the detriment of religion itself. The curés, who prided themselves on their role as defenders of the poor, were further incensed by the frequent failure to leave one twenty-fourth of the tithes to the needy—as required by provincial custom.

Finally, the economic structures of the Church in southeastern France may even have promoted a greater solidarity between the curé and his parishioners. There is evidence, for Upper Dauphiné, that problems involving the tithes were the single most common sources of litigation between clergymen and laymen.[9] Yet in most of the parishes in Dauphiné, the animosities engendered by this ecclesiastical tax were directed not against the curé, but against the non-resident tithe owner. There are, in fact, a number of examples in the eighteenth century of a congruist curé and his parishioners cooperating in a joint suit against this mutual antagonist.[10] Among the curés of Dauphiné, largely disinherited from wealth and status in the Church itself, there would be a particularly strong tendency to identify with the problems of the non-privileged commoners, to internalize the antagonisms of their lay parishioners toward privileged society in general, and to seek recognition not only as men of God but as village notables and public servants.

Common economic problems and a common outside opponent would instill a highly developed *esprit de corps* among the parish priests of Dauphiné and would polarize the clergy to a far greater degree than in most other areas of the kingdom. With relatively few vested interests in existing Church property and institutions, the parish priests of the Southeast would be particularly receptive to schemes for the total transformation of Church finances and the redistribution of Church property.

Throughout the last two centuries of the Old Régime, the various economic problems of the Church in Dauphiné served as the principal impetus for group action among the parish clergy. Already, in a petition concerning the *portion congrue* published in 1664, many of the themes and justifications to be employed in the late eighteenth century were developed at length.[11] Thus, the curés drew a sharp contrast between their own functions, useful and essential for the Church and religion, and the generally useless positions of the absentee tithe owners. The latter were growing ever more wealthy and were enriching their whole families, while the curés, for whom the tithes were originally intended, suffered in base poverty. Richerist themes were also invoked: how unjust it was that the curés, whose office was of divine institution, had been deprived of the tithes, to the benefit of such purely human creations as the canonries and priories *in commendum.* The vile and repulsive material condition in which the curés lived was even perceived as causing some members of the educated classes to shun the parish mass and sacraments altogether.

The edict of 1686, raising the *portion congrue,* and the general fall in prices after 1690[12] were no doubt factors in quieting curé unrest for the next half century. When the economic issue again rose to the fore after 1750, a number of developments during the intervening years had expanded the scope of the grievances and considerably increased the potential for widespread involvement on the part of the curés.

Foremost among these developments was the broad effort by the Catholic Reformation bishops in Dauphiné and in France generally to reform and raise the religious standards of the diocesan clergy. By the beginning of the eighteenth century, seminaries had been endowed and established in all of the episcopal towns of the province, with the exception of Saint-Paul-les-Trois-Châteaux.[13] Perhaps equally important was the organization or reorganization of the parish clergy into rural deaneries—called *archiprêtrés* in Dauphiné—designed as a permanent pastoral link between bishop and parish priest and a means of maintaining and expanding the knowledge and skills obtained in the seminary.[14] The parish clergy of each deanery was to meet at regular intervals in a "conference"—usually held once a month from spring through autumn—to discuss specific moral or theological questions submitted to them by the bishop.[15] In addition to the obvious function of raising the intellectual competency of the parish clergy to a minimal level necessary for pastoral care, the seminaries and rural conferences also had important social effects. Many of the seventeenth-century curés encountered by Cardinal Le Camus of Grenoble during his pastoral visits could scarcely be distinguished from the rural populations in the parishes: dressed in similar fashion, drinking, gambling, and not uncommonly living with "wives" and children.[16] But the priests of the eighteenth century would be sternly trained to remain aloof and apart from their parishioners in their clothing, in their economic and social activities, in their relations with women.[17] They were systematically inculcated with a paternalistic, elitist attitude toward their flocks. The ultimate effect was to reinforce the curés' group consciousness, and to sharpen their sense of elite status in both the Church and the rural communities in which they would serve.

In some French dioceses, the spread of Jansenism during the early eighteenth century was an additional factor in the growth of curé opposition against ecclesiastical superiors. Forced by many of the bishops to renounce their theological convictions—through acceptance of the Bull *Unigenitus*—some parish clergymen were led to put into question the existing system of hierarchical authority. It was in this context that the Richerist position was often adhered to, extolling the divine institution of the curés and requiring their acceptance as the "cooperators" of the bishops, distinctly superior in prestige and authority to such purely human creations as canons, priors, and abbots.[18] Nevertheless, Jansenism as such seems never to have had a major impact on the parish clergy of Dauphiné. After the death of Le Camus, all of the eighteenth-century bishops in the province were firmly opposed to the movement.[19] There was probably never more than a tiny minority of confirmed Jansenist parish priests: perhaps only a few percent, almost entirely confined to the diocese of Grenoble.[20] Whatever the ultimate importance of Richerism in Dauphiné—and, as we have seen, it seems already to have been known in the mid-seventeenth century—it may well have arrived largely independent from the Jansenist controversy.

The new model curé, planted by the Catholic Reformation, continued as a major feature of the ecclesiastical landscape throughout the eighteenth century. Perhaps the most significant change within ecclesiastical society during the century was the growing separation between curé and bishop. This was only in part a social division: in fact, the general social composition of the corps of bishops on the one hand (about ninety to one hundred percent noble),[21] and of the parish clergy on the other (about two to five percent noble),[22] changed very little between the late seventeenth century and the French Revolution. More important may have been the increasing pastoral distance between parish priest and prelate. Numerous French bishops of the early eighteenth century—like Le Camus in the diocese of Grenoble and Berger de Malissoles in the diocese of Gap—worked in close personal contact with their curés through diocesan synods, pastoral visits, and ecclesiastical conferences. But at the end of the century, many bishops never held synods, showed little interest in the conferences, except as administrative organs, conducted pastoral visits merely as formalized ceremonies, and were frequently absent from their dioceses.[23] Few, to be sure, were actually irresponsible or morally reprehensible, and there were many exceptions—Le Franc de Pompignan in Vienne, for example. But, in general, the Catholic Reformation prelate was replaced by a kind of episcopal-seigneurial lord, judiciously administering his temporals, reigning over his diocese from an episcopal palace or from Paris through his agents, the vicars-general. This pastoral distance became a veritable chasm in Dauphiné, when several of the bishops, who were all major tithe owners themselves, emerged in the late eighteenth century as the principal leaders in the efforts to prevent increases in the *portion congrue.*[24] It was in the context of a general loss of confidence in the bishops that many curés chose to seek assistance from such civil authorities as the provincial judiciary or the royal bureaucracy.[25] The curés of Dauphiné would find especially willing allies among the magistrates of the Parlement of Dauphiné, who were only too happy to have the opportunity of attacking the wealth and judicial prerogatives of the upper clergy.[26] The bishops of the province were fully aware of the threat posed to them and to the tithe owners in general by this tentative coalition between Parlement and parish priests.[27]

II

It was probably above all the rapidly rising prices after mid-century which sparked a renewal of curé organization and political activity in Dauphiné.[28] From 1760 through 1768 a veritable flood of letters, petitions, and pamphlets was received by the Agents General of the Clergy and the royal ministers concerning the necessity of raising the curés' salary—writings originating primarily from south and southeastern France.[29] In addition to the direct monetary demands and the traditional justifications supporting them—similar to those of the seventeenth century—the Dauphiné curés also put forward a more comprehensive reform program, including the broadening of curé representation on the diocesan tax boards and the compelling of tithe owners to provide for the upkeep of the church and the maintenance of items required for worship. Even more significant, the ecclesiastical conferences now seemed to be used as the principal mode of political organization. In 1765 a group of curés near Grenoble were apparently soliciting petitions from deaneries in the dioceses of Grenoble, Die, Gap, and Embrun, petitions which they planned to synthesize into a general statement of grievances for the province as a whole.[30] Two years later, by means of "numerous and frequent" curé assemblies in the diocese of Vienne, an appeal to the Parlement of Grenoble was being organized for a unilateral increase in the *portion congrue* throughout Dauphiné.[31]

The royal edict of May 1768, augmenting the curés' minimum salary from 300 to 500 livres per year, put a temporary halt to many of these efforts. But this law, a compromise arranged between the royal ministers and various factions of the General Assembly of the Clergy, served only to further polarize the ecclesiastical society in Dauphiné. In some cases the upper clergy immediately took advantage of the edict to lower their own ecclesiastical taxes and to double or even triple the taxes of the congruist curés.[32] Elsewhere, tithe owners took advantage of a legal technicality to reduce or altogether cease payments to the parishes for many of the articles necessary for the mass.[33] With this turn of events, a number of curés initiated civil suits, inviting the Parlement to step in, as one curé put it, for the protection of the Church against the bishops and tithe owners who were mishandling its affairs, to the detriment of religion.[34] Others used suits or threats of suits to increase the influence of the parish clergy on the tax assessment boards. The curés of the dioceses of Grenoble, Gap, and Vienne even obtained the right to elect their own representation through periodic meetings in their deaneries: thus institutionalizing the ongoing politicization of the rural conferences.[35]

For the period before 1775, it is difficult to identify any one individual or diocese as leading the various protest efforts among the curés of Dauphiné. But the last decade of the Old Régime saw the emergence of just such a leader, Henri Reymond, curé of Saint-Georges in Vienne, who would not only forge a unified political movement among the curés but also crystalize the wide range of problems and grievances into an extensive and cohesive program. From the moment of his nomination to the parish of Saint-Georges, Reymond had become involved in a series of conflicts with the tithe owners, canons, and the archbishop of the diocese. As a result of his experiences and of an independent study of canon law, he published a book entitled *Les Droits des curés et des paroisses* in 1776.[36] The work soon went through several editions and became widely read and influential in the kingdom. Yet it was written above all in response to the immediate and specific problems of the parish clergy of Dauphiné.[37] It was at once a handbook of all the grievances expressed in the province over the previous fifteen years, and an intellectual justification for those grievances. The curés' salaries must be raised and Church wealth more equitably distributed, parish priest representation on tax boards must be instituted, tithe owners must be forced to accept their financial responsibilities in the parishes. To buttress these, and numerous other demands for economic and ecclesiastical reforms, Reymond made ample use of the Richerist doctrine. But he drew simultaneously on the image of the curé as a public servant, popularized by several of the writers of the Enlightenment and promoted, on occasion, by the French government itself.[38] Thus, the older theme of the essential utility of the curés in the Church (as opposed to the generally useless canons, priors, and monks) was enlarged to portray the utility of the curés in lay society. The curés were, after all, "parfaitement citoyens" and love of the "patrie" was, necessarily, one of their foremost convictions. Indeed, "le bonheur des peuples" was the very objective of the curé's ministry. The parish priest was the ideal agent for contact between an enlightened government and the rural population. He was the government's natural ally in the organization of poor relief, and the guardian in the countryside against popular sedition, on the one hand, and irreligion, on the other.[39] A second book, *Les Droits des pauvres,* elaborated a plan for the broad redistribution of the Church's revenues, not only for the support of the curé but for the relief of the village poor, to whom the parish priest was the "natural protector."[40]

Many of Reymond's basic ideas received further publicity in Dauphiné through a series of court suits which he personally argued before the Parlement and of which the results were published and distributed throughout the province.[41] In conjunction with these suits, he entered into correspondence with curés in all of the dioceses of Dauphiné and circulated questionnaires concerning local problems and conditions.[42] In 1779, on the initial prompting of curés in the province of Provence, Reymond requested and was granted permission by the Parlement to organize a meeting of the curés of his diocese for the discussion of problems involving the *portion congrue.* Similar meetings took place in the dioceses of Grenoble, Gap, Embrun, Valence, and Die, and Reymond and a curé from Grenoble were appointed to carry the curés' grievances concerning the salary and a wide range of other problems directly to Versailles.[43] Here, in early 1780, Reymond seems to have obtained a personal interview with Necker himself.[44] He also took the occasion to further publicize his program of reform and to publish a tract for distribution throughout the kingdom.[45] In an effort to put a halt to this "révolution prochaine" among the curés of Dauphiné and Provence, the Agents-general and the archbishop of Vienne finally obtained a royal declaration forbidding all curé assemblies not specifically authorized by the bishops.[46] It would seem, however, that the Parlement of Dauphiné refused to register this declaration.[47]

A relative calm settled over the curés of the province in the mid-1780s. The temporary halt in the long-term inflation, the promise on the part of the government and the upper clergy that the *portion congrue* would soon be raised, the skillful policies of Le Franc de Pompignan in partly disarming opposition in the diocese of Vienne: all may have contributed in appeasing the agitation of the parish clergy. But the turn of national and provincial events after 1787 swept the curés of Dauphiné back into political activity over issues of a far greater scope. Many parish priests closely followed and participated in the local protest movements opposing the edicts of May 1788. A sizable contingent of curés from several dioceses appeared at the Provincial Assembly in Vizilles in July, and numerous others signed municipal statements of support.[48] Some even pronounced political harangues from the pulpit against the "yoke of oppression."[49] Everywhere in France groups of curés were coming to identify many of their own difficulties with the problems of the lay commoners in society in general.[50] But in southeastern France, with its characteristic ecclesiastical structures and the long-developing politicization of the lower clergy, the alliance between curés and Third Estate seemed particularly appropriate and viable. "The interest of the people is inseparable from [that of the curés]," wrote one clergyman of Dauphiné in an especially famous pamphlet: "If the people rise up from their oppression [the curés] will escape the degradation into which [they] have been thrust and so long held down by the upper clergy."[51] It was thus particularly ironic that the curés of this province—unlike the great majority of their colleagues in the kingdom—were to be prevented by political manipulations in the Provincial Estates from electing a single deputy to the Estates-General; nor would they contribute in any way to the official instructions which the Dauphiné deputies were to carry to Versailles.[52]

Faced with these circumstances, a group of curés in the diocese of Vienne, led by Henri Reymond, resolved to compose an independent—and technically illegal—*cahier de doléances* of their own. The text which ultimately emerged was undeniably the work of Reymond himself.[53] But more than any other document written by the curé of Saint-Georges, the *Cahier des curés de Dauphiné* was intended to reflect and respond directly to the views of the curés throughout the province. The committee in Vienne solicited statements of grievances from other curés and groups of curés and made an effort to incorporate many of their ideas. Once a draft had been completed, Reymond himself carried it throughout the province, obtaining signatures of approval from 399 parish priests in eight dioceses (see table below).[54] The signing curés were situated in nearly every area of Dauphiné—both in the Rhône Valley and the Alpine regions—with the major exceptions of the Baronnies (the southern portions of the dioceses of Die and Gap), the Terres Froides (the diocese of Belley and the northeastern portion of the diocese of Vienne), and most of the diocese of Grenoble. Excluding the latter diocese—where the curés had already drawn up an independent cahier of sorts in May[55]—forty-six percent of the curés in seven dioceses signaled their acceptance of Reymond's statement.[56] Thus, despite the dominant role played by Reymond in the composition of the *Cahier,* it can be considered as a statement of the intentions and aspirations, the ideological position of a considerable portion of the Dauphiné parish priests in 1789.

All of the curés' basic economic demands concerning salaries, clerical taxes, church upkeep and decoration, old-age pensions, and many other matters were elaborated once again in the *Cahier des curés.*[57] The National Assembly was to be given full authority to effect a fundamental redistribution of Church wealth for the ample provision-

Curés Signing *Cahier des Curés*

Diocese	No. of Cs. (in Dauphiné)	Cs. signing *Cahier*		Refractory Cs.[1]		Refractory Cs. who signed *Cah.*	
		No.	%	No.	%	No.	%
Vienne	317	143	45	49	15	10	7
Valence	77	31	40	3	4	2	6
Saint-Paul	18	18	100	10	56	10	56
Die	171	84	49	8	5	3	4
Gap	160	53	33	18	11	0	0
Embrun	66	50	76	17	26	12	24
Vaison	18	13	72	3	17	2	15
Grenoble	222	7	3	18	8	0	0
Total	1049	399	38	126	12	39	10
Total, excluding Grenoble	827	392	47	108	13	39	10

Abbreviations for table: Cs.—Curés; *Cah.*—*Cahier*
[1]As of May 1791

ing of both curé and parish poor.[58] Such a redistribution implied a corresponding restructuring of ecclesiastical institutions. All unnecessary and non-utilitarian benefices were to be cut away or greatly reduced. The Gallican Church was to be decentralized, replacing the General Assembly of the Clergy by regional councils; and allowing for the collaboration in the administration of the dioceses between the bishops and their "assesseurs épiscopaux," chosen by periodic synods from among the most experienced members of the parish clergy. Every clerical position, including that of bishop, would be open to any candidate with sufficient experience in pastoral care, and all appointments would be made through the joint decision of the bishop and his *assesseurs.*[59]

But, in addition, the theme of the curé as the perfect citizen was developed far more than ever before. The curés should be the veritable tutors of society at the local level, not only as men of God, but as dominant village notables. They would be the logical agents of central and regional government at the local level, and they might even be endowed with limited police and notorial authority: "No one is more a citizen by profession than a curé. . . . The leader of a parish, a public servant, the curé's personal interests are identical with those of the *patrie*. . . . His day-to-day experience, his ceaseless preoccupation with the public welfare, will necessarily give rise to a patriotism which, all things being equal, is more to be expected in him than in a man of any other profession."[60] They should, in fact, be established in a position of ascendency over all those groups or individuals which might threaten their position as local elites: over municipal officials, over lay confraternities ("those pious mascarades"), over tavern keepers, prostitutes, and the other "ungodly." They denounced "this political insignificance, altogether humiliating for such warm patriots" into which they were now reduced; and they asked that they no longer be considered as merely men of God, as "simple ecclesiastical workers, whose learning and talents are limited to theological knowledge and the instruction of elementary religion."[61]

Throughout the *Cahier*, the various requests and proposals were supported by a curious synthesis of diverse lines of thought—a synthesis which might well be related to what Bernard Plongeron has termed the "Aufklärung catholique."[62] Whenever possible, assertions were justified by an appeal to authority, to Holy Scripture, to the Church Fathers, to the decisions of the Councils. The Richerist tenets were set down once again and developed. Frequent references were also made to the primitive Christian Church as the standard by which present institutions should be judged. But a much more "modern" kind of logic also informed the *Cahier*. The Enlightenment concepts of reason, nature, and progress were invoked. It was through a critical examination of the present system in the light of reason—albeit "la raison éclairée par l'évangile"—that one came to comprehend the injustice, the absurdity, the inefficacy of this system.[63] Once again, it was the principle of utility which served as the fundamental standard of judgment. If only the tissue of abuse could be cut away, how much more valuable the curé's office would be for the state and the society. The curés' civic virtues and public service often seemed to be placed even above their sacerdotal functions in the parish priests' image of themselves. At times, it was the parishioners' happiness, more than their salvation, which seemed to represent the ultimate goal of the curés' labors.

III

A manuscript copy of the *Cahier des curés de Dauphiné* was sent to Versailles in September of 1789, and a printed version appeared in November.[64] By the end of the year, the ecclesiastical committee of the National Assembly was already at work on the new "constitution" for the clergy which would be accepted by the Assembly the following July. In many regions of France the Civil Constitution of the Clergy and the requisite oath of adherence (in early 1791) would give rise to a deep and soul-searching dilemma among the curés. But given the economic problems of the Church in Dauphiné, and given the ideological position and degree of politicization of its parish clergy, the massive affirmation of the curés of this province was perhaps a foregone conclusion.[65] The new legislation seemed directly responsive to a great many of the demands expressed in the *Cahier des curés.* But even where divergencies existed, the Civil Constitution was not fundamentally incompatible with the basic aspirations of the Dauphiné curés.

Thus, among the most notable differences was the National Assembly's suppression of the tithes and expropriation of Church lands.[66] But such innovations were, in a sense, the logical conclusion of the curés' invitation to the legislators to entirely redistribute ecclesiastical wealth and even to eliminate "superfluous" Church possessions;[67] and many parish priests soon came to welcome these changes as positive contributions to the purification and regeneration of the clergy.[68] Most of the curés of Dauphiné had, after all, never experienced any direct benefit from the tithes and glebe. In raising the minimum curé salary, in guaranteeing old-age pensions, and in opening the possibility of advancement in the hierarchy through talent, the Civil Constitution had immeasurably improved the economic situation and social status of the average curé of the province.[69] Indeed, it was a clear boost to his self-esteem that he was no longer to be paid by a pompous non-resident tithe owner, but by the sovereign "French Nation."

Even the lay election of pastors—never mentioned in the *Cahier*—could be viewed as another step in the return to the conditions of early Christianity about which the curés had long been reading and thinking. It might also be argued that such an arrangement was perfectly appropriate to the status of citizen-priest, public servant to the community.[70] To be sure, the National Assembly seemed little responsive to the quasi-theocratic demands concerning the priest's authority in the local community. Yet the Civil Constitution did open up the possibility of overt participation in village and regional government to any clergyman who so desired, and many would, in fact, serve as municipal officers or departmental electors.[71] For a time, the curés would even be the chosen agents of the Nation in the publication of new laws and decrees.[72] The Revolution had made a clean sweep of virtually all of the abuses which in the eyes of the parish clergy had so disfigured the Church and so debased the curé's profession. In early 1791, it was still not impossible to believe that the extensive reforms in ecclesiastical government and discipline might lay the foundation for future, more extensive "moral" reforms.

The long-developing politicization of the Dauphiné curés had, in itself, prepared them to confront the conflicts of authority engendered by the Civil Constitution. Thus, it is of interest that the percentage of curés refusing the oath of 1791 was slightly lower among those who had signed the *Cahier des curés* than for the Dauphiné parish clergy as a whole (see above table). These differences were particularly striking in the three dioceses in which political activities had probably been most intense: Vienne (seven percent refractory among those signing vs. fifteen percent in the diocese generally), Gap (zero vs. eleven percent), and Grenoble (zero vs. eight percent).[73] By and large, the clergy in the Southeast was probably more highly polarized than in any other section of the country. Despite a pervading attachment by many curés to an ideal of the good bishop, a deep suspicion and cynicism had formed toward the existing hierarchy of the Old Régime and all it represented. A large proportion of the curés had already drawn the political and ideological lines on issues which would give rise to such agonizing decisions for many parish clergymen elsewhere in France. They had long grown accustomed to independent collective action, bypassing the bishops and the ecclesiastical hierarchy and appealing directly to various civil authorities for the redress of grievances. By 1789 Henri Reymond and the various local leaders of the curés, organized by rural deanery, had become, more than any of the bishops, the true directors of a large proportion of the parish clergy. The traditional system of ecclesiastical authority had broken down in Dauphiné before the Revolution. In their grievances and in their political activities they had already anticipated the spirit, if not entirely the letter, of the Civil Constitution of the Clergy.

NOTES

1 Among the most important studies in this area are Maurice G. Hutt, "The Curés and the Third Estate: the Ideas of Reform in the Pamphlets of the French Lower Clergy in the Period 1787–1789," *Journal of Ecclesiastical History,* 8 (1957), 74–92; and "The Role of the Curés in the Estates General of 1789," *Journal of Ecclesiastical History,* 6 (1955), 190–220; Edmond Préclin, *Les Jansénistes du XVIIIe siècle et la constitution civile du clergé: Le développement du richérisme: Sa Propagation dans le bas-clergé, 1713–1791* (Paris: Gambier, 1929); Charles-Louis Chassin, *Les Cahiers des curés* (Paris: Charvay, 1882); John McManners, *French Ecclesiastical Society under the Ancien Régime: A Study of Angers in the Eighteenth Century* (Manchester: Manchester Univ. Press, 1960), esp. chs. VIII–XI; Bernard Plongeron *Théologie et politique au siècle des lumières (1770–1820)* (Geneva, 1973), esp. ch. III; Ruth F. Necheles, "The curés in the Estates General of 1789," *Journal of Modern History,* 46 (1974), 425–44; and William H. Williams, The Priest in History: A Study of Divided Loyalties in the French Lower Clergy from 1776 to 1789, Diss. Duke University 1965.

2 This article is an expansion and development of some of the themes in the author's book *Priest and Parish in Eighteenth-Century France* (Princeton, New Jersey: Princeton Univ. Press, 1977). Printed by permission of Princeton University Press.

3 Chassin, pp. 95–107; Préclin, pp. 399–407; Michel Bernard, "Revendications et aspirations du bas-clergé dauphinois à la veille de la Révolution," *Cahiers d'histoire,* 1 (1956), 327–46; also Jean Egret, *Le Parlement de Dauphiné et les affaires publiques dans la seconde moitié du XVIIIe siècle,* 2 vols. (Grenoble: Arthaud, 1942), esp. II, 93–100.

4 The proportion of oaths was initially close to ninety percent, but declined somewhat after a certain number of clergymen retracted: calculated from a wide variety of sources described in Tackett, pp. 271–72. The Old-Régime province of Dauphiné included all or the greater part of the dioceses of Vienne, Valence, Grenoble, Die, Gap, Embrun, and Saint-Paul-les-Trois-Châteaux; and portions of the dioceses of Lyon, Belley, Vaison, Sisteron, and Orange. The Civil Constitution consolidated most of these territories into the three dioceses of Grenoble, Valence, and Embrun.

5 See Tackett, pp. 118–20. The figures available are for the mid-century. With the exception of Valence (forty-one percent) all of the dioceses were over sixty percent and two—Vienne and Grenoble—were over ninety percent. The percentages declined slightly after the royal edict of 1768 which modified certain aspects of the *portion congrue.* The situation seems to have been similar in much of Provence.

6 See Armand Rébillon, *La Situation économique du clergé à la veille de la Révolution dans les districts de Rennes, de Fougères, et de Vitré* (Rennes: Oberthur, 1913), esp. p. cxxi; Charles Girault, *Les Biens d'Eglise dans la Sarthe à la fin du XVIIIe siècle* (Laval: Goupil, 1953), pp. 387–88; Marcel Faucheux, *L'Insurrection vendéenne de 1793, aspects économiques et sociaux* (Paris: Imprimerie nationale, 1964), pp. 86–87.

7 See, for example, a number of grievances by curés of the diocese of Gap in their declarations of revenue of 1772: A.D. Hautes-Alpes, G 2337–39.

8 The expenses incurred by the tithe owners were increased in Dauphiné and Provence by another institutional peculiarity: the absence of endowed parish treasuries (*fabriques*) in most communities.

9 Of seventy-one legal cases involving clergymen brought before the bailliage courts of Gap (1750–90) and Buis-les-Baronnies (1775–90), twenty concerned the tithes or the responsibilities of the tithe owners: A.D. Hautes-Alpes, B 543–79; and A.D. Drôme, B 2185–96 and B 2201–14.

10 See, for example, the *Mémoire pour la communauté de Montjai contre M. Tournu, prieur majeur* (Grenoble, 1782); and the case of curé Martel of Saint-Pierre-d'Avez vs. Sandilleau, commander of Joucas, 1786: A.D. Hautes-Alpes, B 576.

11 *Requête du syndic des curés de la province de Dauphiné* (n.p., 1664). Reference is made in this document to united action by the curés in the diocese of Valence as early as 1635.

12 Pierre Léon, *La naissance de la grande industrie en Dauphiné (fin du XVIIe siècle–1869)*, 2 vols. (Paris: P.U.F., 1954), I, 106.

13 A. Dégert, *Histoire des séminaires français jusqu'à la Révolution,* 2 vols. (Paris: Beauchesne, 1912), I, 178–81, 297–99, 303, 306, 347, 372; and Robert Avezou, "La vie religieuse en Dauphiné du XVIe au XVIIIe siècle," *Procès-verbaux mensuels de la société dauphinoise d'ethnologie et d'archéologie,* 31 (1955), 42, 52. The tiny diocese of Saint-Paul (thirty-four parishes) was never able to afford its own seminary. Many seminaries were used not only for the preparation of young clerics, but also for periodic retreats for veteran parish clergymen.

14 The precise date of the organization of the conferences is often more difficult to determine than that of the seminaries. In Gap they were definitively organized in 1686, just as the seminary was becoming well established: A.D. Hautes-Alpes, G 929. In the diocese of Grenoble Le Camus seems to have established the deanery conferences in 1674, the same year as the seminary: Paul Broutin, *La Réforme pastorale en France au XVIIe siècle,* 2 vols. (Paris: Desclée, 1956), I, 245–46.

15 Broutin, *La Réforme pastorale en France*; Antoine Albert, *Histoire géographique, naturelle, ecclésiastique, et civile du diocèse d'Embrun,* 2 vols., (Embrun, 1783–86), II, 456–57; *Ordonnances synodales du diocèse de Gap,* 2 vols. (Grenoble, 1712), I, 121–35.

16 Jacques Solé, "La Crise morale du clergé du diocèse de Grenoble au début de l'épiscopat de Le Camus," in *Le Cardinal des montagnes, Etienne Le Camus, évêque de Grenoble (1671–1707)* (Grenoble: Presses universitaires de Grenoble, 1974), pp. 179–209.

17 See especially Dominique Julia, "Le Prêtre au XVIIIe siècle," *Recherches de science religieuse,* 58 (1970), 521–34.

18 Préclin, *livres* I and II.

19 Avezou, p. 57.

20 I have checked two of the best sources for Jansenist adherents in France in the eighteenth century: *Table raisonnée et alphabétique des Nouvelles ecclésiastiques, depuis 1728 jusqu'en 1760 inclusivement,* 2 vols. (n.p., 1767) and the supplement for the years 1761–90 (Paris, 1791); and abbé Nivelle, *La constitution Unigenitus déférée à l'église universelle,* 3 vols. (Cologne, 1757). Only seventeen curés, all in the diocese of Grenoble, have been identified as *appelants.* See also Préclin, pp. 84–85 and 124–25; and M. Virieux, "Jansénisme et molinisme dans le clergé du diocèse de Grenoble au début du XVIIIe siècle," *Revue d'histoire de l'Eglise de France,* 60 (1974), 297–321. In the diocese of Gap after 1742 all priests—including the Doctrinaires, sometimes accused of Jansenist leanings—were required to swear their acceptance of the Bull *Unigenitus*: A.D. Hautes-Alpes, G 969.

21 Norman Ravitch, *Sword and Mitre, Government and Episcopate in France and England in the Age of Aristocracy* (The Hague: Mouton, 1966), pp. 69–79. To be sure, the bishops were recruited increasingly from the sword nobility in the course of the eighteenth century.

22 Based on the author's research in wide areas of France to be published in a subsequent article.

23 See the Abbé Sicard, *L'Ancien Clergé de France,* vol. I, *Les Évêques avant la Révolution* (Paris: Lecoffre, 1905), pp. 80–102, 170–82, 283–313, 336–49; somewhat modified by Bernard Plongeron, *La Vie quotidienne du clergé français au XVIIIe siècle* (Paris, Hachette, 1974), pp. 91–112. Compare the *procès-verbaux* of the visits of Le Camus and Malissoles with those of Hay de Bonteville and Narbonne-Lara, their late eighteenth-century counterparts: A.D. Isère, 4 G 271–83, and 4 G 293–96; and A.D. Hautes-Alpes, G 787–88 and G 790. Characteristically, Narbonne-Lara, an *aumônier* in Versailles, felt obliged to ask the king's permission in order to leave the royal palace and visit his diocese. On the dates of synods, see André Artonne, et al., *Répertoire des statuts synodaux de l'ancienne France* (Paris: C. N. R. S., 1963): in six of the seven principal dioceses of Dauphiné there were no synods after 1730 (there was one synod in Saint-Paul in 1751).

24 See, for example, the *mémoire* in favor of the curés of the diocese of Embrun, ca. 1765: A.N., G^{8*} 2518, f° 134–37; also the *mémoire* by the bishop of Gap, Dec. 29, 1784: A.N., G^8 68 (Gap).

25 The minister of foreign affairs, who frequently had authority over the province of Dauphiné, received numerous appeals from the curés: Arch. Af. Et., Mémoires et documents, France, 1388. Both Choiseul and Necker also received appeals: e.g.,

Choiseul to Agents-General, Nov. 11, 1764: A.N., G[8]* 2628, f° 397; and Dailly to Agents-General, Feb. 29, 1780: A.N., G[8]* 2631, f° 287.

26 The Parlement's continual assistance to the curés on the question of the *portion congrue* can be related to the broad assistance given to various rural communities in their efforts to lower the burden of the tithes: see, e.g., the "Etat de situation du diocèse de Gap relativement à ses impositions," 1785: A.N., G[8] 68 (Gap). On the limits of the Parlement's support to the curés, see Egret, *Le Parlement de Dauphiné,* II, 93–100.

27 Bishop Caulet of Grenoble wrote to the Agents-general of the powerful assistance given to the curés by the Parlement: "Le préjugé est formé contre les décimateurs dans quelques mains que soient les dîmes," letter, Sept. 23, 1767: A.N., G[8]* 2524, f° 95–96. The bishop of Gap, Vareilles, wrote in the same vein of the tithe owners: ". . . éprouvant de la part des tribunaux toutes les difficultés, pour ne pas dire les vexations imaginables, tant pour la perception de la dîme que pour les charges extraordinaires qu'on leur fait supporter": *mémoire,* Dec. 29, 1784: A.N., G[8] 68 (Gap). The dangers of a curés-Parlement coalition had been mentioned in the General Assembly of the Clergy as early as 1730: Ravitch, p. 45.

28 See the price curve for wheat in Dauphiné in Léon, vol. I, 287.

29 A list, undoubtedly incomplete, of dioceses from which grievances were sent suggests that the protest came primarily from Dauphiné, Provence, Languedoc, Aquitaine, and the Pyrenees—though some petitions were also sent from northern France: based on a wide variety of sources, particularly A.N., series G[8] and Arch. Af. Et., Mém. et Doc., Fr.

30 This process is described in the *mémoire* by the deanery of Vif: A.N., G[8]* 2524, f° 97–100. The joint petition assembled by the curés of the Grésivaudan has not been located.

31 Statement from the bishop of Grenoble to the Agents-General, Sept. 23, 1767: A.N., G[8]* 2524, f° 95–96.

32 The interpretive decree of July 7, 1768 authorized the redistribution of taxes as a result of the increased curé salaries. In the diocese of Gap, the congruists found their taxes raised by about three-hundred-fifty percent for a salary increase of sixty-six percent: A.D. Hautes-Alpes, G 2485.

33 When the Parlement of Dauphiné registered the Edict of May 1768, it specified that these *menues fournitures* must still be paid by the tithe owners in parishes where there were no *fabriques.* Yet the edict itself freed the tithe owners of just such supplementary expenses.

34 *Mémoire pour la communauté de Montjai contre M. Tournu, prieur majeur* (Grenoble, 1782).

35 In the diocese of Gap after 1772, each deanery chose an elector every third year; the electors, in turn, chose the two deputies to the tax board. The electors might also be given mandates from their constituencies to call the bishop's attention to a wide range of other problems: see A.D. Hautes-Alpes, G 2362–66.

36 *Les Droits des curés et des paroisses considérés dans leur double rapport spirituel et temporel* (Paris, 1776).

37 Reymond makes this clear in his "Notice biographique de Monseigneur Reymond, évêque de Dijon," *Chronique religieuse,* 4 (1820), 366.

38 Reymond was writing while Turgot was in power in the royal government and the curé was well aware of Turgot's policies of collaboration with the curés: see *Droits des curés,* p. 38. Reymond is known to have been influenced by Montesquieu, Voltaire, and the elder Mirabeau: Préclin, p. 400.

39 *Droit des curés,* pp. 30–38, 146–47, 190, 271–72.

40 *Droit des pauvres* (Geneva, 1781).

41 Thus, the Parlement's decision of July 24, 1781 concerning the responsibilities of the tithe-owners: *Recueil des édits et déclarations du roi, lettres patentes et ordonnances de sa Majesté, arrêts et règlements de ses conseils et du Parlement du Dauphiné,* 27 vols. (Grenoble, 1690–1790), XXVI, No. 116.

42 Reymond was circulating letters to the curés of the diocese of Vienne and raising the "standard of revolt" as early as 1773: letter from the archbishop of Vienne to the Agents-General, June 6, 1773: A.N., G^8 661 (Vienne). In c. 1779 he sent a questionnaire to curés throughout the province concerning various economic problems: *Mémoire à consulter et consultation pour les curés de la province du Dauphiné* (Paris, 1780), pp. 100–108.

43 Ordinances of the Parlement of Dauphiné, Apr., June, and Aug., 1779: see the request of the curés of Dauphiné to the king's council: A.N., G^{8*} 2544, no. 323. The two curés went to the capital even though they had been specifically forbidden to do so by the *procureur-général* in Grenoble. When the ministry learned of their place of residence in Paris, the police was sent to order them back to Dauphiné. But by this time, the two had already left: letters from Colaud de la Salcette, *avocat-général,* to the ministry of foreign affairs, Jan.–Mar. 1780: Arch. Af. Et., Mém. et Doc., Fr., 1388, f° 7, 17, 20, 21.

44 Reymond recalled this fact in a letter to Necker, Sept. 30, 1788: A.N., B^a 74 (7).

45 *Mémoire à consulter.*

46 Declaration of Mar. 9, 1782. In fact, it was only a restatement of a long-standing royal policy prohibiting such curé assemblies. See, especially, the note from the Agents-General to De Beaumont, Apr. 10, 1781: A.N., G^{8*} 2620, No. 439.

47 This is suggested in Joseph-Marie Maurel, *Histoire religieuse du département des Basses-Alpes pendant la Révolution* (Digne, 1902), pp. 11–12; and Chassin, p. 110.

48 The 26 curés at Vizille are listed in J.-A. Félix-Faure, *Les Assemblées de Vizille et de Romans en Dauphiné* (Paris, 1887), pp. 345–56. Local curé participation is evident in the municipal deliberations of 1788. Thus, in the diocese of Gap, Archives communales de Veynes, BB 31 (June 23); A.C. Upaix, BB 2 (June 29); A.C. Ribiers, BB 37 (July 6); and *Délibérations du bourg de Corps, 22 juin, 1788* (n.p., 1788).

49 E.g., curés Galland and Goubet in the diocese of Grenoble: Egret, *Le Parlement de Dauphiné,* II, 267 and 313.

50 Hutt, "The Curés and the Third-Estate," pp. 89–92.

51 *Les Curés du Dauphiné à leurs confrères, les recteurs de Bretagne* (n.p., 1789), p. 8.

52 Jean Egret, *Les Derniers Etats de Dauphiné, Romans (1788–1789)* (Grenoble: Arthaud, 1942), pp. 15–16, 28–29, 35. A political compromise allowed each of the three orders to determine its own membership. The dominant upper clergy

allowed only two curé deputies in the Provincial Estates, both to be the tithe-owning curés. The Estates of Dauphiné alone chose all of the province's deputies and drew up a collective "mandate": Gaston Letonnelier, "Les Cahiers de doléances en Dauphiné," *Bulletin de l'Académie delphinale,* 71 (1935), 77–179.

53 The printed version was entitled *Cahier des curés de Dauphiné adressé à l'assemblée nationale et à Messieurs les députés de la province en particulier* (Lyon, 1789).

54 *Cahier des curés,* pp. iii–viii; also Henri Reymond, *Analyse des principes constitutifs des deux puissances* (Vienne and Embrun, 1791), pp. 45–46. Reymond also summarized the lengthy *Cahier* in an eighteen-page manuscript. It was this version—very much like an official *cahier de doléances*—which was actually signed in some dioceses: e.g., A.D. Hautes-Alpes, G 1537. Other priests, however, are known to have read the *Cahier* in its entirety. All but thirty (seven percent) of the curé signatures listed at the beginning of the *Cahier* have been identified by comparison with the *Almanach général de la province de Dauphiné* (Grenoble, 1789 and 1790), and with lists of the clergy in each department who took or refused the oath of 1791: J. Martenelli, Les Serments de 1790 à 1792 dans l'Isère (D. E. S., Université de Grenoble II, 1971); Paul Guillaume, Notes sur l'histoire du clergé du diocèse de Gap pendant la Révolution: A.D. Hautes-Alpes, ms. 399; A.N., D XIX 21 (Drôme).

55 *Assemblée des curés du diocèse de Grenoble* (Grenoble, May 4–5, 1789). It was signed by twenty-two curés, many of whom had mandates to represent the other curés in their ecclesiastical conferences.

56 Reymond indicated he was unable to reach all parts of the province in the time available and that he reached other curés after the night of August 4 when some of the proposals of the *Cahier* no longer seemed relevant: *Cahier des curés,* p. iv.

57 *Cahier des curés,* pp. 72–75, 102–16, 124–26, 140–43.

58 Ibid., pp. 162–90.

59 Ibid., pp. 42–43, 91 n., 130–32, 175–80.

60 Ibid., pp. 118–23.

61 Ibid., pp. 77, 79, 118–23, 126–27.

62 Bernard Plongeron, "Recherches sur l'"Aufklärung" catholique en Europe occidentale (1770–1830)," *Revue d'histoire moderne et contemporaine,* 16 (1969), 555–605.

63 *Cahiers de Curés,* p. 193.

64 It was to be shown to Camus, Grégoire, Agier, and Dillon, as well as to the deputies from Dauphiné: letter from Reymond to Camus, Sept. 1, 1789: B.M. Grenoble, Fonds dauphinois, N 2375.

65 This is not to underestimate the complexity of the decision concerning the oath of 1791: see Bernard Plongeron, *Conscience religieuse en révolution: Regards sur l'historiographie religieuse de la Révolution française* (Paris: Picard, 1969), pp. 22–36; and John McManners, *The French Revolution and the Church* (London, 1969), pp. 47–60. Here, we seek only to understand the near consensus of approval on a province-wide scale.

66 In a footnote added in October 1789, Reymond welcomed the abolition of the tithes, though he initially opposed the nationalization of Church property: *Cahier des curés,* p. 183.

67 Ibid., pp. 114–15, 206–08.

68 See, for example, the ready theological justification for the expropriation offered by curé Chaix of Les Baux in a letter to Dominique Villars, Dec. 22, 1789: B.M. Grenoble, Fond dauphinois, R 10073.

69 The new minimum salary of 1200 livres per year represented a seventy percent increase for the great majority of the curés. In contrast, many curés in northern and western France not only saw their revenues diminished, but were deprived of land and tithing rights which, under the value system of the Old Régime, had invariably contributed to their status in society.

70 The justification of the election of curés by appeals to the conditions of early Christianity is a theme in many of the statements made by priests at the moment of their oaths. See, for example, the speech by curé Nicolas of Ribiers, Jan. 20, 1791: "Le sacerdoce y est rendu à sa dignité première; les glorieuses fonctions que nous remplissons auprès de vous, reprennent toute l'estime qui leur est due. . . . Le droit de choisir vos pasteurs . . . droit inaliénable, la force vous l'avait ravi, la raison et la justice vous le rendent": A.C. Ribiers, D 1.

71 The study of the curé mayors of the early Revolution remains to be made: but they were apparently common in all parts of the kingdom. Some maintained their positions even into the Terror.

72 Albert Mathiez, "La Lecture des décrits au prône," in *La Révolution et l'Eglise, études critiques et documentaires* (Paris: Colin, 1910), pp. 26–65.

73 The sample for the diocese of Grenoble is unfortunately very small. Note, however, that only one of the twenty-two curés signing the statement of grievances for the diocese in May 1789 ultimately refused the oath of 1791.

John Wesley on War and Peace

SAMUEL J. ROGAL

Between John Wesley's birth in mid-June 1703 and his death on 2 March 1791, four British monarchs committed English arms to engagements in at least eight full-scale wars, two serious internal uprisings, a major colonial revolution, and a number of lesser encounters in North America, India, Minorca, French Senegal, Martinique, Grenada, Cuba, and the Philippines. At first glance, it would appear, as with the majority of eighteenth-century Britons, that Wesley's religious and social activities reflected no more than a superficial awareness of and concern for his nation's foreign and colonial policies. Did not the leader of the Methodists and his followers have problems of their own in attempting to establish and then solidify what would become one of the most significant socio-theological movements in the history of modern Western Europe? With the possible exceptions of the Jacobite rebellions of 1715 and 1745, had he or his preachers the opportunity to react to or appreciate the immediacy of death and destruction resulting from battles, campaigns, or sieges? For example, in June 1765, at which time Wesley was traveling through Ireland, a Lieutenant Cook conveyed him from Galway to Ennis; the former had seen considerable action at Fort William Henry, Louisburg, Quebec, Martinique, and Havana, and impressed upon his passenger the fact that he had come through it all without a single wound. The

Methodist patriarch could only comment in his journal, "So true is the odd saying of King William, that 'every bullet has its billet.'"[1]

Nevertheless, such outward lack of enthuasiasm over a soldier's battlefield experiences must not be interpreted as a sign of indifference or decline of patriotic spirit. To the contrary, Wesley could, when occasion demanded, be moved to action in support of king and nation—especially when the political pressures of the moment forced him toward a decision. On 25 February 1744, in the face of imminent invasion by the Young Pretender and impendent war with France, the British government ordered all Papists—both real and reputed—to depart from London and Westminster by 2 March; in addition, suspected individuals were to be confined to their homes, their arms and horses confiscated. Both John and Charles Wesley had long been considered, by those strongly opposed to Methodism, as sworn Papists and even agents of Charles Edward. Thus, the elder brother, in an effort to prove his loyalty, postponed a visit to Bristol so that he might have an opportunity to confront his accusers in London. Then, on 5 March 1744, he drafted a letter to George II, declaring that Methodists "detest and abhor the fundamental doctrines of the Church of Rome, and are steadily attached to your Majesty's royal person and illustrious house." The letter closed on a note of impassioned appeal to the only authority that Wesley could trust: "May He who hath bought us with His blood, the Prince of all the kings of the earth, fight against all the enemies of your Majesty with the two-edged sword that cometh out of his mouth! And when He calleth your Majesty from this throne, full of years and victories, may it be with that voice, 'Come, receive the kingdom prepared for thee, from the beginning of the world!'"[2] However, the letter never left the writer's desk, for Charles feared that such an address would identify the Methodists as a sect distinct from the Established Church. Thirty years later, John Wesley looked back upon the delicate moments in the early history of his movement and concluded, "It is my religion which obliges me to put men in mind to be subject to principalities and powers. Loyalty is with me an essential branch of religion, and which I am sorry any Methodist should forget. There is the closest connection, therefore, between my religious and political conduct;

the selfsame authority enjoining me to fear God, and to honour the king."[3]

Ten years after Cumberland's victory at Culloden, the fear of a French invasion again spread throughout England. The Church declared a national fast for 6 February; Charles Wesley re-issued his *Hymns for Times of Trouble and Persecution* (Bristol, 1745) and published a new volume entitled *Hymns for the Year 1756, particularly for the Fast-Day, February 6,* and George Whitefield, in his *Address to persons of all Denominations,* lashed out at an "insulting, enraged, and perfidious enemy advancing nearer and nearer to the British borders... accompanied with a popish Pretender, and thousands of Romish priests, to invade, subdue, and destroy the bodies and substance, and to blind, deceive, and tyrannise over the souls and consciences of the people belonging to this happy isle."[4] On this occasion, John Wesley decided to do more than merely compose a prayer in support of his nation and sovereign. During the final week of February 1756, the leader of the Methodists had been preaching mostly to soldiers stationed in and around Canterbury; on the 25th, he dined with his friend Colonel Gallatin, who declared, "No men fight like those who fear God; I had rather command five hundred such than any regiment in his Majesty's army."[5] Whether as a result of the colonel's remark or of the fever brought on by a severe cold, Wesley pursued what was, for him, an unusual course. He returned to London on the 27th and, two days later, dispatched a letter to James West, MP for St. Albans and Joint Secretary to the Treasury, containing an offer

> to raise, for his majesty's service, at least two hundred volunteers, to be supported by contributions among themselves; and to be ready, in case of invasion, to act for a year, if needed so long, at his Majesty's pleasure: only within —— miles of London.
>
> If this be acceptable to his Majesty, they beg to have arms out of the Tower, giving the usual security for their return; and some of his Majesty's sergeants, to instruct them in the military exercise.[6]

Fortunately, perhaps, the proposal never materialized; Wesley's attention was diverted to a heated Parliamentary election in Bristol, and the formation of a band of Methodist territorials had to wait until early in the next century.

If war with Catholic France, the haven for Jacobites and traitors, could ignite a spark of militancy within John Wesley, it could also draw forth the more likely response, the reaction of the committed Christian who viewed war as the supreme evil. In that sense, there were no enemies, only human beings who suffered and died. The Seven Years' War was very much a fact of British life during mid-October 1759 when Wesley walked to Knowle, a mile from Bristol, in response to certain rumors about the condition of 1,100 French prisoners interned there. Although reports about unsanitary living conditions, inadequate food, and inhuman treatment proved false, he expressed (in a letter published in *Lloyd's Evening Post* for 20 October 1759) legitimate concern for lack of adequate clothing:

> A great part of these poor men are almost naked: and winter is now coming upon them in a cold prison, and a colder climate than most of them have been accustomed to. But will not the humanity and generosity of the gentlemen of Bristol prevent or relieve this stress? Did not they make a noble precedent during the late war? And surely they are not weary of well doing. Tuesday night [16 October], we did a little according to our power; but I shall rejoice, if this be forgotton through the abundance administered by their liberality, in a manner which they judge most proper. Will it not be, both for the honour of the city and country, for the credit of our religion, and for the glory of God, who knows how to return it sevenfold into their bosom?[7]

On the "Tuesday night" referred to in the letter, Wesley had preached a sermon in Bristol on Exodus 23:9—"Thou shalt not oppress a stranger; for ye know the heart of a stranger, seeing ye were strangers in the land of Egypt"; the congregation contributed £18, and an additional £6 on the following evening. With these sums the Bristol society purchased linen and woolen cloth and made them into shirts, waistcoats, breeches, and stockings. As a result of the appeal in *Lloyd's Evening Post,* the Corporation of Bristol and Methodist societies throughout England sent to Knowle large quantities of mattresses and blankets.[8] Obviously, Wesley proved more adept at clothing the French prisoners than at convincing ministers to arm British Methodists.

Exactly one year later, he had to re-initiate the project. A notice in *The Bristol Chronicle* for Thursday, 23 October 1760 (p. 243), read, "A charity sermon will be preached at the New Room in Horsefair on Sunday evening [26 October] at 8 o'clock, by the Rev. John Wesley for the use of the prisoners at Knowle." The Methodist patriarch stopped at Knowle on Friday, the 24th, on his way from Pensford to Bristol, and found "many of them almost naked again." Once more he took up a collection and directed that the money go toward the purchase of linen and waistcoats. Interestingly enough, the charity sermon for the French was delivered on the day following the death of George II—an event distinctly noted in Wesley's journal.[9] At any rate, he had no further contact with French prisoners of war until October 1779. On Wednesday, the 6th, he preached a sermon at Winchester, remarking that some four thousand prisoners were being held outside the town. "I was glad to find they have plenty of wholesome food, and are treated, in all respects, with great humanity." In fact, he seems to have been more satisfied with conditions at Winchester than with those within the British garrison at Portsmouth. Preaching there the next day and finding no evidence of an army chaplain, he concluded, "The English soldiers of this age have nothing to do with God!"[10]

The relationship between the two instances at Winchester and Portsmouth in October 1779 perhaps provides the clearest insight into John Wesley's real priorities during the years in which England struggled for world dominance. Despite the occasional flirations with militancy, the momentary flashes of anger directed toward Papists and Jacobite usurpers, conflict of any nature—let alone all-out war between or among nations—was alien to everything he taught, to everything that had been taught to him. Essentially, Wesley took his cue from William Law's *A Serious Call to a Devout and Holy Life* (1728), a work that he had read in 1729, shortly after his appointment as Fellow of Lincoln College, Oxford. The straightforward prose of the Anglican nonjuror convinced the twenty-five-year-old tutor "more than ever of the exceeding height and breadth and depth of the law of God. The light flowed in so mightily upon my soul, that everything appeared in a new view. I cried to God for help, resolved, as I had never done before, not to prolong the time of obeying him."[11] In brief, Law communicated clearly the impossibility of being half a Christian; one had to devote himself entirely to God, to give over soul, body, and substance:

> If humility be a Christian duty, then the common life of a Christian is to be a constant course of humility in all its kinds. If poverty of spirit be necessary, it must be the spirit and temper of every day of our lives. If we are to relieve the naked, the sick, and the prisoner, it must be the common charity of our lives, as far as we can render ourselves able to perform it. If we are to love our enemies we must make our common life a visible exercise and demonstration of that love. If content and thankfulness, if the patient bearing of evil, be duties to God, they are the duties of every day, and in every circumstance of our life.[12]

Although Law does not directly take up the issue of foreign intervention and war, the general allusions are of sufficient breadth to allow for an exact decision upon those matters. Wesley took more than one opportunity to fill the gaps.

On 21 April 1790, in his eighty-seventh year, the founder and leader of English Methodism preached a sermon at Halifax, in the West Riding of Yorkshire, on the subject of "The Deceitfulness of the Human Heart." Lashing out against the desperate wickedness within man brought on by pride, self-will, and independence of God, Wesley insists that the love of power, ease, and money pit men against their neighbors and produce ingratitude, revenge, hatred, malice, and envy. "From hence naturally arises a plentiful harvest of all evil words and works; and to complete the whole, that complex of all evils—'That foul monster, War, that we meet, / Lays deep the noblest work of the creation. . . .' In the train of this fell monster, are murder, adultery, rape, violence, and cruelty of every kind."[13] War, in addition to all that causes and all that follows it, he continues, exists not only in pagan kingdoms, but in Christian nations as well; every sin that seemingly roams about only in Roman Catholic countries moves with equal freedom throughout Protestant Germany, Holland, and England. The one remaining hope lies with those born of God and purified by faith, for in the end, faith becomes the only formidable weapon against pride and self-will, the true origins of evil. As is the case with the majority of his pulpit orations, Wesley comes down hard upon man as a basically weak creature; those qualities, natural or acquired, that he displays as principal adornments become the instruments of his subsequent affliction.

Perhaps the one inconsistency observed in John Wesley's character is that, in spite of a long life dedicated to improving the lot of his fellow human beings, in spite of the early influence (e.g. William Law) that formed the core of his Christian ideals, in spite of his own words relating to charity, love, and rational co-existence, he nevertheless permitted himself to be swept away during moments of national excitement. Prior to 1775, he had not ventured far beyond the previously mentioned prayer to his sovereign and the offer to James West, volunteering his embryonic Methodist militia for service against the supposedly invading French. However, Wesley found himself, on the eve of the American Revolution, in a considerably different position from those of 1744 and 1759. Now, he stood at the head of nearly 70,000 British Methodists who, although they had turned away from the state religion, still held firm in their loyalty to king and nation; they needed and expected their leader to provide them with the necessary insights into the delicate political situations of the times. Further, Wesley believed sincerely in his obligations to his followers, one of which was to understand their sentiments and then react accordingly. Thus, when Samuel Johnson set forth his *Taxation No Tyranny; An answer to the Resolutions and Address of the American Congress* (March 1775), the Methodist patriarch took it upon himself to abridge the tract under the title *A Calm address to Our American Colonies. By the Rev. Mr. John Wesley,* M.A. This proved to be a most unfortunate error in judgment, for it left Wesley open to attacks ranging from plagiarism to senility, weakening what eventually emerged as a basically honest position regarding the American question.

Without dwelling too long upon the substance and method of *Taxation No Tyranny,* it would be fair to state that Johnson, with his usual attention to logic and thoroughness, develops the argument as to why the American colonies have no valid right to resist the tax policies of the mother country. All British colonies, maintains Johnson, "however distant, have been, hitherto, treated as constituent parts of the British empire. The inhabitants incorporated by English charters are entitled to all the rights of Englishmen. They are governed by English laws, entitled to English dignities, regulated by English counsels, and protected by English arms; and it seems to follow, by consequence not easily avoided, that they are subject to English government, and chargeable by English taxation."[14] Essentially, Wesley's shorter version paralleled Johnson's thesis of Parliament's right to tax America, contending (as had the latter) that since large sums had been spent in defense of the colonies and of the rights of their inhabitants, it was only reasonable for the Crown to insist that the Americans share the burden. Whether Wesley actually plagiarized Johnson's sentiments is purely academic; in terms of the taxation issue, they both captured the essence of public opinion concerning the matter.

On one point, however, Wesley took his argument one-half step beyond that of Johnson. The Methodist leader contended that the militant resistance to British Colonial taxation originated not so much with the Americans as it did with "determined enemies of the Monarchy" residing in England. In other words, there existed at home a hard core of radicals (obviously Whigs) dedicated to a general undermining of the king and the nation; akin to Milton's Satan, they had managed to steer America to the brink of rebellion, hoping to create an irreparable "breach between England and her colonies." In the end, such madness would bring about the ouster of George and his ministers, to be replaced by "their grand idol, their dear Commonwealth." The thrust of Wesley's thesis bore down upon the idea that the Radical Whigs had duped the Americans into playing a key role in a grand scheme of revolution. He pleaded with the colonists to realize where all of the turbulence would lead; the radicals desired only to "play one against the other in subserviency to their grand design of overturning the English government." In addition, Wesley seemed to recognize that the Americans sought independence from Britain, and thus he attempted to argue them away from that course of action on the grounds that "no subjects are governed in so arbitrary a manner, as those of a Commonwealth."[15]

Finally, Johnson and Wesley differed slightly on the specific measures to be taken by the Crown in preventing both England and America from wallowing in anarchy. Convinced that the colonists had no grounds for rising up against the king's taxation policies, the London sage rested his case on the side of reason and order. "Government is necessary to man," Johnson maintained, "and where obedience is not compelled, there is no government. If the subject refuses to obey, it is the duty of authority to use compulsion. Society cannot subsist but by the power, first of making laws, and then of enforcing them."[16] Certainly, Wesley held to the conviction that the Americans had erred by their resistance, but he also continued to believe that, as naive children, they had been led astray by a band of conspirators in England. Thus, the leader of the Methodists sought to persuade the colonists that their present course of action would produce one of two obvious results, both of them negative: (1) total subjugation by Britain or (2) independence from the mother nation. Peace and harmony would be restored on both sides of the Atlantic once the colonists reverted to their proper roles as loyal Englishmen and renewed their obligation to fear God and their responsibility to honor their sovereign.[17]

Wesley's involvement during the opening months of hostilities in America grew, in part, out of the commitment to advancing the cause of Methodism in that part of the world. The Methodist society there numbered, by 1774, 2,204 members, administered to by seven itinerant preachers. Three thousand miles of ocean made control of that society difficult enough; political separation from England would no doubt carry the society farther away from the influence and direction of its patriarch. However, Wesley's reasons for concern over the situation in America were far from selfish. As late as mid-June 1775, only forty-eight hours before the battle at Bunker Hill, he attempted to convince the Prime Minister, Lord North, and Lord Dartmouth, Secretary for the Colonies, that hostilities between England and her American colonies would serve no real purpose nor solve the difficulties existing between the two parties. In fact, there is evidence that Wesley believed that, in the event of war, the Americans would gain their independence, depriving England of her most valued possessions.[18] At any rate, the letter to Lords North and Dartmouth, written from Armagh, seems worthy of attention, if for no other reason than it stands—far better than the *Calm Address*—as an expression of John Wesley's true sentiments concerning Britain's future course of action in America.

The main argument in the letter focuses not upon the issue of right or wrong in terms of England's colonial policies and the American's unwillingness to accede, but rather on the logic of waging war against the colonies. In the first place, Wesley contends, there is no merit in the notion that the Americans will flee in the face of British regular troops, for "They are as strong men as you: they are as valiant as you; if not abundantly more valiant. For they are one and all enthusiasts; enthusiasts for liberty. They are calm, deliberate enthusiasts."[19] Second, contrary to popular belief within the government, the colonists would present a solid front against Britain, "not in the province of New England only, but down as low as the Jerseys, and Pennsylvania, the bulk of the people are so united that to speak a word in favour of the present English measures would almost endanger a man's life." Finally, in addition to the problem of supplying an army three thousand miles from its native shores—a problem of little consequence for the Americans—the nation would find itself almost defenseless, stripped of everything except an ineffective militia with which to ward off invasions by Spain or France, or to deal with internal uprisings. "All Europe is well appraised of this [condition]; only the English know nothing of the matter! What if they [Spain or France] find means to land but ten thousand men? Where are the troops in England or Ireland to oppose them? Why, cutting the throats of their brethren in America! Poor England in the meantime!"

Lest Wesley be accused of mounting an overly emotional argument against the employment of British arms in America, and lest he be unnecessarily derided for inflating his reasoning with fear tactics, one must realize that he probably knew more of the situations in England and America than did the ministers to whom he wrote. Principally, he traveled some four to five thousand miles per year, not only throughout England, but in Ireland, Scotland, and Wales as well. He truly understood the general temper of the people, especially the poor, and fully realized that a significant commitment in men, war materials, and food supplies to the effort in America would perhaps place too great a strain on the nation's economy and create undue hardships for the masses. Thus, "even now," he continues to North and Dartmouth, "there are multitudes of people that having nothing to do, and nothing to eat, are ready for the first bidder; and that, without inquiring into the merits of the cause, would flock to any that would give them bread." In regard to his statements on America, one need only be reminded that his preachers there—Thomas Rankin, Francis Asbury, George Shadford, John King, James Dempster, Richard Rodda, and Thomas Williams—communicated to him fairly regularly on the state of affairs during the spring of 1775; thus, the Methodist leader probably knew as much, if not more, of conditions across the Atlantic than did either King George's Prime Minister or his Secretary for the Colonies. And so, the conclusion to the letter dated 14 June 1775, although highly charged with the writer's concern for all Englishmen, was not, nor was it meant to be, mere empty enthusiasm: "For God's sake," he pleaded, "for the sake of the King, of the nation, of your lovely family, remember Rehoboam! Remember Philip the Second! Remember King Charles the First!"

From all appearances, the plea to North and Dartmouth should have been John Wesley's final attempt to exert his influence in preventing hostilities between England and her American colonies. Indeed, by summer 1775, he had reconciled himself to the conflict and its inevitable result; all that remained was the hope that God and common sense would win out. Also, it must be noted that during the entire week of 18 June 1775, Wesley was terribly ill, confined to his bed while at Derryaghey, Ireland, drained of his strength and even his memory. By the time he reached Leeds on the 28th, he had recovered sufficiently, and his mind again focused upon the affairs of America. Replying to a request from Thomas Rankin for additional preachers for the colonies, Methodism's leader declared that "you must not imagine, that any more of them will come to America till these troubles are at an end." "The clouds do indeed gather more and more," he wrote to Rankin from London on 13 August, "and it seems a heavy storm will follow; certainly it will, unless the prayers of the faithful obtain a longer reprieve." Then, in early fall, Wesley learned that Rankin and his colleagues determined to carry their mission away from the heart of the conflict and concentrate their efforts in the south, specifically in North Carolina. "... why not into South Carolina too," he asked from London on 20 October 1775. "I apprehend, those provinces would bear much fruit, as most parts of them are fresh, unbroken ground. And as the people are further removed from the din of war, they may be more susceptible to the gospel of peace." In any event, all factions "are already too much sharpened against each other; we must pour water, not oil, into the flames."[20] Obviously, the work in America must, in spite of the unsettled conditions of the times, go forward; perhaps love and charity would eventually heal the wounds between Britain and America, leaving Methodism the ultimate victor.

No doubt Wesley would have turned away completely from the American problem had not he observed, first-hand, the effects of the rebellion upon England. In his view, there existed a general dissatisfaction with the government's determination to put down the uprising by force, and the people appeared ready to vent their anger upon the king. Thus, he sensed a parallel between the England of 1775 and conditions throughout the nation in 1649. Unfortunately, information had reached him, on 22 August 1775, that Lord North and his ministers believed that England was currently basking in the sunshine of flourishing trade and full employment; the following day, Wesley decided once more to approach Lord Dartmouth. Again, as in the letter of 14 June, he attempted to inform the ministry that it was off on an erroneous course. "I aver, that in every part of England where I have been (and I have been east, west, north, and south within these two years) trade in general is exceedingly decayed, and thousands of people are quite unemployed. Some I know to have perished for want of bread; others I have seen creeping up and down like walking shadows."[21] Obviously, Wesley's "walking shadows" had no effect upon the Colonial Secretary—the former probably knew as much before he dispatched the epistle. And so, the seventy-two-year-old man gave up writing letters to government officers and turned his efforts upon one audience that would at least listen to his advice: a congregation gathered in a house of God!

Shortly after returning to London (28 October 1775) from an extensive journey to Ireland and northern England, Wesley was asked to preach a sermon for the widows and orphans of the British soldiers who had fallen at Lexington, Concord, and Bunker Hill. Thus, on Sunday, 2 November 1775, the day following the completion of his *Calm Address,* he stood in the pulpit at St. Matthew's Church, Bethnal Green, and spoke on 2 Samuel 24:17—"Lo, I have sinned, and I have done wickedly: but these sheep, what have they done?" In essence, the sermon—bearing the title "National Sins and Miseries"—exists as a grand summation of Wesley's previously stated arguments relating to the rebellion in America and its effect upon the British nation. Again, he displays, this time for the benefit of his congregation, the current deplorable state of the country: loss of trade and property, unemployment (particularly throughout the west and in Cornwall), the want of food and raiment, and the general distrust in the government. Then, as though remembering the occasion for which he was desired to speak, Wesley attacks the source of this sin and misery:

> And, as if all . . . were not miserable enough, see . . . the fell monster war! But who can describe the complicated misery which is contained in this? Hark! The cannon's roar! A pitchy cloud covers the face of the sky. Noise, confusion, terror, reign over all! Dying groans are on every side. The bodies of men are pierced, torn, hewed in pieces: their blood is poured on the earth like water! Their souls take their flight into the eternal world; perhaps into everlasting misery. The ministers of grace turn away from the horrid scene; the ministers of vengeance triumph. Such already has been the face of things in that once happy land, where peace and plenty, even while banished from a great part of Europe, smiled for near a hundred years.[22]

The real villains of the piece, he claims, are anarchy and confusion masquerading under the banner of liberty, leaving behind them disconsolate widows and desolate orphans.

Certainly, the theme of this sermon aimed directly at the passions; the language seeks primarily to arouse, to excite those who seek guidance for the direction of their enthusiasm. And why should it have been otherwise? Wesley had already set forth reasonable appeals to supposedly reasonable men, yet had received nothing positive in return for his labors. Thus, convinced he is dealing principally with a nation of sinners for whom he continues to hold some hope, the spokesman for all Methodists reaches out to the hearts of his listeners and offers them the one—in his mind the *only*—means by which to halt the plague ravaging throughout England and America. "Show mercy more especially to the poor widows, to the helpless orphans of your countrymen, who are now numbered among the dead, who fell among the slain in a distant land. Who knoweth but the Lord will yet be entreated, will calm the madness of the people, will quench the flames of contention, and breathe into all the spirit of love, unity, and concord. Then brother shall not lift up sword against brother, neither shall they know war any more. Then shall plenty and peace flourish in our land, and all the inhabitants of it be thankful for the innumerable blessings which they enjoy, and shall 'fear God, and honour the king.'"[23]

If the edict to fear God and honor king appears overly simplistic and extremely narrow, it nevertheless constituted the essence of John Wesley's theory of war and peace. In other words, his thoughts relative to the conduct of war or the maintenance of peace strayed hardly at all from the perimeters of British constitutional law or from the ideals set down in Scriptures. Because of his rigorous daily schedule, resulting from his one-man administration of Methodism, Wesley rarely had the opportunity or the luxury of examining carefully the intricate issues affecting decisions in British foreign policy; thus, his thoughts and subsequent actions tended to be dictated by the emotions of the moment. Although generally identified as a staunch supporter of the Crown and the Tory Party, he stood as a spokesman for neither; that left him vulnerable to attacks by those who pounced upon the inconsistencies of his arguments and saw only what they chose to see—a Papist, a Whig, a republican, a traitor, or whatever the opportunity demanded. However, during those occasions upon which Wesley involved himself with political issues, his arguments did indeed evidence consistency and a rigid adherence to the laws of God, the principles of Methodism, and the traditions of his nation. These were lofty ideals that, perhaps, proved too impractical to defend for one armed merely with honesty and enthusiasm. In an age fragmented by tumult and revolution, Wesley asked for peace; in an age chafed from philosophical and political controversy, he tried to apply the healing balm of evangelicalism. In the end, it was Charles Wesley who appended the rhythmic chorus to his brother's impassioned homiletics:

Every stubborn spirit bow,
Turn us, Lord, and turn us now;
Thou who hear'st Thy people's prayer,
End this dire intestine war.

Sprinkling us with Thy own blood,
Reconcile us first to God,
Then let all the British race
Kindly, cordially embrace.

Concord, on a distant shore,
To our countrymen restore;
Every obstacle remove,
Melt our hatred into love.

Gospel-grace to each extend,
Every foe, and every friend,
Then in Thee we sweetly find
Peace with God and all mankind.[24]

NOTES

1 *The Journal of the Rev. John Wesley,* A.M., ed. Nehemiah Curnock (London: Charles H. Kelly, 1909–16), V, 129–30.
2 *Journal,* III, 124.
3 *The Works of the Rev. John Wesley,* A.M., ed. Thomas Jackson, 3rd ed. (London: Wesleyan Conference Office, 1872), XIII, 406.
4 *The Works of the Reverend George Whitefield,* M.A. (London, 1771–72), IV, 265.
5 *Journal,* IV, 149.
6 *The Methodist Magazine,* 3rd ser., 27 (1848), 777.
7 Wesley's *Works,* XII, 266.
8 *Journal,* IV, 355–56.
9 *Journal,* IV, 417.
10 *Journal,* VI, 256.
11 Wesley's *Works,* I, 93.
12 William Law, "A Serious Call to a Devout and Holy Life," Ch. 1, "Concerning

the Nature and Extent of Christian Devotion," in *English Prose and Poetry: 1660–1800*, ed. Odell Shepard and Paul Spencer Wood (Boston: Houghton Mifflin Company, 1962), p. 293.

13 John Wesley, *Sermons on Several Occasions*, ed. Thomas Jackson (New York: Carlton and Phillips, 1854), II, 476.

14 *The Works of Samuel Johnson, LL.D.* (1825; rpt. New York: AMS Press, 1970), VI, 236.

15 John Wesley, *A Calm Address to Our American Colonies* (London: Robert Hawes, 1775), pp. 11–14, 15–16, 17–18.

16 Johnson's *Works*, VI, 257.

17 *Calm Address*, pp. 17–18.

18 See *Journal*, VI, 66–67, n. 3.

19 The complete text of the letter appears in *Journal*, VIII, 325–28; all references to this edition.

20 *The Letters of the Rev. John Wesley*, A.M., ed. John Telford (London: The Epworth Press, 1931), VI, 173, 181, 343.

21 The complete text of the letter appears in *Journal*, VIII, 334–35.

22 *Sermons*, I, 518.

23 *Sermons*, I, 521.

24 *Hymns for the National Fast, Feb. 8, 1782, The Poetical Works of John and Charles Wesley*, ed. George Osborne (London: Wesleyan Methodist Conference Office, 1868–72), VIII, 335.

War and Peace and the British Poets of Sensibility

J. WALTER NELSON

In writing of the British poets of sensibility we refer to those eighteenth-century poets who put feeling first, those who flourished between the Augustans and the Romantics, who are sometimes called the post-Augustans and sometimes the pre-Romantics, but who might more properly, as Northrop Frye has often asserted, be called the poets of sensibility, for they belong to their own aesthetically definable age. And in examining war and peace as a topic for these poets an attempt is made to discover how it was used and to what depth it was probed and presented. The findings are these: first, the British poets of sensibility show no knowledge of the various Enlightenment peace theories; i.e., those of Penn, the Abbé de Saint-Pierre, Leibnitz, Rousseau, and Bentham. Nor do they seem aware of the theories of Cicero, Tertullian, Origen, Augustine, Bernard of Clairvaux, Aquinas, Erasmus, Francesco de Vitoria, Grotius, or Spinoza, in short any of those westerners within or without the Judeo-Christian tradition who presented important ideas on war and our possible avoidance or containment of it. Second, these poets rarely see the topic in depth; that is, with awareness of the hidden motives of men or of the beguiling ironies of warmaking and peacemaking. Third, these poets show little consistency in their thinking about war and peace, even within their own canons, or sometimes within single poems. In fact, war and peace are most commonly used merely to stimulate emotion, any emotion. Fourth, as the century moves along, within this group of poets there may be a trend away from economic and cultural imperialism and toward pacifism. And fifth, the image of the "broken soldier," the soldier as total victim, becomes a common and poignant one.

The Augustan Precedents

Had the poets of sensibility wanted to deal incisively with war and peace, they would have found excellent poetic examples in their immediate predecessors. In his *The Fable of the Bees* Bernard Mandeville shows humorous insight into the ironies of maintaining an army. Standing armies, he writes (somewhat naively at this point), are thoroughly beneficial, for along with courts they are "the greatest schools of breeding and good manners. . . . What officers of distinction chiefly aim at is not a beastly, but a splendid way of living. . . ."[1] Moreover, a wealthy nation like England can afford an army and still have "ease and plenty." But if Mandeville is idealistic concerning the value of the military, he is by no means so about the soldier's motivation. An officer is urged on not by "robustness" but by "the hopes of preferment, emulation, and the love of glory";[2] and any man can be urged to fight by an infusion of "artificial courage." This last is accomplished simply by convincing the soldier of the justice of the cause, telling him his property will be confiscated by the enemy, giving him a distinguishing uniform and a mouthful of slogans, and by breeding in him a fear of the contempt of his peers if he does not fight. Vanity is a large part of every soldier's motivation, so a uniform with some "paltry gaudiness and affected finery" succeeds well. A drum roll helps, and extraordinary honors to the dead "will ever be a sure method to make bubbles [dupes] of the living."[3]

Dryden was well aware of the economic contradictions of a standing army, for in his oft-quoted lines on a paid militia he brands them

"Mouths without hands; maintained at vast expense / In peace a charge, in war a weak defense";[4] and in his imitation of "The First Satire of the Second Book of Horace" Pope spoofs the military enthusiasm of George II and all those who write noisy, martial verses to ingratiate themselves with him. I mention these examples not because they demonstrate that the Augustans thought long and deeply about war and peace, but to show that they penetrated military surfaces and probed men's motivations in warmaking.

The First Poets of Sensibility

Edward Young was a poet of sensibility only in his long and famous *Night Thoughts,* which was not started until late in his writing life. But in his early poems, neoclassical in aim and shape, he wrote much about war and peace, and in his entire canon he probably wrote more on this subject than did any other major British poet in the eighteenth century. What is surprising about his treatment of the topic is the bewildering variety of unexamined ideas he sets forth in poems written within a narrow span of years. In Satire IV of *Love of Fame, the Universal Passion,* a series of seven poems which many consider to be among his best, he shows (perhaps perversely echoing Mandeville) the typical young officer gaining fame by climbing a heap of bodies:

> "Who'd be a slave?" the gallant colonel cries,
> While love of glory sparkles from his eyes.
> . . . .
> But, when indulging on the last campaign,
> His lofty terms climb o'er the hills of slain.[5]

And in Satire VII he seems to be an anti-imperialist berating those who fight to "give mankind a single Lord."[6]

If this were all we had of Young's ideas on war and peace, he would seem consistent at least and perhaps even adroit with a couplet. But in his next poem, "Ocean: An Ode," a work he himself saw as important enough to warrant a lengthy preface proclaiming it to embody a new subject and form in the history of ode writing, we find a common, muscle-flexing, British imperialism:

Let Thebes, nor Rome
So fam'd, presume
To triumph o'er a northern isle;
Late time shall know
The north can glow,
If dread Augustus deign to smile.

The naval crown
Is all his own!
Our fleet, if war, or commerce, call,
His will performs
Through waves and storms,
And rides in triumph round the ball.[7]

Moreover, love of fame, denounced in the seven satires of that title, is now seen as honorific, apparently because it is won primarily in Britain's wars for "honest gain," the only wars Britain ever fights.[8] Seeing the term "honest gain," the reader desires a definition, some analysis, or at least a sign that Young knows that distinctions must be made, but none is offered. And this is the most disappointing observation about these poets in their use of war and peace as topics: they generally avoid even the most elementary distinctions and show no awareness of the second-level questions involved in warmaking and peacemaking.

In his next poem that deals with the subject, *Imperium Pelagi,* Young successively warns England that she must beware the pride of Tyre and the danger of feeding one's young with "human gore," states highmindedly that England's virtue must increase with her wealth, implies that she is divinely destined to trade but must wage defensive war to do so (to assist destiny?), and ends with a panegyric on peace, the ultimate condition of trade.[9] If one reverses the order of the poem, it makes sense: Britain needs peace to carry on trade, an activity for which she is well-situated, but she sometimes seems forced into defensive wars; if so, she should beware the temptation cruelly to misuse her wealth and power. Young's view is not strange, for the poem merely versifies the pacific mercantile policy of the Walpole Whigs. But, alas, we yearn for insight in our poets and in Young some awareness that a policy of defensive wars, as Lactantius demonstrated in the third century A.D. and Augustine in the fourth,[10] quickly becomes a sanction for empire building, for all wars can be seen as defensive and many can be justified on the pretense of defending an innocent ally. He does occasionally show intellectual acuity. For instance, in Satire VII, while writing of war's destruction, he berates those who engage in the more subtle but still dangerous violence of words, and he thus shows awareness of the violence spectrum. He fails, however, to sustain this level of thought. Moreover, one senses in these poems some honest hope that he is furthering the cause of peace. In short, one feels that the urge and capacity to write profoundly on a topic was used but rarely and unfortunately.

Young wrote at least three more poems dealing with war and peace. "The Sea Piece" and "The Foreign Address" repeat several of the ideas expressed in the above-mentioned poems, with the addition in "The Sea Piece" of a notion seen again later in the century, that England fights only defensive wars but is unusually vicious when wronged, as if England were an incarnation of Polonius' advice.[11]

Later in life, in his *Night Thoughts,* the poem from which he achieved international fame, Young briefly presented a more complex view of war, the one set forth by Augustine and Aquinas and the Church generally through the ages which sees war as the mournful, but inescapable, result of the human condition:[12]

> War, famine, pest, volcano, storm, and fire,
> Intestine broils, oppression, with her heart
> Wrapt us in triple brass, besiege mankind.
> . . . .
> Some for hard masters, broken under arms,
> In battle lopt away, with half their limbs,
> Beg bitter bread thro' realms their valour sav'd,
> If so the tyrant, or his minion doom.[13]

Here we see for the first time an image that will become more familiar as the century moves along, that of the "broken soldier" (Goldsmith's term), limbless and begging.

James Thomson is only marginally a poet of sensibility, but in his view of man (in *The Seasons* at least) as a suffering victim of nature, in his interest in the uneducated cottage-dweller, and with his picture of an animus-infused nature, he meets the requirements. It seems strange, then, since we usually think of the men of sensibility as having a feeling for all men, that he provides us with that *locus classicus* of British imperialism, "Rule Britannia!"[14] Many present-day U. S. citizens are Anglophiles who have never considered how outrageous this poem is—most victims of British imperialism have. The opening line states that Britain arose "at heaven's command," and indeed the whole ode sees Britain's commercial life as a perpetual crusade. One should note especially lines 12 and 13, for here Thomson adds to Young's idea (that England is peculiarly vicious when attacked) the further notion that she becomes increasingly vicious with each new offense: "Still more majestic shall thou rise, More dreadful, from each foreign stroke." Britain is Tamburlaine. All of stanza five deserves quoting, for it proclaims that England has proprietary rights to the whole world, apparently for the purpose of creating an international shopping mall:

> To thee belongs the rural reign;
> Thy cities shall with commerce shine:
> All thine shall be the subject main,
> And every shore it circles thine.
> "Rule, Britannia, rule the waves;
> "Britons never will be slaves."[15]

One should not conclude from the above that Thomson has no capacity for ethical discrimination. He is disappointing because, like Young, he occasionally demonstrates this ability. For instance, in the "Autumn" portion of *The Seasons,* where he engages in a diatribe against hunting as a sport, he notes that whereas primitive man hunted from necessity and used what he caught, eighteenth-century Englishmen hunt only for the pleasure of the hunt.[16] There is no great subtlety here, but he goes on to suggest (ll. 474ff.) that if Englishmen must hunt, they should provide a service by killing the fox that raids the sheepfold. Thomson does not see what we do now—that foxes too can be overhunted, but he is at least thinking, discriminating, and suggesting alternatives.[17] Moreover, Thomson is aware of the dark ironies built into the world of nature, for he notes (ll. 418–19) that it is the hare's own scent that betrays it to the hounds and that the wounded stag is cruelly avoided by its own herd. Thomson states these ironies but does nothing with them, as if further thought required too much effort.

In "Winter" Thomson devotes several lines to war and peace, but he seems to be using the topic merely to raise emotion. This in itself is at least explainable if we consider the times, for Thomson was part of a new English desire to feel fully, a love of feeling that continued until a whole epistemology, psychology, aesthetic, Biblical hermeneutic, and even a theology of sensibility developed.[18] But with all of this interest in feeling there was generally the assumption that a poet should select and amend the sentiments, not a recommendation that he arouse contradictory passions and then invite the reader to luxuriate serially in each.[19] Nevertheless this last is precisely what Thomson does in regard to war and peace in "Winter." For instance, he sometimes praises "Peace" (e.g., ll. 344–45) and lauds the Laplanders who "wisely" despise war and lack the "false Desires" and "Pride-created Wants" that breed war (ll. 853–58).[20] But at other times he exalts "Patriots" (ll. 37–38, 383–84, 364–68) and writes honorifically of those who make war. Thus in lines 375–76 he is dismayed at the previous state of the nation's prisons because they destroyed those who might have bled for their country, and in lines 432ff. he writes of the "MIGHTY DEAD . . . who blest Mankind / With Arts, and Arms, and humaniz'd a World." Whether they humanized the world with and through arms or in spite of them we never discover, but we assume Thomson means the former, and if we are right, he sees war (in some parts of the poem, at least) as a civilizing, as well as a commercial crusade, an eighteenth-century "bearing of the white man's burden." Thomson buttresses this idea with the example of Peter the Great, who "Gather'd the Seeds of Trade, of useful Arts, / Of Civil Wisdom, and of Martial Skill" (ll. 980–81) and taught "One Scene of Arts, of Arms, or rising Trade: / For what his Wisdom plann'd, his Power enforc'd" (ll. 995–96). Thomson is for both war and peace in the same poem.

Thomson's confusion is further manifested in his list of the "MIGHTY DEAD," those whom he is to study and hold "high Converse" with. On the one hand he names Numa, by whom he means Numa Pompilius, second King of Rome, a man notable, supposedly, for keeping the peace, Scipio Africanus Major, the humane warrior, famous for his magnanimity in single-handedly saving Hannibal from ruin at the hands of the Romans, and Phocian the Good, the Athenian general who headed the peace party of his day; that is, soldier-statesmen noted for their relatively passive aims and methods. But on the other hand, he also includes Lycurgus, who "bow'd beneath the Force / Of strictest Discipline, *severely wise,* / All human Passions" (ll. 455–47), and Philopemon, who could not cure the luxurious pomp of his day and so subscripted it into the military; that is, men noted for their severity. It makes no difference whether the figure made peace, or war, or peace through war; if he ended up in Plutarch, he is fit for "high Converse."

Some Mid-Century Poets: Getting Emotional about Emotion

William Collins was so in love with various emotions that he wrote poems to several of them, as his "Ode to Pity," "Ode to Fear," and his "The Passions, and Ode For Music" all show. In several of these encomiums he writes of war and occasionally recommends it as a subject for poetry. Thus in his "Ode to Fear" he gratuitously notes that Aeschylus, who first invoked fear's name, disdained this emotion when he grasped "The Patriot's Steel" at Marathon (ll. 30–34),[21] and in his "An Ode on the Popular Superstitions of Highlands of Scotland, Considered as the Subject of Poetry" he sees the "sturdy clans" collecting at the "bugle's call" to meet their "hostile brothers" (ll. 50–53) as part of a general scene peculiarly right for poetry. So also Mark Akenside writes a poem entitled "Ode on a Sermon against Glory," proclaiming that contrary to some clergymen's stance, he desires no "holier place" than Timolean's arms. The latter was one of a long line of Greek and Roman generals who took up arms only at their nation's call and then retired willingly when no longer needed; and thus Akenside is saying that if one picks his generals carefully, he has every right to bask in that hero's glory.

Joseph Warton, the older of the two poet-scholar brothers, was part of this phenomenon of praising the emotions and occasionally recommending emotionally stimulating subjects for poetry; he, too, sees war and soldiering as such subjects. What he otherwise thought about these topics, however, we will never know. Let us consider: in his oft-anthologized "The Dying Indian" he is clearly mocking the Christian soldier in general and the conquistador in particular, he whose spear is dipped in the "double poison" of the European Church and State;[22] but he seems also to be taking delight in the primitive vengeance of the Indian who brags that his "forefathers feast / Daily on the hearts of Spaniards" and whose crown is "deck'd with the teeth / Of that bold christian [note the small c] who first dar'd deflour / The virgins of the sun." Or, if this is not confusing enough, consider that in *The Enthusiast,* in literary terms his most important poem, he pits the peaceful sounds of nature against the "battle-breathing Trumpet" of the world of civilized man,[25] and then just two years later in his "Ode I. To Fancy" writes of the battlefield as a scene to which Fancy, the "Parent of each lovely Muse" should lead him:

> Or sometimes in the fiery car
> Transport me to the rage of war;
> There whirl me o'er the hills of slain,
> Where Tummult and destruction reign;
> Where mad with pain, the wounded steed
> Tramples the dying and the dead;
> Where giant Terror stalks around,
> With sullen joy surveys the ground,
> And pointing to th' ensanguin'd field,
> Shakes his dreadful Gorgon-shield![24]

There is no value judgment on war here. Warton merely desires great British poetry (l. 120); the way to create such poetry is to "O'erwhelm our souls with joy and pain" (l. 108), and one obvious source is battlefield imagery.

War as Romance: The Celtic and Nordic Past

In the poems and essays of Thomas Warton, the younger, Joseph's brother, we find two new eighteenth-century views of war. In the Postscript to his *Observations on the Faerie Queene* he writes of medieval chivalry as an unqualified good in that it "inspired the noblest sentiments of heroism," teaching "gallantry" and "civility" to a rude people and humanizing a "native ferocity."[25] Warton shows here a Mandeville-like respect for the military elite, this time an ancient elite. But the development which most concerns us here is a related one: Thomas Warton, unlike Collins, Akenside, and Joseph Warton, not only calls for a poetry full of sensibility-arousing war scenes but actually writes it, creating battle scenes romantically filtered through the gauze of centuries. Thus, in his "Sonnet IV. Written at Stonehenge," he honors several possible builders of England's "noblest monument," among them the "Danish chiefs, enriched with savage spoil."[26] He makes no value judgments but seems awed by the imagination and strength of these ancient enemies of England. And in "The Crusade" he seems to delight in the violence of the Christians. Blondel, the minstrel of King Richard and supposed composer (along with Richard), recites:

> Syrian virgins, wail and weep
> English Richard plough the deep!
> . . . .
> From Albion's isle revenge we bring.[27]

Later in the poem Warton writes of Calvary "Wet with our Redeemer's gore!" (l. 50) and sees no irony in the fact that the crusaders are about to wet it with Saracen blood. Of course the sentiments are supposedly those of the crusading persona, but Warton has also supposedly selected a poem both he and his readers will enjoy.

In his "The Alliance of Education and Government," a poem which, along with Collins' Preface to the *Persian Eclogues* and Goldsmith's *The Traveller,* seeks to enunciate the notion of general nature modified by geographical differences, Thomas Gray is quite specific but at the same time quite confusing about war and peace. In line 35 he claims that all "by Force repell the Foe," but various climates make some excel in the "polish'd Arts of Peace" (l. 41) and others in "hardy Deeds of Blood" (l. 44).[28] The difficulty is that he seemingly honors all possibilities here while in the final verse paragraph he claims that northerners prevail militarily over southerners and mountain people over lowlanders (ll. 46–70, 94–95) and that the northerners are following "Reason's Light" and "Resolution" (l. 75). Despite this confusion, in much of Gray we continue to see a poetry that delights in the death of ancient warriors. In *The Bard* Gray calls for a prophet-poet to adorn "Fierce War" (l. 126), and we watch the descendants of Edward I suffer fearsome punishment, sometimes in war, for the family's successive war crimes. "The Death of Hoel," "Caradoc," and "Conan" all celebrate the ferocity of primitive people and their willingness to die in battle. "The Fatal Sisters" shows the Valkyries carrying to Wahalla those slain in battle, and "The Descent of Odin" reveals a Gothic hell for all those slain *other than* in battle. True, many of these are translations or paraphrases of Old Welsh and Old Norse odes, but they demonstrate Gray's selectivity, his preference for poems about ancient warriors willingly dying.

In James Macpherson and the tragic child-poet Chatterton we find the same phenomenon, but now with heroes of a humane cast, and thus we get gore and benevolence conveniently combined. Actually, in Macpherson's *Fingal* we get almost every battlefield emotion obtainable. On the one hand we have the warriors who lust Achilles-like for the sport of battle, and on the other we have the many songs of women who wail in loneliness for dead sons, brothers, and lovers. But along with these we get the pagan, but curiously charitable, Fingal, who is chosen to lead the Fianna, not because of his martial skill, but because of his wisdom, generosity, and tolerance, and who at the end of the epic simply frees the invading villain, the Scandinavian Swaran, and allows him to go home. Indeed, the eighteenth-century Scottish rhetorician Hugh Blair suggested that the "moral" of the poem is "Wisdom and bravery always triumph over brutal force; or another, nobler still: that the most complete victory over an enemy is obtained by that moderation and generosity which convert him to a friend."[29] And some of this idea of a soldier of sensibility can also be found in Chatterton's *Aella, A Tragycal Enterlude* in which the title character, a Saxon Lord of Bristol castle, leaves his bride Birtha on their wedding night because he feels honor-bound to help repel an unexpected Danish invasion. While Aella is away fighting, his Saxon rival Celmonde abducts Birtha, but chivalrous Danes find her, kill Celmonde, and escort Birtha back to Bristol. Even the enemies are now men of sensibility. And thus we see a pattern in these mid-century poets: Thomas Warton, Gray, Macpherson, and Chatterton all elicit emotion from battle scenes in northern antiquity, and the latter two portray Celtic and Nordic military figures of high sensibility.

Oliver Goldsmith and the "Broken Soldier"

The pattern is not all-pervasive, however, for in Goldsmith's poetry we find the same contradictions we found in the earlier poets of sensibility. In *The Traveller: or, A Prospect of Society,* as in Gray's "Alliance," Goldsmith discusses universal human nature and its mutations brought on by climate and, like Gray, sees the warrior nations as somehow more noble than the passive ones. The rough climate of Switzerland, he says (ll. 165–70), produces a more "noble" race than does that of Italy even though the only product of the former is soldiers;[30] and the Dutch are seen as a nation of commercial slaves totally unlike their "Belgic sires of old" who had "War in each breast, and freedom on each brow" (11. 313–15). This we read in the 1770 edition of the poem; but in the same year Goldsmith published "The Deserted Village, A Poem," then and now one of the most popular poems of the century, and in it he presents an entirely different view of war and soldiering. Here we find the broken soldier of Young's *Night Thoughts,* not a hero but a victim. In the parson's home

> The broken soldier, kindly bade to stay,
> Sate by the fire, and talked the night away;
> Wept o'er his wounds, or tales of sorrow done,
> Shouldered his crutch, and showed how fields were won.
> Pleased with his guests, the good man learned to glow,
> And quite forgot their vices in their woe.[31]

Two things should be noted here. First, the soldier is broken economically as well as physically; and second, he is broken socially as well, for he is presented as a bore. Notice that the good parson had to "learn" to glow. In short, the soldier is a recipient rather than a bestower of sensibility.

This theme of the broken soldier sometimes involves black humor, as in the anonymous Irish street song of the 1760s, "Johnny, I Hardly Knew Ye." The singer is exclaiming that she hardly recognized her soldier because

> "You haven't an arm and you haven't a leg,
> You're an eyeless, noseless, chickenless egg;
> You'll have to be put with a bowl to beg:
>   Och, Johnny, I hardly knew ye!
>   With drums and guns, and guns and drums,
>   The enemy nearly slew ye;
>   My darling dear, you look so queer,
>   Och, Johnny, I hardly knew ye!"[32]

Some Late Eighteenth-Century Patriots

If the reader thinks these images of the broken soldier signal a wave of pacifism in the late eighteenth-century poetry, he is wrong, for before we get to John Scott, William Cowper, and William Blake, the only real pacifist poets of the century, we find Christopher Smart, Samuel Johnson, and Robert Burns, all of whom exhibit vital forms of patriotism. Actually, Smart's views on war are not clear. At times he appears to be a thoroughgoing Christian pacifist. For instance, in *Jubilate Agno,* his major work, he writes:

> For I bless the PRINCE of PEACE and pray that all guns
>   may be nail'd up, save such as are
>   for rejoicing days.
>
>   . . . .
>
> For I meditate the peace of Europe amongst family
>   bickerings and domestic jars.
>
>   . . . .
>
> For I preach the very GOSPEL of CHRIST
>   without comment and with this weapon will I
>   slay envy.[33]

But in line 38 he says, "For I am ready for the trumpet and alarm to fight, to die, and to rise again," which *may* contradict the previous lines (though, of course, his "fight" may be metaphoric); and throughout the poem Smart honors the militancy of various Old Testament figures, especially Joab, the one-time captain of David's army. Moreover, in "A Song to David" published in 1763, i.e., about the same time *Jubilate Agno* was written, Smart lauds David's violent triumph over Goliath and calls him "valiant" (l. 31). Perhaps, as Albert Kuhn suggests, there is no conflict here—Smart sees himself as a patriot of God: the enemy is the dragon of faithlessness, the fight is the "good fight" of St. Paul, the weapon is the Gospel, and the militancy he lauds in Old Testament warriors is the zest with which he plans to bring the Holy Anglican Empire of the Anglo-Israelis.[34]

Samuel Johnson resisted the sensibility aesthetic all his life, but because he was a dominant literary figure of the time, we should examine his poems involving war and peace. *The Vanity of Human Wishes,* an imitation of Juvenal's tenth satire, and Johnson's most notable poem, is full of antiwar sentiments. Marlborough's campaigns in Austria and Bavaria are seen as all pomp and show that bloodied the Danube and Rhine; Charles XII of Sweden is presented as thinking "Nothing gain'd . . . till nought remain" (l. 202); and Xerxes of old and the more contemporary Charles Albert of Bavaria are also offered as illustrations of the warrior's expensive pride. Moreover, concerning war in general, Johnson comments, "Reason frowns on War's unequal game / Where wasted Nations raise a single name" and "mortgag'd states" go "From age to age in everlasting debt" (ll. 183–86).[35] In all, Johnson offers seventy-nine lines of the poem to antiwar sentiments, often with the acerbic irony of Mandeville, Dryden, and Pope. Yet we know from Johnson's statements outside the poem that he was far from being a pacifist, and he vigorously supported his country's military resistance to the American Revolution. Most likely he was close to the Augustinian stance of his own Church of England, that the Christian must mournfully support a just war and seek divine help in determining precisely which conflicts are just. With his great love for his own country, such a view made him an English patriot, not in the eighteenth-century sense of a follower of Pitt and the expansionist Whigs, but in the sense of one who will vigorously defend his nation when he thinks it has been wronged.

In naming Smart a patriot of the Lord, Johnson a patriot for England, and Burns a patriot for Scotland, I am to some degree merely using a rhetorical ploy for organizational convenience: we are not sure what Smart thought about war, Johnson was a patriot in only one sense of the word (and certainly not in the sense that he himself used it), and Burns's flamboyant Scottish patriotism may have been largely a sensibility pose to further demonstrate that he was one of the folk. Whatever the case, Burns is the apotheosis of the poet of sensibility who uses soldiers and soldiering in any way he can to elicit emotion. For instance, the ever-popular "The Cotter's Saturday Night" ends with a stanza that reads in part:

> O *THOU*! who pour'd the *patriot tide,*
> That stream'd thro' great unhappy WALLACE'S heart;
> . . . .
> (The Patriot's GOD, peculiarly thou art,
> His *friend, inspirer, guardian,* and *reward!*)[36]

Thus Burns humorously places God one hundred percent on the side of Wallace and his guerrilla band against Edward I and his army. Actually, a quick look at the *DNB,* or any scholarly history, shows that Wallace is a figure so clouded in myth that it is impossible to discover his true character or actions. Needless to say, the English hold a view of the man different from that of Burns. And eight years after the publication of "The Cotter" Burns still exhibits a rather ferocious patriotism in his "Scots Wha Hae," a war song which calls Scots, supposedly at the time of Wallace's famous raids, to die or see victory, to "drain our dearest veins" for freedom.[37] But in some subsequent poems, like the "Air. *Tune*—'Soldiers' Joy'" in *The Jolly Beggars: A Cantata,* Burns adopts an entirely different tone. The persona is a *miles gloriosus* who shows his "cuts and scars" wherever he can.[38] But he soon begins to mock himself in such a way that the poem becomes black humor much like that in the anonymous Irish street song examined above:

> I lastly was with Curtis, among the *floating batt'ries,*
> And there I left for witness an arm and a limb;

Yet let my country need me, with Elliot to head me,
I'd clatter on my stumps at the sound of a drum.
Lal de daudle, etc.
. . . .
And now tho' I must beg with a wooden arm and leg,
And many a tatter'd rag hanging over my bum,
I'm as happy with my wallet, my bottle and my callet,
As when I us'd in scarlet to follow a drum.
Lal de daudle, etc. (ll. 37–48)

And in the subsequent "Air. *Tune*—'Soldiers' Laddie'" a now old camp follower sings of her former life in camp, her soldier laddie with "his leg . . . so tight," and her present poverty brought on by peace and the consequent absence of the soldiers, all of this humorously stereotyping the military.

Some Pacifist Poets

In the final quarter of the century we find some notable pacifist poets. John Scott, the Quaker from Amwell, was a friend of Samuel Johnson, attended Mrs. Montagu's parties, and published his poems in the *Gentleman's Magazine*; and his "Ode XIII" is still antholigized:

I Hate that drum's discordant sound,
Parading round, and round, and round:
To thoughtless youth it pleasure yields,
To sell their liberty for charms
Of tawdry lace, and glittering arms;
And when Ambition's voice commands,
To march, and fight, and fall, in foreign lands.[39]

What we have here, of course, is an enumeration of the same recruiting deceptions noted by Mandeville eighty years earlier, this time without the benefits the latter saw. In the second and final stanza of the poem, Scott writes of the "mangled limbs, and dying groans" which Mandeville failed to mention.

William Cowper, that unhappiest of all eighteenth-century Christians, was a self-proclaimed pacifist.[40] In his semi-jest "On a Spaniel, Called Beau Killing a Young Bird," the poet complains that the dog killed what he never intended to eat and that man does the same. But it is in Book IV of *The Task,* Cowper's earlier and major effort, that he sets forth observations similar to those we have seen in Mandeville and Scott and offers a kind of rake's progress of the typical British recruit. Cowper prefaces his description of military mistraining with the generalization

> 'Tis universal soldiership has stabbed
> The heart of merit in the meaner class.
> Arms, through the vanity of brainless rage
> Of those that bear them, in whatever cause,
> Seem most at variance with all moral good,
> And incompatible with serious thought.[41]

Then he describes the gulling of the rustic:

> The clown, the child of nature, without guile,
> Blessed with an infant's ignorance of all
> But his own simple pleasures; now and then
> A wrestling-match, a foot-race, or a fair;
> Is balloted, and trembles at the news:
> Sheepish he doffs his hat, and, mumbling, swears
> A Bible-oath to be whate'er they please,
> To do he knows not what! The Task performed,
> That instant he becomes the sergeant's care,
> His pupil, and his torment, and his jest.
> His awkward gait, his introverted toes,
> Bent knees, round shoulders, and dejected looks,
> Procure him many a curse. (ll. 623–35)

But the most distinctive lines are those describing his return to society:

> And his three years of heroship expired,
> Returns indignant to the slighted plough.
> He hates the field, in which no fife or drum
> Attends him; drives his cattle to a march;
> And sighs for the smart comrades he has left.
> 'T were well if his exterior change were all—
> But with his clumsy port the wretch has lost
> His ignorance and harmless manners too!
> To swear, to game, to drink; to show at home
> by lewdness, idleness, and sabboth-breach,
> The great proficiency he made abroad;

To astonish and to grieve his gazing friends,
To break some maiden's and a mother's heart;
To be a pest where he was useful once;
Are his sole aim and all his glory now. (ll. 644–58)

Cowper goes on to analyze what he sees to be the larger problem, that men joined in groups always lose the virtue of the individual, as blossoms pressed together lose all beauty and life. This is all the analysis presented, and we cannot expect a lot more, for certainly poetry is a form given to feeling or values, and the more analytical a poem becomes the closer it comes to being a mere tract. But we want to know what Cowper expected his beloved England to do were she attacked or what she should do if an innocent ally were attacked; and since Cowper chose to analyze the problem, perhaps we could expect to know his solution.

William Blake, who for much of his life saw himself as a Christian pacifist, produced what is probably the most subtle antiwar poem of the century, the dramatic fragment "King Edward the Third" printed in his *Poetical Sketches,* the only book he ever printed by conventional means. During the course of this drama, Sir John Chandos is, as David Erdman has pointed out, the voice of all Machiavellian schemes to turn defensive battles into wars of imperialism.[42] At one point in the fragment, Chandos counsels:

Courage, my Lord, proceeds from self-dependence;
Teach man to think he's a free agent,
Give but a slave his liberty, he'll shake
Off sloth, and build himself a hut, and hedge
A spot of ground; this he'll defend; 'tis his
By right of nature: thus set in action,
He will still move onward to plan conveniences,
'Till glory fires his breast to enlarge his castle,
While the poor slave drudges all day, in hope
To rest at night.[43]

And Erdman sees "A War Song to Englishmen," printed a few poems removed from "King Edward," as actually being a coda to the drama and a clever parody of William Whitehead's "Verses to the People of England" printed in his *Odes,* 1774. It is, at any rate, a clever parody of chauvinistic poetry, as the fifth stanza shows:

Soldiers, prepare! Our cause is Heaven's cause;
Soldiers, prepare! Be worthy of our cause:
Prepare to meet our fathers in the sky:
Prepare, O troops, that are to fall to-day!
Prepare, prepare.[44]

Blake uses the broken soldier motif more than any other eighteenth-century poet. We find it, for instance, in "London" in *Songs of Innocence and of Experience,* in "Auguries of Innocence" (ll. 77–78), and the "Song of Enion" in "Night the Second" of *The Four Zoas.*

But Blake does more than merely give poetic voice to his revulsion for war—he does precisely what we said Cowper did not do, give poetic form to his pacifist response. In the Prologue to his projected *King Edward the Fourth* he calls for the imaginative voice necessary to answer a world that keeps proclaiming that God and His angels are the ministers of war:

O For a voice like thunder, and a tongue
To drown the throat of war!—When the senses
Are shaken, and the soul is driven to madness,
Who can stand? When the souls of the oppressed
Fight in the troubled air that rages, who can stand?
When the whirlwind of fury comes from the
Throne of God, when the frowns of his countenance
Drive the nations together, who can stand?
. . . .
The Kings and Nobles of the Land have done it!
Hear it not, Heaven, thy Ministers have done it![45]

Blake's answer is, of course, all of his engraved canon with its various calls for "mental fight"; that is, for all men to use their Prophetic Imagination to reunite the universe into the "human form divine." Moreover, if the English Romantics in general present a more satisfying picture of peace and its possibilities than did the eighteenth-century poets of sensibility, this may be the inevitable result of their faith in the Romantic Imagination. At their best the poets of sensibility present themselves as divine men of feeling calling for a world in which each weeps for all, but in their use of war and peace as a topic for poetry they seem merely to be eliciting various emotions for the sheer pleasure they afford. The Romantics, on the other hand, were almost guaranteed at least a peace within and a measure of harmony, however small, with the world about them, for although the concept of Imagination varied with each of them, that concept always embodied, as C. M. Bowra has pointed out,[46] the poet's own harmony with some transcendental order, and this harmony was at first inspired by the world of nature and ultimately helps to explain the appearances of that world.

NOTES

1 Bernard Mandeville in his "Remarks" on l. 180 of *The Fable of the Bees*, ed. Irwin Primer (New York: Capricorn, 1962), p. 85.

2 Mandeville, p. 86.

3 Mandeville, pp. 135–39.

4 *Cymon and Iphigenia*, ll. 401–2, quoted from *The Poetical Works of John Dryden*, ed. Geo. Noyes (Boston: Houghton, 1950), p. 890. This work is an imitation of Boccaccio and may be from the last year of Dryden's life. Dryden was not always this harsh on the military—in his early poems "Heroic Stanzas" and *Annus Mirabilis* he is somewhat of an economic imperialist.

5 Third to the last stanza, quoted from *The Poetical Works of Edward Young* (Westport, Conn.: Greenwood, 1970), II, 94–95. This edition, often the only one available, offers no line numbers.

6 Young, II, 134. At this time Young was desperately trying to find preferment, and since this poem is addressed to Robert Walpole, it may be an obvious attempt to compliment the latter on his pacific foreign policy.

7 Young, II, 142.

8 Young, II, 143–44, 158.

9 Young, II, 335ff.

10 Lactantius, *The Divine Institutes*, Bk. VI in the *Ante Nicene Christian Library*, ed. Alexander Roberts and J. Donaldson (Edinburgh: T. & T. Clark, 1867–87). Augustine, *The City of God*, Bk. IV, 4, 15, in *A Select Library of the Nicene and Post-Nicene Fathers of the Christian Church* (Oxford: Parker, 1890–1900).

11 Young, II, 88.

12 Augustine, *The City of God*, Bk. XIX, 10–13, and Reply to *Faustus the Manichean*, Bk. XXII, 73–76.

13 Young, I, 8–9.

14 The ode is part of the masque *Alfred*, which is the product of both Mallet and Thomson. "Rule Brittania!" is commonly seen to be wholly J. T.'s, however.

15 *The Complete Poetical Works of James Thomson,* ed. J. Logie Robertson (London: Oxford Univ. Press, 1908), p. 423.

16 See lines 400–404 from the 1744 text of "Autumn" in *A Collection of English Poems: 1660–1800,* ed. Ronald Crane (New York: Harpers, 1932), p. 625. Hereafter this anthology will be referred to as "Crane."

17 One could argue, of course, that since sheep were a large part of British mercantilism, Thomson was still being the economic imperialist, but since he commonly shows a large concern for the animal world, we probably should give him the benefit of the doubt.

18 For a handy and helpful discussion of the first three, see chapters IV and V of Walter Jackson Bate, *From Classic to Romantic: Premises of Taste in Eighteenth Century England* (New York: Harper, 1946). For the hermeneutic see Robert Lowth, *De Sacra Poesi Hebraeorum* (London: n.p., 1753). The theology I am referring to is Schleiermacher's.

19 Note, for instance, the title of Adam Smith's influential book *Theory of the Moral Sentiments* (n.l.: n.p., 1759).

20 All line references are to the 1744 edition in Crane.

21 *The Poems of William Collins,* ed. Christopher Stone (London: Henry Frowde, 1907), p. 32. All quotations are from this edition of Collins, though I supply the line numbers.

22 Quoted from *Eighteenth-Century English Literature,* ed. Geoffrey Tillotson et al. (New York: Harcourt, 1969), pp. 929–30. Hereafter this anthology will be referred to as "Tillotson."

23 Ll. 36–42, Crane, p. 748.

24 Ll. 59–68, Crane, p. 763.

25 Quoted from Tillotson, p. 934.

26 Quoted from Crane, p. 813.

27 Ll. 8–9, 18 quoted from *Eighteenth Century Poetry & Prose,* 3rd ed., ed. Louis I. Bredvold (New York: Ronald Press, 1973), p. 1063. Hereafter this anthology will be referred to as "Bredvold."

28 *The Complete Poems of Thomas Gray,* ed. H. W. Starr and J. R. Hendrickson (Oxford: Clarendon, 1966), pp. 94–97. All line references to Gray are to this edition.

29 "Critical Dissertation on the Poems of Ossian," in James Macpherson, *The Poems of Ossian* (Boston: Phillip Simpson, 1853), p. 113.

30 *Goldsmith: Selected Works,* ed. Richard Garnett (Cambridge, Mass.: Harvard Univ. Press, 1967), pp. 593–94.

31 Ll. 155–60, Garnett, p. 611.

32 Ll. 40ff., Tillotson, p. 1525.

33 Ll. 4, 7, 9 (Bond text, B 1), Bredvold, p. 1046.

34 See Albert J. Kuhn, "Christopher Smart: The Poet as Patriot of the Lord," *ELH,* 30 (1963), 121ff.

35 *The Poems of Samuel Johnson,* ed. David Nichol Smith and Edward L. McAdam (Oxford: Clarendon, 1941), pp. 39–40.

36 *The Poems of Robert Burns,* ed. James Kinsley (Oxford: Clarendon, 1968), I, 151–52.

37 Kinsley, II, 708.
38 Kinsley, I, 196–97.
39 Ll. 1–8, Tillotson, pp. 1529–30.
40 See his letter of 16 March 1780 to Joseph Hill in *The Correspondence of William Cowper,* ed. Thomas Wright (London: Hodder and Stoughton, 1904), I, 177.
41 *The Poetical Works of William Cowper,* ed. H. S. Milford (London: Oxford Univ. Press, 1934), pp. 195–96, ll. 217–22.
42 Blake: *Prophet against Empire* (1954; Rev. ed., Princeton: Princeton Univ. Press, 1969), p. 70.
43 Ll. 194–203, quoted from *The Poetry and Prose of William Blake,* ed. David V. Erdman and Harold Bloom (Garden City: Doubleday, 1965), p. 423.
44 Erdman and Bloom, p. 431.
45 Erdman and Bloom, p. 430.
46 *The Romantic Imagination* (Cambridge, Mass.: Harvard Univ. Press, 1949), pp. 12–22.

Cowper's Concept of Truth

JOHN D. BAIRD

William Cowper's poetical activity extended over half a century, from "Verses written at Bath on finding the heel of a shoe," composed in 1748 when he was sixteen, to a scrap of translation from Homer written a few months before his death on April 25, 1800. His contemporary fame, and his present reputation, rest upon the two volumes he published in his early fifties: *Poems by William Cowper, of the Inner Temple, Esq.*, published in 1782, and his masterpiece, *The Task*, published in 1785. While a knowledge of Cowper's concept of truth—more strictly, religious truth—is necessary to a full understanding of all his mature poetry, its importance is most obvious in connection with the first two poems of what may be called Cowper's "major phase," namely, "The Progress of Error" and "Truth," both of which were included in *Poems*, 1782. As an example of the misunderstanding to which they are liable, one may quote Canon Benham, who, in the introduction to his edition of the poems, objects that "The Progress of Error" is a misnomer; we are led, he says, "to expect a philosophical disquisition, whereas we find that the sum of this poem is that operas, card-playing, intemperance, gluttony, reading of bad novels, are the causes of Error; that they who hate truth shall be the dupe of lies. Quite true, of course; but who supposes that this is an adequate account of the progress of Error?"[1] Well, presumably Cowper did, for one. Consideration of the circumstances in which the poem came to be written may help us to understand why.

In 1763 Cowper suffered a complete nervous breakdown (signalized by an unsuccessful suicide attempt), and left London for ever. In the course of his recovery, under the influence of his physician, Dr. Cotton of St. Albans, he became a convinced Evangelical Christian. Nine years later, in 1773, he suffered a yet more drastic collapse. At the height of the seizure he had a dream which haunted him for the rest of his life. Henceforth he believed that God had condemned his soul not to eternal punishment but to annihilation immediately after the physical death of his body; further, that it was God's wish that he should make away with himself at the first opportunity.

This grim conviction weighed upon Cowper's mind every minute of every day. He could obtain relief only by occupying himself with some activity. First his famous pet hares, then gardening, then drawing provided this necessary diversion. Then in 1778 and 1779 he began to write verse again. These little poems are neither gentlemanly love lyrics such as he had written as a young man-about-town in the 1750s, nor are they hymns such as he had composed in the enthusiastic aftermath of his conversion. Instead, they fall for the most part into two groups: moral fables like "The Pine-Apple and the Bee" (always a favourite form with Cowper), or topical poems inspired by the course of the American War. These are loudly patriotic, contemptuous of the Americans and violent against the French. Most of them were not published during his lifetime—he had to suppress two during the preparation of the 1782 volume when it became clear that their confidence had been misplaced—and two were so strident and abusive that they did not appear in print until 1959.[2]

By the spring of 1780, the writing of verse was providing more and more of Cowper's daily "amusement." In May or early June he started to collect his little poems in a manuscript book, and included poems and translations more frequently in letters to his close friends. At the same time, as luck would have it, a new topic of public interest arose to attract his attention.

This was a book called *Thelyphthora or, A Treatise on Female Ruin . . . Considered on the Basis of the Divine Law.*[3] It was written by a leading Evangelical clergyman, Martin Madan, who happened to be Cowper's cousin. Madan was Chaplain of the Lock Hospital, which had been established to care for "fallen women," and he was acutely conscious of the economic and social pressures which brought "ruin" and disease to thousands of unfortunate young women. The thesis advanced in his two thick volumes is reducible to very simple terms: the man who takes a woman's virginity has, by God's law revealed in the Old Testament, married her, and is consequently responsible for her economic support thereafter. *Thelyphthora* was published at the end of May 1780, just before the outbreak of the Gordon Riots—a coincidence deemed significant by some—and set off a controversy which boiled for a full year and was not soon forgotten.

Cowper, although he never read the book through, knew all about it. His friend and spiritual adviser, John Newton, had told him of it long before it appeared, and he kept Cowper informed of his efforts, and those of other Evangelical clergy, to persuade Madan not to publish.[4] (Newton had a few months before moved from Olney to London, as Rector of St. Mary Woolnoth.) But Madan did not listen to them, and so many of his colleagues, in the autumn of 1780, felt compelled to answer him in print. Madan's very real humanitarian concern passed largely unnoticed; he was accused of having advocated polygamy; he found scarcely any defenders, and in the end retired disappointed to the country, where he solaced himself by translating Juvenal and advocating the more frequent imposition of the death penalty.[5]

For his opponents, however, there was one little difficulty. While of course everyone could see at once that *Thelyphthora* was an evil book—for did it not advocate polygamy?—it was by no means clear that anyone could prove its arguments to be false. Madan was not only a learned man; before his conversion he had been a rising young lawyer; he was experienced in controversy, and he knew how to make out his case. Among the fears of Newton and his colleagues not the least, one suspects, was the horrid apprehension that Mr. Madan could not be refuted.

By November the crisis was past. A reviewer called Samuel Badcock published a lengthy refutation of Madan's views which was understood to answer all the points of learning involved.[6] And Cowper, who had written three or four short poems against his cousin's book, was moved to write his allegorical narrative poem *Anti-Thelyphthora.* This marks the beginning of a year of intense poetic activity on Cowper's part.[7]

As soon as *Anti-Thelyphthora* had been despatched to Newton, who undertook to have it published anonymously, Cowper set to work on another poem, to be called "The Progress of Error." Madan is again attacked, this time among a crowd of evil exemplars. This poem was finished in the middle of December 1780, and was at once followed by another, called "Truth," which took about a month to complete. Early in February Cowper added a third long poem, "Table Talk." This was designed to be read as a kind of preface to its predecessors; it concludes with Cowper's declaration of intent as a poet. Religion, he says, has never had a "skilful guide into poetic ground," and the poetic ground itself is well-nigh exhausted:

> And 'tis the sad complaint, and almost true,
> Whate'er we write, we bring forth nothing new.
> 'Twere new indeed to see a bard all fire,
> Touch'd with a coal from heav'n, assume the lyre,
> And tell the world, still kindling as he sung,
> With more than mortal music on his tongue,
> That He, who died below and reigns above,
> Inspires the song, and that his name is love. (732–39)[8]

When we turn, however, to "The Progress of Error" and "Truth" we are liable, like Canon Benham, to be puzzled. The two poems are clearly a pair, intended as the contrast of night with day. But they do not offer any definitions of error and truth; the doctrinal element suggested by these terms is absent. "The Progress of Error" shows us various moral offenders, and shows how their example may corrupt others; "Truth" tells us that those who will be saved—and the hideous alternative is never long out of view—trust in faith, not works, have thankful hearts, and read the Bible. From this they gain a knowledge of "Heav'n's easy, artless, unincumber'd plan" (22), which is so easy, artless, and unincumbered that it can be summed up in just three words: "BELIEVE AND LIVE!" (31). But what it is they believe, and the relation of this belief to virtuous conduct—these things are not explained.

Cowper himself was apprehensive about the way this poem might strike the general reader, one not already Evangelical in outlook, and he asked Newton to write a preface that might coat the pill.[9] In his preface, Newton explains that Cowper's poems commend an "*experimental*" religion. He uses the word "experimental" with obvious caution, and the precise signification which it had for him is not certain; however, it seems to mean both a religion in which personal religious experience is the predominating element, and a religion *proved* by experiment. He writes:

> From this state [of misery] the Bible relieved us—When we were led to read it with attention, we found *ourselves* described.—We learnt the causes of our inquietude—we were directed to a method of relief—we tried, and we were not disappointed.
>
> *Deus nobis haec otia fecit.*
>
> We are now certain that the gospel of Christ is the power of God unto salvation, to every one that believeth. It has reconciled us to God, and to ourselves, to our duty, and our situation. It is the balm and cordial of the present life, and a sovereign antidote against the fear of death.[10]

It is helpful at this point to turn to a later poem, "Conversation," written in the summer of 1781. Tell the world, Cowper writes,

> That while she dotes, and dreams that she believes,
> She mocks her Maker, and herself deceives,
> Her utmost reach, historical assent,
> The doctrines warpt to what they never meant;
> That truth itself is in her head as dull,
> And useless, as a candle in a scull,
> And all her love of God a groundless claim,
> A trick upon the canvas, painted flame. (775–82)

The distinction between "historical assent" and a "lively faith" to which Cowper here refers is of course a common one. It is neatly illustrated by the contrast between Tillotson and Whitefield. Tillotson argues that since we believe in the former existence and deeds of Alexander the Great and Julius Caesar on the basis of written records, so, "if we have the doctrine and history of the gospel, and all the evidence of our Saviour's divine authority, conveyed down to us, in as credible a manner, as any of these ancient matters of fact are, which mankind do firmly believe, then we have sufficient ground to be assured of it."[11] The Calvinist Whitefield, on the other hand, preaching at Bexley on Whitsunday 1739, remarks that "... many now read the Life, Sufferings, Death and Resurrection of Jesus Christ, in the same Manner as learned Men read *Caesar's Commentaries,* or *the Conquests of Alexander.* As Things rather intended to afford Matter for Speculation, than to be acted over again in and by us."[12] Salvation depends not on rational assent but on a personal, subjective, unique experience. And when the truth has been made operative by being "acted over again in and by us," it will be manifest to others in the virtuous life which is the outward sign of a lively faith.

In light of these beliefs, which may reasonably be imputed to Cowper, the problems raised by "Truth" and "The Progress of Error" become less puzzling. They are directed not toward rational conviction but to the creation of a state of mind on the part of the reader. He expounds not what the true believers believe, but the happy results of their believing it—what Newton calls "experimental" religion. And the element of progress in "The Progress of Error" is supplied by the constant emphasis on the spread of moral corruption (evidence of lack of true belief) from a single evil example throughout the nation.

It will be clear, however, that the historical and doctrinal elements of the Christian faith have in these poems, and elsewhere in Cowper's poetry, been so far subordinated as almost to disappear, while the inward experience to which these elements should give rise has grown correspondingly in importance. From this follow two notable consequences.

First, from a biographical point of view, it serves to link the insane, suicidal Cowper with the apparently sane author of the great bulk of Cowper's poetry. Newton argued again and again with Cowper that he could not have committed the unforgivable sin; that God could not wish him to destroy himself; that there was no Scriptural warrant for believing that God would ever condemn a soul to annihilation. Cowper remained unshaken in his conviction, based on his unique experience, that his was a unique case and that God's dealings with the rest of His Creation had no bearing upon it. He had made himself immune to rational argument on this point, no doubt by a perversion of Calvinist theology, but a perversion very hard for Calvinism to correct.

Second, to cultivate the religious affections while emptying them of content is to tend to make them transferable. We can see this process at work in *The Task*: the Olney countryside and its rural life begin to usurp the place of revealed truth as the object of deep emotional commitment and the foundation of moral fervor. And from *The Task* the line of influence is clear to Wordsworth and Coleridge.

NOTES

1 *The Poetical Works of William Cowper*, ed. E. C. Benham (London, 1870), p. xlviii.
2 *The Correspondence of William Cowper*, ed. Thomas Wright (London, 1904), I, 397–98; Charles Ryskamp, *William Cowper of the Inner Temple, Esq.* (Cambridge, 1959), pp. 237–38.
3 *Thelyphthora, or, a Treatise on Female Ruin, in its Causes, Effects, Consequences, Prevention, and Remedy; Considered on the Basis of the Divine Law: under the Following Heads, viz. Marriage, Whoredom, and Fornication, Adultery, Polygamy, Divorce; With many other Incidental Matters*, 3 vols. (London, 1780–81). The third volume (1781) was issued in an attempt to answer criticisms of the first two.
4 I draw here, and in later discussion of Newton's relations with Cowper, on material which will appear in the new edition of Cowper's letters now being prepared by Charles Ryskamp and James King, and shortly to be published by the Clarendon Press.
5 The best account of Martin Madan's career is that given by Falconer Madan, *The Madan Family* (Oxford, 1933), which also includes an extensive bibliography of the *Thelyphthora* controversy.
6 *Monthly Review*, 63 (1780), 273–87; 321–39.
7 The importance of *Thelyphthora* in stimulating Cowper's poetic output is treated (with different emphases) by Lodwick Hartley, "Cowper and the Polygamous Parson," *Modern Language Quarterly*, 16 (1955), 137–41, and by Norma Russell, *A Bibliography of William Cowper to 1837* (Oxford, 1963), pp. 33–36, 38–40.
8 All quotations from Cowper's poetry follow the text of William Cowper, *Poetical Works*, ed. H. S. Milford, with corrections and additions by Norma Russell (London, 1971).
9 Cowper to Newton, 8 April 1781 (*Correspondence*, I, 289–90).
10 *Poetical Works* (see n. 8 above), pp. 650–51.
11 Sermon CCXLII, *Sermons on Several Subjects and Occasions* (London, 1757), XII, 72.
12 "The Indwelling of the Spirit, the common Privilege of all Believers," in *Discourses on the Following Subjects* (London, 1739), not continuously paged.

Criticism, Adaptation, Politics, and the Shakespearean Model of Dryden's All for Love

MAXIMILLIAN E. NOVAK

Of the many critical and scholarly questions posed by Dryden's *All for Love,* few are more perplexing than that raised by the title page, for there, under the title, *All for Love: or, the World Well Lost,* is the description, "In Imitation of Shakespeare's Style." Dryden, of course, referred to his play as "Antony and Cleopatra," which makes the idea of an "Imitation of Shakespeare's Style" even more odd.[1] What would we think but that Dryden regarded Shakespeare's play as an unsalvageable relic of the past? If, as he says in his preface, he took pleasure in drawing the bow, like Ulysses against the suitors of Penelope, in competition with other authors who had written on the theme of Antony and Cleopatra, he must have been thinking of Horace and Lucan among the ancients and of Daniel, Fletcher, Corneille, Sedley, and perhaps a few others among the moderns.[2] If Shakespeare's play served more as an occasional source than as an adaptive model for *All for Love,* it was because Dryden found so much of Shakespeare's *Antony and Cleopatra* useless for the kind of play he wanted to write. The outlines of entire speeches from the original may be found, but for the most part, *All for Love* is the type of adaptation that attempts to consume the original. Insofar as Garrick's lone effort to stage Shakespeare's play during the eighteenth century was a disaster, Dryden achieved a notable success.[3]

Shakespeare scholars have been overly impressed by Dryden's remark in the prologue to *Aureng-Zebe*:

> But spite of all his pride a secret shame
> Invades his Breast at *Shakespeare's* sacred Name:
> And when he hears his Godlike *Romans* rage,
> He, in a just despair, would quit the Stage.
> And to an Age less polish'd, more unskill'd,
> Does, with disdain the foremost Honours yield,
> As with the greater Dead he dares not strive,
> He would not match his Verse with those who live:
> Let him retire, betwixt two Ages cast,
> The first of this, and hindmost of the last.[4]

Aside from the wonderful poetic effect that Dryden was able to achieve by this glance at his relationship to the "Giant Race before the Flood" and to his contemporaries, he manages to say that he remained the best modern playwright (something not all of his fellow dramatists would accept), that he was the only real master of the rhymed heroic play, and that his age was one of greater art, if less inspiration, than the time of Elizabeth and James I.

Aside from the concession of the facts of literary life—that even Elkanah Settle and Thomas D'Urfey could turn out a rhymed heroic play bearing some resemblance to his own product and that the audiences were no longer thrilled by them as they had been—there is not much movement observable in Dryden's critical position.[5] Shakespeare is still the magician of Dryden's prologue to the adaptation of *The Tempest* that he put together with Davenant some eight years before. He is a force of nature, like a tree from whose branches sprang the fruitful images of love that Fletcher borrowed and the wit that Jonson gathered. Admittedly, Dryden is no longer so defiant as he was in the epilogue to the second part of *The Conquest of Granada,* where he accused "the greater Dead" of using their demise as a way of preserving their position in the literary hierarchy and avoiding competition. But he still believes that in any weighing of the Elizabethans against the playwrights of the Restoration, something would have to be added to the writings of Jonson and Shakespeare to make them balance. And there is no reason to believe that he had changed his mind about the list of faults he found in the earlier writers which included: false grammar, misplaced words, redundancy, obscurity, antiquated words, anachronisms, and heavy latinisms.[6]

No matter how hard they tried, critics like Hazelton Spencer and even Ruth Wallerstein had difficulty understanding Dryden's reluctance to admit Shakespeare's overwhelming greatness as an artist.[7] But it was precisely as an artist, as a craftsman, that Dryden felt superior, and that feeling grew out of a larger sense of the refinement of the arts and civilization in the Restoration compared to the times of Shakespeare. In a preface dedicated to an onslaught against Rochester and other wits, we might well think that Dryden's attack on "broad Obscenities in Words" as an offense against "good Manners," and his argument that "Expressions therefore are a modest Cloathing of our Thoughts, as Breeches and Petticoats are of our Bodies,"[8] might be merely an attack on the obscenities of Rochester's poetry, but they also apply to the sexual punning of Shakespeare, who allows Cleopatra to tell Antony angrily:

> I would I had thy inches, thou shouldst know
> There were a heart in Egypt.

Shakespeare's wonderful "serpent of old Nile" can envy the horse that bears Antony's weight and worry that Iras will seduce Antony before she can join him in death. Today we may admire these images, concepts and lines, but we cannot expect that Dryden would appreciate such strokes. We might well think that Shakespeare's Cleopatra has an attractiveness not to be found in Dryden's, but if Dryden was going to make her appealing to his audience, he was going to have to purge her language. He could not give her the purity and dignity of Lee's Statira and Otway's Berenice, but he could try to give her a different kind of stature—a stature that would have been threatened by any hint of the type of playful humor with which Shakespeare surrounded his Cleopatra.

Dryden often remarked that however much Shakespeare had taught Fletcher about writing on love, the student had surpassed his master;[9] and neither understood love so well as the writers of the Restoration. In what must be considered a critical defense of *All for Love,* the "Heads of an Answer to Rymer," Dryden sketched out the possibility of a tragedy based on love and friendship rather than pity and terror.[10] Although he speaks of Rapin, Dryden's main influence here was probably Saint-Evremond, who, in his comments on Racine's *Alexander the Great,* argued for love as a proper subject for tragedy.[11] But if Dryden believed that he understood love better than Shakespeare, it was because of the combination of the analysis of love practiced in seventeenth-century romances and the contemporary libertine treatment of the physiological basis of love. Dryden himself, in spite of gestures toward more spiritual relationships in some of the heroic plays, tended to see love in purely sensual terms, and in adapting his play in the direction of what might be called libertine tragedy, the bulk of Shakespeare's play had to go.

Numbers of eighteenth-century critics commented on the pernicious moral of Dryden's play, but only John Dennis put his criticisms in a political context. Quoting the last lines of the play, "No Lovers liv'd so great, or dy'd so well," he complained:

> Was ever any thing so pernicious, so immoral, so criminal, as the Design of that Play? . . . And this encomium of the Conduct and Death of *Antony* and *Cleopatra,* a conduct so immoral, and a Self-murder so criminal, is, to give it more Force, put into the Mouth of the High Priest of Isis; tho' that Priest could not but know, that what he thus commended, would cause immediately the utter destruction of his Country, and make it become a Conquer'd and a *Roman* Province. Certainly never could the Design of an Author square more exactly with the Design of *White-Hall,* at the time when it was written, which was by debauching the People absolutely to enslave them.[12]

Dennis sees Dryden's revision of Shakespeare, then, as deliberately directed toward inculcating a message of libertinism and absolutism, as if Dryden were acting on the orders of the court to transform the relative purity of Shakespeare's moral vision into a celebration of the manners of the libertine court of Charles II and Shakespeare's suspended judgment on Roman history into an argument for placing the activities of monarchs beyond the reach of ordinary political values.

Dennis was certainly correct in thinking that the literature of the seventies revealed an unsympathetic treatment of monogamy and a distinct interest in various forms of sexual pleasure. In a poem like *Gallantry A-la-Mode* (1674), for example, there is a treatment of seduction that is as fervent and sensuous as Keats' *Eve of Saint Agnes,* with only an element of satire preventing it from slipping into pornography, and manuals on love and seduction were commonplace at the time.[13] The popularity of Lee's *The Rival Queens,* with its glorification of homosexual love and his half sympathetic portrayal of polygamy was surely no accident.[14] Perhaps Charles II grew tired of seeing himself in an Almanzor or a virtuous Aureng-Zebe and decided that he would like to see his relationship with the Duchess of Portsmouth dramatized in a kindly light. Portsmouth was certainly compared to Cleopatra at times;[15] and how apt to have a compliment to her in a play dedicated to her political ally, the Earl of Danby.[16] And would not the compliment to Charles be similar to that in the beginning of *Absalom and Achitophel?*

What *All for Love* lacks may be as significant as what is actually present in the play. It is far from being a defense of the court against the enemies of Charles II in the manner of Neville Payne's *Siege of Constantinople* (1675), but very little is said about luxury, a common theme in plays treating Cleopatra. But the fact is that, in seventeenth-century iconography, the luxury of Cleopatra was a popular and glorified theme. The scene of the first meeting of Antony and Cleopatra as well as that in which Cleopatra dissolved a pearl in a glass of wine as an act of conspicuous consumption were painted in great detail.[17] This was, after all, the age of Louis XIV and the glories of Versailles. Dryden's play constitutes a defense of the magnificence of monarchy in general, and in choosing to present a sympathetic account of the world's most luxurious couple, he was turning the attacks on the court of Charles II to the court's advantage. Not that the implied portrayal of Charles and Portsmouth as Antony and Cleopatra was intended to win over the citizens of a London about to plunge into the anxieties of the Popish Plot, but it must have made sense to the court and its friends. In bolstering the court through images of myth and historic grandeur, Dryden was always preaching to the converted.

Also lacking is the common theme of the threat to Rome's liberties implicit in the victory of Octavius over Antony. The Antony of Thomas May's play on this subject offers to restore all power to the Senate and the people if he is victorious.[18] Dryden alone has a seemingly unpolitical Antony whose passion is a victory in itself. As he goes out to fight Octavius after his reconciliation with Cleopatra, he says:

> I'm eager to return before I go;
> For all the pleasures I have known, beat thick
> On my remembrance! how I long for night!
> That both the sweets of mutual love may try,
> And one Triumph o'er *Caesar* ere we dye.[19]

The future triumph over Octavius seems to be more in the bedroom than in the battlefield.

There was critical precedence for such an attitude toward his character in Saint-Evremond, who argued:

> When a Passion is generally known, we ought to ascribe as little as we can, to the Character of the Person. For Instance, if you were to describe *Mark Antony,* after he had abandon'd himself to his Love, you ought not to pain him with those shining Qualities which Nature bestowed upon him. *Antony* besotted with *Cleopatra,* is not *Antony* the friend of Caesar. Of a brave, bold active Man, he is become a weak effeminate, lazy, whining Wretch. Of a Man who had in no respect been wanting, either to his Interest, or to his Party, we find him wanting to himself, and utterly undone by himself.[20]

If such a judgment influenced Dryden, it would explain some of the reasons for Antony's lack of resolution—his passivity. But it would not explain why we view him as a man who lost the world for the right reasons.

Much the same is true of Cleopatra. Sedley shows her fighting in the field to help Antony,[21] but Dryden was intent on isolating his hero and heroine from politics. Nor need we pay very much attention to Dryden's moralizing about the presence of Octavia dividing the pity of the audience. Later in the century, Cleopatra was played by the sensual Mrs. Barry with the virginal Bracegirdle as Octavia, but in the original performance, Cleopatra was played by Mrs. Boutel, who is described by Curll as small and "Childish" in appearance. He added that "her Voice was weak, tho' very mellow; she generally acted the *young Innocent Lady* whom all the Heroes are mad in Love with."[22] On the other hand, Mrs. Corey, who played Octavia, was a large woman who specialized in playing shrewish wives.[23] Can anyone doubt who was supposed to be the innocent? The Cleopatra who remarks in the fourth act,

> Nature meant me
> A Wife, a silly, harmless, household Dove,
> Fond without art.[24]

is only announcing what the audience would have known from her appearance on the stage and her first speech.

Of course, in writing a tragedy around sexual love and friendship, Dryden took risks. Hazelton Spencer questioned, "Why does Dryden's pathos so frequently put the reader in mind of comic situations?"[25] And with some justification. Mr. Limberham, the "Kind Keeper" of Dryden's next play, is a man whose strength of character is undercut by his fondness for his unfaithful mistress. Woodall, the rake and contrasting character to Limberham, jumps into bed with every available lady, is advertised as being sexually capable of peopling an Ile of Pines, and treats women with some of the same sexual contempt that Ventidius shows to Cleopatra. Certainly the man who is attracted to a woman to the point of gullibility and total preoccupation might be considered more of a candidate for comedy than a tragedy.

Without going over to Bruce King's concept of Dryden's heroic plays as partly comic and extending the idea to his first blank verse tragedy, I believe it might be argued that Dryden did attempt certain ambiguous effects in *All for Love.*[26] For example, Antony's scene with Octavia, in which the hero is temporarily won over by the appearance of the children he has had with Octavia, has often been criticized for its sentimentality,[27] but the idea of a hero being driven from what he considers to be a love of superhuman proportions by the cries of his children—a love which caused him to sacrifice half the world—may have been intended rather as a moment of embarrassment for Antony. If, as seems likely, Dryden took his suggestion for the scene from Shakespeare's *Coriolanus,*[28] one has only to turn to contemporary comments on that general who gave up his chance to conquer Rome on the appeal of his mother, wife, and children, to see that the gesture was considered an example of an incredible blunder.[29] At a later moment, when Antony thinks of his future with Octavia and fears the time when she will berate him and threaten him with Octavius' anger, we are very close to a serious version of a typical situation from Restoration comedy. If Cleopatra is protected from hints of the comic, Antony is not.

Yet Dryden attempts to convince us, and for the most part successfully, that losing the world for Cleopatra is an act worthy of a hero. He achieves this by suggesting a childlike innocence about the lovers. Cleopatra compares her feelings to those of "harmless infants," Antony's "golden dream" of love and friendship implies a boy's view of the world rather than a man's, and Ventidius's lengthy speech likening all human activity to the play of children leaves the suspicion that love might rank among the most innocent of such activities. The smile on Cleopatra's face at the end, which

> Shows she dy'd pleas'd with him for whom she liv'd,
> And went to charm him in another World,[30]

manages to convey a sense of satisfaction that is sexual, eternal, and without sin.

In remaking Antony and Cleopatra in this new image, Dryden had little need of Shakespeare's plot. What he had to say of history plays in "The Grounds of Criticism in Tragedy,"[31] where he objected that "they were rather chronicles represented than tragedies," would apply to *Antony and Cleopatra.* But in the "Heads of an Answer to Rymer" Dryden attempted to argue against the importance of plot in tragedy.[32] A year later, and this time in a public document, "The Grounds of Criticism in Tragedy," he surrendered the point completely, praising the criticism of Le Bossu with its arguments on the central importance of the fable and its moral, but in the sketch of his reply to Rymer, he had defined tragedy as being more than an artistic construct for moving pity and terror—as a work to "reform manners by delightful representation of human life in great persons, by way of dialogue."[33] If Ruth Wallerstein is right about the many discoveries that Dryden made in writing *All for Love,* it might also be argued that he made some errors as well. The emphasis on dialogue and discourse suggests that some of his ideas went in the direction of a drama of pure argument and debate. Indeed, without Alexas and his intrigues, *All for Love* has some of the same static quality that makes Otway's *Titus and Berenice* so deadly.

But if Dryden abandoned Shakespeare's fable, characters, manners, and thoughts as unsuitable for the kind of tragedy he was writing, he did make an effort to draw on Shakespeare's language, or, to use the terms of Dryden's Aristotelian catalogue, "words." By the time he came to write the preface to *Troilus and Cressida,* he was no longer defending Shakespeare's language and concentrated exclusively in his "thoughts."[34] While continuing to praise the rendering of the quarrel between Brutus and Cassius in Shakespeare's *Julius Caesar,* upon which he had modelled the dialogues between Ventidius and Antony in *All for Love,* Dryden condemns much of Shakespeare's imagery and language. He concluded his attack with the comment that if "Shakespeare were stripped of all the bombast in his passions and dressed in the most vulgar words, we should find the beauties of his thoughts remaining; if his embroideries were burnt down, there would still be silver at the bottom of the melting-pot."[35] Interestingly enough, Dryden uses "we" to refer to those who made the mistake of imitating Shakespeare's language rather than his substance. The mistake, if it was that, was made in *All for Love.*

Plainly enough, when he jotted down his "Heads of an Answer to Rymer," he did not think it was a mistake. Taking up the question of language at the end of his comments, he quotes Rapin to the effect that "the discourses when they are natural and passionate" are the true beauties of tragedy. After that he simply wrote, "So are Shakespeare's."[36] The echoes from Shakespeare in *All for Love* occasionally approach pastiche. Several variations on Macbeth's "she should have died hereafter" are employed to evoke a sense of lost opportunities. For Antony's jealousy, pieces of *Othello* and *A Winter's Tale* are used; for

Antony's adopting the role of Timon, a bit of *Hamlet*; for a description of Cleopatra's beauty, a dash of *Romeo and Juliet.* [37] Some critics have treated such echoes as if they were allusions attempting to call up the original passage and their contexts. Nothing could have been further from Dryden's purpose. He had simply come to believe that Shakespeare's "magic" inhered in given phrases and speeches.

David Vieth has suggested that *All for Love* might be viewed as a "giant metaphysical conceit in which elements of Shakespeare's sprawling play are yoked by violence together with the tighter concept of the three unities."[38] But, except for the language, there is little left of the original that is not in Plutarch and a number of other plays. And Dryden's borrowings from Daniel's and Sedley's plays, along with a tragedy on a very different theme, Milton's *Samson Agonistes,* have been well documented.[39] When he does use a speech of Shakespeare, he will sometimes attempt to make his original sound more like his idealized conception of the Shakespearean model. Take some of the most famous lines of Shakespeare's play, Enobarbus' reluctant praise of Cleopatra:

Eno. I saw her once
Hop forty paces through the public street;
And having lost her breath, she spoke, and panted
That she did make defect perfection,
And breathless, pow'r breathe forth.
Maec. Now Antony
Must leave her utterly,
Eno. Never, he will not:
Age cannot wither her, nor custom stale
Her infinite variety. Other women cloy
The appetites they feed, but she makes hungry
Where most she satisfies; for vilest things
Become themselves in her, that the holy priests
Bless her when she is riggish. (II, II, 229–40)

Dryden makes this speech into a statement which characterizes Cleopatra in a way which is not borne out by the knowledge we have of her in the play. While adding to our admiration of her beauty, it functions more directly as an insight into Ventidius, who delivers the parallel speech in *All for Love*:

> I pity *Dolabella,* but she's dangerous:
> Her eyes have pow'r beyond *Thessalian* Charms,
> To draw the moon from Heav'n; for Eloquence,
> The Sea-green Syrens taught her voice their flatt'ry;
> And while she speaks, Night steals upon the Day,
> Unmark'd of those that hear: Then she's so charming
> Age buds at sight of her, and swells to youth:
> The holy Priests gaze on her when she smiles,
> And with heav'd hands, forgetting gravity,
> They bless her wanton eyes: Even I, who hate her,
> With a malignant joy behold such beauty,
> And, while I curse, desire it.[40]

So far from his usual cutting of Shakespeare's images and metaphors,[41] the toning down which he felt necessary for adapting *The Tempest* and *Troilus and Cressida,* he actually adds metaphors.

In passages like this, Dryden tried to imitate Shakespeare's style, that is to say, to write the way he thought someone with Shakespeare's imagination might have written had he been so fortunate as to have been born into a more refined age than his own, namely, the Restoration. The implication is that such a reborn dramatist would have recognized the failings of his plots and written more or less like Dryden himself. In the preface to *All for Love,* he complimented Shakespeare by remarking how amazing it was that Shakespeare "should by the force of his own Genius perform so much that in a manner he has left no praise for any who come after him."[42] There is not a slight touch of complaint in such a remark, but for one play at least, Dryden put aside his rivalry with the dead long enough to teach himself to write brilliant dramatic blank verse.

NOTES

1 See John Dryden, *Of Dramatic Poesy and Other Critical Essays,* ed. George Watson (London, 1962), II, 205, 207.

2 For some surveys of Dryden's non-Shakespearean sources, see J. Douglas Canfield, "The Jewel of Great Price: Mutability and Constancy in Dryden's *All for Love,*"

ELH, 42 (1975), 33–47; and H. Neville Davies, "Dryden's *All for Love* and Thomas May's *The Tragedie of Cleopatra Queen of Egypt*," *N&Q*, N. S. 12 (1965), 140–41.

3 For Garrick's attempt at staging Shakespeare's play and some explanation of his failure, see George Odell, *Shakespeare from Betterton to Irving* (1930; rpt. New York, 1966), I, 367.

4 John Dryden, *Dramatic Works*, ed. Montague Summers (London, 1932) IV, 87. All quotations from *All for Love* will refer to this edition.

5 For discussions of the decline of the heroic play, see Eric Rothstein, *Restoration Tragedy* (Madison, 1967); and Maximillian E. Novak, *The Empress of Morocco and Its Critics* (Los Angeles, 1968), pp. iii–vii, xvi.

6 See "Defence of the Epilogue: or an Essay on the Dramatic Poetry of the Last Age," Watson, I, 169–83.

7 See Hazelton Spencer, *Shakespeare Improved* (Cambridge, Mass., 1927), pp. 210–20; and Ruth Wallerstein, "Dryden and the Analysis of Shakespeare's Techniques," *RES*, 19 (1943), 165–85.

8 *Dramatic Works*, IV, 182.

9 Watson, I, 69, 247, 260.

10 Watson, I, 212.

11 *Works* (London, 1700), I, 197. Ruth Wallerstein first suggested the relevance of some of Saint-Evremond's criticism to Dryden's position in the essay cited in n. 7 above.

12 *Critical Works*, ed. Edward Hooker (Baltimore, 1938–43), II, 163.

13 *Gallantry-A-la Mode* was only one of a number of works written during the 1670s propounding libertine views in opposition to traditional values of marriage. For a manual on love, see *The Art of Making Love* (London, 1676).

14 See *All for Love*, ed. David Vieth (Lincoln, Nebraska, 1962), p. xxiv.

15 Specifically in a series of poems supposedly written under a portrait of Portsmouth. The first of the poems has been ascribed to Dryden. See *Poems on Affairs of State* (n.p., 1704), III, 132; and John Dryden, *Poetical Works*, ed. George Noyes (Boston, 1950), p. 928.

16 See Andrew Browning, *Thomas Osborne, Earl of Danby* (Glasgow, 1951), I, 236.

17 Some of the better-known paintings were by Tiepolo, who painted an entire series of frescoes, Lorrain, Steen, Schoonjans, Knupfer, Voorhout, Elliger, and Naiveu.

18 Thomas May, *The Tragedie of Cleopatra Queen of Egypt* (London, 1639), sig. B9v (Act II).

19 *Dramatic Works*, IV, 216.

20 *Works*, I, 36.

21 Sir Charles Sedley, *Antony and Cleopatra* (London, 1677), pp. 37–42 (VI, ii–iv). In Sedley's play Agrippa laments the coming time of tyrants.

22 Edmund Curll, *The History of the English Stage* (London, 1741), p. 21.

23 Harold Wilson, *All the King's Ladies* (Chicago, 1958), pp. 132–33.

24 *Dramatic Works*, IV, 232.

25 Spencer, p. 217.

26 *Dryden's Major Plays* (New York, 1966), pp. 10–13. I agree with Anne Righter's argument that Restoration tragedy and comedy shared common attitudes and situations, but I am not so convinced, as she appears to be, that the results were so

destructive for tragedy. See "Heroic Tragedy," in *Restoration Theatre,* ed. John R. Brown and Bernard Harris (Stratford, 1965), pp. 134–58.

27 See for example Arthur Kirsch, *Dryden's Heroic Drama* (Princeton, 1965), pp. 129–31.

28 See D. T. Starnes, "Imitation of Shakespeare in Dryden's *All for Love,"* *Texas Studies in Literature and Language,* 6 (1964), 44–46.

29 See Virgilio Malvezzi, *Considerations upon the Lives of Alcibiades and Coriolanus,* trans. Robert Gentilis (London, 1650), pp. 217, 234, 243. Swift selected Coriolanus' decision as one of the great embarrassments of world history. See Jonathan Swift, *Prose Works,* ed. Herbert Davis et al. (Oxford, 1938–68), V, 86.

30 *Dramatic Works,* IV, 261.

31 Watson, I, 243.

32 Watson, I, 216, 219. Dryden quotes Rapin for justification at this point, perhaps retreating to critical authority where he felt uncertain. See Robert Hume, *Dryden's Criticism* (Ithaca, New York, 1970), pp. 114–17.

33 Watson, I, 213.

34 Watson, I, 259.

35 Watson, I, 259–60.

36 Watson, I, 220.

37 See for example T. P. Harrison, Jr., "Othello as a Model for Dryden in *All for Love," Texas Studies in English* 7 (1927), 136–43; and D. T. Starnes, "More about Dryden as an Adapter of Shakespeare," *Texas Studies in English,* 8 (1928), 100–106.

38 *All for Love,* ed. Vieth, p. xix.

39 Morris Freedman, "*All for Love* and *Samson Agonistes,*" *N&Q,* 201 (1956), 514–17.

40 *Dramatic Works,* IV, 236–37.

41 See *The California Edition of the Works of John Dryden,* ed. Maximillian E. Novak (Berkeley, 1971), X, 337–38.

42 *Dramatic Works,* IV, 187. W. Jackson Bate seems to believe that Dryden recognized the inferiority of his own age to that of Shakespeare and the great Elizabethans and accepted it with wisdom and good humor. This strikes me as a complete misrepresentation. When he wrote to Congreve that "The present Age of Wit obscures the past," there was nothing in that statement that cannot be found elsewhere in his criticism. The comedies of the Restoration were, to Dryden's mind, far superior to those of Shakespeare and Jonson, and with Congreve and Vanbrugh in the 1690s that style of comedy reached its height. Of Shakespeare's comedies, only *The Merry Wives of Windsor* was considered actable, and Jonson's comedies were not popular on the contemporary stage. Dryden struck off some magnificent lines about his relationship to the poetry of the past, but it would be a mistake to read them as anything but great poetry. See *The Burden of the Past* (London, 1971), pp. 25–26.

Radical Physicians and Conservative Poets in Restoration England: Dryden among the Doctors

HUGH ORMSBY-LENNON

. . . as in Physic, so in Poetry
Charles Gildon, *Miscellaneous Letters and Essays*

I

"With what do you prepare yourself . . . when you write?" Bayes asks Smith in the Duke of Buckingham's satiric play *The Rehearsal.* "Prepare myself! What the Devil does the Fool mean?" Smith wonders. Literary critics have been wondering ever since, for the answer given by Bayes (who personates Dryden) appears to have little relevance to what is now generally accepted about Dryden's literary practice: "Why, I'l tell you, now, what I do. If I am to write familiar things, as Sonnets to *Armida,* and the like, I ever make use of Stew'd Prunes only; but, when I have a grand design in hand, I ever take Physick, and let blood; for when you would have pure swiftness of Thought and Fiery flights of Fancy you must have a care of the pensive part. In fine, you must purge the Belly."[1] Is Buckingham's allusion to the two therapeutic cornerstones of Galenic medical practice—blood-letting and purging—a shaft of misdirected irony, or does it have a point? That other enemies of Dryden, Shadwell for example, made the same jibe has merely confirmed for modern commentators the way in which such seemingly baseless libels assume an ineradicable life of their own.[2]

Yet further corroboration, albeit late, for Dryden's peculiar medico-literary habits has come from the essayist Charles Lamotte. "I once thought that this was pure Waggery and Banter by the Author of that diverting Play," he writes, initially as sceptical as many of his twentieth-century successors. "But," he adds, "I have been told since, by a Person of good Credit, and who was acquainted with Mr. *Dryden*, that it was actually true, and that when he was about any considerable work, he used to purge his Body, and clear his Head, by a Dose of Physic."[3] Most recently, marginalia in the hand of one who had an intimate knowledge of Restoration literary mores have come to light in the Van Pelt Fourth Quarto of *The Rehearsal.* "Dryden's own words," our as yet unidentified expert on the period's drama writes next to what we had thought was Buckingham's banter about *Armida*, Stew'd Prunes, and the Fiery flights of Fancy.[4]

In physical distress, no less than in his unorthodox search for inspiration, Dryden was sure to turn to the time-honored Galenic remedies: the mundane remnants of Dryden's personal correspondence which have survived indicate that the poet was, at least in later life, something of a valetudinarian, and we frequently see him "deep in doctors, 'pothecaryes & Nurses."[5] After he had caught an ague during a particularly trying coach journey, he writes to Mrs. Steward that he took "twice the bitter draught, with Sena in it, & [loosed] at least twelve Ounces of blood by Cupping in my neck."[6] Apparently concerned about his bowel movements, Dryden asked his publisher Tonson to pass on a message to his wife: ". . . for feare the few Damsins should all be gone, desire her to buy me a Sieve full."[7] Buckingham's waggery about the Stew'd Prune is confirmed.

Must we convict Dryden on a charge of "pseudo-science and credulity" in the era of William Harvey, whose discovery of "The *Circling* streams, once thought but pools, of blood" Dryden himself had celebrated?[8] Modern critics generally agree with Jean Riolan, Harvey's Galenic opponent from the ultra-conservative Parisian Faculty of Medicine, that the discovery of the circulation had collapsed the venerable therapies of bleeding and purging.[9] Yet, as we shall see, the poet's own recourse to the Galenic *methodus medendi* (for physical ailments if not for poetic inspiration) is not only consonant with the theory of medicine that can be gleaned from his writings, but also with the accepted medical practice of his age.

II

Two years before Harvey's *De motu cordis* was printed in Frankfurt (1628), John Donne surveyed the progress of scientific knowledge, and observed, somewhat pessimistically, that "we look upon Nature, but with *Aristotles* Spectacles, and upon the body of man, but with *Galens,* and upon the frame of the world, but with *Ptolomies* spectacles."[10] But, less than half a century later, it seemed even to Crites, Dryden's most conservative spokesman in *An Essay of Dramatic Poesy,* "that almost a new nature has been revealed to us." "Is it not evident," he asks, "that more errors of the school have been detected, more useful experiments in philosophy have been made, more subtle secrets in optics, medicine, anatomy, astronomy, discovered than in all those credulous and doting ages from Aristotle to us?"[11]

With the overthrow of what Dryden criticized in "To Dr. Charleton" as "The longest Tyranny that ever sway'd," that of Aristotle and his followers, it seemed that a "new nature" had indeed been revealed.[12] Only curmudgeonly eccentrics like Alexander Ross and Henry Stubbe looked to the past and continued to champion Ptolemy; after a brief flirtation with the Tychonic cosmology, other English scientists embraced the Copernican hypothesis. But in the conservative College of Physicians Galen maintained his authority, even though Dryden numbered the Fellows Harvey, Ent, and Charleton among "th' *Assertors* of free Reason's claim."[13]

Galenic therapists like John Twysden could not accept the Neoterics' contention that physiological and climatic changes had brought about "the introduction of a new Nature into Men and Diseases."[14] Although he praises "the later Hippocrates" Harvey, Twysden also insists, in his *Medicina Veterum Vindicata,* that "*New discov-*

eries alter not nature" and stoutly refuses "to alter the ancient tryed method, practised for many Ages."[15] The neoclassical critic Thomas Rymer argued very similarly in a literary context when he objected to those "*Stage-Quacks* and *Empericks* in Poetry" who justified their modern practice by arguing "that *Athens* and *London* have not the same Meridian." "Certain it is, that *Nature* is the same, and *Man* is the same," Rymer insists: "he *loves, grieves, hates, envies,* has the same *affections* and *passions* in both places, and the same springs that give them *motion.* What mov'd *pity* there, will *here,* also produce the same effect."[16]

"Whatever *Hippocrates* might do in *Greece* or *Galen* who practised in *Greece* and *Rome*," the Neoteric Marchamont Nedham complained, "is no example for us not only in regard of the differences of Climates but in respect of the Alteration of Time and Diseases themselves."[17] The discovery of the circulation, Nedham maintained, had demonstrated "the insufficiency and Uselessness of meer *Scholastick Methods* and *Medicines*" based as those were on the four humors.[18] Literary moderns like Dryden seem no less sceptical about the consequences of Rymer's uniformitarianism than were the Neoterics about the *sequelae* of Twysden's.[19] "The climate, the age, the disposition of the people," maintains Dryden in his *Heads of an Answer to Rymer,* "may be so different that what pleased the Greeks would not satisfy an English audience."[20] Even though he endorses Rymer's neoclassical qualification that "nature . . . is the same in all places, and reason too the same," Dryden stands by the literary (if not the medical) modernism of his medical conception of literature when he declares that dramatists have necessarily prescribed for "the genius of the age and nation in which they lived."[21]

As one of the first members of the Royal Society, Dryden seems, then, to have subscribed to the three "central or primary ideas" which animated, according to R. F. Jones, the progress of science in seventeenth-century England: scepticism, observation and experimentation, and the inductive method of reasoning.[22] For Dryden, the "subtle secrets" of poetry and drama were no more inscrutable than those of anatomy and medicine; literary criticism entailed an exercise of the natural philosopher's *scepsis scientifica,* a necessary tentativeness in the face of literary as well as natural phenomena. "Why," asks Dryden, who had assented to the Society's motto *Nullius in Verba*, "should there be an *Ipse Dixit* in our poetry any more than in our philosophy?"[23] The translator must also employ the objectivity of the medical scientist, as the poet notes in his discussion of the saltier parts of Lucretius: "If nothing of this kind is to be read, physicians must not study nature, anatomies must not be seen."[24] Acknowledging that "the modest inquisitions of the Royal Society" influenced his early rejection of dogmatism in literary criticism, Dryden cast his *Essay of Dramatic Poesy* in the dialogue form which was popular with such Fellows as Walter Charleton (who proposed the poet for membership in the Society) and the more celebrated Robert Boyle.[25] Indeed, from Charleton's dialogue on *The Immortality of the Human Soul* (for which he probably wrote the "Advertisement to the Reader") Dryden derived congenial theories of the genius of the age and of a new medical nature as well as the civilized form of modest inquisition which he uses in the *Essay*.[26]

But Dryden was also quick to recognize that the *Essay* "was sceptical according to the way of reasoning which was used by Socrates, Plato, and all the Academics of old, which Tully and the best of the Ancients followed."[27] Strategic equivocation as to the respective influence and importance of the old and the new can be found throughout Dryden's poems, plays, and criticism: even during the exhilaration of the scientific sixties we can see that Dryden's support of the moderns was qualified. Notwithstanding, Dryden never doubted that "a man should be learn'd in severall sciences . . . to be a compleat and excellent poet."[28] But as to the sources of his metaphors and figures of speech, he was an opportunist: although responsible in 1668 for the first stage allusion to the circulation of the blood, he did not hesitate to revive the ancient tidal doctrine when the need arose thirty years later.[29] "An heroic poet," Dryden argued pragmatically, "is not tied to a bare representation of what is true."[30]

The tension between ancient and modern strained more than the dramatist's working choice of imagery: Dryden actually prepared himself for the composition of poems in which he celebrated the Royal Society and its revelation of a new nature by submitting to a *methodus medendi* which this very revelation disproved. Such cognitive dissonance cannot be explained away by "pseudo-science and incredulity": it reflects, rather, an unresolved tension between anatomical discovery and medical practice which also perplexed many contemporary doctors. Like Dryden, they championed the new science but sought the old remedies. On his deathbed Harvey himself requested that he be "lett blood in the Tongue"; Dryden's own determination to submit solely to the Galenic remedies may well have resulted in the fatal spread of gangrene.[31]

III

Polished, epitomized, and elaborated over the centuries by countless Arabic and Western commentators, Galen's complex physiological theories had come to represent, for the progressive seventeenth-century scientist, another aspect of that scholastic vermiculation which Dryden dismissed as "Hard words seal'd up with *Aristotle's* arms."[32] In his *De motu cordis* Harvey also refused to "*swear Allegiance to Mistris Antiquity*"; rejecting such "custome and doctrine once received and deeply rooted (as it were another Nature)" he insisted that his new anatomy was derived "*from Dissections and from the fabrick of Nature.*"[33] To most twentieth- (and not a few seventeenth-) century eyes, Harvey's discovery of the circulation presaged the end of the Galenic *methodus medendi* which had lauded the efficacy of bleeding and purging in terms of the tidal theory of the blood and a humoral physiology.[34] Harvey's discovery indicated that "breathing a vein" merely reduced the *volume* of blood in the body and not the flow of (imaginary) "peccant humors" to the disordered member; it did not, paradoxically, lead to that collapse of the traditional theory which Jean Riolan had feared. Harvey's own "therapeutique way" seems to have been unaffected by his experimental research.[35] "Daily experience satisfies us," he maintained, "that bloodletting has a must salutary effect in most diseases, and is indeed foremost among all the general remedial means. . . . This indeed nature teaches, and physicians at all events propose to themselves to imitate nature."[36] In his equivocations about nature (changeable or uniform?) Harvey shows himself a man of his century.

How did the legatees of Harvey's experimentalism, the strong contingent of Physicians in the Royal Society, manage to reconcile their attendance at the meetings of a society whose motto was *Nullius in Verba* (during which they inspected a "new nature" under one of Hooke's microscopes) with their medical practice in which they obeyed the *Ipse Dixit* of a doctor who had been dead for well over a thousand years?[37] The paradox was even more marked within the College of Physicians which was itself a center of experimental research as well as the bastion of therapeutic conservatism.

"In the Colledge of *Physicians* in London," Charleton wrote with a fashionable allusion to Bacon's New Atlantis, "you may behold *Solomon's House* in reality."[38] Nevertheless, as Owsei Temkin succinctly observes of the College, "its members could still summarily be called Galenists, because the fall of the Galenic science of medicine was not identical with the fall of the Galenic practise of medicine."[39] Thus the medical reformer Noah Biggs passionately denounced the "*Rialto,* or Palace Royal of *Galenical* Physick" in which the Physicians had "crown'd [Galen] with the title of Parent and Monarch thereof."[40] Sensitive to the incompatibility of this Palace Royal with Solomon's House, Charleton and other collegiate assertors of free Reason's claim set out to justify the ancient *methodus medendi* in terms of that "incomparable invention of Dr. Harvey"; in time, they developed the iatromechanical hypothesis in which the discoveries of Harvey, Boyle, and Borelli described ever more dazzling epicycles around bloodletting and purging.[41]

The neoteric assertors of free Reason's claim who were outside both Royal Society and College had a surer eye for this inconsistency between discovery and therapy. After applauding Harvey's discovery of "that wonderful secret of the blood's circulary motion" the educational reformer John Webster complained that, although it had "brought great satisfaction to a speculative understanding," it had done little in "practice and application for the more certain, safe, and easie cure of diseases."[42] George Thomson railed against the College's "sanguinary way of curing Diseases" and his colleague George Starkey promised "to perform all my cures without bloudletting [or] purging by any promiscuous purge."[43] "It is high time," insisted Nedham, "to look towards other Principles to direct us in the inventory of Medicine proper for the Age wherein we live."[44]

When these three doctors set their names to the Society of Chymical Physitians' call for "the Improvement of that most laudable and necessary Science of Physick, only by *Hermetick* or *Chymical Medicaments,*" they proclaimed their allegiance to the great medical revolutionaries Paracelsus and van Helmont who had both railed against "the ignorant Natural Philosophy of *Aristotle* and *Galen.*"[45] The English Paracelsians' defense of their novel pharmacopoeia was often conducted with great conceptual brilliance but, lacking both an infective theory and a sophisticated pharmacological grasp of disease, medicine could not accommodate their chemical theories to successful practice.[46] Meanwhile, the Galenists quietly appropriated the most effective of such Chymical Medicaments to reinforce their own "Galenicals" (herbal decoctions) in the College's *Pharmacopoeia Londinensis,* even though they openly disparaged the originators as "Mountebanks, Empericks, and rash Psudochemists."[47]

The radical Neoterics who laid siege to the Palace Royal of Galenical Physick during the Interregnum and Restoration sought to destroy more than the traditional *methodus medendi* upon which the College had set its *imprimatur*: they also strove to break the College's monopoly of medical licensing in London and established the Society of Chymical Physitians as a rival professional organization.[48] In Galen, the College physicians rediscovered a leader who could protect their privileges and they were determined not to witness another regicide. A classical education still represented the *entrée* to this lucrative profession, for "the classical tag," as Hugh Kearney has remarked, "was a class shibboleth of unerring simplicity."[49] Despite the College's distinguished program of research, its Fellows were careful to retain the traditional examination system which demanded from prospective members extraordinary mnemonic feats with the works of Galen but left their proficiency in anatomy, pharmacology, and therapy essentially untested.[50]

Marchamont Nedham complained that such doctors still attained "their Journey's end of Scarlet, and Worship, and Profit without so much as welting, or smutching, or burning a finger."[51] The Galenist who had traditionally delegated the manual tasks to apothecary and barber-surgeon dismissed his unlicensed rival as an "empiric," "a practitioner in physicke that hath no knowledge in Philosophy, Logick or Grammar, but fetcheth all his skill from bare and naked experience."[52] Not infrequently, of course, the real empiric proved quite as murderous as the polemical butt of this Galenist's abuse! By the mid-century, however, when the scientist's laboratory began to replace the scholar's library as the center of research, "experience," its cognate "experiment," and even "empiricism" became more respectable, as the scientific community came to realize, with Thomas Sprat, "*the advantages of an Experimental education.*"[53] As Fellows of the Royal Society and of Solomon's House, the Physicians approved the smutching of fingers in experiments and preferred "the language of Artizans, Countrymen, and Merchants, before that, of Wits, or Scholars"; as defenders of the Palace Royal of Galenical Physick, they celebrated "polite Latinists, accurate Grecians, eloquent Oratours" and jeered at their empirical opponents (who worked manually and used the vernacular in their treatises) as "Foot-Men, Gun-Smiths, Heel-Makers, and Butchers."[54]

With experiment and empiricism becoming scientifically more respectable, the Galenists resolved to tar the Neoterics with the brush of political radicalism. "Entermedlers in state affairs" had often been figuratively attacked as "empiricke Phisicions, brought up onely in an experimental prentiship" and the College worked to convert this metaphor of the body politic into historical actuality.[55] "We have to deal," wrote Charles Goodall, "with a sort of men not of Academical, but Mechanick education . . . either actually engaged in the late rebellion or bred up in some mean and contemptible trades."[56] And there is no doubt that the Christian iconoclasm of Paracelsus rendered the chemical pharmacopoeia particularly attractive to his English followers.[57] In their fight against the College's "Polyarchical *Government* in the *Galenical* way," the Neoterics denounced Aristotle and Galen as "ignorant, wicked, malicious and blind *Pagans*" and George Starkey spoke for many of them when he proclaimed himself "sent from God, for pulling down this rotten ruinous building of the Galenists method."[58] Nevertheless, some of the chymical physitians succeeded after 1660 in accommodating their religious and social radicalism to a strategic royalism and were successful in being preferred at Court by the Duke of Buckingham (who scoffed at Dryden's Galenism in *The Rehearsal* and was in turn ridiculed as "Chymist, Fidler, Statesman and Buffoon").[59] Confronted by the success of their enemies, the Galenists exploited with a new urgency the polemical relationships they had established between illiteracy, medicine, and political radicalism: still, they need not have feared the temporary advantage gained by the Neoterics.

When the Plague struck London in 1665, the Galenists followed their rich clients (among them Dryden) into the safety of the country, from which they abused the Paracelsians and contented themselves with advocating traditional remedies for the pest: "Pull off the feathers from the Tails of living Cocks, Hens, Pigeons or Chickens, and holding their Bills, hold them hard to the Botch or Swelling, and so keep them at that Part, until they die, and by this means draw out the Poison."[60] The Neoterics, meanwhile, tended the capital's diseased and dying "by Art *Chymical,* as is not borrowed out of former *Authors,* but agreeably devised and fitted to the nature of the present *Pest,* which in many things differs from the *Pests* of former times."[61] When Dryden himself introduced the new medicine as an analogy for his discussion of modern literary requirements, we should remember that he wrote *An Essay of Dramatic Poesy* "in the country when the violence of the last plague had driven me from the town": to his contemporaries the analogy would have been far more than mere literary embellishment.[62]

When the members of the College of Physicians returned to their London headquarters, they discovered that the plague had succeeded where they had failed: many of the chemists had been silenced forever. But skirmishes between the Galenists (increasingly bolstered by their iatromechanical hypothesis) and their critics continued, if on a much smaller scale, until the last years of the century, during which the

College's altruistic plan to open a Dispensary for the issue of cheap drugs to the London poor brought medical controversy to fever pitch yet again.[63] Although the apothecaries (former allies of the chymical physitians) were opposed to the Dispensary, the most vitriolic disputes occurred within the College itself, where the "Apothecaries physicians" were led by the poetaster Sir Richard Blackmore while the "Dispensarians" found their literary voice in Samuel Garth. In his immensely popular *Dispensary* Garth not only developed the tradition of branding the College's enemies as crazed political innovators but also clinched for his friend Dryden the relationship between bad poetry and bad physic.

To the aging Dryden the century seemed "all, all of a piece throughout." In Dryden's youth, the Royalist poet-physician William Chamberlayne had attacked the "hyperbolical" and "impudent" language in the "big bulk'd volumes of *Physick* . . . by these *indigent* Vermin" the Paracelsians, who, even worse than the "squint-ey'd sectaries," threatened to cry down all good learning and fine expression.[64] As a new century began, another young poet-physician, Samuel Garth, launched a new attack upon the "barren Superfluity of Words," "Vile terms of Art," and the fustian poetry of the College's enemies who now connived both inside and outside its walls.[65] In his last poems Dryden also returned to explore this parallel betwixt poesy and physic.

IV

Dryden's frequent allusions to the debate between the Neoterics and Galenists reveal his "familiarity with the keenest battle of the war which the moderns carried on against the ancients."[66] Unlike Donne, who generally used his medical learning for intellectual effect, Dryden deploys his medical references as analogies for, or at his most subtle, as embodiments of, a sophisticated reconciliation of the contrary demands of a "new nature" and ancient practise.[67] In an early consideration of the act of creation there is an emblematic juxtaposition of new philosophy and Galenic physiology: should the "native sweetnesse" of

Sir Robert Howard's verse be attributed to the "hidden springs within the Engine" or to "The curious Net that is for fancies spread," Galen's *rete mirabile* whose existence in the brain Vesalius had disproved over a century before?[68]

In his references to medicine Dryden is, then, far from simply affirming that progressive sympathy for the Neoterics which R. F. Jones discerns in his writings: Dryden's personal reconciliation of the discovery of the circulation with the old *methodus medendi* actually has more in common with Sir William Temple's sceptical conclusion that the innovations of both Copernicus and Harvey "have been of little use to the world, though perhaps of much honour to the authors."[69] If Dryden modeled his own intellectual scepticism on "the modest inquisitions of the Royal Society," then he derived his need for intellectual stability from "the dogmatical way of the *Galenists.*"[70]

In many of his medical allusions, Dryden reaffirms the familiar analogy between the mountebank and the bad poet or politician, albeit with a new (if conservative) edge: political and literary stability is associated with the Galenic physicians, anarchic innovation with the "Emp'rique politicians" who "use deceipt, / Hide what they give, and cure but by a cheat" and "th' illiterate Writer" who, "Emperique like, applies / To minds diseas'd unsafe, chance, Remedies."[71] The subversive activities of the "Fanaticks in Physic," whether they be unscrupulous empirics or radical chemists, are as destructive of the realm's political fabric as the scribblings of the "Phanatick in Poetry" and the "leveller in Poetry" are deleterious to its literary fabric.[72] Dryden designs his poetic kingdoms to be analogies for the "body politic," and supports in each the Galenic equation between "antient wit" and "nature." "With some respect to antient Wit proceed"—he bids the innovators in poetry (mimetically breaking couplet and metrical decorum) lest

> . . . when you lay Tradition wholly by
> And on the private Spirit alone relye
> You turn Fanatics in your Poetry.[73]

Using "Huddled Atoms" to "build their poems the *Lucretian* way," these "haughty Dunces" of London imitate the Neoterics' casual use of atomism in the campaign against the Galenists, and eschew the rules of method to rely upon the luck of the solipsist:

> And if they hit in Order by some Chance
> They call that Nature which is Ignorance.[74]

Given these parallels betwixt bad physic, politics, and poesy, it was only to be expected that "Quack Maurus"—the hack poet-physician Blackmore—should write against Garth and the Dispensarians as well as use "His Cant, like *Merry Andrew's* Noble Vein / [To] Cat-Call the Sects, to draw 'em in for gain."[75] Dryden sneers that "our Mountebank" cannot even make his verse "dull by rule" because of what another contemporary called his "affected contempt of the Ancients, and supercilious derision of transmitted knowledge."[76] Blackmore's heroic poems and medical prescriptions are both composed in the canting measure of the empiric:

> At leisure Hours in Epique Song he deals,
> Writes to the rumbling of his Coaches Wheels,
> Prescribes in hast, and seldom kills by Rule,
> But rides Triumphant between Stool and Stool.[77]

The other anti-Dispensarians are equally unmethodical in their pharmaceutical preparations:

> Th' Apothecary-Train is wholly blind.
> From Files a Random-Recipe they take,
> And Many Deaths of One Prescription make.

With such swoopstake practitioners Dryden contrasts the skillful Collegiate Physicians "lab'ring for Relief of Humane Kind."[78]

The true poet has also learned from the rules of the ancients how to gauge the effects of his carefully chosen literary medicines. Most appropriately, it is in the epic—the highest genre that the poet can attempt—that the literary "Galenicals" work most potently:

> To raise, and afterwards to calm the passions, to purge the soul from pride by the examples of human miseries, which befall the greatest; in few words, to expel arrogance, and introduce compassion, are the great effects of tragedy. Great, I must confess, if they were altogether as true as they are

> pompous. But are habits to be introduced at three hours' warning? Are radical diseases so suddenly removed? A mountebank may promise such a cure, but a skilfull physician will not undertake it. An epic poem is not in so much haste: it works leisurely; the changes which it makes are slow; but the cure is likely to be more perfect. The effects of tragedy, as I said, are too violent to be lasting. If it be answered that, for this reason, tragedies are often to be seen, and the dose to be repeated, this is tacitly to confess that there is more virtue in one heroic poem than in many tragedies. A man is humbled one day, and his pride returns the next. Chemical medicines are observed to relieve oftener than to cure: for 'tis the nature of spirits to make swift impressions, but not deep. Galenical decoctions, to which I may properly compare an epic poem, have more of body in them; they work by their substance and their weight.[79]

The Galenic remedy works elsewhere, too, even if not so thoroughly. We are, for example, unduly familiar with the satirist as the "short-gowned barber surgeon of Renaissance metaphor": in his satire, Dryden renounces the surgical knife (recourse to which might, incidentally, have saved his life in 1700).[80] Although no enemy to controlled blood-letting, Dryden, like the monarch whom he advises in *Absalom and Achitophel,* prefers to administer "physic to the great" on Galenic principles:[81]

> The true end of *Satyre,* is the amendment of Vices by correction. And he who writes Honestly, is no more an Enemy to the Offendour, than the Physician to the Patient, when he prescribes harsh Remedies to an inveterate Disease: for those are only in order to prevent the Chyrurgeon's work of an *Ense rescindendum,* which I wish not to my very Enemies. To conclude all, If the body politique have any Analogy to the Natural, in my weak judgment an Act of *Oblivion* would be as necessary in a Hot, Distemper'd State, as an *Opiate* would be in a Raging Fever.[82]

Thus the true statesman is also a Galenist. Even the successful Cromwell had been praised by Dryden for easing the country's "consumption" by a judicious venesection (for which image Dryden was later to suffer):

> He fought to end our fighting, and assaid
> To stanch the blood by breathing of the vein.[83]

The poet's next choice of politician-doctor was itself more judicious: General Monck's skilful handling of political events on the basis of the humoral physiology made the Restoration possible and continued the best therapeutic traditions of the College of Physicians:

> Wise Leeches will not vain Receipts obtrude,
> While growing pains pronounce the humours crude;
> Deaf to complaints they wait upon the ill
> Till some safe *crisis* authorise their skill.[84]

Finally, Dryden was able to extol Charles himself as the *roi thaumaturge*—most appropriately, since touching for the King's evil was again introduced after 1660.[85] As the Fire of London rages in *Annus Mirabilis,* the Royal Doctor prays for divine intervention to save his stricken capital and reflects on his past care for the body politic:

> Be thou my Judge, with what unwearied care
> I since have labour'd for my People's good:
> To bind the bruises of a Civil War,
> And stop the issues of their wasting bloud.[86]

Faced, during the Exclusion crisis, by a diseased rabble of "state-empirics" which included medical freaks like "Tapski" Shaftesbury, blasphemous parodies of the *Christus medicus* like Titus Oates, and fiddling chemists like Buckingham, Charles accepted the advice of his faithful courtiers ("who shew'd the King the danger of the Wound"), stood firm, and finally succeeded in allaying the fever in the body politic with the minimum amount of blood-letting.[87]

Being "naturally inclin'd to Scepticism in Philosophy," however, Dryden tempered his faith in the magisterial authority of politician, physician, poet with a scepticism about the value of tradition and stability which was occasionally far closer to cynicism than to "the modest inquisitions of the Royal Society."[88] It was not simply that Dryden doubted the wisdom of the College of Physicians. "To use blasphemy" in comedy, he observes tartly during a diatribe against trumpery wit, "is a kind of applying pigeons to the soles of the feet: it proclaims their fancy as well as their judgement to be in desperate condition."[89] It was not simply that the London theater-going public did not appreciate the comic medicines that Dryden prescribed for them but, in their ignorance, preferred the farcical nostrums of his rivals: "In short, there is the same difference betwixt farce and comedy as betwixt an empiric and a true physician: both of them may attain their ends; but what the one performs by hazard, the other does by skill. And as the artist is often unsuccessful while the mountebank succeeds; so farces more commonly take the people than comedies. For to write unnatural things is the most probable way of pleasing them, who do not understand nature."[90]

It was that the ancient wits themselves, who had first revealed "nature" to Dryden, could prescribe like the unruly empirics: Horace's satiric method brings his reader a "pleasant cure, with all the limbs preserved entire; and as our mountebanks tell us in their bills without keeping the patient within doors for a day."[91] Worse still, it seemed to Dryden that his own popular success depended upon the conjunction of the poet's luck and the listener's whim, rather than the operation of judgment in either:

> But, after all, a Poet must confess
> His Art's like Physick, but a happy ghess.
> Your Pleasure on your Fancy must depend.[92]

Does Dryden, at his most pessimistic, see *himself* as a mountebank? "*Thespis,* the first Professor of our Art," he concedes, "At Country Wakes, Sung Ballads from a Cart," adding that Horace himself believed Aeschylus to be "the first Mountebank that trod the Stage."[93] Recognizing the contemporaneity of this ancient family resemblance between dramatist and mountebank, Dryden occasionally envisaged himself as a "Tinker empirical to the Body of Man" who merely "administers Physic with a Farce": his eloquent arguments for a Galenic theory of literature notwithstanding, Dryden confessed, not unlike the Society of Chymical Physitians, that "my chief endeavours are to delight the age in which I live."[94]

Such self-doubts must be qualified by reference to events over which Dryden had no control. In the extraordinary confusion that surrounded the poet's funeral, one fact stands out: Walter Charleton and Samuel Garth, his oldest and youngest doctor friends, arranged for Dryden to lie in state in the College of Physicians.[95] That the poet who did "ever take Physick, and let blood" should at last join the monarch Galen in his "Palace Royal" was only fitting.

NOTES

1 *The Rehearsal, As it is now Acted at the Theatre-Royal. The Fourth Edition with Amendments and large Additions by the Author* (London: R. Bentley and S. Magnes, 1683), II, ii. In the shorter 1672 version of the play the scene ends without any inkling of this medical humor.

2 See *The Medal of John Bayes* (London: Richard Janeway, 1682), sig. A2[r] and James M. Osborn's discussion of the apparent mutual dependence of such allusions; *John Dryden: Some Biographical Facts and Problems* (New York: Columbia Univ. Press, 1940), pp. 160–61.

3 *An Essay upon Poetry and Painting,* 2nd ed. (Dublin: Thomas Bacon, 1742), p. 103 n.

4 Some conclusions as to the possible identity of the author will appear in my "*The Rehearsal* Revisited: Seventeenth-Century Annotations in the University of Pennsylvania Van Pelt Library Fourth Quarto." It should be noted that the marginalia are quite independent of Sam Briscoe's "A Key to *The Rehearsal,*" which first appeared in 1704 and was appended to most subsequent editions of the play. In the "Key" which I consulted—appended to *Two Plays written by his Grace George Late Duke of Buckingham* (London: J. Poulson and R. J. and B. Wellington, 1731)—the only pertinent medical gloss is to Bayes' remark "be sure you never take snuff, when you write . . . it spoil'd me once, I Gad, one of the sparkishest Playes in all England" (Q4, II, ii). Briscoe: "He was a great Taker of Snuff, and made most of it himself" (p. 81). Dryden's other medical vagaries go unannotated.

5 *The Letters of John Dryden,* ed. Charles E. Ward (Durham: Duke Univ. Press, 1942), p. 24.

6 *Letters,* p. 104.

7 *Letters,* p. 58.

8 Osborn, *John Dryden,* p. 160; "To my Honour'd Friend, Dr Charleton," in *The Poems of John Dryden* (Oxford: Clarendon Press, 1958), I, 33. (Hereafter referred to as *Poems.*)

9 On Riolan, the only critic whom Harvey deigned to answer, see Gweneth Whitteridge, *William Harvey and the Circulation of the Blood* (London: Macdonald, 1971), Ch. 8.

10 *Sermons on the Psalms and Gospels,* ed. Evelyn Simpson (Berkeley: Univ. of California Press, 1967), p. 222. Since this comment is from a sermon "preached at the funerals of Sir William Cockayne," Donne's pessimism is to be expected.

11 *Of Dramatic Poesy and other Critical Essays,* ed. George Watson (London: Dent, 1962), I, 26. (Hereafter referred to as *Essays.*)

12 "To my Honour'd Friend, Dr Charleton," *Poems,* I, 32.

13 Ibid.

14 *Medicina Veterum Vindicata* (London: John Crook, 1666), p. 111. On this debate, see Lloyd Stevenson, "'New Diseases' in the Seventeenth Century," *Bulletin of the History of Medicine,* 39, (1965), 1–21. Twysden has been defended against such

modern critics as R. F. Jones by Lester S. King, *The Road to Medical Enlightenment 1650–1695* (London: Macdonald, 1970), pp. 154–60.

15 *Medicina Veterum Vindicata,* pp. 54, 38, 40.

16 "The Tragedies of the last Age consider'd and examin'd by the Practice of the Ancients, and by the Common Sense of All Ages," *The Critical Works of Thomas Rymer,* ed. Curt A. Zimansky (New Haven: Yale Univ. Press, 1956), p. 19.

17 *Medela Medicinae: A Plea for the Free Profession, and a Renovation of the Art of Physick* (London: Richard Lownds, 1665), p. 389. On Nedham's theory of medicine (for and against) see R. F. Jones, *Ancients and Moderns,* 2nd ed. (Gloucester, Mass.: Peter Smith, 1975), pp. 206–10, and King, *The Road to Medical Enlightenment,* pp. 145–154.

18 *Medela Medicinae,* title page; for Nedham's discussion of the impact of the circulation upon the humoral physiology, see pp. 257–60.

19 For a succinct account of Dryden's response to Rymer and its intellectual implications, see Robert D. Hume, *Dryden's Criticism* (Ithaca: Cornell Univ. Press, 1970), Chs. 3–5.

20 *Essays,* I, 214.

21 Ibid.

22 "Science and Criticism in the Neo-Classical Age of English Literature," *The Seventeenth Century* (Stanford: Stanford Univ. Press, 1951), p. 42. Dryden was proposed, elected, and admitted to the Royal Society in 1662; already in arrears with his dues in 1663, Dryden was finally ousted from the Society in 1665. (The relevant sections from Thomas Birch's *History of the Royal Society* are reprinted by Claude Lloyd, "John Dryden and the Royal Society," *PMLA,* 45 [1930], 967–76. But see also the ensuing correspondence from Louis Bredvold et al. *PMLA,* 46 [1931], 951–62.) Nevertheless, laudatory references to the Society continue to appear in his writings, although the degree of his commitment to the new science remains tantalizingly elliptic. Phillip Harth provides the most extensive account in *Contexts of Dryden's Thought* (Chicago: Univ. of Chicago Press, 1968), Ch. 1, which contains an important redefinition of scepticism.

23 "Preface to *An Evening's Love,*" *Essays,* I, 148.

24 "Preface to *Sylvae,*" *Essays,* II, 27.

25 "A Defence of An Essay of Dramatic Poesy," *Essays,* I, 123. Boyle's most notable dialogue, *The Sceptical Chymist,* was published in 1661. Sprat, Evelyn, and many others assert, more generally, the crucial importance of civilized *conversation* to corporate scientific endeavour.

26 Osborn suggests that Dryden may have written this "Advertisment" to Charleton's *The Immortality of the Human Soul* (London: Henry Herringman, 1657) even though Herringman's name appears under it: "Was Dryden in Herringman's Employ?" *John Dryden,* pp. 174–75. If Dryden actually "turn'd a journey-man t'a Book-seller [Mr. Herringman, *who kept him in his House for that* purpose]," as Shadwell sneers in the text and notes of *The Medal of John Bayes* (p. 8), he may well have had a hand in the despatch of real "Emp'rique Wares, or Charms" (as he himself describes patent intellectual medicines—"Hard words seal'd up with *Aristotle's* arms"—in "To Dr Charleton") to the country, since booksellers acted as

mail-order pharmacists: ". . . for more convenience to those that live remote," a puff for Buckworths' "famous Lozanges or Pectorals" tells us, "quantities of [Lozanges] sealed up with their Coat of Armes are left constantly at the house of [among others] Mr. H. Herringman at the Anchor in the New Exchange." (This advertisement appears on the last page of Sir Kenelm Digby's *A Late Discourse*, 2nd ed. [London: R. Lownds, 1660].) "Every Age hath its peculiar Genius," concludes Charleton's Athanasius after the long discussion of medical progress in England (*Immortality*, p. 49). Charles Webster sets Charleton's valuable account of medical research in London (which Dryden surely read) in its full intellectual context in "The College of Physicians: 'Solomon's House' in Commonwealth England," *Bulletin of the History of Medicine*, 41 (1967), 393–412.

27 "A Defence of An Essay of Dramatic Poesy," *Essays*, I, 123.

28 "Postscript" to "Notes and Observations on *The Empress of Morocco*," *The Works of John Dryden*, ed. E. N. Hooker et al. (Berkeley: Univ. of California Press, 1956—), XVII, 182. (Hereafter referred to as *Works*.)

29 *An Evening's Love*, V, i, 80–81 (*Works*, X, 296); *Love Triumphant*, V, i, *Works of John Dryden*, ed. Sir Walter Scott and George Saintsbury (Edinburgh: William Paterson, 1884), VIII, 467. See the discussion by Herbert Silvette, *The Doctor on the Stage: Medicine and Medical Men in Seventeenth Century England* (Knoxville: Univ. of Tennessee Press, 1967), pp. 237, 242.

30 "Of Heroic Plays: An Essay," *Essays*, I, 161.

31 John Aubrey's *Brief Lives*, ed. Oliver Lawson Dick (Harmondsworth: Penguin Books, 1962), p. 215; Ned Ward, The *London-spy*, 3rd ed. (London: J. How, 1706), pp. 422–23. Dryden's death (like so much in the life preceding) is shrouded in mystery, and Ward's account is not necessarily the one which we would most desire.

32 "To Dr Charleton," l. 8.

33 *The Anatomical Exercises of Dr. William Harvey . . . Concerning the Motion of the Heart and Blood*, English trans., 2nd ed. (London: Richard Lowndes and Matthew Gilliflower, 1673), sig. A4^r, p. 49, sig. A4^r.

34 Recent helpful discussions of the rationale for bleeding include Rudolph E. Siegel, "Galen's Concept of Bloodletting," *Science, Medicine and Society in the Renaissance*, ed. Allen G. Debus (London: Heinemann, 1972), I, 243–74, and (less daunting for the non-specialist) Silvette, *Doctor on the Stage*, Ch. 2.

35 Aubrey, *Brief Lives*, p. 215. "I have heard him say," Aubrey also notes, "that after his Booke of the *Circulation of the Blood* came out, that he fell mightily in his Practize, and that 'twas beleeved by the vulgar that he was crack-brained" (p. 214). Notoriety (rather than any change in *practise*) occasioned this "falling-off" in patients: see further, Audrey B. Davis, "Some Implications of the Circulation Theory for Disease Theory and Treatment in the Seventeenth Century," *Journal of the History of Medicine*, 26 (1971), 28–39.

36 William Harvey, "On Generation," *The Works*, trans. Robert Willis (London: Sydenham Society, 1847), p. 391.

37 "Nearly a fifth of the 115 original Fellows held the degree of M.D., and it has been reckoned . . . that 55% of the scientists amongst them were physicians or

surgeons: in 1698, the proportion was still about the same." Peter Laslett, "The Foundation of the Royal Society and the Medical Profession in England," *British Medical Journal,* July 16, 1960, p. 167. What such head-counting proves is still disputed: see, most recently, A. Rupert Hall, "Medicine and the Royal Society," *Medicine in Seventeenth-Century England,* ed. Allen G. Debus (Berkeley: Univ. of California Press, 1974), 421–52. Charles Webster reveals the complex web that bound experimental philosophy and medical therapy in *The Great Instauration: Science, Medicine, and Reform, 1626–1660* (London: Duckworth, 1975), s.v. "College of Physicians."

38 *Immortality of the Human Soul,* p. 34.

39 *Galenism: Rise and Decline of a Medical Philosophy* (Ithaca: Cornell Univ. Press, 1973), p. 165.

40 *Mataeotechnia Medicinae Praxeως: The Vanity of the Craft of Physick. Or a New Dispensatory* (London: Giles Calvert, 1651), "Epistle Dedicatory to the Parliament," sig. A4^{v}.

41 *Immortality of the Human Soul,* pp. 37–38. The later fortunes of this early resolution of Charleton's are followed by Theodore M. Brown, "The College of Physicians and the Acceptance of Iatromechanism in England, 1665–1695," *Bulletin of the History of Medicine,* 44 (1970), 12–30.

42 *Academiarum Examen* (London: Giles Calvert, 1654), p. 74.

43 *Galeno-Pale or A Chymical Trial of the Galenists* (London: Edward Thomas, 1665), p. 48; *Nature's Explication and Helmont's Vindication* (London: Thomas Alsop, 1657), "Epistle Dedicatory," sig. A2^{v}.

44 *Medela Medicinae,* p. 458.

45 "The Copy of the Engagement" of the Chymical Physitians appeared in Thomas O'Dowde's *The Poor Man's Physician* (London, 1665) and is reprinted by Sir Henry Thomas, "The Society of Chymical Physitians," *Science, Medicine, and History,* ed. E. A. Underwood (London: Oxford Univ. Press, 1953), II, 62–63; *Van Helmont's Workes . . . wherein the Philosophy of the Schools is Examined, their Errors Refuted, and the whole Body of Physick Reformed and Rectified,* trans. John Chandler (London: Lodowick Lloyd, 1664), Ch. 7. The medicine and philosophy of Paracelsus and van Helmont were far from interchangeable but, as in the case of Aristotle and Galen (where disciple had also criticized master), a mid-seventeenth century apprenticeship to the values of one usually entailed a similar commitment to the system of the other.

46 The writings of Walter Pagel, notably *The Religious and Philosophical Aspects of van Helmont's Science and Medicine* (Baltimore: Johns Hopkins Univ. Press, 1944), discuss the conceptual brilliance of these chemists in great detail; Sir Charles Dodds has shown that the doctors of the seventeenth and eighteenth centuries lacked "a knowledge of the infective nature of most diseases" as well as "an adequate variety of powerful drugs" and so were unable to exploit the revolutionary discovery of the circulation: "A Riddle of the Seventeenth Century," *British Medical Journal,* July 16, 1960, p. 187.

47 Webster, *The Great Instauration,* pp. 311–14; George Starkey refutes such Galenical name-calling, *Nature's Explication,* p. 48.

48 The College continued to place its imprimatur upon approved works during the Interregnum and its Fellows were horrified by the unlicensed appearance of vernacular medical works. In addition to Thomas, "Society of Chymical Physitians," see Charles Webster, "English Medical Reformers of the Puritan Revolution: A Background to the 'Society of Chymical Physitians'," *Ambix,* 14 (1967), 16–41, and P. M. Rattansi, "The Helmontian-Galenist Controversy in Restoration England," *Ambix,* 12 (1964), 1–23.

49 *Scholars and Gentlemen: Universities and Society in Pre-Industrial Britain, 1500–1700* (London: Faber and Faber, 1970), p. 118.

50 See Sir George Clark, *A History of the Royal College of Physicians of London* (Oxford: Clarendon Press, 1964), I, 99–100, 179–80; this examination system was carefully retained in the Statute Revisions of 1647: I, 279.

51 *Medela Medicinae,* pp. 249–50.

52 John Cotta, *A Short Discoverie of the Unobserved Dangers of severall sorts of ignorant and inconsiderate Practisers of Physicke in England* (London: R. Field, 1612), p. 10.

53 For the background to the redefinition of these terms, see Christopher Hill, *Change and Continuity in Seventeenth-Century England* (London: Weidenfeld and Nicolson, 1974), pp. 256–58; *The History of the Royal Society of London* (London: J. Martyn and J. Allestry, 1667), p. 329.

54 *History of the Royal Society,* p. 113; Charles Goodall, *The Royal College of Physicians of London . . . And An Historical Account of the College's proceedings against Empiricks and unlicensed Practisers in every Princes Reign from their first Incorporation to the Murther of the Royal Martyr, King Charles the First* (London: Walter Kettilby, 1684), sig. Pp3[r]. William Johnson, Ἀγυρτο-μάστιξ (London: Henry Brome, 1665): quoted by Thomas, "Society of Chymical Physitians," p. 67.

55 Edward Forset, *A Comparative Discourse of the Bodies Natural and Politique* (London: John Bill, 1606), p. 85.

56 *The Royal College of Physicians,* "Epistle Dedicatory," sig. A4[r].

57 P. M. Rattansi, "Paracelsus and the Puritan Revolution," *Ambix,* 11 (1963), 23–32.

58 Thomson, *Galeno-Pale,* p. 105; Webster, *Academiarum Examen,* p. 75; *Pyrotechny Asserted and Illustrated, To be the surest and safest means for Art's Triumph over Nature's Infirmities* (London: Samuel Thomson, 1658), p. 149.

59 See Rattansi, "Helmontian-Galenist Controversy"; "Absalom and Achitophel," *Poems,* I, 231.

60 "Necessary Directions for the Prevention and Cure of the Plague in 1665. With Divers Remedies of Small Charge by the College of Physicians," in *A Collection of Very Valuable and Scarce Pieces Relating to the last Plague in the Year 1665* (London: F. Roberts, 1721), pp. 54–55. This well-established cure had been popular since at least the Middle Ages and was used for a variety of ailments: from Pepys we learn that it was used for the Queen's spotted fever (*Diary,* Oct. 19, 1663). The new science was again pressed into service to justify an ancient therapy: see Digby's justification of the practice by the atomic hypothesis, *A Late Discourse,* pp. 64–65.

61 "An Advertisement from the Society of Chymical Physitians, Touching Medicines by them prepared, in pursuance of his Majesties Command, For the

Prevention, and for the Cure of the Plague." (Broadsheet) Facsimile in Thomas, "Society of Chymical Physitians," p. 57.

62 "Epistle Dedicatory," "Of Dramatic Poesy: An Essay," *Essays,* I, 13.

63 See Clark, *History of the Royal College of Physicians,* II, Chs. 20, 22, 23; F. H. Ellis, "The Backgrounds of the London Dispensary," *Journal of the History of Medicine,* 20 (1965), 199–212.

64 "Secular Masque," *Poems,* IV, 1764; *Pharonnida* (London: Robert Clavell, 1659), "To the Reader," sigs. A6^{v}–A7^{r}.

65 "The Dispensary," *Poems on Affairs of State, 1697–1704,* ed. F. H. Ellis (New Haven: Yale Univ. Press, 1970), Canto 2, l. 84; Canto 3, l. 71, etc.

66 Jones, "Science and Criticism," p. 48.

67 On Donne's use of medical imagery, see D. C. Allen, "Donne's Knowledge of Renaissance Medicine," *JEGP,* 42 (1943), 322–42.

68 "To my Honoured Friend Sir Robert Howard," *Poems,* I, 13. Dryden specifically glosses "the Curious Net" as the *rete mirabile.* For Galen's extravagant praise of the *rete mirabile* (which was probably observed in a pig!), see *Galen on the Usefulness of the Parts of the Body,* trans. and ed. Margaret Tallmadge May (Ithaca: Cornell Univ. Press, 1968), I, 430–32; for Vesalius' discovery that it was not to be found in man, see *Works,* I, 209.

69 "An Essay upon the Ancient and Modern Learning," *Five Miscellaneous Essays,* ed. S. H. Monk (Ann Arbor: Univ. of Michigan Press, 1963), p. 57; Dryden anticipates the attitudes of Temple, Swift, et al.—see Lester S. King, "Attitudes towards 'scientific' Medicine around 1700," *Bulletin of the History of Medicine,* 39 (1965), 124–33.

70 The phrase is George Starkey's *Nature's Explication,* p. 11.

71 Writers who had explored the analogy before Dryden included Ronsard, Sidney, Reynolds, and (by ironic imitation of "Sir Emp'ricks tone") Cleveland. "To my Lord Chancellor," *Poems,* I, 30; "Prologue to the University of Oxford," *Works,* I, 146.

72 Johnson, 'Αγυρτο-μάστιξ, cited Thomas, "Society of Chymical Physitians," p. 67; Postscript to "Notes and Observations on *The Empress of Morocco,*" *Works,* XVII, 182; "Of Dramatic Poesy: An Essay," *Essays,* I, 21.

73 "Prologue to *Oedipus,*" *Poems,* I, 168.

74 "Prologue to the University of Oxford," *Works,* I, 146; Twysden criticizes Nedham's use of atomism, *Medicina Veterum Vindicata,* pp. 84–89.

75 "Prologue to *The Pilgrim,*" *Poems,* IV, 1758–59. This is, of course, pure libel: Blackmore was an Oxford graduate, a member of the Church of England, and a celebrated society physician.

76 Ibid., 1759; criticism of Blackmore cited by Thomas Noxon Tunney, "Sir Richard Blackmore," *Annals of Medical History,* 4 (1922), 186.

77 "Prologue to *The Pilgrim,*" *Poems,* IV, 1759.

78 "To my Honour'd Kinsman, John Driden of Chesterton," IV, 1532.

79 "Prefixed to the *Aeneis,*" *Essays,* II, 227.

80 Mary Claire Randolph, "The Medical Concept in English Renaissance Satiric Theory," *SP,* 38 (1941), 126; Ward, *The London-spy,* pp. 422–23.

81 "Postscript to the *Aeneis,*" *Essays,* II, 259.
82 "Absalom and Achitophel: To the Reader," *Poems,* I, 216.
83 "Heroique Stanza's," *Poems,* I, 8; Shadwell, *Medal of John Bayes,* p. 8.
84 "Astrea Redux," *Poems,* I, 20.
85 See Marc Bloch, *Les Rois Thaumaturges* (Strasbourg: Max Leclerc, 1924), esp. pp. 375ff., 443ff.
86 "Annus Mirabilis," *Poems,* I, 98.
87 On Shaftesbury (whose "suppurating hydatid abscess of the liver . . . was irrigated daily through a silver drainage pipe"), see Kenneth Dewhurst, *Dr. Thomas Sydenham, 1624–1689* (Berkeley: Univ. of California Press, 1966), pp. 37–38; on the "Monumental Brass" Oates (in whose anti-typology *Numbers* 21:9 and *John* 3:14–15 are negated), see Stephen N. Zwicker, *Dryden's Political Poetry* (Providence: Brown Univ. Press, 1972), p. 97; "Absalom and Achitophel," *Poems,* I, 240. On the disease imagery of the poem in general, see Bernard Schilling, *Dryden and the Conservative Myth* (New Haven: Yale Univ. Press, 1961), s.v. "Imagery: disease and madness."
88 "Preface to *Religio Laici,*" *Poems,* I, 302.
89 "Prefixed to *The Assignation,*" *Essays,* I, 187. This familiar remedy (see above, note 60) had become a minor literary *topos* in the seventeenth century which was used by Webster, Donne, and Cleveland among others.
90 "Preface to *An Evening's Love,*" *Essays,* I, 187.
91 "A Discourse Concerning Satire," *Essays,* II, 138; Dryden does add, however, "What they promise only, Horace has effectually performed."
92 "Epilogue to *Aureng-Zebe,*" *Poems,* I, 157.
93 "The Prologue at Oxford, 1680," I, 211. In this poem, Aristotle again becomes a shibboleth in the struggle against fanatical innovators.
94 The proximity (both physical and metaphorical) of the mountebank's stall to the travelling actor's stage (and, by extension, to the legitimate theatre and preacher's pulpit) fascinated writers so diverse as Ned Ward, Samuel Garth, and Jonathan Swift. See also Sybil Rosenfeld, *The Theatre of the London Fairs in the Eighteenth Century* (Cambridge: The University Press, 1960), "Index" s.v. "Merry Andrew." Samuel Butler, "A Mountebank," *Characters* (Cleveland: Case Western Reserve Univ. Press, 1970), pp. 181–82; "Defence of An Essay of Dramatic Poesy," *Essays,* I, 110.
95 William Munk, *The Roll of the Royal College of Physicians of London* (London: Longmans Green, 1861), I, 457; Clark, *History of the Royal College of Physicians,* II, 472.

The Femininity of Moll Flanders

KATHLEEN McCOY

Defoe's *Moll Flanders* is not only a document by which to mark the development of English prose fiction, it also introduced into English literature a new and apparently unprecedented female character. Moll Flanders emerges full-blown and highly specified without any readily recognizable literary antecedents in the character types of the previous century. The book has been linked formally to the spiritual autobiography and to the criminal biography or confession, but neither of these influences can account fully for the complexity and difficulty which recent controversy about the novel and its heroine seems to indicate.

The last two decades of critical discussion of *Moll Flanders* have established only that the novel is not so simple to read nor so easy to assess as earlier readers assumed. It has become impossible to dismiss it, as Leslie Stephen did in the last century, as a mere accumulation of dull facts. It is equally inadequate to call it "indisputably great," the praise of Virginia Woolf. In 1957, Ian Watt,[1] arguing that Moll Flanders' values were probably very similar to Defoe's, concluded that although Defoe was "a master illusionist," nevertheless he was not a founder of the novel because his works lacked "a controlling moral intention." He also felt that Moll was essentially not feminine. Ten years later, having marked the rise of critical interest in *Moll Flanders*, Watt sorted out the areas of disagreement.[2] The central issue was irony—intentional or unconscious, sustained, intermittent, or none at all. Most of those who credited Defoe with a high degree of artistic awareness found the novel consistently ironic. Those who continued to believe him naive saw that Defoe, not Moll, was the one whom the reader must laugh at and whose values the reader must reject. Watt also raised again the question of Moll's femininity. He still doubted "whether there really is such a thing as a specifically feminine character."[3] However, this time he allowed the women to answer. He deferred to the judgments of Virginia Woolf and Dorothy VanGhent that Moll is authentically a woman. While such a critical maneuver demonstrates that Watt is a gentleman, it does little by way of answering the question, What makes a literary character feminine or not feminine?

Woolf and VanGhent essentially disagree about Moll Flanders. Woolf, who supposed that Defoe was an "unconscious artist," found in Moll an early desire for romance which was never allowed to flower, mostly because Moll is never allowed to settle down into a "subtle domestic atmosphere." Her lack of delicacy is a product of her situation, which demands instead ambition, imagination, and a "robust understanding." That is, she would be more feminine if she could. But just as Moll can waste no time on "refinements of personal affection," so Defoe himself "never lingers or stresses any point of subtlety or pathos."[4] Although the hard conditions imposed by Moll's circumstances do not permit her feminine nature to develop fully, Woolf implies that it might have developed as a leaning toward domesticity, refinement, affection, and emotional subtlety.

By contrast, VanGhent calls Moll an "Earth Mother" and follows this nomination with a list of horrendous progeny "suitable to a waste-land world." Moll is female, rather than feminine, "a lusty, full-bodied, lively-sensed creature" with no "subjective life" but an insanely narrow focus on "financial abstractions."[5] Like many critics who see the novel as essentially ironic, VanGhent was much less charmed by Moll than was Woolf. Thus in Moll we can read either the lusty creature or the thwarted romantic. Arnold Kettle is able to see both. He has defended Moll on grounds that she "becomes a criminal because she is a woman." She is "immoral, shallow, hypocritical, heartless, a bad woman, yet Moll is marvelous."[6] Because she aspires to personal relationships of a high level, higher than that of a servant, she deserves sympathy.

Since 1967, the intensity of discussion and disagreement has not abated. Michael Shinagle has demonstrated the importance and continuity of Defoe's concept of gentility in his book, *Daniel Defoe and Middle-Class Gentility.*[7] James Sutherland, who does not believe that *Moll Flanders* is consistently ironic, nonetheless finds Moll a good character, "both warm-hearted and hard-headed." Conflicts of heart and head make her more realistic than inconsistent, and "sexually, at any rate, Moll has the characteristics of a normal woman."[8] This normality seems to be demonstrated for Sutherland in Moll's last whoring episode, wherein she clearly has her eye on the man's money and coolly lets the sexual action happen.

Several recent studies have reflected a new emphasis. Understanding Moll's mind rather than Defoe's intentions or limitations has become the focal point. A part of this shift in emphasis moves in the direction of defining her nature as a sexual being.

Douglas Brooks, for example, explores the incest motif. Having been married off to the younger brother while still desiring the elder, the young Moll commits imaginary incest during her first marriage. Later she unknowingly marries her half-brother and they remove to Virginia where the incest is discovered by their mother. Moll is repelled by it, but her husband-brother suffers a serious mental and physical decline. Moll escapes back to England, having achieved, says Brooks, a "revenge through this ritualistic reenactment of the first episode." He also cites many echoes and correspondences with the originally incestuous marriage, so that all of Moll's sexual relationships seem to have been tainted with incest except that with Jemmy, whom she loved in a "normal" way.[9]

Similarly, William Krier waives the irony question in favor of an attempt to clarify the "book's reality." He finds Moll initially in the "feminine situation," reliant on others and unable to act. After her second marriage, to the gentleman-tradesman, and her subsequent experience in the Mint, Moll decides to act, thereby shifting into the "masculine situation." She then picks out a likely man to exploit and, with the help of the captain's wife, effectively ensnares him. (Surely there are many readers who would call *this* action typically feminine.) After her Newgate conversion, wherein Moll accepts responsibility for her own actions, there is some shifting back from or modification of the masculine situation. In the end, as a mother benefiting from her son's work, she comes to rest in a middle position of semi-independence.[10]

But positions of relative dependence or self-reliance do not adequately define the sexual nature of a character. It is relevant to notice that two of Moll's husbands, each one supposing her to be rich, employ seductive strategies and false suggestions of their own wealth which are quite parallel to Moll's campaign in each case. Jemmy, in particular, gambles on a display of equipage to gain security in winning Moll's hand. Although Moll has taken up the feminist attack on the importance of money in the marriage market, it clearly works both ways. A fortune hunter's tactics include a good deal of sham no matter which his sex.

Curt Hartog, writing for *Literature and Psychology,* has compared Defoe's expressions of submission and aggression in *Robinson Crusoe* and *Moll Flanders*. For Crusoe, the conflict of these inner tendencies is an anxious one, and this conflict achieves solution only in fantasy when, through religious conversion, Crusoe represses his will and submits to the will of God. Subsequently, Hartog finds, Defoe was able to cope more successfully with the expression of aggression by using the feminine point of view. That is, Moll's femininity "makes possible a freer expression of aggression" and "disperses moral judgments, shifting guilt away from the protagonist" because the conflict against authority is diffused among many male antagonists and because Moll's feminine vulnerability seems to make her more clearly a victim of necessity. But, "Moll is less than a perfect portrait of a woman, and clearly reflects a great deal of her creator's personality." Her passivity is apparent, not real. What Hartog finds more characteristically feminine is Moll's need of a supporting friend and confidante and her simultaneous tendency to be secretive, even of her own identity. Defoe never reveals to us Moll's real identity because, ultimately, she has "no self."[11] While Defoe's reticence might as easily be explained on formal or on historical grounds,[12] Hartog's Freudian analysis brings us back very close to Krier's assumption that overt aggression is masculine and deviations from that norm indicate femininity. Truly feminine characters are covert, or passive. It is a common enough idea.

The specifically sexual behavior of Moll has been examined by Juliet McMaster. She traces the consequences of Moll's first affair, which taught Moll to equate love with gifts of money. Unlike Defoe, who held the Puritan view that a merely commercial and loveless marriage is legal prostitution, Moll purposely manages all her subsequent affairs with financial gain as her primary object. But the symbolic linkage of gold with sex remains potent, so that Moll experiences the "real consummation" of her affair with her Bath lover when he fills her lap with guineas. Money is the sexual bait used by both Jemmy and Moll. When they are reunited years later, "they still do their courting by offering each other money." McMaster finds Moll increasingly cool about sexual activity after her first affair, to the point where she can adopt a masculine disguise. "One sees why several critics have found her unfeminine, curiously neutral in sex."[13]

Several, but not all. There is as much disagreement about the femininity, womanliness, or normal sexuality of Moll Flanders as there has been about the degree, level, or kind of irony in *Moll Flanders*. It is difficult to find a consistent thread because primary assumptions about sexuality and its manifestation in a character of fiction are seldom made explicit. As with the irony question, critics who most identify Moll's personality with Defoe's tend to see her feminine qualities as false or weakly conveyed. Others who credit Defoe with more imaginative force see the tricks of Moll, her lapses and inconsistencies, as part of her feminine image. Neither position is without some limitations.

Furthermore, the irony debate and the femininity question are linked. Unstated assumptions about typical or normal feminine behavior can lead the reader to suppose, when the expectations are not met, that the author is being ironic,[14] or that the book can be read as ironic whether the author meant it so or not. Formally, the book asserts the inherent importance and interest of the events of the life of an ordinary criminal woman. As she retells her life, the enormous egocentricity of Moll Flanders, her expectation that we should know and will care how much linen and plate she had on hand at one time or another, this egocentricity seems a breach of decorum so great that it could only have been made ironically by a satirist or ignorantly by a parvenu. If assertion is masculine, Moll is a failure as a character, a mere economic man in drag. If victimization and submission are the essence of the feminine, why will she not sit still and keep quiet?

Many female characters both before and since Defoe have been active and vocal. Definitions of femininity must be referred back to the historical and literary tradition from which the character is drawn. The question cannot be illuminated by informally consulting the critic's notions of how women behave. This problem becomes obvious with *Moll Flanders* because Moll, like Defoe, is in several ways outside the pale.

First, Moll clearly exists far from the realm of the courtly or the ideal. Even her modest aspirations to the status of gentlewoman are futile. She achieves outward gentility only partially, temporarily, or as disguise. It is no part of her character to endure suffering with patience, to hold aloof from temptation, or to sacrifice self. Her instincts are for mundane survival. Unlike the ambitious courtesan Roxana, Moll desires nothing more lofty than a secure marriage to an amiable gentleman. She is no female fop in a world of manners.[15] While her social status, opportunism, and exploitation of sex link her with comic female characters, her basic situation is not comic. Happy marriages are ended by bankruptcy, death, or the revelation of incest.

If it is difficult to place Moll in any of the traditional kinds, it is impossible to be sentimental about her. Although she is frequently in dire straits and does not hesitate to ask for our sympathy, she also demands our admiration of her daring, her ingenuity and persistent ability to survive by controlling and using others. She herself is a model of clear-eyed lack of sentiment. "Tis something of relief even to be undone by a man of honour rather than by a scoundrel,"[16] rings with worldliness and wit. Moll does not prefigure Pamela or her daughters, who stake everything on the heart of one man.

Moll's own story—a life of adventure and wickedness abandoned after a change of heart and ending in happy rewards—is sentimental enough in its outlines, especially if she were a masculine character reformed. But her tone is bold, flat, plain. Her emphasis on remorse is less than adequate to convince, as even the "editor" is forced to admit in his Preface. Guilt pales in comparison to her interest in the valuable knowledge that her wicked life has given her, knowledge which she now enjoys sharing. The satisfaction she once gained from doing she now gains from tutoring the reader in how it is done. This is the attitude which colors her style and controls the narration.

In the manipulation of her various husbands and lovers, she shows an artful combination of outright lies, half truths, concealment of motives, and "woman's rhetoric"[17] (tears). It is customary for her to manage affairs so that a man finds himself begging her to reveal what she is really very eager to tell him or admitting that she has not deceived him even though he has been disastrously deceived. The same pride, deftness, and skill in handling dupes is evident in her account of her later career as thief. Her vanity is inflated by her ability to steal gold watches; she is able to invent occasions.

This incident is typical. Having interviewed a loose-tongued footman about the family of two young ladies strolling the Mall, Moll approaches the elder:

> I saluted her by her Name, and the Title of Lady Betty; I ask'd her when she heard from her Father? When my Lady her Mother would be in Town and how she did?
>
> I talk'd so familiarly to her of her whole Family that she cou'd not suspect but that I knew them all intimately: I ask'd her why she would come Abroad without Mrs. Chime with her (that was the Name of Her Woman) to take care of Mrs. Judith that was her Sister. Then I enter'd into a long Chat with her about her Sister, what a fine little Lady she was, and ask'd her if she had learn'd French, and a Thousand things to entertain her, when on a sudden we see the Guards come, and the Crowd run to see the King go by to the Parliament-House.
>
> The Ladies run all to the Side of the Mall, and I help'd my Lady to stand upon the edge of the Boards on the side of the Mall, that she might be high enough to see; and took the little one and lifted her quite up; during which, I took care to convey the gold Watch so clean away from the Lady Betty, that she never felt it, nor miss'd it, till all the Crowd was gone, and she was gotten into the Middle of the Mall among the other Ladies.
>
> I took my leave of her in the very Crowd. . . .
>
> . . . so having drop'd the two little Ladies, and done my business with them, without any Miscarriage, I kept hurrying on among the crowd, as if I

> run to see the King . . . I bestowed a coach upon myself, and made off; and I confess I have not yet been so good as my word (viz.) to go and visit my Lady Betty.[18]

In her "long chat" with the reader, Moll is just as clever. The ironic inquiry into the absence of Mrs. Chime is reminiscent of the famous passage wherein Moll admonished the careless parents of the child coming from dancing school unattended and wearing an expensive necklace.[19] Here, the final sardonic joke at the expense of her aristocratic victim suggests the pleasure of the aged Moll reflecting on her skill and nicety of conduct in risky circumstances. She boasts that she was much better at the trade than any of those who tried to collaborate with her, that she surpassed all others in the acquaintance of her Governess in being "exquisitely keen," and that she "always had most Courage when I was in most danger."[20] Finally, she congratulates herself that she has managed so well that she can spend her remaining years comfortably in London, enjoying "sincere Penitence."

There are a number of ways for a character to be female, but femininity traditionally includes a strong element of apparent docility and indirect means. Moll boasts that she has used the feminine means well, with ease and daring. But she boasts, which is not feminine, and she mocks others—the careless, the foolish, the unwary. She tells us that they are her victims partly through their own faults. One purpose of her story, repeatedly claimed, is to shift the reader from a state of ignorance, potential victimization, to a state of active vigilence and courage to resist.

The value of an ordinary person's private experience, as it unfolds through a lifetime, is Defoe's main fictional idea. Far from believing that "most women have no characters at all," his Puritanism leads him to assume that each soul, each person, is equally and individually accountable to God. Character exists as the memory of a meaningful series of actions and thoughts continuing through time. Self-examination for the purpose of self-knowledge and evaluation is part of the duty of each one. Accordingly a woman must also be responsible for her own state of soul. Family and religious councilors could be useful guides and supports, especially for women or youths, but Moll has had to do without these for the most part. She has obeyed the essential laws of nature first, by finding ways to survive.[21] Having survived, she re-examines her life, weighing good against bad, intentions against performance, necessity against inclination to crime, and giving herself passing marks. She has found much to repent of, but she has also found much to celebrate and much that is of use in her personal history. In this, she is not different from a male character. The evidence of George A. Starr,[22] linking Defoe's narrative method to the spiritual autobiography, tends to make all characters alike; all souls are independent and subject to the same passage through sin to redemption. The sameness of the Christian experience makes each autobiography useful for others and excuses drawing attention to oneself, to the trivia of one's means of existence.

Therefore, what is feminine is not first. One's primary being is asexual—the individual acting according to the demands of necessity and the obligations of religious law. Sexuality is secondary, imposing limitations of situation and dictating means. The vitality of Moll shows in her minimal acceptance of the limitations and adroit exploitations of the means. Moll belongs more to the tribe of her class than to the tribe of her sex. She can endure to disguise herself as a man better than as a beggar woman. The term feminine, with its connotations of the passive, the indirect and the covert, is more readily applied to her self-deceptions than to her self-knowledge and self-aggrandizement. That is, we will allow that she is skilled, that she knows how to trick, how to steal, how to seduce. But her sense of accomplishment seems too gross, even sometimes to herself. It is not nice, it is not "feminine."

Moll's character is a product of a set of vital ideas, lower middle-class dissenting Protestant ideas, which are extra-literary but through which Defoe found an original concept of characterization. The concept still disconcerts, because the modern reader continues to put gender identity first.

NOTES

1 *The Rise of the Novel* (Berkeley: Univ. of California Press, 1957), p. 131.

2 "The Recent Critical Fortunes of *Moll Flanders*," *Eighteenth-Century Studies,* 1 (1967), 109–26.

3 Watt, pp. 112–13.
4 "Defoe, *The Common Reader,* 1st ser. (London: Hogarth Press, 1938), pp. 124–27.
5 *The English Novel: Form and Function* (New York: Harper & Row, 1953), pp. 51–59.
6 "In Defense of Moll Flanders," in *Of Books and Humankind: Essays and Poems Presented to Bonamy Dobree,* ed. John Butt (London: Routledge and Kegan Paul, 1964), 55–67.
7 Cambridge, Mass.: Harvard Univ. Press, 1968.
8 *Daniel Defoe; a Critical Study* (Cambridge, Mass.: Harvard Univ. Press, 1971), pp. 181–85.
9 "*Moll Flanders:* An Interpretation," *Essays in Criticism,* 19 (1969), 46–59.
10 "A Courtesy which Grants Integrity: A Literal Reading of *Moll Flanders,*" *ELH,* 38 (1971), 397–410.
11 "Aggression, Femininity and Irony in *Moll Flanders,*" *Literature and Psychology,* 22 (1972), 121–38.
12 Gerald Howson, "Who was Moll Flanders?" *TLS,* No. 3438 (January 18, 1968), 63–64.
13 "The Equation of Love and Money in *Moll Flanders,*" *Studies in the Novel,* 2 (1970), 131–44.
14 For a discussion of tests for irony, see Wayne C. Booth, *The Rhetoric of Irony* (Chicago: Univ. of Chicago, 1974), pp. 49–76.
15 Contrasting Roxana and Moll, Paula Backscheider finds Roxana "always more the woman" because of Roxana's greater vanity and longing to be well-dressed. See "Defoe's Women: Snares and Prey," *Studies in Eighteenth-Century Culture,* vol. 5 (Madison, Wis.: Univ. of Wisconsin Press, 1976), p. 109.
16 *Moll Flanders,* ed. Edward Kelly (New York: Norton, 1973), p. 118. Subsequent citations from the novel refer to this edition.
17 Ibid., p. 236.
18 Ibid., pp. 201–2.
19 Ibid., pp. 151–52.
20 Ibid., pp. 209–10.
21 Maximillian Novak, *Defoe and the Nature of Man* (New York: Oxford Univ. Press, 1963), pp. 78–79.
22 *Defoe and Spiritual Autobiography* (Princeton: Princeton Univ. Press, 1965), pp. 14–17.

Toward a Generic Theory of Restoration Comedy: Some Preliminary Considerations

BRIAN CORMAN

Treating a time-bound body of literature generically presents two basic sets of problems to the critic—problems arising from the necessity for defining the genre itself and problems arising from the necessity for defining the unique features of its actual embodiments in a particular age. Restoration comedy has a history and identity of its own within the larger history and identity of comedy in general. Its definition depends in part on a definition of comedy, a requirement that at best provokes skepticism in most critics. Moreover, in a highly traditional form with a long history, formal changes are gradual, not sudden, piecemeal, not wholesale. The origin and development of Restoration comedy are thus so difficult to isolate that many critics doubt that they can be isolated profitably at all.

Extraordinary similarities have nevertheless always been observed among Restoration comedies. An educated reader or theatergoer can encounter a play for the first time and identify it not only as a comedy but as a comedy of the Restoration. From such shared and common experiences follow what R. S. Crane calls "the two complementary ideas of ages and traditions,"[1] the structural realities of literary history. As a result the generic critic of Restoration comedy must anticipate the scope of the theorist who demands an awareness of the comedy of other periods; a time-bound theory will be of little generic significance. At the same time the critic must prepare for the scrutiny of the historian who insists on a thorough knowledge of the period; a theory which pretends to deal with Restoration comedy must account for more than Etherege, Wycherley, and Congreve. Since my immediate goal is an answer to the question "What is Restoration comedy?" a strictly generic approach is not appropriate. Generic theory helps place Restoriation *comedy* in the comic tradition and provides a useful vocabulary for inquiry. But specifying the distinguishing features of *Restoration* comedy is essentially a historical problem.

I also have a second goal—to investigate the development of Restoration comedy—a goal, I suspect, behind most discussions of Restoration comedy. The concept of the age is thus all the more important. Anne Righter claims that Restoration drama is "positively schizophrenic," that the "disjunction" between comedy and tragedy is one "for which no precedent existed in any earlier theatre"—and the separation of critical studies into studies of comedy and studies of tragedy would tend to substantiate her claim.[2] Yet few writers produced either form exclusively, and most also indulged in mixed forms, much to the chagrin of critics of Restoration drama for three hundred years. Thus a central figure like Dryden enters the standard histories of Restoration comedy through the side door, often with apologies. Comic plots are excised from *Secret Love* or *The Spanish Friar* and treated in isolation.

Restoration comedy cannot be understood fully without a knowledge of the other forms of Restoration drama, not only because their histories are parallel but because their shared conventions help explain all genres. Recognizing that the Dorimants and the Almanzors are in many ways different versions of the same character type, for example, clears up a number of potential interpretive difficulties in the comedies and in the heroic plays, and provides an approach to mixed forms as well. More concretely, Alithea's loyalty to Sparkish continues to puzzle critics of *The Country Wife* who cannot take seriously her straightforward appeal to her honor. Her statements make more sense when set alongside of Almahide's similarly puzzling loyalty to Boabdelin:

Almahide. This day
I gave my faith to him, he his to me
. . . .
Whate're my secret inclinations be,
To this, since honor ties me, I agree.
Alithea. The writings are drawn, Sir, settlements made;
'tis too late, Sir, and past all revocation
. . . .
I wish my Gallant had his person and
understanding:—
[Nay if my honour— [*Aside.*][3]

This juxtaposition may not make Wycherley's artistry any better on generic grounds, but at least his limitations can be explained on historical grounds.

Generic approaches to Restoration comedy have been almost exclusively of two kinds, usually identified as, on the one hand, "historical," "empirical," or "preconstructional," and, on the other hand, "dialectical," "modal," or "postconstructional."[4] The remainder of this paper will discuss these two approaches as well as a third, what I call, after Crane, the constructional approach. A "historical" approach focuses on the artist and those sources and traditions that directly influence artistic production, such as conceptions of literary history or commitments to critical principles. Claudio Guillén is probably right to argue that for the artist genre provides "a contemporary model or a 'working hypothesis'"; he is also right to complain that most genres discovered by critics postdate the works themselves.[5] But this should not imply, as it sometimes does for Guillén, that the work of the literary historian ends with reproducing the perspective of the artist in question. The business of the literary historian is to explain how the individual artist used the compositional principles of the genre in unique ways.

A literary historian is grateful to have recorded Dryden's sense that his predecessors left him "scarce an humour, a character or any kind of plot, which they have not blown upon."[6] Similarly, his famous exchange with Shadwell about Ben Jonson's place in Restoration comedy provides the essential raw material of literary history:

> *Dryden:* I declare I want judgment to imitate him and should think it impudence in myself to attempt it.
> *Shadwell:* I am so far from thinking it impudence to endeavour to imitate him that it would rather, in my opinion, seem impudence in me not to do it.[7]

Conscious motivation is, of course, of central importance, but it can be misleading; theory and practice are seldom one. Moreover, literary history as perceived by Dryden and Shadwell is no more "historical" (and therefore pure) than twentieth-century literary history. One need not read much Dryden and Shadwell to realize that a knowledge of Ben Jonson (or Shakespeare or Beaumont and Fletcher) is of limited value in explaining their plays.

Gerard Langbaine's *Account of the English Dramatic Poets* remains an invaluable treasury of sources and analogues for Restoration drama. But no source study can adequately describe, not to mention evaluate, Restoration comedy. Knowledge of sources does not yield understanding of the new plays based on them. Yet replace Langbaine's accusations of plagiarism with, say, Wycherley's view that "tho' the Matter that a Writer treats of be not new, the Disposition, Method, or Uses of it may be new; as it is the same Ball which good and bad Gamesters play with, but one forces or places it better than Another, by a different Art, Use, or Disposal of it,"[8] and what remains resembles most standard twentieth-century definitions of Restoration comedy.[9]

Critics often return to the debates between Dryden and Shadwell or Dennis and Steele on the respective places of pleasure and instruction, particularly in comedy. For example, Charles O. McDonald begins his examination of Restoration comedy in reprimanding Thomas Fujimura for using "the historical method throughout [his] book . . . only to end with an analysis of the effect of the comedies based on modern aesthetic theory."[10] Yet the repeated inability of Horatian commonplaces, even in the hands of a Samuel Johnson, to explain Restoration and eighteenth-century literature provides eloquent testimony to their inadequacy. Shadwell was—fortunately—unable to practice what he preached: had he done so critics would not now be bothered by the injustice of *MacFlecknoe.* And Dennis is surely at his worst when he feels compelled to pursue the moral instruction offered by *The Man of Mode*: he is reduced to treating Etherege's masterpiece with *Volpone* as two of a kind. Furthermore, if McDonald is pressed about the moral of *The Man of Mode,* he is forced into either the banality of Dennis ("Loveit . . . is a just caution to the fair sex never to be so conceited of the power of their charms . . . as to believe they can engage a man to be true to them to whom they grant the best favor without the only sure engagement") or the absurdity of Rymer when he facetiously provided a moral for *Othello.*[11] Surely Fujimura's is the sounder approach; he makes full use of "historical" material without allowing it to limit inquiry.

Yet any dialectical view like Fujimura's applies ends to Restoration comedy that are derived from some external ideal, sometimes contemporary (and hence quasi-historical), sometimes not. Here "distinctions of genre" are not drawn from "historically determined conventions" but rather from "general qualities or complexes of qualities which are often identified as peculiarly characteristic of one or another of the recognized forms but not restricted to it."[12] A. H. Scouten's complaint about scholars of Elizabethan drama who have written histories of Restoration drama provides a familiar example. The partisan scholars hold up Elizabethan drama as the ideal against which Restoration drama necessarily falls short.[13] Their evaluation may well be correct; their methods must nevertheless be rejected. The Elizabethan template prohibits accurate judgment and understanding of the special qualities of Restoration drama.

Norman Holland provides a thematic example of dialectical criticism when he argues that "the dialectic between inner desires and manners . . . informs the comedies" of the Restoration; that is, "the discrepancy between 'appearance' and 'nature'" provides a theme that "is distinctly and specially a Restoration theme."[14] It is indeed often illuminating to recognize that a discrepancy between appearance and reality can be found in most if not all Restoration comedy as, for example, David Vieth has shown in a discussion of *The Country Wife* that seems more fruitful than Holland's.[15] But Holland carries his thesis too far when he claims that the treatment of appearance and nature makes Restoration comedy what it is. This claim can be made for any literary form from Homeric epic to the *nouveau roman.* Holland's theory fulfills the demands of neither literary history nor genre theory.

A final example is provided by Fujimura, who uses a "historical" method to find that Restoration comedy reflects "the temper of the times" or "*Zeitgeist*" epitomized by the "naturalistic" philosophy of Hobbes.[16] He performs a valuable service in pointing out Hobbes's importance for understanding Restoration drama, but he distorts both Hobbes and the comic writers to make Hobbesian thought the defining characteristic of Restoration comedy. Moreover, his speculations encourage a number of new and ultimately unsatisfactory critical dualisms such as William Myers' polarization of Hobbes and Locke to distinguish Etherege and Wycherley from Congreve.[17] "Hobbesian" and "Lockean" are useful metaphors; taken literally they produce a new, oversimplified prescriptive dialectic. Perhaps Fujimura was aware of these limitations for, as McDonald observes, he departs from "historical" analysis in the later parts of *The Restoration Comedy of Wit.*

A more important objection, though, is not that Fujimura abandons the historical, but rather that he retains the dialectical in constructing his genre, "the comedy of wit." Since the distinguishing traits of wit comedy are Fujimura's, they remain idiosyncratic and highly contentious. Historically minded critics like Scouten and Robert Hume rightly dismiss "the comedy of wit" on empirical grounds; it simply does not explain the comedy of the period. But Fujimura goes further: he dismisses works from his genre because they violate his construct, as if his dialectically determined genre were empirically valid. Congreve's *The Double-Dealer,* for example, "has many characteristics of the comedy of wit, but it is a poor example of this type."[18] The notion that it may be an excellent example of some *other* type does not occur to him, because his dialectic necessarily blinds him to such a possibility.

My use of the terms "preconstructional" and "postconstructional" for the historical and dialectical varieties of genre criticism implies the existence of a third, preferable, "constructional" approach such as that proposed by Crane. For Crane, the business of the critic is to argue

> from completed works to the specific artistic ends and problems they presuppose; from the ends of problems to the reasoning implicit in the particular choices and combinations of means affected by writers in relation to them; from the means as used to the antecedent events and circumstances implied by the writers' preference for these means over others as well or better suited, theoretically, to their ends; and from the ends as chosen to the previous happenings, in the minds of the writers and in the general situation, necessitated hypothetically by their choice.[19]

The constructional critic thus subsumes while fully benefitting from the findings of both preconstructional and postconstructional critics. And the same method of inquiry that applies to individual works provides explanatory generalizations for the canon of a given author, the members of a given school, or the literature of a given age. The special value of a sense of species is that it provides relevant criteria for the analysis of a given work, author, or period in question. An attempt to determine species is thus an attempt to formulate the appropriate questions for understanding the work and its parts. It is an attempt to methodize the intuitive analysis most readers or audiences apply to an unfamiliar play: "What kind of play is this? Where does it fit in the larger context of literary history?"[20] Genres are, for the constructional critic, inductively known species of works heuristically conceived in terms of artistically selected elements and principles of construction.

In practice this means that one starts with a constructionally determined hypothesis about a work, author, or period and tests its ability to explain the literary event in question. *The Adventures of Five Hours, An Evening's Love,* and *The Rover* are traditionally referred to as Spanish intrigue comedies, yet a Spanish source and setting is all they have in common. Similarly *The Plain Dealer, City Politiques, The Squire of Alsatia,* and *Amphitryon* share little more than a tendency to embarrass formulators of a comedy of wit or a comedy of manners. A constructional approach forces the critic to recognize that no single generic formulation can be all-inclusive for Restoration comedy. At the same time it points to the finite, determinable number of species of comedy and the still more limited number of species actually present in the Restoration period. A remarkable feature of Restoration comedy is the range of expression possible within the limited number of genres. The great writers of Restoration comedy are those who perfect existing forms, not those who invent new ones. While variations within that limited range may be as numerous as the individual plays themselves, plays like Shakespeare's *Tempest* and *The Shoemaker's Holiday* are not to be found, and others, like the plays of Brome, are to be found in revivals only. Moreover, an extremely limited number of types predominate, and that dominance is not stable throughout the forty-year period.

A generic theory of Restoration comedy based on Crane's *Principles* would attempt to analyze the comedies of the Restoration by determining their peculiar artistic ends and judging them according to their success or failure in realizing those ends. The distinct analyses of individual plays would ultimately facilitate a full "narrative-causal history" of Restoration comedy. Such a history, ideally, would be written in terms of four factors: (1) shifts in the artistic or formal ends of different writers throughout the period, (2) changes in the materials through which these ends were realized, (3) discoveries of new and more effective devices or techniques, and (4) "successive actualizations" of these possibilities in "artistically valuable or historically significant works."[21]

Such a theory would attempt to account for the emergence after the Restoration of new kinds of comedy, yet comedy strongly in the tradition of pre-Commonwealth England, especially of Beaumont, Fletcher, and Jonson. It would attempt to isolate the body of dramatic conventions common to most Restoration comedy and to show how these conventions were adapted and modified by various comic writers to produce the major achievements of the 1670s; at the same time it would recognize that even within this remarkably coherent common heritage plays such as *The Man of Mode, The Country Wife,* and *The Virtuoso* remain unique, individual achievements. Problems of shared conventions would inevitably lead to consideration of plays that do not clearly fall into standard generic categories yet reveal striking similarities to plays that do, especially since they are often written by the same playwrights—plays like *Marriage à la Mode, Love in a Wood,* and *The Libertine.* It would also explain the gradual changes that continue to occur resulting in, by the 1690s, the significantly different comedies of (late) Shadwell, Cibber, Congreve, Vanbrugh, Farquhar, and (early) Steele.

A good test case for such a theory would be its ability to deal with *The Way of the World.* Congreve's masterpiece is generally considered the greatest comedy of the Restoration. At the same time it is unique in evoking through the common materials of post-1660 comedy a moral seriousness otherwise unknown in Restoration comedy.[22] Congreve's achievement must be seen first in the changes and developments of formal ends that distinguish *The Way of the World,* then in the changes in materials necessary to accomplish those ends (with a recognition of those materials that remain unchanged). From this it becomes possible to see *The Way of the World* as the culmination of Congreve's career as a comic writer and to see his place in the dramatic tradition to which Dryden proclaimed him heir.[23]

The great advantage, then, of a "narrative-causal history," is that because of its constructionist generic approach, it allows the fullest possible appreciation of a play like *The Way of the World* in its own right, in the career of its author, in the historical context of its age, and in the history of literary endeavor, which is surely the collective goal of all critical attempts at literary history. To understand the intrinsic limitations of purely historical or dialectical methods will make possible a beginning.

NOTES

1 "Critical and Historical Principles of Literary History," in *The Idea of the Humanities and Other Essays Critical and Historical* (Chicago and London: Univ. of Chicago Press, 1967), II, 152.

2 "Heroic Tragedy," in *Restoration Theatre,* ed. John Russell Brown and Bernard Harris (London: Edward Arnold, 1965), p. 139.

3 *The Conquest of Granada,* part 1, in *Selected Dramas of John Dryden,* ed. George R. Noyes (Chicago and New York: Scott, Foresman & Co., 1910), III.i.395–96, V.iii.186–87; *The Country Wife,* in *The Complete Plays of William Wycherley,* ed. Gerald Weales (Garden City, N.Y.: Anchor Books, 1966), pp. 279, 281.

4 See Crane, II, 47–56, and David H. Richter, "Pandora's Box Revisited," *Critical Inquiry,* 1 (1974), 453–78.

5 *Literature as System: Essays toward the Theory of Literary History* (Princeton, N.J.: Princeton Univ. Press, 1971), p. 130.

6 *Of Dramatic Poesy: An Essay,* in "*On Dramatic Poesy*" *and Other Critical Essays,* ed. George Watson (London: J. M. Dent, 1962), I, 85.

7 "Preface" to *An Evening's Love,* in Watson, I, 148; "Preface" to *The Humorists,* in *Critical Essays of the Seventeenth Century,* ed. J. E. Spingarn (1908–9; rpt. Bloomington and London: Indiana Univ. Press, 1957), II, 158.

8 *The Posthumous Works of William Wycherley Esq.; in Prose and Verse* (London: A. Bettesworth, 1728), pp. 7–8.

9 For example, "This comedy of manners is a peculiar, intangible sort of thing. In plot and in character it was not much of an innovation. Fletcher's *The Wild Goose Chase* . . . contains a good deal of its atmosphere. Jonsonian personages abound in Etherege and in Congreve. The intrigue of the Spanish school is to be marked in almost every plot. Molière and his companions of the French stage gave merely a touch to the wit and to the theme" (Allardyce Nicoll, *A History of English Drama, 1660–1900,* Vol. I: *Restoration Drama 1660–1700* [4th ed.; Cambridge, Eng.: Cambridge Univ. Press, 1952], p. 196). Catalogs of sources and conventions ultimately can do little more than reveal that Restoration comedy is, as Nicoll so candidly admits, a "peculiar, intangible sort of thing."

10 "Restoration Comedy as Drama of Satire: An Investigation into Seventeenth-Century Aesthetics," *Studies in Philology,* 61 (1964), 522.

11 "Defence of Sir Fopling Flutter," in *The Critical Works of John Dennis,* ed. Edward Niles Hooker (Baltimore: Johns Hopkins Univ. Press, 1939, 1943), II, 241–50; "A Short View of Tragedy," in *The Critical Works of Thomas Rymer,* ed. Curt A. Zimansky (New Haven: Yale Univ. Press, 1956), p. 132.

12 Crane, II, 52.

13 "Notes toward a History of Restoration Comedy," *Philological Quarterly,* 45 (1966), 69.

14 *The First Modern Comedies: The Significance of Etherege, Wycherley, and Congreve* (Cambridge, Mass.: Harvard Univ. Press, 1959), p. 4.

15 "Wycherley's *The Country Wife*: An Anatomy of Masculinity," *Papers on Language and Literature,* 2 (1966), 335–50.

16 *The Restoration Comedy of Wit* (Princeton, N.J.: Princeton Univ. Press, 1952), pp. 39–57.

17 "Plot and Meaning in Congreve's Comedies," in *William Congreve,* ed. Brian Morris (London: Ernest Benn, 1972), pp. 73–92.

18 Fujimura, p. 170.

19 Crane, II, 102.

20 See Sheldon Sacks, "The Psychological Implications of Generic Distinctions," *Genre,* 1 (1968), 106–15.

21 Crane, II, 81–82.

22 See my "*The Way of the World* and Morally Serious Comedy," *University of Toronto Quarterly,* 44 (1975), 199–212.

23 "To My Dear Friend Mr. Congreve, On His Comedy, Call'd *The Double-Dealer,*" in *The Complete Plays of William Congreve,* ed. Herbert Davis (Chicago and London: Univ. of Chicago Press, 1967), pp. 123–24.

Rhetoric versus Truth: Diderot's Writings as an Illustration of Stability and Innovation in Eighteenth-Century Literature

HUGUETTE COHEN

Is *philosophy* to be equated with *truth*, as the Enlightenment wants it, and *poetry* with *rhetoric* (or deception, if we accept the derogatory attributes given to both rhetoric and poetry by the *philosophes*)? A study of Diderot's writings over a period of forty years shows that the problem is of far greater complexity for this particular *philosophe*. In a strange transference, *truth*, with Diderot, has a way of reaching out for *poetry*, while *rhetoric* comes closer to *philosophy*. He professes repeatedly to be a seeker of truth; but perhaps more than finding truth, it is the search for truth that he prizes most. And he discovers very early in his literary career that classical rhetoric may indeed be an obstacle to this search—not that he is willing to forego completely structure and order in the literary form that he adopts. The basic dualism of order and disorder found by Lester Crocker[1] in Diderot's inquiries into metaphysics, morals, aesthetics, and politics can also be applied to his theory of literature.

At the onset of his literary career, Diderot is aware of a basic type of opposition between the philosopher and the poet. Human knowledge in the *Encyclopédie* is divided into *Histoire* related to memory, *Philosophie* stemming from reason, and *Poésie* born from imagination. In his own writings, Diderot often lumps in the same category *poésie* and *éloquence.* [2] This parallel is interesting because in the eighteenth century, the terms *éloquence* and *rhétorique* are virtually interchangeable; we can thus infer that in Diderot's mind, *poésie* and *éloquence* are united by the same artificiality stemming from rhetoric. This does not prevent him from expressing his regret about the disappearance of poetry, following the progress of the Enlightenment: "... plus de grands poèmes, plus de ces morceaux d'une éloquence sublime; plus de ces productions marquées au coin de l'ivresse et du génie; tout est raisonné, compassé, académique et plat."[3] As a humanist, Diderot is hesitant to sacrifice individual expression to the philosopher's dream of a world ruled and described by reason alone.

There is an aspect of Diderot's attitude towards poetry that is more puzzling, given his position as the official spokesman of the Enlightenment. He often associates the poet and the genius as originators of truth; both terms become interchangeable in his vocabulary. Rameau's nephew, the abortive genius who "secoue, agite... fait sortir la vérité,"[4] is one of these bizarre individuals, endowed with uncommon sensitivity and disorganized creative gifts, whom he chooses as spokesmen for his most personal and daring theories in his dialogues and his novels. It can be assumed that, in his own mind, the place of honor of the *philosophe* fighting for the progress of Truth, is often taken by the genius-poet speaking his *own* truth. This has, of course, profound implications for literary expression, as it foreshadows the abandonment of traditional linguistic patterns and rules for a more personal style, a "rhetoric of nature."

Seventeenth-century classical linguistic theories were still prevalent in Diderot's time. The *grammairiens-philosophes* contend in their *Encyclopédie* articles that the role of language is to reflect thought clearly and logically. No room is left for the expression of feeling, emotions, or the irrational. They remain faithful to the rational criteria applied to language in the seventeenth century by Descartes and the Port-Royal logicians in their *Grammaire générale et raisonnée.*[5] Dumarsais and Beauzée, the two most important contributors of linguistic articles to the *Encyclopédie,* are convinced of the need for a general grammar which would describe once and for all the universal features of all languages. The paradox of this doctrine is that those same *philosophes* who are dedicated to progress are equally committed to the "freezing" of language for all eternity.

The spread of empiricism and its doctrine that all knowledge is derived from the senses made inevitable the emergence of another theory of language based on the emotive power of words. According to Condillac, language does not emerge through human reason, but from the need of men to communicate their feelings and emotions. Consequently, language has to take into account impressions received through the senses. Thought and language are conditioned by the environment instead of by pre-established norms. Condillac contends that "le style, dans son origine, a été poétique, puisqu'il a commencé par peindre les idées avec les images les plus sensibles. . . ."[6]

Diderot's two major pronouncements on the theory of language mirror these two conflicting trends.[7] In the article "Encyclopédie" of 1753, he is the faithful disciple of the *grammairiens-philosophes,* and throughout his literary career, he never wavered in his position as to the importance of the *Grammaire générale et raisonnée.* Any thought of evolution in his attitude must be discarded outright.[8] He goes even further than the *grammairiens-philosophes,* and wants language to be fixed not only grammatically, but also semantically and phonetically. This idea of a "universal dictionary" haunts him to the very end of his life. He expresses the wish "qu'il n'y ait rien de vague dans l'expression. Il serait mal dans un livre philosophique d'employer les termes les plus usités, lorsqu'ils n'emportent avec eux aucune idée fixe, distincte et déterminée; et il y a de ces termes, et en très grand nombre. Si l'on pouvait en donner des définitions, selon la nature qui ne change point, et non selon les conventions et les préjugés des hommes qui changent continuellement, ces définitions deviendraient des germes de découvertes."[9]

This opposition to change is all the more striking because in the *Lettre sur les sourds et muets,* written two years before the "Encyclopédie" article, Diderot expresses an equal concern for the restraint imposed by language on the mobility of the mind. Like Condillac, he realizes that a language which is solely the product of reason is unable to convey things beyond the border of logic and reason. The poet who speaks and writes about those things uses a faulty instrument. Diderot makes a truly remarkable attempt to define poetic expression:

> Il passe alors dans le discours du poëte un esprit qui en meut et vivifie toutes les syllabes. Qu'est-ce que cet esprit? j'en ai quelquefois senti la présence; mais tout ce que j'en sais, c'est que c'est lui qui fait que les choses sont dites et représentées tout à la fois; que dans le même temps que l'entendement les saisit, l'âme en est émue, l'imagination les voit, et l'oreille les entend; et que le discours n'est plus seulement un enchaînement de termes énergiques qui exposent la pensée avec force et noblesse, mais que c'est encore un tissu d'hiéroglyphes entassés les uns sur les autres qui la peignent. Je pourrois dire en ce sens que toute poésie est emblématique.[10]

Like the Egyptian hieroglyph, then, poetic language can be made to *show* and *tell* at the same time. Diderot is rather vague about how this synthesis is to be achieved by the poet: he mentions some examples, taken from his favorite authors, of imitative harmony—sound and rhythm—in conjunction with vocabulary and subject matter. We have here an implicit admission of failure for the logical language of the Encyclopedists to convey anything else but truth of a general and impersonal nature.

How does theory influence practice in Diderot's writings? Forever present in his mind are two antagonistic theories of language, and this is bound to have some effect on the structural characteristics of his works and his style. And in view of these conflicting theories, what are Diderot's specific reactions to the contradiction of rhetoric and truth? We may perhaps apply to the literary craftsman in Diderot Wayne Booth's statement about the fiction-writer: "The author cannot choose to avoid rhetoric, he can choose only the kind of rhetoric he will employ."[11] It is my thesis that in Diderot's practice as a writer, we find classical rhetoric and a "rhetoric of truth" combined in a complex manner, unparalleled in his century. (The term *rhetoric,* as it is used here, includes the whole organization of works as well as the selection of specific stylistic devices.)

If we look into Diderot's choices of specific literary media—dialogues, letters, *pensées détachées*—we must keep in mind his rigorous classical training. Traditional rhetoric continued to dominate education in Diderot's time. It was studied not only as theory, but as a practical guide for future writers. In more than one way, the writer in Diderot was a man of order, a classic. He was exposed through his early training to constant contact with the masters of Greek and Latin literature. His enthusiasm for the French classic writers of the seventeenth century, themselves faithful followers of the Ancients, proves his genuine attachment to continuity in literature.[12] From his studies of the Ancients, he inherited above all a desire for the restructuring of reality according to an ideal order more satisfying to the mind. In his writings on drama, he stresses the importance of the three unities of time, place, and action advocated by the Ancients. In his art criticism, he develops his favorite idea of the *modèle idéal,* a reversion to a purely Platonic concept. The *Paradoxe sur le comédien* confirms the extent of his classical heritage. The thesis that the great actor should strive to be cool-minded and rational instead of giving way to his own personal emotions is rhetorical in intent. It implies an artificial display of emotion in the actor, just as rhetoric teaches the speaker to express emotion even if he does not feel it. It is perhaps in the *Paradoxe* that we see best at work the extent of Diderot's involvement in the dialectics of rhetoric and inner truth.

The *dispositio* of classical rhetoric is indeed present even in Diderot's seemingly most disorderly works. He is a man of the Enlightenment, conscious of his audience (even when this audience is restricted to some "happy few"). One of his first collections of essays, *De l'Interprétation de la nature,* is made up of disjointed thoughts, so to speak, but its didactic intent is obvious in the dedication: "Jeune homme, prends et lis."[13] At the same time, however, Diderot does not wish to appear openly as a persuader. His favorite writer is the one who "doit entrer furtivement dans l'âme de son lecteur, et non de vive force." Diderot goes on to say: "C'est le grand art de Montaigne qui ne veut jamais prouver et qui va toujours prouvant. . . ."[14] Seneca, another of his favorite writers, is an orator who does not compose but "exhorts" nevertheless. Diderot searches for a medium best adapted to this coexistence of naïveté and persuasion. He finds it first in the form of the *pensées* and the letter, then in the dialogue, which he uses consistently in the latter part of his literary career. The three media stress the spoken word, which Diderot deems more effective than written rendering as a tool of persuasion, again a rhetorical reason.

The dialogue, adopted by Diderot after his ill-fated experiments in the drama, is probably the best illustration of the dialectics of rhetoric and truth in his choice of a medium. It is strongly rhetorical in intent and at the same time translates a genuine inner conflict within Diderot himself. Let us recall the famous statement of his inner moral dilemma: "J'enrage d'être empêtré d'une diable de philosophie que mon esprit ne peut s'empêcher d'approuver et mon coeur de démentir."[15] In other words, he finds materialism strongly antagonistic to his moral standards. In adopting the dialogue form, Diderot follows the tradition of the Socratic and Platonic dialogues, resumed in the seventeenth century for the popularization of philosophical ideas. The dialogue replaces the treatise as a device to convince a non-specialized audience. Although it compels the reader to think for himself, it is still rhetoric in the sense that it wants to please and persuade. If we take at random any of Diderot's dialogues, we find them to be treatises in disguise. The *Entretiens sur Le Fils naturel,* a dialogue between a calm *Moi* and an eloquent and enthusiastic Dorval, turns out to be mere propaganda for Diderot's pet idea of the *drame bourgeois.* In the *Paradoxe sur le comédien,* the two interlocutors are not even named, signaling their total abstraction. One interlocutor dominates the discussion by expounding Diderot's ideas on the actor's need to remain cool and impassive, the second is a mere echo. This chorus effect, which gives liturgical tones to the dialogue, emphasizes its artificial character. This same effect appears in the *Rêve de d'Alembert*: the two main interlocutors seem engaged in an operatic duet, in which Bordeu, the spokesman and exponent of Diderot's materialistic philosophy, clearly dominates his female interlocutor. The digressions woven around d'Alembert's dream are also a didactic device. They serve a twofold purpose: to illustrate the mobility of the mind, a corollary of materialistic philosophy, and to clothe abstract concepts in an anecdotal form more palatable to the audience.

When Diderot attacks religion or religious life, we are faced with pure rhetoric of the classical brand. In the *Entretien d'un philosophe avec la Maréchale de* ———, we have a clearly defined rhetorical situation. The *philosophe* attempts to work particular effects upon his interlocutor, a devout Catholic lady, to convince her that atheists can and do practice virtue. He does so by utilizing a complete array of stock devices: philosophical tirades, sets of liturgical responses to lull the interlocutor's attention, rhetorical questions, feigned naïveté, disguised syllogisms, apologues to illustrate a difficult point. The relaxed tone of urbane conversation hardly conceals a tightly structured philosophical argument. *La Religieuse,* a novel which turns out to be a vigorous plea against religious life in the convents, also fits in the category of classical rhetoric. We are faced again with a clearly rhetorical situation: a young nun attempts to work specific effects, with feigned naïveté, on a would-be protector, by writing him a letter on the evils of convent life. This is pure *éloquence du barreau* with all the tricks attendant to it. The tightly structured progression of the narrative underlines Diderot's ability to "compose" when the subject matter demands it, a point which confirms the place of rhetoric in his writings.

If we now turn our attention to *inventio,* the poetic side in Diderot seems to dominate here: if there is innovation in Diderot's theory of literature, we find it more in his stylistic idiosyncrasies than in his choice of a literary medium. The artist and poet in him rebels against a faulty instrument which tends toward generalization. How can the writer transform a shabby and lifeless collection of words into a dynamic instrument? Diderot's answer is a *langue d'accents.* What are these *accents*? They constitute a new "rhetoric of nature" based on immediacy, direct imitation, that breaks the barrier of conventional expression with its array of semantic, grammatical, and syntactical rules. They exploit all the possibilities of linguistic illusion to counteract the discontinuity of language which freezes the fluid processes of thought.

Not that Diderot is willing to sacrifice completely purity of style for the sake of spontaneity: he remains too much of a classic for that. He recommends to new writers to polish their style and acknowledges that he knows, when he wants to, how to make his own sentence harmonious. He is a fervent admirer of Racine's style, one of the most polished and artificial in French literature. In his own writings, the *langage d'esprit* used by the *philosophes,* a sonorous classical period heavily adorned with clichés, often coexists with the *langage du coeur,* more lively and abrupt. His prose can be oratorical and bristle with rhetorical figures and tropes, when he is the *philosophe,* the crusading Encyclopedist preaching the ideology of the Enlightenment. Diderot's philosophical tirades, with their seemingly unending flow of anaphoric sentences and rhetorical questions, are there to prove his ability to use *le beau style.* I have particularly in mind the two celebrated tirades in *La Religieuse,* against convents and religious life, one of which I will quote to illustrate my point:

> Voilà l'effet de la retraite. L'homme est né pour la société; séparez-le, isolez-le, ses idées se désuniront, son caractère se tournera, mille affections ridicules s'élèveront dans son coeur; des pensées extravagantes germeront dans son esprit, comme les ronces dans une terre sauvage. Placez un homme dans une forêt, il y deviendra féroce; dans un cloître, où l'idée de nécessité se joint à celle de servitude, c'est pis encore. On sort d'une forêt, on ne sort plus d'un cloître; on est libre dans la forêt, on est esclave dans le cloître. Il faut peut-être plus de force d'âme encore pour résister à la solitude qu'à la misère; la misère avilit, la retraite déprave. Vaut-il mieux vivre dans l'abjection que dans la folie? C'est ce que je n'oserais décider; mais il faut éviter l'une et l'autre."[16]

The young nun, become orator, is apparently familiar with all figures of speech taught in treatises of rhetoric: tropes (the metaphor of the "ronces dans une terre sauvage"), *figurae verborum* (the parallelisms and antitheses of life in the forest and in the convents), *figurae sententiae* (the concluding rhetorical question). The passage is carefully structured to produce a cumulative effect, starting with a general statement on the harms of isolation, then proceeding to compare life in the wilderness and in convents, in a crescendo of parallelisms. The reader is flattered into believing that he is solving a riddle by himself: is convent life worse than life in the wilderness? The orator feigns to ignore the answer and leaves it to the reader to conclude, a classic rhetorical trick. In another passage, the young nun actually reveals the rhetorical intent of her orations by remarking that one of them had, at first, too much *esprit* and not enough *pathétique*,[17] a statement which brings to mind Plato's parallel of oratory and cookery in his *Gorgias!*

No rhetorical effect is more favored by Diderot than the threadbare metaphor, which he obviously did not create himself. In spite of his often-repeated preference for *la belle action* over *la belle page*, he does use an inordinate amount of facile images which stem from his classical training. We find the recurring image of the labyrinth, the philosopher is a Titan scaling the sky, the passions are deceitful Sirens, the controversial artist is a gladiator in the arena.[18] These trite images seem to invade his style when he is the Encyclopedist talking of virtue, tolerance, justice: thus, the most artificial aspect of his style appears when he speaks of Truth.

Coexisting with this oratorical flourish is the expression of Diderot's *own* truth. How does he express the verbal *hiéroglyphe* meant, in his thinking, to delete the time element from speech, and make *mots* and *choses* coincide? His artistic training with the *Salons* proved to be a momentous influence on his style. He started very early to assimilate writing to painting, and declared in the *Salon de 1767*: "C'est sur un grand mur que je regarde, quand j'écris," and "Il faut avoir vu, soit qu'on peigne, soit qu'on écrive."[19] He actually *sees* his favorite structure, found in his dialogues and novels alike, as "une chaîne d'expériences dispersées d'espace en espace, entre des raisonnements, comme des poids sur la longueur d'un fil suspendu par ses deux extrémités."[20] His use of visual imagery is found in bold metaphors that bring together hidden relationships. Paradoxically, his scientific treatises are the richest of all in visual imagery. The *Rêve de d'Alembert* has the often-quoted Diderotian metaphors of the memory as a harpsichord with vibrating strings, and the brain as a spider. I find the images in *De l'Interprétation de la nature*, a treatise on experimental philosophy, even more striking, since they emerge as miniature *tableaux*. Innate ideas without relationship to nature are likened to "ces forêts du Nord dont les arbres n'ont point de racines. Il ne faut qu'un coup de vent, qu'un fait léger, pour renverser toute une forêt d'arbres et d'idées."[21] The work of the experimental scientist, alternating between reasoning and the senses, evokes a beehive: "On a battu bien du terrain en vain, si on ne rentre pas dans la ruche chargée de cire. On a fait bien des amas de cire inutile, si on ne sait pas en former des rayons."[22]

Every non-linguistic device becomes desirable to supplement language. We may recall at this point Diderot's ideal situation for the production of creative expression: a man deprived of a sense, eyesight, hearing or speech, and forced to supplement it by gestures. He used to plug his ears in a theater, finding a good actor's gestures more meaningful than his speech. Inspired by these experiments with the stage and his art criticism, he paints small *tableaux* in his fictional works, showing his characters in silent poses, like this composition in *La Religieuse,* a novel that he himself describes as full of *tableaux pathétiques,* which should be perused by artists: "C'était dans l'hiver. Elle était assise dans un fauteuil devant le feu; elle avait le visage sévère, le regard fixe et les traits immobiles; je m'approchai d'elle, je me jetai à ses pieds et je lui demandai pardon de tous les torts que j'avais."[23]

Diderot transfers style beyond language, into the *accent,* i.e. intonation and imitative harmony. Rhythm becomes "l'image même de l'âme rendue par les inflexions de la voix."[24] One of Diderot's stylistic discoveries is his *style coupé.* It is a breathless, tense style, the utmost symbolization of thought by sentence structure, produced by a sequence of short sentences, making use of interjections, exclamation points, interrogations, asyndeton, and repetitions, generally accompanied by descriptions of gestures. Diderot uses it every time he wants to convey emotion in his dramas and novels. Here is a typical monologue by a worried father, from Diderot's play, *Le Père de famille*:

> Je n'entends plus rein. *(Il se promène un peu, puis il dit)* Asseyons-nous. *(Il cherche du repos; il n'en trouve point et il dit)* Je ne saurais . . . quels pressentiments s'élèvent au fond de mon âme, s'y succèdent et l'agitent! . . . O coeur trop sensible d'un père, ne peux-tu te calmer un moment! . . . A l'heure qu'il est, peut-être il perd sa santé . . . sa fortune . . . ses moeurs. . . . Que sais-je? . . . sa vie . . . son honneur . . . le mien . . . *(Il se lève brusquement, et dit)* Quelles idées me poursuivent![25]

Diderot's plays failed to gain acceptance with the public, but his *style coupé* remained one of his legacies to nineteenth-century playwrights.

At the extreme limit and close to silence is the literary cry, which Diderot admires in the dramas of Racine, Corneille, and Shakespeare. For him, this is an instance of the *sublime*, which he tries to emulate in *La Religieuse*, with the confession of the deranged Mother Superior, surrounded by silence: "Mon père, je suis damnée. . . ."[26]

Sound effects can also fill the gap between *words* and *things*. There is an often-quoted scene in *Jacques le fataliste* where an innkeeper's lengthy tale is constantly interrupted by outside interference from the inn. This may be the first instance in French of *littérature concrète*—whole books composed of mere words, images, the collective whispers of crowds—just as we speak of *musique concrète*. For Diderot, the spoken word must be framed by a whole system of surroundings in order to become meaningful.

This leads us to the stylistic expression of mobility. Diderot was a man in constant motion, as his contemporaries have often testified. Leo Spitzer has aptly remarked that Diderot's ". . . nervous system, philosophical system and stylistic system are exceptionally well-attuned."[27] He was first to use the refrain in prose to suggest automatism triggered by intense emotion. The process is associated with highly emotional characters like Rameau's Nephew and the deranged Mother Superior in *La Religieuse*. There is a very striking passage in *Le Neveu de Rameau*, where the Nephew is carried away by visions of the glory he would like to reach in the world of music. Words unleash patterns of repetition and gestures:

> Et c'est ainsi que l'on te dirait le matin que tu es un grand homme; tu lirais dans l'histoire des *Trois Siècles* que tu es un grand homme; tu serais convaincu le soir que tu es un grand homme; et le grand homme, Rameau le neveu, s'endormirait au doux murmure de l'éloge qui retentirait dans son oreille; même en dormant, il aurait l'air satisfait: sa poitrine se dilaterait, s'élèverait, s'abaisserait avec aisance, il ronflerait comme un grand homme; et en parlant ainsi, il se laissait aller mollement sur une banquette; il fermait les yeux, et il imitait le sommeil heureux qu'il imaginait. Après avoir goûté quelques instants la douceur de ce repos, il se réveillait, étendait ses bras, bâillait, se frottait les yeux, et cherchait encore autour de lui ses adulateurs insipides.[28]

Accumulations of verbs denoting movement are put to their most effective use when associated with essentially mobile characters like

Rameau and the Mother Superior. Past tenses shift to present without transition, to convey immediacy in *La Religieuse.* We must keep in mind that all the processes just described may seem commonplace to us, but they were a novelty in eighteenth-century French literature, which still favored the classical free-flowing longer period.

Diderot's role as a trailblazer in style is perhaps even better described as an affinity for stylistic commotions, which jolt the reader out of his intellectual comfort. They are the verbal rendition of Diderot's inner vision of a chaotic universe, ruled by chance, a vision which permeated his works of later years, *Le Neveu de Rameau* and *Jacques le fataliste.* Here we find Diderot's authentic self, at long last completely freed from the shackles of rhetoric. There seems to be no more effort to persuade, move, or teach. A recent critic calls these processes *variants aberrants,*[29] improbable combinations, deviations which make up the true definition of style. In a Diderotian text, these processes of rupture have in common an abruptness with a ring of sincerity unparalleled in the eighteenth century. *Jacques le fataliste,* this anti-novel with seemingly "missing pages," like its main character's conversation, contains some of the best examples. The basic process consists in an outside interference, which breaks up crystallized speech. The plot is built on the principle of interruption which life, i.e. chance, forces upon two minds with rigid convictions: the fatalist Jacques and the Master obsessed by his fixed memories of the past. The jolt in the reader's mind can be provoked by a sudden thought association, like the one occurring in the first lines of the novel. After stating, out of the blue, that "chaque balle qui partait d'un fusil avait son billet . . . ," Jacques declares, "Que le diable emporte le cabaretier et son cabaret!"[30] Jacques' memory has made the *saut étonnant* that so fascinated Diderot and shocks the reader: the bullet reminds Jacques of the tavern where he got drunk, which forced him to enlist in the army to avoid his father's punishment.

The list, or abrupt juxtaposition of items without obvious relationships, is a favored means to render the absurd. The list of Jacques' masters, with its accumulation of relative clauses, ("C'est lui qui me donna au . . . qui me donna à . . . qui me donna à . . ."[31]) is very effective in conveying the condition of the *Ancien Régime* valet, reduced to the status of object. Verbal disjunctions are also favored by Diderot for rendition of the absurd. A crowd description in a few words tells it all: ". . . et les voilà mêlés dans la foule, regardant tout, et ne voyant rien, comme les autres."[32] Or this succinct description of convent life in *La Religieuse*: ". . . elle est devenue folle, et elle est enfermée; mais la supérieure vit, gouverne, tourmente, et se porte bien."[33]

Of all the processes of disjunction, none is more favored by Diderot than the bold metaphor that helps make the *saut étonnant,* and brings together unforeseen *rapports.* In the middle of an otherwise sober discussion of the role of the actor in the *Paradoxe sur le comédien,* and without warning, Diderot's imagination takes flight: "Rien . . . ne ressemblerait tant à un comédien sur la scène ou dans ses études, que les enfants qui, la nuit, contrefont les revenants sur les cimetières, en élevant au-dessus de leurs têtes un grand drap blanc au bout d'une perche, et faisant sortir de dessous ce catafalque une voix lugubre qui effraie les passants."[34] To me, this is pure Baudelaire, in the middle of Enlightenment rhetoric.

Diderot's obsession with *rapports cachés* goes even beyond Baudelaire, and is sometimes closer to surrealism and all post-Freudian literature. Let us recall the definition of surrealism, a literary movement which "repose sur la croyance à la réalité supérieure de certaines formes d'associations négligées jusqu'à lui, à la toute-puissance du rêve, au jeu désintéressé de la pensée."[35] Diderot's own major interest in dreams dates back to one of his earliest literary works, *Les Bijoux indiscrets,* where he gives his strikingly modern definition of the function of dreams "qui, rapprochant des objets qui ne se tiennent que par des qualités fort éloignées, en composent un tout bizarre."[36] For him, as for the surrealists, it remains the function of the poet, the seer, to reveal these secret associations. The occult function attributed by Diderot to the poet seems to dwell more in this power of association than in his ability to create the *hiéroglyphe* of the *Lettre sur les sourds et muets,* which is not far removed from imitative harmony . . . and rhetoric. These nightmarish visions crop up unexpectedly in any Diderotian text, ambiguous, uncertain shapes, half-human, half-animal: fingernails swell and stretch to cover a human hand and form a horse's hoof,[37] a dog's head grows on a woman's body.[38] A fantastic world unfolds where humans appear with fingers stretched in compass shape, heads looking like globes, snails in place of eyes.[39] Some dream images seem obsessive to the point of appearing at different periods of Diderot's writing career: the dream motif of the inflated giant, with his head in the skies and outstretched legs and arms around the globe, appears within an interval of twenty years in three different texts.[40]

If Diderot tortures language to translate his innermost urges, he also describes at length the torture inflicted on the sensitive writer by words unfit for expression: this capitulation in front of language becomes a major Diderotian theme. This feeling of helplessness is never more acute for Diderot than when he is in front of a painting. His art criticism expresses his utter frustration as a writer to report what he sees. He is known as one of the creators of art criticism, yet he never ceases to question it. Rather than trying without success to report what he sees, he remakes the paintings with his own words. But nowhere is his pessimism more genuine than when it expresses the hopelessness, for human beings, of communicating with one another. Language is one of the major themes of his fictional works *Le Neveu de Rameau* and *Jacques le fataliste.* Both Rameau and Jacques, uncommonly talkative and emotional characters, are equally uncomfortable with words, and comment at length about their feelings. Diderot understands that a novelist cannot pretend to experiment with moral truths without sooner or later introducing the problem of language. The dialogue in *Le Neveu* is literally built on a series of semantic misunderstandings. Words, when passing from one interlocutor to the other, assume a different meaning, giving a new twist to the dialogue. Abstract passwords like *paix, génie, éducation* become objects of dispute. The philosopher uses abstract moral words in their generally accepted meaning, while Rameau gives them a new shade of meaning adjusted to his own vision of society, divided between masters and slaves. Here is an example of misunderstanding around the word *paix*:

> *Moi:* C'est sa mère qui se mêle de son éducation; car il faut avoir la paix chez soi.
>
> *Lui:* La paix chez soi? Morbleu! on ne l'a que quand on est le serviteur ou le maître, et c'est le maître qu'il faut être.[41]

For the *philosophe* (Moi), peace is the result of wisdom and mutual concessions; for Rameau, peace can only be the outcome of a fight. This is how the Nephew sums up the semantic gap: "... il pourrait arriver que vous appelassiez vice ce que j'appelle vertu, et vertu ce que j'appelle vice."[42] While the *philosophe* prides himself to tell only the truth, Rameau envies his linguistic facility, but only as an instrument of self-concealment: he reads the classics to find in them models of what one must *do* and not *say*, since he wishes to remain what he is, but to speak as society expects. Language becomes costume, mask, a protective wall for vice. The theme of language is so central to the fabric of the dialogue that it becomes the basis of moral metaphors: "... il y a une conscience générale, comme il y a une grammaire générale, et puis des exceptions dans chaque langue. ..."[43]

The dialogue between Jacques the fatalist and his Master is also doomed to failure, as each tells his own truth. The Master admits total capitulation in front of language when he orders to his servant: "... dis comme toi, je t'écouterai comme moi, et je t'en croirai comme je pourrai."[44] Jacques, the embodiment of Diderot's own dilemma, adores words as much as he mistrusts them. He is an inveterate speaker, aware of the falseness of language. As the novel unfolds, the tales told by the characters illustrate the vanity of all communication. The major tale by the innkeeper is a masterpiece of concealment, as she blends the story of Mme de La Pommeraye's revenge against an unfaithful lover with her own vision of a woman unhappy in her marriage, at the same time protesting that she tells things as they happened, without omitting or adding anything. Here again, the problem of language becomes the essence of the novel. Thus, Diderot's two major fictional dialogues end nowhere and illustrate the futility of language: the dialogue between universal Truth, Enlightenment rhetoric (the *philosophe*, the Master) and expressionism (the Nephew, Jacques) ends in an admission of failure. Communication breaks down and each side remains unchanged.

Nowhere is Diderot closer to the preoccupation of contemporary French linguistic theorists than when he lends these words to Jacques, ordered by his Master to say things as they happened: "Cela n'est pas aisé. N'a-t-on pas son caractère, son intérêt, son goût, ses passions, d'après quoi l'on exagère ou l'on atténue? Dis la chose comme elle est! . . . Cela n'arrive peut-être pas deux fois en un jour dans toute une grande ville."[45] Translated into the language of modern semanticists, Jacques is preoccupied by the gap between *signifiant* and *signifié.* The French semanticist Pierre Guiraud puts it this way: "Nous révisons nos concepts cependant que les mots gardent la trace de croyances anciennes et reflètent une idée de l'univers, et de l'univers et de l'homme qui n'est plus la nôtre."[46]

Thus, Diderot seems to combine in his theory and practice of style what looks to us, twentieth-century readers, like the best and the worst of the Enlightenment. In this he does not differ much from his contemporaries. To some degree they were all conscious of the linguistic resources of poetry, restrained by the demands of philosophy. However, Diderot's reaction to this dilemma is different in the sense that, instead of trying to find a compromise solution or ignore the problem, he brings it into the open. He uses it as the central theme of his major fictional works. And his style is, at times, so unusual and so interesting to us precisely because of the phenomenon of rupture brought about by an interference of the two trends, which can give birth to a poetic image in the middle of a scientific treatise.

Another remark comes to my mind by way of conclusion. In Diderot, theory and practice do not seem to coincide. He seems much more adventurous in his experiments with style than he is in his theories of language. His frequent mention of *rapports cachés* and his obsession with dreams point to a definite interest in the surreal. Had he been familiar with Freud, Diderot might have written the *Manifeste du surréalisme.* Like the surrealists, he groped for the essence of poetry. He was under the delusion of having found the key to poetry in the *hiéroglyphe* described in the *Lettre sur les sourds et muets.* Significantly, it is in a treatise on experimental science that he seems to have come closest to defining the true essence of poetry. The "esprit de divination" he attributes to the experimental scientist is built upon the perception of "des oppositions ou des ressemblances si éloignées, si imperceptibles, que les rêves d'un malade ne paraissent ni plus bizarres, ni plus décousus."[47] This is very close to the surrealists' search for striking images through sudden associations. In their search for the essence of poetry, which represents a return to innocence, a nostalgia for the primitive in ourselves, both Diderot and the surrealists discovered the resources of automatism. Diderot's opening statement in one of his works may be the first statement of *écriture automatique* in French: "Je laisserai les pensées se succéder sous ma plume, dans l'ordre même selon lequel les objets se sont offerts à ma réflexion, parce qu'elles n'en représenteront que mieux les mouvements et la marche de mon esprit."[48] This to me is the formulation by Diderot himself of the particular Diderotian essence, which seems so elusive to critics. However, as a spokesman for the Enlightenment, he could only oscillate from one pole to the opposite, from rhetoric to truth.[49]

NOTES

1 See his *Diderot's Chaotic Order* (Princeton: Princeton Univ. Press, 1974).

2 *Oeuvres complètes,* ed. R. Lewinter (Paris: Club français du livre, 1969–73), II, 482, 507; hereafter designated as O.C.

3 *Oeuvres romanesques,* ed. H. Bénac (Paris: Garnier, 1962), p. 717; hereafter designated as O.R.

4 O.R., p. 397.

5 Noam Chomsky borrows from the Port-Royal logicians his own theory of a "deep structure" underlying all languages. See his *Cartesian Linguistics* (New York: Harper and Row, 1966), pp. 31–51.

6 *Essai sur l'origine des connaissances humaines* (Paris: A. Colin, 1924), p. 149.

7 For a very perceptive study of Diderot's dilemma in front of language, see Herbert Josephs, *Diderot's Dialogue of Gesture and Language* (Columbus: Ohio State Univ. Press, 1969).

8 Some twenty years later, he stresses again the importance of the *Grammaire générale et raisonnée* in his *Plan d'une université,* for the Empress of Russia. See in O.C., XI, 785.

9 O.C., II, 458.

10 *Diderot Studies* (Geneva: Droz, 1965), VII, 70.

11 *The Rhetoric of Fiction* (Chicago: Univ. of Chicago Press, 1961), p. 149.

12 He never wavered on the importance of a knowledge of the classics for the future man of letters. For his position in later years, see O.C., XI, 792.

13 *Oeuvres philosophiques,* ed. P. Vernière (Paris: Garnier, 1964), p. 175; hereafter designated as O.P.

14 *Oeuvres complètes,* ed. J. Assézat and M. Tourneux (Paris: Garnier, 1875–77), II, 272–73. Hereafter designated as A.T.

15 *Correspondance,* ed. G. Roth and J. Varloot (Paris: Minuit, 1955–70), IX, 154.
16 *O.R.*, p. 342; for the other tirade on convents, ibid., p. 309.
17 Ibid., p. 309.
18 Eric Steel has methodically catalogued these images. See his *Diderot's Imagery* (New York: Corporate Press, 1941), pp. 48–77.
19 O.C., VII, 105, 219.
20 *O.P.*, p. 184.
21 Ibid., p. 185.
22 Ibid.
23 *O.R.*, p. 252.
24 *A.T.*, XI, 268.
25 O.C., III, 277.
26 *O.R.*, p. 383.
27 "The Style of Diderot," in *Linguistics and Literary History* (Princeton: Princeton Univ. Press, 1948), p. 135.
28 *O.R.*, p. 407.
29 Michael Riffaterre, *Essais de stylistique structurale* (Paris: Flammarion, 1971), p. 73.
30 *O.R.*, p. 493.
31 Ibid., p. 657.
32 Ibid., p. 622.
33 Ibid., p. 319.
34 *Oeuvres esthétiques,* ed. P. Vernière (Paris: Garnier, 1968), p. 309. Hereafter designated as *O.E.*
35 André Breton, *Manifestes du surréalisme* (1924–30; rpt. Paris: Gallimard, n.d.), p. 37.
36 *O.R.*, p. 160.
37 *O.P.*, p. 187.
38 *O.R.*, p. 162.
39 Ibid., p. 60.
40 Ibid., p. 117; *O.E.*, p. 308; *O.P.*, p. 334.
41 *O.R.*, p. 419.
42 Ibid., p. 449.
43 Ibid., p. 425.
44 Ibid., p. 544.
45 Ibid.
46 *La Sémantique* (Paris: P.U.F., 1965), p. 91.
47 *O.P.*, p. 197.
48 Ibid., p. 177.
49 *Sincerity* might have been a better word than *truth,* for this study. Henri Peyre puts it this way in his *Literature and Sincerity* (New Haven: Yale Univ. Press, 1963), p. 12: "*Truth* presupposes an adequacy with some objective criterion, or at least an inner coherency among our views on an exterior reality, which sincerity does not."

A Sweet Disorder: Atomistic Empiricism and the Rococo Mode of Vision

PATRICK BRADY

In the present essay, "vision" will not be taken as a synonym of "sight"; on the contrary, "sight" and "vision" will be taken as referring to two antithetical approaches to reality: representation (imitation, mimesis) and transformation (compensation, euphemization). In the domain of cultural periodization, each period style does not so much elaborate a view *of the world* as it creates a world *of its own,* which it presents to us as a coherent and self-consistent vision; and yet—we can scarcely say that this vision has been quite divorced from our manner of perceiving external reality.

Both poles, the representative and the transformative, are present in the rococo aesthetic, and indeed their co-existence is central to that aesthetic and explains why it is so complex and difficult to approach and has never yet been adequately interpreted. The rococo mode of transformation is the sugary coating on the rather bitter pill of empiricism (seen as threateningly reductive), and when, some half-century later, Cochin invents the term "rococo" in 1755 to complain that the confection of Louis Quinze furniture is altogether too fussy and "pretty,"[1] he is expressing the new attitude of a decade marked by the appearance of the *Encyclopédie,* Rousseau's *Discours,* the Lisbon earthquake, and *Candide.* It is in this critical half-century, the first part of the eighteenth century, that the rococo spirit developed. Two features of the rococo actually combine the two chief aspects of the style (reduction and compensation) in single synthetic manifestations; these are: in the plastic arts, the flowering of the *rocaille,* and in literature, the recourse to metonymy, to which we shall return later.

I shall first characterize the rococo mode of vision as ascertainable from a study of the visual arts, and secondly indicate the intimate relationship between this mode of vision on the one hand and rococo literature and the empirical, sensualist philosophy of Locke and his followers on the other. To clarify the historical framework, the Age of Rococo will be taken as roughly corresponding to the last seventy years of the life of Fontenelle (1687–1757).[2] Indeed, Fontenelle represents the rococo age to a remarkable degree, and not least through his combination of straightforward empirical approach to phenomena with rococo manner and embellishments.[3]

Symbiosis, Random Distribution, Loss of Hierarchy

When we examine the furnishing and interior decoration of the rococo, for which the term was first coined, we are struck by the remarkable degree of blending and melding of all elements into an unbroken whole which defies analysis. The rococo is essentially a symbiotic style, and a rococo interior is a seamless garment of many—but subtly interwoven—hues and textures. There is an elimination of the traditional hierarchy among the elements of the whole: table and wall are no longer distinguishable, each separately and each from the other, for the table is grafted onto the wall, the table is a part of the wall, the table *is* the wall: who is to say whether a two-legged rococo console is a table or a wall-ornament?[4] And does it matter? This of course is an insidious question, which challenges the received notion consecrating the importance of distinction, classification, and hierarchy.

Between 1719 and 1725, England saw the birth of the rococo garden, under the influence of Swift, Addison, and the author of *The Rape of the Lock,* that poet too often termed "Augustan" and too rarely called "rococo," Alexander Pope. The essence of the new approach is to leave "the contours of Nature untampered with,"[5] but this was interpreted as meaning abandoning "fine sett gardening" and replacing it by "as many Twinings and Windings as [a site] will allow."[6] This, of course, is precisely the same tendency as that which, in furnishing, will provoke Cochin's ridicule in the 1750s.

In rococo painting,[7] the disposition of figures in landscape settings is characterized by free distribution.[8] Moreover, the powerful dominance of the mythological-biblical-historical tradition represented by Poussin and Lebrun (and later by David) is rejected in the rococo—a development which constitutes an important further illustration of the tendency to eliminate notions of hierarchy. It is no doubt significant that both Watteau and Chardin were received into the Academy, whose categories were anachronistic, as masters in minor genres—the *fête galante* for Watteau and, in the case of Chardin, the *nature morte.* The inclusion of Chardin in the rococo may seem provocative—I have always excluded him myself, restricting the rococo to the more decorative style of Watteau, Pater, Lancret, Boucher, and Fragonard. But we must come to a deeper understanding of the rococo, both as an international aesthetic including artists like Hogarth and Tiepolo, and above all as a style made up of two components of which the decorative is only one, and a compensatory one, the other being a metonymic and realistic perspective represented by Watteau's "Enseigne de Gersaint" (an exception in his production) and the work of Chardin. This explains, among other things, the fact that Chardin limited himself to the pastel palette of the rococo—and it solves the hitherto insoluble mystery of his place in eighteenth-century painting.

When we come to literature, we find that the elimination of hierarchy typical of the rococo is characteristic of a work like Marivaux's *Vie de Marianne,* which offended the classicizing taste of critics like Desfontaines by combining subtlety and finesse of observation with what were considered disgustingly realistic elements ("éléments ignobles").[9] Another element of similar significance is what Desfontaines calls the excessive emphasis on subordinate features (again in reference to the work of Marivaux): "Ces moralités ne doivent être que l'accessoire, et elles sont le principal, contre toutes les règles de la nature."[10] There is a random look about the choice, disposition, and distribution of the constitutive elements. An aristocrat is not a more interesting object of study than is a coachman or a laundress; indeed, in rococo literature in general, a man is often less interesting than his brocaded lace, his fancy snuff-box, and his clouded cane, from which he derives most of his colour and visual appeal (the only appeal he has)—less interesting in fact to a lady than her lap-dog. The reduction of cultivated man (the aristocrat) to coachman on the one hand or to foppish clothes-horse on the other represents different modes of metonymic substitution. The destruction of hierarchy brings an emphasis on (and glorification of) the trivial, which in order to avoid ridicule generates an affectation of negligence. This studied negligence marks the poetry of the imitators of La Fontaine, such as Chaulieu, and La Fare. Finally, the free, plant-like development of the rococo arabesque is mirrored in the rococo prose style of Marivaux (which employs the meandering sentence of psychological exploration) and in his free manner of plot-construction.[11]

What are the philosophical bases of such as aesthetic? The rococo of the early eighteenth century is both preceded and followed by modes of the Classical aesthetic with their emphasis on order, system, hierarchy (Louis Quatorze furnishing and the painting of Lebrun, Louis Seize furnishing and the painting of David). In the realm of philosophy, the same evolution may be seen, with Cartesian deduction being dominant in the late seventeenth century (contemporary with French Classicism) and a return to system-building evident in the late eighteenth century (contemporary with the return to the neo-Classicism of David) in the thought of Rousseau and Kant. The interval is filled by the rococo in aesthetics, and in philosophy by the empiricism and sensualism stemming from Locke. What is more interesting is the fact that the tendencies we have discerned in the rococo aesthetic correspond closely with features of this philosophy. Empiricism, in its rejection of the guiding function of fundamental axioms and deductive method, attempts to observe reality rather than order it. It is true, of course, that empiricism also means Newton and Newton means an ordered universe: but the order implicit in the empirical perspective is so flexible and sophisticated that, like the rococo, it produces an impression, an illusion, of haphazard organization (or lack of organization, lack of system), free from order and restraint, from notions of hierarchy.

It is also true that Polignac's defense of Descartes (*Anti-Lucretius*) appeared as late as 1747, and that the dissemination of Locke's ideas in France is generally attributed chiefly to Voltaire's *Lettres philosophiques* (1734), followed by significant works like La Mettrie's *L'Homme machine* (1758), Diderot's *Lettre sur les aveugles* (1749), and Condillac's *Traité des systèmes* (1749) and *Traité des sensations* (1754). The late dates of these works tend to link French conversion from Cartesian to Lockean thought to the mid-century Enlightenment. The truth is, however, that the mid-century marks not the beginning of the triumph of inductive over deductive thinking but rather the completion of that triumph: it is in the *Discours préliminaire* (1751) of the *Encyclopédie* that d'Alembert declares: "Le goût des systèmes . . . est aujourd'hui presqu'absolument banni des bons ouvrages." This triumph of empiricism presages a swing to the other pole, represented by the reappearance of rationalistic, deductive thought in the work of Rousseau, which replaces sensation with sentiment.[12] The traditional division of the century into reason and sentiment is much less valid than a division into sensualistic empiricism followed by sentimental rationalism. Moreover, Locke's thought was both familiar and influential in France much earlier than this: his *Essay Concerning Human Understanding* was translated in 1700 (by Coste) and Le Clerc's *Abrégé de l'Essai* dates from even earlier.

Euphemization, Elongation, and Miniaturization

The rococo style has often been associated with the *rocaille*, a form of ornamentation which gives free reign to the imagination and whose strange shapes (not based on "distortion," as no point of departure in reality can be detected) suggest the visionary: "The forms in detail seem to be incessantly changing, splashing up and sinking back. What are they? Do they represent anything? Sometimes they look like shells, sometimes like froth, sometimes like gristle, sometimes like flames."[13] Is the rococo, then, essentially free, creative, tied to transcendence and the visionary?

In many ways, the contrary is true. The *rocaille,* in fact, while it is compensatory in shape (that is, as an autonomous whole), is essentially metonymic in function (that is, as part of a greater whole): while it appears to float about and settle at random, it actually comes to rest in places where it serves to conceal the structural organization of the architecture, as if to deny the latter's necessarily studied rationality.[14] The distinction, the hierarchy between wall and ceiling is thus denied. And of the two ways of viewing the *rocaille,* we have seen that the perspective central to the rococo mode of vision is that which subordinates the part to the whole—a perspective which consequently valorizes the metonymic rather than the compensatory role of the *rocaille.*

As the *rocaille* does in the plastic arts, so metonymy in the literary at first strikes us by its quality of lush and figurative evocation. Representing the whole by its most colourful part, it gives us a society in which man and woman, reduced to the social stereotypes of the Beau and the Coquette, are then replaced by their own exquisite garments and assorted knick-knacks like snuff-boxes and fans, clouded canes, tweezer-cases, scarlet plumes, flaxen wigs, and so on. There is a proliferation of exquisite objects and accessories rendered ephemeral both by the vagaries of fashion and their own intrinsic fragility. The visual effect is breathtakingly sumptuous and elegant.

Close examination, however, shows that this aspect of the use of metonymy is essentially compensatory—that is, euphemizing—for the prime thrust is not transformation but reduction. The emotional impoverishment characteristic of the rococo is typified by the obsession with toy pets (parrots, cats, lap-dogs, monkeys) with their guarantee of automatic response to affection. This is closely related to the obsession with *objets d'art.* Whereas poverty produces tribalization—dependence on human relations, especially of the family type—wealth produces isolation and alienation, and a preference for substitute relationships, the gradual erosion of true relationships being reflected in the movement from monkey to lap-dog to parrot to furniture (as in Gay's poem *To a lady on her passion for old china*). This alienation is caused not by a fetishism of the market (bourgeois) but by a fetishism of the object (aristocratic).

The human form as presented in rococo painting and sculpture is based, for its proportions, not on the Classical canon (the six heads of the "neo-Grec") but on the slender, elongated version characteristic of mannerism (ten heads)—a precursor of the rococo in several other ways as well.[15] The mannerist canon is ectomorphic:[16] it reduces the amount of flesh on the figure, and this absence signifies a devaluation of the fleshly, of the sensual aspect of Man.[17] (The opposite pole would be represented by the fleshy baroque figures used by Rubens.) This elongated canon may be used, as we find brilliantly done by El Greco, to exploit the reduction and hollowing of the flesh (which is taken to a much greater extreme [1-1-7 or 1-2-7][18] than in the rococo) to convey spirituality; but this is by no means the only type of suggestion which may be conveyed by the mannerist canon. When we come to Watteau, for instance, we find a more moderately ectomorphic canon (3-2-5) used in a rather different manner: its particular valorization of the slender, elongated body tends to suggest to us a world in which man is fragile and ephemeral—as are, by extrapolation, his sentiments, reflected in so many *Apologies de l'inconstance.*

A further tendency of the rococo is miniaturization, which finds expression on several different levels. Palace living is replaced by a more comfortable, informal life in *hôtels particuliers*; rooms are reduced in size so as to be cozy (as in the *petits appartements* introduced into Versailles by Louis XV); furniture is made lighter and smaller; more attention is given to tiny personal accessories which do not seem to threaten to dominate the wearer (although, as we have seen, they *did* come to outweigh him in importance); and paintings grew smaller in size from Watteau on. In the works of Pillement and Fragonard man is dwarfed by his surroundings (in Fragonard, an open landscape like the "Fête de Saint-Cloud"; in the earlier but more radical Pillement, the magnified plants and insects upon which he sits and plays). In sculpture we have the charming terra cotta miniatures of Clodion.

In literature, man's newly modest dimensions in relationship to the universe are reflected in works like *Gulliver's Travels* and *Micromégas*, both of which suggest not only that sometimes his smallness is quite evident but also that even when he appears a giant it is an illusion: all dimensions are relative. Moreover, literary works themselves grow smaller, whether *contes* or *vers de circonstance*. The fragile, ephemeral character of *compliments galants* and clay figurines reflects a fragmentation—a "miniaturization"—of *time* at this period, best expressed of course in those arts in which the temporal dimension is central, namely literature and music; in the plastic arts, this is expressed by the choice of the most rapid modes of execution, whether clay modelling or Watteau's exquisite sketches.

These further elementsof the rococo also relate to the philosophy of empiricism or sensualism:

Metonymy and a compensatory euphemization are natural companions for a way of thinking which proposes that we control our philosophical elucubrations and realize that the mind is the prisoner of the senses.

The slender figures which can be seen strolling or frolicking in rococo artworks have a fragility which suggests their lives and loves are as ephemeral as the delighted glance of the voyeur in the paintings of Fragonard, as fleeting as the *contact de deux epidermes* which will consummate their *amour-goût*. Miniaturization reflects a newly modest view of man's place in the endless universe which dwarfs him and whose vast expanses reduce to nothingness the micro-passions of rococo men and women. So keen is this new feeling of man's smallness, evanescence, and ultimate irrelevance that insignificant plants are magnified to tower above him. There are compensations here, too, however, for the severe and grave responsibilities of the erstwhile "Lord of Creation" have been exorcised and man finds himself surrounded by playfellows of equal insignificance: these giant grasses and insects which surround him intend no threat—they are playful equals in a new Eden, a Golden Age.

The rococo mode of vision is characterized by symbiosis and random distribution, by elongation and miniaturization. These tendencies may be observed in rococo interiors (the Hôtel de Soubise, the Amalienburg, the Palazzo Carignano in Turin), in a painting by Watteau or Fragonard, a statue from Vierzehnheiligen. There is a general devalorization of previously received socio-aesthetic values such as autonomy, order, hierarchy, moderation, and responsibility.

The relationship between such a mode of vision and a certain philosophical standpoint is already suggested in the empiricist's injunction "Observe before interpreting," as expressed in Fontenelle's story of *La Dent d'or,* which emphasizes the visual as against the intellectual. The Copernican revolution is completed by the Lockean: after the theocentrism of the Middle Ages, the anthropocentrism of the Renaissance in its turn is sceptically scrutinized and radically diluted, metaphysics is discredited, rationalistic deduction with its intuited axioms is abandoned, and primacy is now given to the phenomena registered by the senses, giving an unheard-of prestige to surface sense-impressions and shallow sensuality. In the face of this rejection of both reason and sentiment in favour of sensations, there developed a coldly realistic view of reality accompanied by desperate or cynical attempts to compensate by a hedonistic aesthetic of frothy voluptuousness. It is this double character of the rococo aesthetic which provides the clue to an understanding of the relationship between atomistic empiricism and the rococo mode of vision.

NOTES

1 "Le mot *rococo* . . . a été . . . employé pour la première fois en 1755 par le graveur Cochin" (*Encyclopédie des arts,* dir. L. Réau [Paris: Baschet, 1960], p. 318). See also *Enciclopedia Italiana* (Rome, 1949), p. 534: "Il nome rococo si trova per primo nel linguaggio corrente in Francia: Cochin a Parigi si vantava d'avere 'couvert le partisan du rococo d'une assez bonne dose de ridicule' " Cochin was no doubt referring to his articles in the *Mercure de France* in the early 1750s, such as his famous "Supplication aux orfèvres. . . ."

2 This period is suggested particularly for France: 1687 is the date of publication of Fontenelle's *Histoire des oracles* (relativism) and of Perrault's *Le Siècle de Louis le Grand* (modernism); another significant date is 1697, which saw Fontenelle elected Secrétaire perpétuel de l'Académie and the publication of Bayle's *Dictionnaire historique et critique* (skepticism). The dates vary somewhat, of course, from art to

art and from country to country: in poetry, for instance, the rococo appears earlier in England, later in Germany.

3 These two poles of his inspiration are represented by *La Dent d'or* on the one hand, with its emphasis on empirical observation as the only source of reliable information on reality, and his poetry and theatre on the other, with their links to the *précieux* and to Marivaux. The two tendencies are combined in a work like the *Entretiens sur la pluralité des mondes habités* (1686), where the content is modern in its scientific character while the manner and style are modern (i.e. rococo) in their urbane informality, so typical also of writers like Addison and Pope. Fontenelle's "scientific" position here is of course Copernican but also Cartesian, and as such rapidly superseded by Newton's *Principia* (1687); it is rather in a work like *La Dent d'or* that his espousal of empiricism makes him appear a proponent of the philosophy of the new century.

4 See Patrick Brady, "Rococo and Neo-Classicism," *Studi francesi,* 8, No. 1 (Jan.–April 1964), 34–49.

5 Desmond Fitz-Gerald, "Irish Gardens of the Eighteenth Century II: The Rococo," *Apollo,* NS 87, No. 79 (Sept. 1968), 206.

6 Fitz-Gerald, p. 204.

7 See Patrick Brady, "Rococo Painting: Some Points of Contention," *Studi francesi,* 16, No. 2–3 (May–Aug. 1972), 271–80.

8 See Wylie Sypher, *Rococo to Cubism* (New York: Random House, 1960), pp. 28–30.

9 See Patrick Brady, "Rococo Style in French Literature," *Studi francesi,* 10, No. 3 (Sept.–Dec. 1966), 428–37. In this novel, Marivaux may thus be said to combine the aesthetic of Watteau with that of Chardin.

10 Quoted in the Deloffre edition of Marivaux's *La Vie de Marianne* (Paris: Garnier, 1963), p. lxvii.

11 See Patrick Brady, "Rococo Style in the Novel: *La Vie de Marianne,*" *Studi francesi,* 19, No. 2 (May–Aug. 1975), 25–43.

12 The importance of this change is well brought out in Walter Moser, "De la signification d'une poésie insignifiante," *Studies on Voltaire and the Eighteenth Century,* 94 (1972), 277–415. Rousseau's manner represents a return to that of d'Urfé and Shaftesbury—pastoral, didactic, sentimental, regular, harmonious. In this we may perceive, to some extent, a Romantic return to certain tendencies of the Baroque era. Certainly, the replacement of sensation by sentiment as central principle indicates a rejection of Lockean sensualism which will be confirmed in the full flowering of the Romantic movement.

13 Nicolas Pevsner, *An Outline of European Architecture* (London, 1953), p. 195.

14 J. Philippe Minguet, *Esthétique du rococo* (Paris: Vrin, 1966), p. 157. See also Ernest Mundt, "The Rocaille in Eighteenth-Century Bavarian Architecture," *Journal of Aesthetics and Art Criticism,* 26, No. 4 (Summer 1968), 501–13.

15 The ectomorphic rococo canon here referred to is that used by Watteau, Lancret, Pater, Natoire, Gravelot, Lépicié, and in Germany by Rugendas and Nilson (Augsburg) and Peters (Cologne). Boucher, on the other hand, used an endomorphic canon (4-4-3, 5-4-3). Tiepolo prefers the mesomorph, but keeps the

tapered calf of the rococo. See Winslow Ames, "Some Physical Types favoured by Western Artists," *Gazette des Beaux-Arts,* 44 (Sept. 1954), 110–11 and elsewhere.

16 The characterization of any particular somatotype as endomorphic (dominance of the digestive), mesomorphic (dominance of the muscular), or ectomorphic (dominance of the nervous and sensory) is derived from William Sheldon's *The Varieties of Human Physique* (New York, 1940) and *The Varieties of Temperament* (New York, 1942).

17 Mannerist painting can convey sensuality, but only through a compensatory nudity (in which the flesh is emphasized not by its mass but by its exposure); it can be erotic, but for this it must depend on situations instead of forms.

18 These triple figure-clusters reflect the share of endomorphy, mesomorphy, and ectomorphy (each scored out of a maximum of seven) visible in the type under discussion.

Parodies and Imitations of Johnson in the Eighteenth Century

WILLIAM KENNEY

By labeling Johnson "Pomposo" and "Pensioner Sam," Charles Churchill and John Wilkes did much to develop the negative response to Johnson in his own time.[1] They were among the most talented of those who were hostile to Johnson, for their abuse has style and wit. They were followed by men vastly inferior to themselves like William Kenrick and James T. Callender, whose invective often bordered on madness. Indeed most of the abuse heaped upon Johnson in hundreds of attacks was singularly mindless. The parodists, however, were sometimes an exception. Since parody attempts to imitate cleverly an author's style, it imposes certain restraints that a writer interested merely in personal abuse does not know. The parodist cannot vent his hostility in denunciation; he must control it and carefully study his author if he is to imitate his manner with any success.

Parody is based upon imitation, but are all imitations parodies? The distinction is usually made that, while an imitator merely reproduces a manner, a parodist distorts it in order to amuse. Imitation has been called the highest form of flattery; often a beginning writer, wishing to develop his own voice, chooses for practice the style of some author that he greatly admires. Fanny Burney, as will be shown, was deeply influenced by Johnson and imitated him to some degree. Sir Joshua Reynolds, longing to hear his deceased friend's voice once more, nostalgically reproduced Johnson's conversational manner in dialogue form.

Parodists, on the other hand, have as their underlying purpose a desire to make fun of a writer. Their tones vary from gentle teasing to savage ridicule, depending upon their attitudes toward their subjects. A friend of an author may use a little good-natured raillery as he lightly exaggerates some mannerism. Another may wish to burlesque a style or travesty a particular work. Mrs. Barbauld, for example, wrote a delightful travesty of one of Johnson's *Ramblers* and his attitude toward romances. An enemy, on the other hand, may try to make an author look foolish by trivializing his ideas or blowing them up out of all proportion. Archibald Campbell, detesting Johnson's style, wildly inflated it.

Johnson defines parody as "a kind of writing, in which the words of an author or his thoughts are taken, and by a slight change adapted to some new purpose."[2] He himself was skilled in the art of ridicule. Through parody he deflated the pretensions of political figures, critics, and translators. Well known is his little rhyme making fun of the ballad-writing efforts of Percy and Warton. He applied simple diction to an inane subject to get his effect:

I put my hat upon my head,
And walk'd into the Strand,
And there I met another man
Who's hat was in his hand.[3]

Johnson was parodied very early in his career. In March, 1738, he published an Ode praising Edward Cave in the *Gentleman's Magazine* and condemning his detractors.[4] The next month one of the detractors published an answering Ode in the *London Magazine.*[5] But real parody did not begin until the *Rambler* had established his fame. In 1752 Bonnell Thornton parodied Johnson's tendency to use allegory and personification. He wrote a mock *Rambler,* numbered it 99999, and described in pompous terms the human body from the brain to the feet.[6] The longest parody of the *Rambler,* indeed one of the most elaborate and savage treatments of any of Johnson's works, was Archibald Campbell's *Lexiphanes.* Campbell, nicknamed Horrible because of his personal appearance, was a purser in the navy. During a long voyage he had plenty of time to read through a stack of *Ramblers,* the only diversion available to him. He was intensely bored and wrote *Lexiphanes* to castigate Johnson for the heaviness of his style, claiming that the purpose of his attack was to return English to its original purity. It is set in the form of a dialogue in which Johnson bores everyone with his nearly unintelligible rhapsodies. The repulsive climax comes when he is given an emetic that forces him to vomit up most of his hard words. This passage was inspired by the screech-owl of *Rambler* No. 59:

> From this assemblage of festivity we will unanimously extrude those screech-owls whose only care is to crush the rising hope, to damp the kindling transport, and allay the golden hours of gaiety with the hateful dross of grief and suspicion. Such is Suspirius, whom I have now known fifty-eight years and four months, who has intercepted the connubial conjunction of two hundred and twenty six reciprocal hymeneal solicitors by prognostications of infelicity, and has never yet passed an hour with me in which he has not made some attack upon my tranquillity, by representing to me, that the imbecillities of age, and infirmities of decrepitude are coming fast upon me. Indeed to those whose timidity of temper subjects them to extemporaneous impressions, who suffer by fascination, and catch the contagion of misery, it is extreme infelicity to live within the compass of a screech-owl's voice.[7]

The elements of Johnson's style usually parodied were the diction, the long sentences, the parallelism, the tendency toward allegorizing and personifying, the alliteration, and the inversions. Campbell had a certain feeling for sentence structure and balance, and he used some of Johnson's phrasing. But his lumping together of hard words was something Johnson rarely did, and it soon becomes wearying. Interestingly enough, *Rambler* No. 59 is less formal than some of Johnson's other essays. It is straightforward, and the diction is relatively simple. A crucial point that Campbell and other parodists missed is that Johnson had not one style but many, depending upon occasion and subject. Campbell published an even less effective parody three months after *Lexiphanes* called *A Sale of Authors.*

The main dilemma facing parodists of Johnson was that, while they might understand his manner, they could not grasp the complexity of his thinking. In our time discussions of style usually do not separate form from content, but in the classical period the distinction was an accepted one. While parodists might imitate Johnson's diction, his long sentences, his varieties of parallelism, they could not understand his mind. As Edmund Burke exclaimed to Boswell over an imitation, "It has all his pomp without his force; it has all the nodosities of the oak without its strength."[8] Only one parodist was singled out by Johnson for special praise. Letitia Aikin, better known as Mrs. Barbauld, wrote a mock-*Rambler* called "On Romance. An Imitation." Of it Johnson said, "She has imitated the sentiment as well as the diction."[9]

So close indeed is the essay to his thought and manner that many have suggested that he could have inserted it among his *Ramblers* without any difference being noted. Yet there is the exaggeration that makes it definitely a parody, although, unlike Campbell's, it is a good-natured one. It echoes several essays in which Johnson tries to account for the popularity of fantasy over more realistic forms of literature, but Mrs. Barbauld, with delicious irony, selects as her primary target *Rambler* No. 121, in which Johnson warns of the dangers of imitation. Johnson writes:

> It might be conceived, that of those who profess to forsake the narrow paths of truth every one may deviate towards a different point, since though rectitude is uniform and fixed, obliquity may be infinitely diversified. The roads of science are narrow, so that they who travel them, must either follow or meet one another; but in the boundless regions of possiblity, which fiction claims for her dominion, there are surely a thousand recesses unexplored, a thousand flowers unplucked, a thousand fountains unexhausted, combinations of imagery yet unobserved, and races of ideal inhabitants not hitherto described.[10]

Mrs. Barbauld uses his diction and sentence structure as she gently mocks his ideas:

> The gloom of solitude, the languor of inaction, the corrosions of disappointment, and the toil of thought, induced men to step aside from the rugged road of life, and wander in the fairy land of fiction; where every

> bank is sprinkled with flowers, and every gale loaded with perfume; where every event introduces a hero, and every cottage is inhabited by a Grace. Invited by these flattering scenes, the student quits the investigation of truth, in which he perhaps meets with no less fallacy, to exhilarate his mind with new ideas, more agreeable, and more easily attained: the busy relax their attention by desultory reading, and smooth the agitation of a ruffled mind with images of peace, tranquillity, and pleasure: the idle and the gay relieve the listlessness of leisure, and diversify the round of life by a rapid series of events pregnant with rapture and astonishment; and the pensive solitary fills up the vacuities of his heart by interesting himself in the fortunes of imaginary beings, and forming connections with ideal excellence.[11]

The single most popular form of parody involved the ransacking of Johnson's *Dictionary* for large words and the stringing of these together in paragraphs or stanzas. This type was doubtless so popular because it was so easy. It takes no imagination to pull words out of context and use them in ways Johnson never intended; one does not need to have much knowledge of his works. Again and again words like *adscititious, ablactation, concatenation, pedestrious,* and *salsamentarious* were put into letters, dialogues, essays, and poems as a means of ridiculing Johnson's vocabulary. Often hard words were applied to trivial subjects. Typical was the person who took the name Mimos in the *Monthly Miscellany* of March, 1775, for "A Pedestrious Ramble from Hyde-Park Corner, to Farnham. Written for the Encouragement of Johnson's Dictionary." This parody and others like it quickly deteriorated into monotonous collections of polysyllables.

The best parody of the *Dictionary* trivialized Johnson's language and his seriousness of purpose, but it did so in an amusing way. Boswell praised the result. George Colman, the dramatist and essayist, drew up mock proposals for a dictionary of "Colloquial Barbarisms," as opposed to the formal words of Johnson's work. He asserts that unless the scholar knows the meaning of low terms, he will never be able to understand contemporary culture: "The Ebullitions of Convivial or Epistolary Humour, and the Sallies of Dramatick Hilarity, the Lucubrations of the Periodical Essayist, the Sportive Vein and Dry Intelligence of our Diurnal, Nocturnal, and Hebdomadal Historians, are almost totally unintelligible for want of an adequate interpretation."[13] He goes on to make fun of the apologetic tone of Johnson's own proposals: "Annexed to this letter is a short specimen of the Work, thrown together in a vague and desultory manner, not even adhering to alphabetical concatenation. The whole will be comprised in two Folio Volumes, and will appear some time within the ensuing twenty years."[14]

He ridicules Johnson's definitions by taking low words and giving their meanings in formal language. "Higgledy-piggledy" he renders as "Conglomeration and Confusion." "See-Saw" becomes "Alternate Preponderation," while "Tit for Tat" is defined as "Adequate Retaliation."[15]

The *Rambler* and the *Dictionary* were drawn on for most parodies, but other works also received attention. In the *Scots Magazine* in 1783 appeared a moderately successful take-off of *A Journey to the Western Islands of Scotland.* The author has Johnson in Ireland, leaving Dublin in a coach with two high-born ladies and a clergyman to visit the villa of one Colonel Marlay at Celbridge. The Scottish journey is often echoed; laurel trees, for example, are the only evergreens at Celbridge. Johnson's sense of history is suggested in references to Swift and Vanessa. More important, the author catches Johnson's feeling for the poor: "The poverty of the lower class of people in Ireland is generally imputed to laziness; but sagacity will not rest satisfied with a solution, especially when it is considered that the risk of a halter is intuitively preferable to the certainty of famine, and that the rags of these miserable bipeds might be mended with less trouble than they are worn; and in a shorter time than, if they are shaken off, they can again be indued."[16] But the author weakens his effect by resorting to heavy-handed burlesque. He has Johnson, while exploring the Liffey, fall in and escape drowning only by a hanging on to the tail of a cow.

The best-known parody of the *Lives of the Poets* was a book-length effort by John Young, Professor of Greek at Glasgow. Young pretended that Johnson was writing an elaborate critique of Gray's *Elegy.* Critical opinion was sharply divided in evaluating Young's effort. Boswell called it "the most perfect imitation of Johnson."[17] Sir Walter Scott agreed.[18] Horace Walpole, on the other hand, found it confusing and working at cross-purposes.[19]

Young's method was to take Johnson's critical approach—which combined generalizations with close attention to concrete aspects of imagery and diction—and push it to absurdity. He thus made Johnson a quibbler and, ultimately, a bore. The cleverest lines in the whole long work may be those that echo Johnson's comment on the personification of the Thames in the Eton Ode. Johnson said: "His supplication to father Thames, to tell him who drives the hoop or tosses the ball, is useless and puerile. Father Thames has no better means of knowing than himself."[20] Young, referring to the Owl's complaining to the moon, writes, "The idea of the Owl's *complaining* is an artificial one; and the views on which it proceeds absurd. Gray should have seen, that it but ill befitted the *Bird of Wisdom* to complain to the Moon of an intrusion, which the Moon could no more help than herself."[21]

More typical of the work is this tedious passage, in which Young parodies Johnson's criticism of Gray's language:

> When I am told that 'all the Air a solemn stillness holds,' I hestitate, and endeavour to discover which of the two is the holder, and which is the held. If it is the *Air* that holds the stillness, too great liberty is taken with the verb; and if it is the stillness that holds the Air, the action is too violent for so quiet a personage: but the sound was necessary, to assist the bell-wedders to complete the lulling of the *folds*.[22]

Some interesting parodies and imitations were composed by members of Johnson's own circle. Boswell, prompted by a growing dislike of Mrs. Piozzi, struck at her by ridiculing the style of Johnson's occasional verse, which she delighted in printing as part of her memorabilia.[23] While Boswell struggled to write his *Life* in the years following Johnson's death in 1784, Mrs. Piozzi published with comparative ease her *Anecdotes* and letters. Boswell was made jealous by evidence of the closeness of her relationship with Johnson and angered by the fact that she hardly mentioned him at all. He decided to ridicule her by adding to a mock epithalamium that he had written in 1781, the day after Henry Thrale's funeral, in which he had depicted, with a shocking lack of taste, Johnson courting the widow. He updated and developed this poem, calling it *Ode by Dr. Samuel Johnson to Mrs. Thrale upon her Supposed Approaching Nuptials.* He published it in 1788 but had it predated four years to give it verisimilitude. Although Boswell campaigned energetically to make it known, he had no success.

Boswell's *Ode* is mean-spirited. Johnson's occasional verse never meant to wound. It was light and often whimsical as he took for subjects Mrs. Thrale's birthday, Queeney's new dress, or the coming-of-age of Mrs. Thrale's wayward nephew. Boswell's *Ode,* on the other hand, crudely sacrifices Johnson's dignity as it attacks a woman whose hospitality Boswell himself had often enjoyed. Neither jealousy nor the frustrations over the writing of the *Life* can excuse the reference to Johnson's long dead wife in the third stanza:

> To rich felicity thus rais'd,
> My bosom glows with amorous fire;
> Porter no longer shall be prais'd;
> 'Tis I MYSELF am *Thrale's Entire!*[24]

The styles of Fanny Burney and Johnson were so similar that they were sometimes wrongly thought to have collaborated. Undoubtedly he influenced her, but it must be noted that in her first novel, *Evelina,* she already shows many of the formal traits that parodists usually associated with him. *Cecilia* is generally acknowledged to be the novel that reflects the most Johnsonian influence. The last paragraph, for example, not only reproduces Johnson's sentence structure and parallelism, but also imitates his sentiments. Enduring happiness is nowhere to be found:

> The upright mind of Cecilia, her purity, her virtue, and the moderation of her wishes, gave to her in the warm affection of Lady Delvile, and the unremitting fondness of Mortimer, all the happiness human life seems capable of receiving:—yet human it was, and as such imperfect! she knew that, at times, the whole family must murmur at her loss of fortune, and at times she murmured herself to be thus portionless, tho' an HEIRESS. Rationally, however, she surveyed the world at large, and finding that of the few who had any happiness, there were none without some misery, she checked the rising sigh of repining mortality, and, grateful with general felicity, bore partial evil with chearfullest resignation.[25]

Late in his life Sir Joshua Reynolds developed a desire to imitate Johnson's talk. The result was two dialogues that he circulated among friends.[26] They certainly rank with the very best imitations, probably because Sir Joshua had heard Johnson speak so often that he could reproduce his very tone and cadence. The dialogues concern David Garrick, whom Johnson considered so much his property that only he could blame or praise him. The first dialogue shows Johnson censuring Garrick and is called "Johnson against Garrick." The second, filled with praise, is "T' Other Side." Reynolds leads into the subject by goading Johnson into speaking. He slyly pretends that he has a "weighty matter"—which turns out to be predestination—on which he merely wants Johnson's opinion. Johnson immediately examines his motives:

> No, Sir, you meant no such thing; you meant only to show these gentlemen that you are not the man they took you to be, but that you think of high matters sometimes, and that you may have the credit of having it said that you held an argument with Sam Johnson on predestination and free will; a subject of that magnitude as to have engaged the attention of the world, to have perplexed the wisdom of man for these two thousand years; a subject on which the fallen angels, who *had yet not lost all their original brightness,* find themselves in *wandering mazes lost.* That such a subject could be discussed in the levity of convivial conversation, is a degree of absurdity beyond what is easily conceivable.[27]

Here is Johnson in all his glory: the bow-wow manner, the learned references to *Paradise Lost,* the hatred of cant, the strong belief that certain matters should not be brought up in conversation. Most important, Reynolds shows that Johnson's conversation did not arise spontaneously. He had a tendency to remain silent unless he was goaded into speaking.

Parody is at best a minor literary form. A lesser writer tries to make fun of a greater one, and often he does not succeed too well because he cannot comprehend the genius of his intended victim. Johnson, like Shakespeare, is difficult to ridicule because what makes him great is beyond imitation. Parodists cannot reproduce the complexity of his thinking or the variety of his styles. Yet, however weak they are, they do serve a purpose. They testify to his fame and give us some ideas about his manner. And they did begin a tradition that has lasted to the present time. Modern parodists have called on Johnson for his posthumous views on such diverse figures and topics as Wordsworth and Coleridge,[28] Bernard Shaw,[29] and American Prohibition.[30]

NOTES

1 For a thorough study of eighteenth-century attacks on Johnson see Helen Louise McGuffie, "Samuel Johnson and the Hostile Press," Diss. Columbia Univ. 1961. For a listing of stylistic studies of Johnson, including important ones by the late W. K. Wimsatt, see James L. Clifford and Donald J. Greene, *Samuel Johnson: A Survey and Bibliography of Critical Studies* (Minneapolis: Univ. of Minnesota Press, 1970), pp. 190–93.

2 *A Dictionary of the English Language* Vol. II (London: Knapton, etc., 1755).

3 *Poems,* ed. E. L. McAdam, Jr., with George Milne, *The Yale Edition of the Works of Samuel Johnson* (New Haven: Yale Univ. Press, 1964), VI, 269.

4 *Poems,* pp. 40–42.

5 *Poems,* pp. 42–43.

6 *Have at You All, or The Drury Lane Journal,* 30 Jan. 1752, pp. 69–71.

7 *Lexiphanes, A Dialogue Imitated from Lucian and adapted to present times* (London: J. Knox, 1767), pp. 9–10.

8 *Boswell's Life of Johnson,* ed. G. B. Hill, revised and enlarged by L. F. Powell (Oxford: Clarendon Press, 1934), IV, 59.

9 *Life,* III, 172.

10 *The Rambler,* ed. W. J. Bate and Albrecht Strauss, *The Yale Edition of the Works of Samuel Johnson* (New Haven: Yale Univ. Press, 1969), IV, 282.

11 J. and A. L. Aikin, *Miscellaneous Pieces, in Prose* (London: J. Johnson, 1775), pp. 42–43.

12 *Life,* IV, 387–88.

13 George Colman, "Letter from LEXIPHANES," *Prose on Several Occasions* (London: T. Cadell, 1787), II, 92–93.

14 Colman, II, 93.

15 Colman, II, 94.

16 "A Tour to Celbridge, in Ireland," *Scots Magazine,* October, 1783, p. 518.

17 *Life,* IV, 392.

18 *The Croker Papers. The Correspondence and diaries of . . . John Wilson Croker,* 2nd ed., rev. (London: J. Murray, 1885), II, 34.

19 *Horace Walpole's Correspondence with William Mason,* ed. W. S. Grover Cronin, Jr., and Charles H. Bennett, *The Yale Edition of the Correspondence of Horace Walpole* (New Haven: Yale Univ. Press, 1955), XXIX, 308.

20 "Gray," *Lives of the English Poets,* ed. George Birkbeck Hill (Oxford: The Clarendon Press, 1905; rpt. New York: Octagon Books, 1967), III, 434–35.

21 John Young, *A Criticism of the Elegy Written in a Country Church Yard; Being a Continuation of Dr. J–n's Criticism on the Poems of Gray* (London: G. Wilkie, 1783), p. 17.

22 Young, p. 19.

23 For a study of the relationship see Mary Hyde, *The Impossible Friendship: Boswell and Mrs. Thrale* (Cambridge, Mass.: Harvard Univ. Press, 1972).

24 As quoted in Hyde, p. 131.

25 *Cecilia, or Memoirs of an Heiress* (London: T. Payne, 1782), V, 398.

26 "Sir Joshua's Two Dialogues Illustrating Johnson's Manner of Conversation," *Portraits by Sir Joshua Reynolds,* ed. Frederick W. Hilles (New York: McGraw Hill, 1952), pp. 101–19.

27 Reynolds, pp. 105–6.

28 Edmund Blunden, "Lives of the Poets: If Dr. Johnson Had Lived Rather Longer," *Times Literary Supplement,* May 20 and 27, 1955, pp. 276, 292.

29 F. L. Lucas, "Literary Trifling," *Nation-Athenaeum,* November 16, 1929, pp. 249–51.

30 Owen Wister, *Watch Your Thirst: A Dry Opera in Three Acts, with a Preface by Samuel Johnson* (New York: Macmillan, 1923).

Faith in the Enlightenment: Voltaire and Rousseau Seen by Michelet

OSCAR A. HAAC

Even should it be true, as E. D. Hirsch asserts, that later critics are more apt to discover the truly valid meaning of works of literature than even their authors themselves,[1] Michelet would hardly appear today as one of these superior modern critics; however, like many members of the romantic generation inbued with the thought of the Enlightenment, raised reading the *philosophes,* his portrayals of Rousseau and Voltaire, his debt to them, his description of their importance within the context of French history, did much to keep them before the public eye at a time when many opinions were negative.[2] More than that, his enthusiasm and powerful evocations did much to preserve their influence and constitute an important chapter in their afterlife.

His activity is naturally divided into two periods, separated by a personal crisis (1839–45) which greatly affected his evaluation of the past. Our discussion will similarly be in two parts: the first devoted to his readings, early references, and developing philosophy (for some years he planned a career of teaching both history and philosophy) and to the events which altered his orientation; the second will study the later years which include most of his discussion of the *philosophes,* in the *Histoire de la Révolution française* (1847–53) and later in his account of the eighteenth century, in volumes 15, 16, and 17 of the *Histoire de France* (1863, 1866, 1867). We shall find that by this time Rousseau and Voltaire have become symbols, foci of his ideology, keys to his philosophy of history; his descriptions evoke their life and, at the same time, express his world-view; they do this so effectively because, for the most part, his references are extensive, concrete, well-informed, never denuded of reality even when they clearly transcend it.

Michelet's affection for the *philosophes* can be traced back to the early days when, at the *pension Mélot,* he and his close friend, Poinsot, were carried away by their intellectual interests, and to the days at the *lycée Charlemagne,* where the frail, poverty-stricken boy took refuge in academic excellence; when his work for the *lycée* was done, he steeped himself in his beloved books and took long walks to meditate and converse with his favorite authors. We are not surprised to find that the *Journal de mes lectures* of 1819–20 bears witness to his methodical reading of Rousseau and Voltaire, first concurrently, then with a concentration on Voltaire who is represented by over twenty titles.[3] This indicates an increasing interest in history more than an absolute preference, for, by temperament, Michelet stood closest to Rousseau. Like him he kept a diary and the day he undertook to expand it into a full narrative, in his *Mémorial* (dedicated to Poinsot, who died), he proposed that Rousseau should not remain the only individual known to the world.[4] A religious conversion, in 1816, had brought him close to the spirit of the *Profession de foi du vicaire savoyard* and the course in philosophy he taught at the Ecole Normale Supérieure in 1827 still grows directly out of this influence which, by then, has been reinforced by the idealism of the Scottish philosophers, Reid and Stewart, and the anti-Cartesian orientation of Vico.[5]

In this course, Michelet distinguishes the self, i.e., the individual, and the non-self, i.e., society. Like Rousseau, he introduces conscience as the moral guide and as the supreme evidence of the immortality of the soul. This is so important because of the essential role he assigns to moral philosophy: "La philosophie . . . est la science de la nature de l'homme. C'est enfin l'art d'améliorer et de diriger l'homme individuel et l'espèce humaine."[6] By way of his conscience, man, he asserts, has access to eternal truth and senses the mandates of Providence. Rousseau affirms: "Si les vérités éternelles que mon esprit conçoit pouvaient souffrir quelque atteinte il n'y aurait pour moi nulle espèce de certitude";[7] so Michelet: "J'aimerais mieux . . . croire à toutes les absurdités, que renoncer aux vérités fondamentales qui se cachent sous ses formes."[8] This idealism found support also in Voltaire, whose remarks appended to the *Essai sur les moeurs* conceive of history as "l'histoire de l'esprit humain."[9] Thus Rousseau's social concerns, identified with the classical motto, *vox populi vox dei,* merge with Voltaire's activism, supported by Vico's concept of man shaping his destiny, of man as his own Prometheus. Rousseau provides the concepts of *sociabilité* and *peuple* (the non-self) and Voltaire that of the power of reason and of the individual (the self) which is in turn strengthened by Rousseau's divine voice in us (conscience). In all this "esprit" and "raison," the heart and the mind, are seen as complementary and not antithetical. In the *Journal de mes idées* of 1829, Rousseau is likened to Abelard and Voltaire to Erasmus.[10]

Naturally, references to the *philosophes* are scarce in the historical works of this period, the *Précis* for use in secondary schools, the *Histoire romaine,* the history of France in the Middle Ages. Meanwhile tragedy entered Michelet's life. The death of his wife Pauline (1839), who had never been his intellectual associate and who had floundered in despondency and drink, caused Michelet to blame himself intensely. Then came the death from cancer of Madame Dumesnil, the first woman to share his interests and deep affection (1842). Just before her death she reverted to the Church and her Jesuit confessor, the abbé Coeur; she showed Michelet her crucifix and called herself *la religieuse.*[11] All this constitutes a traumatic experience which accounts for the violent attacks first against the Jesuits—in the course he taught jointly with Quinet in 1843[12]—then against priests and confessors who abuse the confidence of defenseless women—in *Du Prêtre, de la femme et de la famille* and in the course of 1845. As Michelet put it during the trip to Germany he undertook just after the death of Madame Dumesnil to overcome the shock, "L'action, l'action, l'action, voilà le seul consolateur! Nous devons non seulement aux hommes, mais à toute la nature inférieure qui monte vers l'homme, qui a sa pensée en lui, de continuer vivement la pensée et l'action."[13] Athénaïs Mialaret, who was to become his second wife in 1849, first came to know Michelet through her correspondence in which she discussed *Du Prêtre* and similar experiences with confessors.

The haunting theme of death propelled Michelet into further polemics, especially in the wave of enthusiasm for democratic freedom which foreshadowed the revolution of 1848. We find expressions of this in the *Journal*, in *Le Peuple* (1846), where the historian comes to speak of his humble origins and their common cause, then in the *Histoire de la Révolution française.*

An early illustration of this new activist spirit, indebted to the *philosophes,* is found in the *Journal* of 1846, where Michelet meditates about the death of his father, Furcy, who had lived under the same roof with him for almost fifty years. Recalling his early days in Furcy's printing enterprise (his press published pamphlets, some by Babeuf; it was closed down by Napoleon in 1812) he admits: "Toujours je retrouvais mon père, c'est-à-dire la vieille France de Voltaire et de Rousseau."[14] Michelet's father is often called a "Voltairien," but this means an agnostic, not one who discussed the *philosophes* with his son. Indeed, Furcy's letters show him to have a simple, non-intellectual spirit which had little in common with the vibrant commitment of Jules.[15] Our citation merely proves that his vision transforms reality, that he literally sees Voltaire and Rousseau as two mainstays of freedom and the tradition of France, of *le peuple,* as incarnated by his father.

An almost mystical tone enters his work, evident in the way he defines his task as a historian. In *Le Peuple* he speaks of the teachers of his student days and says: "Ces grands historiens ont été brillants, judicieux, profonds. Moi, j'ai aimé davantage."[16] Later, in *l'Amour* (1858) he again comments on the theme of death: "J'ai des pleurs dans mon coeur et pour plus d'une chose. Ce n'est pas impunément que tant de fois je passai (dans l'histoire) le Styx, le fleuve des morts. Je ne suis pas insensible à mon temps et j'en sens les mortelles blessures."[17] The experience of death in his personal life (to the deaths of 1839, 1842, 1846 already mentioned, let us add those of his infant son in 1850, and of his daughter and son from his first marriage in 1855 and 1862) is repeated over and over again in his work as a historian, witnessing the shadows of the past and lending them a new life, "resurrection" as he was to call it. History, as the record of cataclysmic reversals,[18] brings not only progress (e.g., of *le peuple* and freedom) but also untold suffering, injustice which must never be condoned. Was not the Revolution undone by Robespierre and abolished by Napoleon? In this context Michelet turns to Voltaire; he seeks inspiration from the anti-fatalist who, in the *Lettres philosophiques,* condemns Pascal for seeking refuge in other worlds. Voltaire who saved Calas becomes a true hero. In 1845 Michelet calls out: "Qui brisa l'échafaud? Un persécuté, Voltaire, à qui on doit associer Buffon, Montesquieu, Rousseau, Fréret. La philosophie victorieuse sauve le protestantisme qui la détestait. Vous savez la terrible aventure de Calas."[19] An extensive passage of the *Histoire de la Révolution* takes up this theme: "Vieil athlète, à toi la couronne!" Outliving Montesquieu, Buffon, Diderot, Rousseau, Voltaire continues the battle for humanity, never weary, never discouraged: "Tu défends Calas et la Barre, tu sauves Sirven, tu brises l'échafaud des protestants. Tu as vaincu pour la liberté religieuse, et tout à l'heure pour la liberté civile, avocat des derniers serfs, pour la réforme de nos procédures barbares."[20] We cite but a brief portion of this tribute which honors first Rousseau, then Voltaire.

Apostrophes and invocations like these become frequent. The two *philosophes* appear as patrons of the rising bourgeoisie,[21] as the true kings of Europe,[22] the incarnation of "la pensée philosophique," as "les grands docteurs de la nouvelle église."[23] The *Convention* deserves our gratitude for having honored them with tombs in the Panthéon as the true sons of Descartes.[24] Voltaire is the guardian against terror and hypocrisy,[25] while Rousseau's principles of education produced an "éruption du génie," the great leaders of the Revolution.[26] Michelet feels solidarity with all "génies sublimes" whose ardent faith mocks man's fears: "O mes pères, ô mes frères, Voltaire, Molière, Rabelais, amis chéris de ma pensée . . . génies sublimes chargés de porter le dépôt de Dieu, vous avez donc accepté, pour nous, ce difforme martyre d'être les bouffons de la peur."[27]

Michelet has a tragic, even a grotesque conception of satire, of what he calls the "comedy" in history. This becomes strikingly clear in the most unusual passage we shall cite, taken from Book III of his *Révolu-*

tion where he discusses his method and comes to speak of Catherine Théot, a religious fanatic who believed she was the Virgin, the mother of God. Imprisoned, released, then denounced to the Comité de sûreté générale for harboring reactionaries, she was acquitted only after the fall of Robespierre; she died in prison, nonetheless, but the fact she had not been sent to the guillotine appeared to Michelet as a victory of humanism, due to the intercession of the spirit of Voltaire and to his powerful weapon, satire:

> Pendant que les faux Rousseaux prouvent à la Convention, au nom des principes, qu'elle doit s'exterminer elle-même, pendant qu'elle baisse la tête et n'ose dire: Non. . . . Voici un accident grave: Voltaire ressuscite.
>
> Béni sois-tu, bon revenant: tu nous viens en aide à tous. Nous étions bien embarrassés sans toi, personne ne pouvait arrêter la mort déchaînée au hasard. Les philosophes du moment ont guillotiné la clémence. Ils ne savent plus eux-mêmes avancer ni reculer.
>
> Le procès voltairien de la mère de Dieu (Catherine Théot), tombé dans la Convention, y soulève un rire immense . . . . Miracle! ces morts qui rient . . . . L'invincible torture du rire lui donnant la question, suscite au fond de ses entrailles ce qui eût semblé éteint, l'étincelle de Voltaire . . . . Disons mieux, la flamme immortelle de la France . . . . Rire sacré, rire sauveur, qui vainquit la peur et la mort, rompit l'horrible enchaînement.[28]

Michelet is saying: while Robespierre and Saint-Just ("les faux Rousseaux") incite members of the *Convention* to denounce even each other and send each other to the guillotine ("s'exterminer") and while no one dares resist the vicious cycle ("l'horrible enchaînement"), the spirit of Voltaire, his satire, overcame not only the fanaticism of Catherine Théot but that of those who believed in her execution, and this was a miracle indeed in which the eternal flame of the French spirit was rekindled, for laughter defeats man's inhumanity to man! Thus Michelet appeals to the grand tradition of the *philosophes*; if it saved Catherine and the *Convention* (let us note that just before being arrested, Robespierre had accused six more of its members of treason, without naming them), it can save France again! Michelet uses Voltaire's name much as Voltaire invoked Socrates, Plato, Confucius, and others, in the greetings he added to his letters, sending salutions in the name of the great heroes of the past to defeat "l'infâme." Michelet singles out Voltaire's laughter and gives it universal proportions. It becomes a symbol of hope, an essential contribution of France to the cause of freedom.

Much in the same way, Michelet identifies with Rousseau's faith in Providence, with his ideal of a just society:

> Montesquieu écrit, interprète le Droit. Voltaire pleure et crie pour le Droit. Rousseau le fonde.
>
> Beau moment où, surprenant Voltaire accablé d'un nouveau malheur, le désastre de Lisbonne, Voltaire aveuglé de larmes et ne voyant plus le ciel, Rousseau le relève, lui rend Dieu, et sur les ruines du monde, proclame la Providence. . . .
>
> Où prit-il son point d'appui? . . . Il le prit en ce qui vous a trop défailli. . . . Dans le coeur. Il lut au fond de sa souffrance, il lut distinctement ce que le moyen âge n'a jamais su lire: *Un Dieu juste.*[29]

Michelet finds in Rousseau the confirmation of his own need to believe in Providence and justice.

Such, at least, was his view up to 1850, when a negative note enters his comments on Rousseau.[30] In order to define its object, we shall study Michelet's commentaries to 1867 as a group. It should be emphasized, from the start, that none of the objections extinguish Michelet's fundamental love for Rousseau. He had identified with him too long for that to happen.

Book VII of the *Histoire de la Révolution* (1850) begins with the events of August 10, 1792, the seizing of the Tuileries palace and the King. The radical leaders of the Revolution were now in power and the foreign invasion was soon to propel the guillotine into action. We cannot help but feel that Robespierre and Saint-Just, as "disciples" of Rousseau quoting the *Contrat social,* are one element in Michelet's reassessment.[31] He later explains: "Il [Rousseau] veut qu'on ait dans chaque Etat un code moral qui contienne les bonnes maximes que chacun soit tenu d'admettre. Il faut que chacun déclare, confesse, articule sa foi (et sous peine de mort, dans le *Contrat social*)."[32] Michelet has in mind the famous passage demanding that a citizen who refuses to obey the general will "be forced to be free."[33] Bertrand Russell and some other modern critics see Rousseau for this reason as the direct precursor of Hitler.[34] Michelet has more sense and does distinguish between Rousseau and his disciples. Speaking of

Malesherbes, who was sent to the guillotine—Michelet admires him as the protector of Diderot and of his heroic enterprise, the *Encyclopédie*—he comments: "Qu'aurait dit Rousseau, bon Dieu! si on lui avait annoncé que ses inintelligents disciples tueraient le bienveillant censeur, le propagateur de l'*Emile*, au nom même de ses doctrines!"[35] Still, the association exists; Robespierre appears as a "faux Rousseau," and it is by way of a compliment that Michelet says of Danton, his revolutionary hero *par excellence*, "lui seul ne dérive pas de Rousseau."[36]

There are a number of other explanations for Michelet's apprehensions. His resolute anticlerical stance makes some of Rousseau's ideas suspect. Wolmar's conversion to Christianity in the *Nouvelle Héloïse*—Michelet believes Rousseau's letter to Vernet which speaks of it[37]—makes Rousseau into a defender of the Church and, as such, a traitor to the cause of the *philosophes*.[38] Similarly, Robespierre's cult of the Supreme Being is described as a compromise with the Church, not as a substitute for Christianity.[39] Once again a parallel appears between Robespierre and Rousseau.

The image of Rousseau as a traitor to the *philosophe* cause sounds like the propaganda of the pseudo-memoirs of Madame d'Epinay. Michelet admits that Rousseau suffered, that Grimm behaved toward him as a boor, that Madame d'Epinay unfairly chased him from the *Hermitage* in the midst of winter, but even so he calls Rousseau "le judas du parti [philosophique]."[40] We may speculate that Michelet was affected by the *Mémoires de Madame de Montbrillant* (d'Epinay). The fact is that just at the time when doubts enter Michelet's mind concerning Rousseau, Diderot emerges in a new light. He becomes Pantophile, Panurge, and Prométhée all in one,[41] a *philosophe* of diversitarian concerns as compared to Voltaire, who stands for the unity of reason.[42]

Finally Michelet makes the charge that Rousseau, like Mably, stands for the extreme ideal of Spartan virtue, primitivism, and community property.[43] Michelet belives that Rousseau's contacts with Mably are responsible for the negative attitudes of the *Discours sur les sciences et les arts* and later the *Discours sur l'inégalité*, even though, admittedly, they do not mention Mably. Once again Rousseau is opposed to Diderot, for Michelet cannot believe that Diderot would also have chosen the negative argument in the first *Discours*; he advised Rousseau to take that side for *his* sake, or for the sake of paradox.[44] With Mably, and contrary to Diderot, Rousseau stands accused of "ostentation de pauvreté"[45] and of forsaking the essential cause of progress in history.

As the all-important corrective for the critique outlined in the last paragraphs, we hasten to repeat: Michelet's love for Rousseau remains alive, and so does his enthusiastic admiration of the accomplishment of this genius able to produce three masterpieces at one time, the *Nouvelle Héloïse, Emile,* and the *Contrat social.* In order to reconcile his mixed reactions, Michelet even invents two Rousseau's, two styles: the *style noué* of Rousseau-Mably in the *Discours* and the *Contrat,* and the *style dénoué* of the *Nouvelle Héloïse,* the *Confessions,* the *Rêveries,* conceived by the Rousseau who was formed by Madame de Warens and reformed by Madame d'Houdetot.[46] Since the negative side is merely *one* aspect, Michelet lets stand his warmest tribute in the early pages of the *Histoire de la Révolution* (1847) and merely adds a footnote, in 1868, explaining that his early judgment must be compared to more recent opinions.[47] So we must balance a passage cited earlier, the tribute to Rousseau's faith which flows from his heart,[48] against the later statement that had Palissot not attacked him in his comedy *Les Philosophes*—where Rousseau appears on all fours—he was in danger of becoming "le coryphée du parti dévot,"[49] for at times he seems to aspire to Christian fatalism: "Le mépris de la sagese, la haine du libre arbitre, le renoncement à l'action, violà l'enseignement de Julie. . . . toutes les sottises que Voltaire a pulvérisées dans ses réponses à Pascal trente années auparavant (1734)."[50] Notwithstanding this, Michelet recalls "le grand, l'immense succès . . . celui de l'*Héloïse*. . . .Ce ne fut pas chose de mode. Les moeurs en restèrent changées. Le mot d'*amour,* dit Walpole, avait été pour ainsi dire rayé par le ridicule, biffé du dictionnaire. On n'osait se dire amoureux. Chacun, après l'*Héloïse,* s'en vante, et tout homme est Saint-Preux."[51] No question then that Michelet admires Rousseau's work even later when he voices certain objections. His love dominates. He speaks of "la belle lettre contre le poème de Lisbonne," he states that the *Nouvelle Héloïse,* though it may seem dull today, hit upon a new chord which makes it superior to all novels of its day. Everyone was looking for a Julie; Madame de Pompadour was trying to find one for the King! *Emile* likewise carried its readers away: one actress, unsuited for nursing her child, did so for the sake of Rousseau.[52] Michelet feels for him as he compares him to Mirabeau: "Rousseau et Mirabeau partirent du désespoir. . . . Rousseau naît de ce jour (1756) où, délaissé de ses amis et de lui-même, il fut seul, sans famille, rejetant ses enfants, fort de sa liberté, de sa pauvreté solitaire, pour couver ses trois fils immortels, ses trois livres."[53] In the end Michelet remains positive. In *Nos Fils* (1869) Rousseau appears as the educator for the future, for the Revolution.[54] Paul Viallaneix is quite right when he feels that the idea of the sovereignty of *le peuple,* stressed in Michelet's famous preface of 1869, goes back to both Voltaire and Rousseau.[55]

Throughout the historian's work, Voltaire remains the voice of the future, one of those calling mankind back to nature, like Montaigne and Vico; in the later volumes of the *Histoire de France* he no longer appears as the continuator of Cartesian rationalism, for Descartes is no longer Michelet's prophet.[56] What is most surprising is to find Voltaire's life and work in ever so many chapter headings or subheadings in the last three volumes (1863–67). Even Voltaire would have been astounded by this image of an entire century revolving around him. Michelet makes a methodical if not always successful attempt to link Voltaire's works to the major political developments. We might ask, are *Oedipe* and *Brutus* really warnings to the kings that their rule has passed?[57] Is the admittedly "pale" *Henriade* immortal because it combines grand satire—it castigates the St-Barthélémy—with compassion for Henri IV?[58]

The last chapter of book X, "le credo du dix-huitième siècle," defines the Enlightenment as a philosophy of action, with Voltaire and Diderot in the forefront. Voltaire is praised once again for rejecting Pascal in his *Lettres philosophiques*: "Ce terrible livre, comme un esprit qui rit des portes et des serrures, s'envole de lui-même."[59]

Meanwhile Diderot, in his *Pensées,* exclaims: "Elargissez Dieu!"[60] Both transcend Christianity and aspire to a better future.

Michelet is especially moved by Voltaire's sensibility. He speaks of *Zaïre* stirring audiences to tears, of Adrienne Lecouvreur acting in *Oedipe* before her untimely death. Besides, Michelet praises the *Histoire de Charles XII* for its reasoned argument ("réfléchi") and Voltaire's correspondence with Frederic II, for it would convince the King that man is free.[61]

Lest it be said he is uncritical, Michelet takes pains to point out that he is a stern judge; he proudly tells us that he is critical of Voltaire's pro-English views[62] and of his support of Choiseul, whom Michelet identifies with the Austrian danger. Michelet claims that Voltaire was able to buy Ferney due to the protection of Choiseul and of Madame de Pompadour; at that point he is a "roi d'Yvetot" depending on Versailles.[63] Such criticism is strange indeed. It expresses Michelet's hatred of English materialism and economic predominance and of the anti-revolutionary activities of Maria Theresa and Marie Antoinette; as he described them, these culminated exactly nine months before the birth of each of Marie Antoinette's children, ill moments indeed for the cause of liberty![64] When Malesherbes and Turgot lose power due to the Austrian influence, Voltaire weeps![65] In this last instance, Voltaire chose the anti-Austrian side and is exonerated. Michelet's partisan attitude is simplistic and a full study of his portrait of English and Austrian politics would be a peculiar and all too consistent document; yet there is a nobler side to this: Michelet defends himself by saying that his history must be subjective; it will make no foul compromise between the cause of good and the cause of evil![66]

An eloquent chapter is devoted to Voltaire's fight for Calas, i.e., for the end of serfdom.[67] Voltaire stands for progress, like the *Encyclopédie*: "Elle fit table rase d'un monde de vieilleries."[68] History is the battle of freedom against its enemies, now as before,[69] except that Michelet's nature studies, his discovery of determinism, of biological (and economic) forces to be reckoned with, have forced him to modify his definition of freedom, and of the spirit ("esprit") that strives for freedom. It is remarkable to find Michelet reinterpreting Voltaire to make him into his precursor even here. He starts out by explaining that, unlike some less advanced minds, he has accepted determinism and does not postulate universal freedom:

> Un espirit plus systématique [que moi] eût suivi exclusivement cette tendance qui donne tout à la liberté. Moi, au contraire, j'accordai place égale aux deux principes [liberté et déterminisme] dans le mouvement alterné des choses humaines. Et, au prix d'une inconséquence apparente, je marchai, comme le monde marche, par cette voie géminée, sur deux ailes. Notre maître Voltaire nous a donné l'exemple. Tout en faisant grande part à la matière, il l'a mobilisée, vivifiée par l'esprit. De sorte qu'en paraissant et se disant matérialiste, il introduit dans son matérialisme un si vif mouvement, une si souple élasticité, que les lourds attraits de la matière échappent. Il semble que tout soit esprit.[70]

The vocabulary indicates that Michelet holds to the idealism of the past. Matter is a dead weight ("lourd") while the spirit is alive and gives life ("vivifie"); but accepting the inevitable, Michelet is pliable and elastic. He welcomes modern science, only he insists that his hero Voltaire has understood nature the same way, as spiritualized, as ruled by the force of the spirit.

Voltaire is hope, not perfection. When this last passage was composed (in 1870–71), utopia was not at hand. Michelet knew this as much as Voltaire, who saw the golden age as that of Louis XIV, not the present. Beset by what he considered the tyranny of Napoleon I (to be described in his last three volumes) and of Napoleon III, suffering under the debacle of the Franco-Prussian war, Michelet was anxious to insist on the triumph of the spirit he associated with Voltaire, catastrophies and determinism notwithstanding.

Thus, accepting what defeats history might bring with it, he maintains his hopes, he upholds freedom, the principles of the Revolution. In this struggle he looks for allies and finds them in Vico, in Rousseau, in Voltaire. He considers their idealism akin to his own, and that of Voltaire, as René Pomeau has defined it, is indeed not unlike that of Michelet: "Un humanisme révolutionnaire comme celui de Ferney ne sera jamais entièrement vérifié ni absolument contredit par les faits. Mais cette attitude trouve sa justification hors de l'histoire, dans la valeur morale de l'optimisme qui l'inspire. Quoi qu'on en dise, c'est une saine philosophie, celle qui persuade aux hommes qu'il dépend d'eux d'édifier une cité meilleure."[71] Such an outlook judges the past with a constant moral objective in mind. Michelet's originality lies not only in his images and style, but in such a visionary conception appropriate to the necessarily subjective nature of the historical account.

Michelet was no literary critic, but a historian honoring his intellectual forebears. He is an intensely personal author, one who did not so much set out, as Ranke did, to find "how things actually were,"[72] but rather one who describes the past to recapture "the flame which burned in the hearts of our fathers."[73] He sought to inspire social action by means of historical comment and spoke through those who, before him, had likewise fomented action, above all Voltaire and Rousseau.

NOTES

1 *Validity in Interpretation* (New Haven: Yale Univ. Press, 1967), p. 43 on Blake, p. 137 on *Hamlet.* I rather agree with Hans-Georg Gadamer, *Wahrheit und Methode* (Tübingen: J. C. B. Mohr, 1965), p. 184, who says that the variety of interpretations puts into question the possibility of *one* valid meaning of a text. Hirsch, pp. 245–64, attacks Gadamer; Gadamer defends himself against similar attacks by Betti.

2 Raymond Trousson, *Rousseau et sa fortune littéraire* (St.-Médard-en-Jalles: Guy Ducros, 1971), p. 103; cf. pp. 88–92 on Michelet; R. S. Ridgway, *Voltaire and Sensibility* (Montreal: McGill-Queens Univ. Press, 1973), pp. 264–73.

3 *Ecrits de Jeunesse* (Paris: Gallimard, 1959), pp. 305–21.

4 Ibid., p. 125 (of 1820).

5 Paul Viallaneix, *La Voie royale* (Paris: Delagrave, 1959), pp. 171–74. Descartes is still Michelet's hero in the *Histoire de la Révolution* (see n. 24), but not later (see n. 56).

6 Oscar A. Haac, *Les Principes Inspirateurs de Michelet* (Paris: Presses Universitaires de France, 1951), p. 111.

7 *Emile* in *Oeuvres complètes* (Paris: Gallimard, 1969), IV, 617.

8 Haac, p. 118 (of 1827).

9 *Essai sur les moeurs* (Paris: Garnier, 1963) II, 815, 818, 905–6, 954; cf. Viallaneix, pp. 198, 206, 213.

10 *Ecrits de jeunesse,* pp. 244–45.

11 *Journal* (Paris: Gallimard, 1959) I, 394 (of 12 April 1842); cf. *Jules Michelet, lettres*

inédites, ed. Paul Sirven, (Paris: Presses Universitaires de France, 1924), p. 46, favorable to the abbé Coeur.

12 Michela Magó, *Nationalism as a Secular Religion: The Evolution of Michelet's Historical Thought, 1840–46* (Diss. Cambridge Univ. 1974), ch. 1, esp. pp. 6–7.

13 *Journal* I, 431.

14 Ibid., 657.

15 Sirven, pp. 317–41.

16 *Le Peuple* (Paris: Flammarion, 1974), p. 71.

17 *L'Amour* (4e éd., Paris: Hachette, 1859), p. 256.

18 Hayden White, *Metahistory* (Baltimore: Johns Hopkins Press, 1973), p. 155; on Michelet, pp. 135–62.

19 *Cours 1845* (Clermont-Ferrand typescript to be edited by Paul Viallaneix), p. 69, cf. Magó, p. 250.

20 *Histoire de la Révolution française* (Paris: Gallimard, 1952, henceforth *HR*) I, 60.

21 *HR* I, 431.

22 *HR* I, 617.

23 *HR* I, 738, also 52.

24 *HR* II, 636, cf. n. 5.

25 *HR* I, 497, 576–77.

26 *HR* I, 429, 465.

27 *HR* I, 40.

28 *HR* I, 301–2.

29 *HR* I, 57–58.

30 Haac, p. 135 (of 1848); *Journal* I, 694 (of 1849), still favorable.

31 *HR* I, 283 (on Robespierre), 302, 479, 1270; II, 54–57, 428–29; Sirven, p. 197 (of 1853).

32 *Histoire de France* (Paris: Hetzel, n.d., henceforth *HF*), V, 430.

33 *Contrat social*, livre I, ch. 7; *HR* II, 125, 196.

34 *History of Western Philosophy* (London: Allen and Unwin, 1946), p. 711.

35 *HR* II, 118.

36 *HR* I, 1025, cf. II, 406, 446.

37 *HF* V, 433, cf. 435 (Book XI, chs. 4–5). Rousseau writes Vernet: "Sa conversion est indiquée avec une clarté qui ne pouvait souffrir un plus grand développement sans vouloir faire une capucinade." Cited in *Oeuvres complètes* (Paris: Gallimard, 1961), II, 1812 from the *Correspondance générale* (ed. Dufour-Plan), VI, 158.

38 *HF* V, 428, 430, 436 ("qu'est-il au fond? Chrétien."), cf. n. 40.

39 *HR* II, 428–29.

40 *HF* V, 429 (Book XI, ch. 4).

41 *HF* V, 407 (Book X, ch. 21).

42 *HF* V, 407, 409.

43 *HF* V, 410, 427. Rousseau appears as a "souffre-douleur" who denies private property and finds his ideal in "la barbarie de l'état sauvage," *HF* V, 371–72, 383–84 (Book X, chs. 16, 17, 19); on the right to property also *HF* V, 431, 481 (Book XI, chs. 4, 14).

44 *HF* V, 409–10 (Book X, ch. 21). Diderot is mentioned as early as 1820 in *Ecrits de jeunesse*, p. 266, but the warm tributes are of 1866–67.

45 *HF* V, 430.
46 *HF* V, 427, 431 (Book XI, ch. 4).
47 *HR* I, 57.
48 Ibid., see n. 29.
49 *HF* V, 435–36 (Book XI, ch. 5). Palissot is associated with the "parti bienpensant" (although he did not attack Voltaire).
50 *HF* V, 432 (Book XI, ch. 4); cf. p. 431: "Il désespère de la raison. Il inaugure la rêverie, ce narcotisme qui depuis a été toujours croissant."
51 *HF* V, 427.
52 *HF* V, 430 (Lisbon), 432 (superior novel), 436–37 (Julie).
53 *HF* V, 519 (Book XI, ch. 19).
54 Comment from *Nos Fils* cited in Viallaneix, p. 114, and Trousson, p. 91. In 1861 Michelet defends Rousseau against the severe judgments by Lamartine, Sirven, p. 285.
55 Viallaneix, p. 307. However in *Le Tyran,* a preface to the *Histoire de la Révolution* of 1869, directed against Robespierre, only Voltaire appears as a champion of *le peuple* and Rousseau is again associated with Robespierre, *HR* II, 1016, 1019.
56 *HF* V, 131–32 (Book 9, Preface); for Descartes as a hero see nn. 5 and 24 above.
57 *HF* V, 187 (Book IX, ch. 7).
58 *HF* V, 266–67 (Book IX, ch. 25).
59 *HF* V, 322 (Book X, ch. 9).
60 *HF* V, 275, 408 (Book 10, preface and ch. 21).
61 *HF* V, 313 (Book X, ch. 7 on *Zaïre*), 301, 304–5 (Book X, ch. 5 on Adrienne Lecouvreur), 404 (Book X, ch. 21 on Frederick). Michelet points out that Madame de Genlis was so moved she saw "le coeur" in Voltaire's eyes, 313, and calls Frederick "le caractère le plus complet du XVIIIe siècle, 395.
62 *HF* V, 321 (Book X, ch. 9).
63 *HF* V, 423–26 (Book XI, ch. 3). Michelet adds that Choiseul needs the support of Ferney, 448 (Book XI, ch. 7).
64 Austrian caresses, July 14, 1774, *HF* V, 473; first pregnancy, Madame d'Angoulême, March 18, 1778, 485; second pregnancy, Jan. 22, 1781, 492; third pregnancy, Louis XVII, June 1784, 495; the king is "le nègre de la reine," 492; dates are nine months prior to each birth (Book XI, chs. 11–12, 14–16).
65 *HF* V, 480 (Book XI, ch. 8).
66 *HF* IV, 70–71 (Book IV, conclusion) (of 1856).
67 *HF* V, 448–53 (Book XI, ch. 8), cf. nn. 19–20 above. Michelet says that Voltaire and others admired Catherine the Great for her efforts to free the serfs, but that they shuddered when they saw her portrait, 449; Michelet mistook a portrait of Maria Theresa to be that of Catherine which Voltaire was to have seen; see J. Pommier, *Michelet interprète de la figure humaine* (London: Athlone Press, 1961), pp. 11–12.
68 *HF* V, 481 (Book XI, ch. 8).
69 *HR* I, 3 (of 1847).
70 MS. note of 1871–72 cited by Viallaneix, p. 245. Michelet also opposed Voltaire's idea of freedom to the "fatalism" of race theories like that of Augustin Thierry.

71 Preface to Voltaire, *Oeuvres historiques* (Paris: Gallimard, 1957), p. 74.
72 Gadamer, pp. 192–93, speaks of Ranke's philosophy of freedom, but it is a freedom of choice, while Michelet conceives freedom in the framework of democratic ideology. On their relations see Werner Kaegi, *Michelet und Deutschland* (Basel: Schwabe Verlag, 1936) and Haac, pp. 180–81, 205–6.
73 *HR* I, 609.

Executive Board, 1977–78

President: J. G. A. POCOCK, Professor of History, The Johns Hopkins University

Past Presidents: GWIN J. KOLB, Professor of English, University of Chicago

VICTOR LANGE, John N. Woodhull Professor of German, Princeton University

First Vice-President: PHILLIP HARTH, Merritt Y. Hughes Professor of English, University of Wisconsin, Madison

Second Vice-President: MADELEINE B. THERRIEN (1977), Professor of French, University of Maryland, College Park

Executive Secretary: PAUL J. KORSHIN, Professor of English, University of Pennsylvania

Treasurer: JEAN A. PERKINS, Susan Lippincott Professor of French Literature, Swarthmore College

SHIRLEY A. BILL (1978), Professor of History, University of Illinois, Chicago Circle

ROBERT DARNTON (1980), Professor of History, Princeton University

WALTER GROSSMANN (1979), Professor of History and Director of Libraries, University of Massachusetts, Boston

ROBERT HALSBAND (1978), Professor of English, University of Illinois, Urbana

JAN LaRUE (1980), Professor of Music, New York University

JEANNE R. MONTY (1979), Professor of French, Tulane University

Institutional Members

of the American Society

for Eighteenth-Century Studies

National Library of Australia
Byrn Mawr College
University of Calgary
University of California, Berkeley
University of California, Davis
University of California, Irvine
University of California, Los Angeles/William Andrews Clark Memorial Library
University of California, Riverside
University of California, San Diego
Carleton University
Case Western Reserve University
The Catholic University of America
University of Cincinnati
City College, CUNY
Claremont Graduate School
Cleveland State University
Colonial Williamsburg
University of Colorado, Denver Center
University of Connecticut
Dalhousie University
University of Delaware
Delta State University
Detroit Institute of Arts, Founder's Society
Institute of Early American History and Culture
Emory University
Fordham University
Librarie Gason, Verviers, Belgium
University of Georgia
Georgia Institute of Technology
Georgia State University
Herzog August Bibliothek, Wolfenbüttel
University of Illinois, Chicago Circle
University of Illinois, Urbana
The Johns Hopkins University
University of Kansas
University of Kentucky
Lehigh University
Lehman College, CUNY
The Lewis Walpole Library
University of Maryland
University of Massachusetts, Boston
McMaster University/Association for 18th Century Studies
The Metropolitan Museum of Art
University of Michigan, Ann Arbor
Michigan State University
Middle Tennessee State University
The Minneapolis Institute of Fine Arts
University of Minnesota
University of Mississippi
Mississippi State University
Université de Montréal
Mount Saint Vincent University
University of New Brunswick
State University of New York, Fredonia
State University of New York, Oswego
Noel Foundation Library, Shreveport, La.
University of North Carolina, Chapel Hill
North Georgia College
Northern Illinois University
Northwestern University
Ohio State University
University of Pennsylvania
University of Pittsburgh
Princeton University
Purdue University

Rice University
University of Rochester
Rockford College
Smith College
University of South Carolina
University of Southern California
Southern Illinois University
University of Southern Mississippi
Stanford University
Swarthmore College
Sweet Briar College
University of Tennessee
University of Texas
Texas Tech University
Tulane University
University of Tulsa
University of Utrecht, Institute for Comparative and General Literature
University of Victoria
University of Virginia
Virginia Commonwealth University
Washington University
Washington and Lee University
Washington State University
Wayne State University
West Chester State College, Pennsylvania
Westfälische Wilhelms—Universität, Münster
West Virginia University
The Henry Francis du Pont Winterthur Museum
University of Wisconsin, Madison
University of Wisconsin, Milwaukee
The Yale Center for British Art and British Studies
Yale University

Sponsoring Members

of the American Society

for Eighteenth-Century Studies, 1977–78

Margaret E. Adams
Georgia Robison Beale
W. B. Carnochan
Chester Chapin
Donald Greene
Walter Grossmann
Paul J. Korshin
Michael Morrisroe, Jr.
Edgar V. Roberts
Joseph E. Stockwell
Calhoun M. Winton

Index